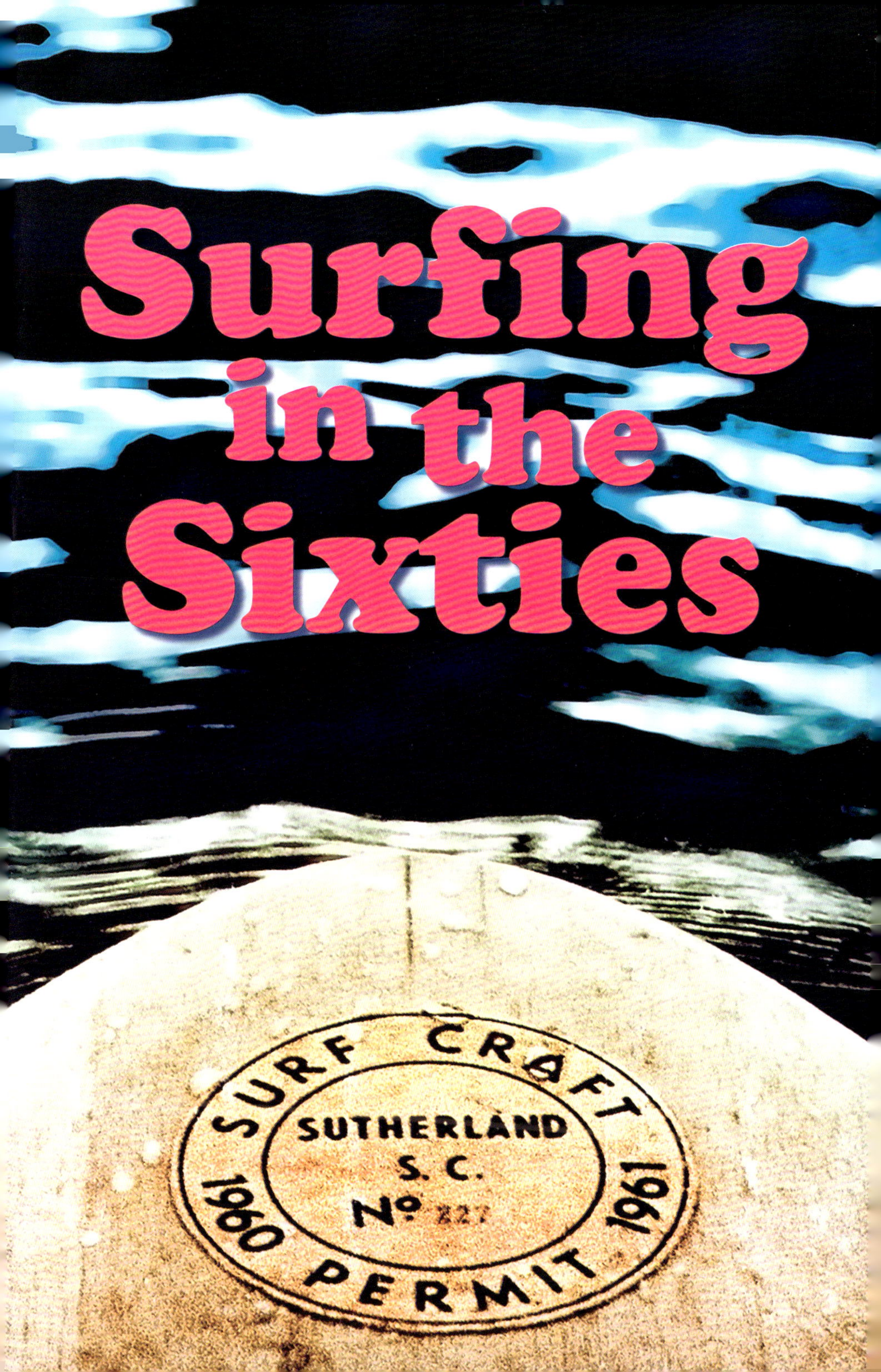

Surfing in the Sixties
SURF CRAFT
SUTHERLAND
S. C.
Nº 227
1960 PERMIT 1961

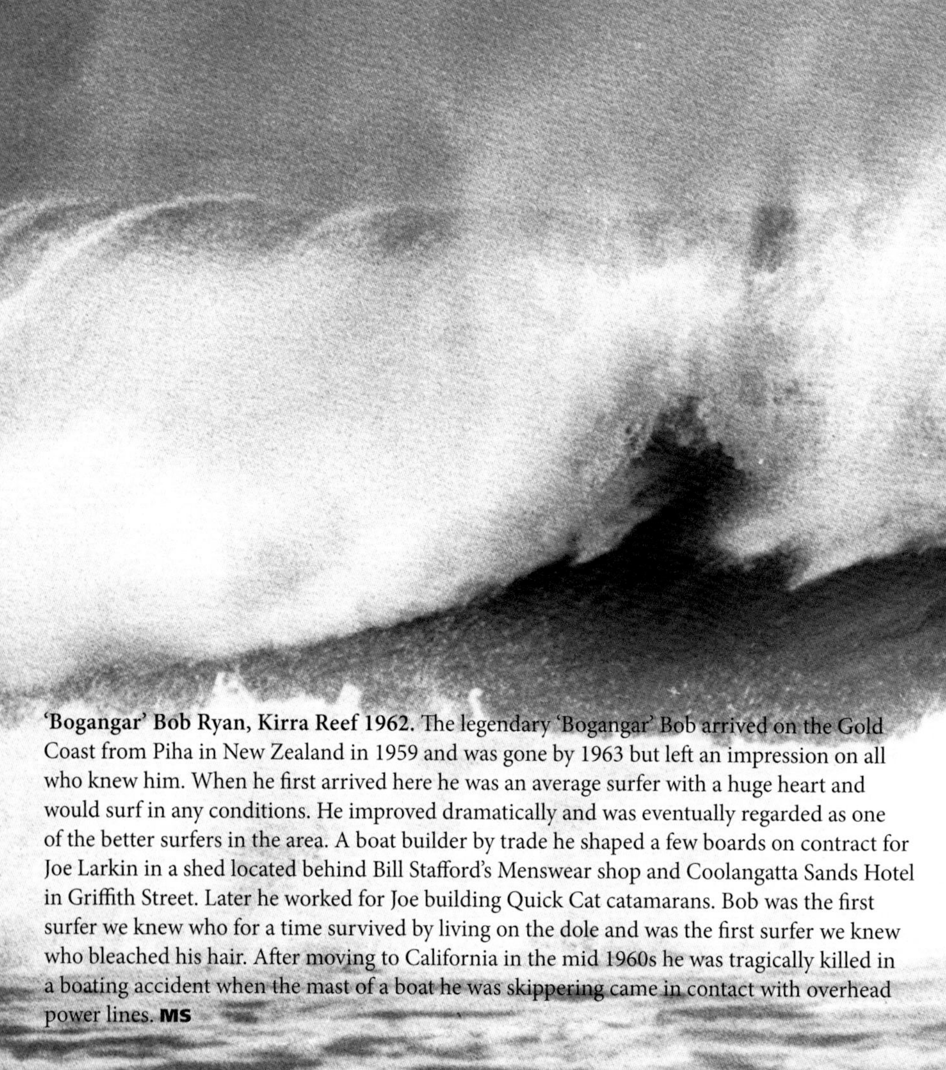

'Bogangar' Bob Ryan, Kirra Reef 1962. The legendary 'Bogangar' Bob arrived on the Gold Coast from Piha in New Zealand in 1959 and was gone by 1963 but left an impression on all who knew him. When he first arrived here he was an average surfer with a huge heart and would surf in any conditions. He improved dramatically and was eventually regarded as one of the better surfers in the area. A boat builder by trade he shaped a few boards on contract for Joe Larkin in a shed located behind Bill Stafford's Menswear shop and Coolangatta Sands Hotel in Griffith Street. Later he worked for Joe building Quick Cat catamarans. Bob was the first surfer we knew who for a time survived by living on the dole and was the first surfer we knew who bleached his hair. After moving to California in the mid 1960s he was tragically killed in a boating accident when the mast of a boat he was skippering came in contact with overhead power lines. **MS**

Surfing in the Sixties

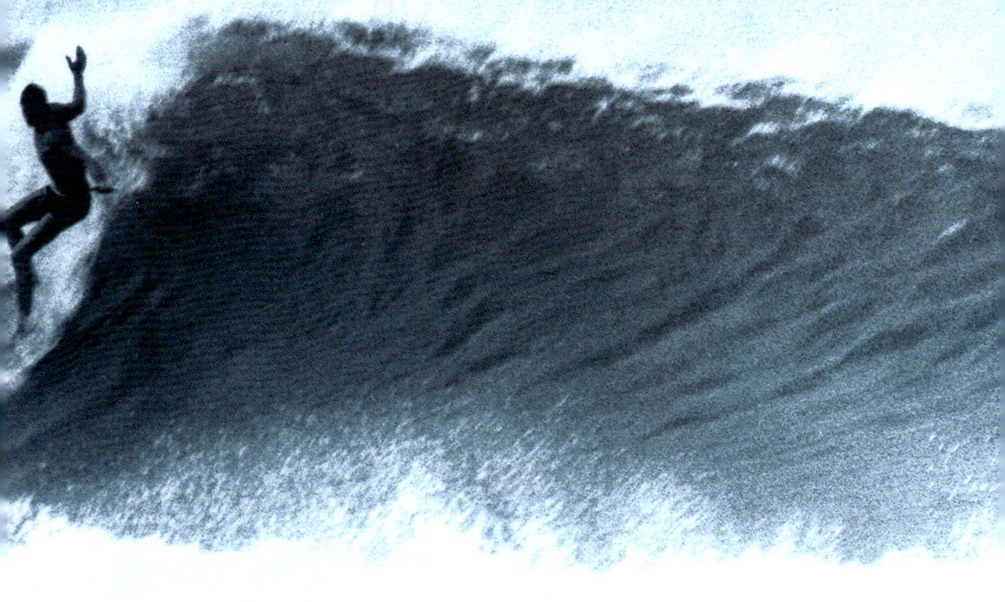

The photography of
Mal Sutherland, John Pennings, Barrie Sutherland & Bob Weeks

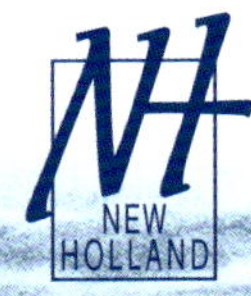

Gordon Merchant before Billabong, early 1960s. **JP**

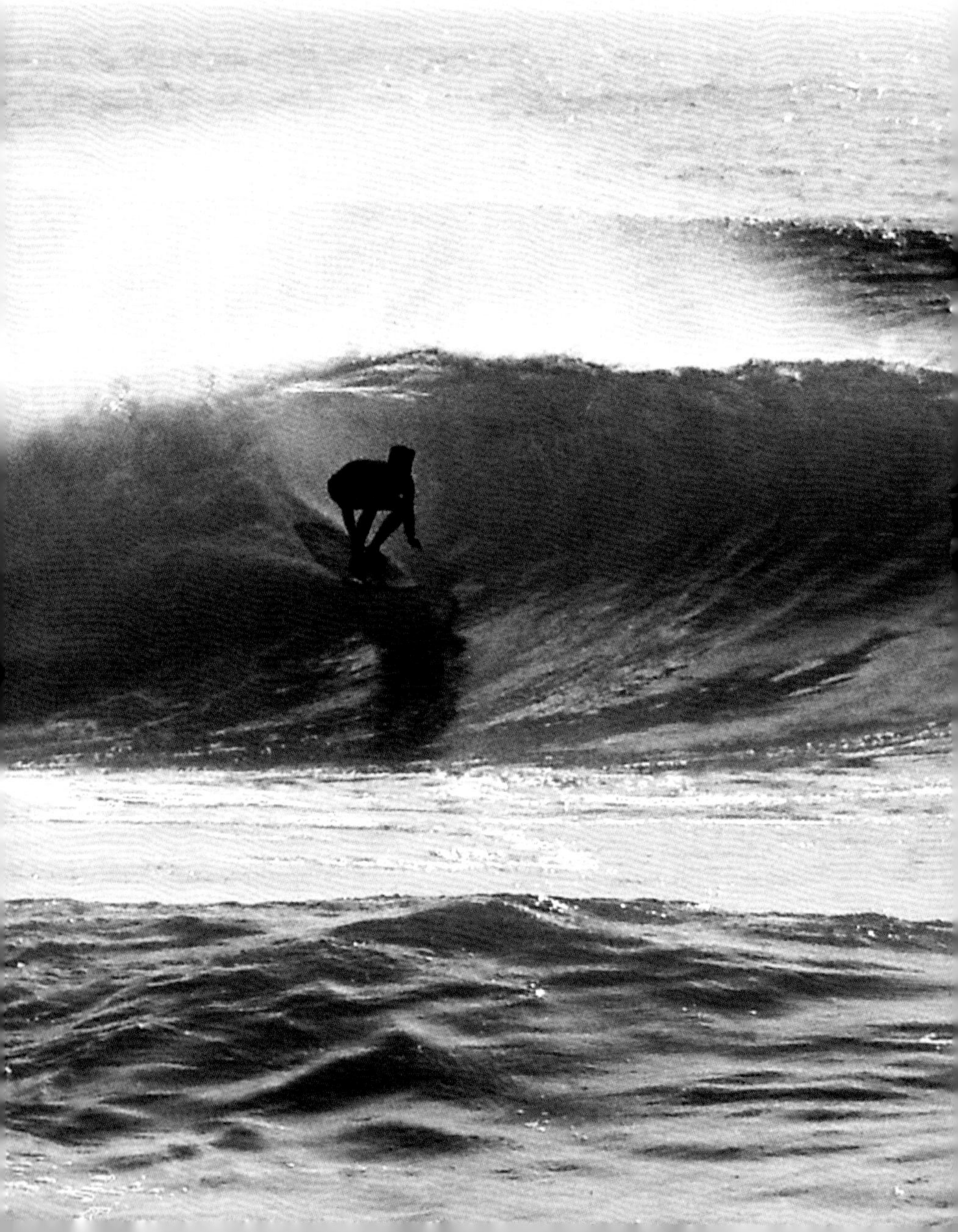

Contents

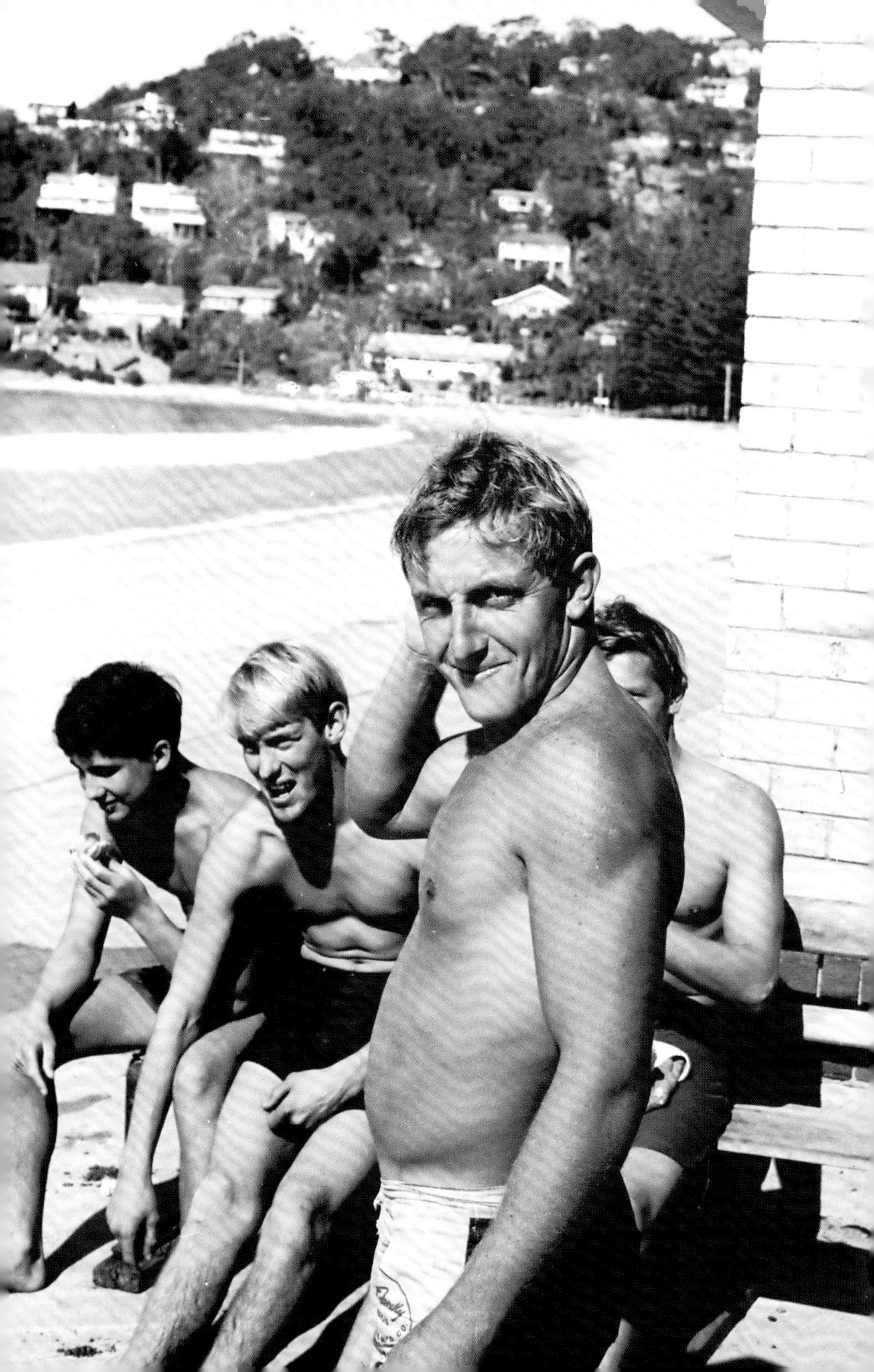

Foreword

Contrasted with this era when the whole planet goes surfing, in Australia in the sixties, riding a surfboard was the exclusive domain of either the very poor, or the wealthy. Why? Because they were the only ones who had the time to master this new and difficult sport. Consequently, many of us chose the poverty path, throwing our fate to the winds, rejecting the post-war consumerism and the suburban, *Saturday Evening Post* dream. We just went surfing, with no thought to tomorrow.

Consequently, our cars were old jalopies crammed with bodies and boards, to share the petrol pennies around. Our wardrobe was goodwill – and sparse. At one stage I had one pair of shorts I surfed in, slept in, and shaped surfboards in. Our diet was high on cheap carbs (fresh bread and bananas) and low on style. Alcohol was pretty much in excess, but only once or twice a week. Pub nights happened when we could afford it. No drugs. Our dreams were of next day's surf, which meant five or six hours of paddling, take-offs, speed trim thrills, and attempting new manoeuvres as they were developed. We made better and better boards as our skill level quickly increased.

Hunting for new surf spots was a major part of our culture, both along Australia's massive coastline, and soon broadening out to our surrounding lands like New Zealand and Indonesia. We were penniless, but mobile.

We surfers of the era, and you the reader of today, are so fortunate that a few guys had cameras, and a talent for capturing the essence of a situation. Bob Weeks hung out with the tribe from southern Sydney; Mal Sutherland the warm Queensland crew; Victoria was Barrie Sutherland's beat; and John Pennings covered Sydney's northside. Together they covered the original tribal territories of the Aussie surfers of the sixties. What an era! What a fine portrayal is captured on these pages!

The era has passed but the adventurous spirit and sheer joy of surfing that shines through these great photographers work lives on for our pleasure!

Bob McTavish, Byron Bay

Opposite: **Bob McTavish.** Relaxing after a session at Palm Beach in 1964 with Chris Beecham, Peter Hammel, Dave Letts in the background. **JP**

Following spread: **Bob McTavish, Bells Beach Easter contest final, 1966. BS**

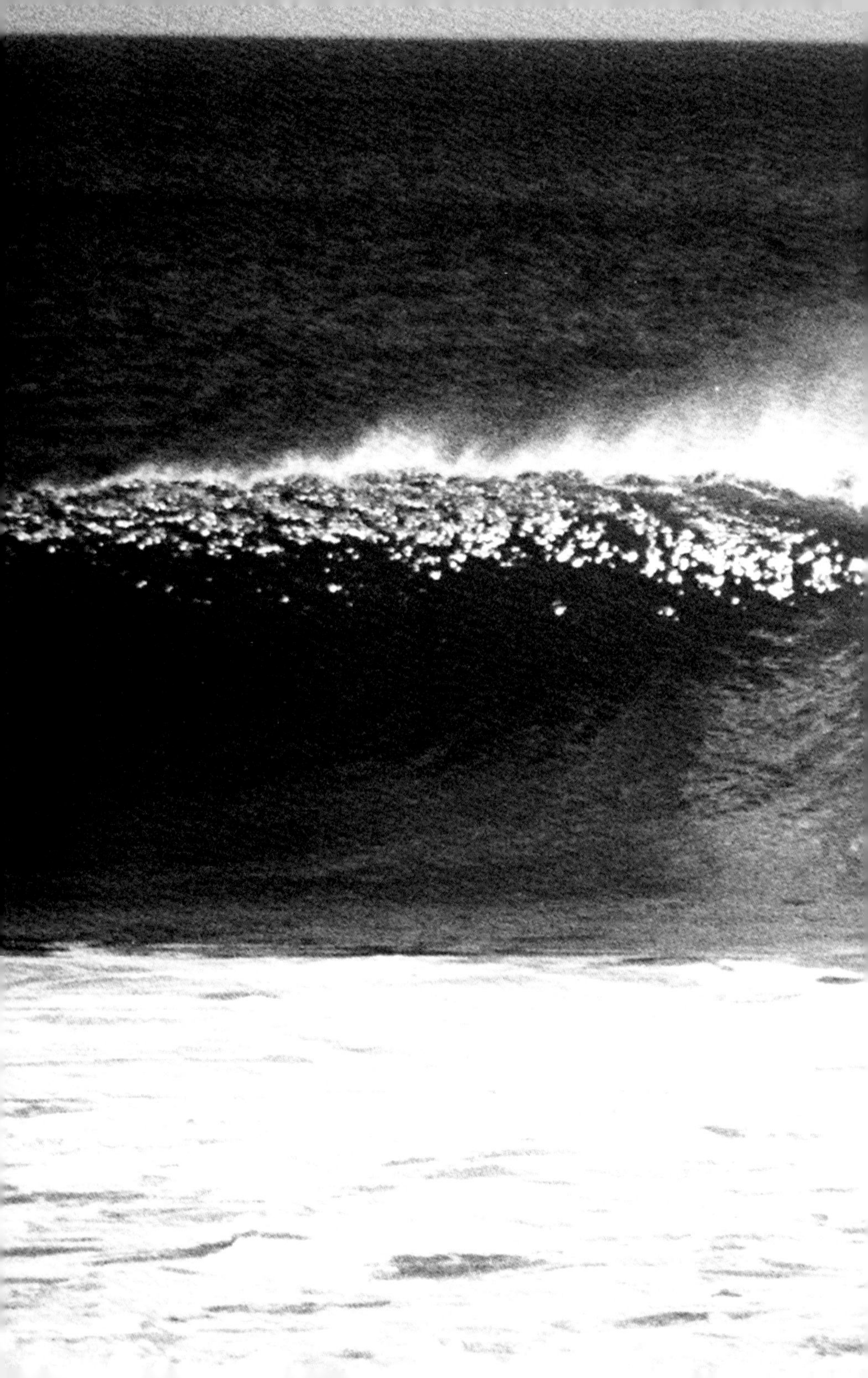

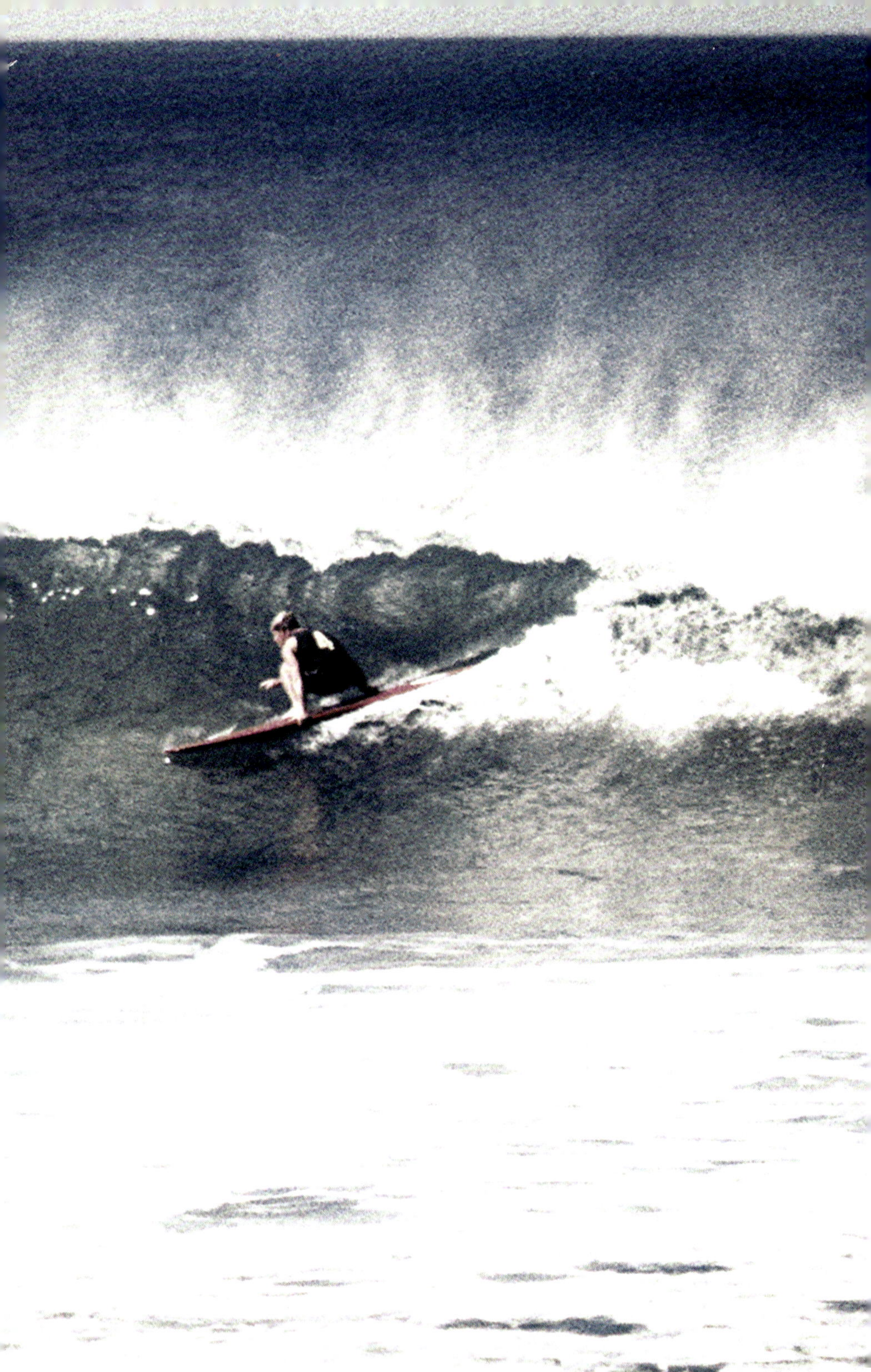

Snapper Rocks, 1963 Even before the construction of the Tweed River training walls and sand pumping the surf normally broke off Snapper Rocks as it does today, but shifting sands sometimes created the peak shown in this photo.

The object in the foreground is a money-in-the-slot telescope overlooking Jack Evans' 50m swimming pool. Built in the 1950s as a public salt water pool Jack installed two porpoise that had been trapped by net fisherman. Locals of the time would train in the pools with the porpoise swimming around and underneath them.

Extra pools were added later and became the site of the original porpoise shows before Jack constructed the purpose-built pool (now demolished) at the mouth of the Tweed River.

The concrete wave break wall and pumping station walls are the only sections of the original structure standing today. **MS**

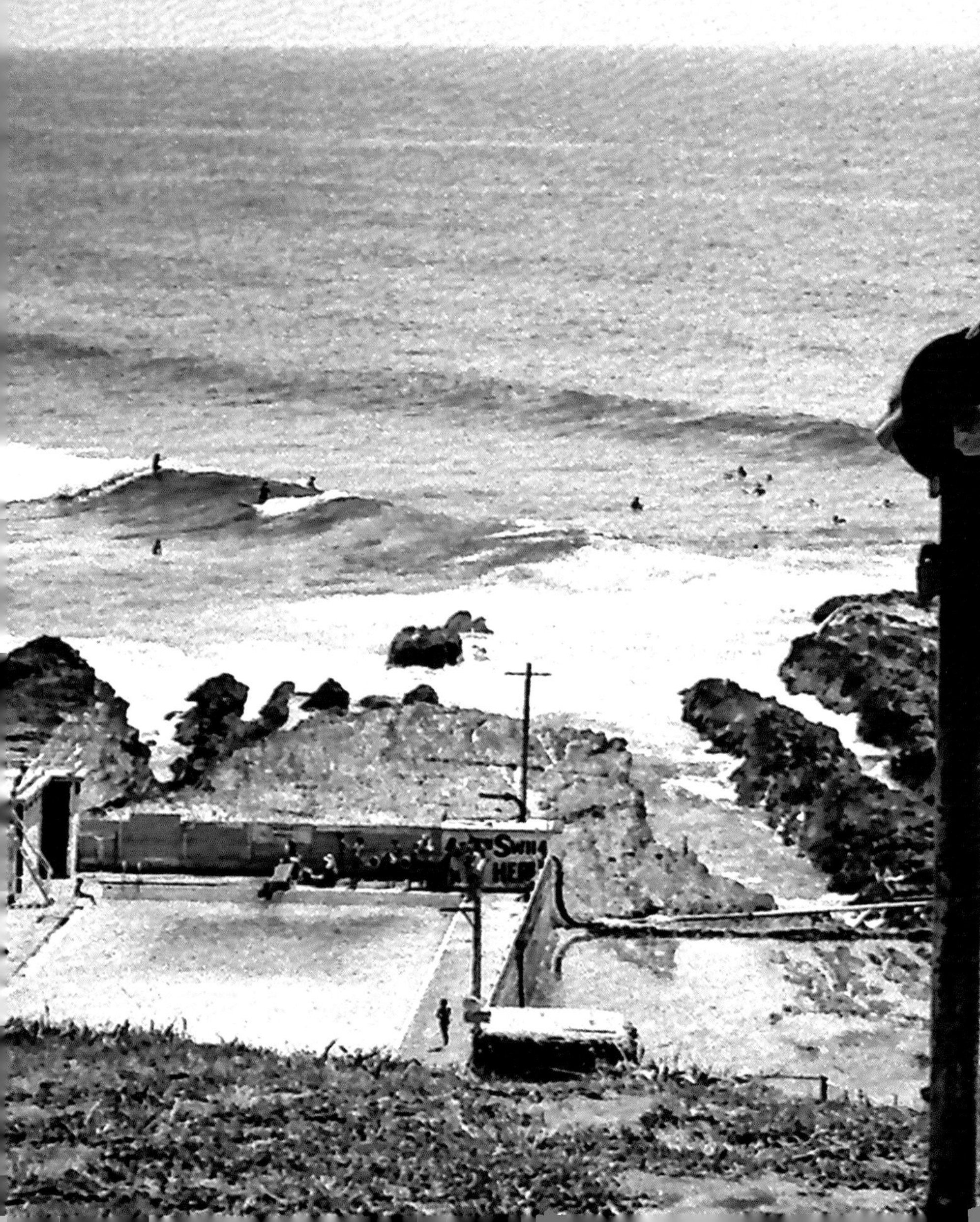

Mal Sutherland

I grew up on Kirra Beach and whether it was fishing with Dad or wallowing around in the shallows on a surfoplane my life revolved around the ocean. My first surfboard was a 17-foot monster that at 13 years of age I could hardly carry so when Malibus came on the scene in late 1956 I couldn't get hold of one quick enough.

I have been very fortunate to have been in the right place at the right time to have witnessed and been part of a developing sport and to be able, because of my interest in photography, (accidently) document its progression. Never in our wildest dreams could those of our era have imagined that surfing would, for better or worse, become the giant it has become today.

When I was asked to be part of this book I was skeptical at first, but then came to realise that it was an opportunity to get our photos out there to showcase what it was like in the 1960s. Otherwise, the images would have languished in a bottom drawer never to be seen. Also I saw it as an opportunity to leave a legacy for my grandchildren.

Fortunately, there is a growing awareness among the surfing fraternity that what we had in the late 1950s early 1960s is worth preserving. I hope that those who read this book can appreciate the photos and relive the 'stoke'.

Surf 'til you drop.

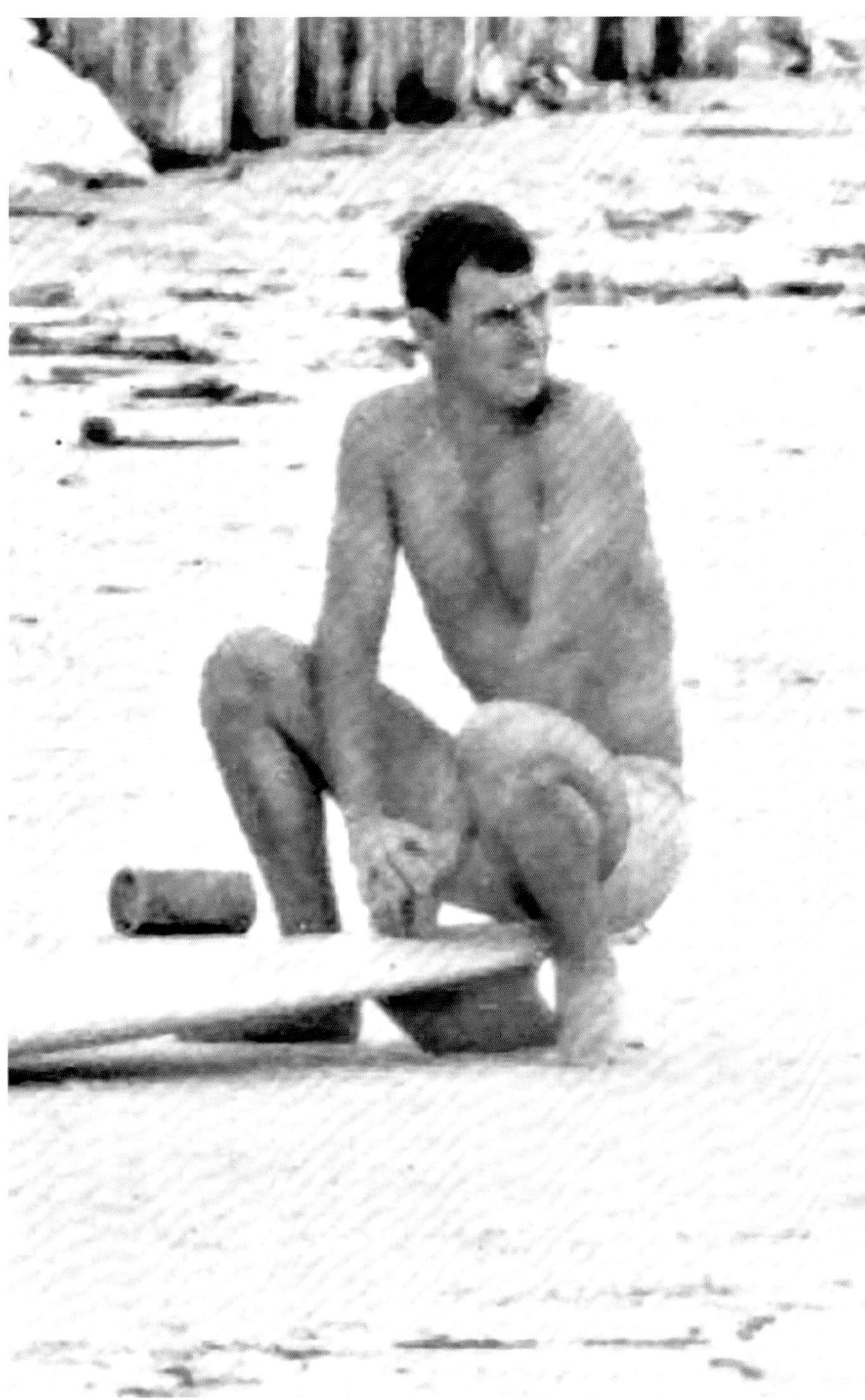

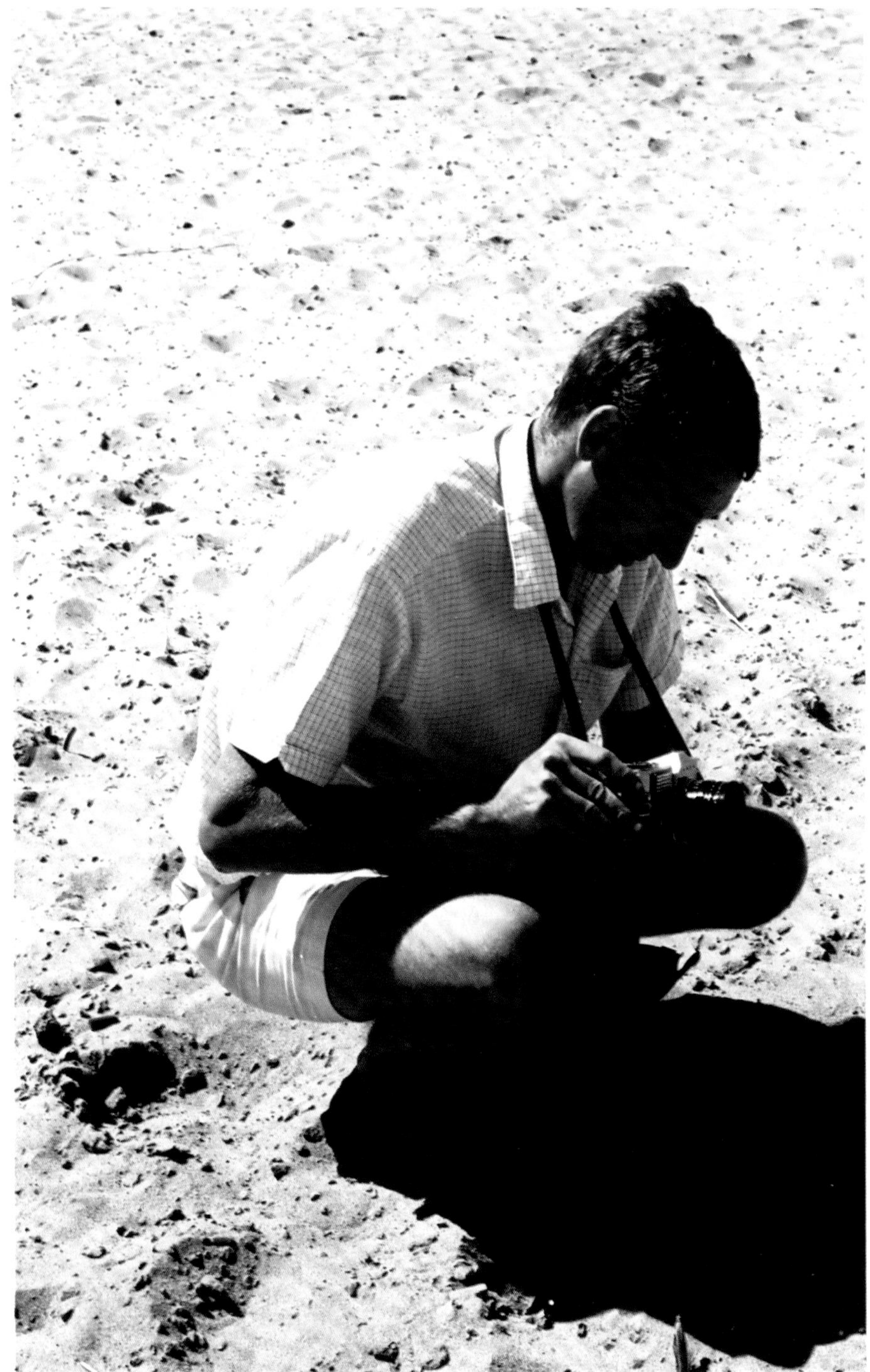

John Pennings

My interest in surfing began in 1956 after watching a display of board riding by US lifeguards at Avalon Beach. I purchased my first board from Roger Keiran, a 'pig' shape – heavy balsa, absolutely fantastic, a completely new experience – this was around 1959.

My interest in surf photography began a year later when a good friend of mine, Bob Commys, started taking photos with a small telephoto lens and getting good results. With the launch of *Australian Surfer* magazine in 1961 I saw a good spread of Bob's surfing photos published – this certainly sparked my interest.

I used to run into Bob Evans on the beach quite regularly after a surf. Bob had just started *Surfing World* magazine and stated to me that he may find it difficult to gather enough material to print 12 issues a year. That meeting with Bob prompted me to purchase camera equipment. This was in the late months of 1962. My camera consisted of a 35 mm SLR Pentax, with a 400 mm Novaflex lens and came with a 200m m extension screw-fitting lens – I guess very basic equipment certainly by today's standards – however, I was absolutely stoked. So my association with *Surfing World* commenced. I was fortunate enough the following year to be on hand to photograph a classic North Narrabeen day in April of 1963. One photo of a wave with local surfer Jim Fordham in the slot gained a lot of recognition, and I was commissioned to have a 6 foot by 4 foot framed mural to hang in the Narrabeen surf club hall for the Saturday 'stomp' nights. My passion for surf photography definitely increased. Of course there was very little money paid for surf photos – the meagre amount paid by the magazines covered the cost of film and printing – not too much over. However, the self-satisfaction I got out of photography more than compensated for that.

Besides *Surfing World*, I contributed regularly to *South African Surfer* magazine, had several articles published in *American Surfer* magazine and *International Surfing*. My photo of Wayne Lynch's cutback during the 1968 Australian surfing championships was used on a poster to advertise Paul Witzig's movie, *Evolution*.

Barrie Sutherland

I grew up swimming and playing with paddle boards at Portarlington in Port Phillip Bay, Victoria. I wasn't interested in photography. Mum and Dad were into sport and always encouraged me to join them and participate. I was never pressured. When my grandparents built a house in Torquay and my cousin's parents built next door, the doorway opened to ocean beaches and the waves. I couldn't have had better locations to play! Calm bay waters allowed me to beg or borrow wooden paddle boards and have fun around the pier. Torquay took it to the next phase where I learned to bodysurf and ride surfboards.

The 1956 Melbourne Olympics was a life-changer when I attended (with thousands of others) the Olympic demonstration sport (surfing) carnival. I'd just turned 14 years and was fascinated watching the visiting American team, who were mostly life guards, ride balsa Malibu boards at Torquay Point. The experience stimulated my desire to do the same.

In February 1959, I made my first visit into Bells. It took 45 minutes from Torquay via the now Great Ocean Road and bush tracks. At the time I had commenced my first year of study in civil engineering. Wednesday afternoons was sport time so in summer we took off for Torquay. I was captivated with Bells. It was quiet, beautiful, no footprints on virgin sands, birds singing and no waves! I knew I'd return.

Fast forward to 1963 graduation and with my first pay packet I purchased a new surfboard and VW. Madeleine and I were free to go surfing. I don't know what prompted me but I thought I'd buy a camera to take photographs of this new venture. I had no photographic skills apart from holding the camera and pressing the shutter. Early results were primitive with my second hand 35mm Practika. I traded it back and opened the doorway to better options – Pentax, Nikon and Minolta. I chose the Minolta SR1 and joined the Geelong Camera Club.

Under the tutelage of the members and competition judges – renowned commercial photographer Ian Hawthorne and Ralph Williams (my former art teacher at Geelong High School) I rapidly developed my photographic skills. Throughout those fabulous 1960s I combined surfing and photography with the Minolta and its lenses – 55mm, 135mm and 400mm. I used Ilford FP3 film, developed it and printed the images on my own enlarger in home laundries at night! Prints were washed in the shower or laundry trough.

In 1966 I purchased a Nikonos underwater camera and began taking photos from the water. I wanted to capture the intensity in the water that

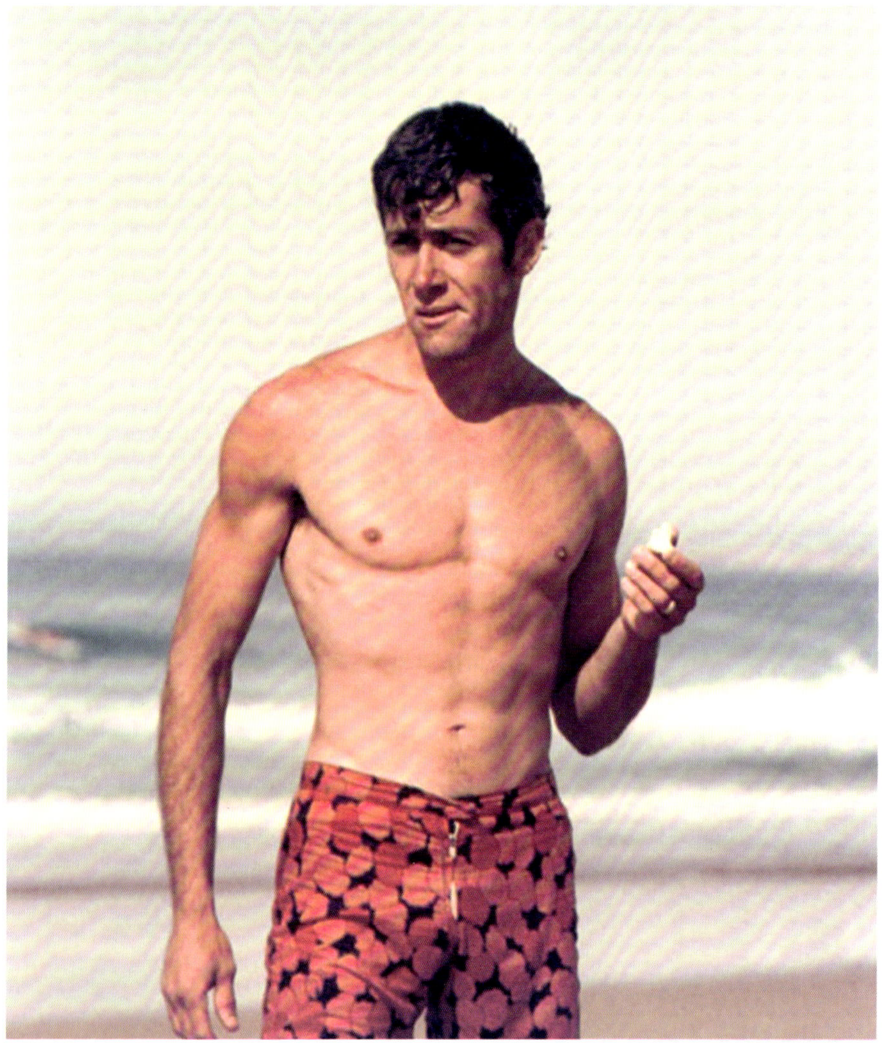

wasn't apparent from the beach. It was a ground-breaking experience, first paddling out on my surfboard, secondly standing in the water ducking under small waves, then swimming out to the breaking zone.

After 30 years in W.A. Madeleine and I returned to Torquay to open Watermarks Photo Gallery which is devoted to my black and white photography. I've been writing my memoirs for many years and this book has provided the first step to showcase my work.

Without Madeleine by my side checking, editing and critiquing my work throughout the years, we wouldn't be where are today with this wonderful collection of photographs and stories. She's a gem!

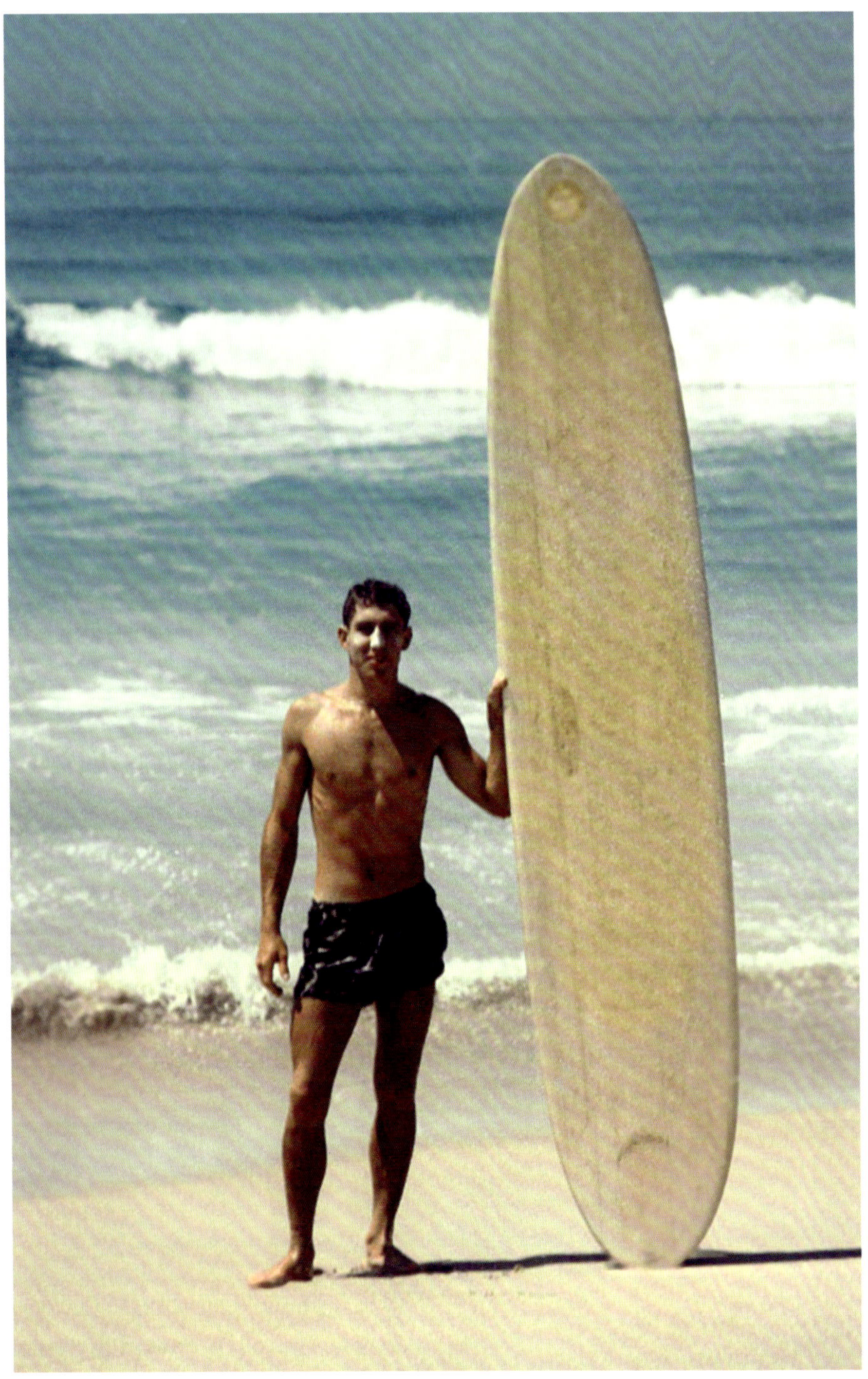

Bob Weeks

Growing up in Sydney and surfing with my mates on the south side, in a time of 'mal' riding and surfing innocence, we all lived for the surf. I still remember my first 'love hit' with surfing. It was in December 1953, and having finished the school year mid-morning I caught a train to Cronulla which was about an hour away. It was a pleasant warm day and I was still in my school clothes. Sitting on the sand and watching the waves, I clearly remember my mind going off on a high. This was the beginning of an addiction that is still imbedded in my psyche today.

After many winter surf safaris up the north coast, we fell in love with the quiet uncrowded beaches and the warm winter waves. The mood changed however, not just with surfing becoming popular, but we were all starting to get married and surfing became 'just for fun' as real life took over. After our first child was born in 1970 it made me consider moving north to a quiet environment to raise a family. We moved to Woolgoolga in 1971 just after our daughter was born seeking the country lifestyle for our family. My son was born in 1973 and I soon had a surfing mate.

I was one of the original members of the Woolgoolga Longboard Club and became the first life member in 1990. I swim the local beach every morning all year round and hop on my board whenever good quality waves are breaking.

Over the years, my 1960s surfing images have been published in many books and magazines. My continuing passion for photography paid off and because of the demand I became a professional photographer in 1989.

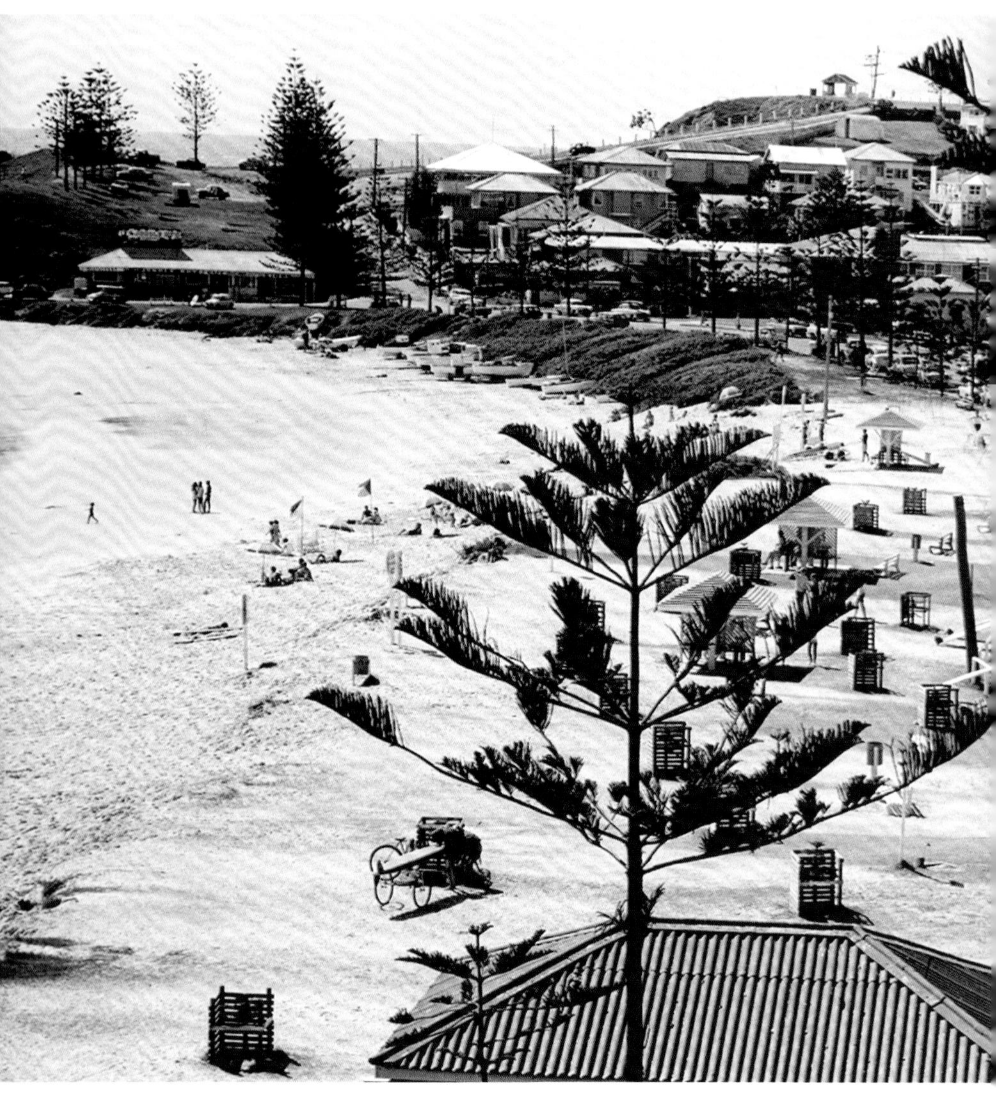

Rainbow Bay, 1965. Rainbow Bay before high-rise units and the Rainbow Bay SLSC. The kiosk shown in the photo has since been demolished.

Old single cylinder diesel fishing boats are lined up at the base of the sandhills and were launched from the beach directly into the surf.

The bicycle trailer for the transport of boards to the left of the roof was probably owned by the Deane brothers. **MS**

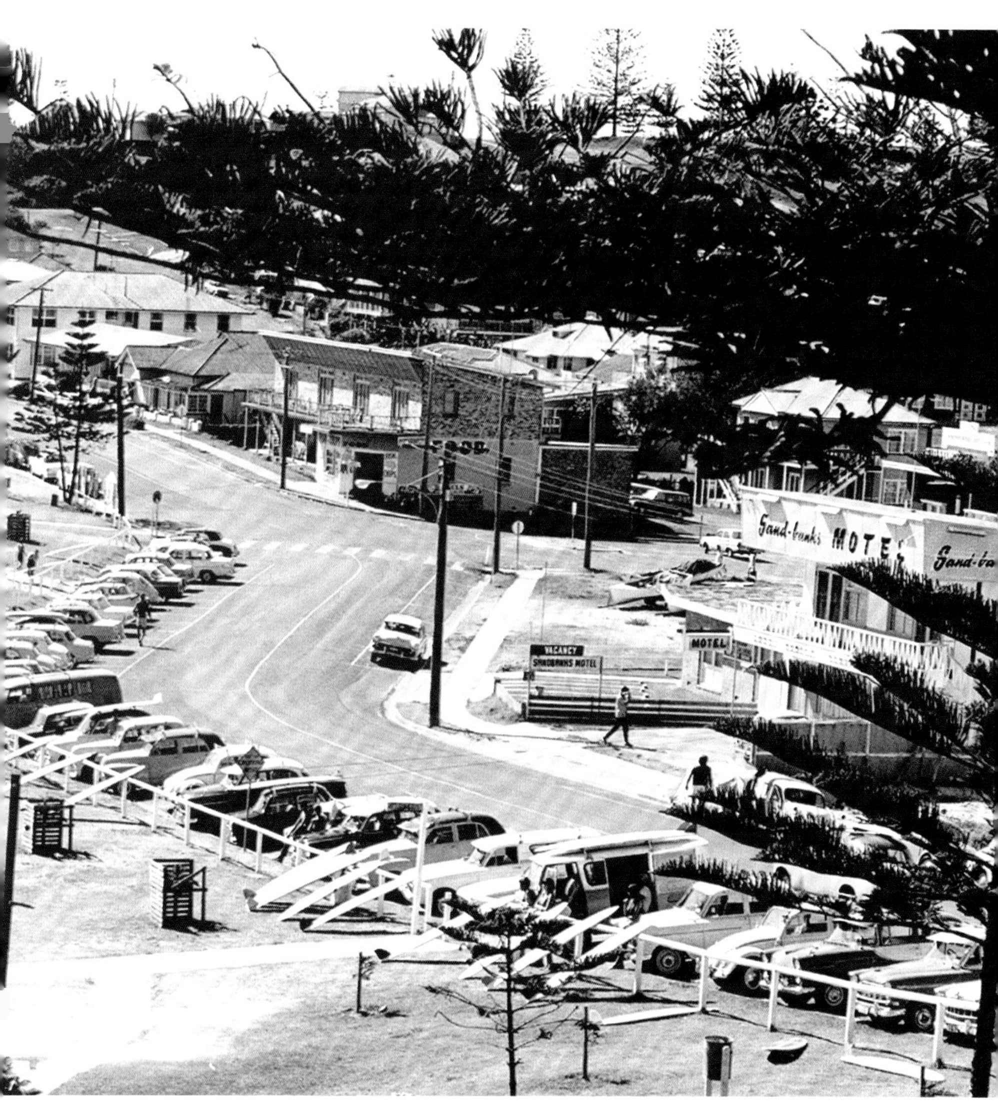

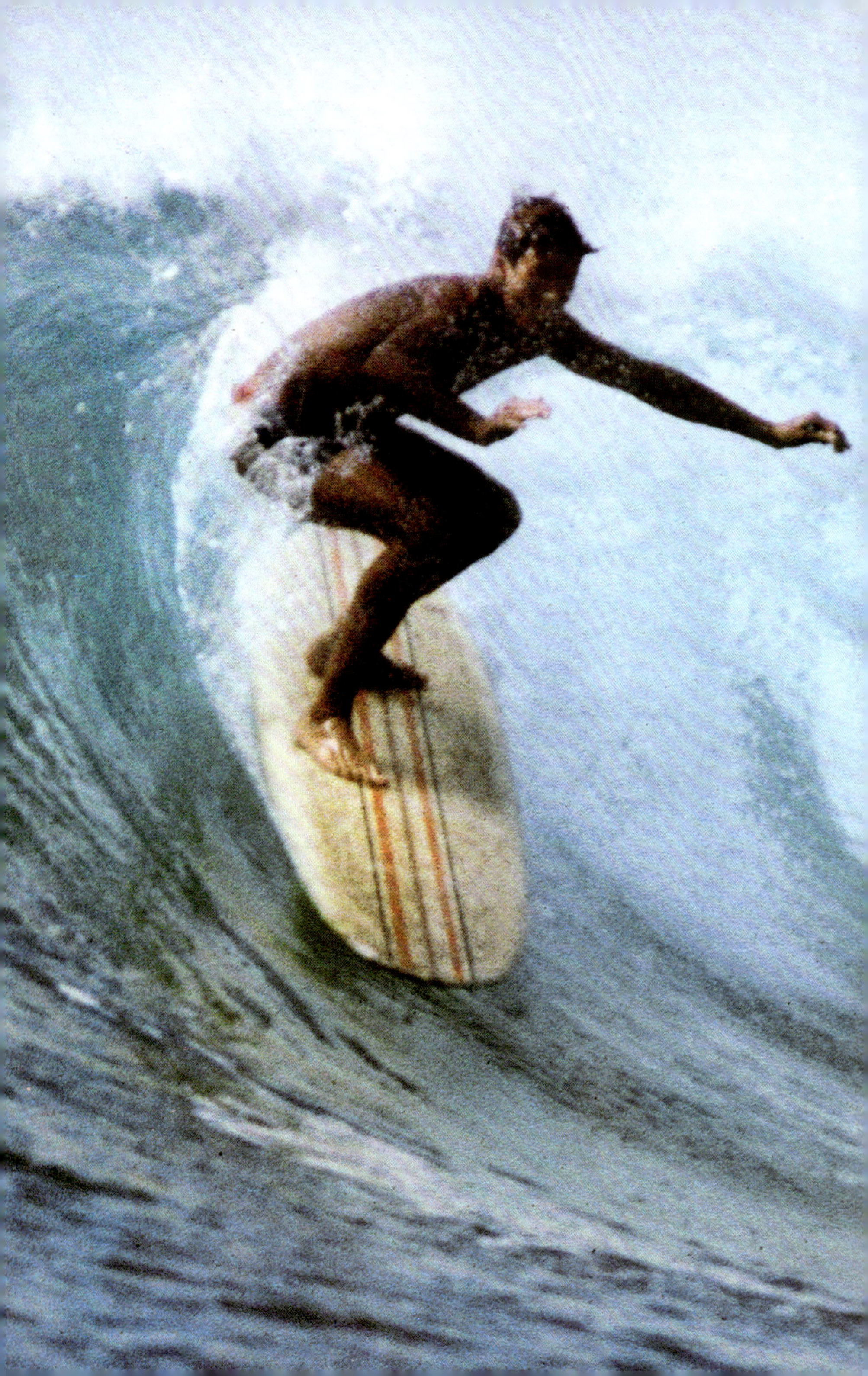

Surfing in the Early 1960s

Since it all began, surfers have been trying to describe and explain 'the feeling'; that intangible joy that surfers feel when riding a wave. Yet to this day, words cannot do the pastime justice. Modern surfing culture has only existed for a relatively short period of time: from surfers with boards that would trim along the face of the wave to ultimately, by 1970, short surfboards that would allow surfers to ride in the womb of the wave – the tube. Within the spectrum of colours that are the five or six decades of modern surfing, there is one decade that will always have a hue all its own, the 1960s.

This book represents a snapshot into the imagery of the time, a time now known as 'the golden era of surfing'. These photographers were paid (a pittance) by the fledgling surfing magazines of the era, either *Surfing World* or *Surfabout*. There were no other magazines and there was not one dedicated surfing magazine in Australia before 1960. There were perhaps a dozen committed surfing photographers (total) in the 1960s, so this book represents a significant portion of the 35mm film shot in Australia through this decade, making *Surfing in the Sixties* an even more valuable record.

Surfing in the 1960s was a counterculture all to itself, attracting some flamboyantly colourful characters who collectively, yet unconsciously, changed the face of modern surfing with their far out surfing style and surfboard innovations. Surfing and surfers were very much on the fringe of society, not interested in a conventional job and the mainstream way of life. The 1960s are often glorified and romanticised, yet, without being sentimental, surfing is part of the folklore. Surfers were a personification of everything that the counterculture was pursuing – freedom, exploration, innovation, change and discovery – all in bare feet and boardshorts!

Cronulla Point, 1964. Unknown surfer. **BW**

These photographers were there and they lived through it, travelling the coast with the best surfers and honing their craft with 35mm film, sadly an artform that barely exists in the digital age. This book spans the decade of the sixties and what is intriguing is that we can basically date a photograph by the

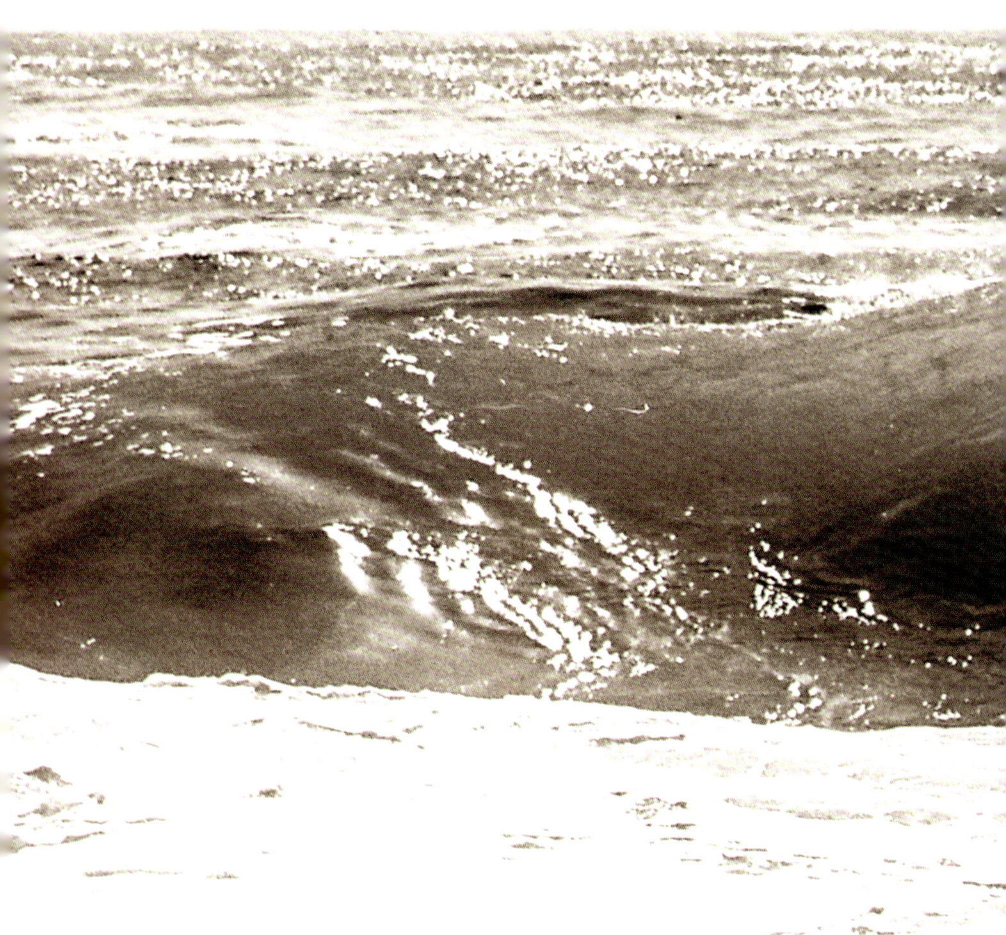

Unknown surfer taking off on a critical section and hopping forward on his longboard. **JP**

surfboard fin, which was revolutionised in 1965 by American surfer/inventor/innovator George Greenough. In the 1960s, 35mm colour film was a serious luxury, so let's take a walk back in time into the world of Australia's early surfing culture, an era that will always have a special place in surfing history.

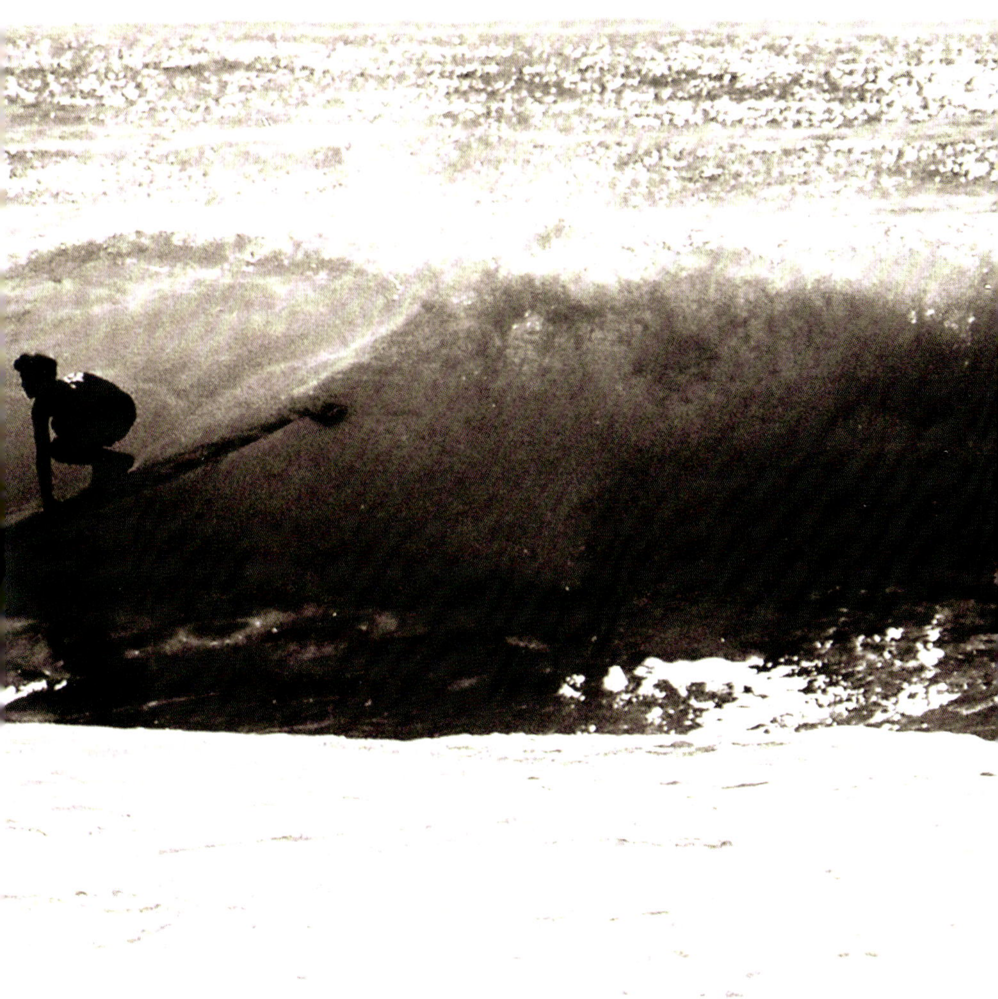

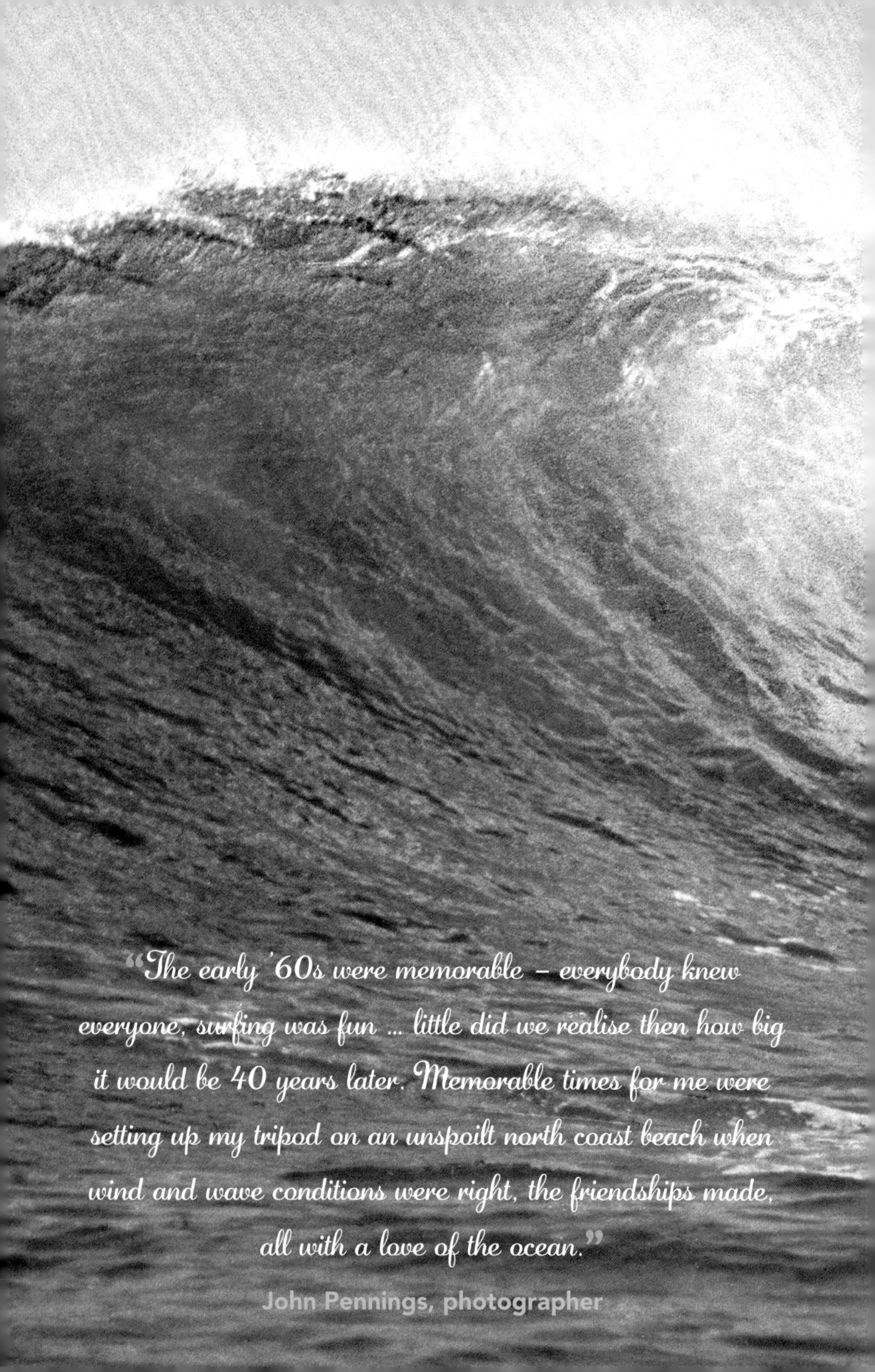

"The early '60s were memorable – everybody knew everyone, surfing was fun ... little did we realise then how big it would be 40 years later. Memorable times for me were setting up my tripod on an unspoilt north coast beach when wind and wave conditions were right, the friendships made, all with a love of the ocean."

John Pennings, photographer

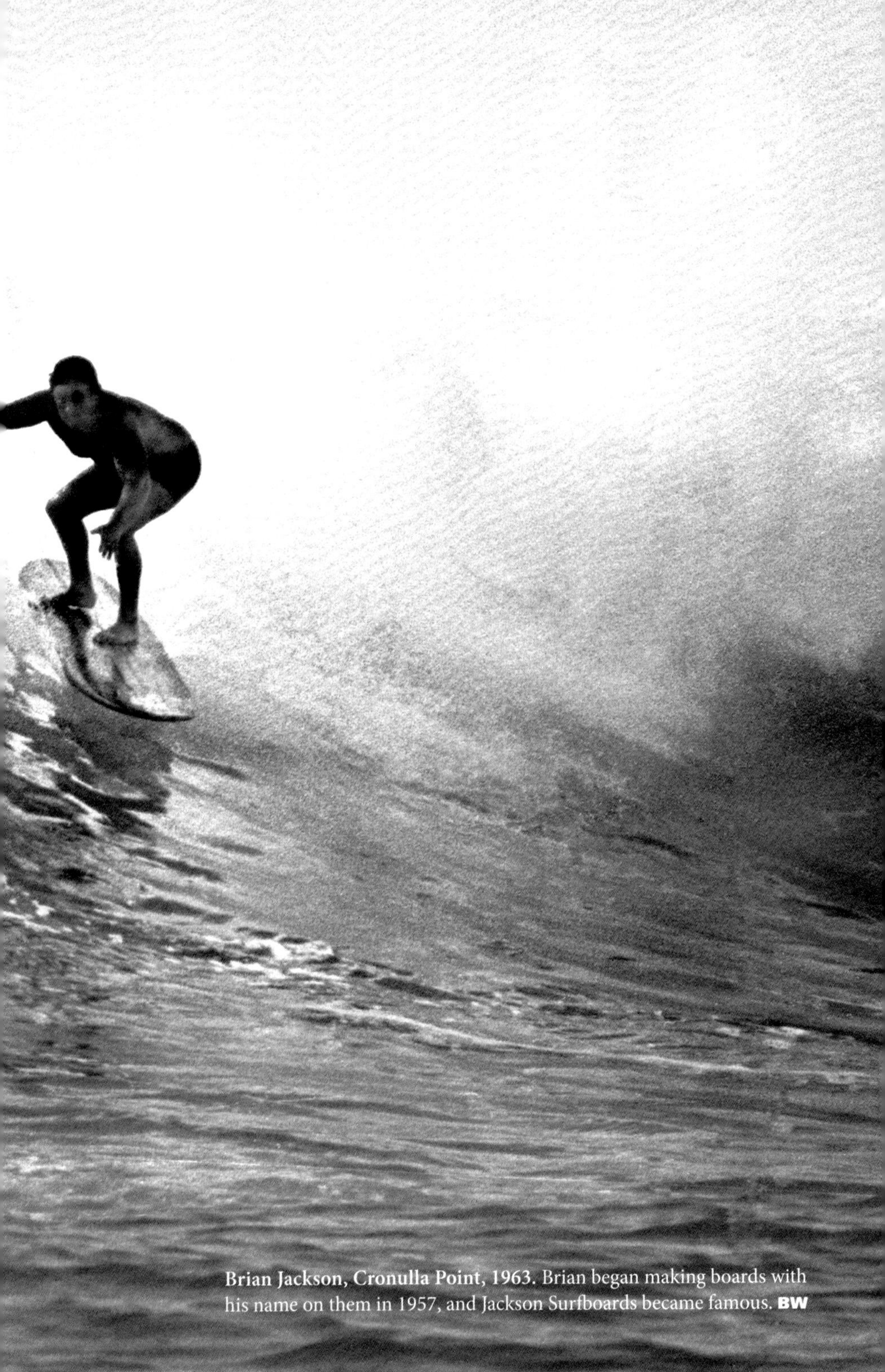

Brian Jackson, Cronulla Point, 1963. Brian began making boards with his name on them in 1957, and Jackson Surfboards became famous. **BW**

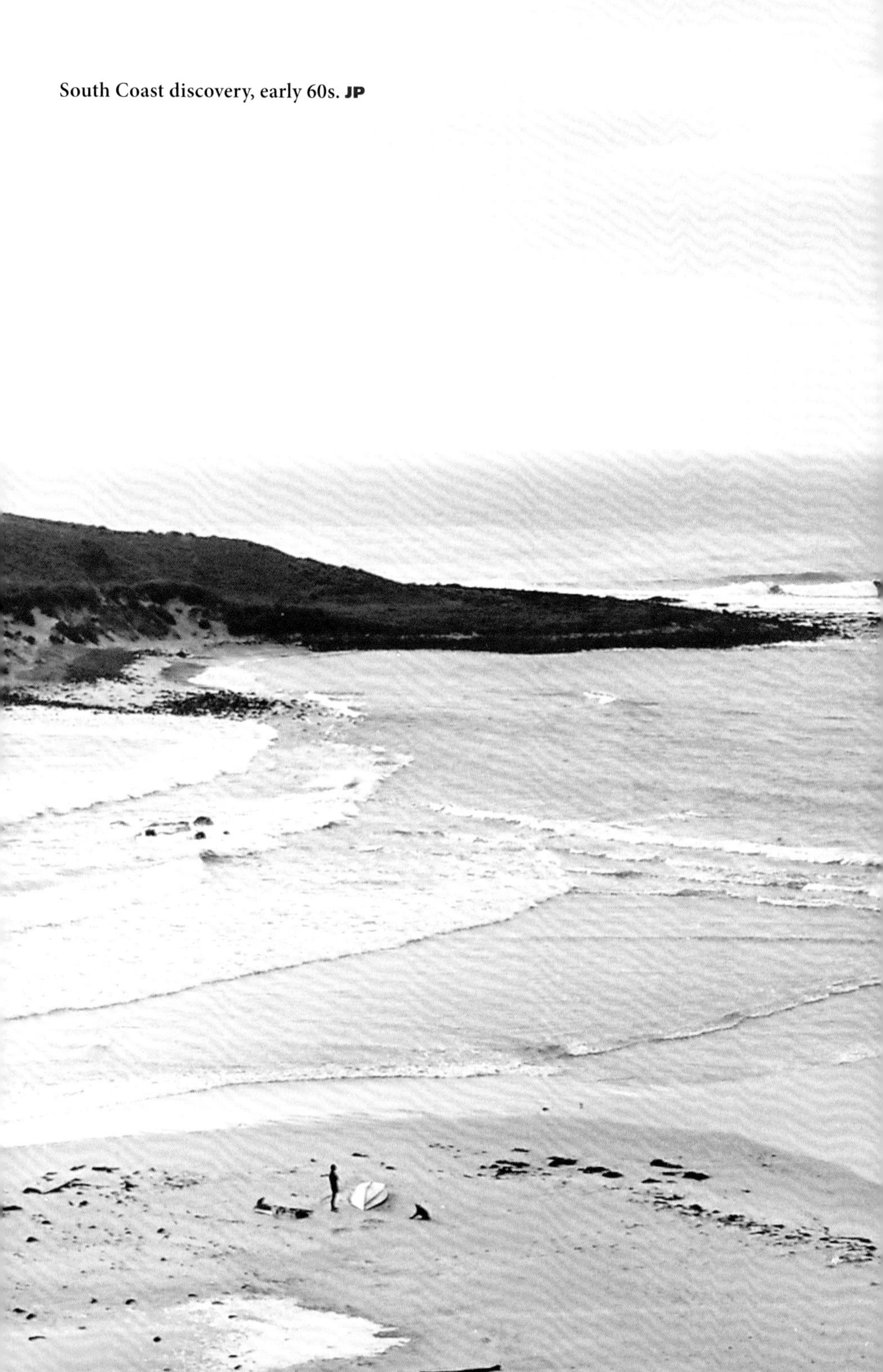

South Coast discovery, early 60s. **JP**

"One of the original attractions with surfing was the voyage of self discovery that it involved. It was worth it and you knew it at the time that it was worth it. Those people who shunned you because you never wore shoes, never shaved and had secondhand clothes and an old car with no stereo ... it was okay because they had what they wanted and you had what you wanted. That was fine with me."

Bob Cooper, US expat, pioneer surfer and surfboard designer

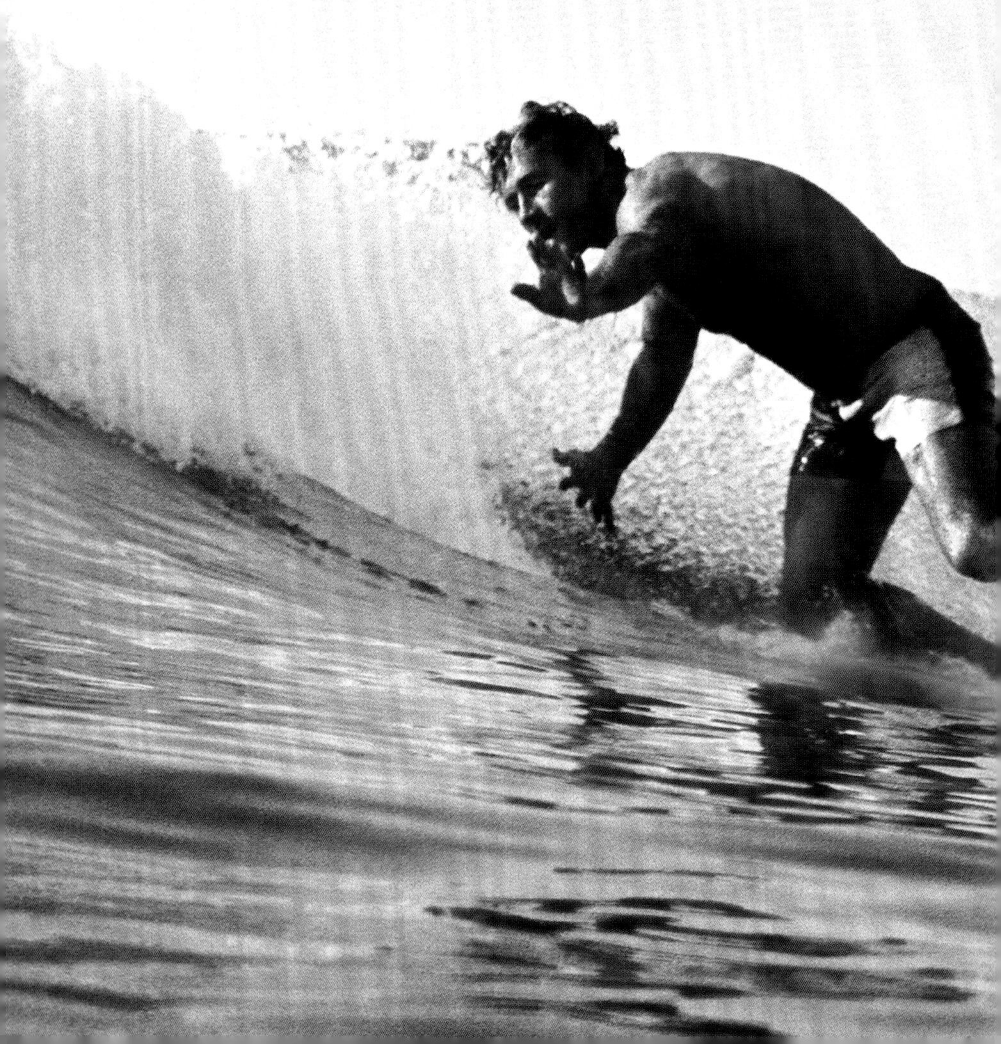

Barry 'Chubby' Kirkham at a surf break near Cronulla Point. Cronulla Point was nicknamed 'Sandshoes' in the early 1960s because many surfers wore the footwear for protection from sea urchins on the sea floor. **BW**

"Back in those days it was all laughs and joy. Craziness in the carparks, painting our cars, putting soap on your mate's board, cutting your fins down in the back of the car on the road so you could turn easier, cutting old boards down that had gone on the rocks a million times, making the boards small enough so we could carry them."

Michael Cundith, pioneering surfboard designer

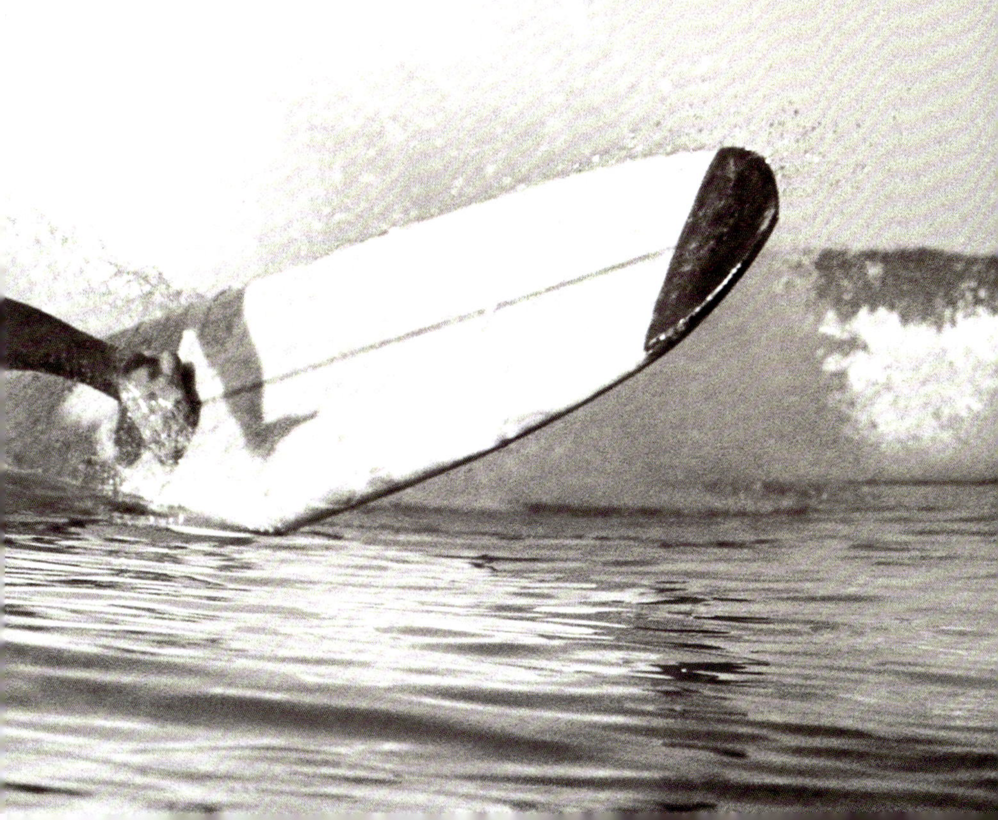

"We just cherished our freedom and made sure we didn't lose it. We saw that the society of the '60s was due to be changed and we were a generation that could achieve it. At least achieve something. It wasn't just surfers, it was the whole mood of the era that had as much to do with the student movement in Paris, the festivals in the US like Woodstock and other movements around the world. It was an era of great change and we understood that, and we relished [it]. In terms of creative endeavours, it was a great time to make movies. We didn't have any money and we didn't have any budgets – we just got out there and did it. There was an attainable freedom and we made sure we attained it. There was a really creative opportunity involved for surfers, filmmakers and musicians. A lot of good stuff has come out of that period and a lot of it has lasted. Many people look back on that era as if it was something special and it was, I think! We were all pioneers in our own way."

Paul Witzig, surfer and filmmaker

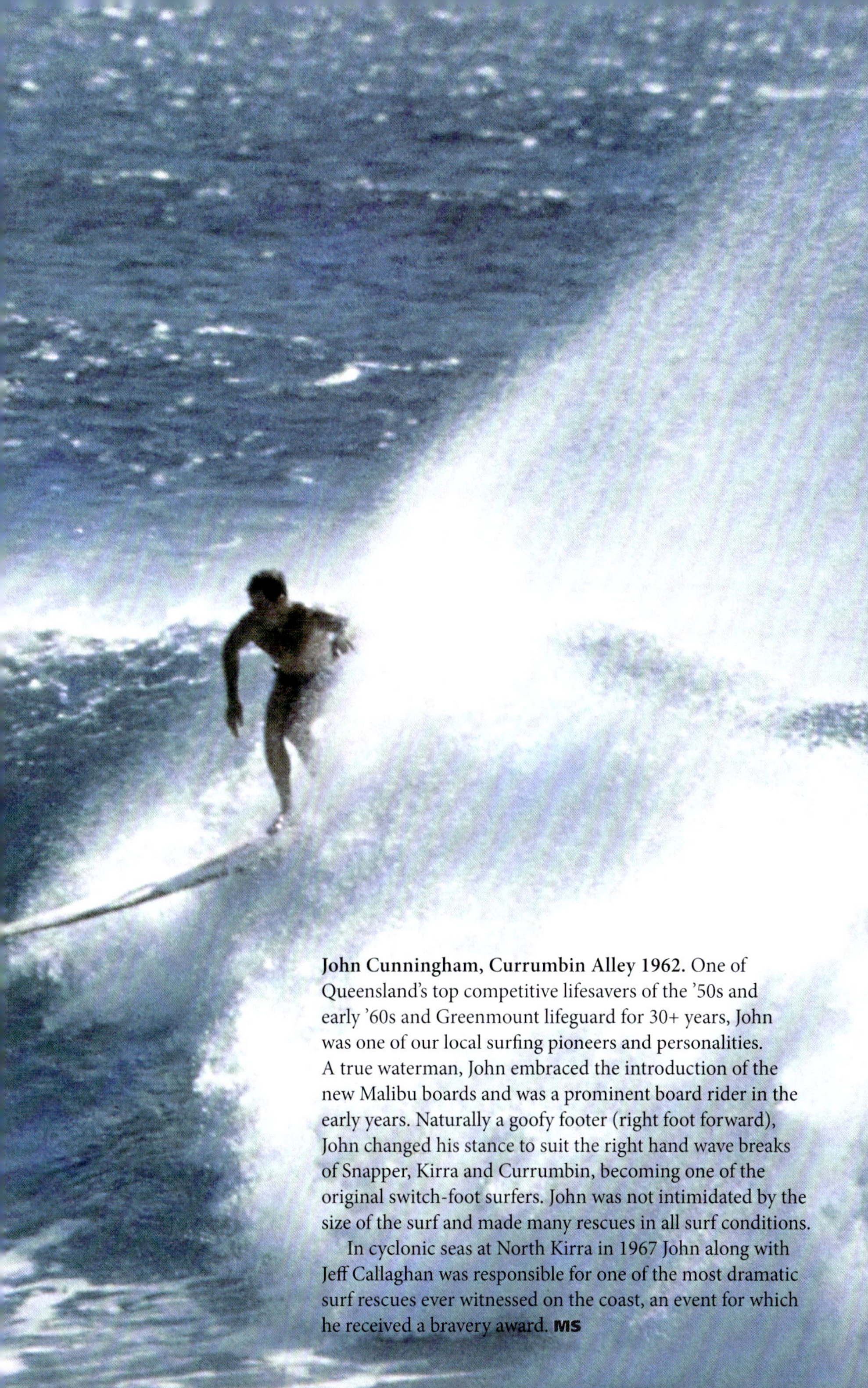

John Cunningham, Currumbin Alley 1962. One of Queensland's top competitive lifesavers of the '50s and early '60s and Greenmount lifeguard for 30+ years, John was one of our local surfing pioneers and personalities. A true waterman, John embraced the introduction of the new Malibu boards and was a prominent board rider in the early years. Naturally a goofy footer (right foot forward), John changed his stance to suit the right hand wave breaks of Snapper, Kirra and Currumbin, becoming one of the original switch-foot surfers. John was not intimidated by the size of the surf and made many rescues in all surf conditions.

In cyclonic seas at North Kirra in 1967 John along with Jeff Callaghan was responsible for one of the most dramatic surf rescues ever witnessed on the coast, an event for which he received a bravery award. **MS**

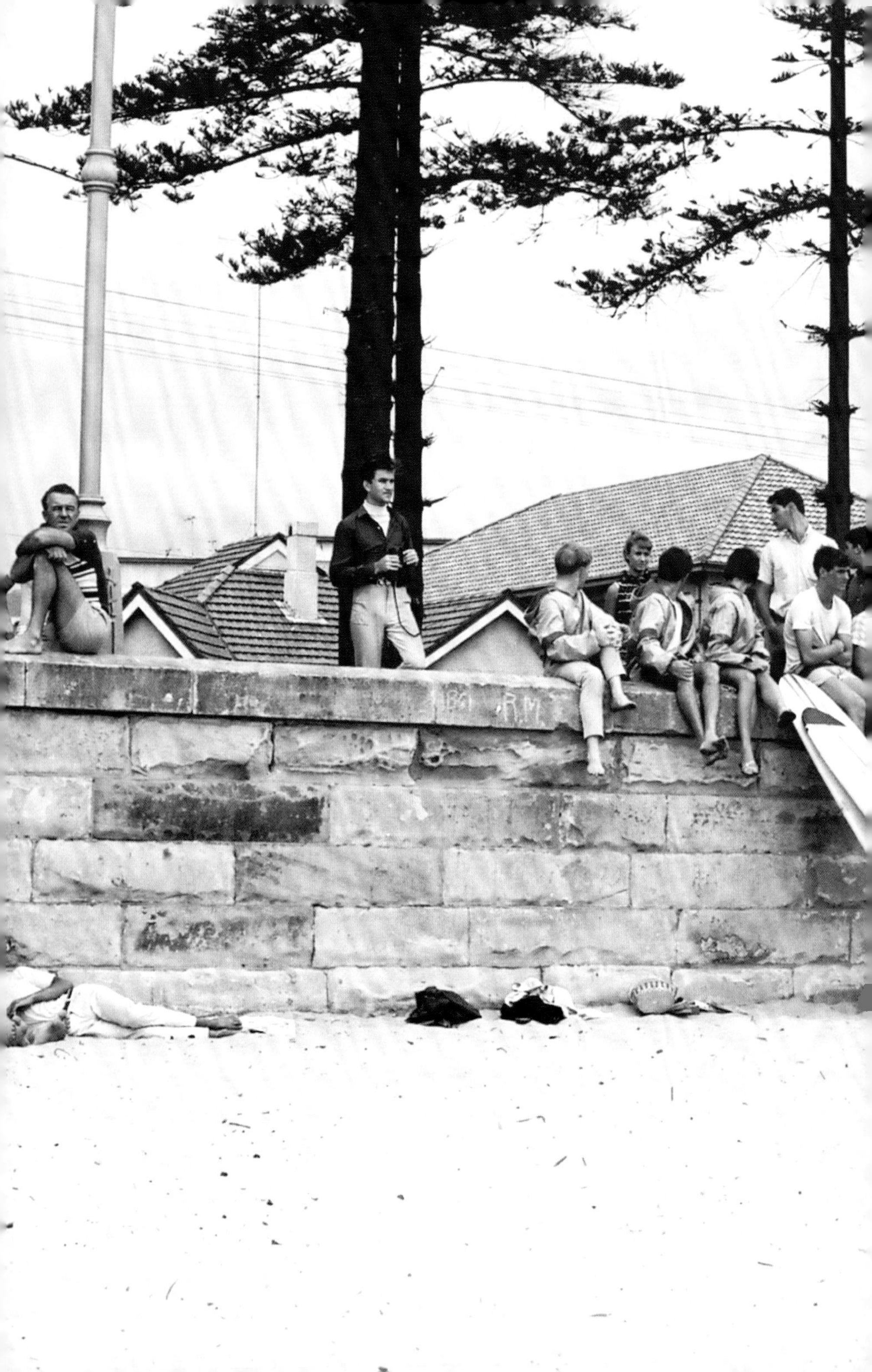

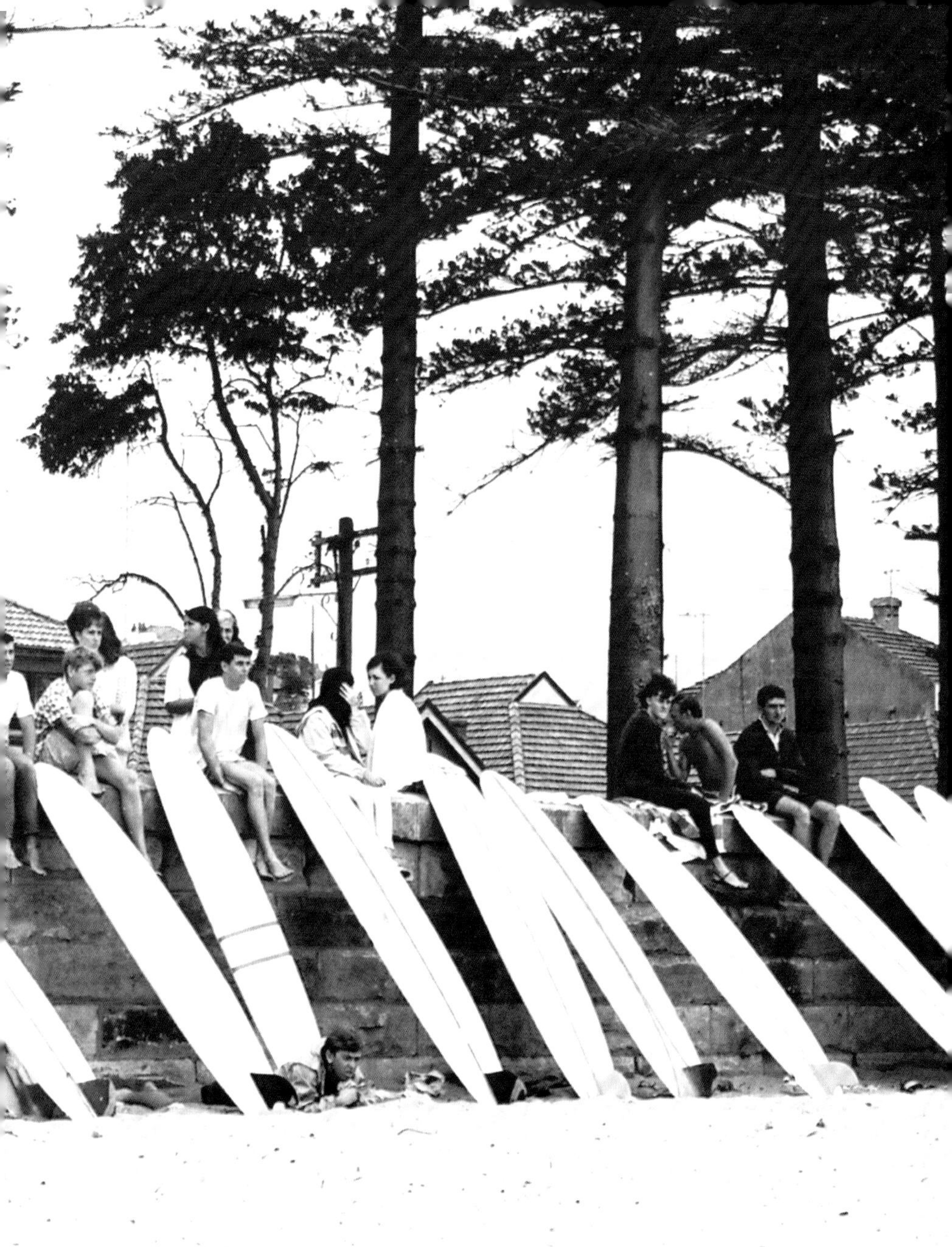

Boards on the sea wall at Manly. Note the long 9'6" boards all have a D-shaped fin. **JP**

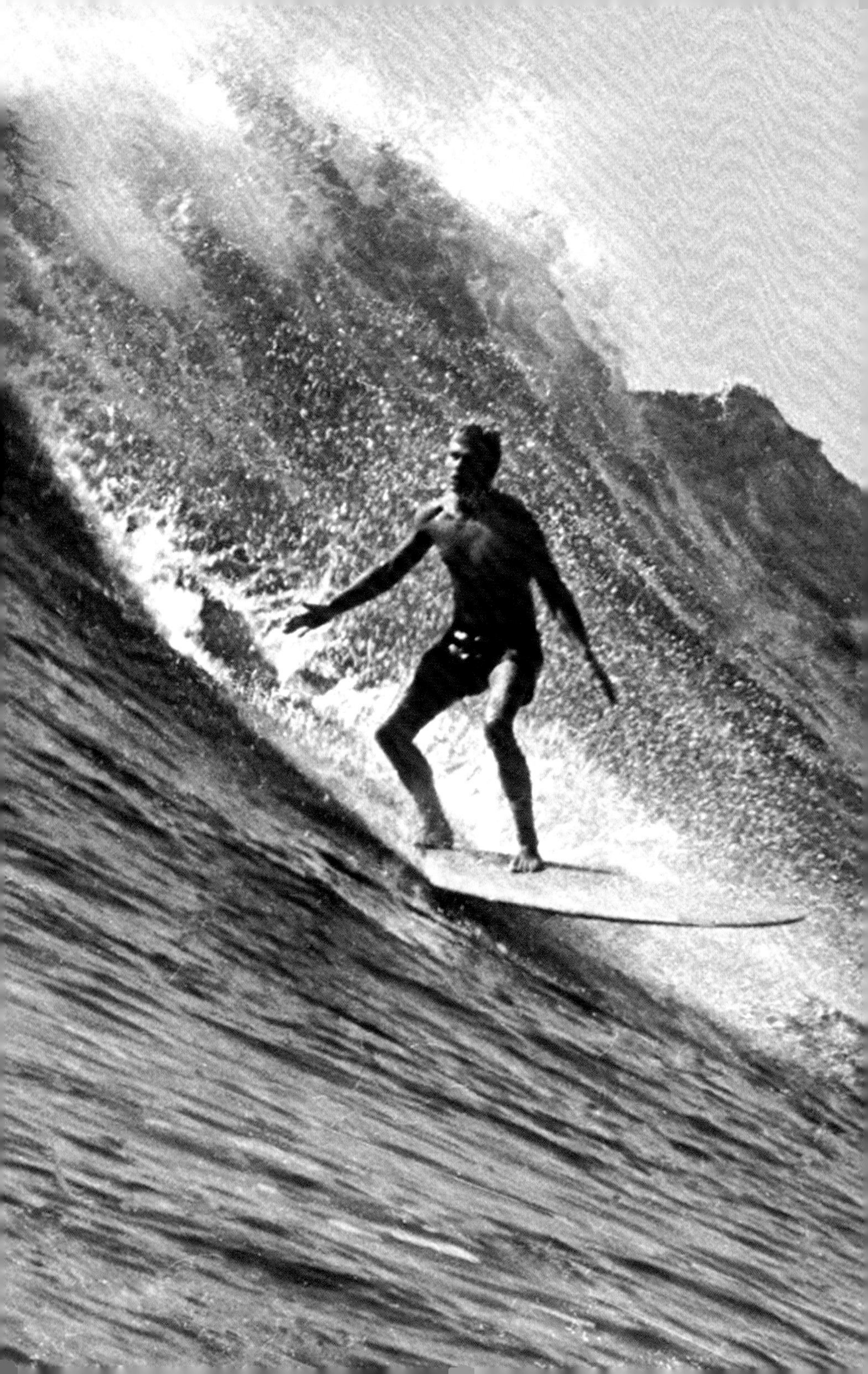

The Malibu Era

The surfers in the 1950s surfed on a board that was 16 foot long, made of timber and colloquially known as a 'toothpick'. With no fins, square rails and averaging between 14 foot to 17 foot in length these boards were hard to manoeuvre and the surfer generally just rode the wave straight to shore. This was to change virtually overnight after the Americans introduced the balsa 'Malibu' board at the International Surf Lifesaving Carnival held in conjunction with the 1956 Melbourne Olympic Games. For those surfers who witnessed the Americans' performance, it was if someone had just turned on the light.

Surfers were demanding this new type of board but because balsa was not available in long lengths in Australia at the time the manufactures constructed hollow ply versions. These 10 foot hollow ply versions became known as 'Okanui' boards and were only made for a short period of time until balsa became available. The introduction of polyurethane foam in the early 1960s changed board construction forever and today foam and fibreglass is still the preferred method of construction. By 1962 most surfers had abandoned balsa and timber in favour of foam.

The 'Okanui' was replaced by the 'Malibu' (or 'Mal' for short) and to this day most Australians refer to their longer surfboard as a 'Malibu', whereas the Americans simply call them a longboard. A 'Malibu' was a foam/fibreglass laminate with a redwood stringer, 9 ft to 10 ft 6" in length. Extra features included multiple stringers, tail blocks and pigment colours. Fins were either fibreglassed, timber or solid fibreglass. Common fin shapes were the 'Standard D', 'Square' or 'Reverse D', but all this was soon to change, yet again. The surfboard design was in a state of rapid innovation. In the early 1960s surfing really took off in Australia, the demand for surfboards and equipment spiked and this trend continued for the next ten years. With more and more surfers entering the water, most of them learning how to surf on a 10-foot long cumbersome longboard, things started to get dangerous at the popular beaches.

In Sydney, seaside councils introduced a registration policy where surfboard riders had to pay an annual subscription fee to license their longboard, complete with a registration sticker and zoning, the sticker placed 12 inches from the nose of the board. Surf club members were exempt from the fee. The authorities had the power to confiscate surfboards and they started to isolate 'problem surfers', the 'authority at the beach' no doubt escalate the tensions of the burgeoning youth movement who, by the late '60s, had finally found their voice.

Terry Steen, Cronulla Point, 1962. **BW**

and the process was quite a risky operation needing government regulation and safety standards. Of course the surfers avoided these sorts of formalities right through those fledgling days of trying to work out the way the process should be done. By 1962, with foam blanks becoming the industry norm, and timber construction in the rear view mirror, surfing was experiencing a boom and everyone wanted a shorter 9-foot 6-inch foam surfboard. Mainstream manufacturing entered and competed with the cottage industry. Surfers could go to high street sports stores and get a foam surfboard off the rack from brands such as Ron Surfboards and Pacific Star, by sporting giant Dunlop.

Hayden Kenny established himself with Hayden surfboards (1962) on the Sunshine Coast (Alexandra Headlands) and attracted some of the best surfers and shapers to work for him, names like Bob McTavish, Kevin Platt, George Greenough and Bob Cooper were all lurking around the factory in the early days. His factory and showroom hold some of the vital surfboard innovations of this period. Kenny was quite alone up on the Sunshine Coast in Queensland in the early '60s, until Cord Surfboards was established in Caloundra in 1965.

There was plenty of action happening on the Gold Coast with Sydney's Joe Larkin moving north and establishing the iconic Larkin Surfboards at Kirra. In 1963, Laurie Hohensee became an institution at Mermaid Beach with his Safari Surfboards label, teaching many of the young kids, including Michael Peterson, how to shape a surfboard. Graeme Merrin (1964) opened in Tweed Heads, Bob Clapp was set up in Surfers Paradise by 1962 and Mick Carey set up in Currumbin in 1965. Up the road Ray Woosley and Ken Adler operated successfully out of Brisbane from 1962 and 1964, with Ken Adler later setting up the San Juan label in the then sleepy whaling town of Byron Bay in the late 1960s.

The Victorian surfboard makers were definitely out on their own, the tyranny of distance providing them with a history all of their own. One cannot make a surfing book that references the 1960s and surfboard making without the inclusion of Vic Tantau, George Rice, Fred Pyke, Klemm Bell, John Saffron, Max Gill, The Young Brothers [Bill and Bob], Peter Davies and Pat Morgan.

If the Victorian history is often under-exposed, the history of surfing in South Australia and Western Australia are firmly in the shade; but the names Jay Bee, Don Burford, John Arnold, Peter Crofton, Greg Frost, Wayne Dale, Gregg Webb and others do live on in the folklore of South Australian surfing and Cordingley Bros Surfboards, Hawke Surfboards and Len Dibben Surfboards are notable pioneers from Western Australia.

The big name in surfboard building in Australia in the 1960s is Barry Bennett (born 1932). Barry, a Brookvale institution, became the hub and the driving force behind the industry through the 1960s and he still is to this day. With the inception of foam blank surfboards replacing timber, Barry Bennett placed himself well to supply the blanks to surfboard manufacturers all over Australia, he had a virtual monopoly on the industry. This was a giant change

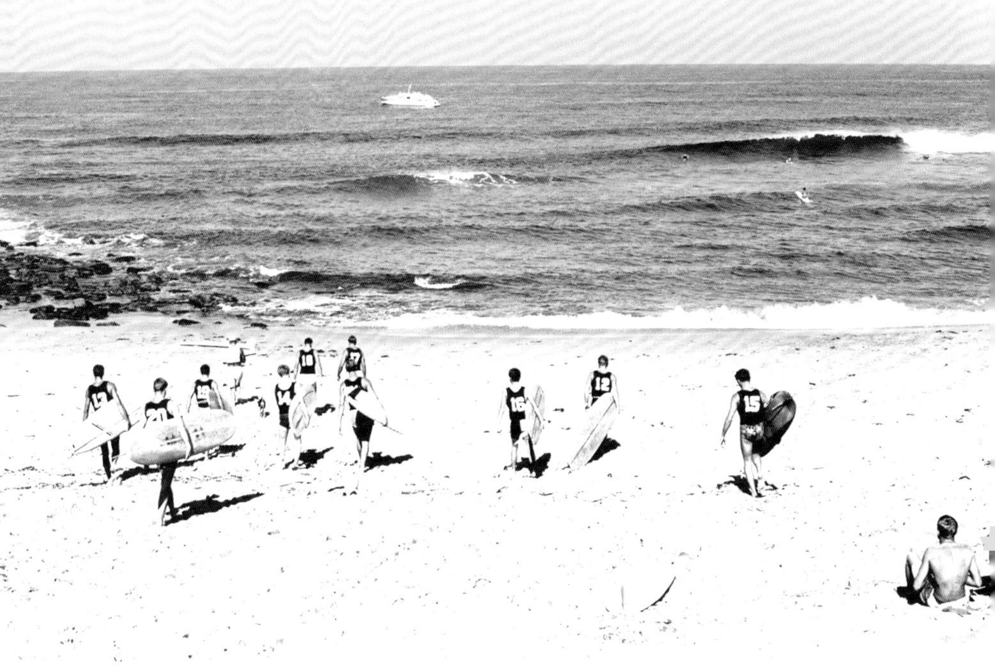

North Avalon, 1963. Competitors prepare for a heat at the Interstate Surf Meet. **BW**

The most notable surfboard shapers of the early '60s, the surfers who put
Australian surfboard manufacturing on the map, were Gordon Woods (now
90 years old at the time of writing), Bill Wallace (89), Scott Dillon (89) and Joe
Larkin (85) and it all occurred in Sydney. These four gents started out in the
1950s making 16-foot longboards (toothpicks) and paddleboards from plywood
in a backdrop that can only be described as a back-yard cottage industry. They
then ventured into balsa wood construction and the iconic 'Okanui' board,
complete with a fiberglass coating. These early surfboard building pioneers
then explored fin dynamics, foam blank mouldings and later… the shortboard.
They saw every step of the longboards' evolution; from a 16-foot plywood
construction that used to hang up in surf clubs via a metal hook attached to the
surfboard, to the modern professional surfer who has 64 wafer-thin foam board
replicas (all under 6 feet in length) delivered to their rented apartment at every
world contest stop. How surfboard design has changed through the decades!
Other prominent names from Sydney and NSW in this era are Sam Egan, Garry
Birdsall, Bill Clymer, Danny Keyo, Graham Ferris, Brian Jackson, Norm Casey,
Wally Carle, Mick Dooley, Shane Stedman and Roger 'Duck' Keiran. Australian
surfing owes them all a debt of gratitude.

Denny Keogh and Greg McDonagh put some serious bricks in the wall
for the *foam manufacturing* in Australia and one could write a book about
their exploits, experiments, failures and successes while investigating foam
production. In fact, 'blowing blanks', the manufacture of foam, the chemicals

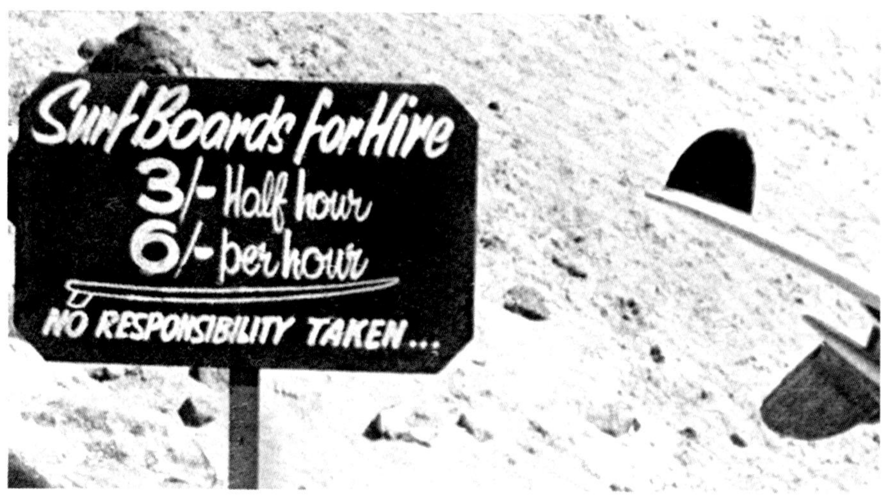

for the industry and his brand called Dion Chemicals became the go-to place for all surfboard makers to get their blanks, much like Hobie Alter and Grubby Clark had established in America.

A Good Samaritan for the industry, Barry didn't use his monopoly-like position solely for financial gain, rather he helped many a fledgling shaper stay in business. Winter is always a quiet time for everyone in the surfing industry and in those early days many a surfboard shaper would have closed its doors if it were not for Barry Bennett allowing them 6–12 months' gratis on their stock supply. Legend indeed.

Midget Farrelly (1944–2016) led the way for famous and world-class surfers who made their surfboards. He set up his own shaping bay and showroom in Sydney, a brand all to himself. Farrelly Surfboards was born with an ethos of quality at the core of the business model and it still exists today. Midget, who died in 2016, inspired many other surfers to follow his lead, most notably Ken Adler who, after seeing Midget's surfboard building business in Sydney, took the brave step to open his own showroom in the quiet town of Byron Bay. Adler opened San Juan Surfboards in the late 1960s and it quickly became a melting pot of design innovation, attracting the world's best surfers to visit, surf and shape surfboards.

Above: **Board hire sign, Red House, 1963. BW**

Opposite: **Frank Latta, Cronulla, 1963. BW**

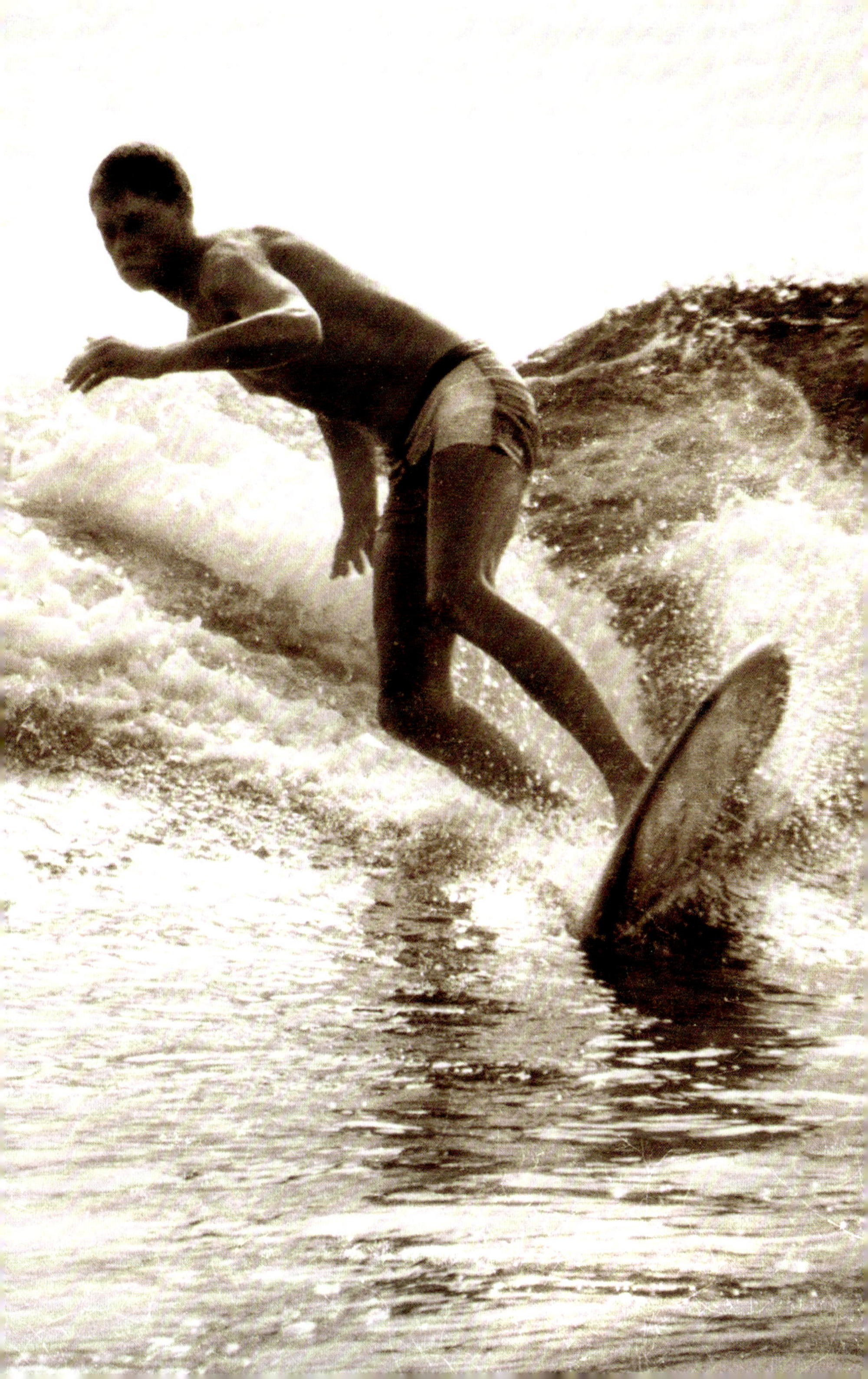

Coolangatta, 1966 Australian Titles. Everyone that was there still talks about a young Peter Droyn who won the junior division. If he had surfed the seniors, he would have won it too. A pivotal moment in the changing styles of Australian surfers. **JP**

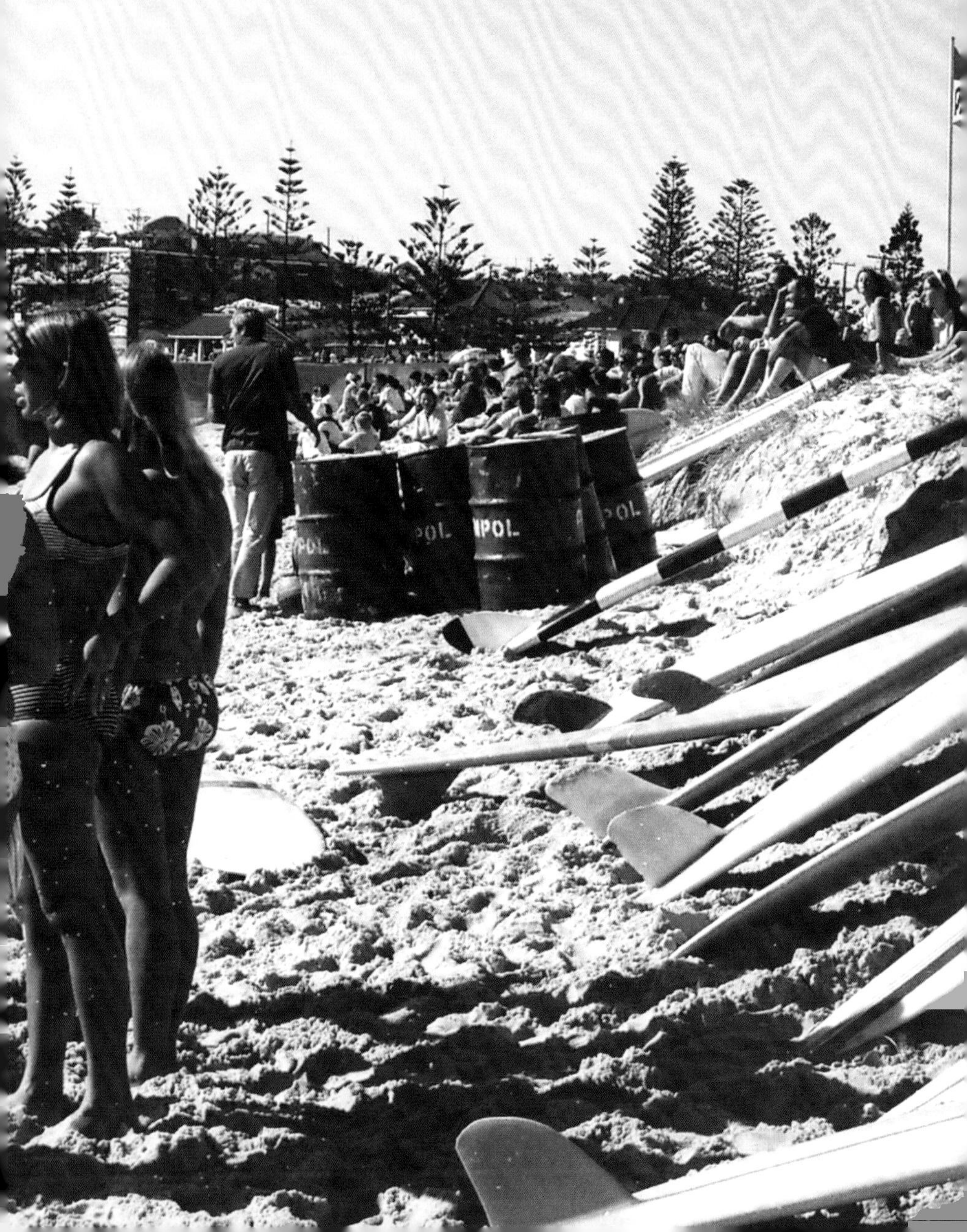

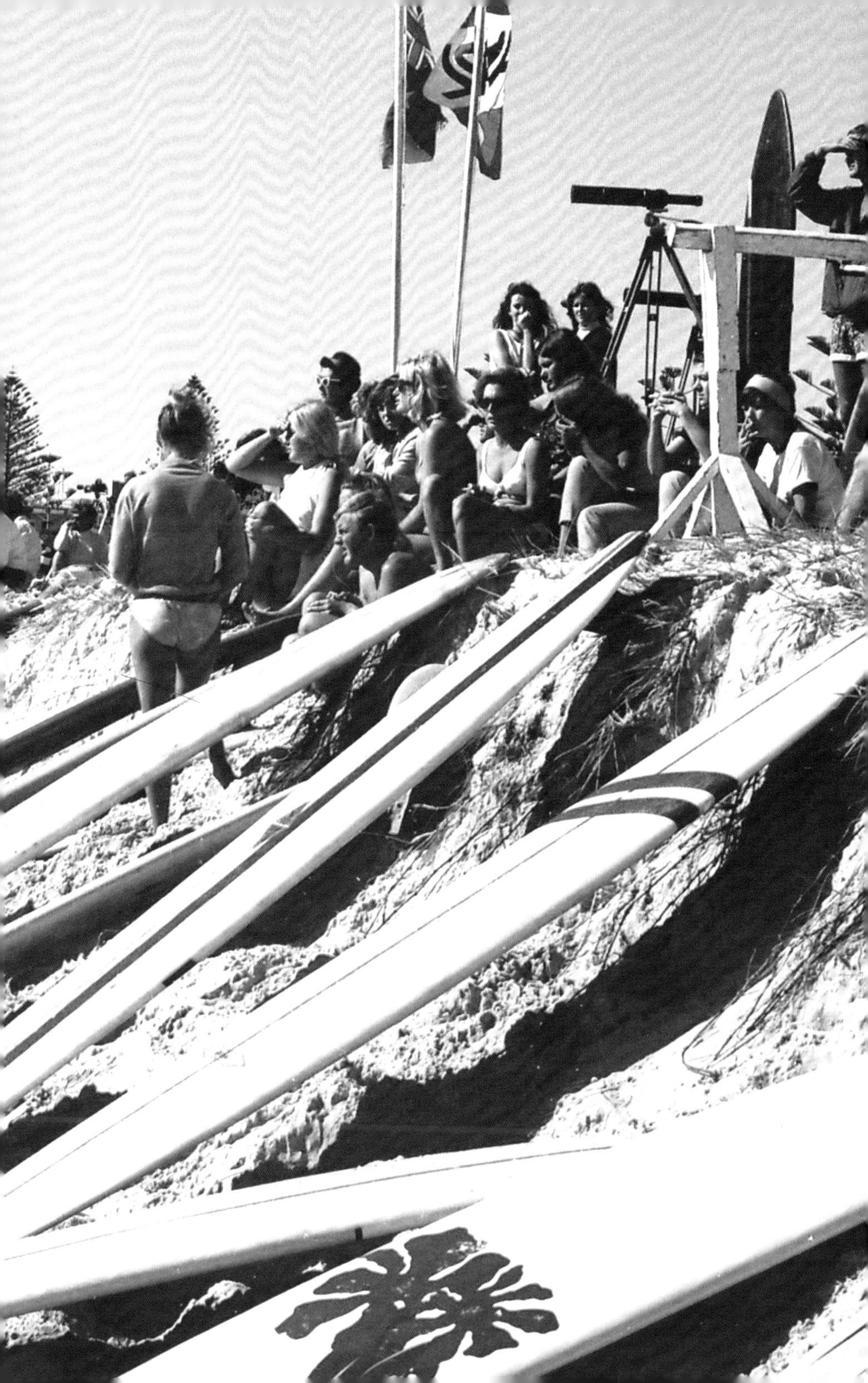

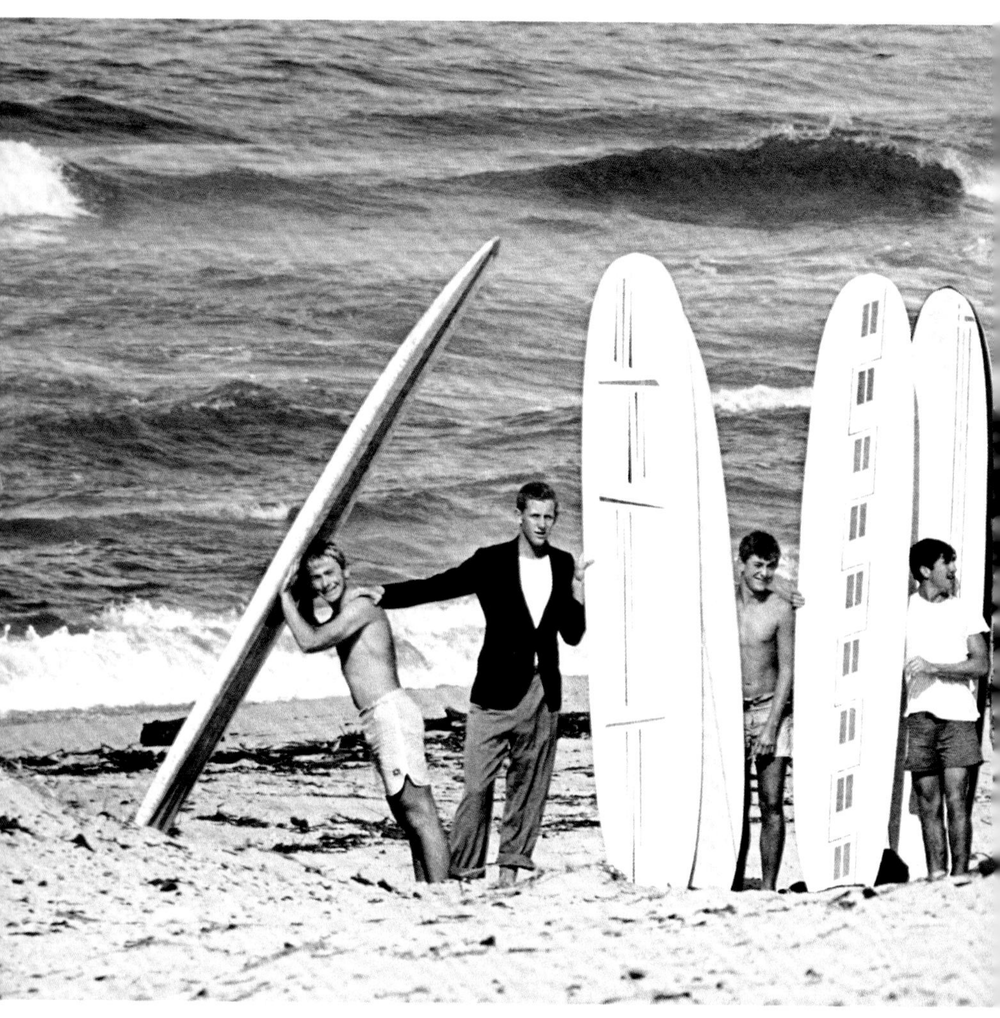

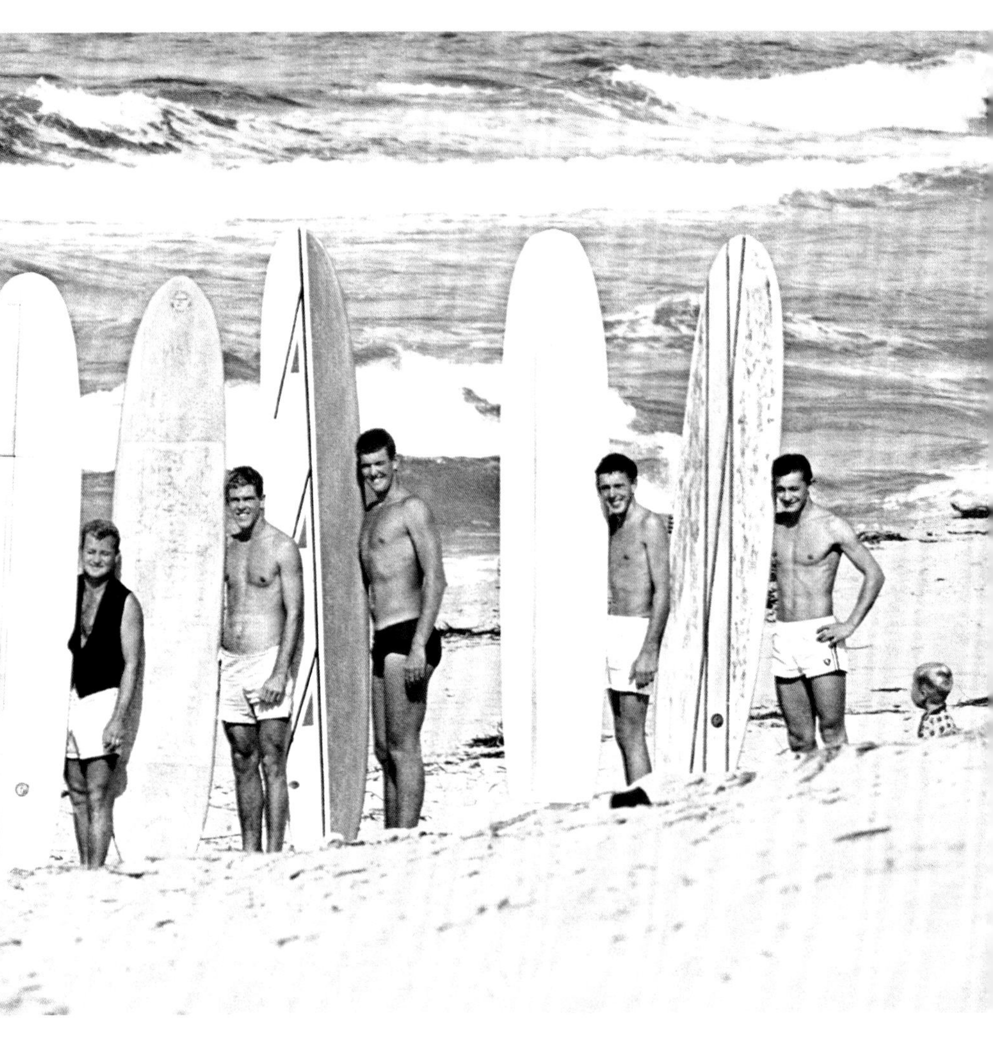

The 'Midway Crew' in 1962. Midway was very isolated in those days and we often had the waves to ourselves. The break is between North Cronulla and Wanda and is now the site of the Elouera Surf Club. **BW**

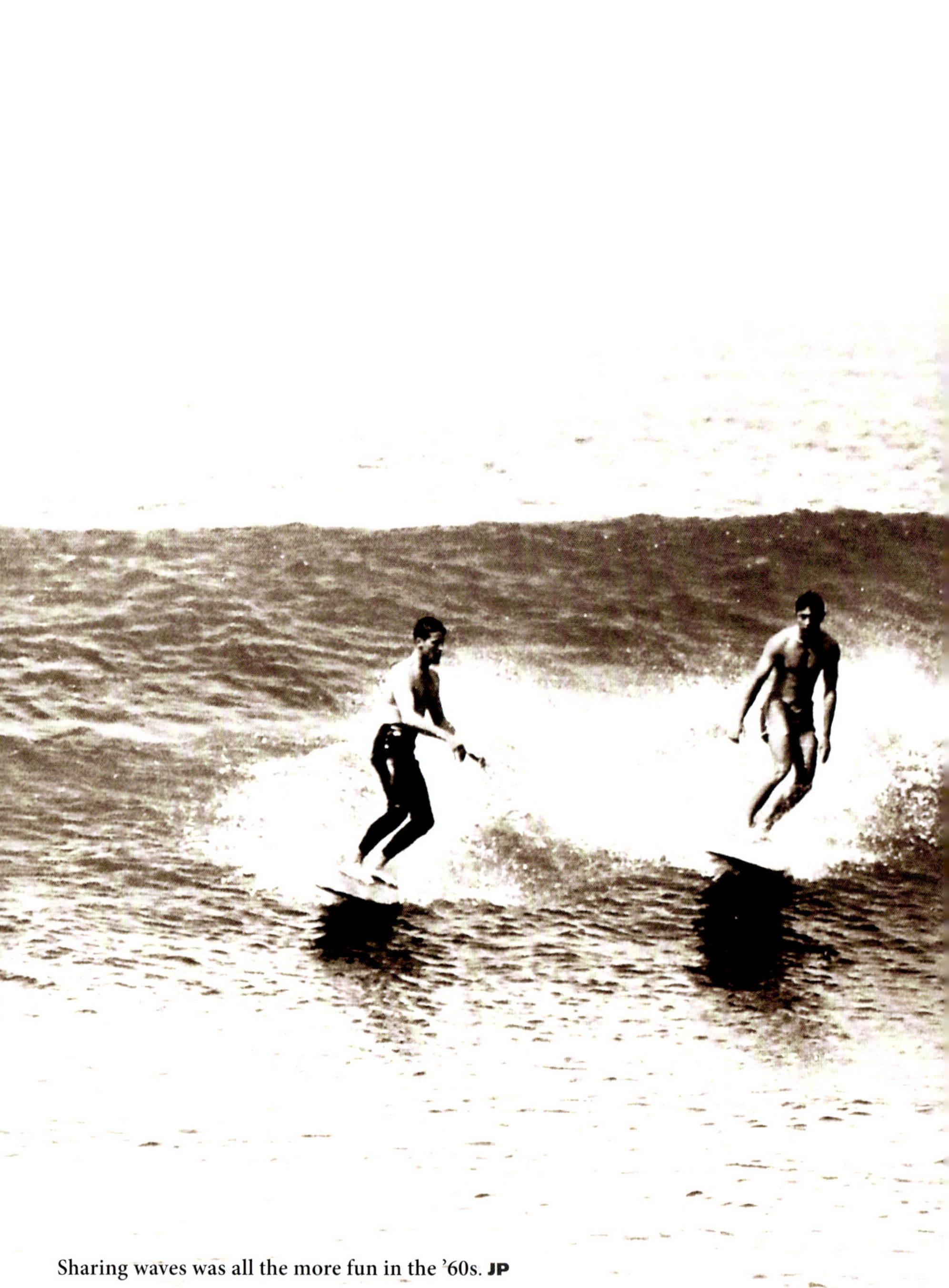
Sharing waves was all the more fun in the '60s. **JP**

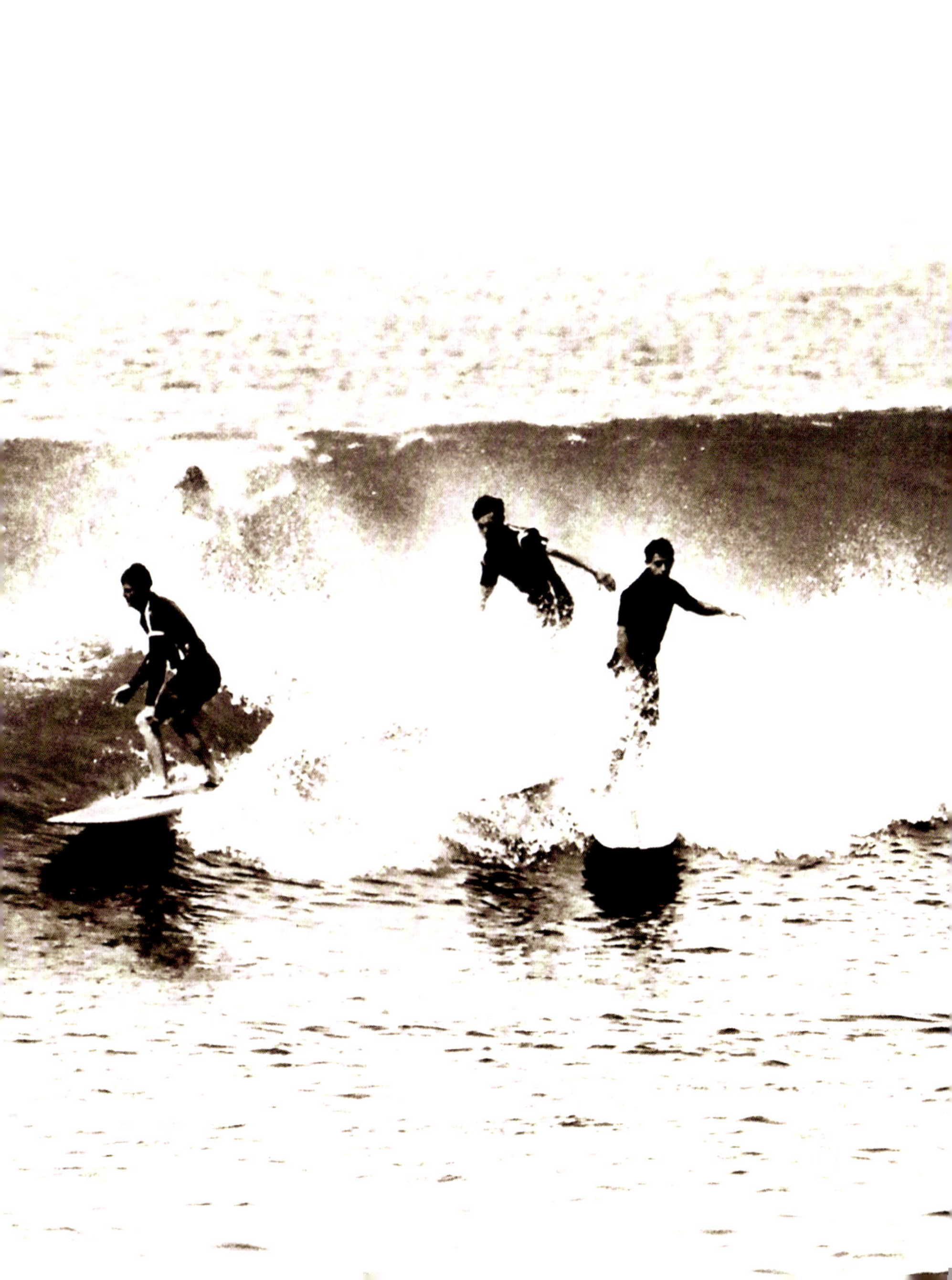

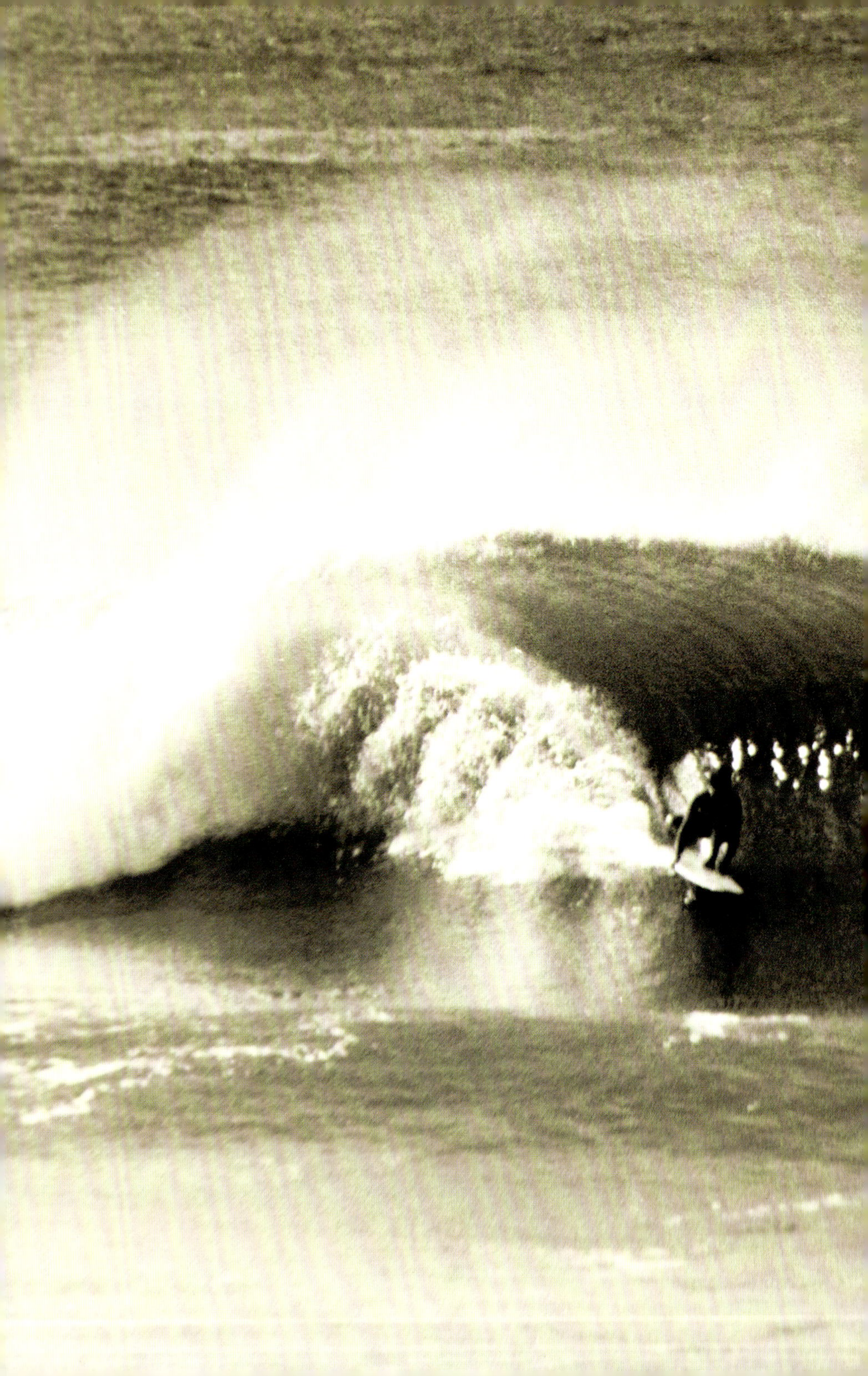

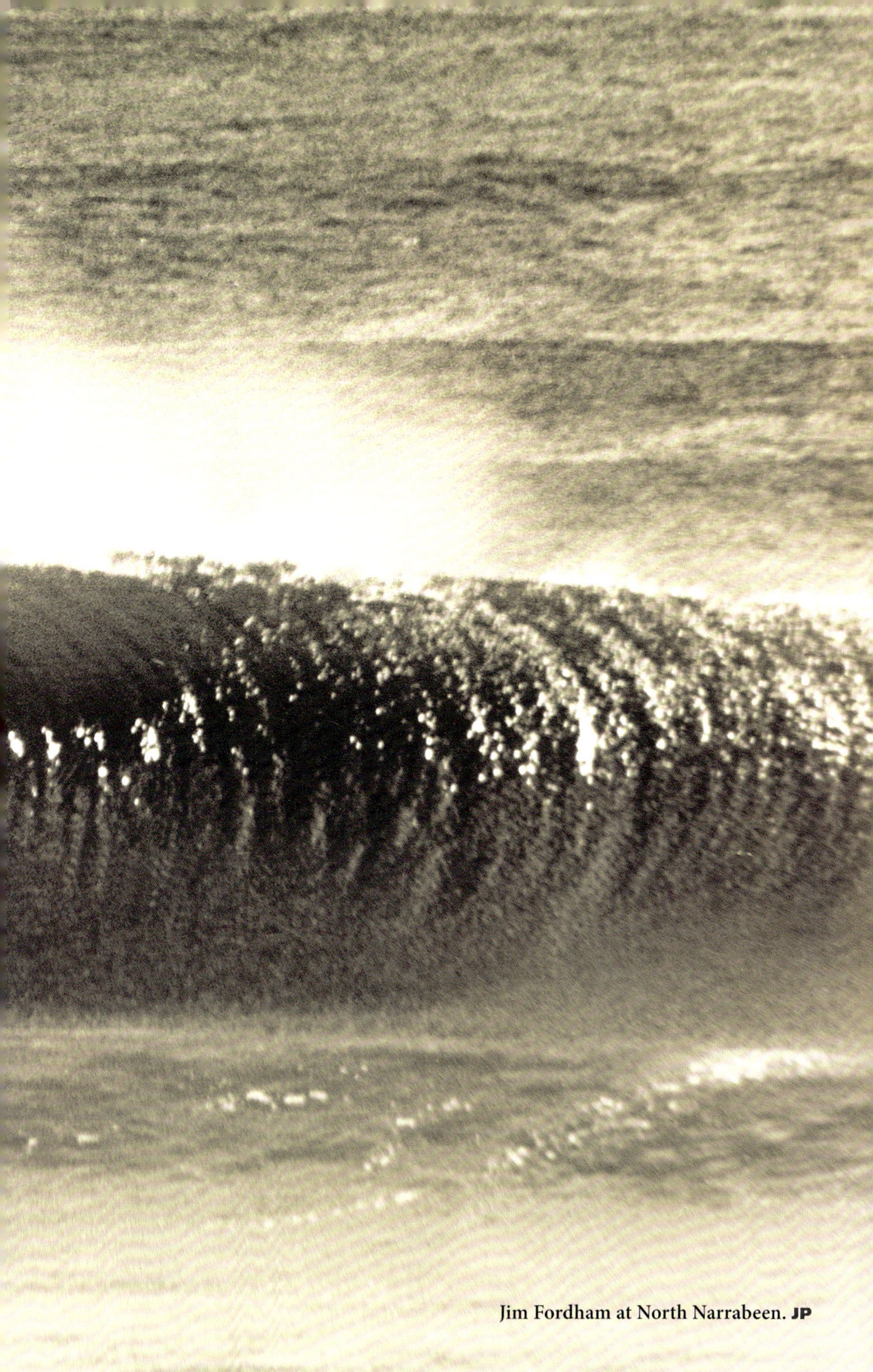

Jim Fordham at North Narrabeen. **JP**

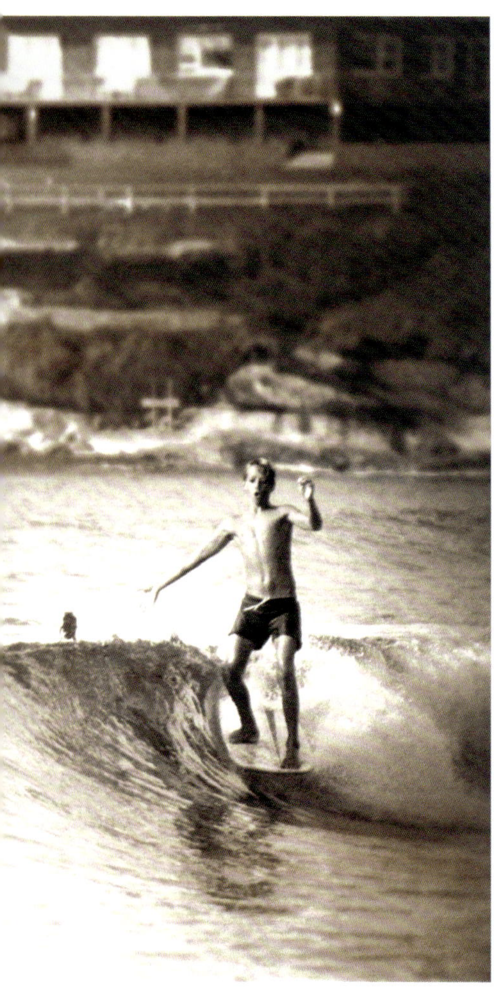

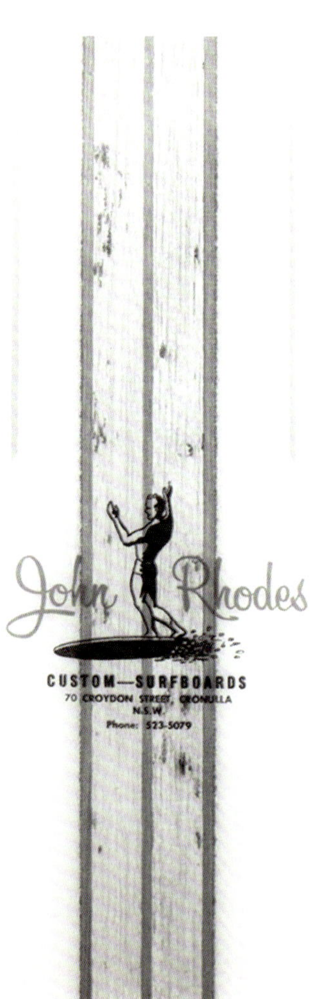

Left: **Bobby Brown 'hangin' five' at the Alley, Cronulla, 1962. BW**

Right: **John Rhodes classic, early Sixties design, 1963. BW**

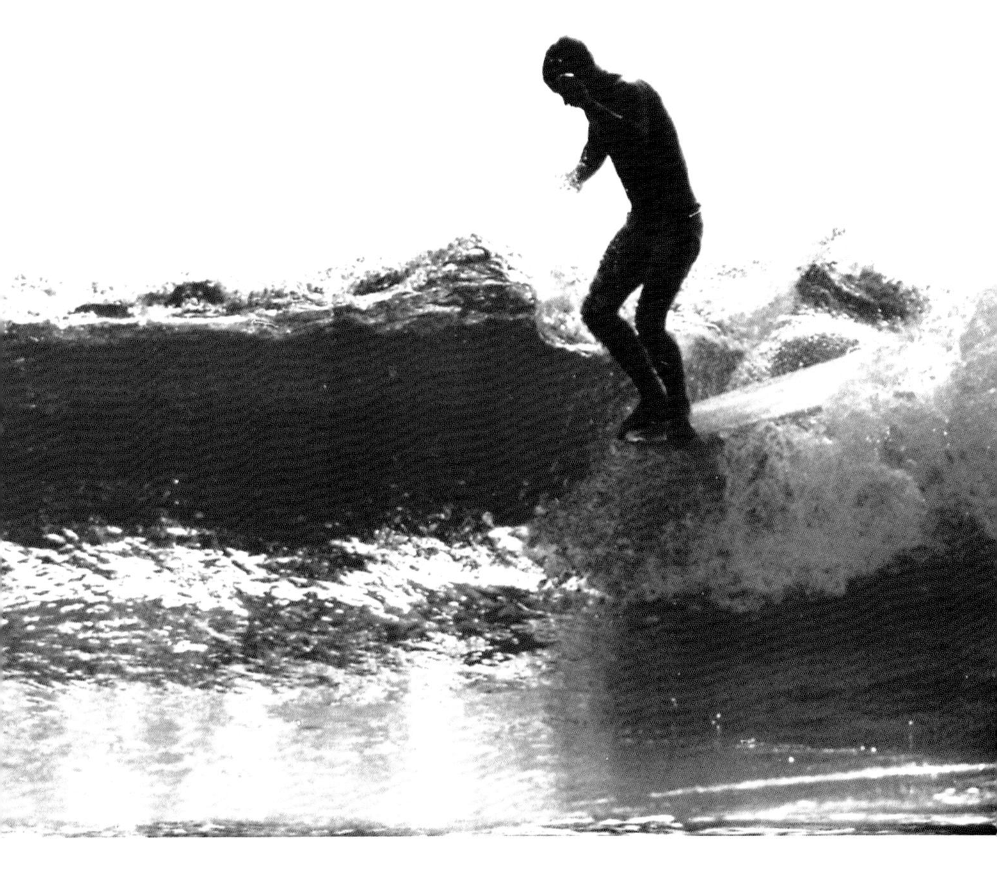

Wayne Cowper hanging ten. Early morning Palm Beach. **JP**

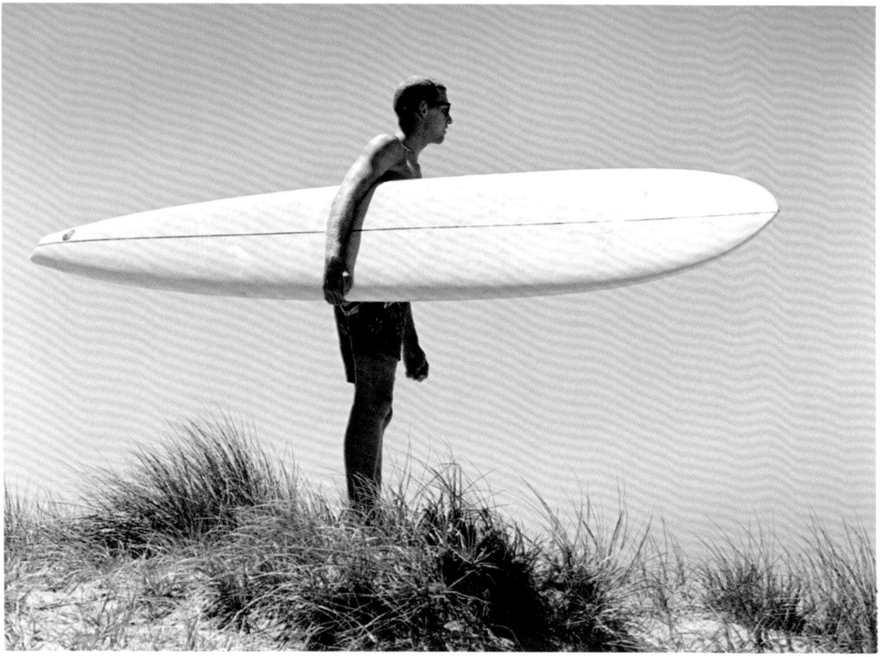

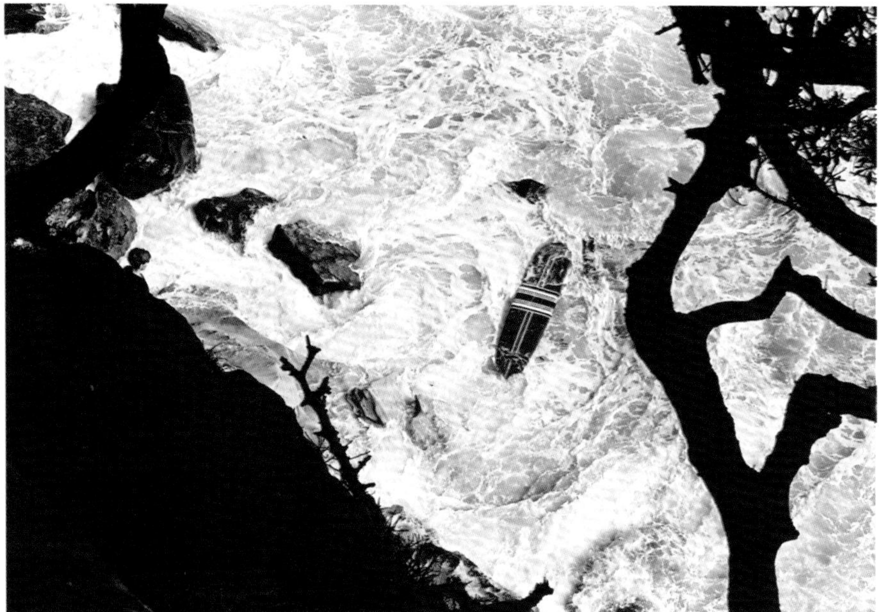

Above: **Bill Dews and his 'gun', Cronulla, 1963.** Billy was a big guy and loved riding his gun on big waves. **BW**

Below: Surfer lost his board in a big swell Sydney Harbour. **JP**

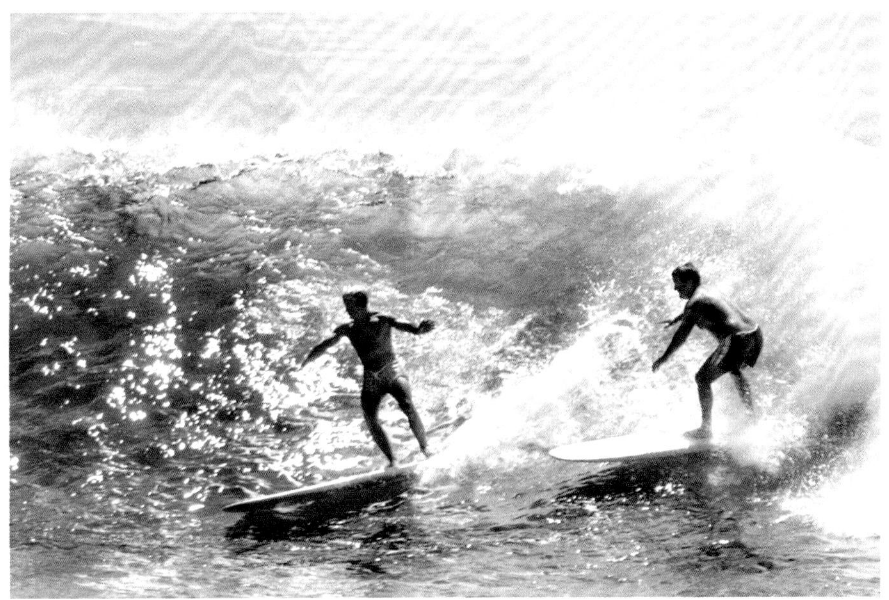

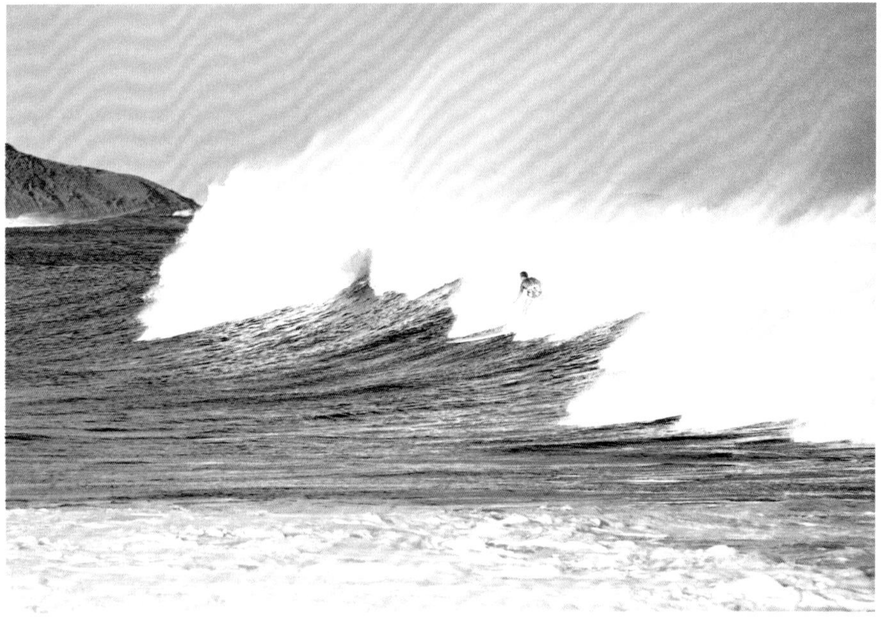

Above: **Dorman and Jacko, 1961.** Alan Dorman and Brian Jackson share a wave at Cronulla Point in 1961. **BW**

Below: **Dave Jackman at Dee Why Point, 1962.** Dave was a big wave rider and is famously remembered for riding one of the largest waves ever at the Queenscliff Bombora in 1961. **BW**

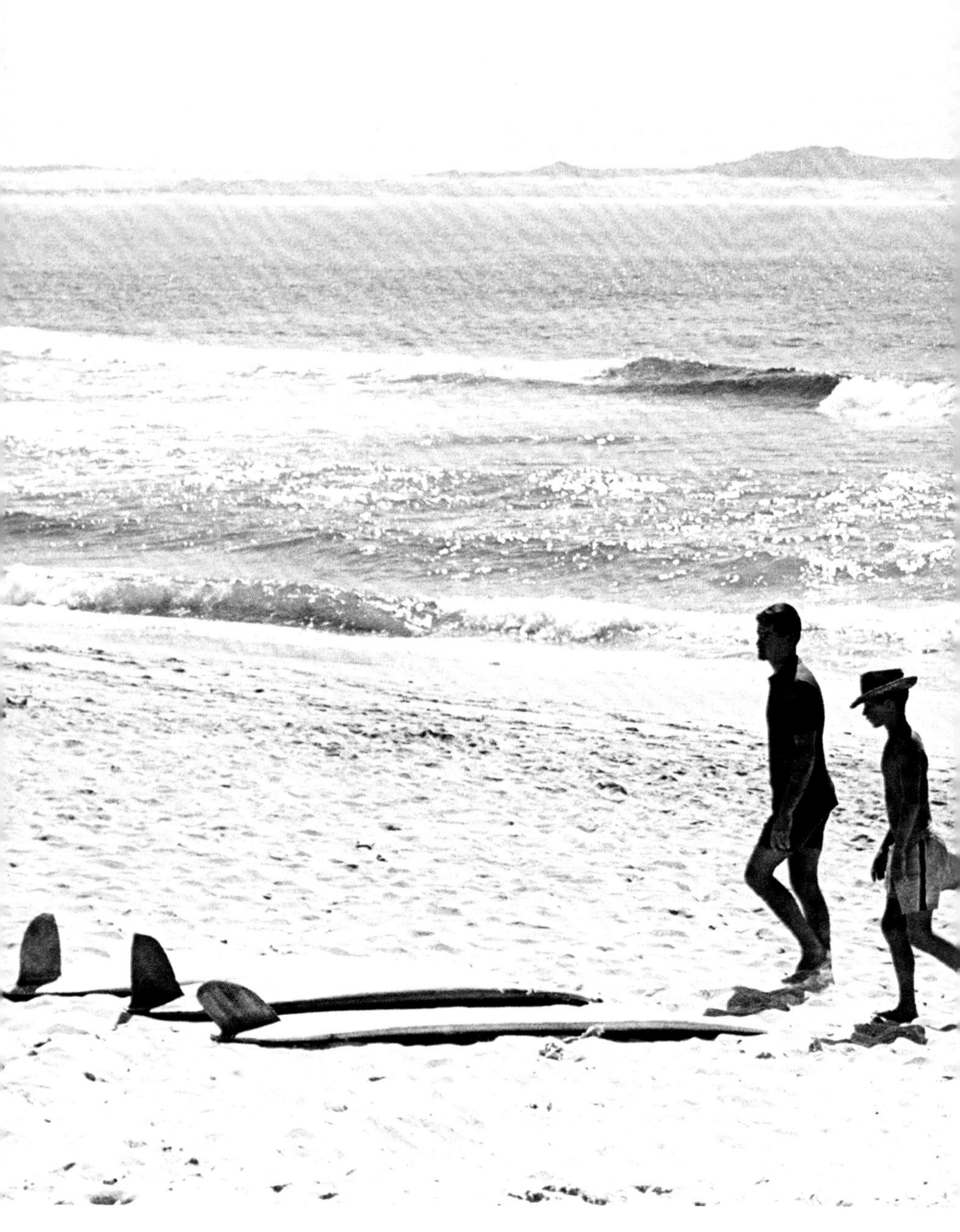

Red House, Cronulla, 1963. Bob Findow, Ian Selig and a
young assistant setting up the boards for a day's hiring. **BW**

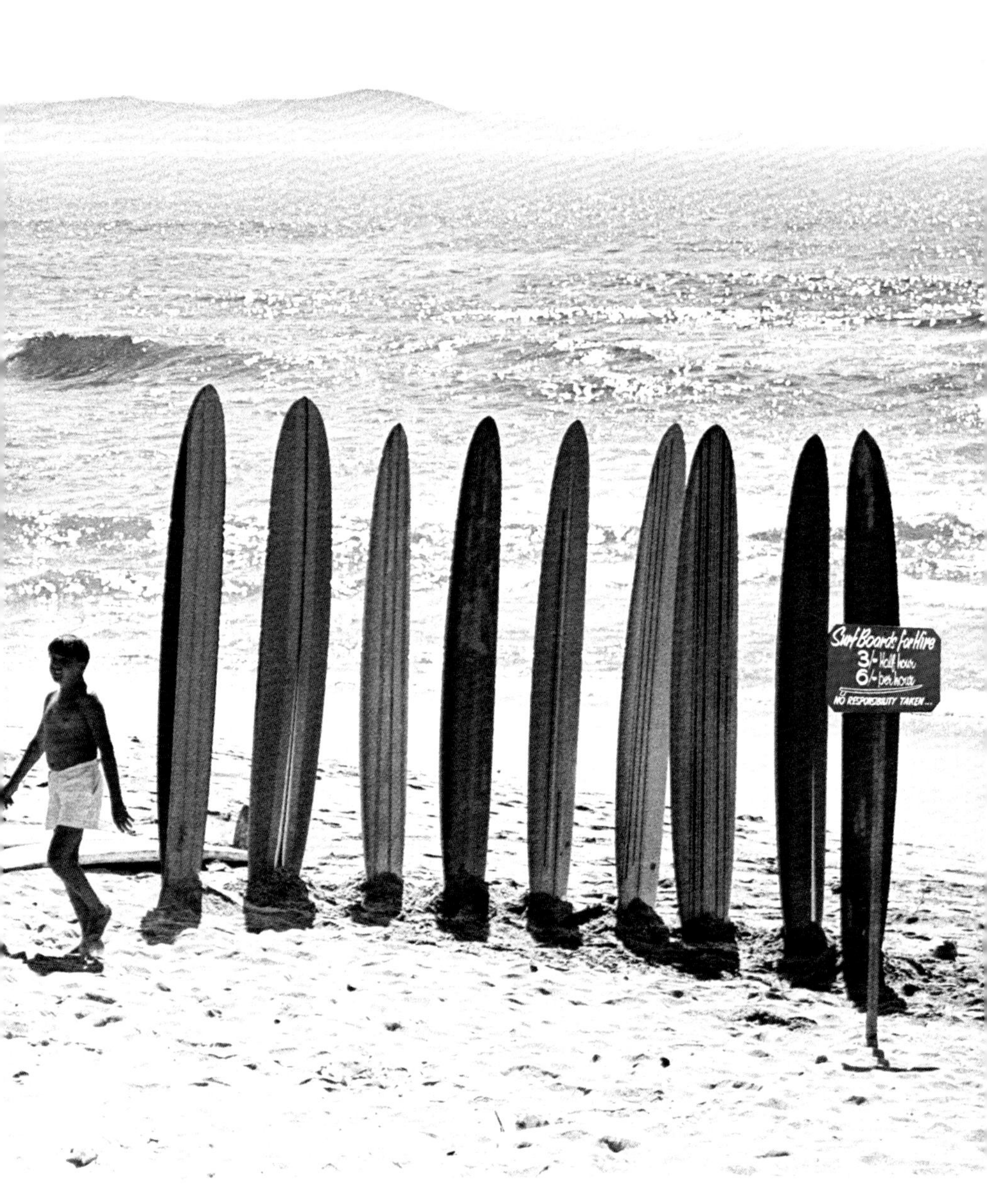
Surf Boards for Hire
3/- Half Hour
6/- per hour
NO RESPONSIBILITY TAKEN ...

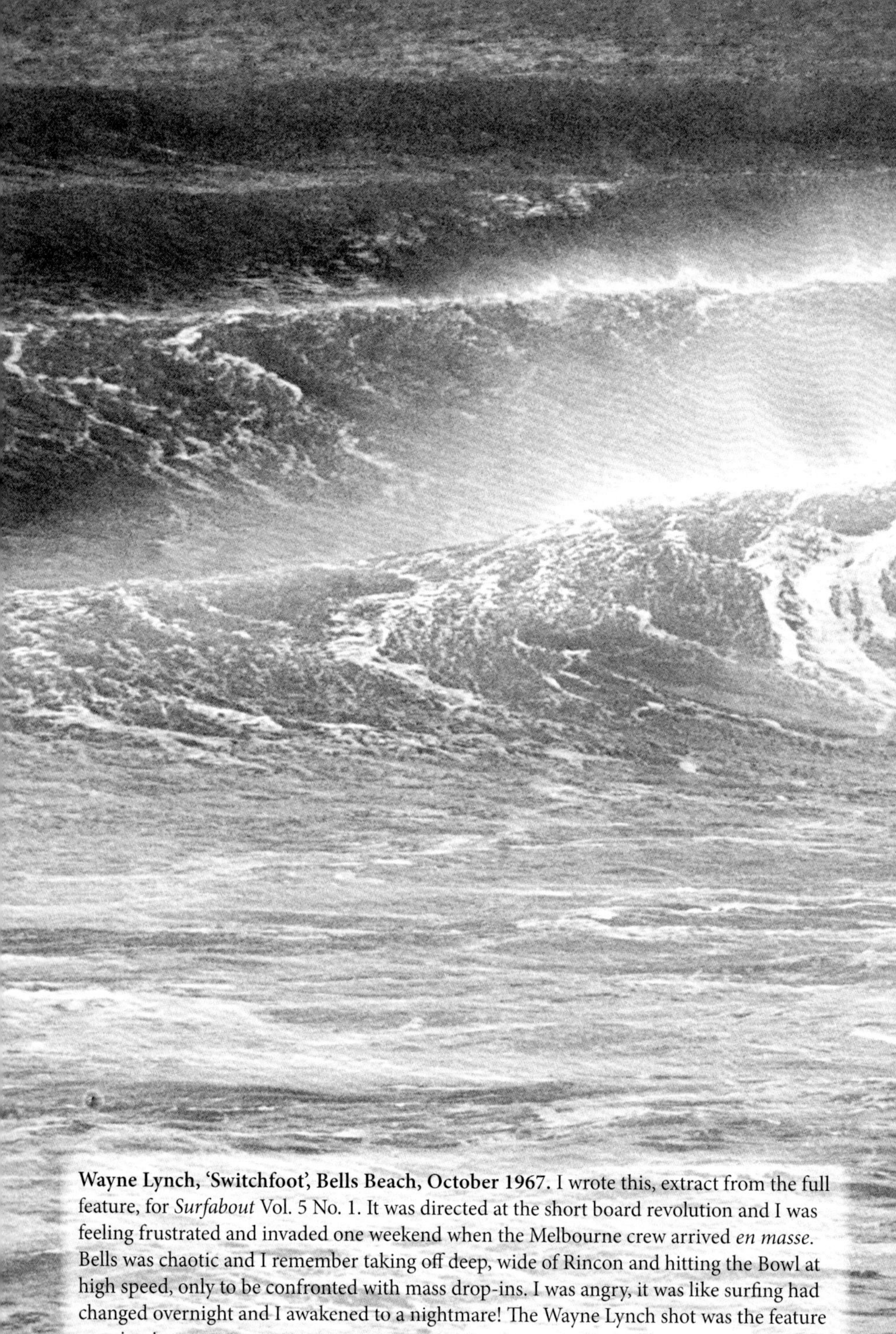

Wayne Lynch, 'Switchfoot', Bells Beach, October 1967. I wrote this, extract from the full feature, for *Surfabout* Vol. 5 No. 1. It was directed at the short board revolution and I was feeling frustrated and invaded one weekend when the Melbourne crew arrived *en masse*. Bells was chaotic and I remember taking off deep, wide of Rincon and hitting the Bowl at high speed, only to be confronted with mass drop-ins. I was angry, it was like surfing had changed overnight and I awakened to a nightmare! The Wayne Lynch shot was the feature opening image. **BS**

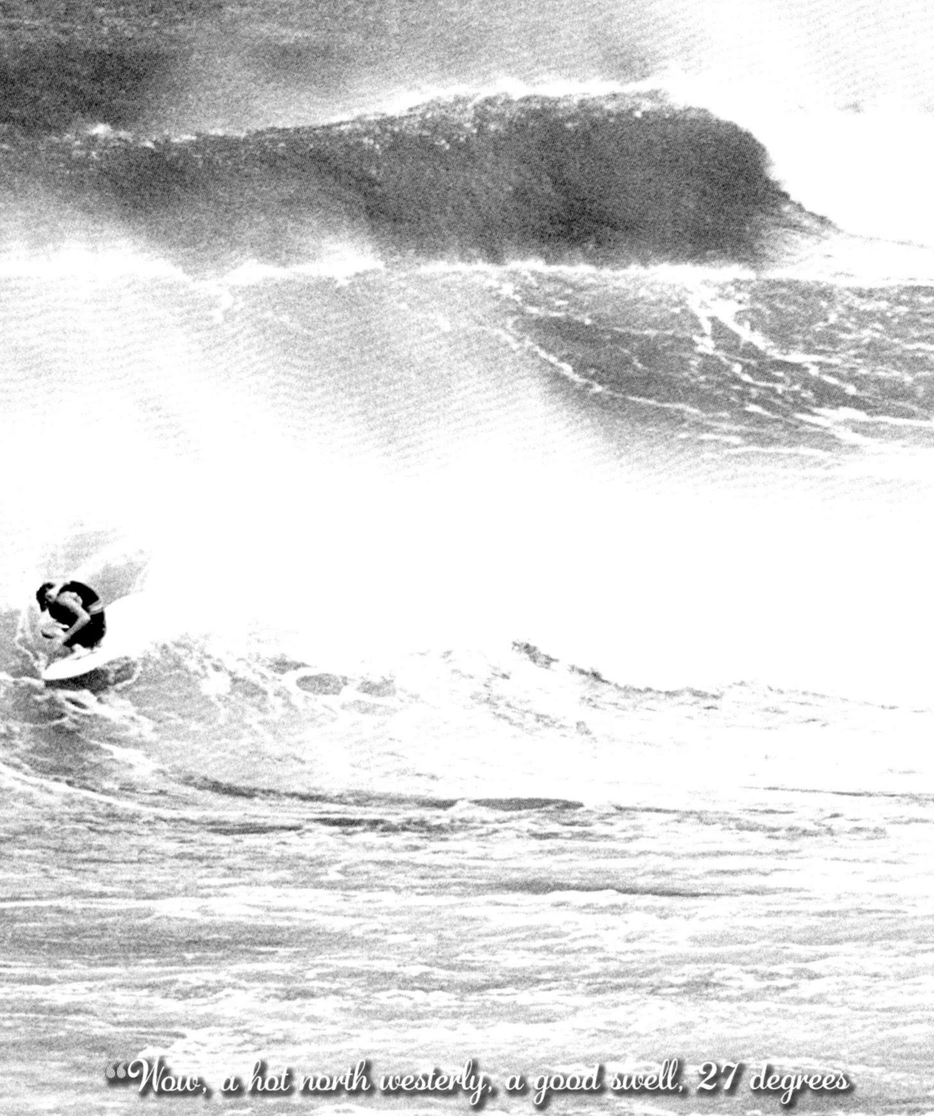

"Wow, a hot north westerly, a good swell, 27 degrees plus, and with a bang summer and the jet-set just dropped in. Barbecues, fast cars, fast living, psychedelic boards and gear and the result – an endless rat race. What do you do? Paddle out and drop in on the first wave, regardless of how many surfers are already on it. It is a battle for every wave."

Barrie Sutherland

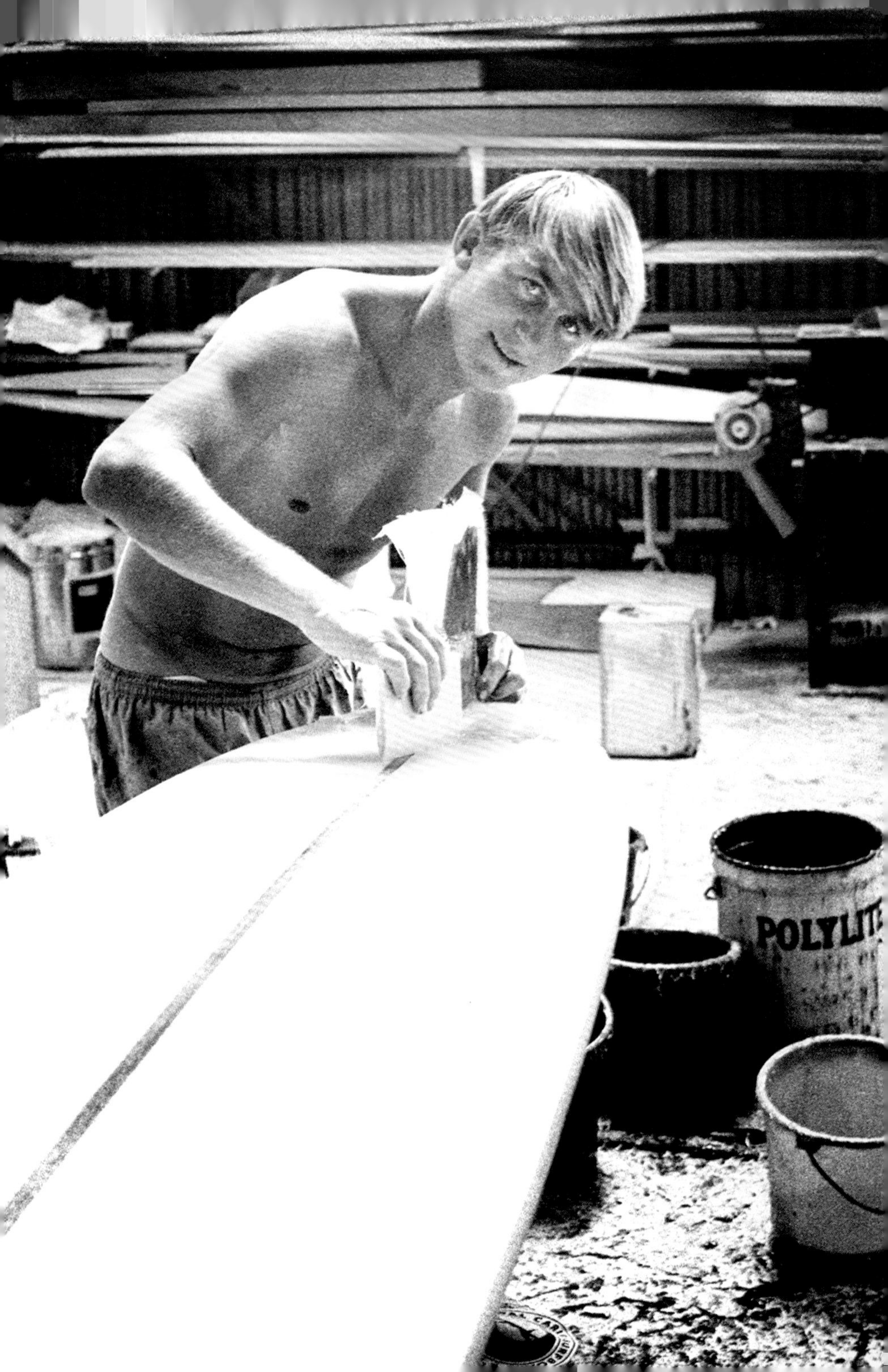
POLYLIT

Early Board Manufacturers

Prior to the early 1960s the only recognised board manufacturer on the Gold Coast was Roger Kieran who was making balsa boards at Burleigh Heads. All other local boards, whether they were hollow ply or balsa, were generally 'one offs' made by boat builders, skilled tradesman or hobbyists. Gus Green, a Tweed Heads boat builder, had made a number of 16-foot paddle boards and Owen Cowlishaw a Kirra SLSC member made six hollow-ply okanuiis for Kirra and Greenmount club members.

Most surfers ordered their boards directly from the Sydney manufacturers of the time who were, Gordon Woods, Bill Wallace, Barry Bennett, Norm Casey or Scott Dillon.

Sydney board manufacturers were experimenting with polyurethane foam trying to perfect the process and stabilise the foam. Most manufacturers had their share of disaster during this period such as fires and explosions and, because of the expense, were only producing enough to fill their own orders. All of the polyurethane foam boards were coming from Sydney via manufacturers' agents on the Gold and Sunshine Coast.

As Barry Bennett and Gordon Woods finally perfected the foam making process they started to produce more blanks and began selling to the general market. This prompted a number of locals to open factories or to manufacture boards under their house names.

Some of the early manufacturers were Joe Larkin, who arrived from Sydney and set up at Kirra, Graeme Merrin in Tweed Heads, Geoff Godby and Laurie Hohenesee in the Miami/Mermaid Beach area, Al Kirton at Main Beach, Ray Woolsley in Brisbane, and Hayden Kenny at Alexandra Headlands.

Multi Plastics Industries (MPI) were experimenting with injection-moulded boards based on a mould taken from a Gordon Woods board. Their boards were not generally accepted as surfers wanted their boards custom made.

Most, if not all, of the best surfers in Australia were shaping their own surfboards through the 1960s and into the 1970s, some of them created their own businesses off the back of their skills, most notably Midget Farrelly, Bob McTavish, Geoff McCoy, Ken Adler, Wayne Lynch, Dick Van Straalen and later Mark Richards. Surfers shaping their own surfboards was unique to the 1960s era. By the 1970s, most of the best surfers were getting their surfboards from a professional shaper and through this era Geoff McCoy was the biggest name in surfboard manufacturing in Australia. The McCoy name was so successful that McCoy relocated to the US and opened a factory, this was all before

Nigel Dwyer glassing a surfboard at Norm Casey's board factory at Taren Point, Sydney, 1964. Nigel moved to New Zealand and opened a board factory in New Plymouth on the North island. The business is still operating. **BW**

commercial textile companies reflected the surfing culture and the fashion trends.

By 1966 there was real change in the air with surfboard design. Shorter surfboards were being experimented with and a revolution in surfing style was around the corner. This ultimately left the longboard as an obsolete piece of history, discarded at the local rubbish dump – replaced by something 3 feet shorter and far more manoeuvrable, with a dorsal fin inspired by the Thomas Edison of surfing, George Greenough. While the finely-crafted longboards of the early 1960s had been left in the garage or at the rubbish dump, they did experience a radical comeback in the early 2000s with surfers and hipsters wanting the old feeling. The original 9'6" early 'D' fin surfboards are now commanding a price tag previously unheard of. Modern replicas are painstakingly following 1960s construction methods, complete with a bygone-era timber fin.

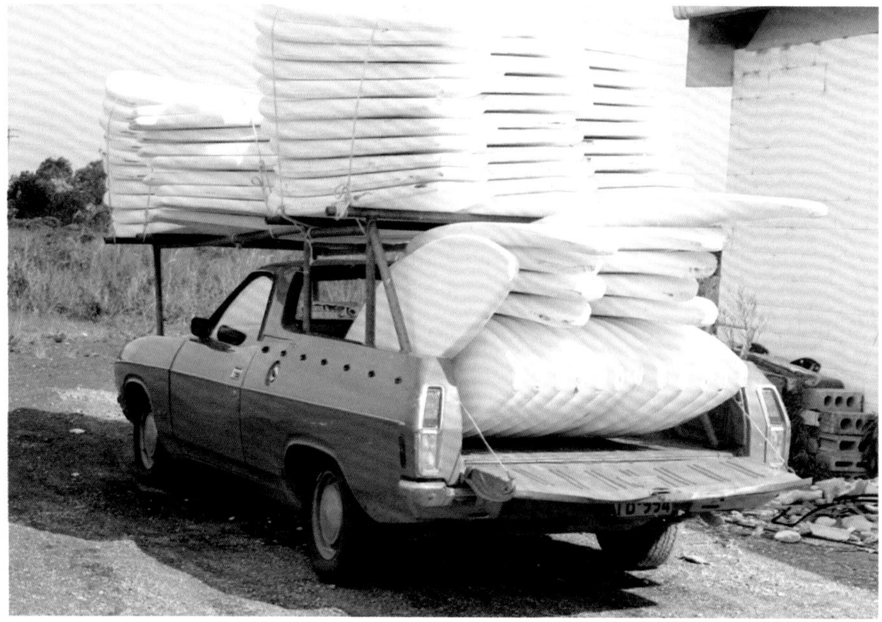

Above: **Surfboard blank delivery.** These were strapped to the roof in Sydney at Barry Bennett's and driven to Byron Bay. Simpler times. **DICK HOOLE** (COURTESEY OF HODADDY)

Opposite: **John Gudgeon, Chris Wood, Rod Brooks,** Mates party wave, from the water (1st at Winky Pop), May 1966. **BS**

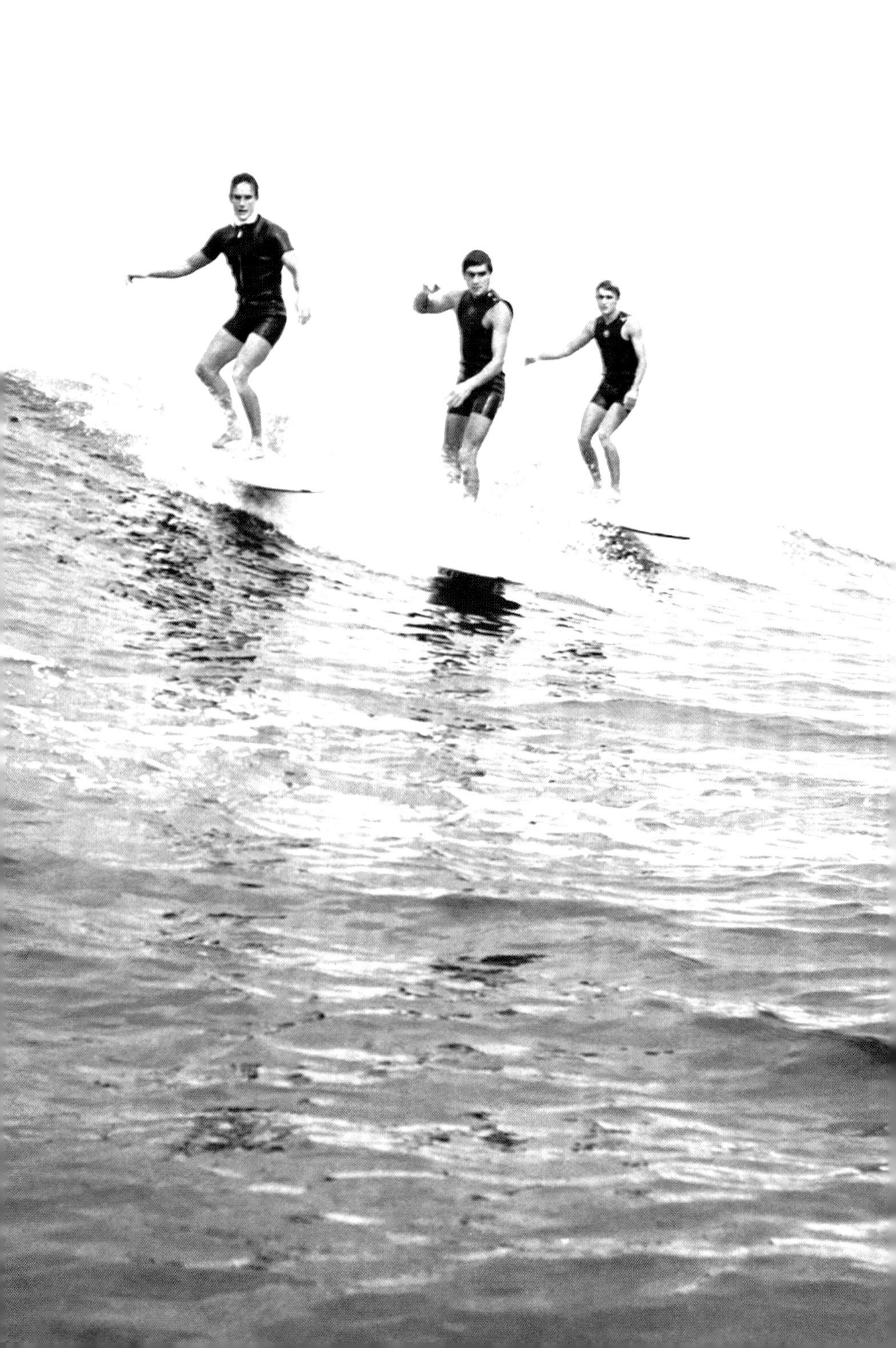

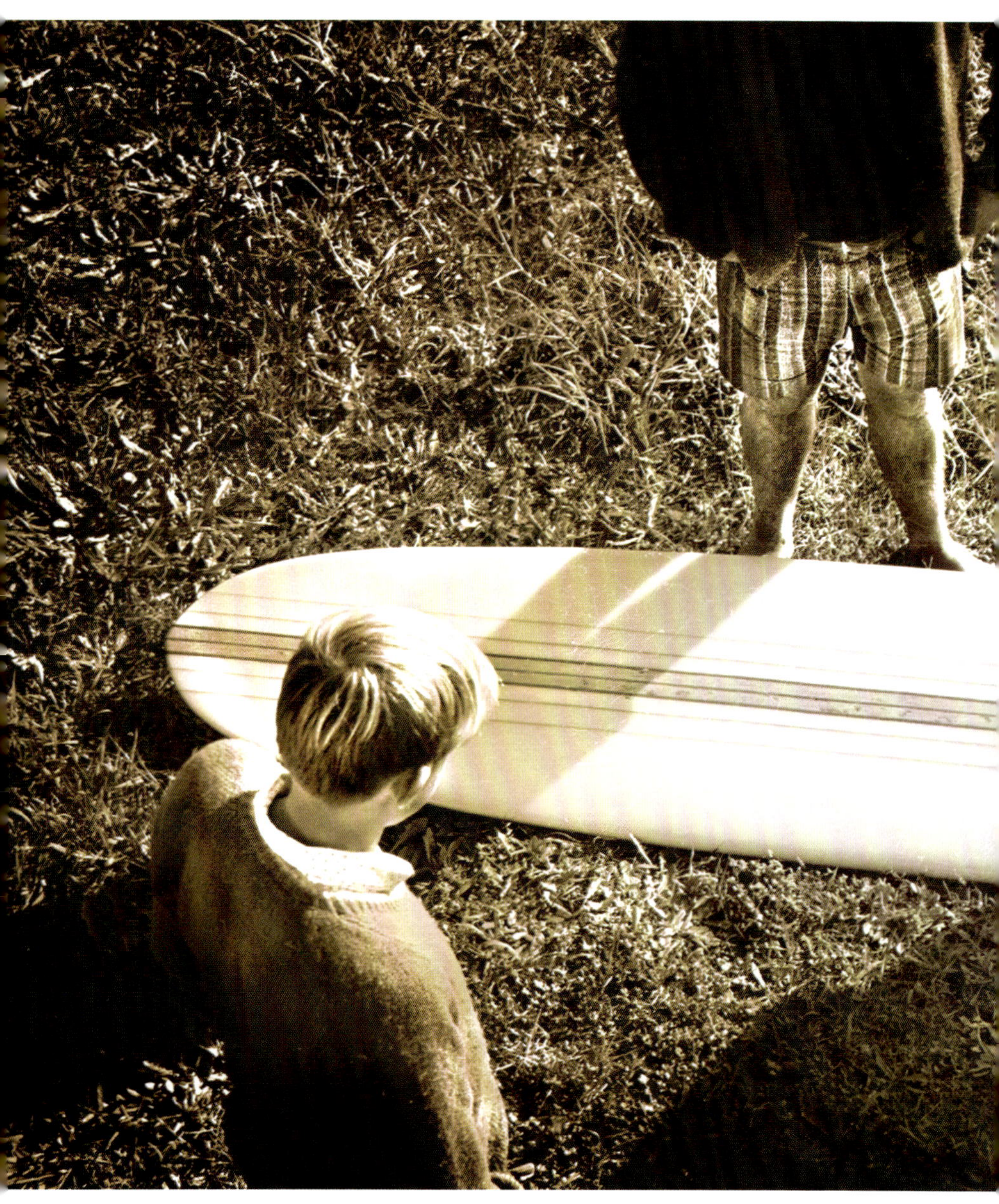

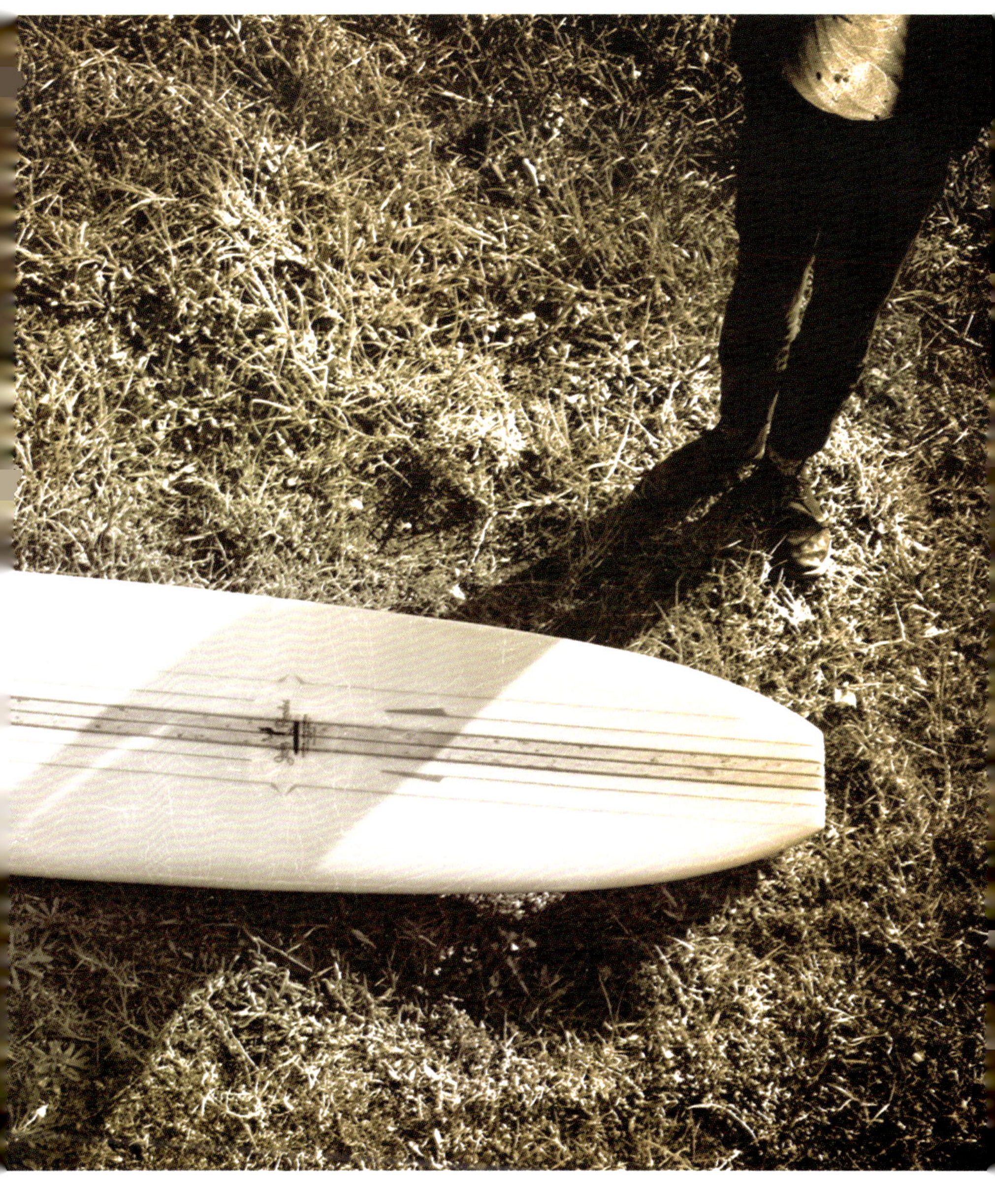

Surfers admiring a John Rhodes classic, early Sixties design, 1963. **BW**

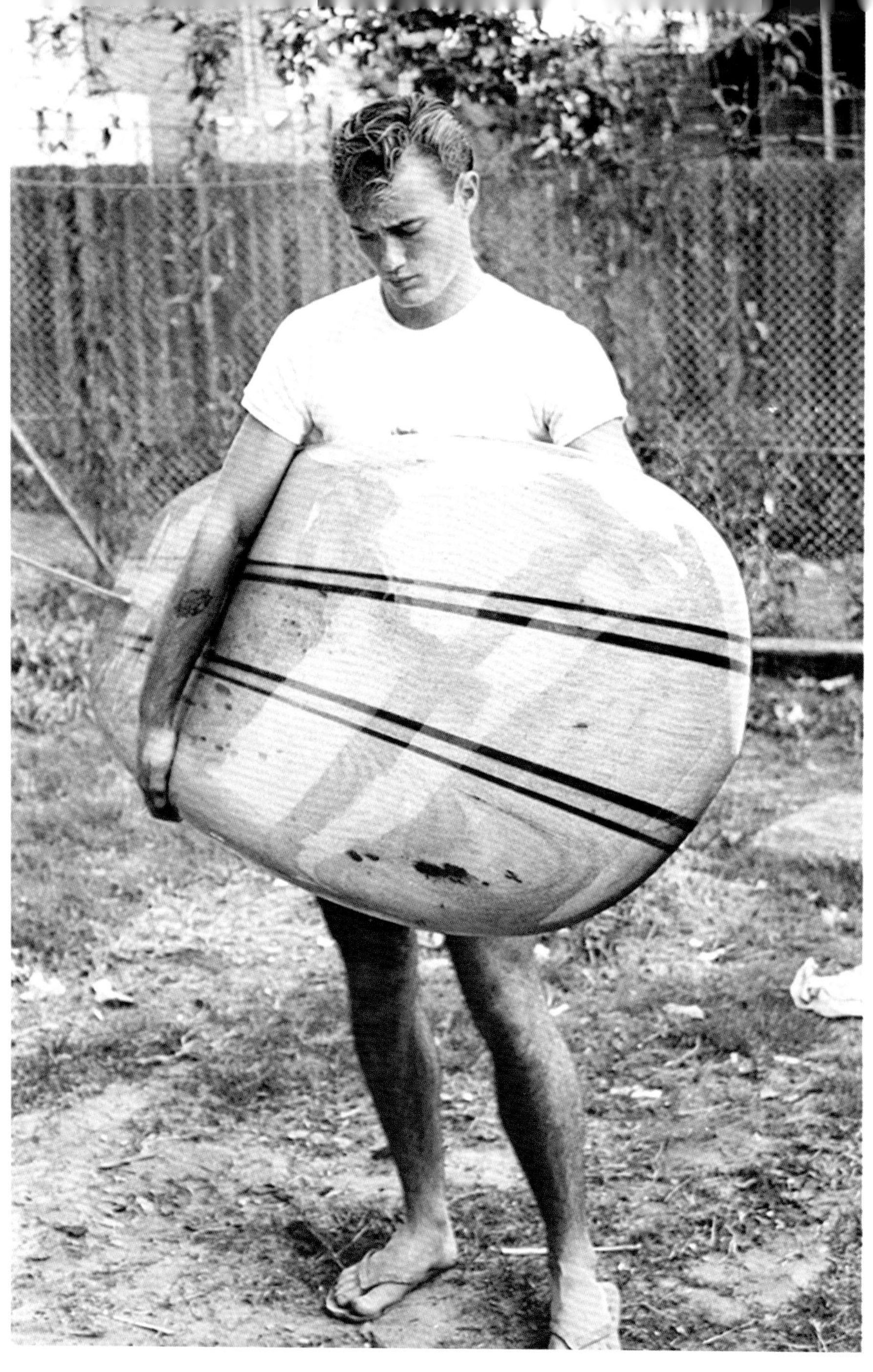

Above: **John Rhodes with a beautiful balsa board, 1963. BW**

Opposite: **John Rhodes outside his surfboard shop in Cronulla, 1963. BW**

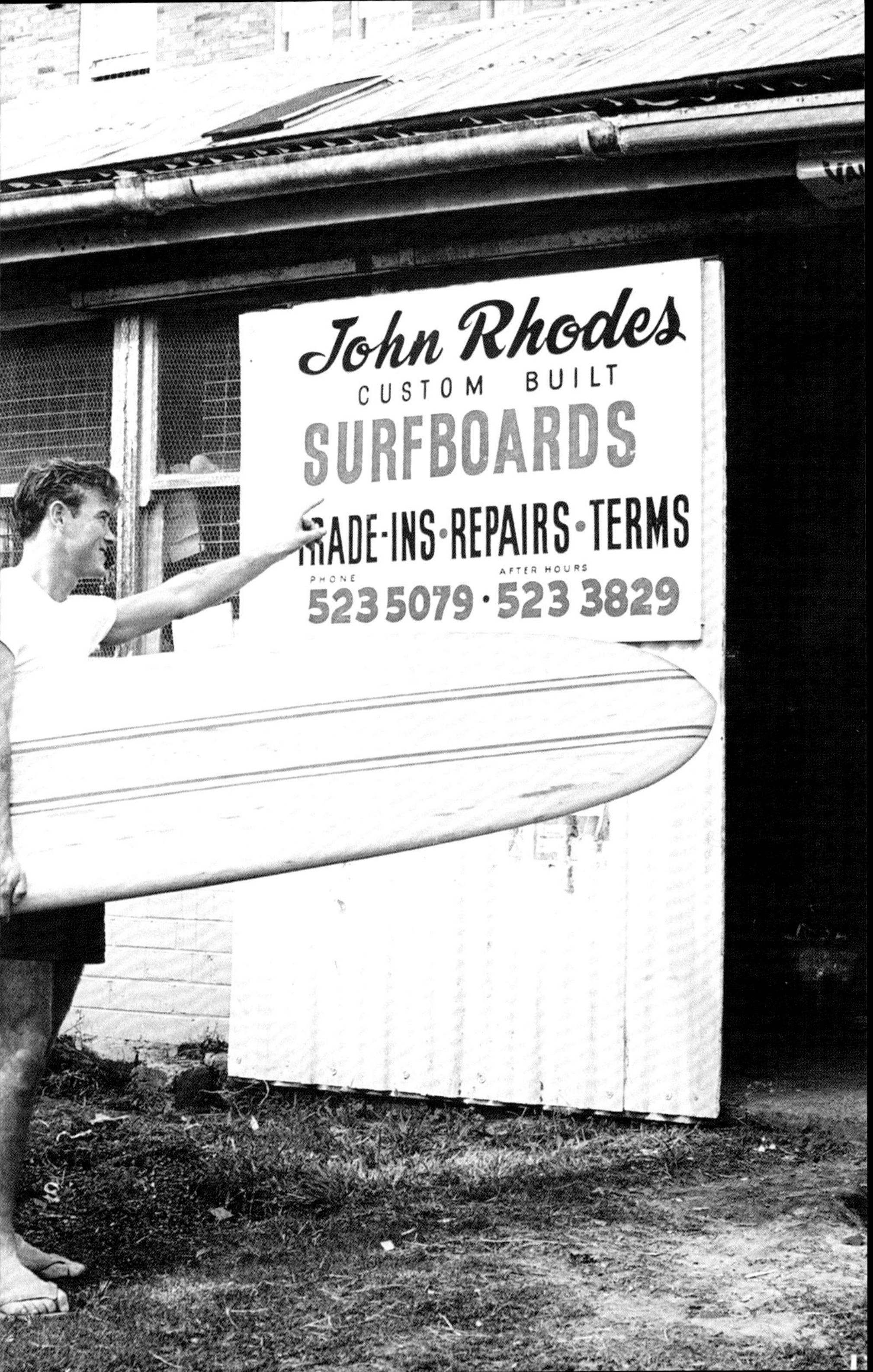
John Rhodes
CUSTOM BUILT
SURFBOARDS
TRADE-INS · REPAIRS · TERMS
PHONE
AFTER HOURS
523 5079 · 523 3829

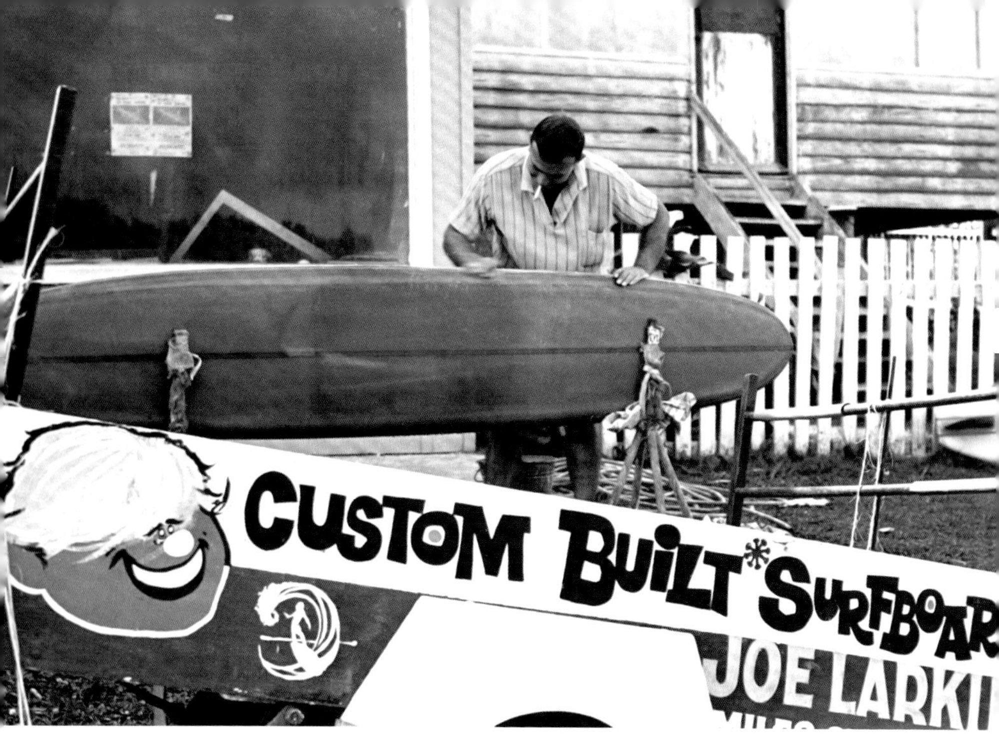

Joe Larkin. Pioneer, innovator, beach inspector, surfer, board manufacturer, master craftsman, larger-than-life character and living legend, all of these titles describe Joe.

Joe grew up in Freshwater Sydney and has been around the ocean all his life. He was a recognised surfer in the 16ft paddle board era and after the Americans introduced us to the balsa boards in 1956 became one of Australia's pioneers, not only in surfing, but in the manufacture of the Malibu board.

When balsa was unavailable to construct boards similar to the American boards he commenced making hollow ply 'Okanuii' versions under his parents house, later he worked for both Gordon Woods and Barry Bennett, shaping both balsa and foam boards.

In 1962 Joe moved to Coolangatta and opened a factory in Miles Street Kirra, this factory became the centre of surfing on the southern end of the coast. The list of notable surfers who worked for Joe in the '60s reads like a who's who of surfing, names like Peter Thomas, Bob McTavish, Garry Birdsall, Brian 'Furry' Austen, Terry Fitzgerald, Michael Peterson, Darryl 'Rooster' Dell, Algie Grud, Gordon Merchant and many others.

In 1964 Joe was elected manager of the Queensland team to compete at the 1st World Titles and was one of the appointed judges for the contest. Now retired and living at Cabarita, Joe occasionally makes one of those fabulous 10ft hollow ply Okanuii boards that were unique to Australia.

In 2004 Joe was inducted into the Surfing Hall of Fame in two categories for his contribution to surfing. **MS**

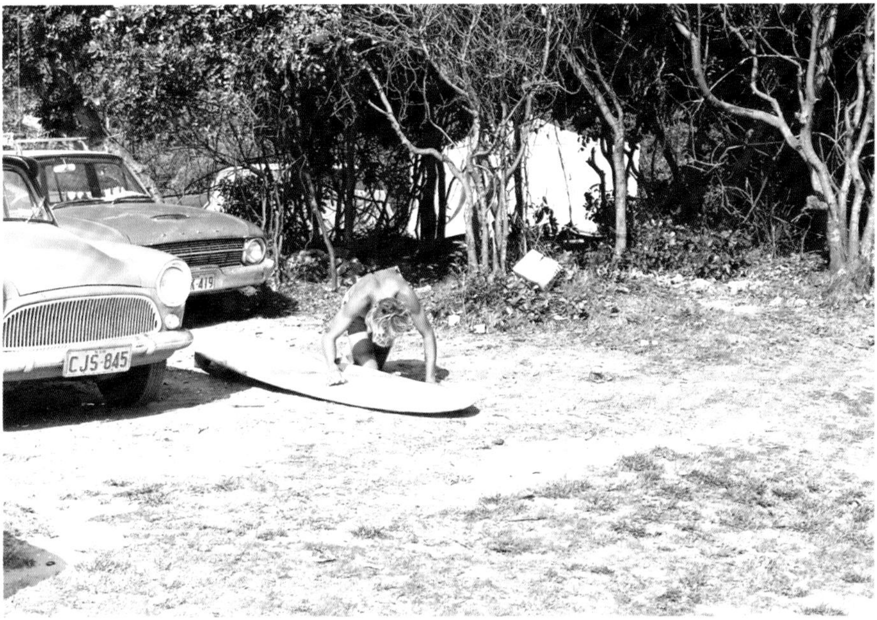

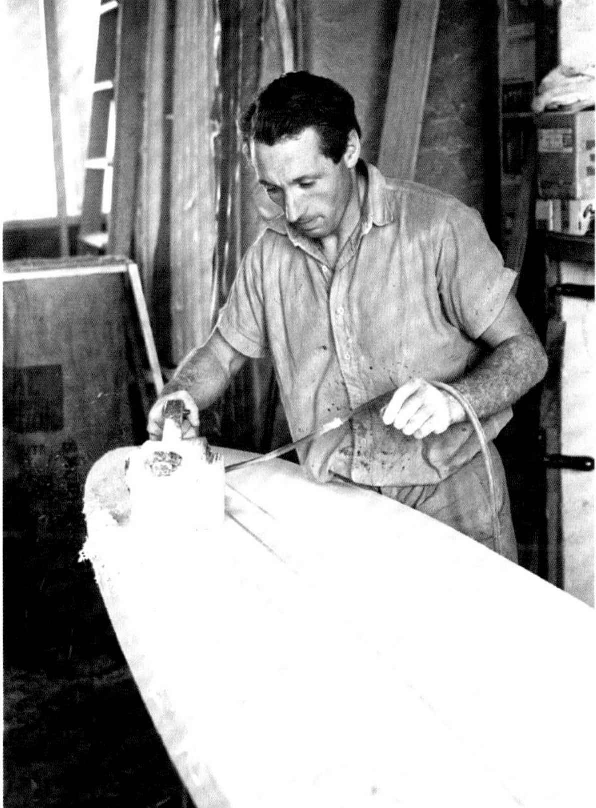

Above: **Waxing up. JP**

Right: **Master Victorian craftsman Fred Pyke. BS**

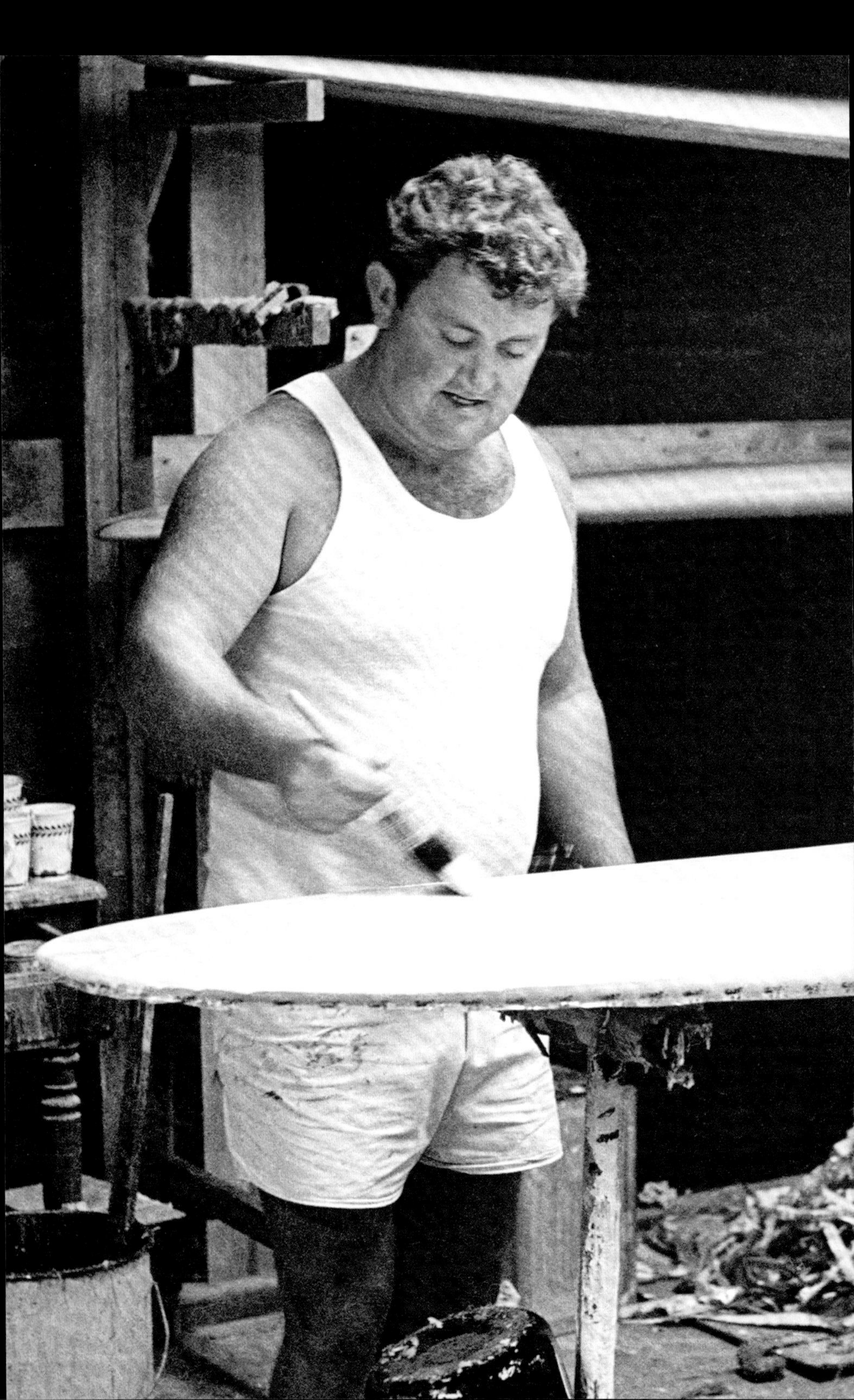

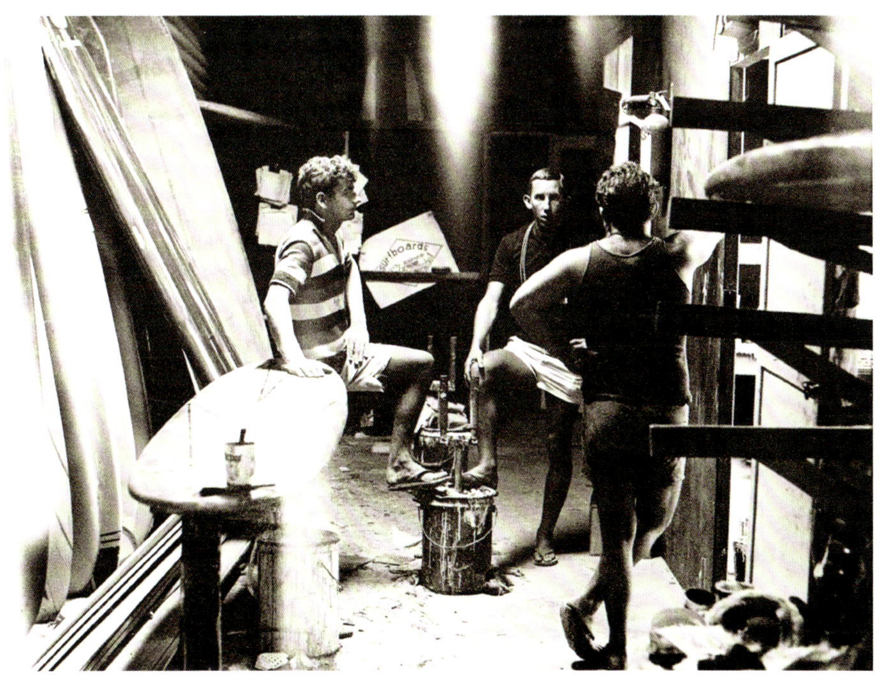

Above: **The crew inside Jackson and Cansdell's Surf Shop, 1962. BW**

Opposite: **Cronulla, 1962.** Brian Jackson smoothing the resin on a newly-glassed board in his factory. **BW**

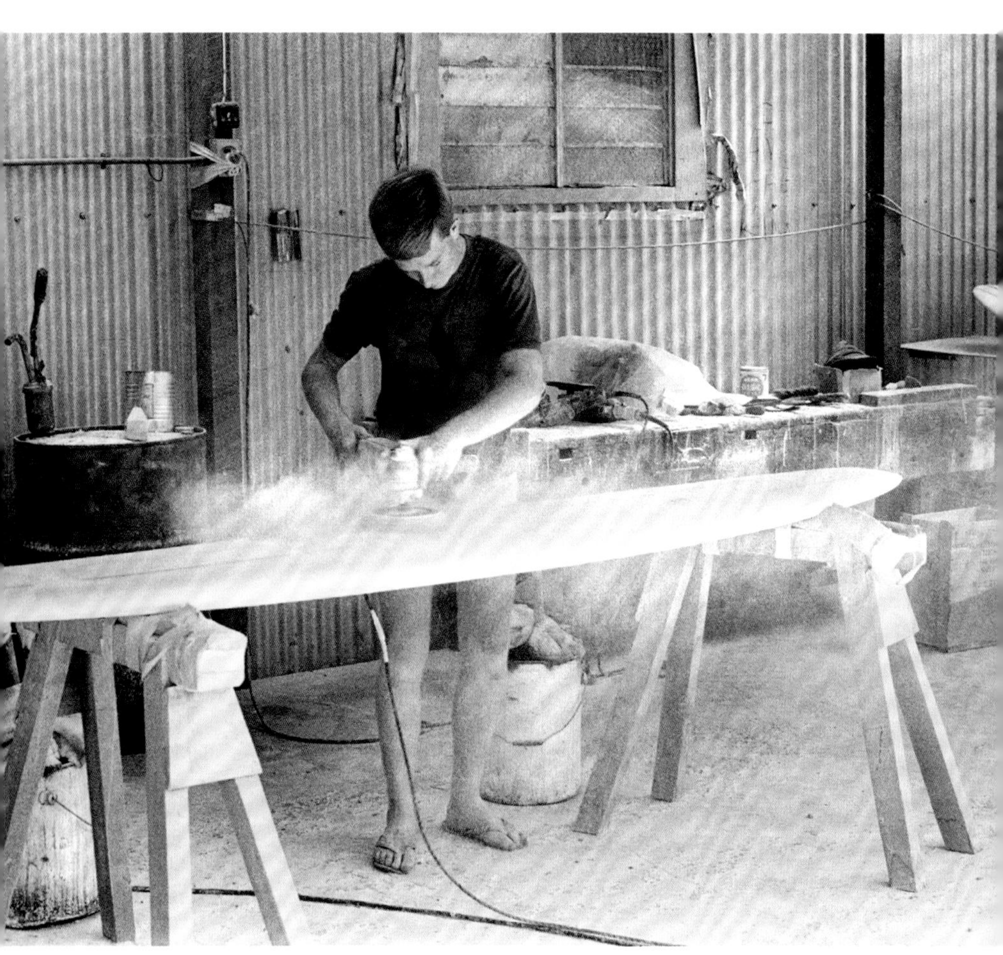

Ross Longbottom sanding at Norm Casey's in Taren Point, 1964. **BW**

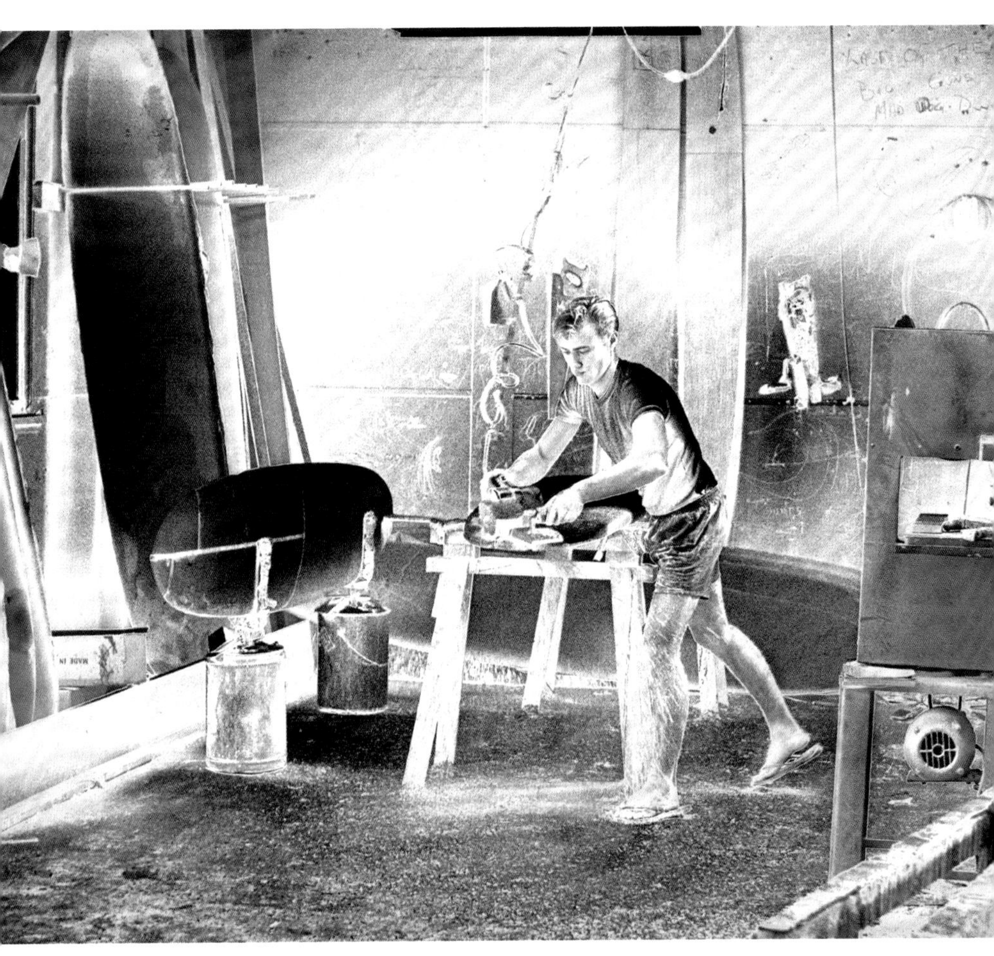

John Rhodes shaping a board in his surf shop at Cronulla, 1963. **BW**

On the Beach

In the 1960s, ordinary, everyday Aussie teenagers caught the wave of enthusiasm for the beach, via Hawaii, all the way from the America's west coast. As the baby-boomer generation born at the end of World War II entered their teenage years they embraced the music, fashion, language and culture of the beach – the music of The Beach Boys and Jan & Dean, the Gidget and Beach Party films of the era and the clothes, hats and sunglasses favoured by their peer group. There also was a revolution happening in the shape and make of the surfboards.

Alan Sharp, Cronulla Point, 1964. **BW**

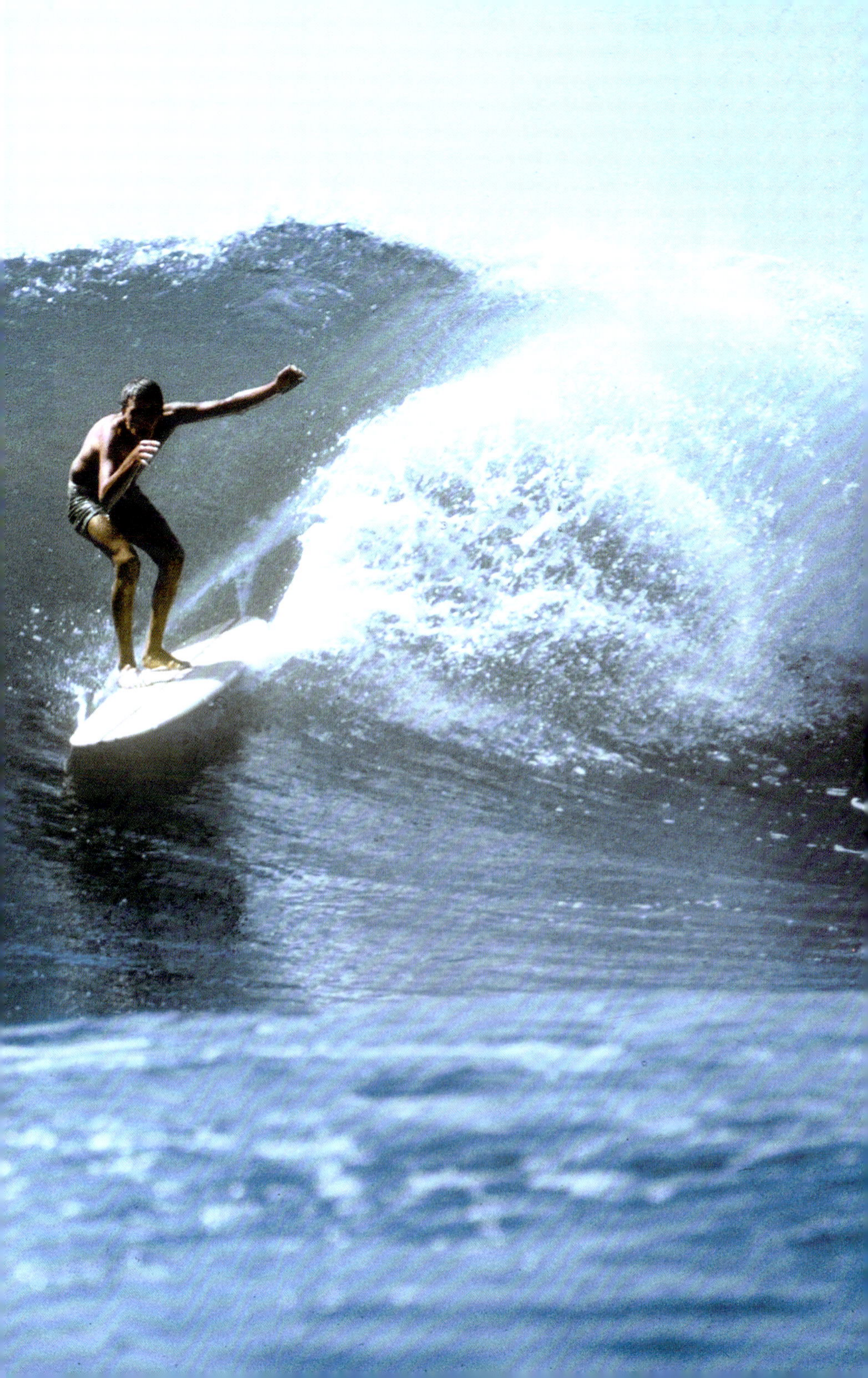

Early surfboards were made out of plywood and were of hollow construction and they took a lot of maintenance. They had to be varnished regularly to keep them from splitting, but once the boards were made from foam and fibreglass maintenance wasn't that big an issue because fibreglass is so easy to fix. Foam-mould boards were also lighter and easier to turn and manoeuvre … they rode in the surf much better than the balsa 15 footers.

Recalls Mal Sutherland: 'Most of the areas where I surfed, for example Kirra Point in Queensland, riders were forever damaging their boards because we had no leg ropes at that time and there no way to stop the board from washing up on the rocks. You knew if you lost your board you were in trouble …

Countless hours were spent waxing boards to give surfers the best possible grip out on the waves. Boards needed to be maintained to keep the water out of them. When the move went towards fibreglass, it was simple as mixing up a hot batch of resin and then waiting an hour and sanding it back before going out again after patching up a board. A lot of surfers carried their own repair kits with them and did their own repairs.

Local riders hit the beach at dawn, taking advantage of having the waves to themselves and the conditions where the wind was yet to pick up. They would surf until 9 o'clock and then go home and have breakfast and then go down back to the beach for the rest of the day. But then there were very few board riders on the beach at the start of the decade – it was is estimated that there were no more than 1500 surfboard riders on the east coast of Australia in 1960 – and even then they were quite a tightknit group. And parochial! Surfers had their 'home' beach of course but there was a camaraderie in the early days among the riders.

'Surfing was tribal, because the surf clubs were tribal,' says Mal Sutherland. There was little angst, however, as there were so few of them that they tended to get along pretty well. There was very little conflict or competition in the early days but when the beaches started to be 'invaded' that's when surfers became territorial. 'After having the beaches pretty much to ourselves for so long, we got pretty shitty when the crowds came, I can tell you … "we don't go to Brisbane to play football in your front yards," we would say to the influx of visitors, "what are you doing down in surfing in our front yard?"'

It was only natural that surfers who had grown up in that culture sought to protect their space and lifestyle. And that was the attraction … if you loved the surf, you found the beach, any beach, somehow. Every group of riders had their 'secret surfing places' says Mal. 'Cabarita, on the north coast of New South Wales, was a particular favourite and we kept it to ourselves for quite a while.

Many of the best beaches of the era were hidden in remote parts of the coast surrounded by coastal scrub and accessible by seldom-used bush tracks. Over the years, coastal township appeared with local 'mixed businesses' and designated 'milkbars' (another American influence from the 1950s) sprouting up to cater for the summer influx of surfers.

Whenever you get a group of fit young men you will find girls. Being seen 'on the beach' was as much a lifestyle for the girls as it was for the guys. 'It was the same for the girls who followed the surf lifesaving clubs,' says Mal Sutherland. 'The 'clubbies' had a tremendous female following except the girls were not allowed to compete until much later. They weren't even allowed inside the surf clubs in the early 1960s.'

Although reticent at first, girls soon started to ride surf boards … and when organised competition started among the surfing fraternity there was also female competition. 'There may not have been too many competitors but they included them from the start and that was something surfing had over the lifesavers … we included the girls in competition,' says Mal Sutherland. He takes great pride that his home beach Kirra also produced the first Australian world champion, Phyllis O'Donell.

The girls had to put up with quite a bit in the early 1960s, Mal admits. 'They weren't encouraged to get into the water at all at first – but a lot of us guys had a heap of respect for the girls, and there were some quite good girl surfers up here. There was a certain group who believed they shouldn't be in the water in the first place but that thinking soon faded.'

Nev, Scott, Mal, Kirra, 1963. The board Mal is sitting on was the big gun that Scott took to Hawaii that year. **MS**

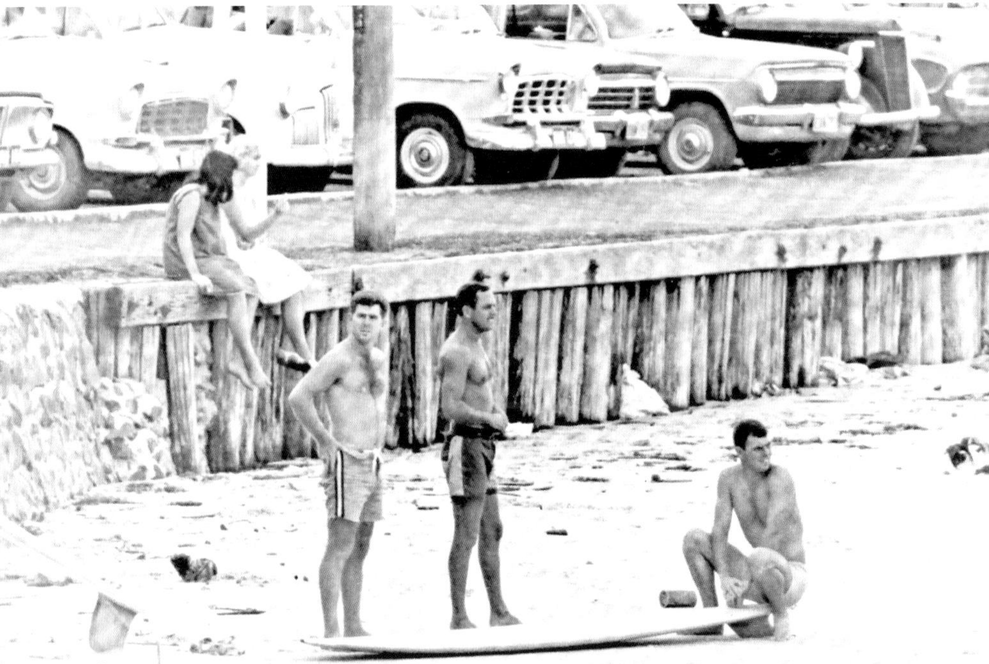

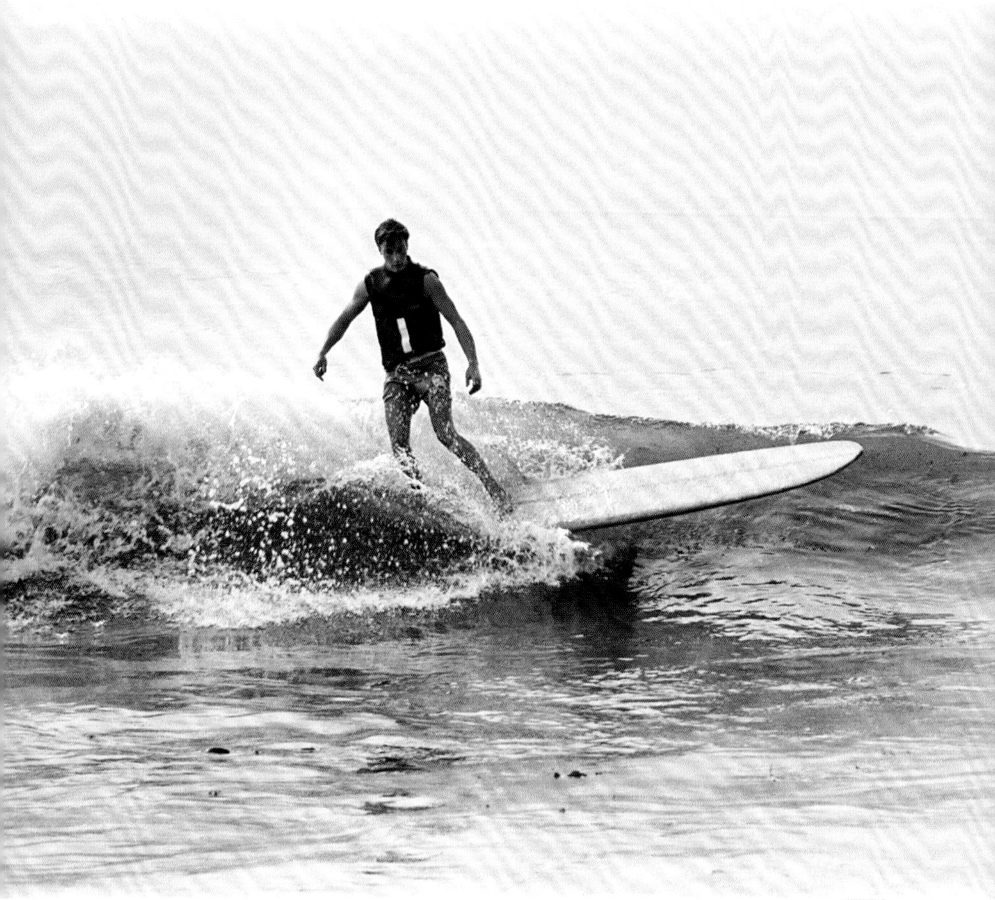

Brian Singer, ASA contest, Lorne Beachbreak, 1966. **BS**

Surfers were also safety conscious, given they often charted unpatrolled beaches. 'You always accessed the danger before you went out on the waves,' says Mal Sutherland. 'If the conditions were too dangerous you didn't go out.' They knew where the rips were, and if the conditions were unsurfable … and they watched out for each other. 'We were always surfing in twos or threes – not in the hundreds that crowd beaches today.'

Then there was always the spectre of sharks. 'Sharks were there all the time,' says Mal. 'They didn't seem to worry us and we didn't worry them. We have all had our experiences with sharks, but if I was to tell the story of every shark I encountered (I fell on top of one once) people would think I was making it up so I don't generally talk about it. Certain types of sharks are dangerous

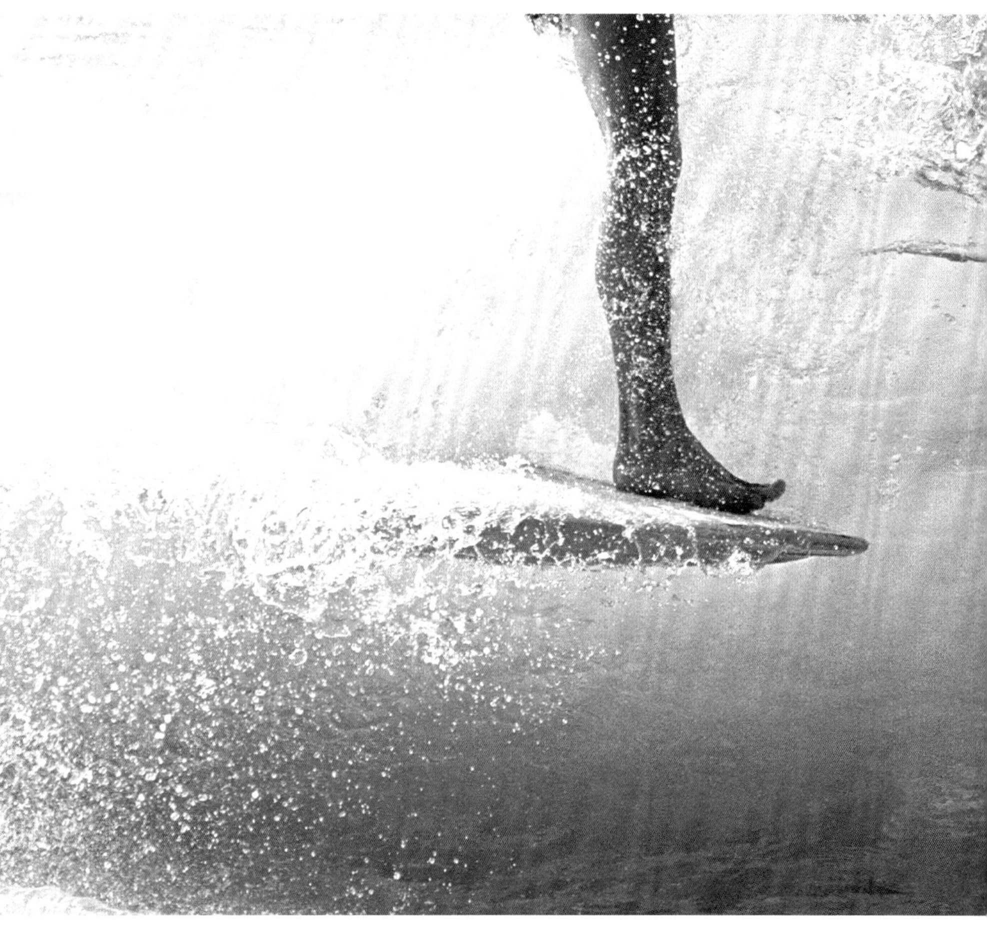

Curly toes at North Cronulla, 1962. The toes belong to Dave Coppleson. **BW**

at any time – tiger sharks, white pointers – but mostly they leave you alone because they are just as frightened of you as you are of them.'

We'll take his word on that.

'We mainly surfed points and beach break, not reefs (reefs attract fish, fish attract sharks). Where people are surfing now among reefs you almost have expect sharks to be there.'

Surfers looked out for one another, especially when they lost their board and faced a half-mile swim into the beach to collect it again. It's a fair swim, so riders would shadow swimmers and take them in to collect their boards if they got into difficulty. 'Your mate kept an eye on you,' says Mal.

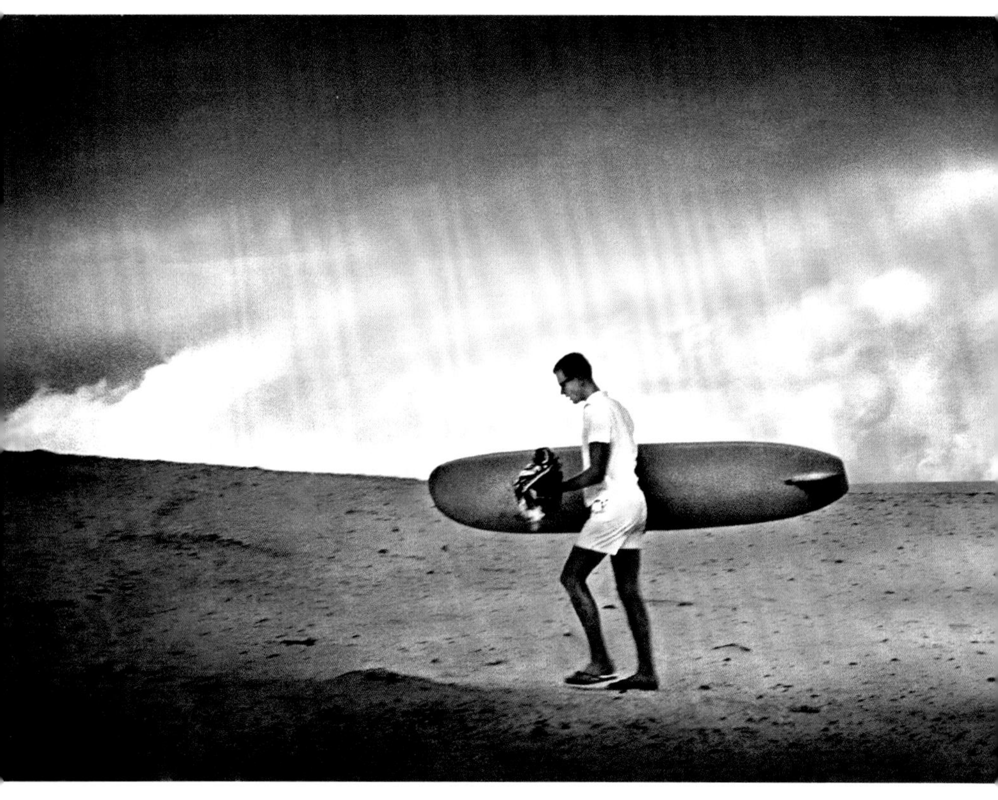

Heading home. Billy Dews (left) and a friend on
the sandy trek to the Cronulla car park, 1962. **BW**

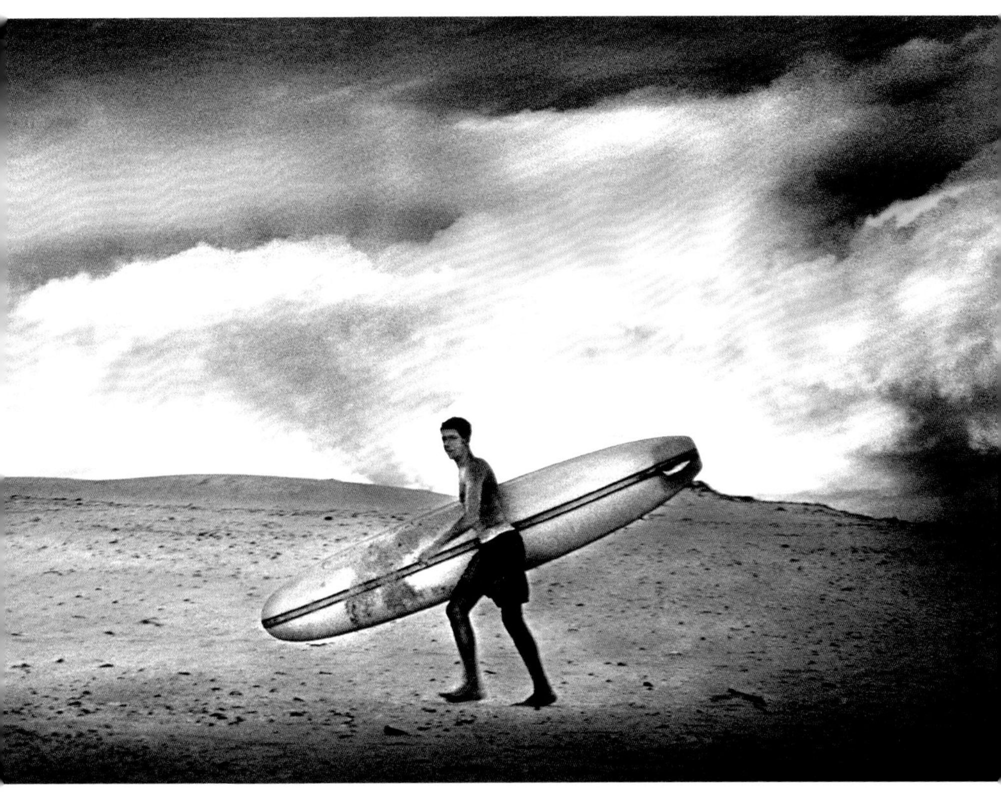

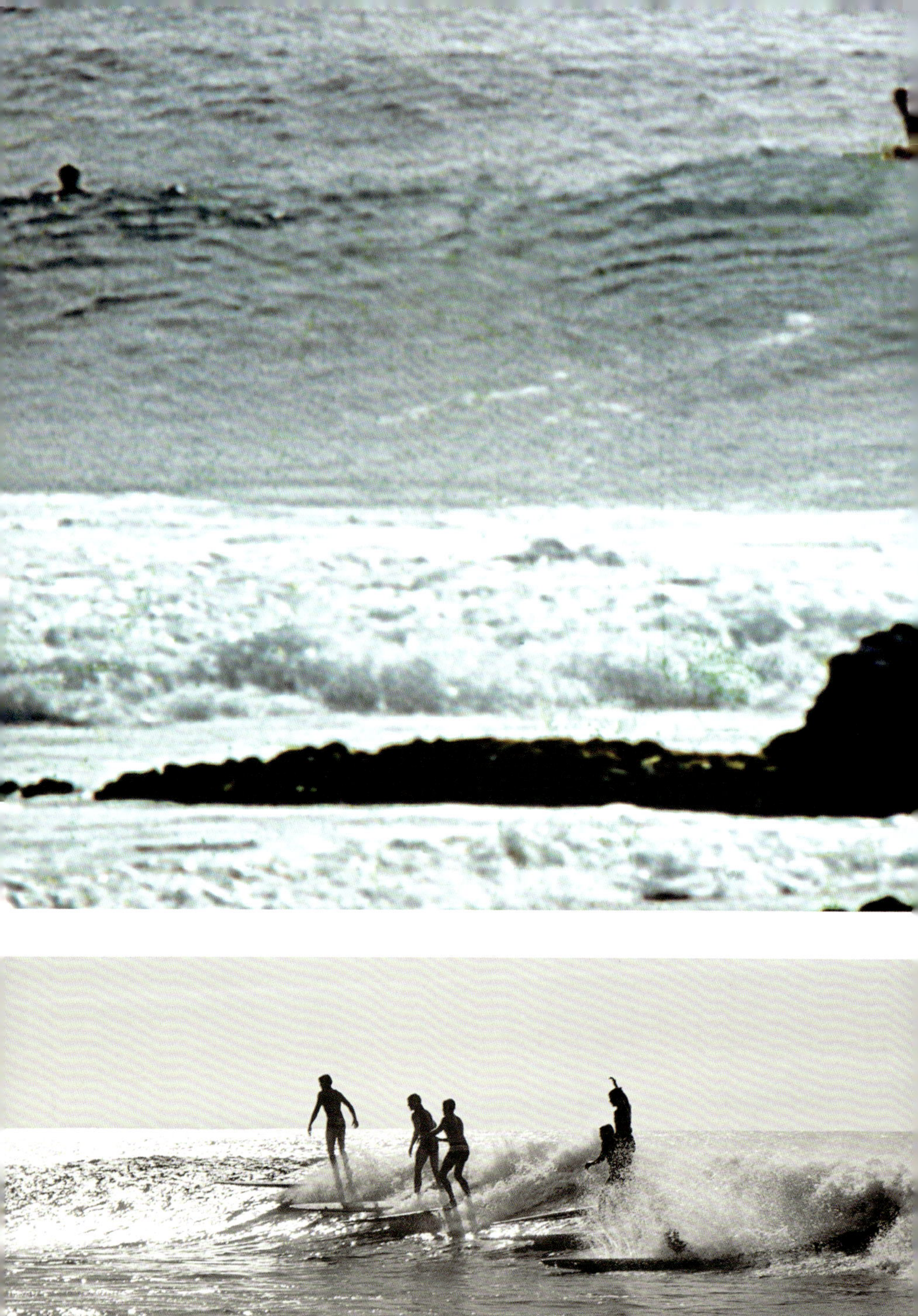

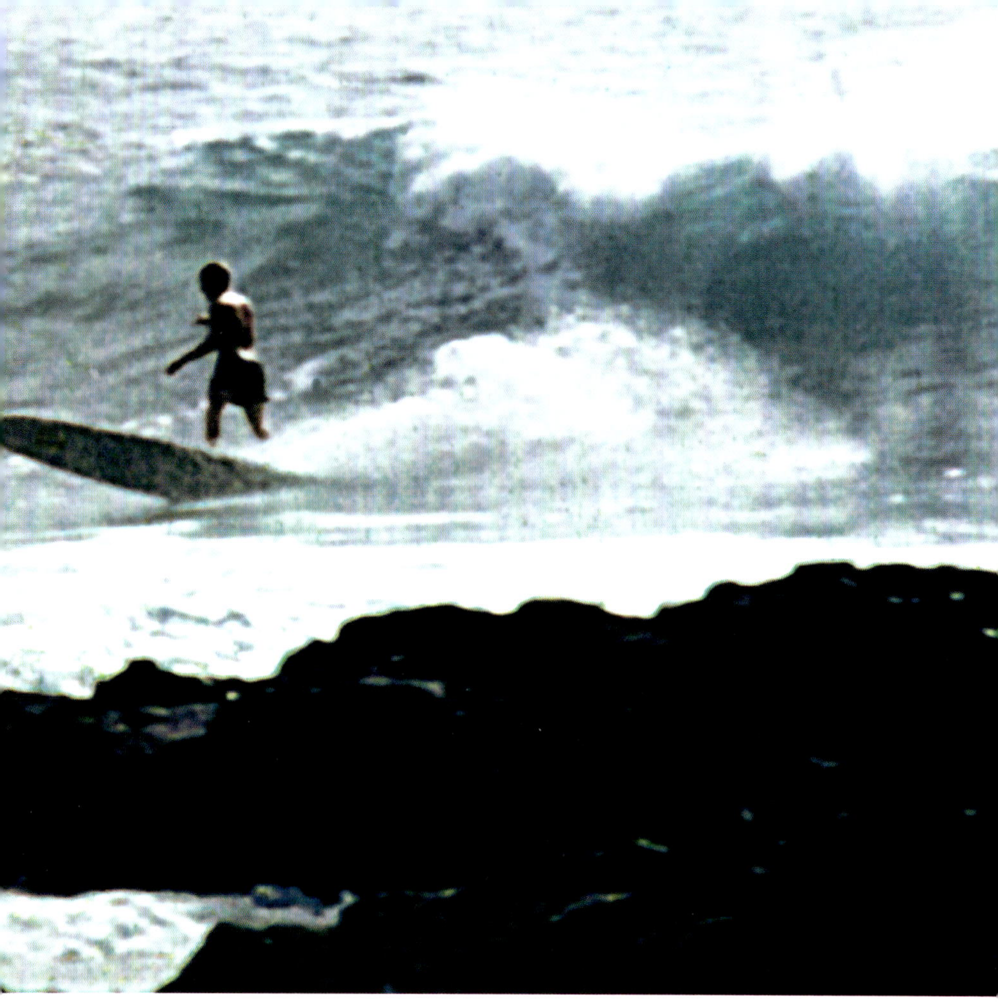

Above: **Bob McTavish Surfing's Free Spirit.** Bob's life and achievements have been extensively covered in surfing magazines over the past 40 years and his exploits have been recorded in two books. In the early 60s Bob wandered the coast living hand to mouth, doing whatever was needed to allow him to spend maximum time in the ocean.

He made headlines in 1963 when he and David Chidgee successfully stowed away on a ship bound for Hawaii where they spent six weeks before being arrested by the FBI and deported.

He won the Queensland Open Men's Title in 1965 which started a string of contest wins for him, but eventually he retired from competitive surfing because it was too restrictive. During the mid '60s he worked at Hayden's factory on the Sunshine Coast and with influence from George Greenough and Nat Young as a test pilot became the innovator of the short board revolution and modern surfing as we know it today. **MS**

Opposite: Unidentified surfers, Crowded wave, Winky Pop, January 1966. **BS**

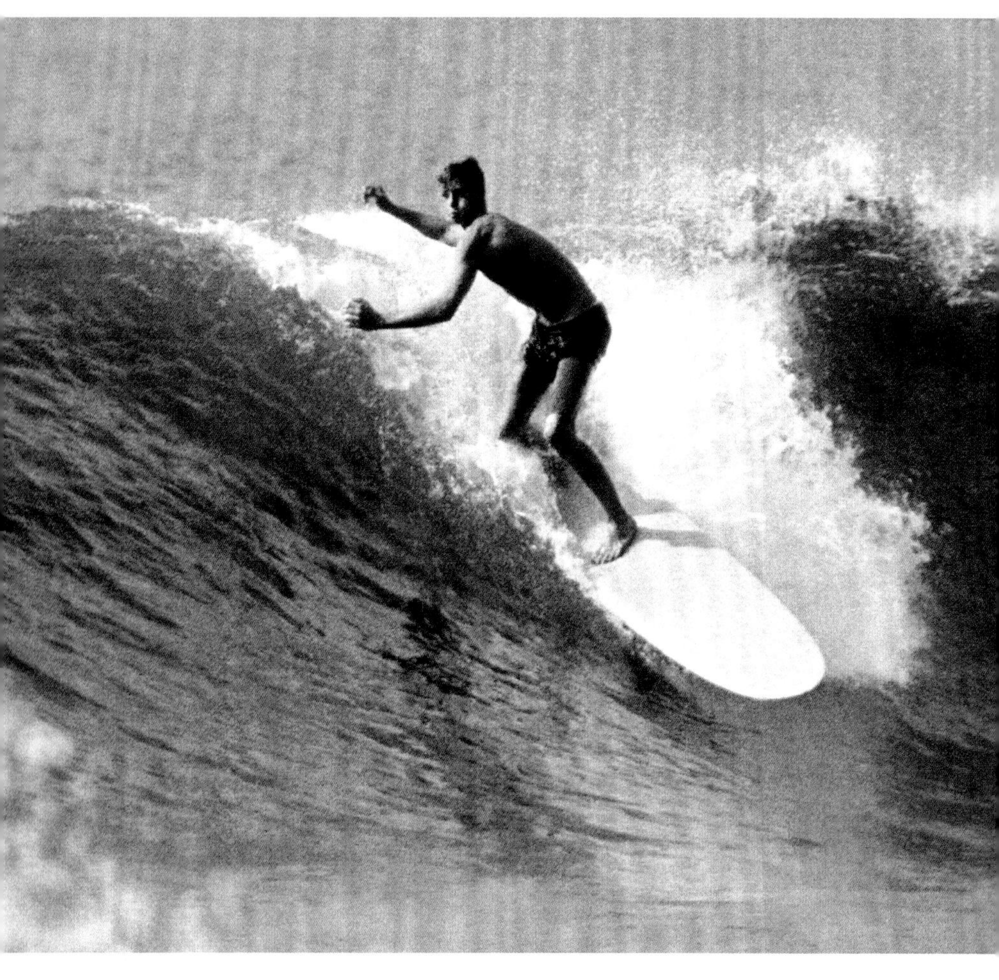

Frank Latta (1947–2010), surfing at Sandshoes, 1964. Frank grew up surfing at Cronulla and was a well-known and talented long board rider in the Sixties and won many surfing awards. He began designing and shaping boards at Jackson's Surfboards around the age of 19.

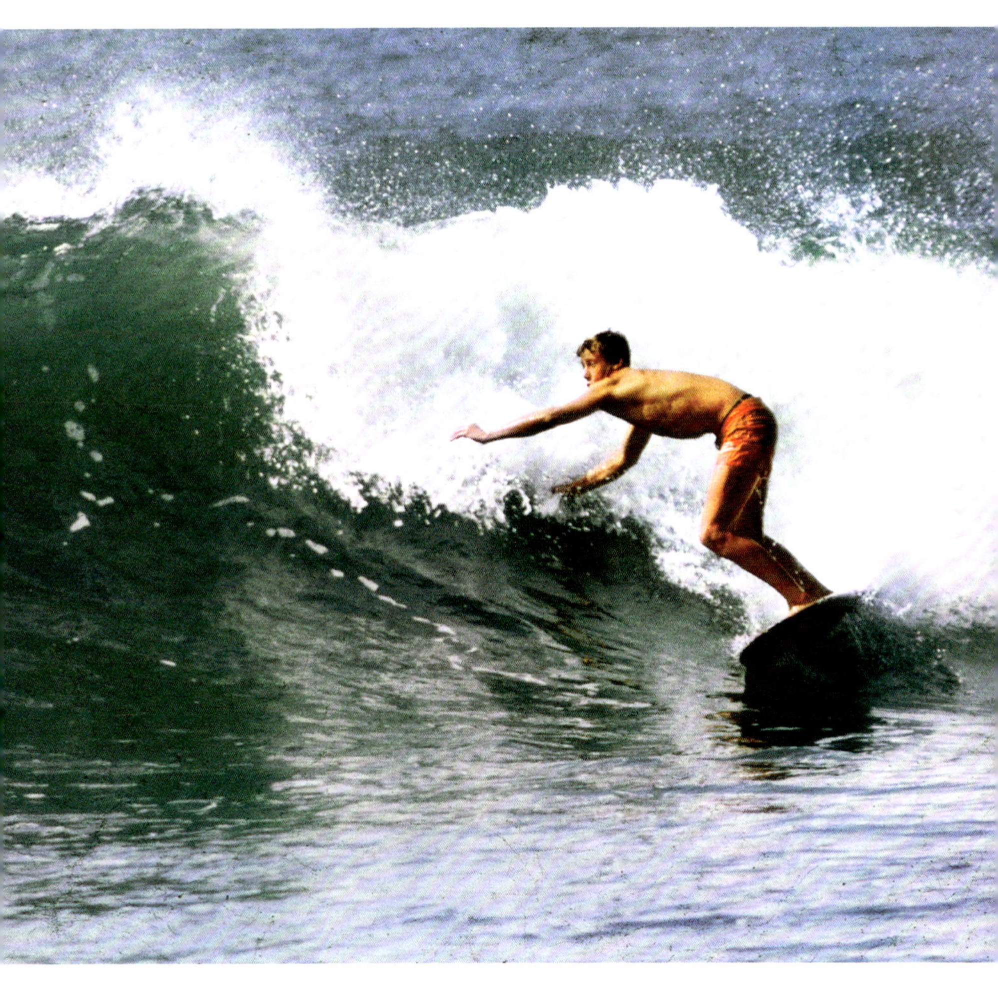

His boards were much sought-after and in 1991 he began shaping boards for John Skipp in Wollongong for several years. He had to give it up because of a hip problem and he died in the surf at Valla Beach aged 63. **BW**

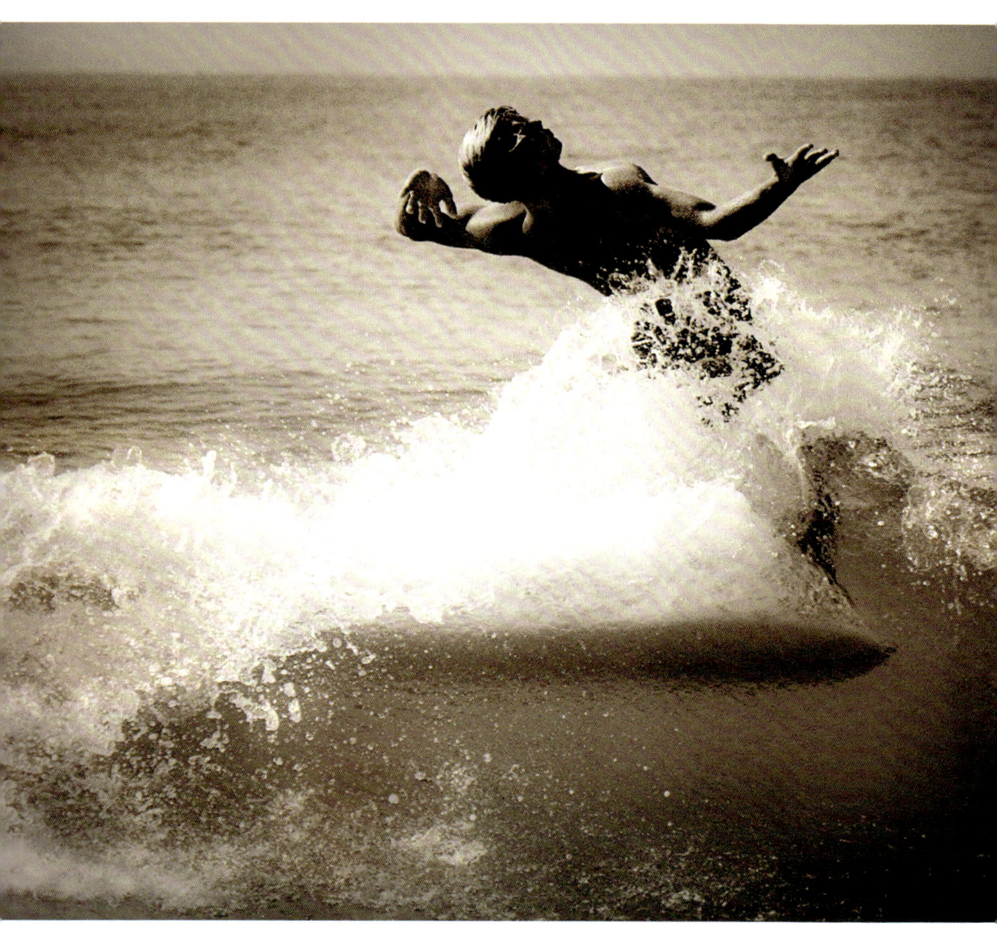

Above: **North Cronulla, 1962.** Noted board builder John Rhodes performing a classic arch on the shorebreak. **BW**

Opposite: **Midway, 1962.** Cronulla's best dressed surfer Billy Dews. **BW**

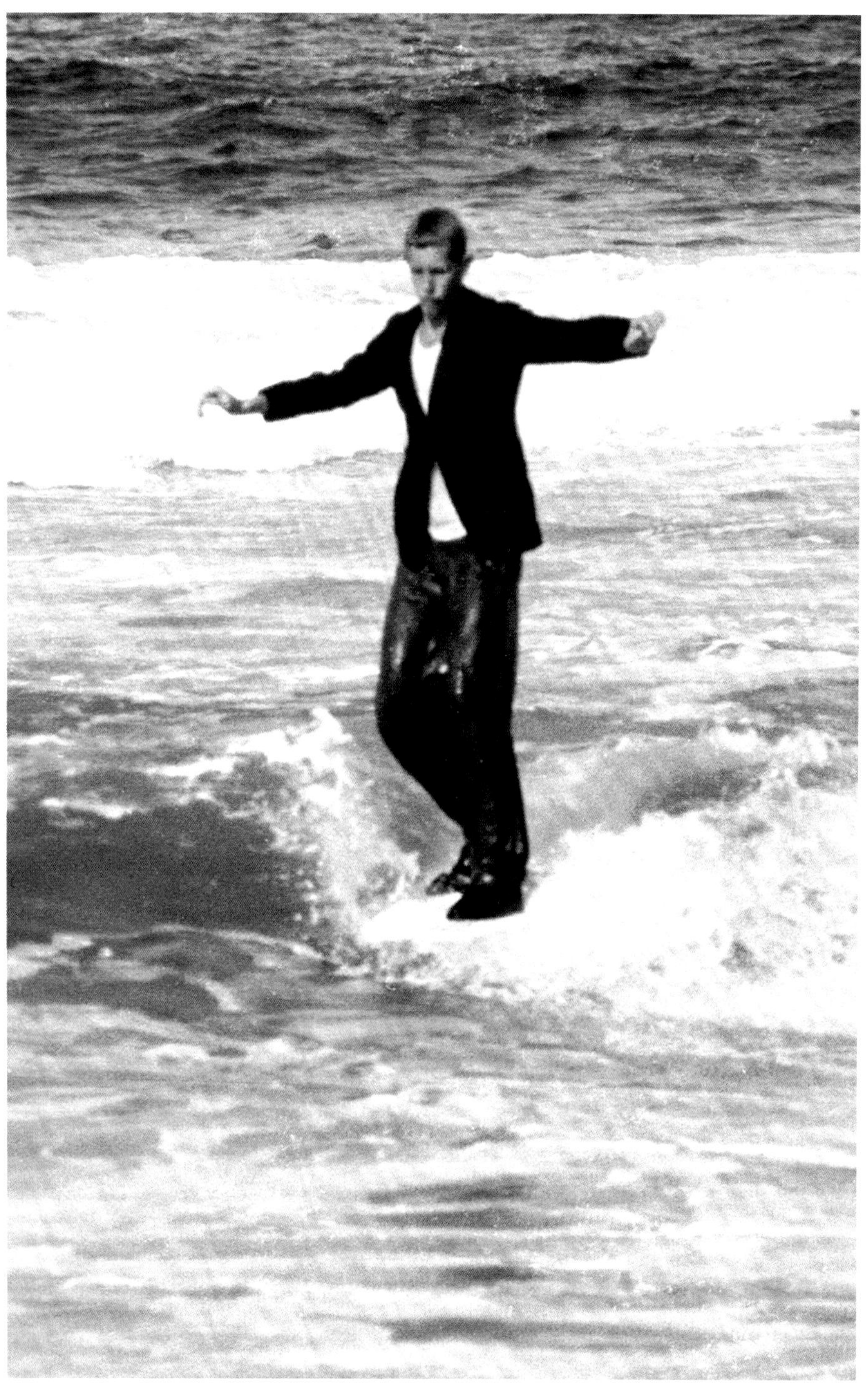

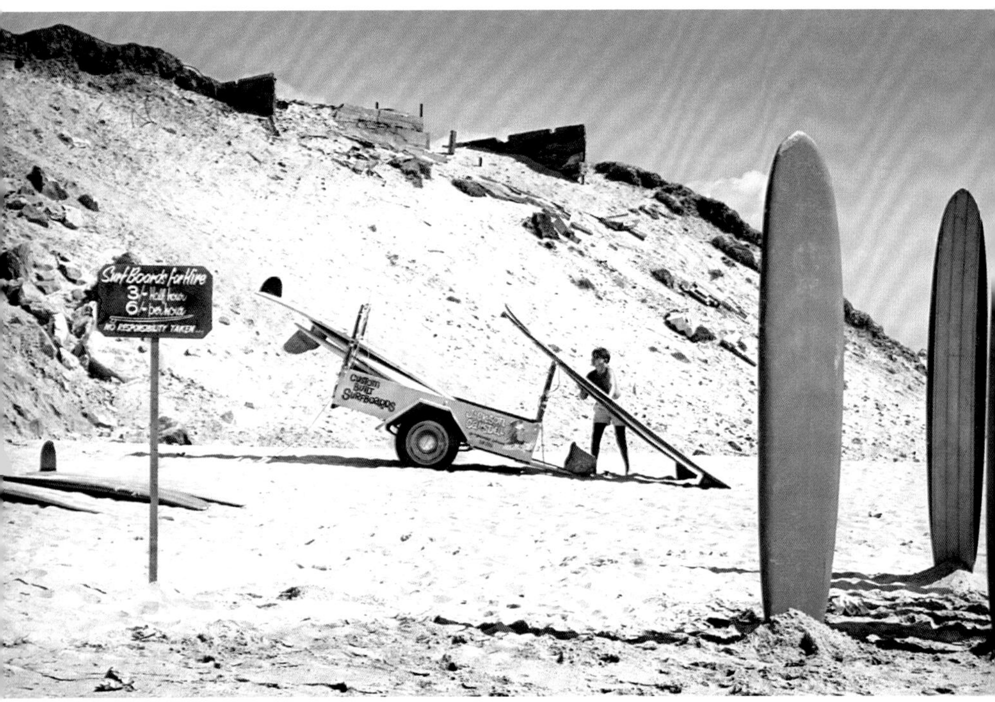

Board Hire, Cronulla, 1963. **BW**

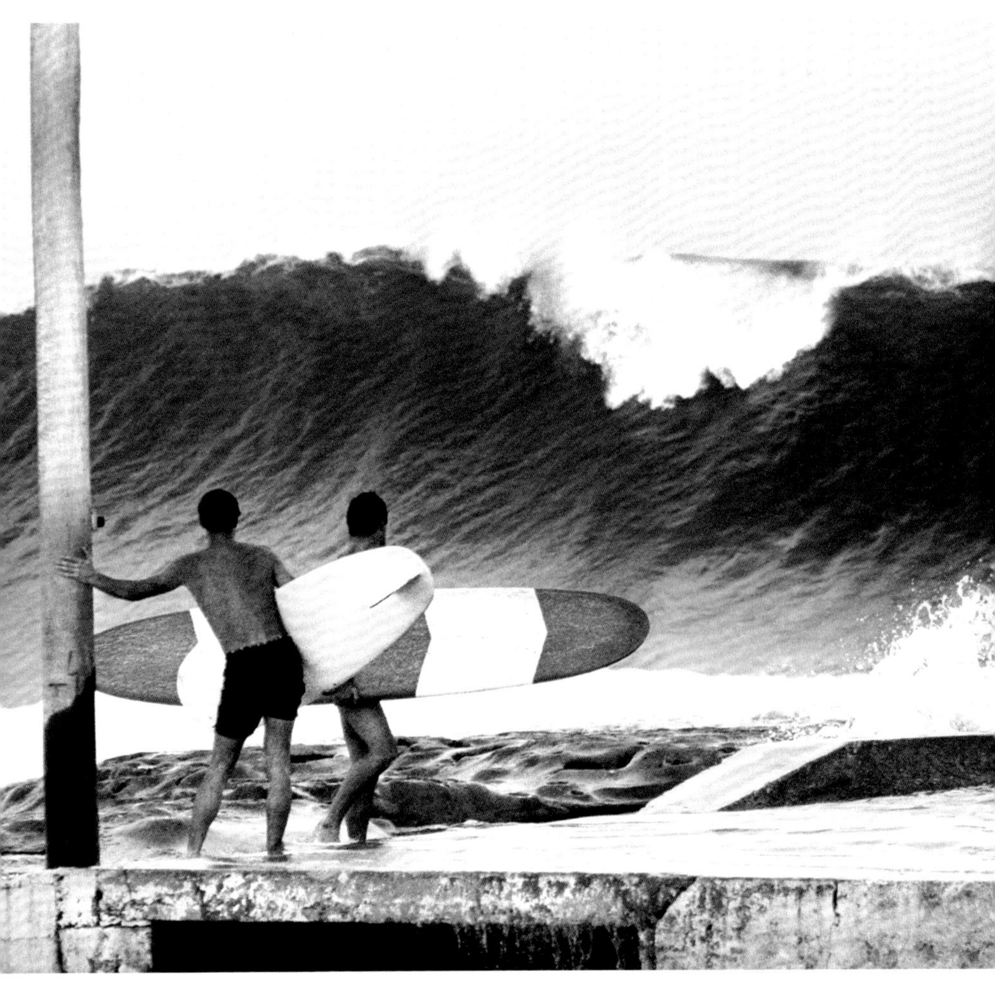

Maybe after this one, Dee Why Point, 1962. Two surfers waiting for a lull to allow them to hop off the rocks and paddle out … the lull never came. **BW**

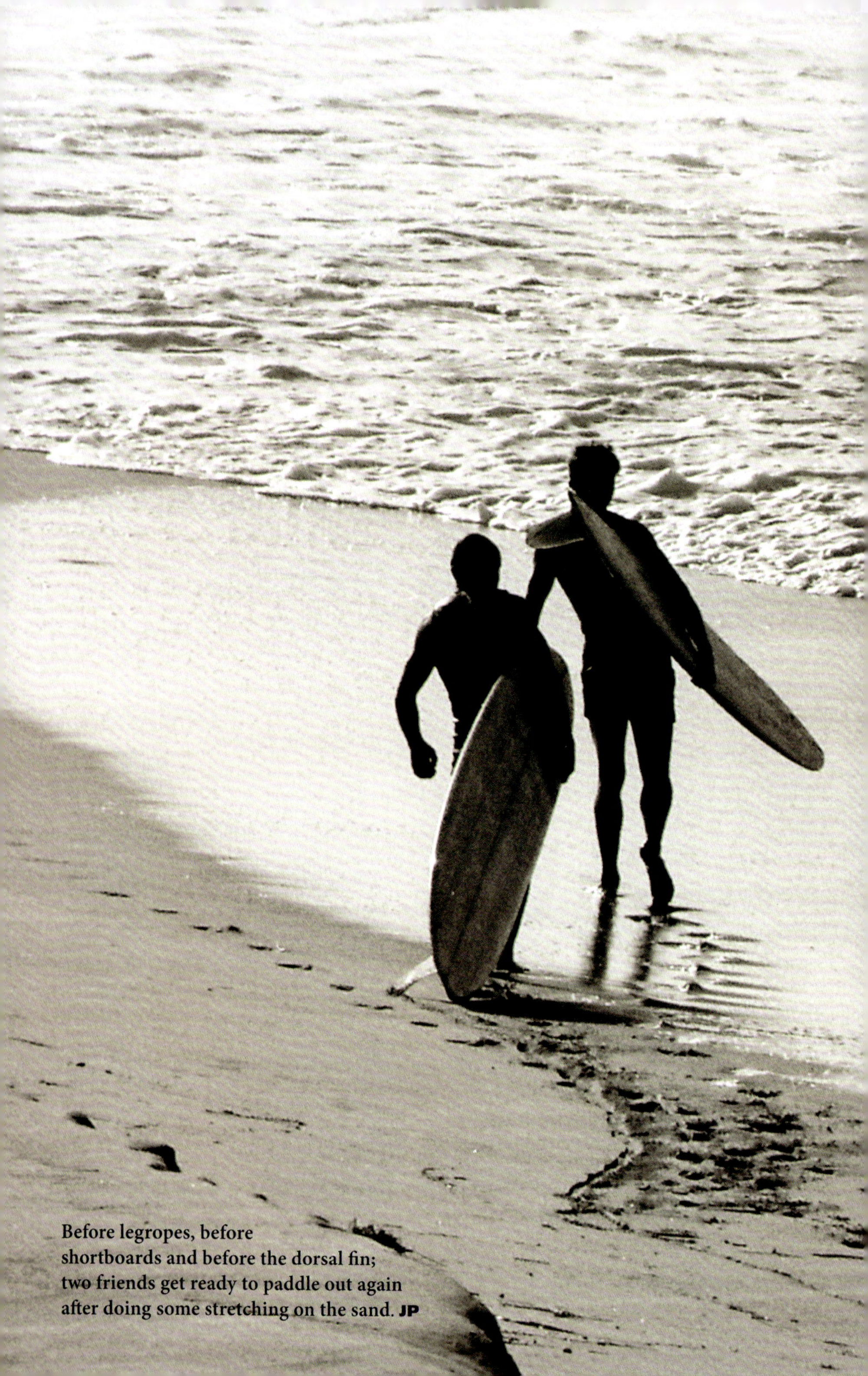

Before legropes, before
shortboards and before the dorsal fin;
two friends get ready to paddle out again
after doing some stretching on the sand. **JP**

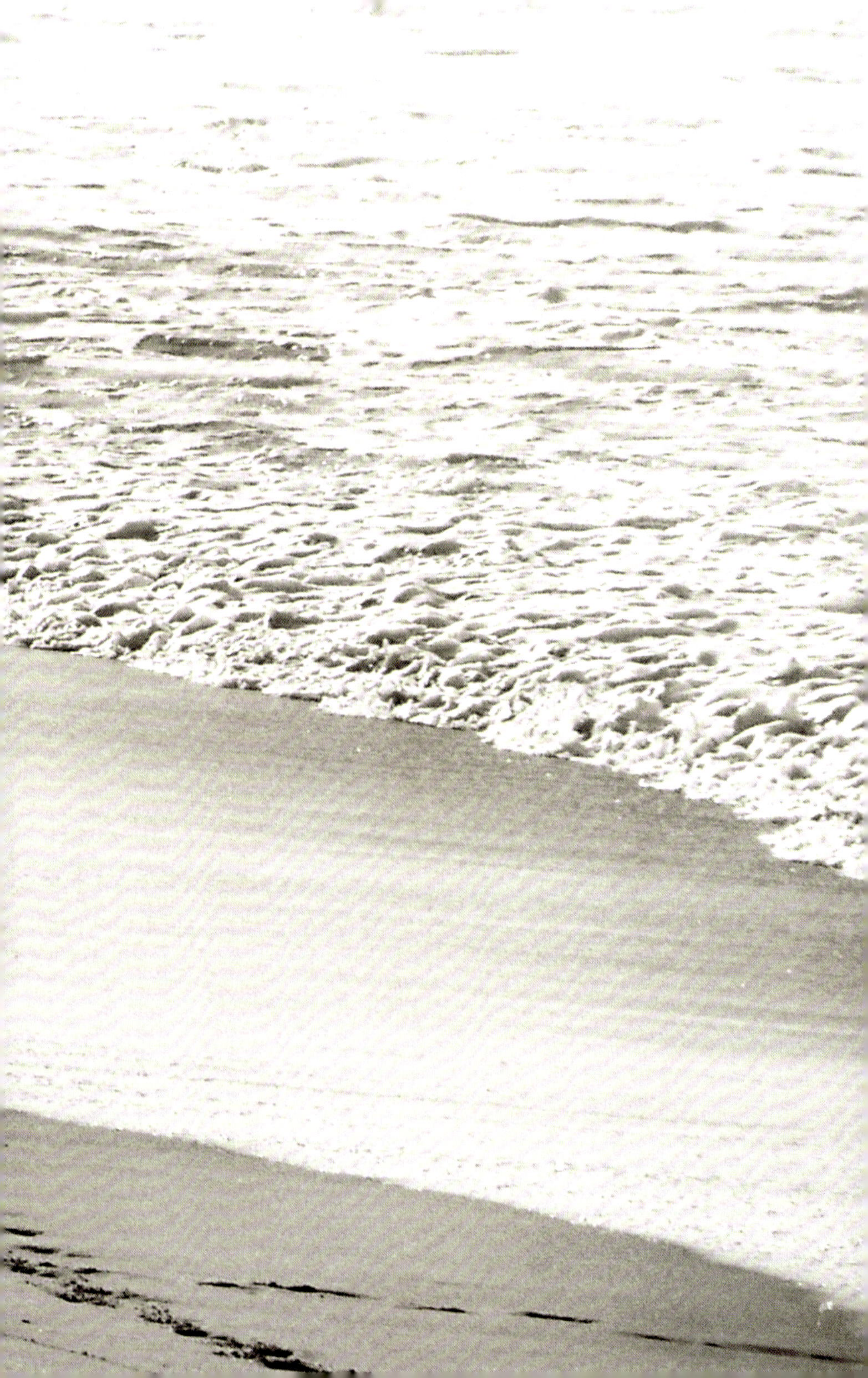

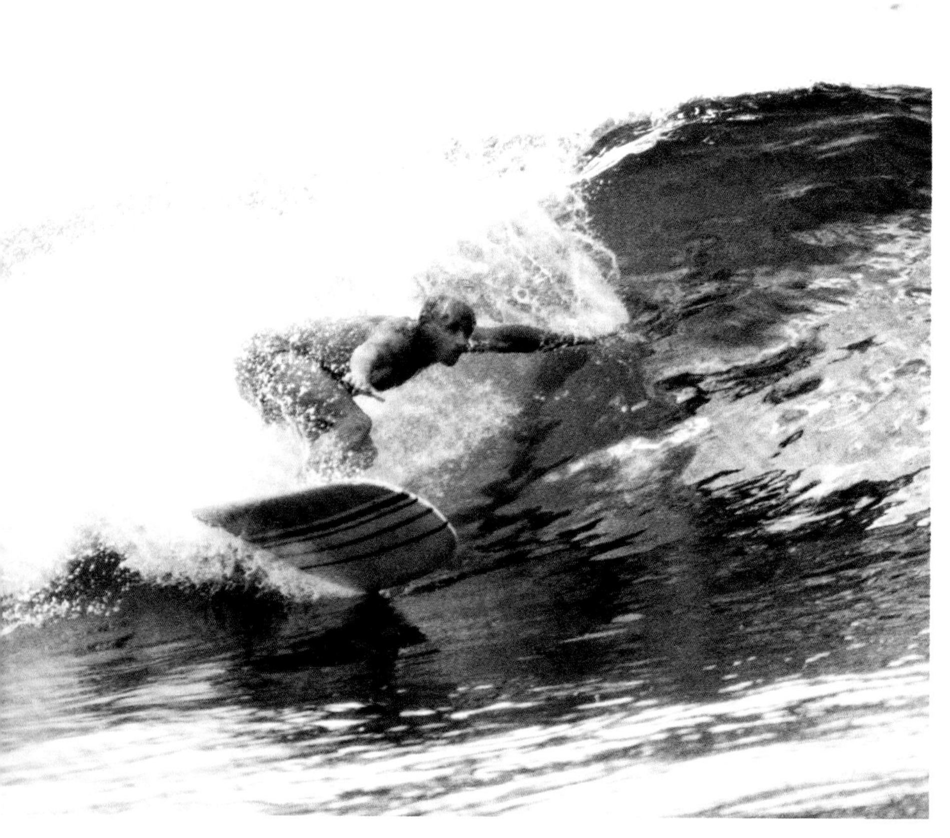

Warwick Smith, Collaroy, 1962. **BW**

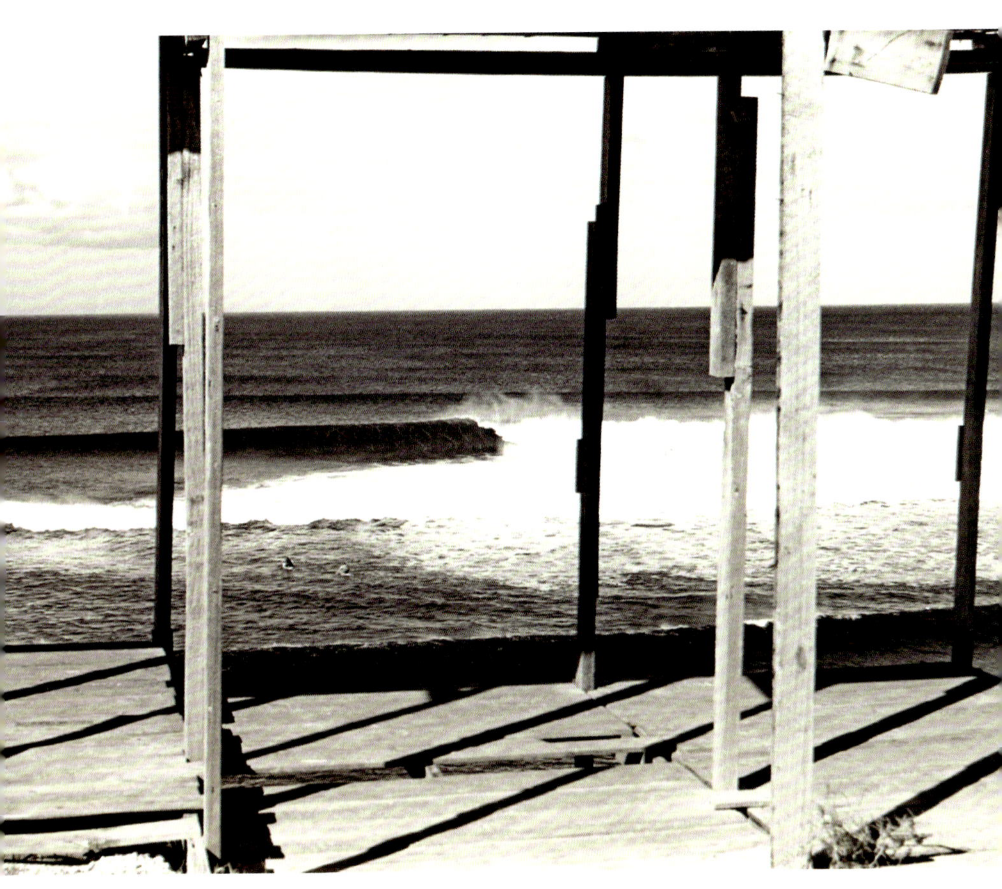

Surfers seen through the vacant judges' stand at Bells Beach. **BS**

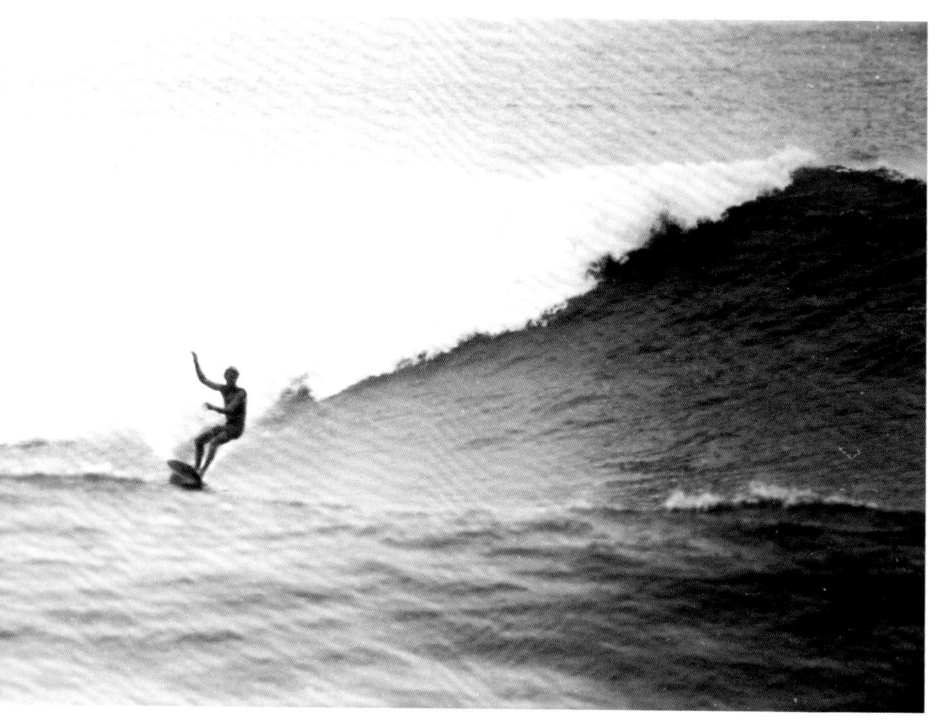

Above: Going left, Midget Farrelly riding one of his own shapes. Midget was the heartbeat of Australian surfing in the early 1960s. He went on to be the first world champion (1964) and a prolific surfboard designer who hugely influenced the transition to shorter surfboards. Bells Beach. **JP**

Opposite: **Solitude, 1961.** Terry Tumeth's calming stance near the completion of his ride at Cronulla Point. **BW**

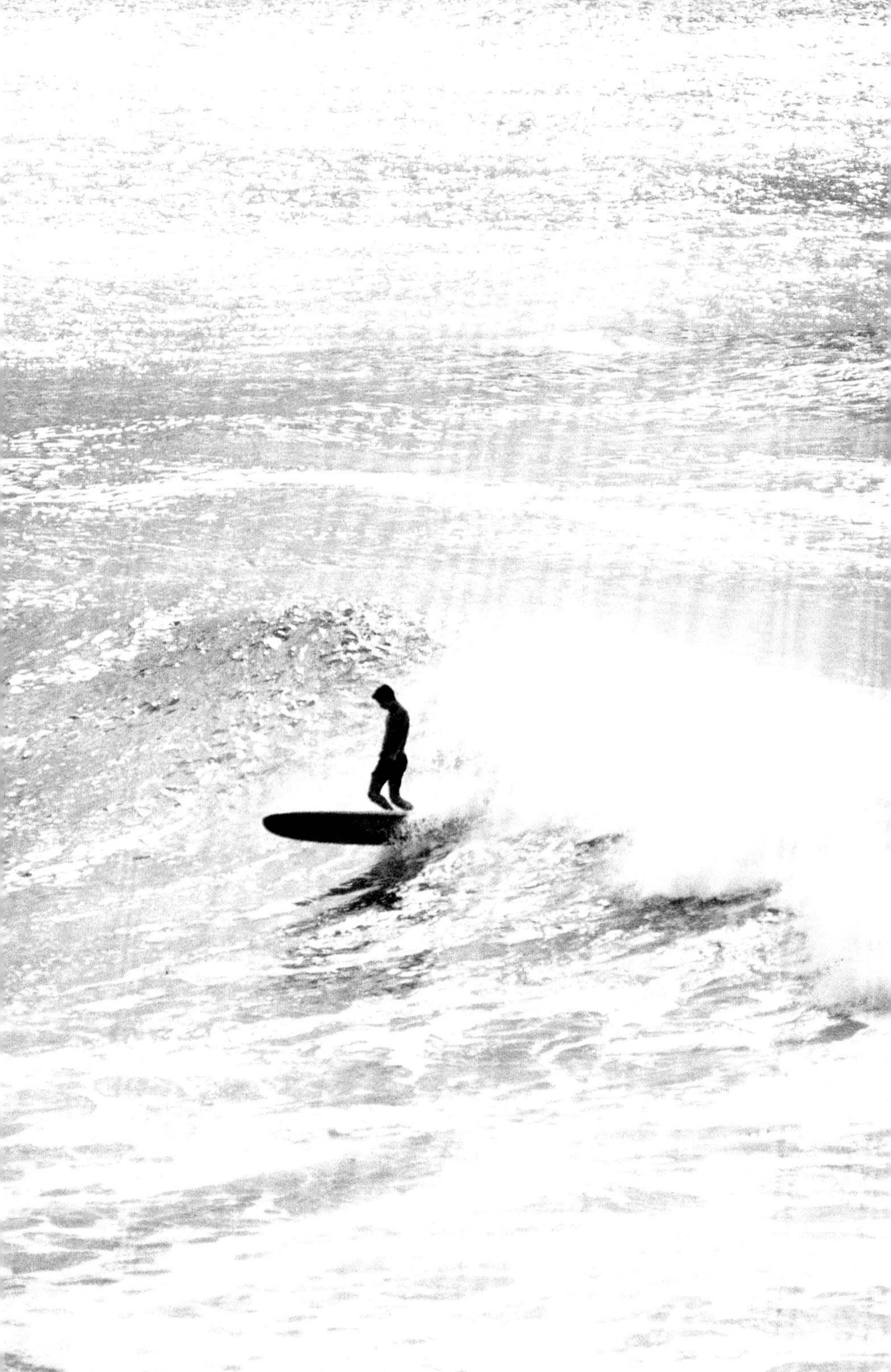

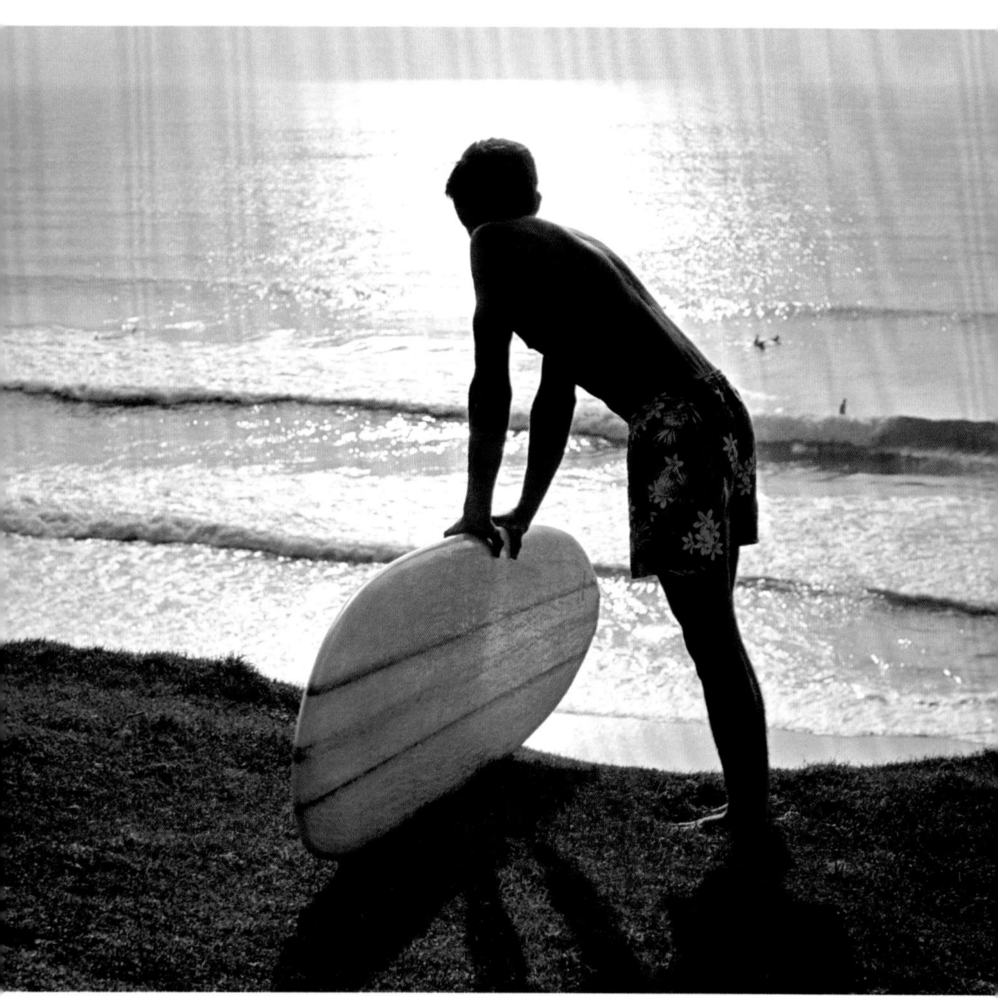

Gordon Hill, 1964.

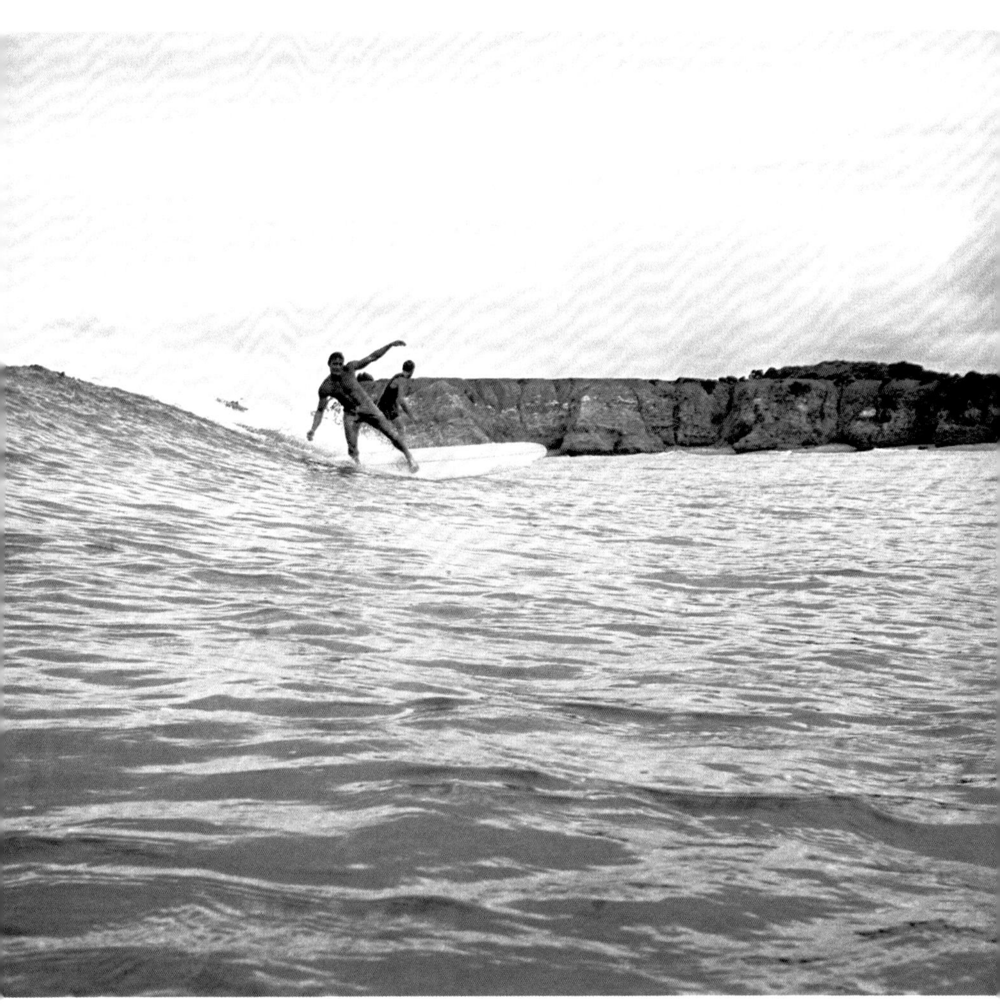

John Gudgeon, from the water, Torquay Point, 1967. **BS**

"*My earliest recollection of learning to surf was in the 1950s with my cousin Ian Von Einem at Torquay Front Beach. We'd walk from my grandfathers' house at 60 Anderson Street, down to the Front Beach. Apart from the demolition of the old houses over the years, and their replacement with larger homes or units, the street always looks strangely familiar to me. The most significant feature is the combination of grassed verges, some sections with gravel pathways, others none at all. The wooden groynes were there, adjacent to the bathing boxes. There was no seawall and no Norfolk Island pines. The beach sand mingled around the bathing boxes with tracks leading up to The Esplanade. It was an idyllic childhood period for us in the early 1950s. We were free to roam down to the beach to play and swim in the small, safe surf.*"

Barrie Sutherland

Barrie Sutherland, Bells Bowl on his new Gordon Woods surfboard, February 1963. **BS**

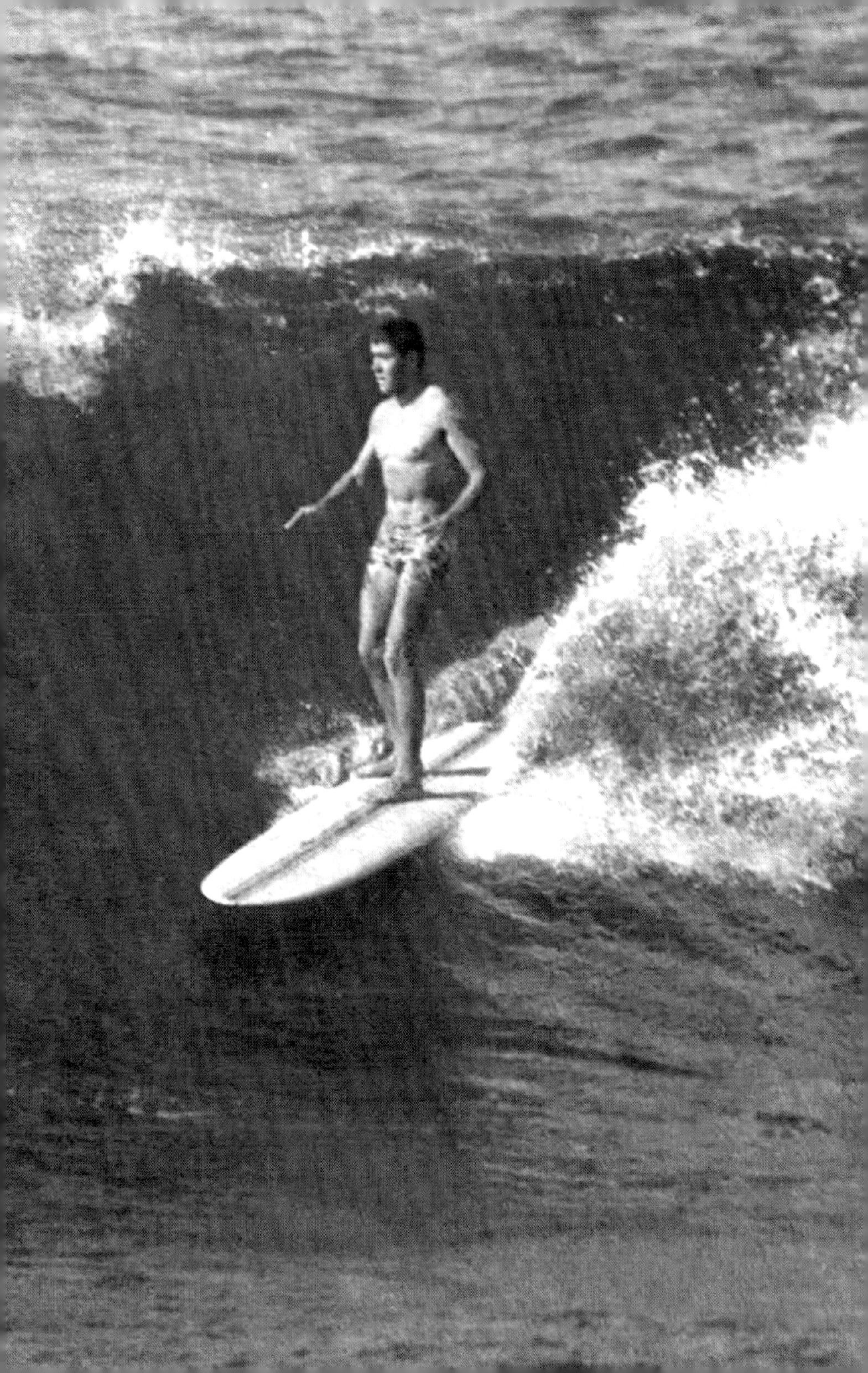

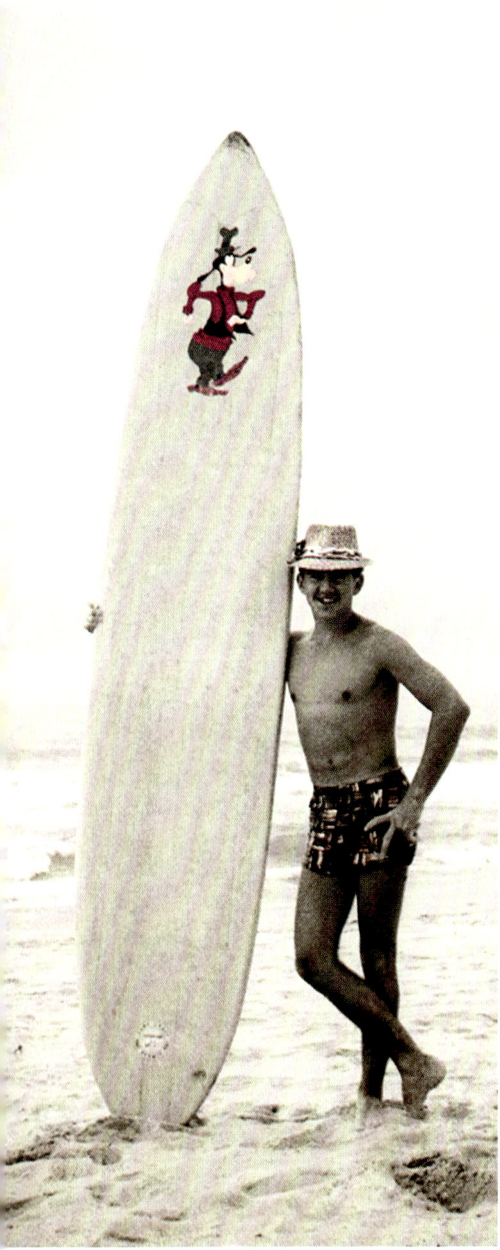

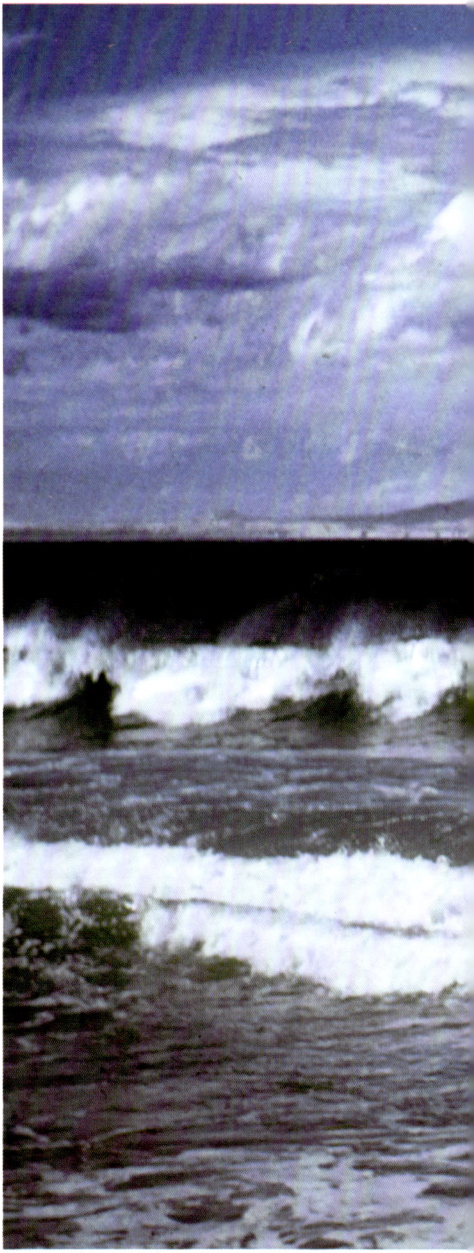

Midway, 1960. Gordon Hill
with his arty balsa board. **BW**

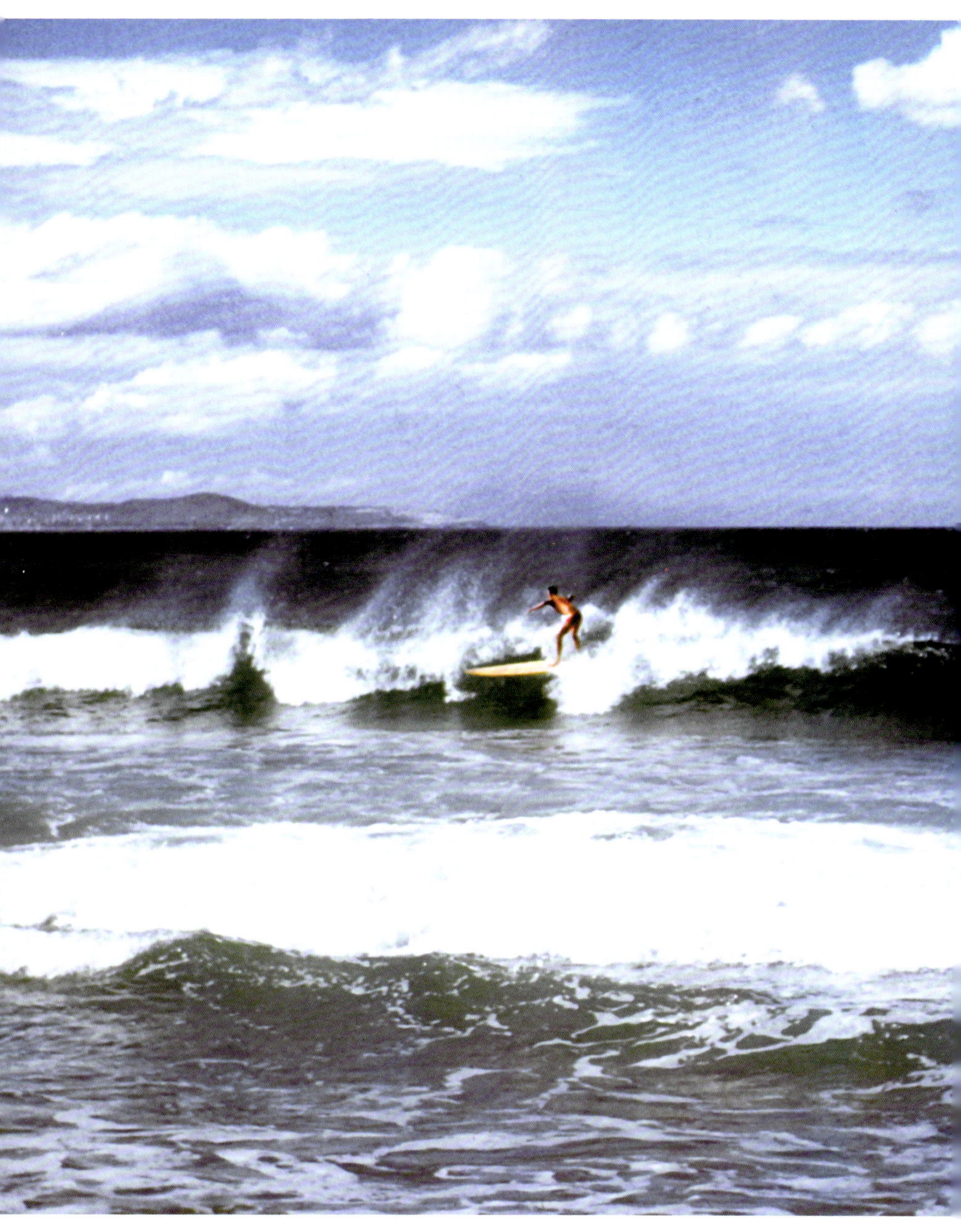

The Alley, May 1960. This is the very first surfing photo that I took before I began surfing. I was wandering around with a small camera not long after my family moved to a nearby Cronulla suburb and this is the result. **BW**

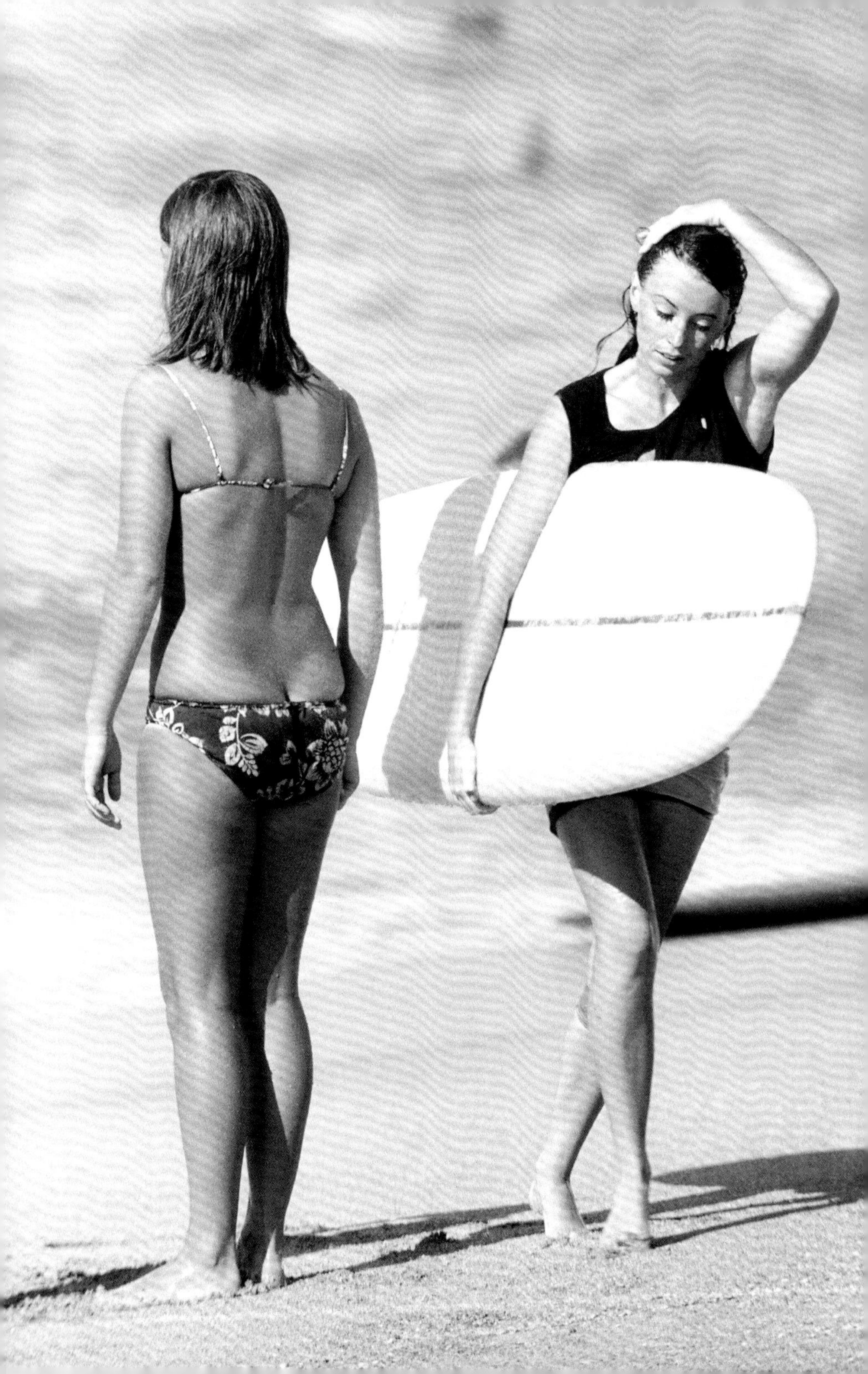

Beach Fashion

As Australia entered a new decade, swimwear reflected the conservative nature of the 1950s which, for the most part, had been geared towards adult needs rather than the humble teenager. All that changed in the 1960s, however, as baby-boomers found a fashion style that favoured low-cut bathing suit boardshorts (called 'boardies' or 'baggies') and the increasing popularity of the bikini. Female bathing suits – once cut straight across the top of the leg to form a 'modesty apron' to hide the separate matching fabric crutch in young women – all of a sudden looked decidedly old-fashioned. The bikini was sexy, permissive and here to stay!

A French fashion innovation from as far back as 1946, the two-piece bikini (so named after Bikini Atoll in the Pacific, which had been used for atomic bomb tests) found instant fame when Brigitte Bardot starred in the 1952 film *Manina, la fille sans voile* (*Manina, the Girl Unveiled*). A decade later, actress Ursula Andress stepped out of the blue crystal ocean (and into the collective fantasies of the western male) wearing a stunning white bikini (not to mention the matching white knife belt) in the first James Bond movie, *Dr No*.

Fashion designers from around the world began to focus on the tastes and styles preferred by the ever-growing youth market. Designs created for the younger generation in Europe and America quickly found their way to Australia through the popularity of beach-culture-associated media. A change in fabric to Nylon and Lycra gave swimsuits the stretchable quality needed for the beach. American brand jeans were hugely popular with both sexes, as were that ubiquitous fashion accessory – sunglasses – while casual shoes ranged from rubber souled tennis or beach shoes to sandals and thongs.

Spending prolonged periods in the sun resulted in another minor revolution in regards to headwear. In 1963, bikinis and headscarves were all the rage after the release of the *Beach Party* film starring Annette Funicello. 'Beach Party' head scarves, a long strip of patterned fabric tied around the hairline, added a splash of colour and style as well as protecting women's hair from the elements. Straw beach hats also led the resurgence in head apparel, serving both a functional and fashionable role.

Dianne Milling (left) checking the action as Lyn McCarthy leaves the water after completing her heat, Wanda 1966. **BW**

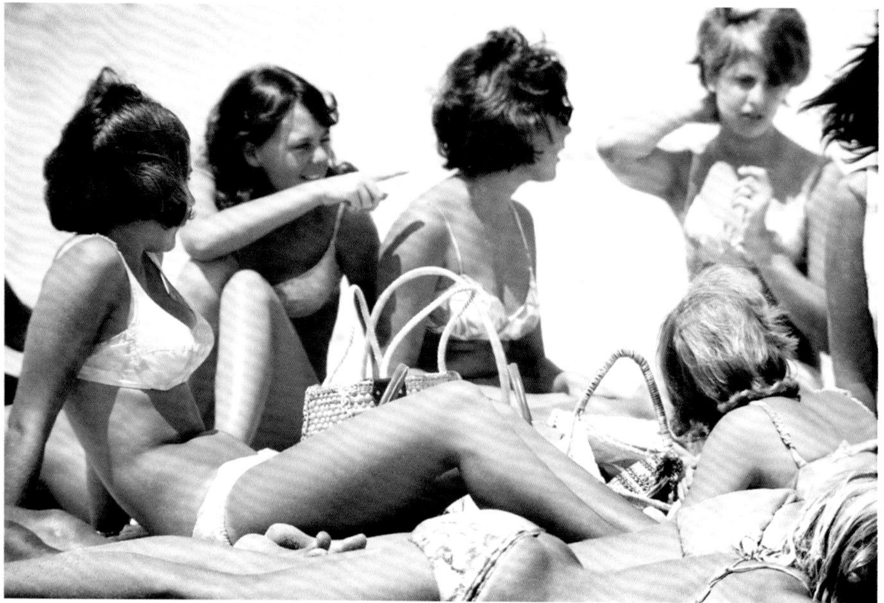

Wanda girls, 1964. **BW**

A lone boardrider, wearing the latest bikini fashion, paddles out to the waves. **JP**

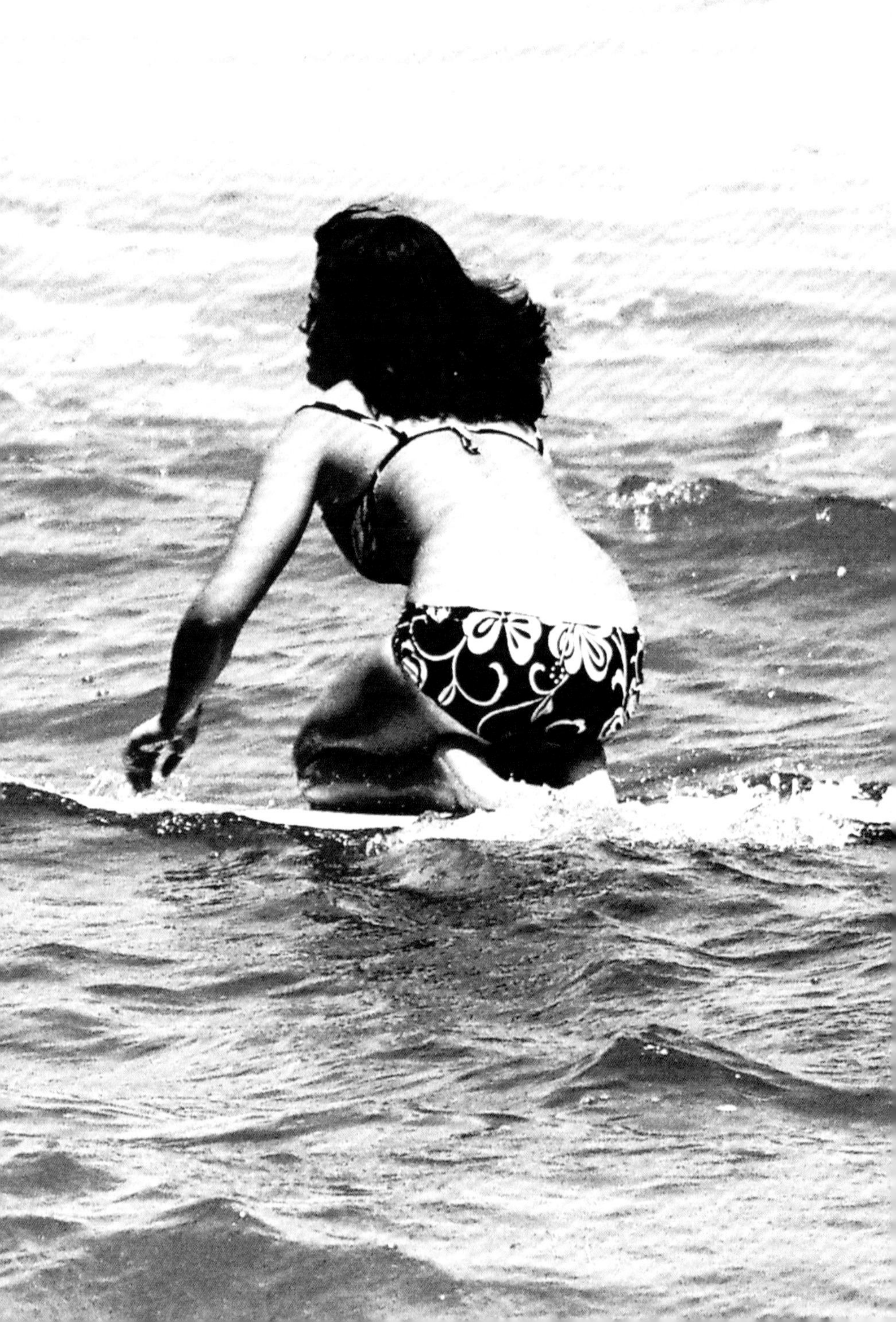

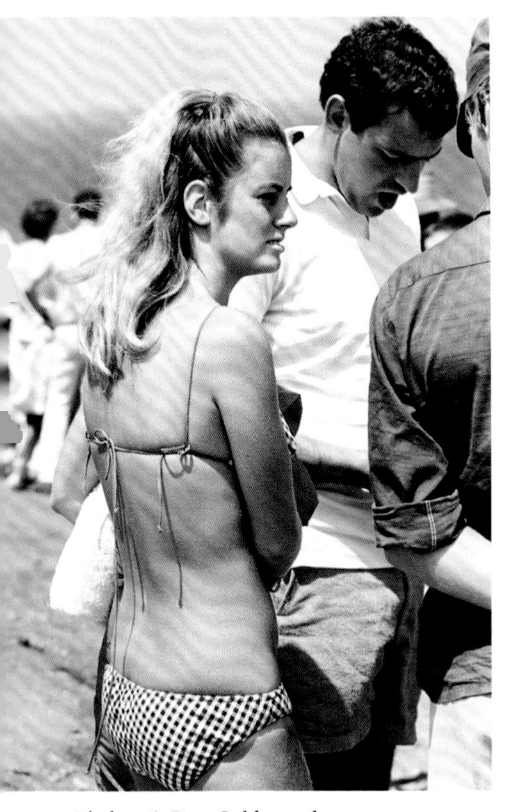

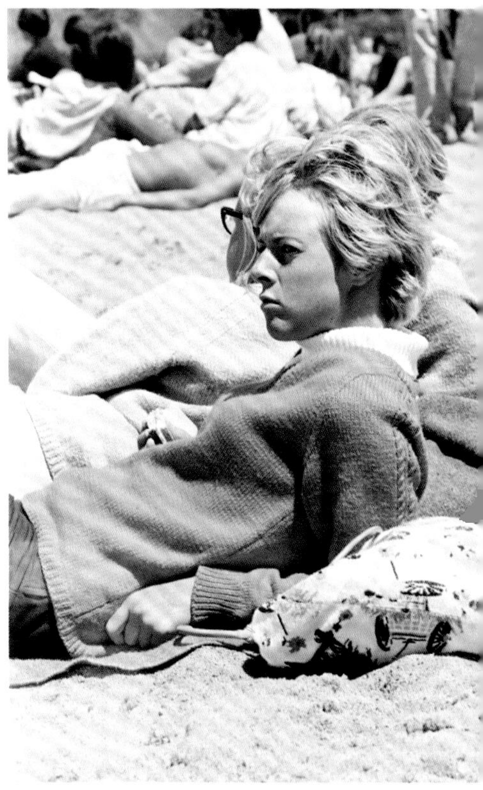

Thelma & Ron Goldsworthy. **BS**

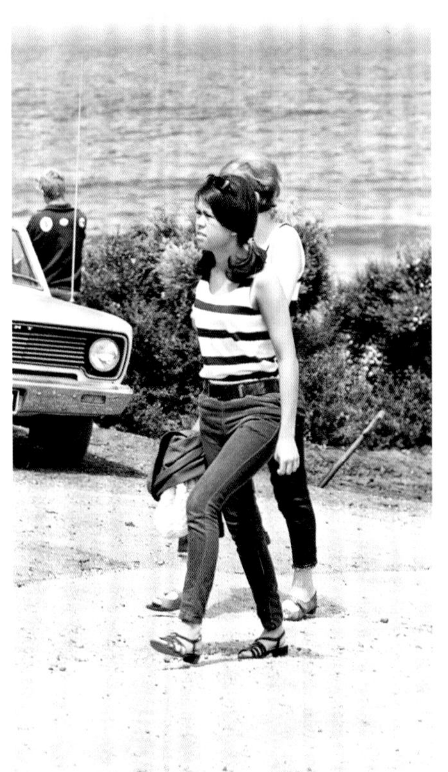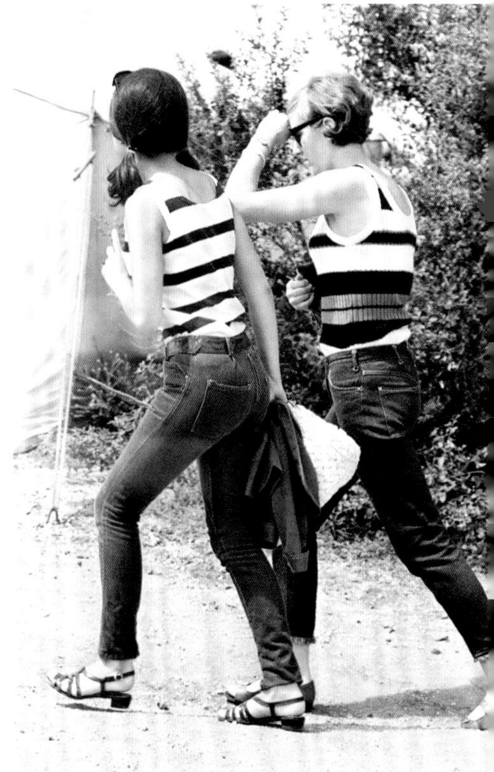

At the Victorian Titles, Bells Beach, February 1967. **BS**

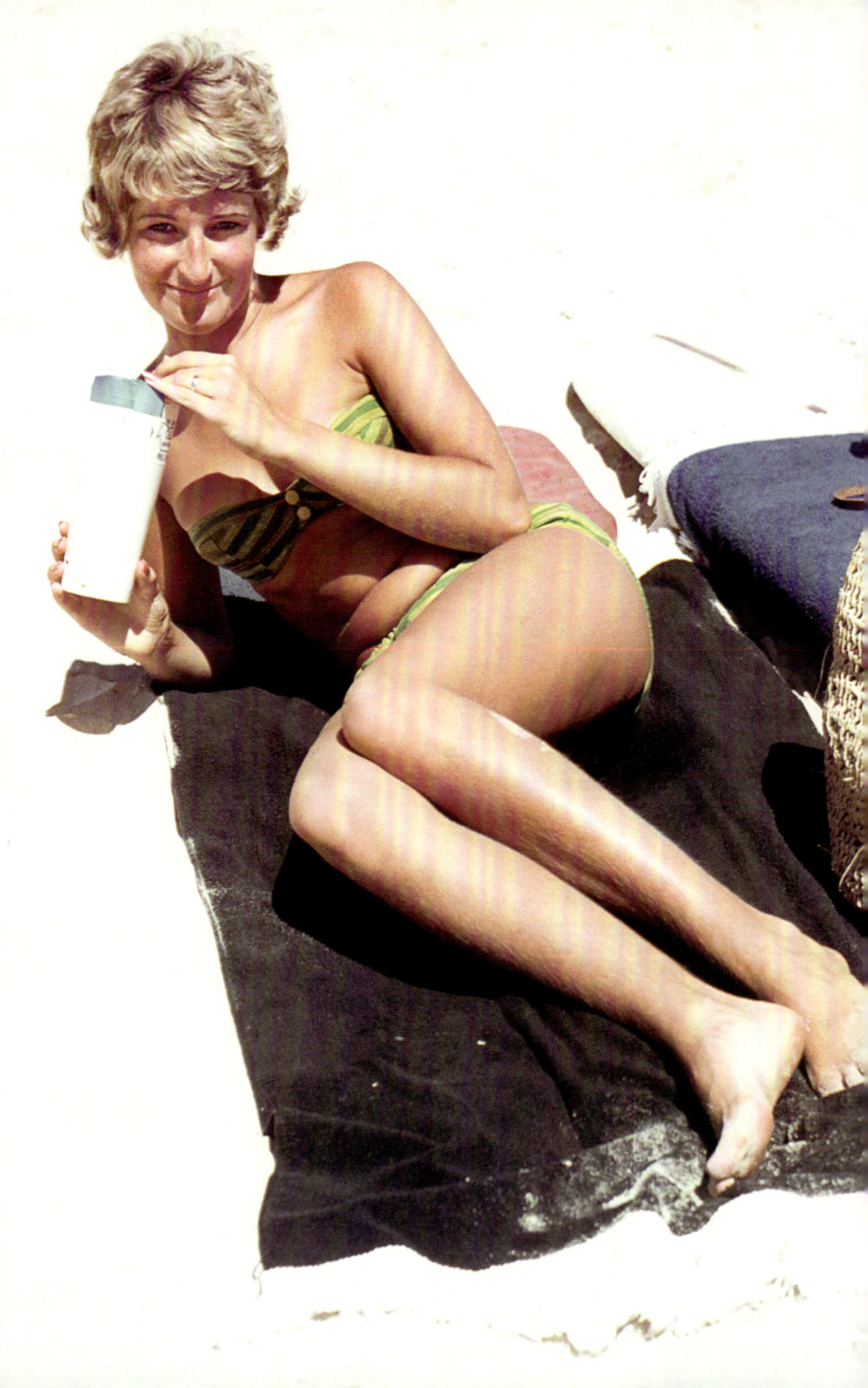

Do-It-Yourself

I designed and sewed my clothes from an early age and apart from some very basic sewing classes at high school I was self taught, so many of my efforts resulted in reconstructed mistakes that often turned out to be fabulous. I learned to be creative because of this. Much of my material was from unpicked garments that were hand me downs or my father's shirts, dinner suit pants, hessian bags ... whatever caught my eye!

By the time I left school and was earning my first weekly wages I had the luxury of shopping for fabrics which I often hunted out of the remnant bins. Although I didn't follow or read the patterns correctly I managed to fit my pattern pieces on the cloth, despite not always having enough. It taught me to think outside the box and I never tossed away a mistake ... I somehow fixed it with innovation and ideas.

I wish I had been confident enough to go to a dressmaking or design school to learn properly and save myself countless hours of frustration and distress. I laboured late into the night trying to fix many mistakes or fit the pattern pieces together properly.

Shopping for clothes in the '50s and '60s was difficult for anyone as slight as I was, probably between a size 6 and 8, and unlike today's options, choice was limited and price tags prohibitive. There was no Target or KMart!

I loved owning unique outfits that creating and sewing afforded me.

My bikinis were made by covering underwire bras and a cut down briefs pattern. As I recall, bought bikini patterns only had triangle tops which did nothing for my 32B cup size. I never learned to draft a pattern ... it was too daunting for me as I was hopeless with maths and numbers ... it all seemed too hard.

The pics featured here show some of the pieces I made to take on my honeymoon to the Gold Coast in 1965. I had several sets of matching 3/4 pants and bikinis, with contrasting tops and triangle head scarves, which must have been the rage for the surfie girls. Kerchiefs I think we called them.

The white terry towelling which kept fraying was a brute to sew and annoyed me so much as I tried to keep the bikini small. I laugh now at the bulk of it compared with the micro designs so available these days. My blue and white gingham top and head scarf went with this.

Yellow 3/4 pants were worn with my homemade silky Paisley style shirt, or a tank style top of white with large yellow spots and matching head scarf. Yellow bikini from the same cotton fabric as the pants.

Madeleine, Coolangatta Beach, April 1965. **BS**

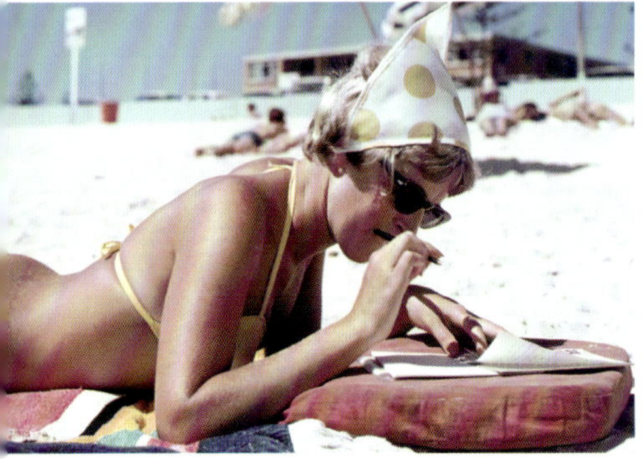

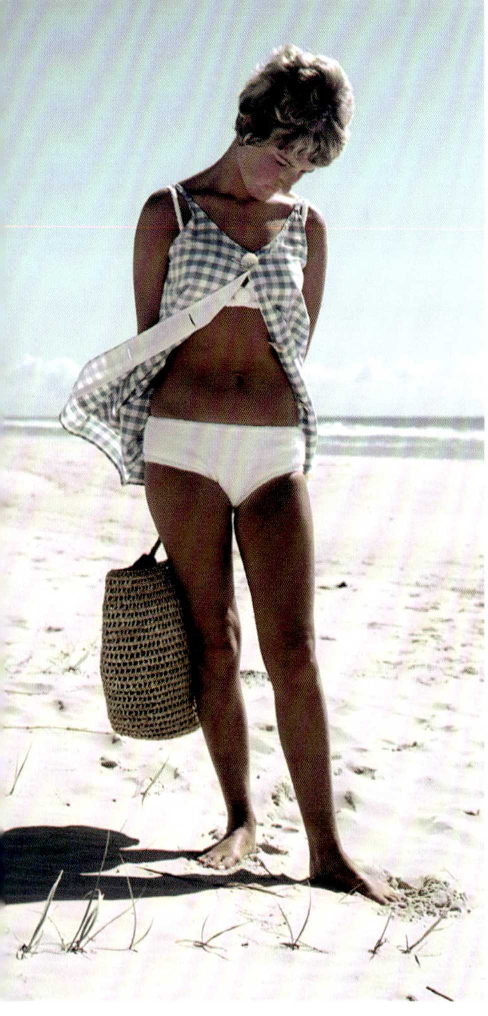

Lime green and yellow striped bikini also had the 3/4 matching pants and head scarf and a chartreuse/lime silky tank style top went with that.

A veritable trousseau of leisure wear!

Considering the meagre wage of the day, I managed to have a good wardrobe collection because of my interest in sewing.

Woven raffia beach bags were in vogue in the sixties and although useless in the sand, were a fashion must-have, along with the fabulous knitted cotton tops in a natural colour. These were popular for males and females.

I cut and sewed a pair of Bermuda shorts out of a couple of hessian bags I begged from my father's shed. They teamed well with these knitted cotton tees or better still ... with a black t shirt ... the very trendy beatnik colour of the day!

I cut up my bamboo hula hoop to make handles for a large black corduroy bag I sewed when I was fifteen. Did I say innovative? Another beach bag for my collection.

Creativity grows out of necessity and some of my friends also made themselves items they wanted and couldn't buy.

MADELEINE SUTHERLAND

Madeleine, Palm Beach, April 1965. **BS**

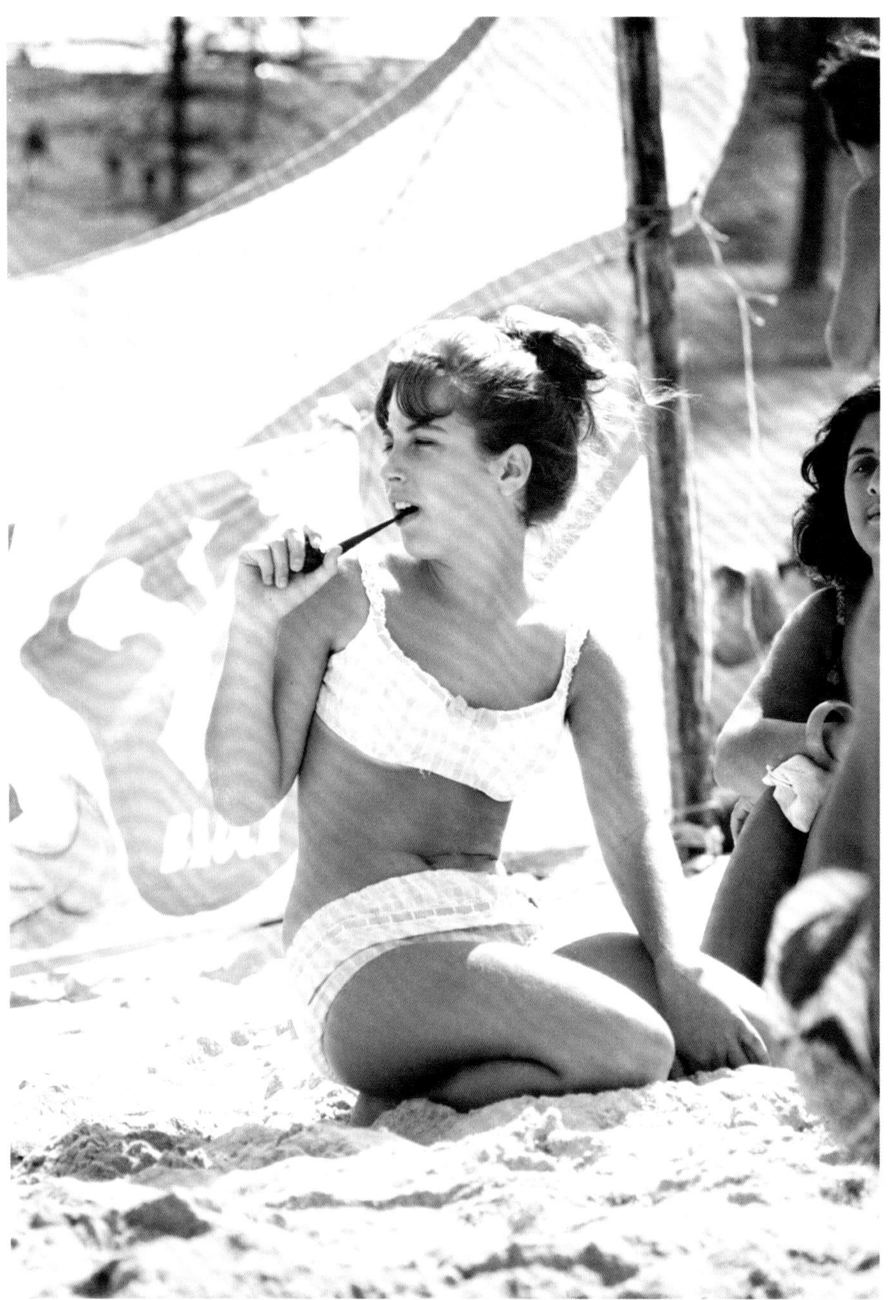

Unidentified girl, Bondi Beach 1963. While photographing the Ladies' Invitational Championships at Bondi that year, I spotted this young lady smoking a pipe! A quick click captured the chick! **BW**

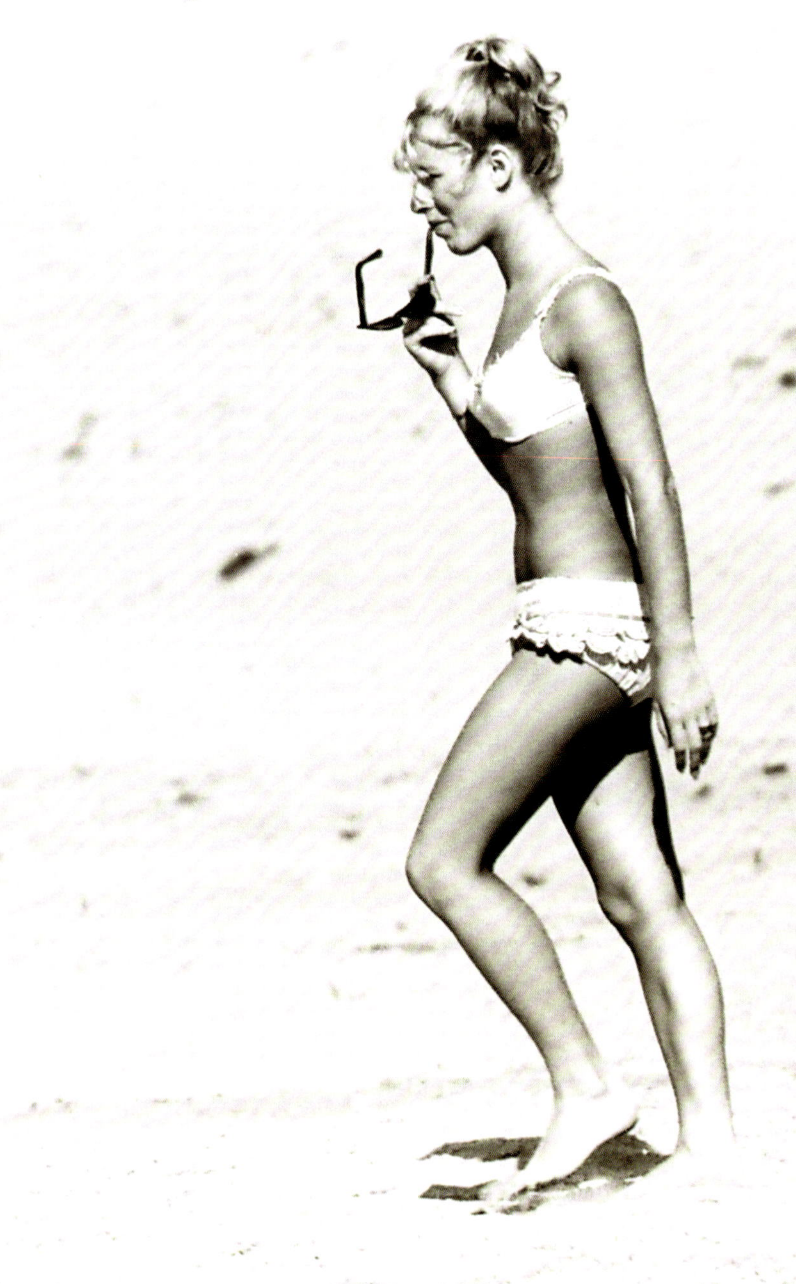

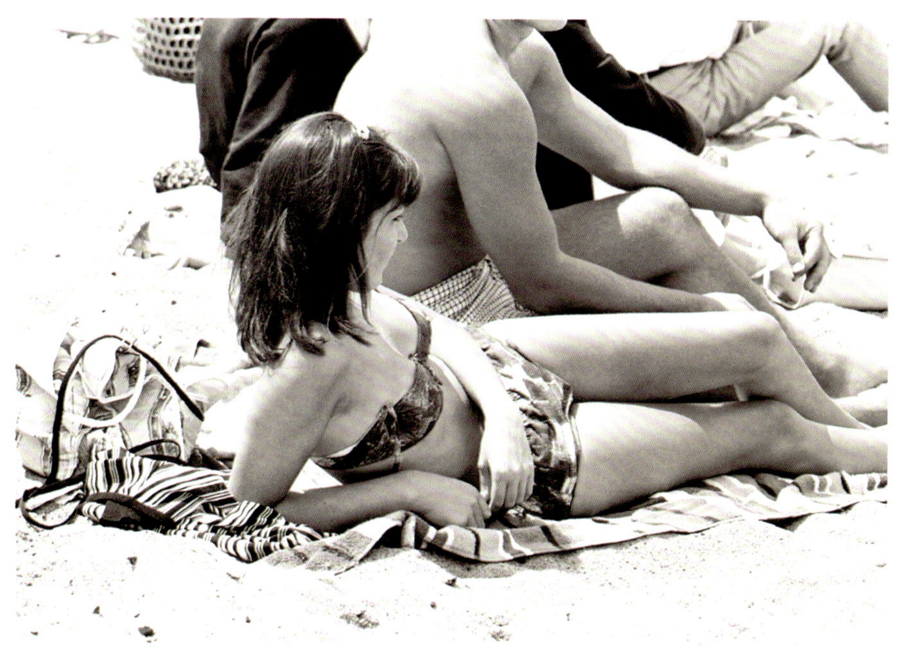

Above: A young lady with all the fashion accessories needed for a day at the beach ... **BS**

Opposite: A bikini girl with the ubiquitous pair of sunglasses walks across the sand at Wanda in a pensive mood. **JP**

Spectators and surfers flocked to Bells Beach for the 1967 state titles. The first day we had a reasonable ground swell messed up with a cross south easterly one. Second day the cross swell had expired and the ground swell decreased. Not exciting but the show must go on! Unable to take any decent photos I decided to wander around the beach and carpark in search of people to photograph. The wind was a cool onshore southerly, the surfing mundane apart from Wayne Lynch surfing outside the judging criteria of the day. Controversially he lost the junior final after executing re-entries, floaters and radical backhand turns in the shore break. The other finalists rode small, slow, sloppy waves aggregating points on length of ride. Amazing! I thought Wayne had won easily but the judges were locked into a time warp long since passed. Contest judging was never the same again and had to change to stay abreast of the shortboard revolution. We still talk about it today! **BS**

Below right: I was photographing on Cronulla Point in 1963 when I noticed this young lady with a serious look on her face listening to her transistor radio. **BW**

Below left: **Unknown girls on the beach.** I saw them looking happy and click! Victorian State titles February,1967. **BS**

Opposite: **Unknown girl on the beach.** I liked the pose, framed with mum and dad (perhaps), click! Victorian State titles February 1967. **BS**

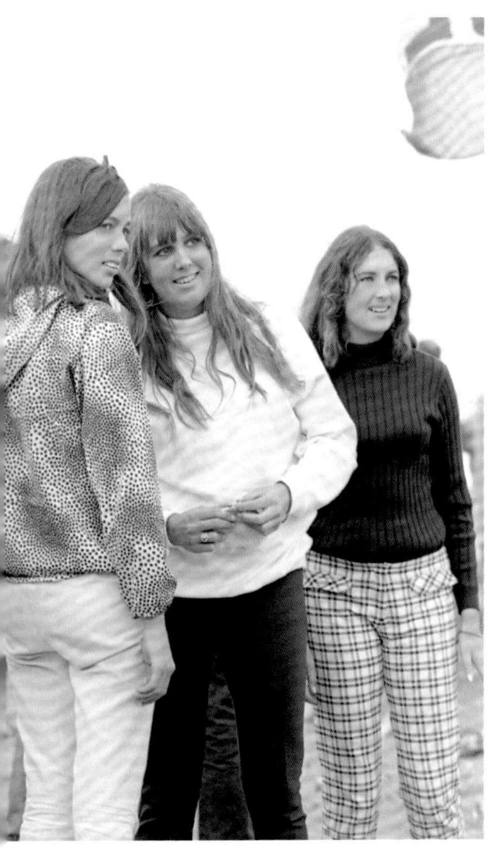

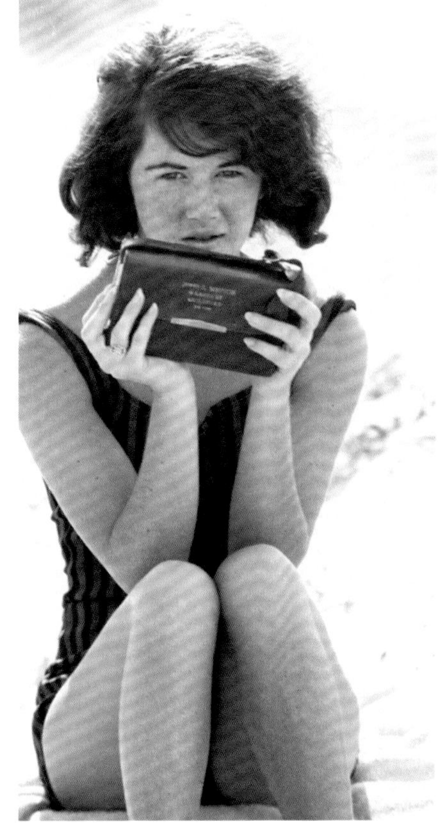

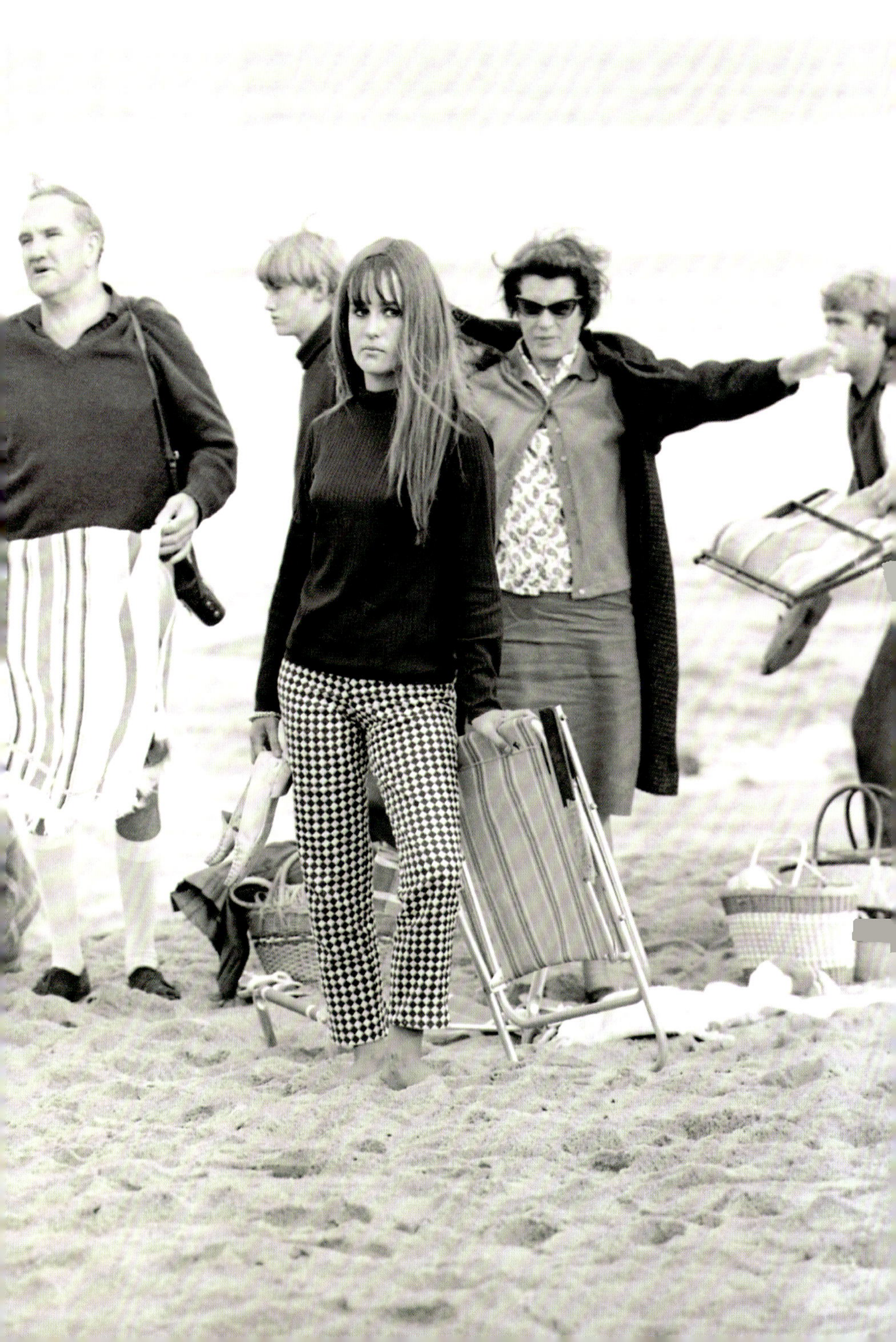

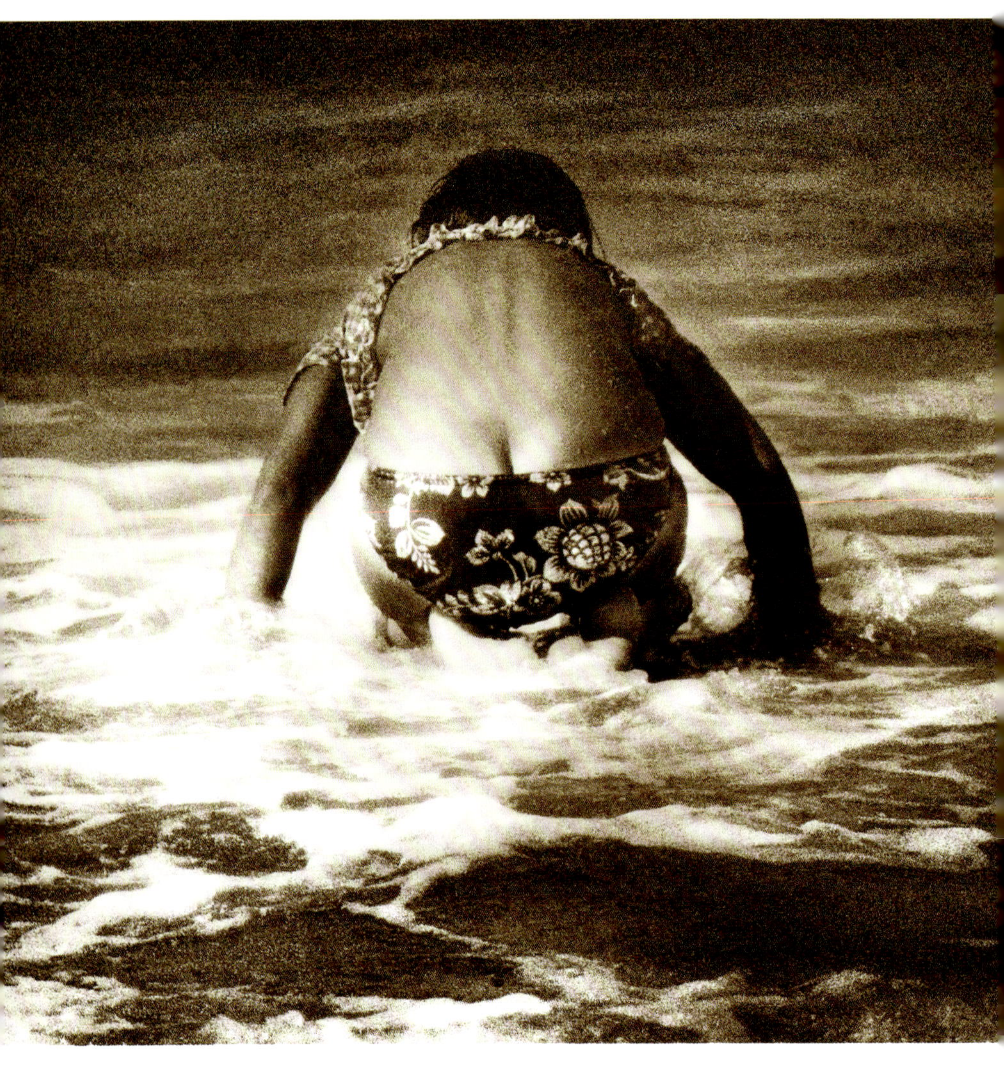

Cronulla girl, 1966. It was a very rare sight in those days for a girl to be surfing in a bikini! **BW**

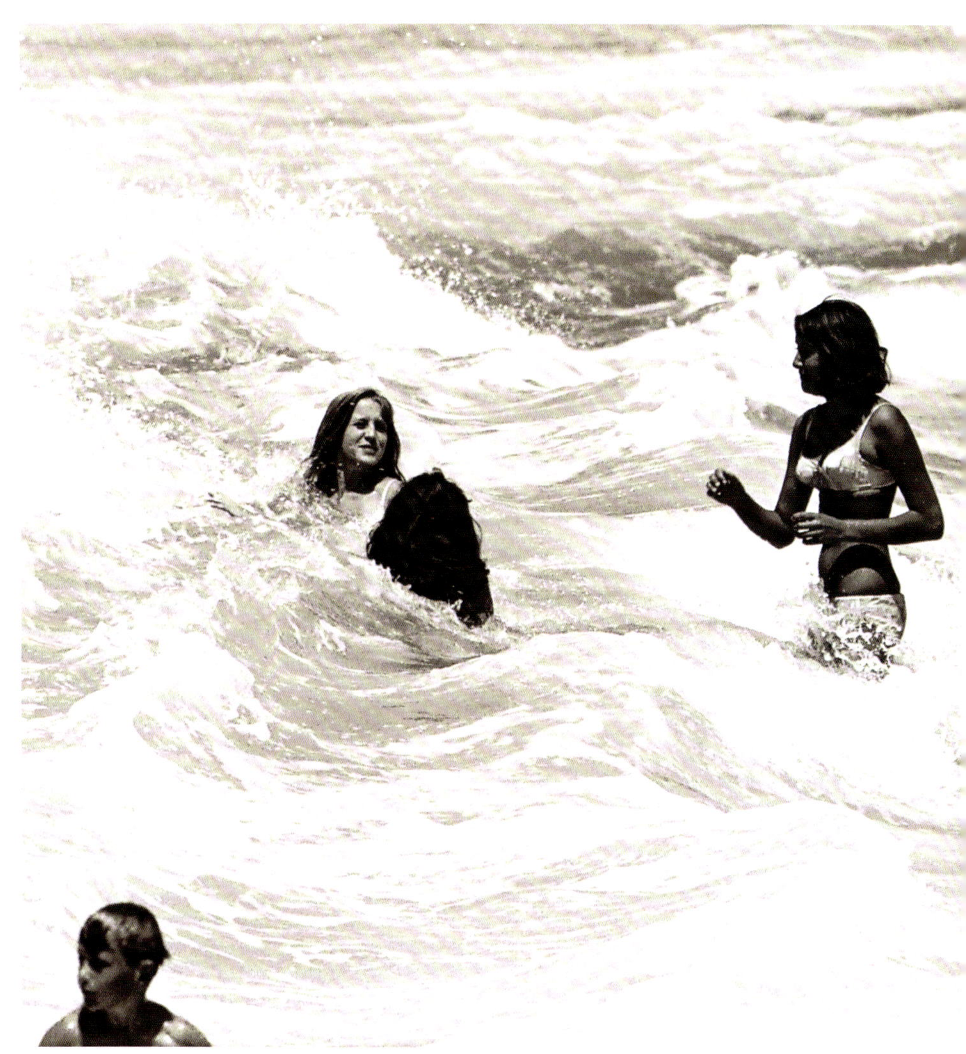

Girls taking on the waves wearing the latest gear. **JP**

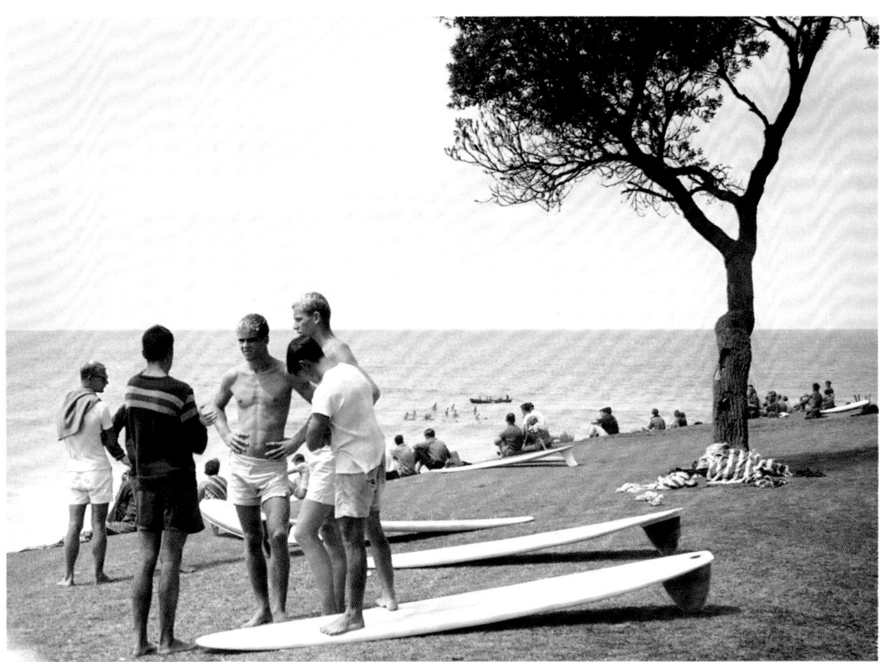

Above: **Cronulla Point, 1962.** Casual men's beach fashion on display. **BW**

Opposite above: **Torquay Surfer Supplies advertising photo shoot, Drainos, Torquay, April 1965.** This custom surfwear advertisement later featured in *Surfing World* magazine (*below*). **BS**

On the 20th July 1962 Don and Faye Loveless opened a shop in Gilbert Street, Torquay, trading as Loveless Television. Faye commenced making board shorts and parkas which became very popular with the local surfers. Before long the demand was so great that they started Victoria's first surf shop known as Torquay Surfer Supplies. A few years later Don asked me to photograph some local surfers wearing his garments. I obliged and he chose Rodney 'Fatty' Long, Rodney Marks and Malcolm Brough for his models. We chose the eastern end of Torquay Surf beach at Drainos reef break. It was a favourite spot for the Torquay grometts, a small wave high tide location. Someone brought their dog so we included it in the advertising shoot. Retrospectively, when I look back, the photos are kind of cute and innocent – the genesis of branding and Torquay's massive surf industry we have today. **BS**

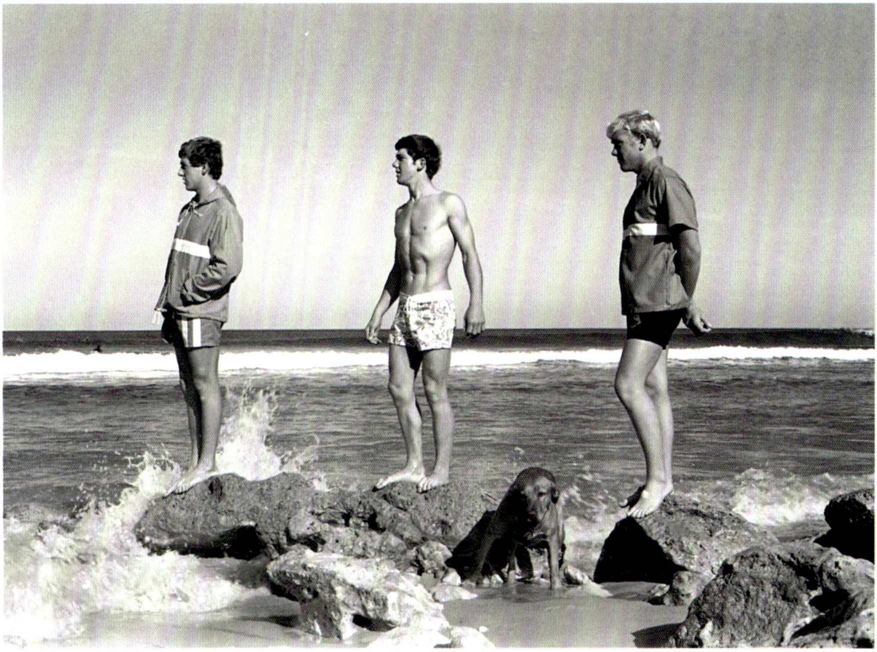

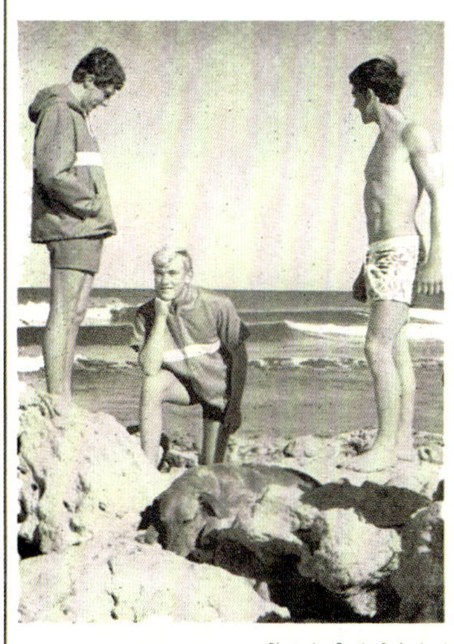

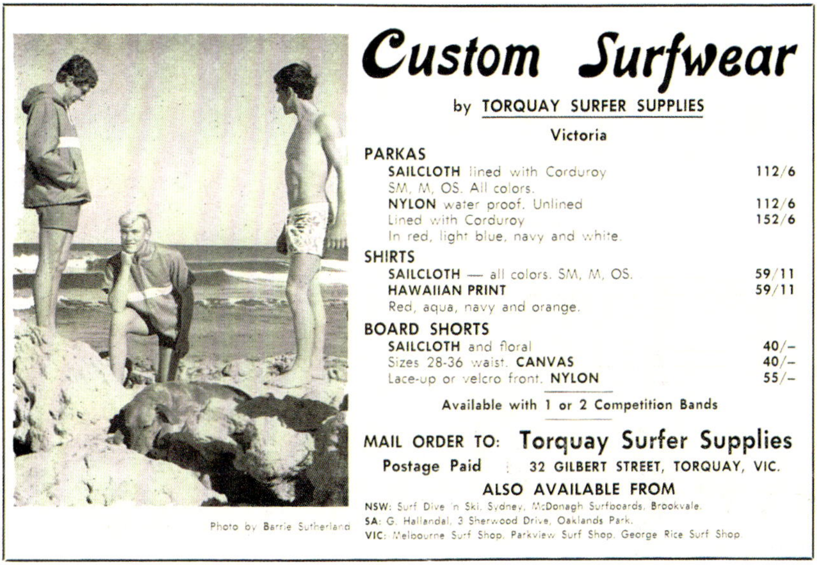

Custom Surfwear

by <u>TORQUAY SURFER SUPPLIES</u>

Victoria

PARKAS
  SAILCLOTH lined with Corduroy   112/6
  SM, M, OS. All colors.
  NYLON water proof. Unlined   112/6
  Lined with Corduroy   152/6
  In red, light blue, navy and white.

SHIRTS
  SAILCLOTH — all colors. SM, M, OS.   59/11
  HAWAIIAN PRINT   59/11
  Red, aqua, navy and orange.

BOARD SHORTS
  SAILCLOTH and floral   40/—
  Sizes 28-36 waist. **CANVAS**   40/—
  Lace-up or velcro front. **NYLON**   55/—

Available with 1 or 2 Competition Bands

MAIL ORDER TO: Torquay Surfer Supplies
Postage Paid   32 GILBERT STREET, TORQUAY, VIC.

ALSO AVAILABLE FROM

NSW: Surf Dive 'n Ski, Sydney, McDonagh Surfboards, Brookvale.
SA: G. Hallandal, 3 Sherwood Drive, Oaklands Park.
VIC: Melbourne Surf Shop, Parkview Surf Shop, George Rice Surf Shop.

Photo by Barrie Sutherland

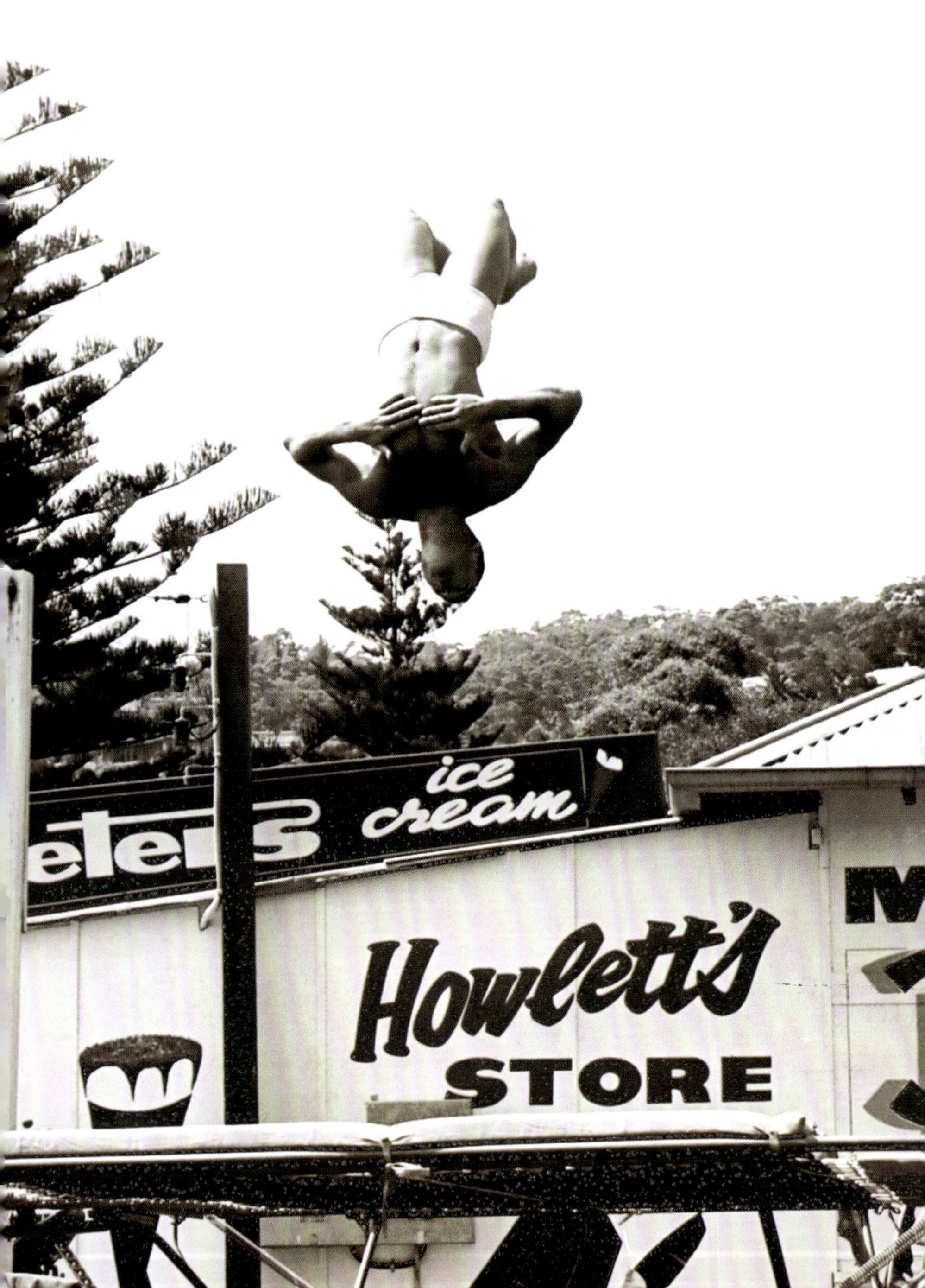
ice
cream
eter's
Howlett's
STORE

Lifestyle

The fact that Australia is surrounded by pristine beaches and the majority of the population live close to the sea has made the beach lifestyle a magnet for people. Most people are exposed to the beach from an early age – wallowing in the shadows, fishing with their fathers and grandfathers, even raised on beach culture. The Australian beach lifestyle offered something for everyone.

The actual idea of standing on top of a huge balsa board in the late 1950s and then balancing on top of a wave, caught the imagination of some teenagers. 'The first surfboard I got my hands in in 1952 was 17 feet (5.2m) long,' recalls Mal Sutherland. 'Then there was a 15 footer, and when the "Yanks" brought out the shorter Malibu board in the early 1960s we jumped on that straight away.'

Beach culture, particularly surfing, exploded in Australian suburbs in the early 1960s. The dream of catching the perfect wave was not limited to those teenagers who lived in seaside suburbs … in Sydney and Melbourne, kids from the outer western suburbs caught trains, trams, buses and even pooled their resources to buy cars in search of that dream.

In Post-war urbanised Australia, leisure time became an integral part of middle class reality. Healthy, youthful beach-goers from this demographic were targeted by advertisers … jeans, sunglasses, hats, hairstyles, surfboard manufacturers, beach accessories, soft drinks, food, beer and even sex! The baby boomer generation would dominate the sixties because of their social and commercial assertiveness and the sheer weight of their numbers.

Soft drinks – especially American brands such as Coke, Pepsi and Fanta – were immensely popular on the beach, but there was very little alcohol around in those days. Consuming alcohol on the beach was difficult because of the inability to keep drinks cold for long periods of time (the esky was just coming in but it was also difficult to find commercial quantities of ice for sale). Teenagers favoured buying a cold drinks from local beach kiosks, vendors and milkbars.

The shot of liquid sugar was essential for the board riders, who were on the whole incredibly health conscious for the time. As Mal Sutherland explains, 'Anyone who spends a lot of time around the ocean has to be health conscious because you have to be pretty fit to start with to ride a surfboard. It's hard work riding waves all day!'

Australia's beaches in the early 1960s were not egalitarian, however. The beach would see the 'battle of the sexes' played out in an ever-changing decade. At the beginning of the decade girls played a very passive role in the

Trampolining outside a surfside milkbar, 1960s. **JP**

beach lifestyle – and very few surfed because the boards were just too big and heavy – but the 'fairer' sex were included in surfing competitions. As boards became lighter, girls found their own independence on the beach, although the battle for universal acceptance would not be won until the 1970s and 1980s. But in the Sixties, this wasn't the only source of conflict on the beach.

The rise and popularity of 'surfies' – tanned, often blond (bleached or naturally) surfboard riders – brought them into direct confrontation with 'bodgies and widgies' – male and female 'rockers' who were the last remnants of the Elvis-dominated 1950s. This was particularly the case in beachside suburbs such as Cronulla, south of Sydney, and in Greenmount, on Queensland's Gold Coast, where standoffs between rival groups sometimes degenerated into rumbles and brawls on Friday and Saturday nights outside beachside shops and hotels.

The clashes between the two cultures were a case of the past meeting the present … a working-class tradition crashing head on with middle and upper-class kids who had the time, education and financial resources to pursue the surfing lifestyle. There was also a class war happening on some beaches … in Sydney the more 'affluent' kids tended to frequent the northern beaches of Newport, Avalon, Whale Beach and Palm Beach while the working-class kids gravitated to Bondi, Coogee and Maroubra. Western Sydney kids flocked to Cronulla, much to the dissatisfaction of the locals in the Shire, because it was the only Sydney beach accessible by train.

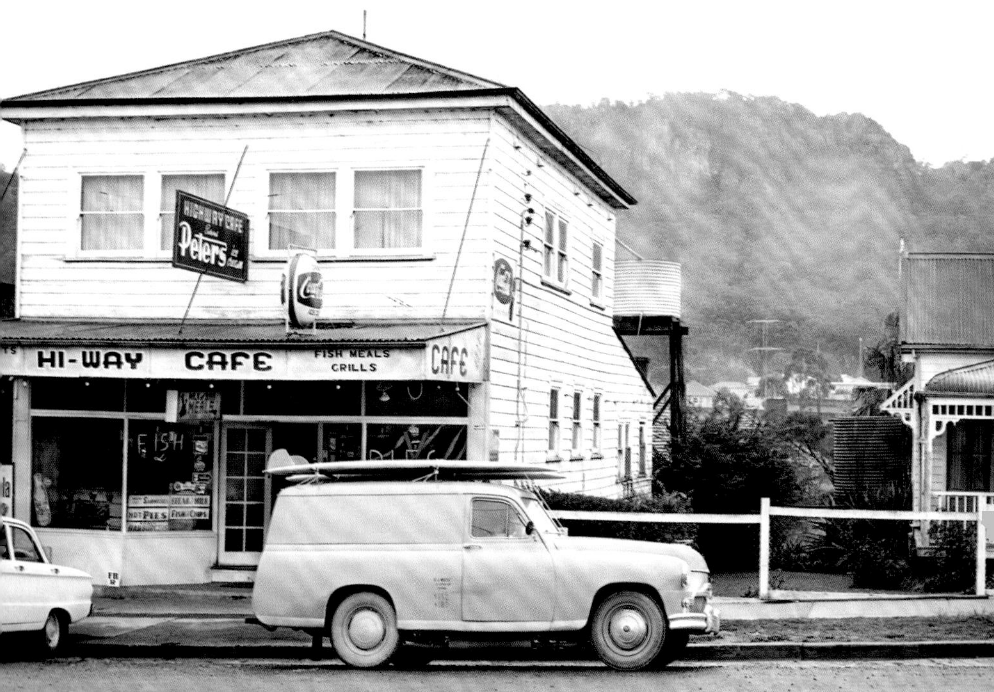

Beach language became increasingly exclusive and signified subculture membership to the exclusion of 'outsiders'. You would need an entire glossary to cover all the language derived from beach culture. Terms such as 'doing a 360', 'catching the A-frame' and avoiding the 'beach chowder' were all but incomprehensible to outsiders. A 'beach bunny' was a non-surfing beach girl, a 'hodad' was a non-surfer who hangs around the beach, and a 'woodie' was a wood-sided station wagon used by surfers to cart their boards to and from the beach. As one writer noted in 1964, the conversation of local surfers' was 'larded' with Australian and American slang.

For a time 'surf' records regularly topped the hit parade and teenagers who've never been on a surfboard before packed out screenings of American surf movies. Teenagers bought the latest American surf magazines and they increasingly identified themselves with the US beach scene.

Other aspects of surf culture to develop during the decade included a number of other sports including water or board skiing, body and body board surfing and even skateboarding. The Australian beach scene was alive with activity.

Opposite: **Bulahdelah Hi-way Café, 1964.** After travelling north from Sydney with a surfing mate we stopped for breakfast at this old building on the Pacific Highway at Bulahdelah. **BW**

Below: **Mal's brother Barry at Currumbin Alley, early 1960s. MS**

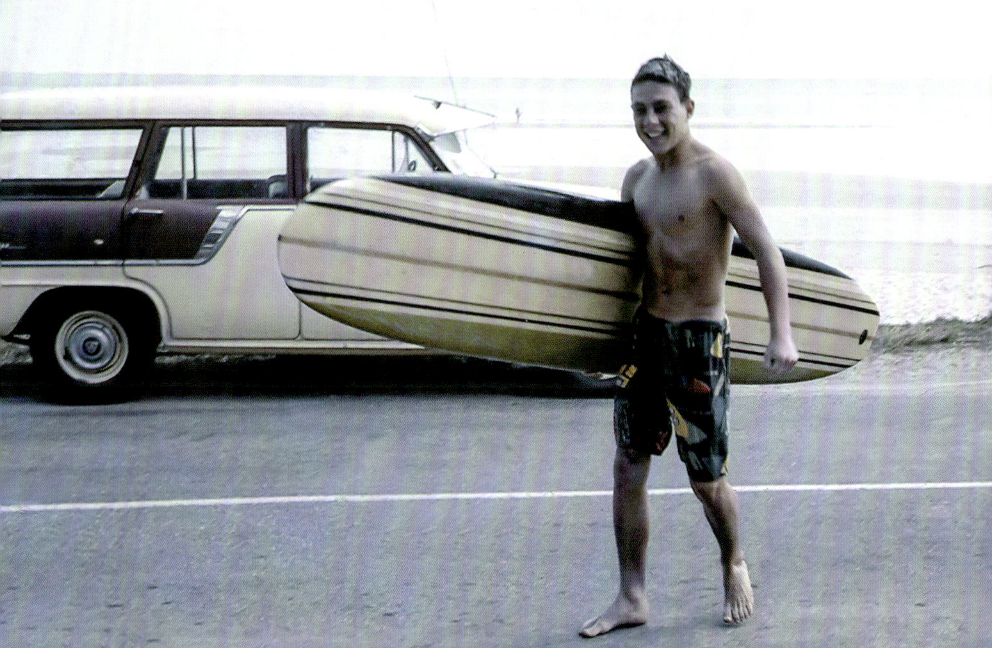

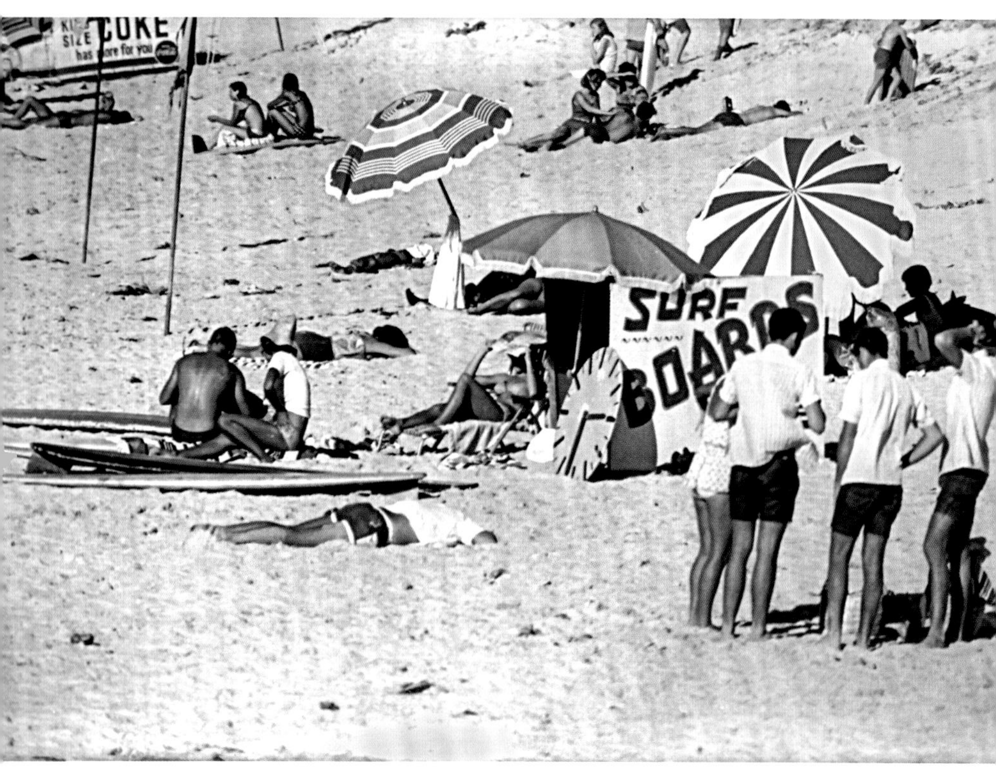

Coolangatta, 1965. Col Taylor and his wife had the beach concession to hire boards on Coolangatta in the 60s. Here a group of young tourists are deciding whether or not to hire a board. **MS**

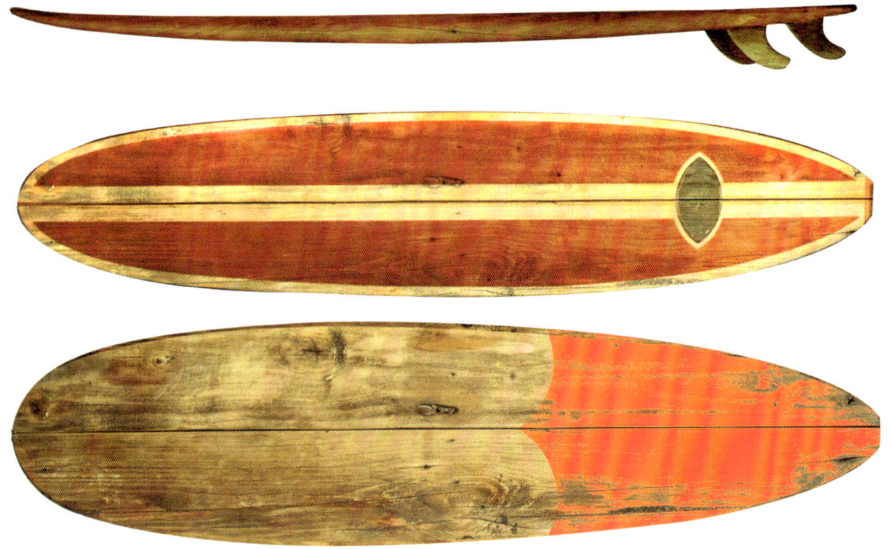

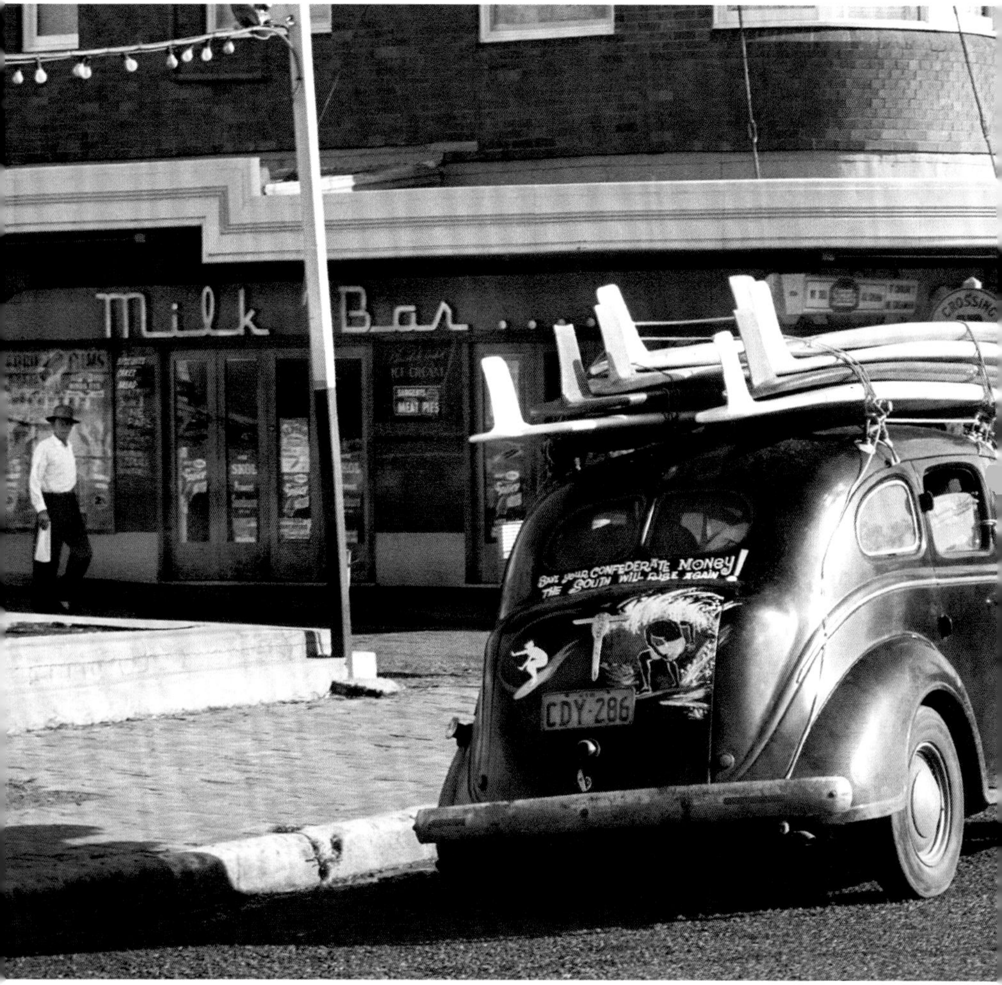

Surfmobile, 1962. A crowded Desoto loaded with boards and the Cronulla Crew leaving South Cronulla in search of some quality waves. **BW**

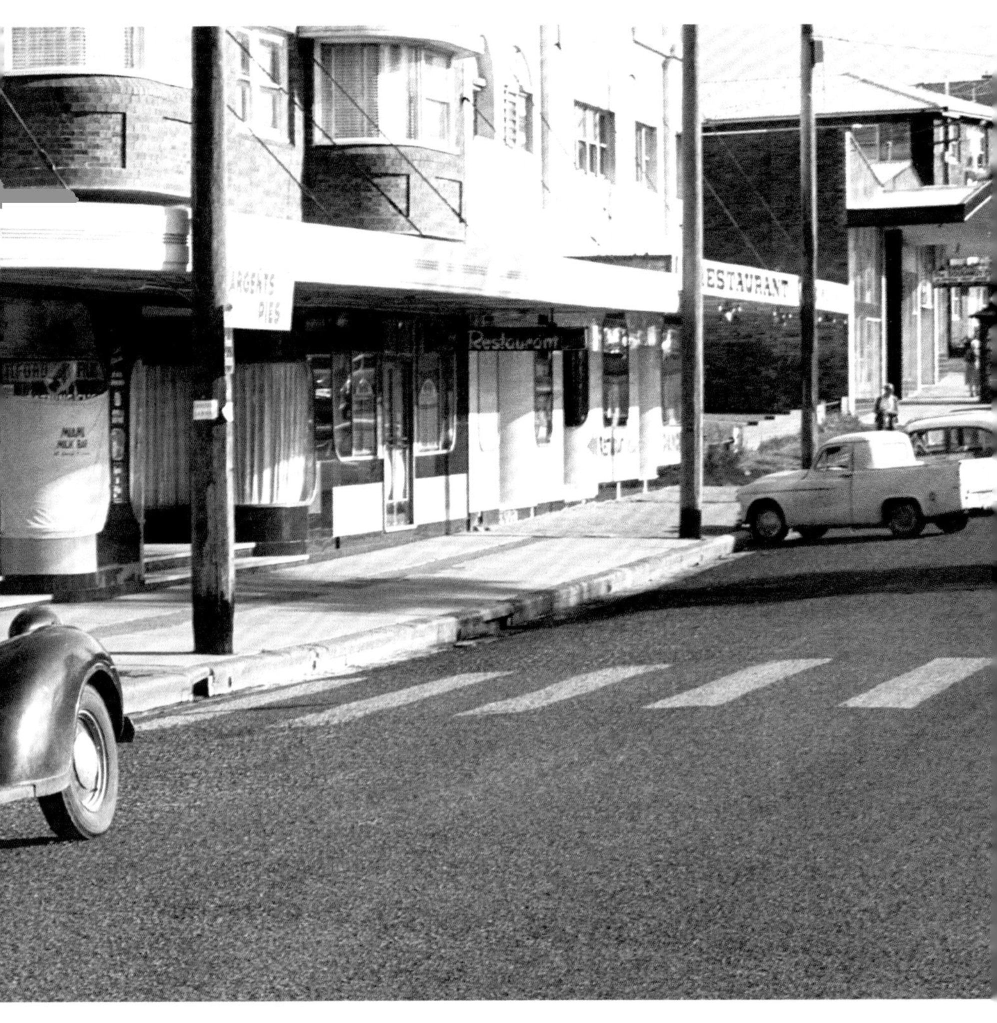

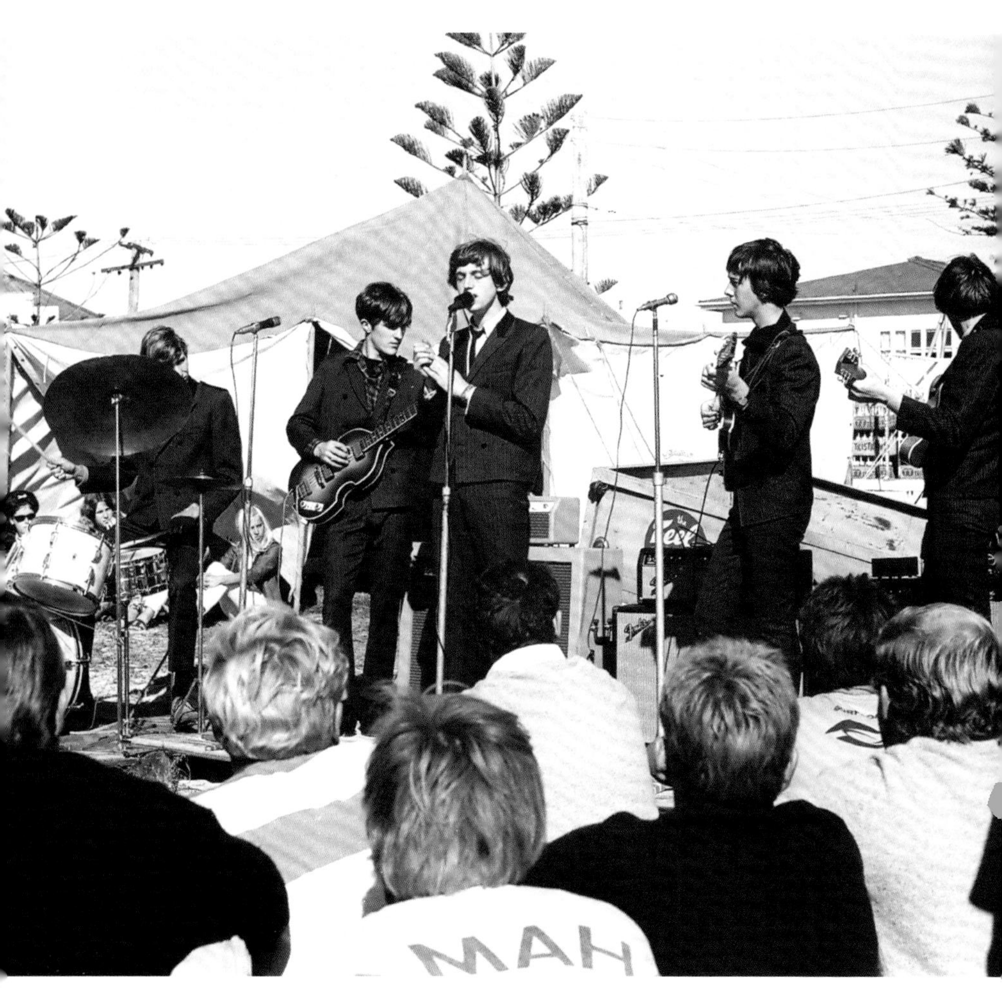

Coolangatta. The Feelgoods band playing 1966 Australian Titles contest. **JP**

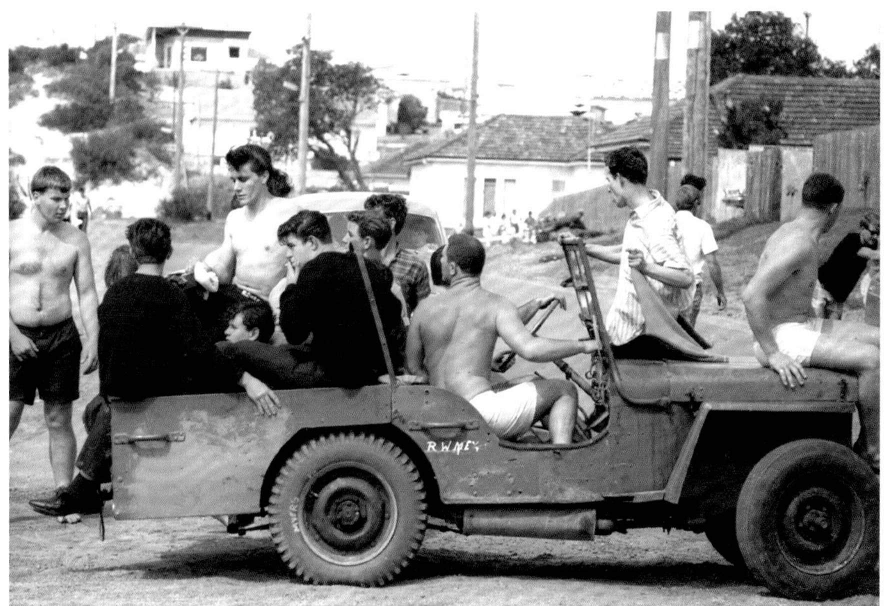

'Rockers' in a Jeep, Cronulla 1965. A larger number of 'rockers' – '50s rock and roll fans, the antithesis of clean cut surfers in the early 1960s – arrived by train one day and proceeded to walk the sandhills north of Wanda Beach. Bob Findon brought some back in his Jeep, so fortunately they weren't aggressive. **BW**

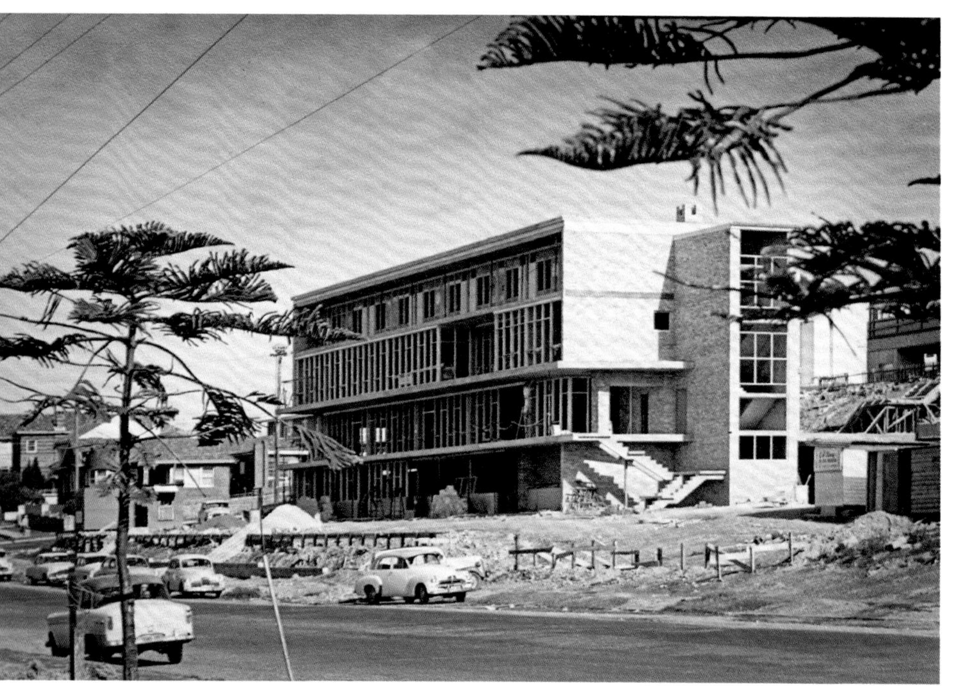

Above: Northies Hotel at North Cronulla, under construction in the early '60s. **BW**

Opposite: **Beach walk, Cronulla 1963.** Ian Nolan and Terry Steen heading down the beach to find the best waves. **BW**

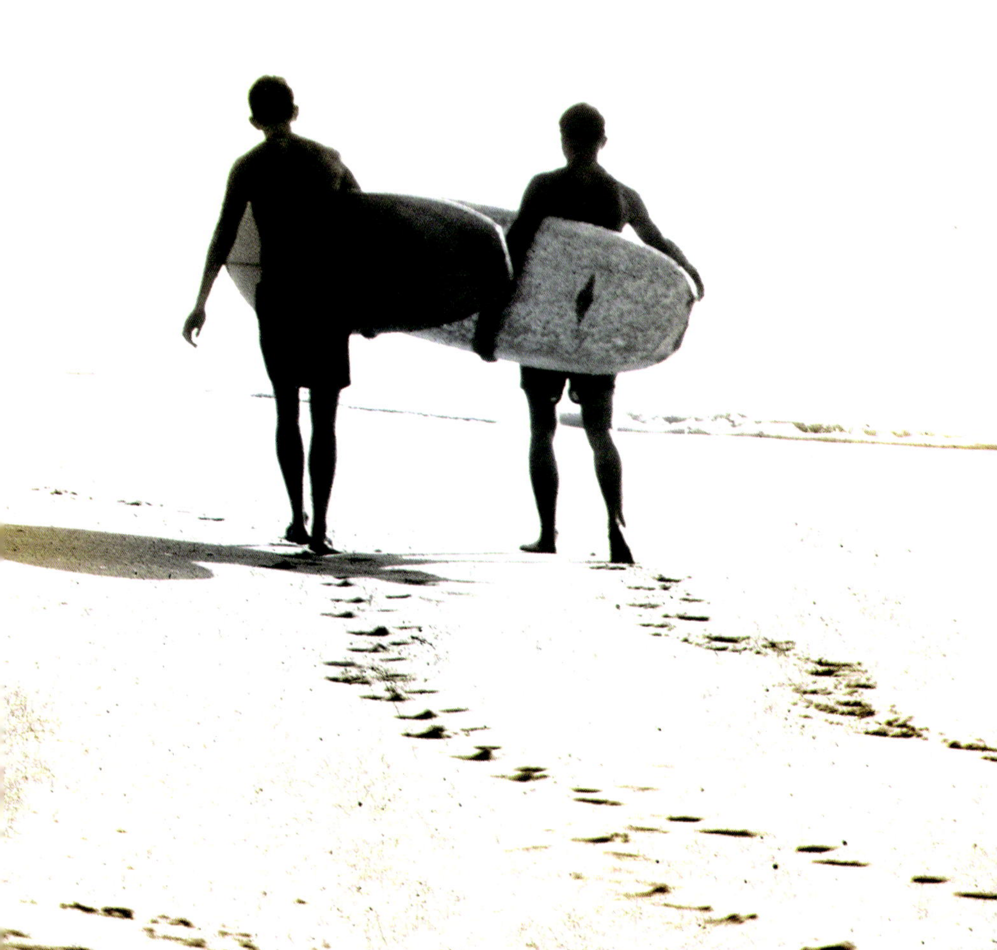

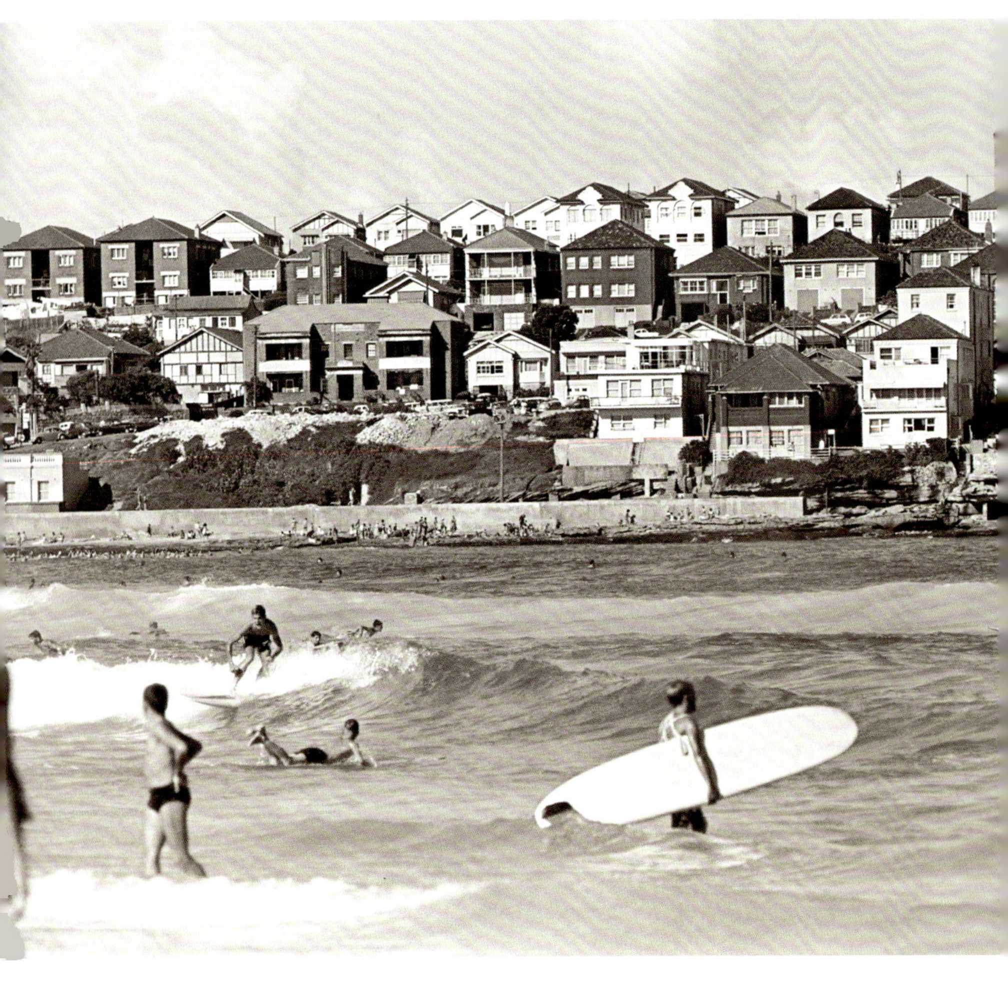

Bondi Beach, with apartments in the background, 1962. **BW**

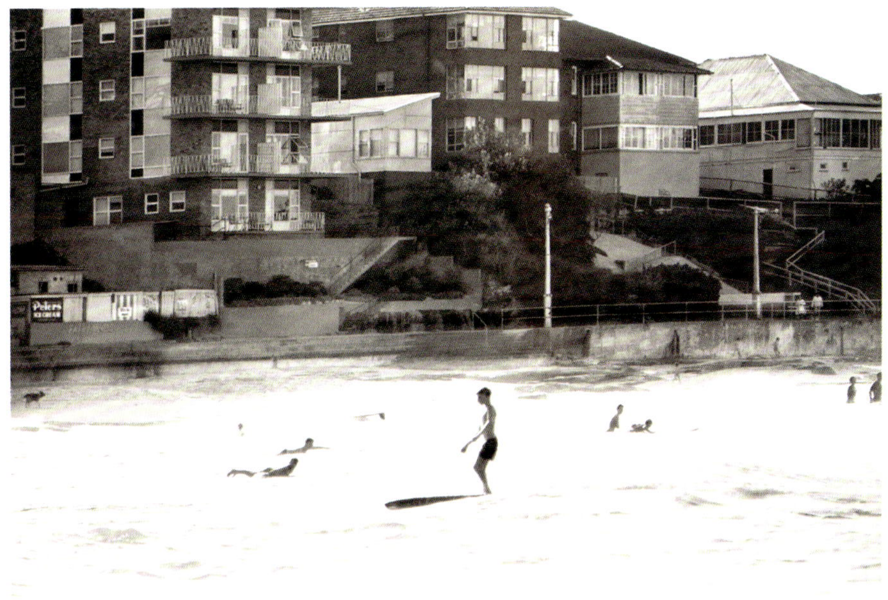

A young Bobby Brown surfing at South Cronulla in 1962. **BW**

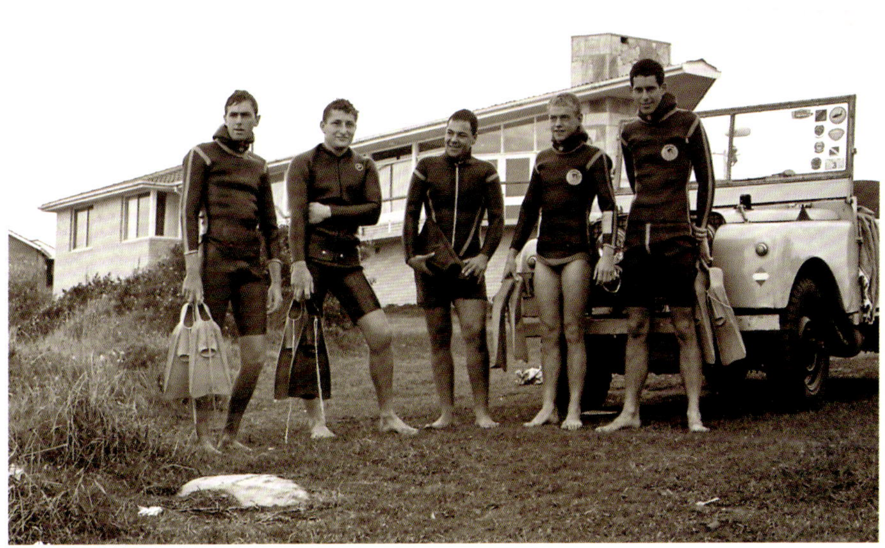

Bodysurfing was an integral part of surfing culture in the '60s. Most surfers had fins, flippers and they were strong swimmers. Pictured here is (left to right) John Holden, Adrian Parsons, Dennis Markson, John Dunn, Paul Collier at Little Avalon in 1964. **JP**

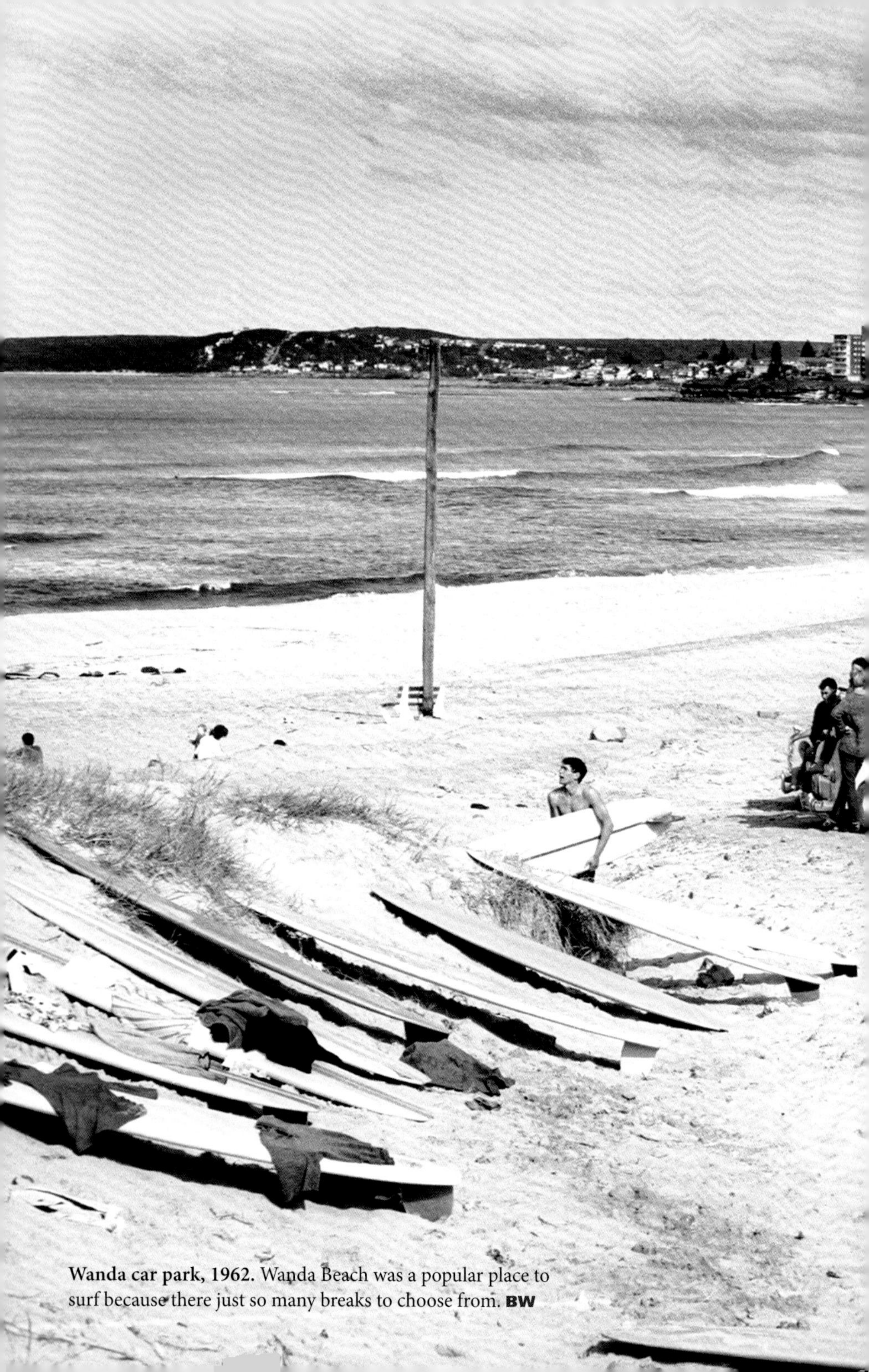

Wanda car park, 1962. Wanda Beach was a popular place to surf because there just so many breaks to choose from. **BW**

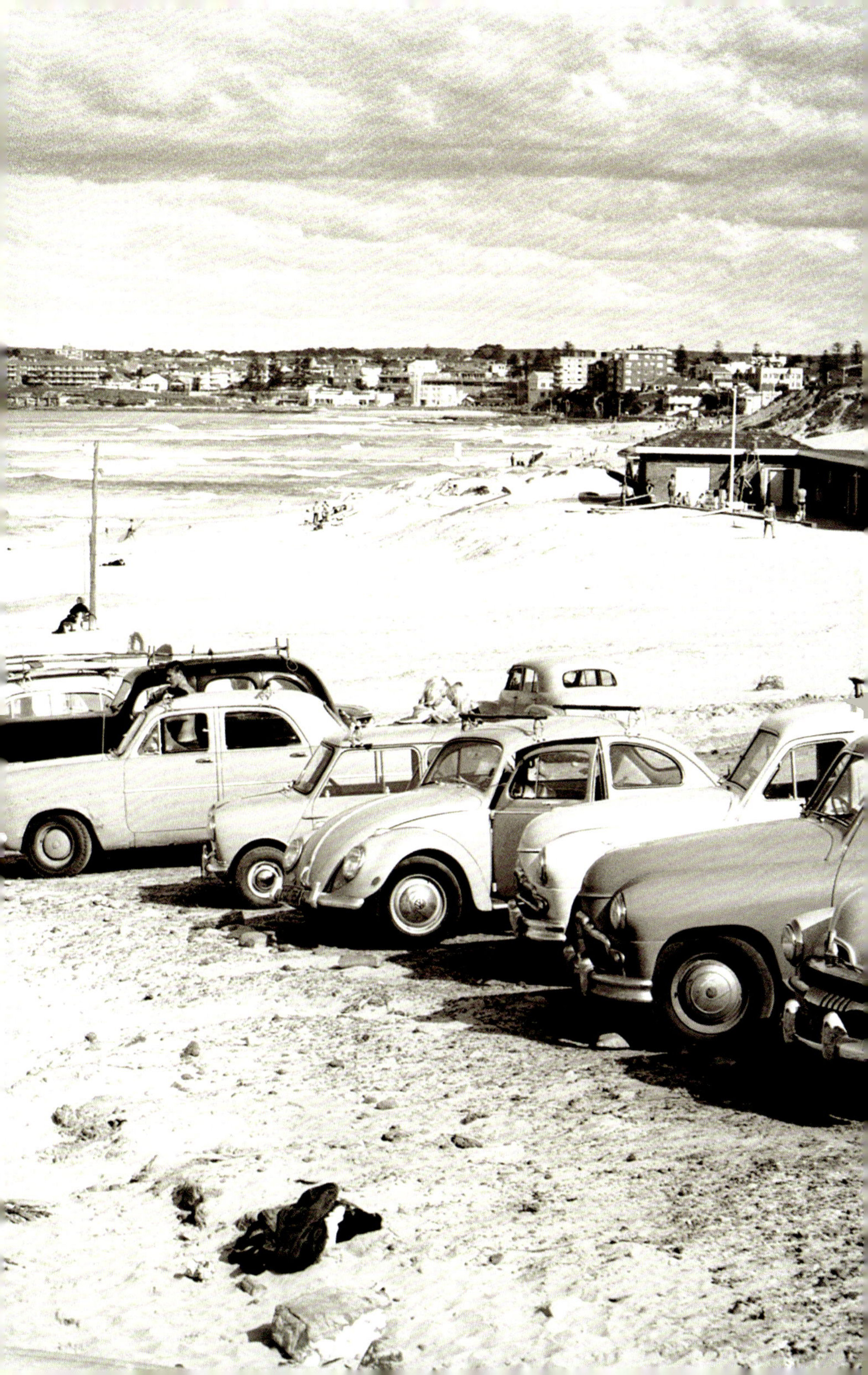

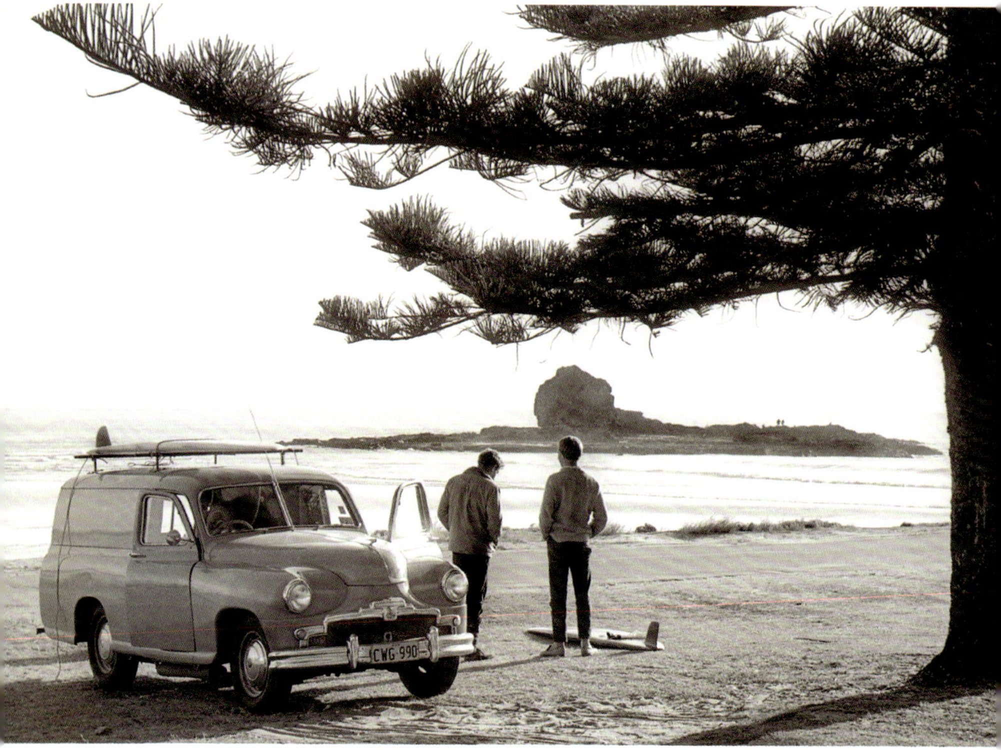

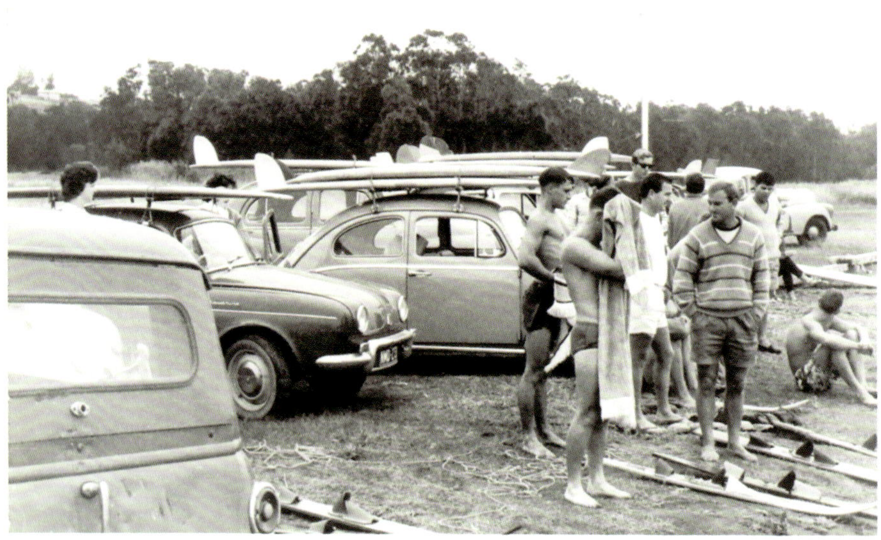

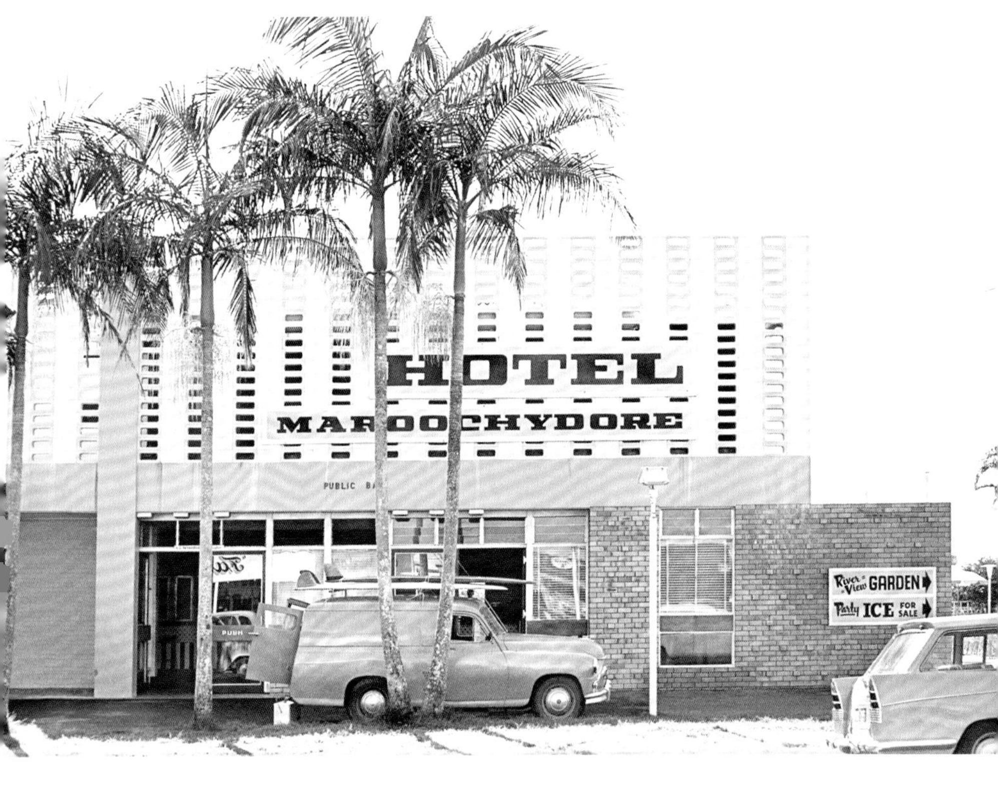

Above: Restocking the bar in my Vanguard at Maroochydore Hotel, Queensland, 1964. **BW**

Opposite above: Bob Weeks and Ross Longbottom at Currumbin, Queensland, on a surfing trip up north in 1964. **BW**

Opposite below: **Dell Periotts Water Ski Gardens, Banora Point, 1962.** When the surf was flat we did other things. Dell was a pioneering surfer, water skier and founding member of the ASAQ now Surfing Queensland who operated a Water Ski school at Banora Point in the late 1950s and 1960s (water skiing developed on a parallel to surfing).

Featured in the photo are: Vinny Ford with towel, Col Taylor behind, Ralph Pullinger in white shirt, Ray Blackman in sunglasses, John Burns back on, Joe Larkin hands in pockets, Darryl 'Fungus' Bulunk behind Joe, Peter Moore sitting. **MS**

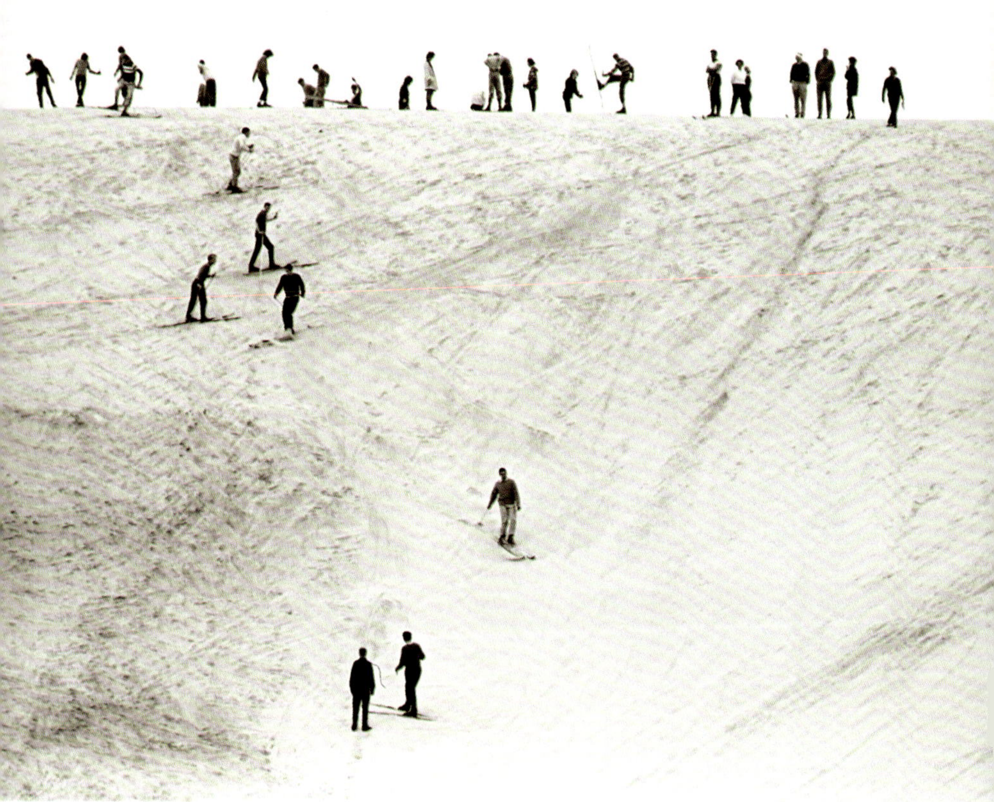

Skiing on the sandhills near Cronulla Beach, 1962. **BW**

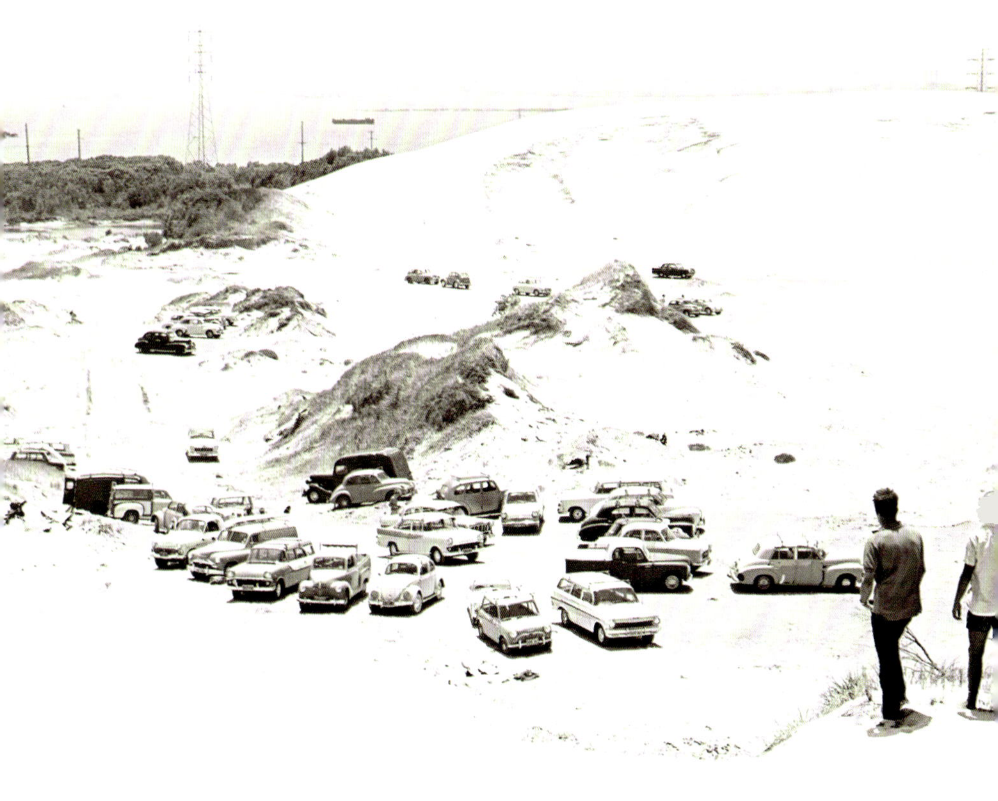

Greenhills carpark near Kurnell in 1964. It was a long walk
over the sandhills to the surfbreak from here. **BW**

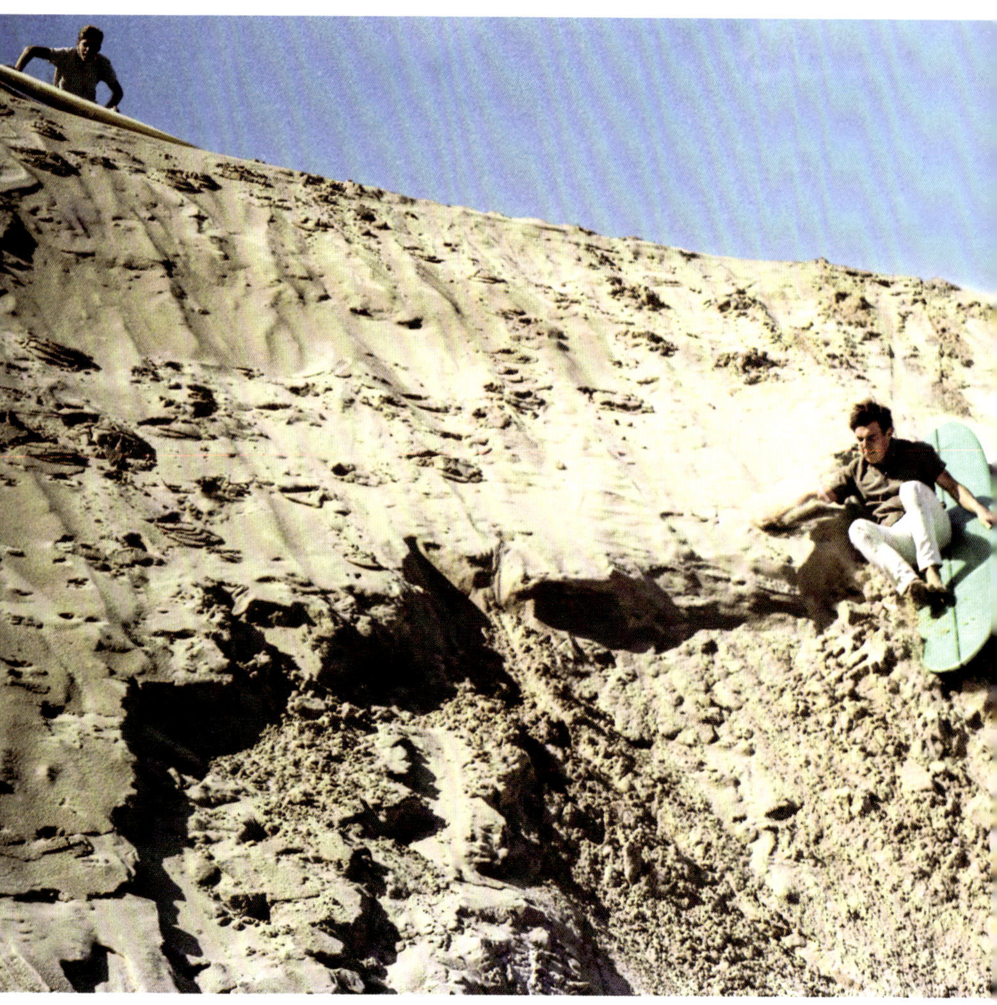

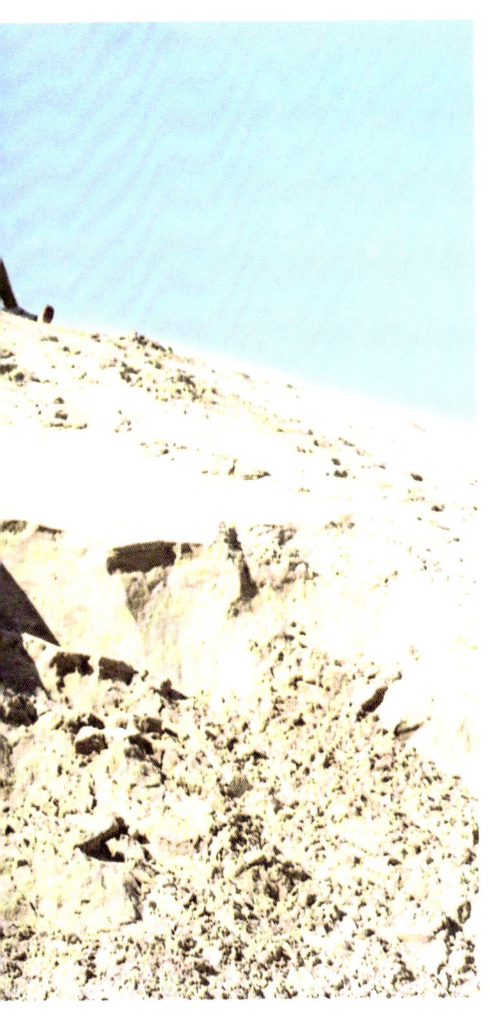

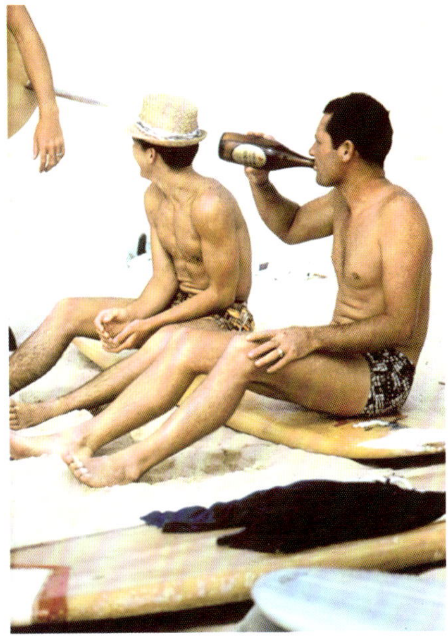

Above: **Midway, Cronulla, 1962.** A thirsty session. **BW**

Left: **When the surf was flat.** We also had the option of sandhill surfing on the huge dunes that once existed at Fingal until mineral sand mining flattened them. **MS**

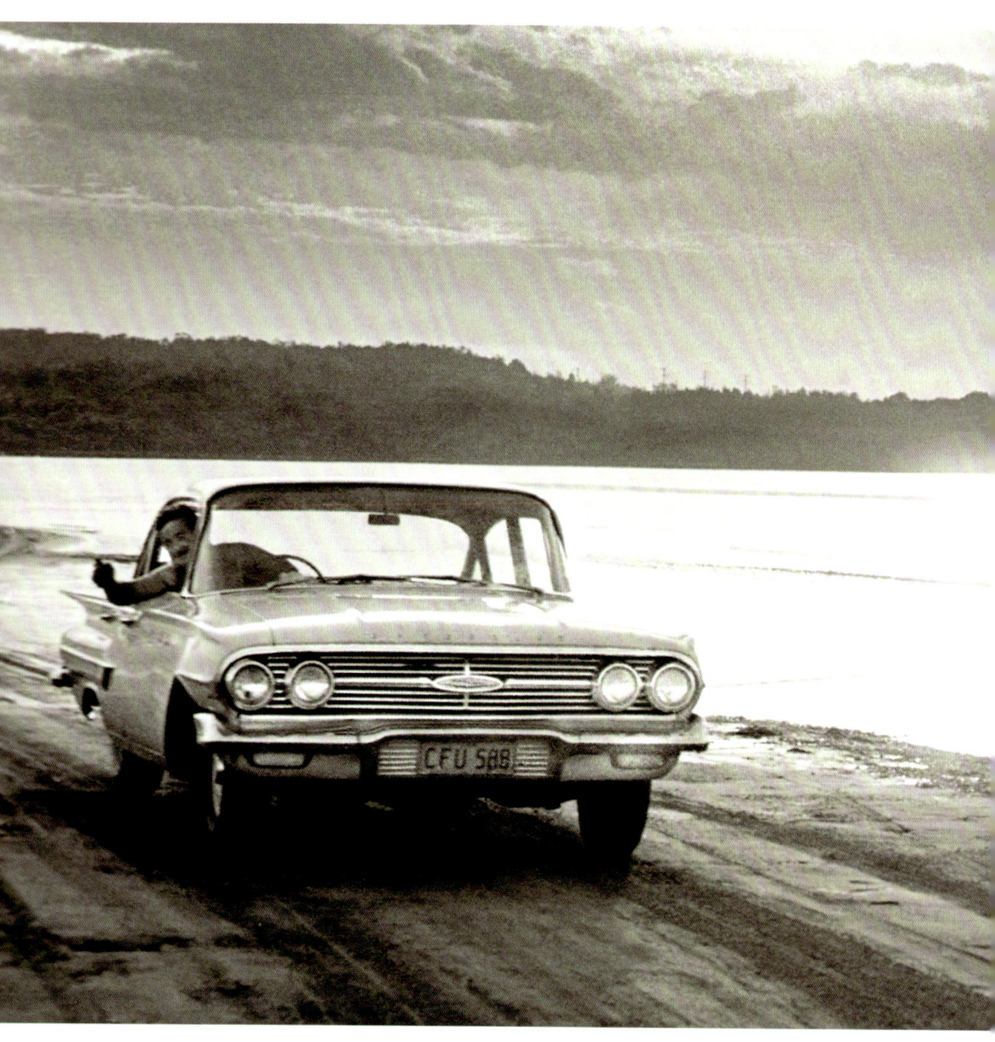

Freeboarding at Weeney Bay, 1964. Weeney bay is a short distance from Cronulla on the road to Kurnell and is a tributary of famous Botany Bay. At low tide it was quite easy to drive a vehicle on hard stand beside a deep channel for quite a distance while towing a surfer. In this photo, Brian Jackson is driving while Bob Findon is carving up the water. **BW**

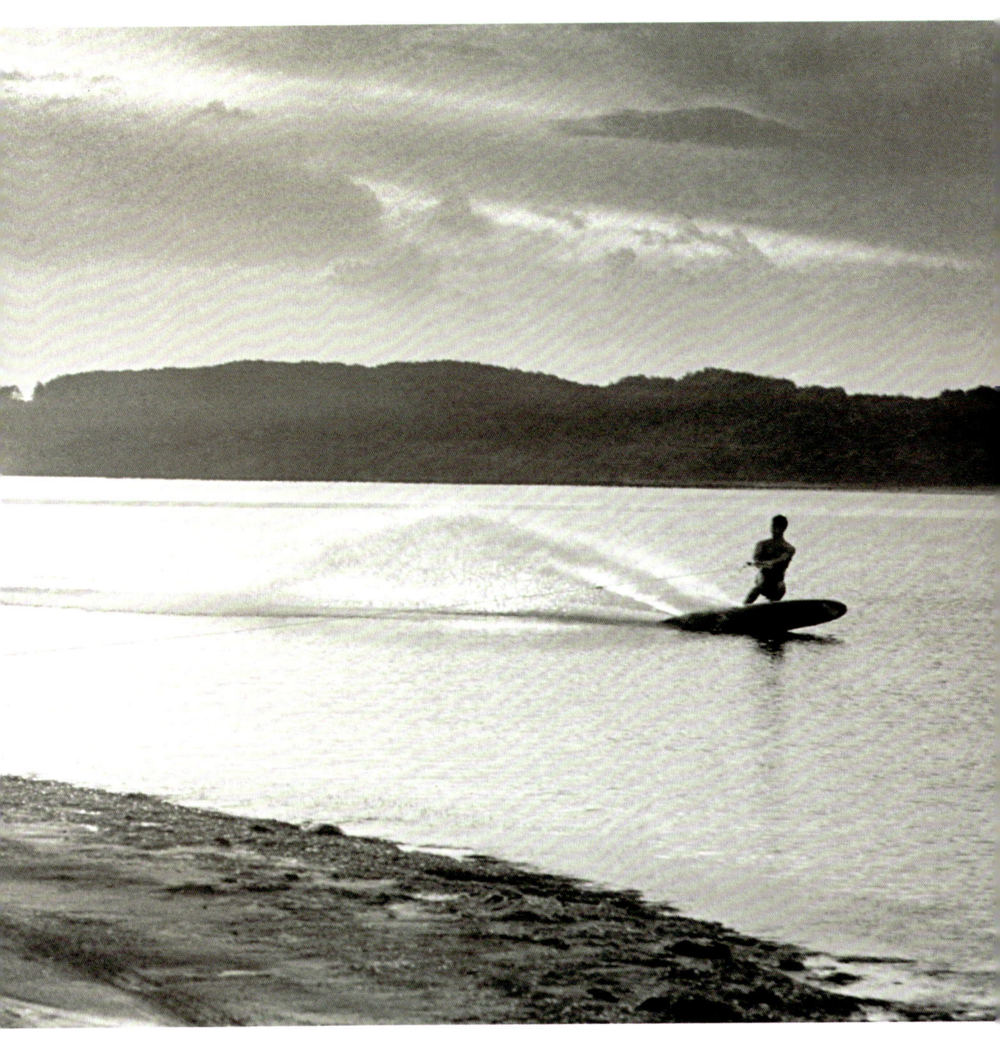

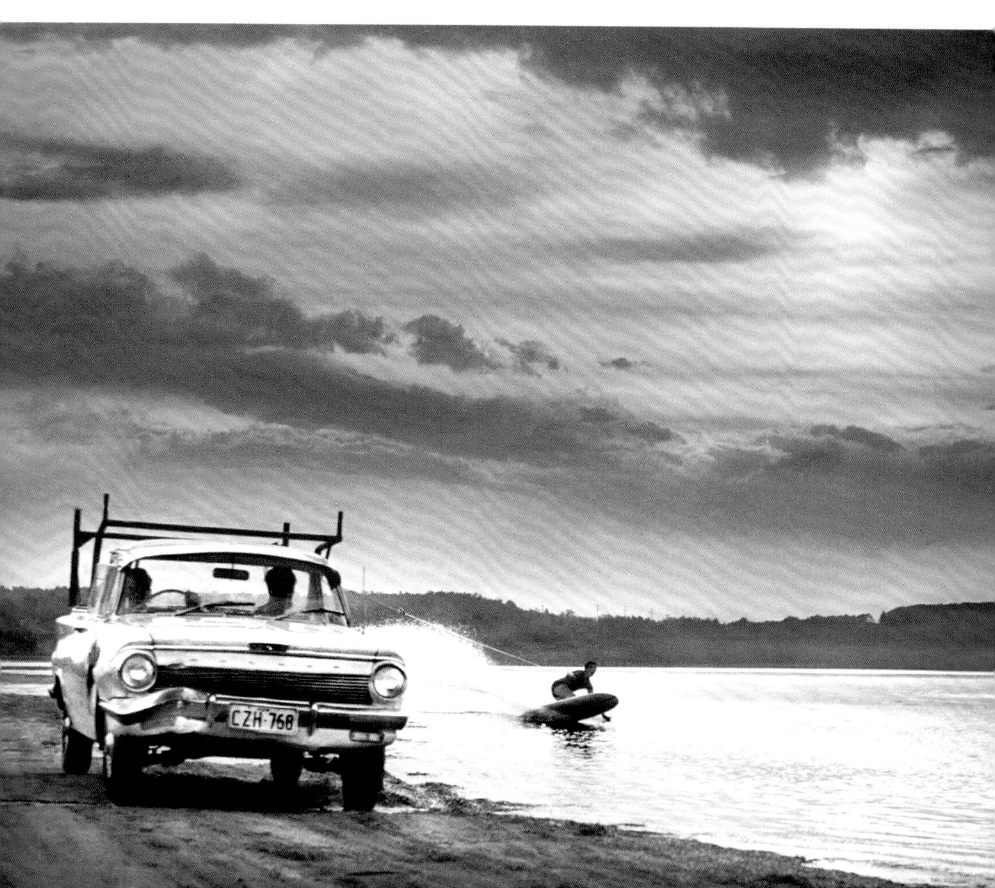

A Holden ute towing a freeboarder on a cloudy afternoon in 1964. **BW**

Opposite above: **Peter Thomas at Dell Periotts Water Ski Gardens, Tweed River, 1962.** The Barneys Point lift-up bridge has since been demolished and replaced by the new freeway. **MS**

Opposite below: Freeboarder slicing through the water at Weeney Bay, 1964. **BW**

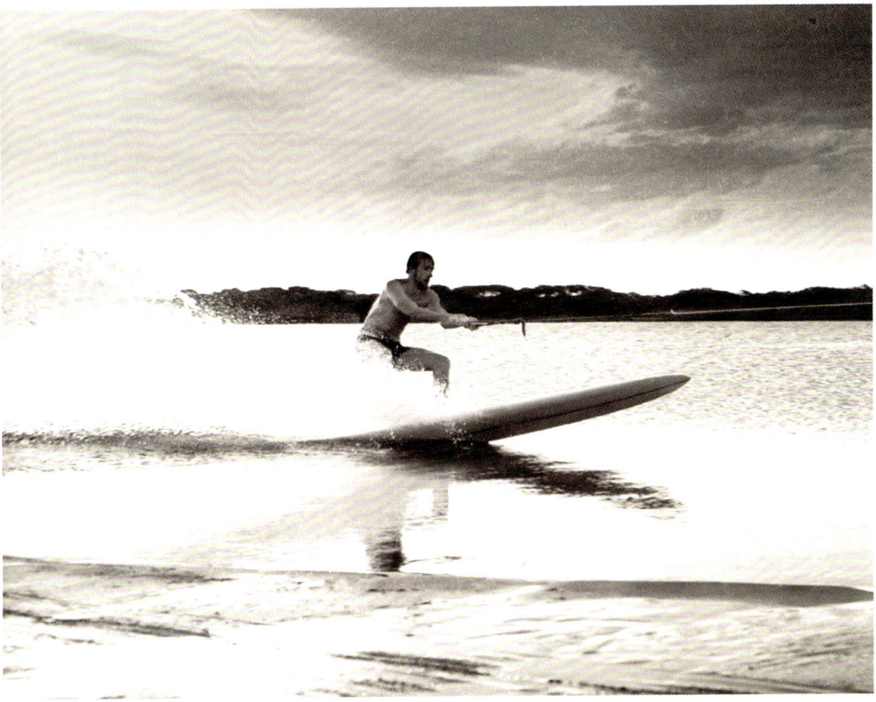

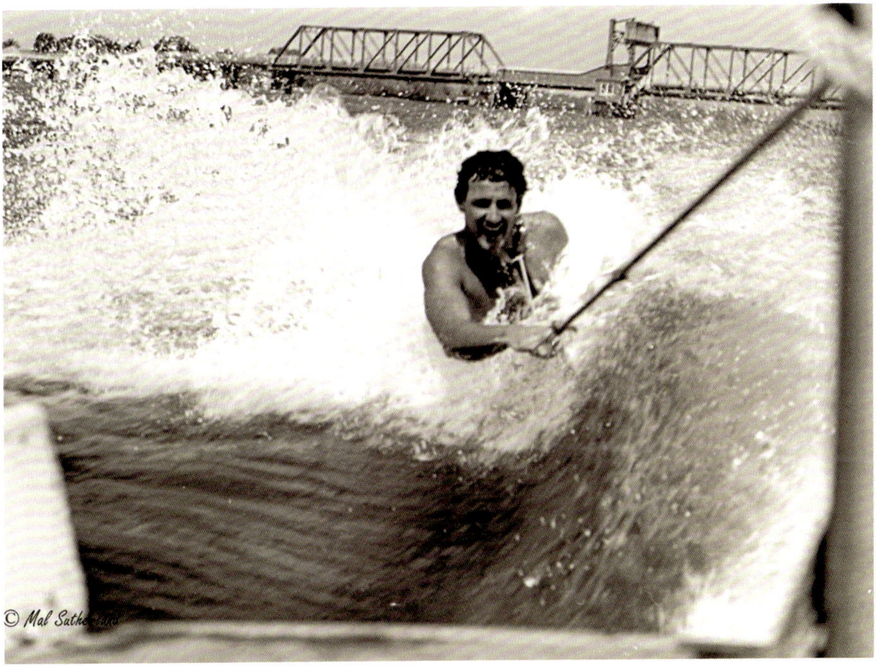

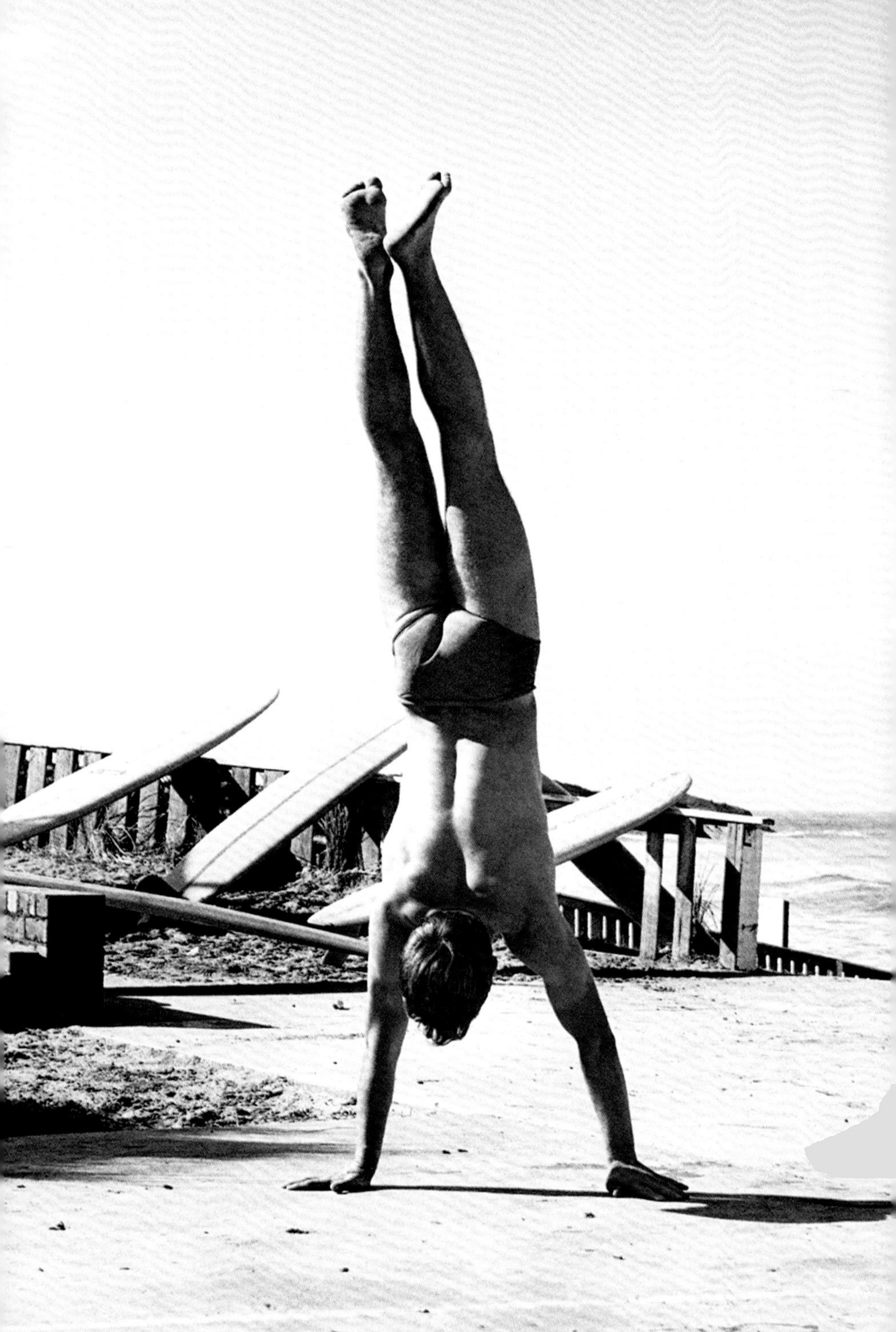

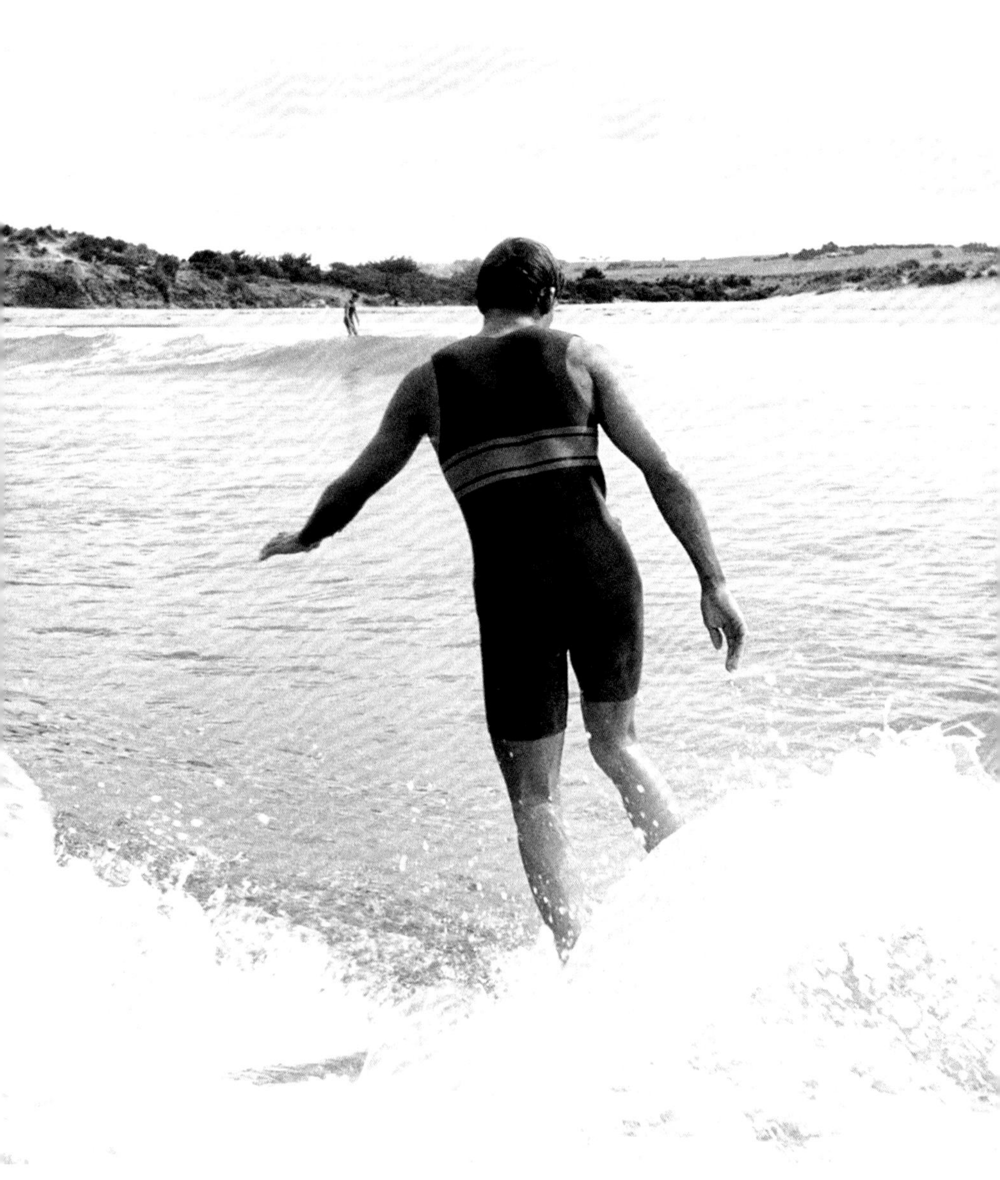

Above: John Panozzo, Shorebreak left hander, from the water, Torquay Point, September 1967. **BS**

Opposite: Rod Brooks doing a handstand, Torquay Surfclub, July 1965. **BS**

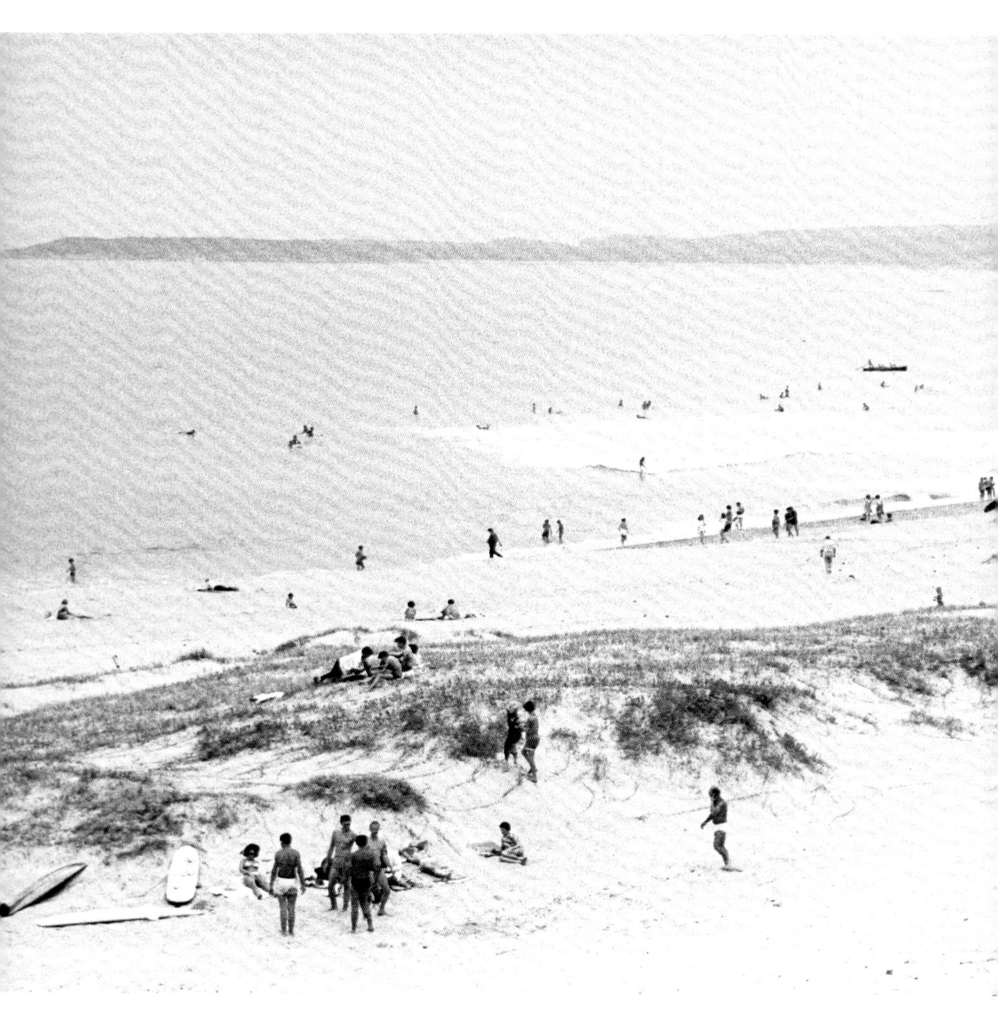

This photo was taken in 1962 where Eluoera Surf Club
is now situated. It was all sand back then. **BW**

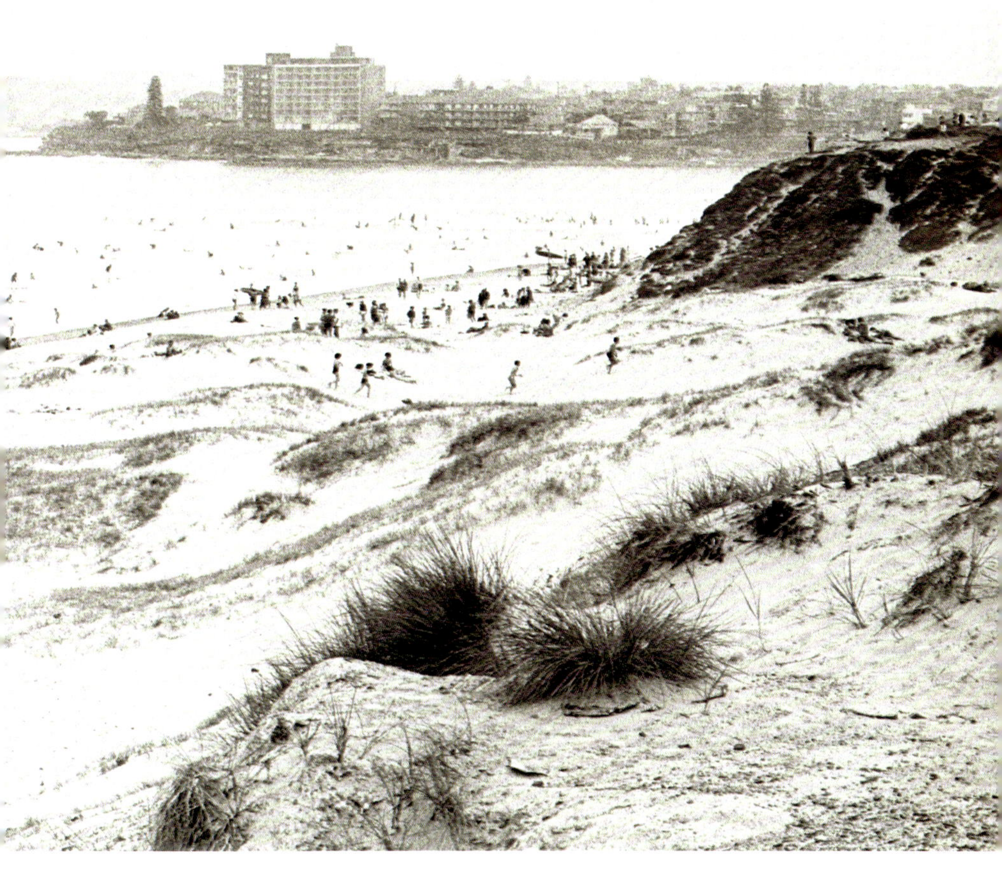

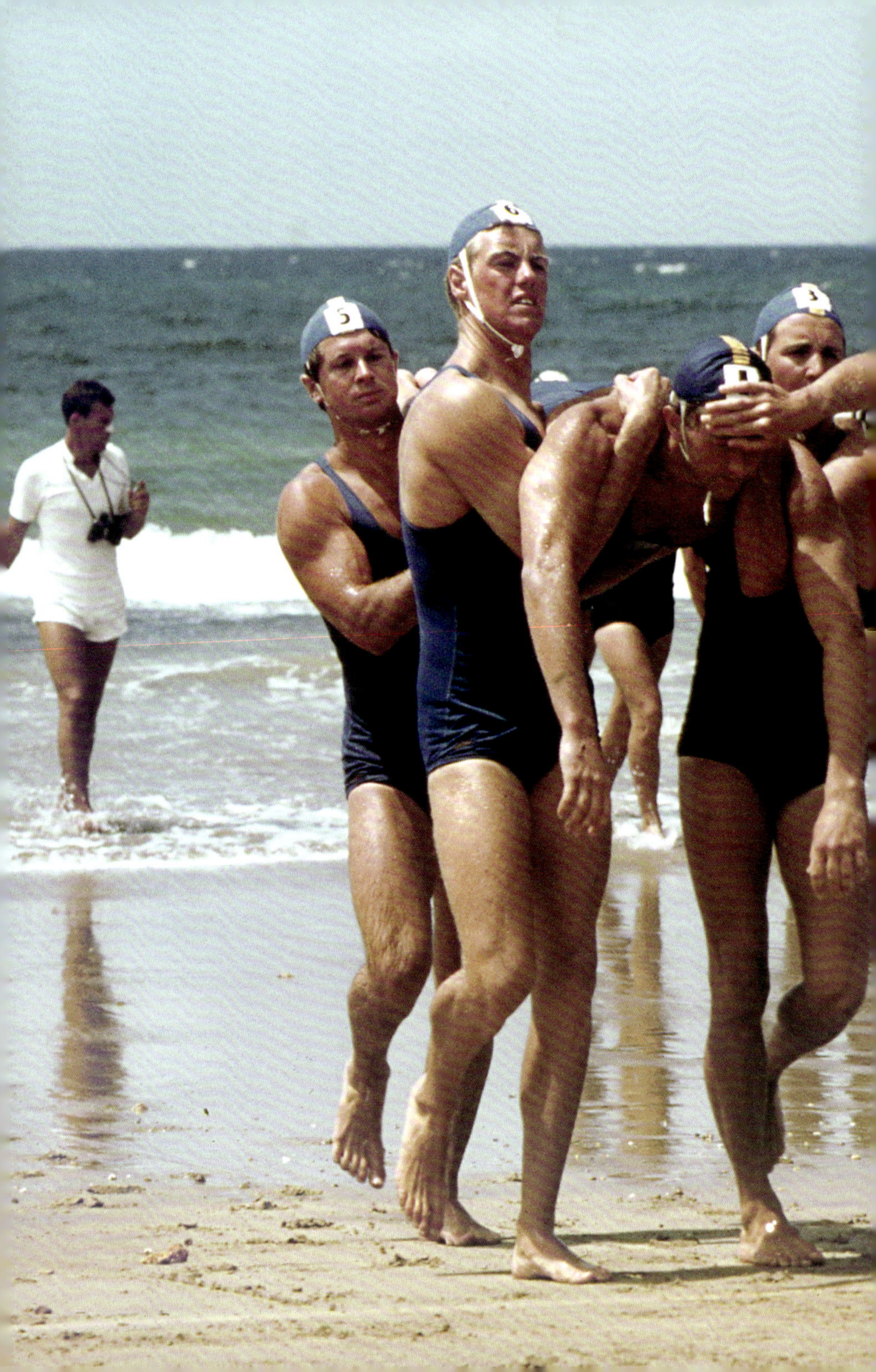

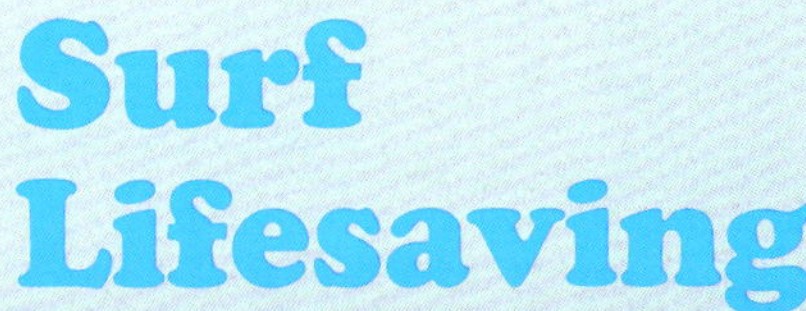

Before surfboards dotted the beach horizon, there was surf lifesaving. By the 1960s, the surf lifesaving movement had become entrenched part of the Australian way of life. The first surf lifesaving club in the world had been formed at Sydney's famous Bondi Beach in 1906 (although neighbouring Bronte disagrees), servicing the millions of people who frequented Australia's public beaches. Sun and surf 'bathing' were already national past-times when Hawaii's Duke Kahanamoku introduced surfing at Freshwater Beach in 1917. By that time the various surf life-saving clubs had formed the NSW Surf Bathing Association (later Surf Life Saving Australia, or the SLSA) and had started inter-club competition to foster the ideals of the association and to encourage membership growth.

Surf Life Saving Carnivals, held a different beaches around the country, see members of rivals clubs compete in sports associated with surf rescue – these include the opening 'march past', 'ironman' races, longboat rescue, surf ski and board events, as well as rescue and resuscitation, first aid and patrol competition. Carnivals are conducted at state and interstate level and have also

State R&R team patient carry, Australia Day carnival, South African invitational, Torquay Surf Beach, January 1967. **BS**

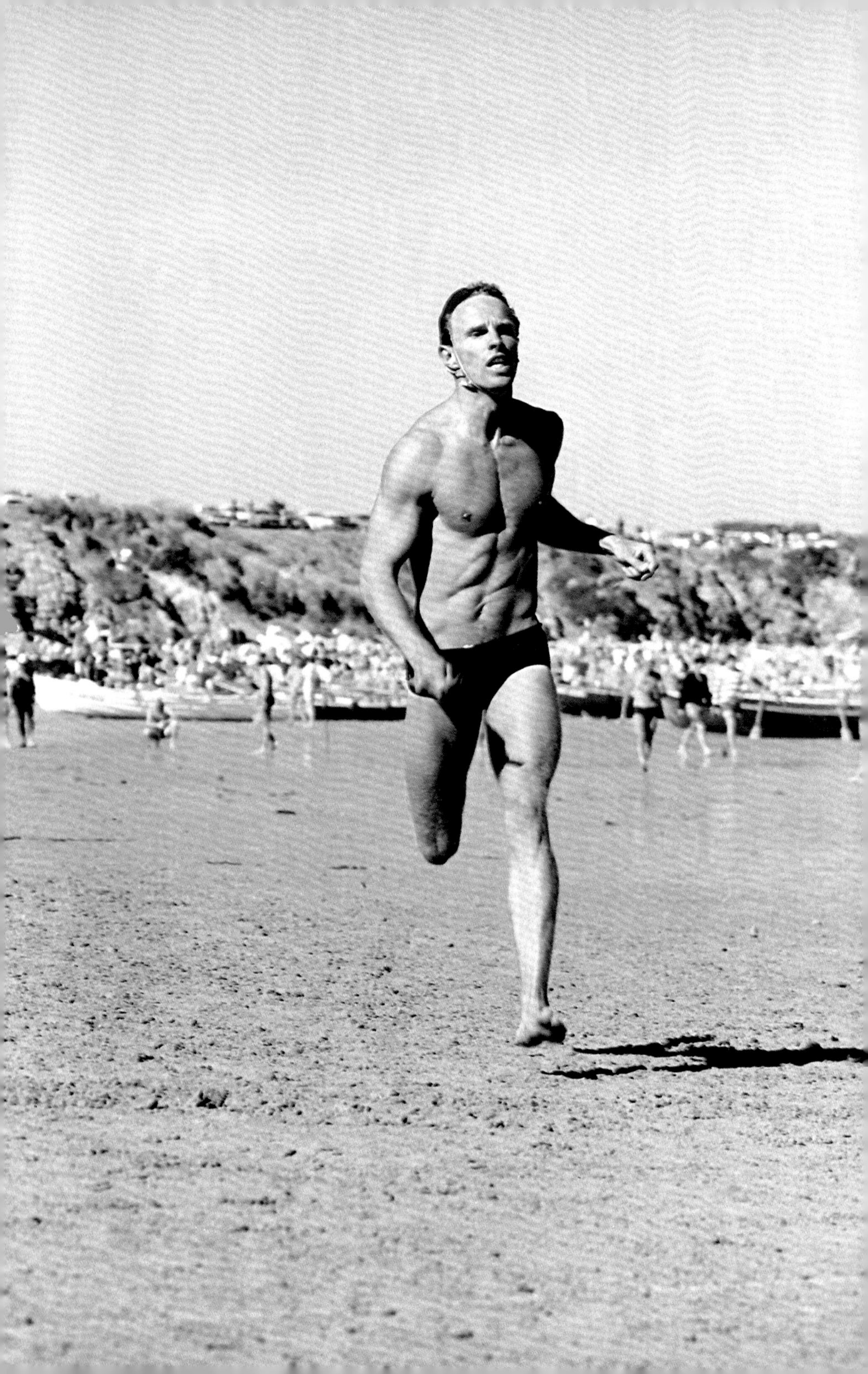

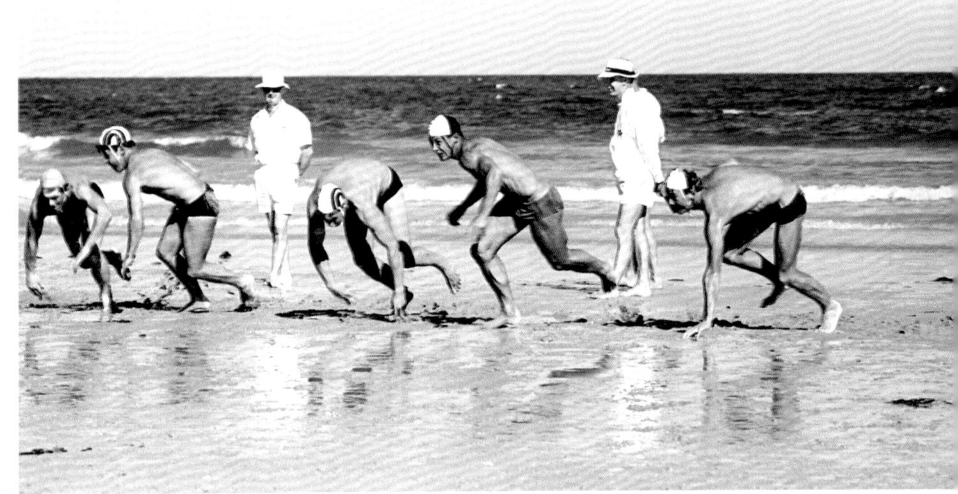

featured international competition between clubs from New Zealand, South Africa and Great Britain.

In the 1960s, there was a distinct lifestyle clash between the 'surfies' and 'clubbies', however. Many surfboard riders wanted to maintain a separate identity to the members of the surf club. The board riders 'did their own thing' and didn't want to be regimented by surf club rules, which were geared towards the surf lifesaving movement and inter-club competition. Most surfers were already involved in surf clubs … often they had to be involved in the local surf club in order to ride a surfboard at the beach.

'When I became interested in surfing, at Kirra (near Coolangatta, Queensland) I was quickly told I had to join the surf club if I wanted to ride my board there,' recalls Mal Sutherland. 'They also wanted you to join the club to boost their competition numbers. A lot of my group were 'clubbies' first, and it wasn't until that we got the freedom of riding Malibus that we branched out on our own. At least with being part of the surf club you had your boards transported to wherever the carnivals were being held … when the boards became shorter we had our own transportation and it didn't feel as if we needed to be tied to the surf club anymore. When I left the club in 1961 and my name was mud … several people didn't want to talk to me. It was very parochial.'

Above: **Flag race final start, Torquay Beach, January 1967.** Dr Barry Kaufman (South African champion 2nd from right, 1st place). **BS**

Opposite: **Billy Johnston, beach sprint, South African Carnival, Torquay Beach, January 1967. BS**

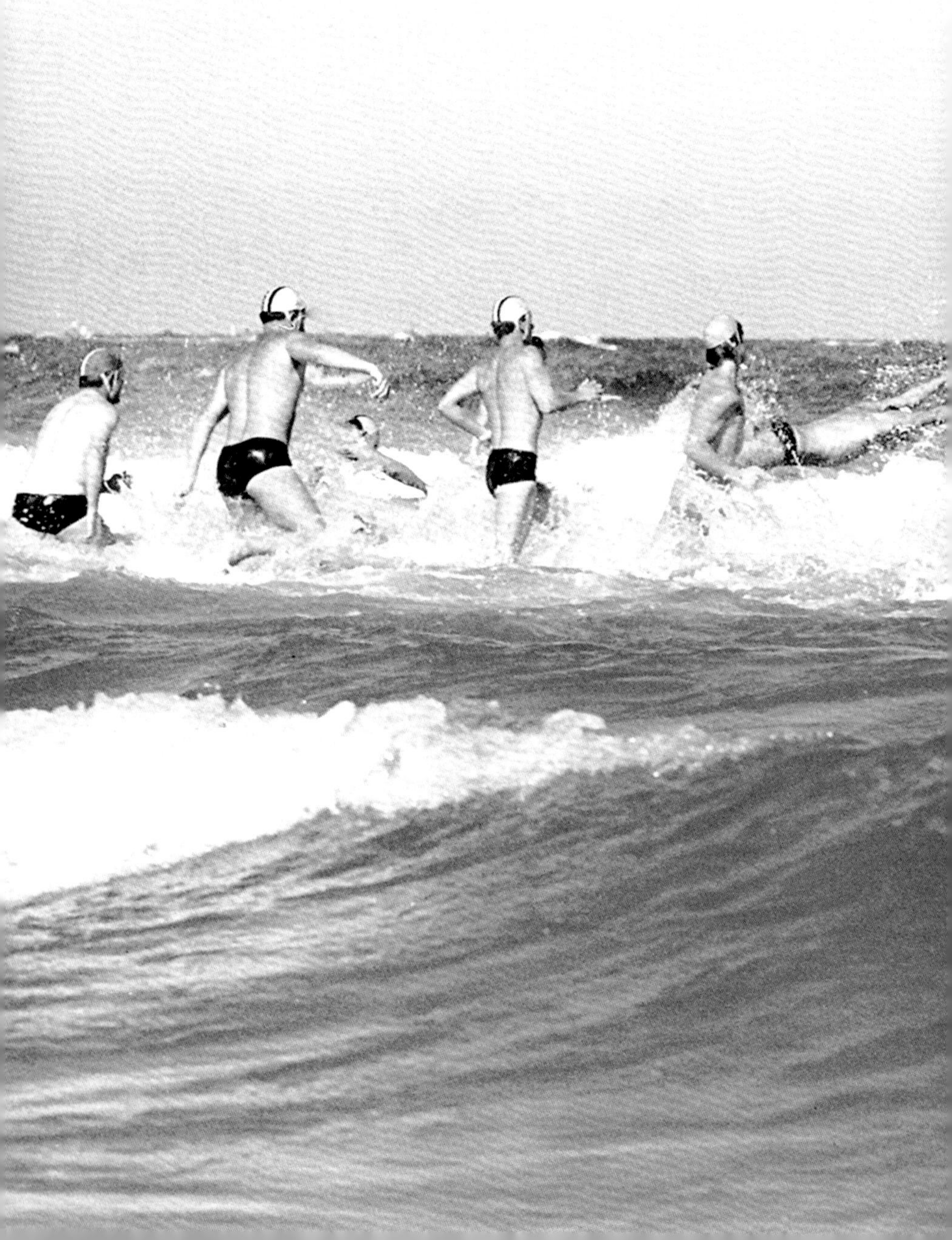

Torquay SLSC invitational carnival for South African visit, January 1969. **BS**

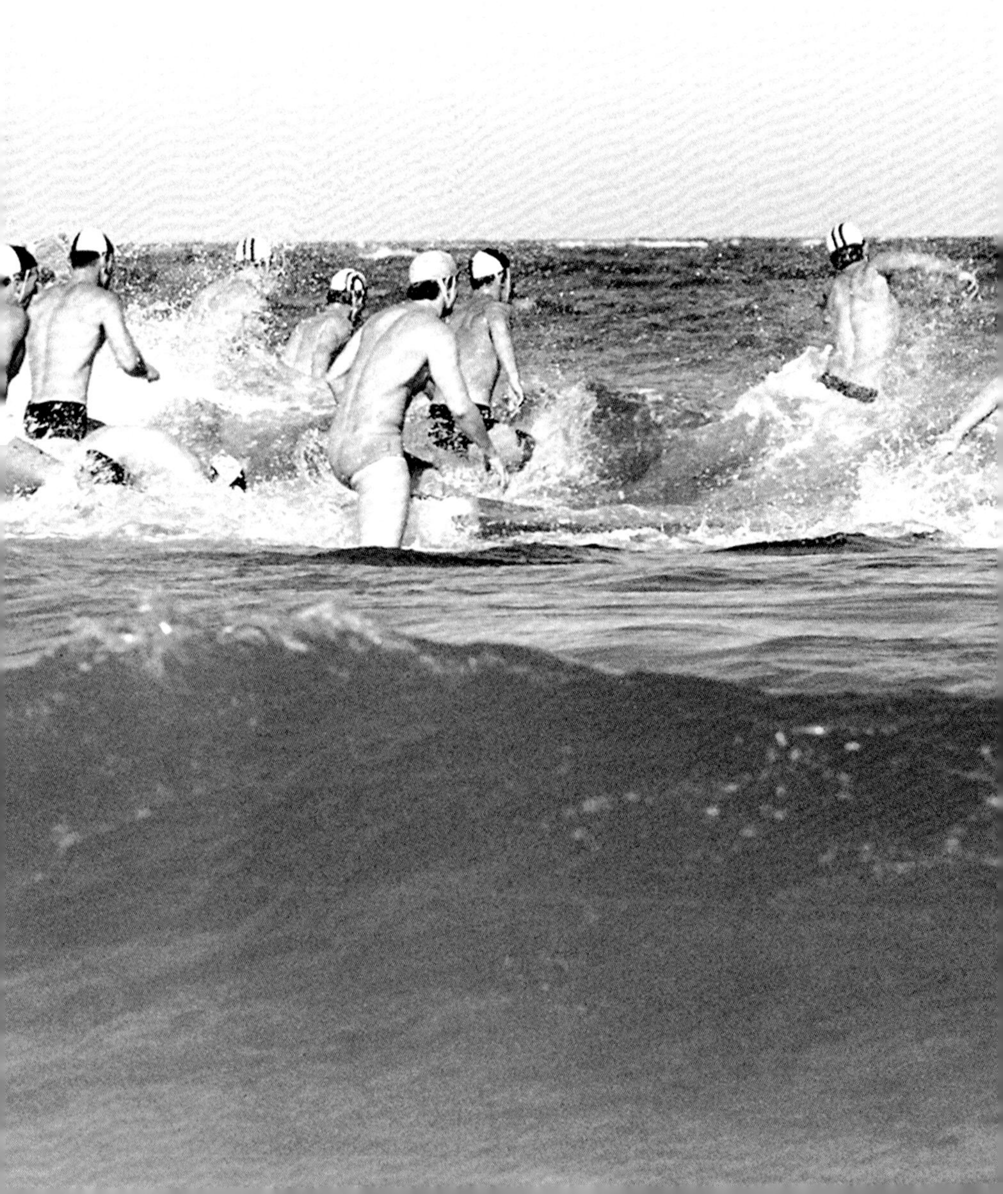

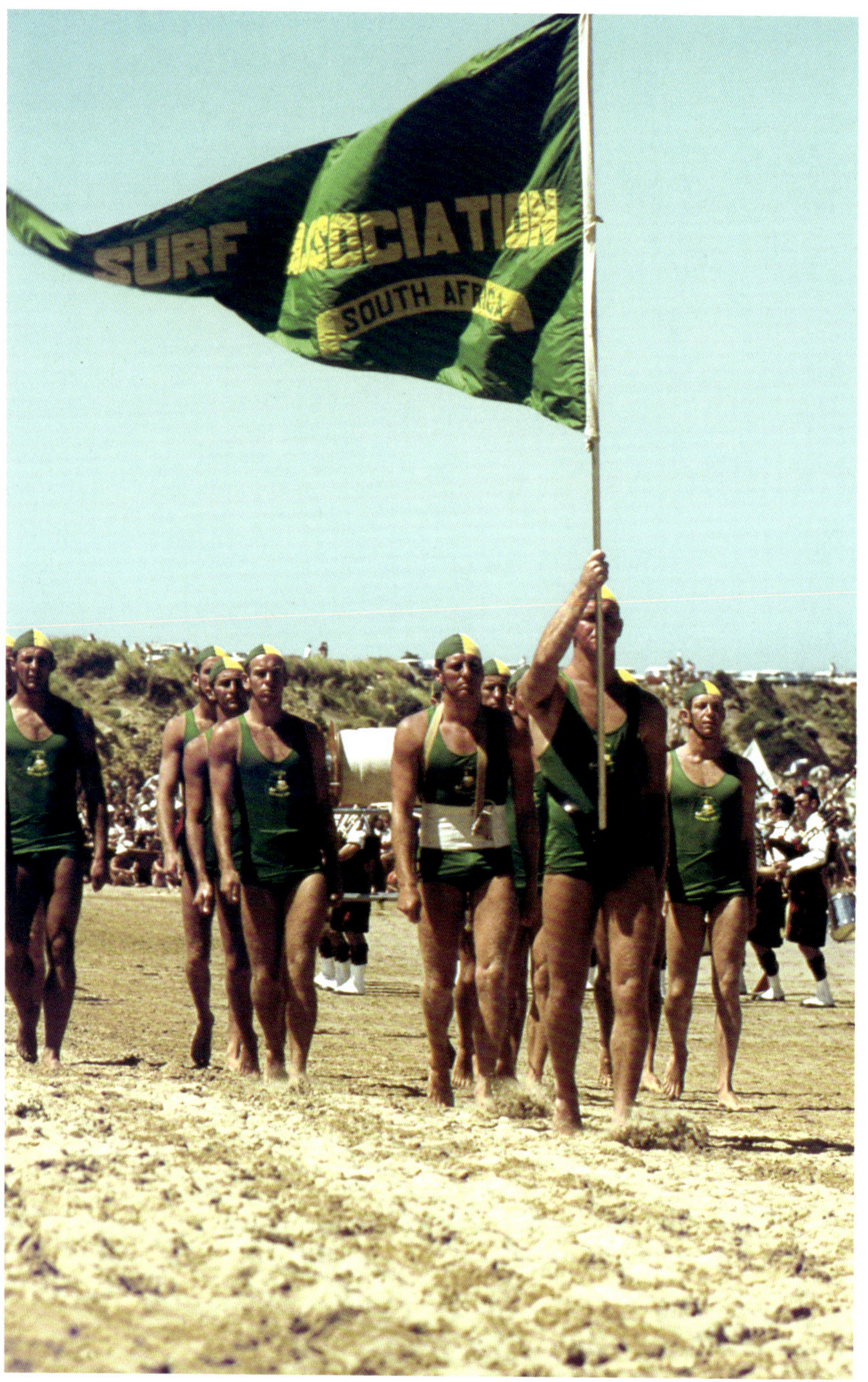
SURF ASSOCIATION
SOUTH AFRICA

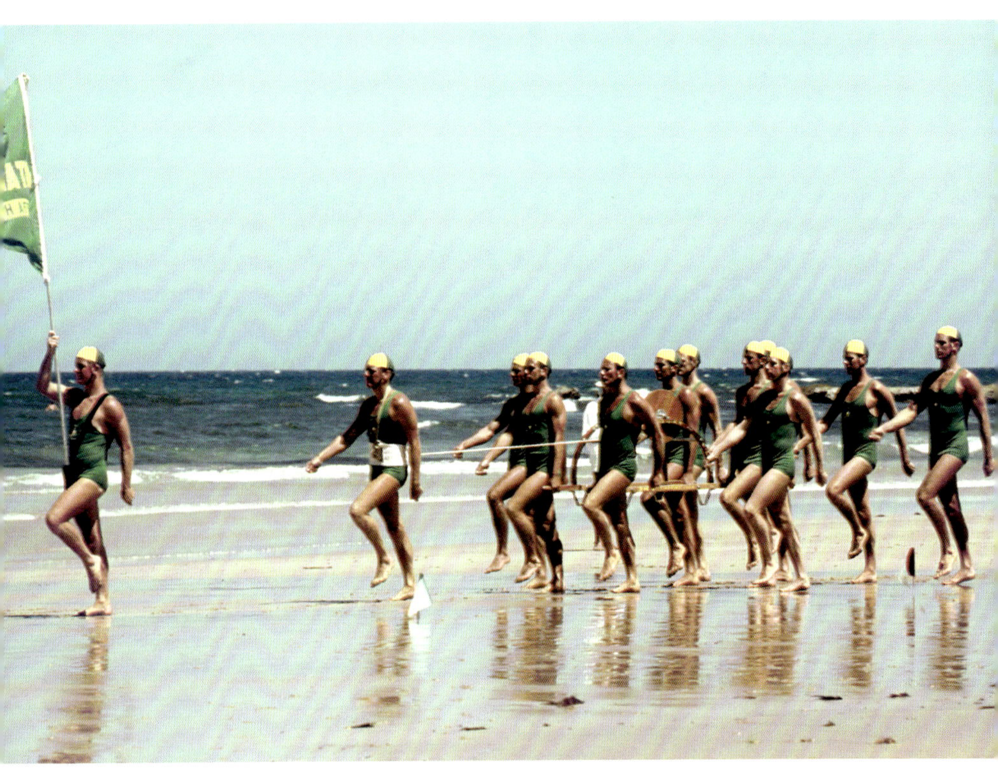

South African march past team, 1969. It was the last time South Africa competed in Australia before apartheid bans were activated. **BS**

Victorian surf culture

Unlike their interstate counterparts, Victorian surfers were not disengaged from the surf life-saving clubs. Early Victoria board-riding grew out of the surf clubs, particularly Torquay. Its foundations were body surfing and board riding. It was common from the late 1940s, after the club was formally created, to see surf skis, surf boats and wooden longboards cruising off Torquay Point. He rolling waves wrapping around Rocky Point into the bay provided the perfect haven for surfing to prosper.

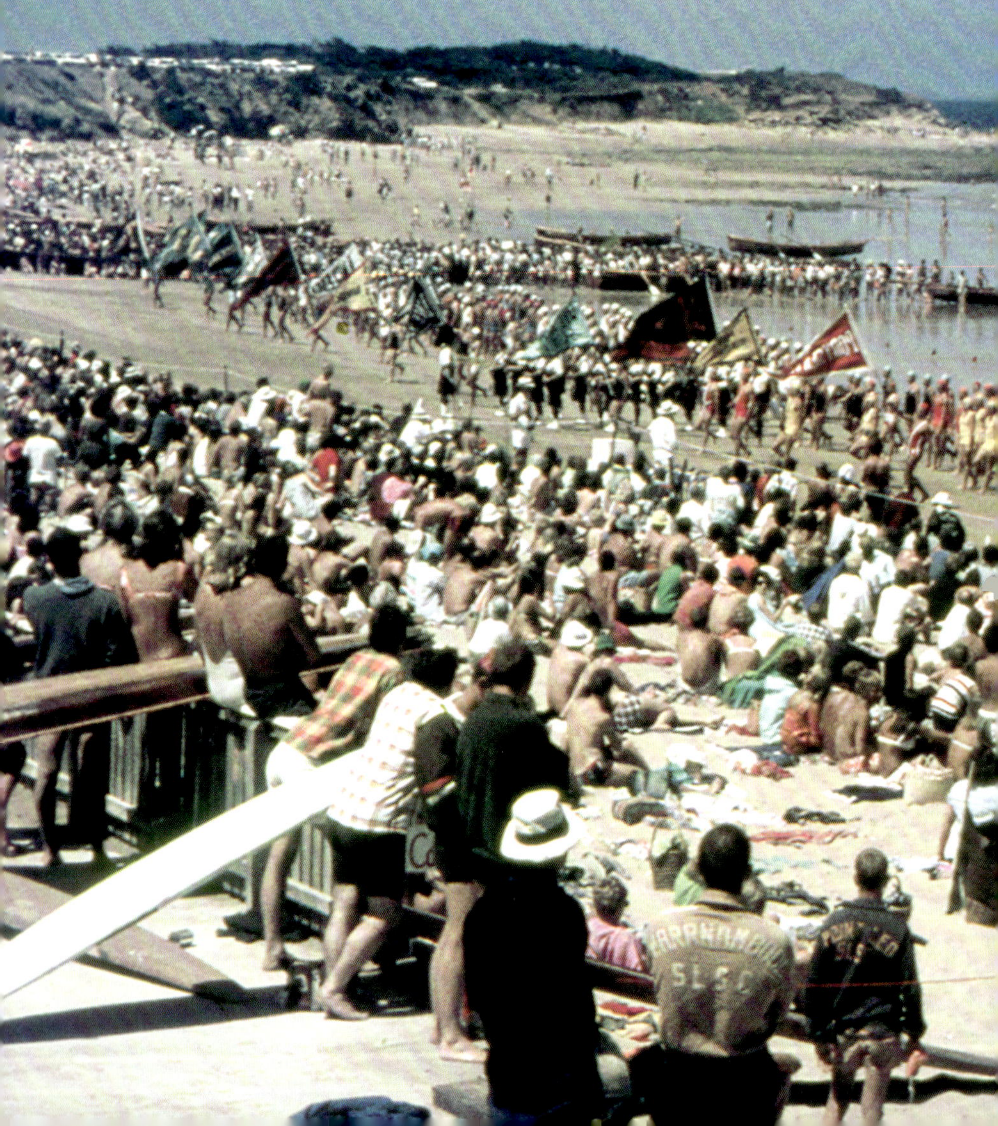

Board riders had the Point and swimmers the beach adjacent to the surf club. Boards (now called toothpicks), skis and boats were stored underneath the surf club for easy access to the water, few travelled outside their home beach, and at Torquay the predominantly Melbourne surfers stayed in the adjacent camping ground. The Club culture enabled the two groups to utilize the waves in harmony.

Beach crowd, Australia Day carnival, South African invitational, Torquay Surf Beach, January 1967. **BS**

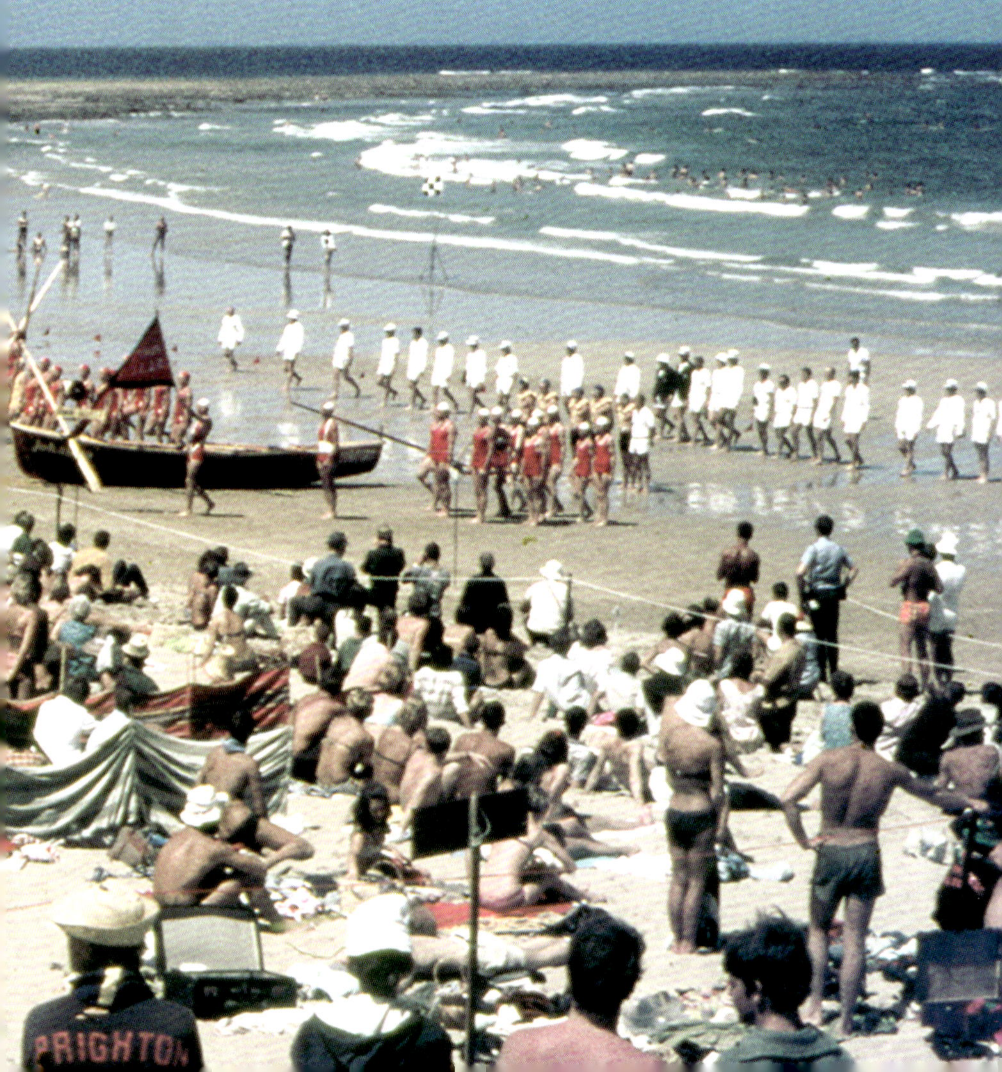

The 1956 Melbourne Olympic Games facilitated significant change after thousands of visitors made the trip to Torquay to attend the Olympic demonstration sport (surfing) carnival. I was there with my cousin and family and had just turned 14 years. Watching the visiting American team, which were mostly life guards, ride balsa Malibu boards off the Point fired my desire to do the same.

With the rapid growth of board riding and local board manufacture by pioneer Vic Tantau, modern surfing exploded. Increasing crowds and the search for more challenging waves led to the discovery of Bells Beach, a few kilometers along the coast west of Torquay, which was close enough for Torquay ski and paddle board surfers and boat crews to take a cruise along the coast. They quickly found Bells intimidating and their equipment unable to handle the intensity of the waves.

Bells was pioneered throughout the late 1950s by two groups – Torquay board riders under the leadership of Peter Troy and a Geelong boxing and gymnasium group led by Marcus Shaw. There will always be arguments over who was the first to consistently surf Bells, but in the context of Victorian surfing culture it doesn't matter. Marcus was dubbed the King of Bells by his peers. In 1962 Troy and Tantau ran the first Bells Beach Board Rally which became the Rip Curl Pro. In the middle '60s Peter then led the way in surf exploration around the world, introducing modern surfing to Brazil and discovering Lagundri Bay in Nias, Indonesia. His book of letters home, *To the Four Corners of the World* is a classic.

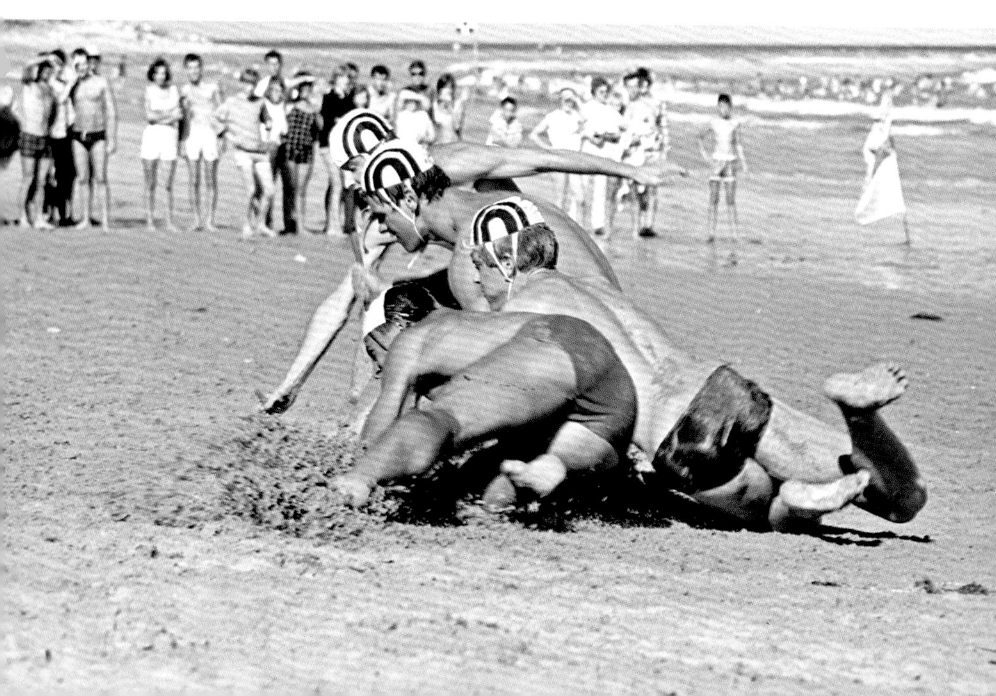

An aspect of Victorian surfing culture was the distance of the ocean beaches from Melbourne. Either way it was about 1½ hour's drive to the east and west coast beaches. To get to Torquay and the Great Ocean Road, Melbourne-based surfers had to drive through Geelong's CBD. Throughout the 1960s Melbourne surfers either did a day trip or departed Friday for the weekend. Later, in the 1970s many moved to Torquay and became the builders of its surfing industry so they could live by the ocean, and created what is now the 'Surf Coast'.

Surfing in the cold Southern Ocean waves bred hardened surfers where for many, the surf lifesaving club bonds provided places to stay or hang out as they surfed during the winter months. The need for decent wet suits drove the early surf industries. Beach crowds were not an issue for the coastal shires. They were far from the madding crowd in their approach to managing the new wave of surfing and left it largely to the surf clubs. There was no licensing system for surfboards, and little cultural angst between surfers and 'clubbies'. During the '60s specialist surfers and also surfing clubs then developed as the freedom of the new mobility was appreciated and the organization of the Australian Surfriders Association emerged.

BARRIE SUTHERLAND

Flag race final finish, South African Carnival, Torquay Beach, January 1967. **BS**

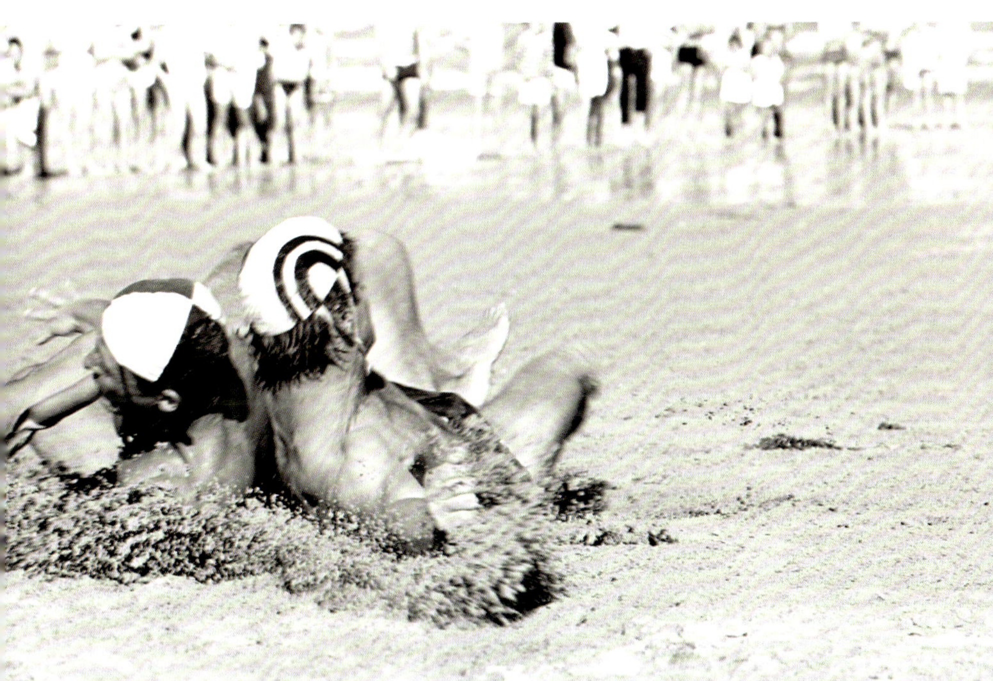

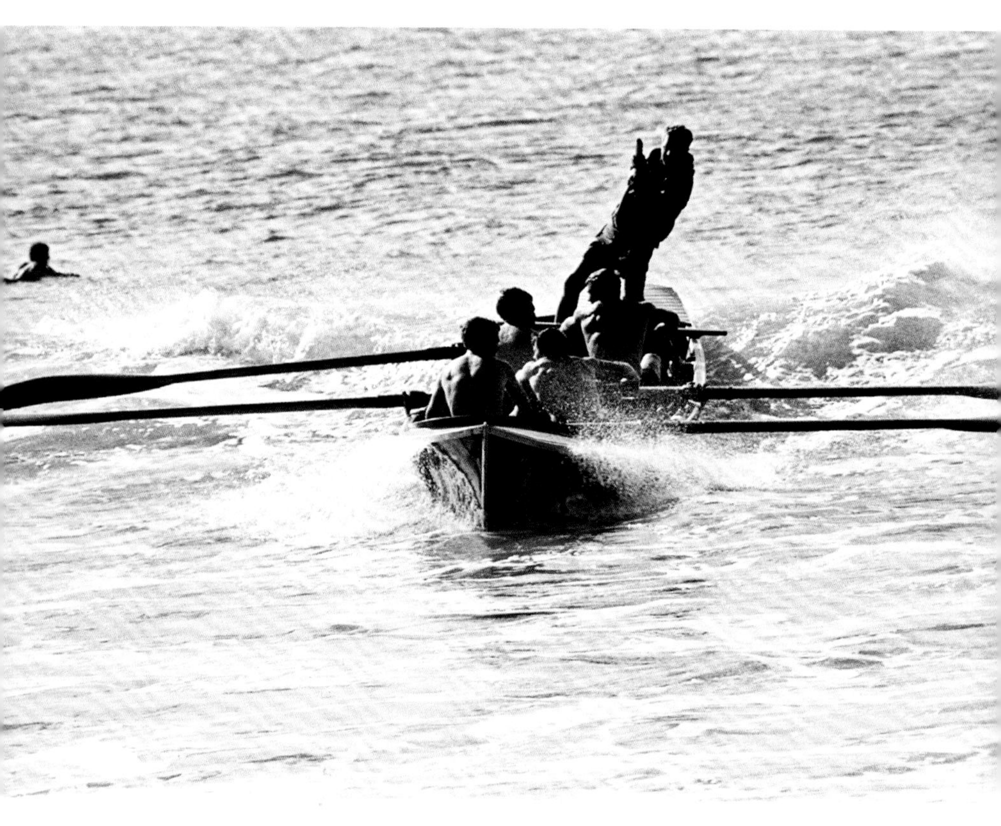

South African Carnival, Torquay Beach, January 1967. BS

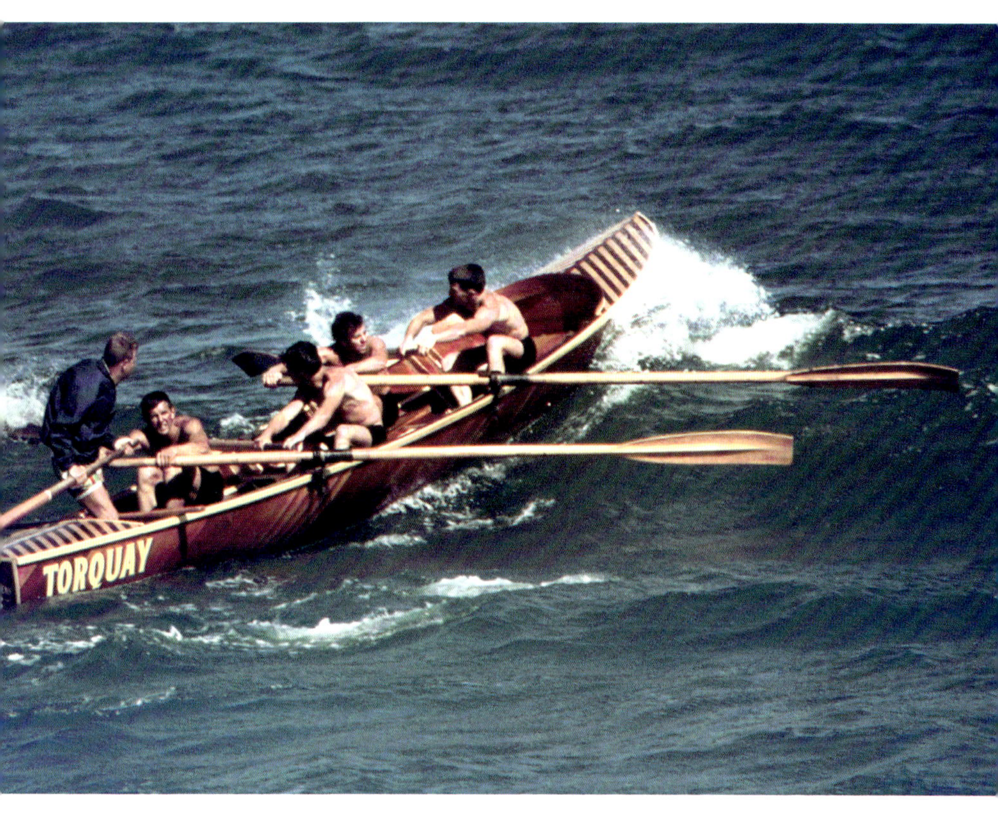

Johanna – Torquay A crew, Australia Day carnival, South
African invitational, Torquay Surf Beach, January 1967. **BS**

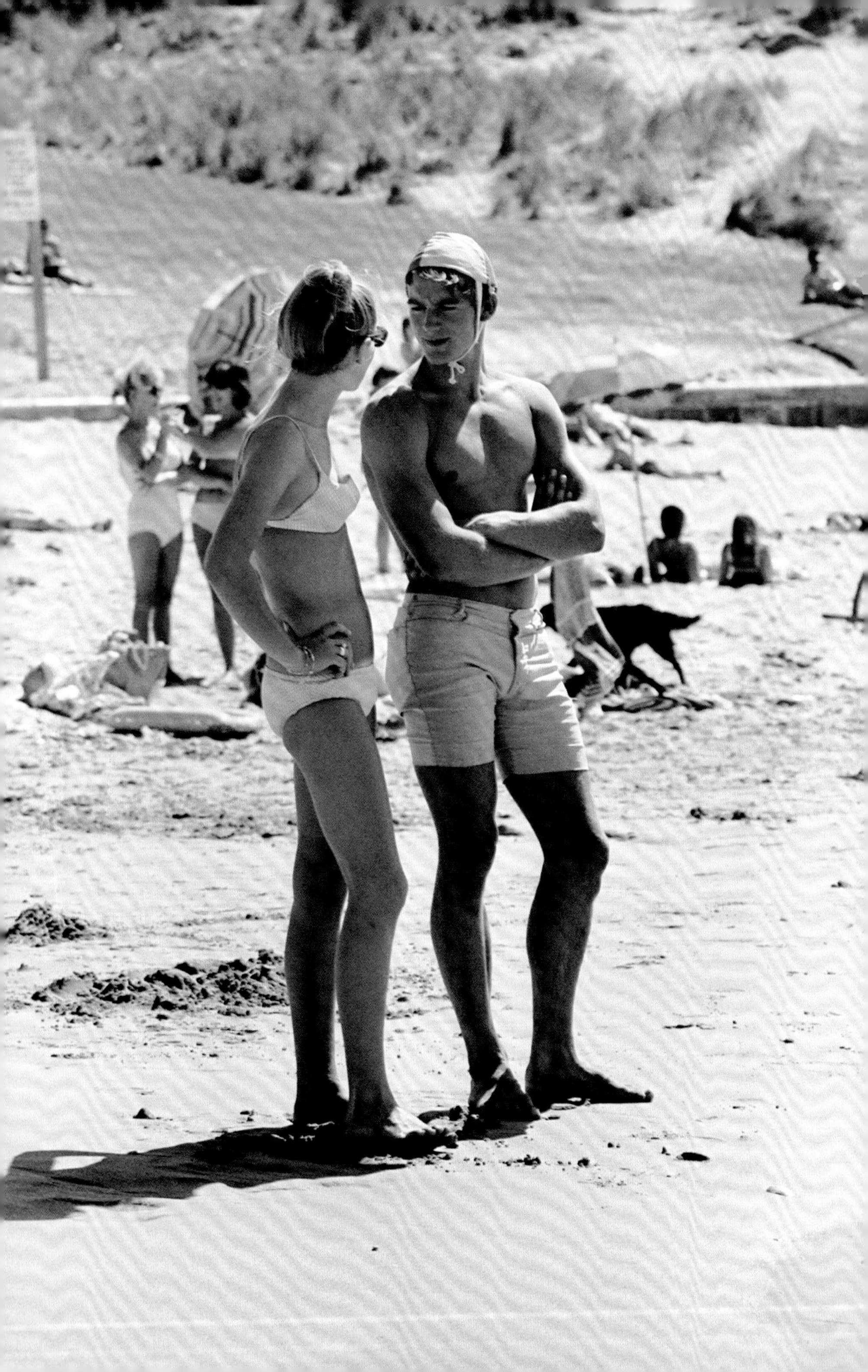

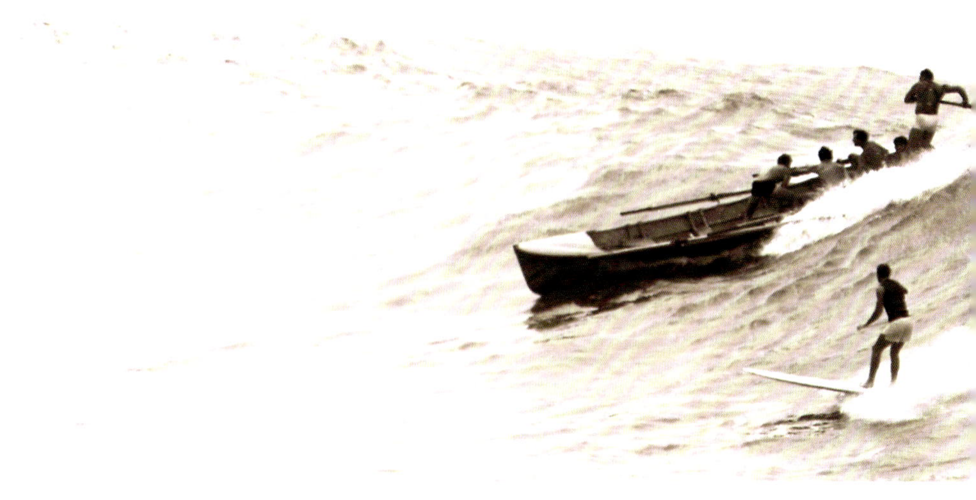

Above: There was a tension between the surfers and the 'clubbies'. This photo illustrates the surfboat thinking they have right of way. **JP**

Opposite: John Gudgeon & Glynis Milne, Patrol captain, Torquay, February 1966. **BS**

Competitions

In the 1960s, surfing was either a complete way of life for a select few and a pleasant recreational pastime for thousands. The sheer exhilaration of surfing on an ocean wave, however, found its full expression in organised competitions on popular Australian beaches. By the mid-1960s, thousands of surfing fans packed events in Queensland, NSW and Victoria to crown the newest surfing champion – both male and female, junior and senior.

Competitive surfing in Australia started with the Australian Surfers Association, the amateur body to which most surfing clubs were affiliated. Surfing clubs were by their very nature fairly loose affairs early in the decade, with plenty of social activity complementing the competition. However, these clubs provided the means by which surfers could enter state, national and eventually international championships. There were seven divisions of amateur

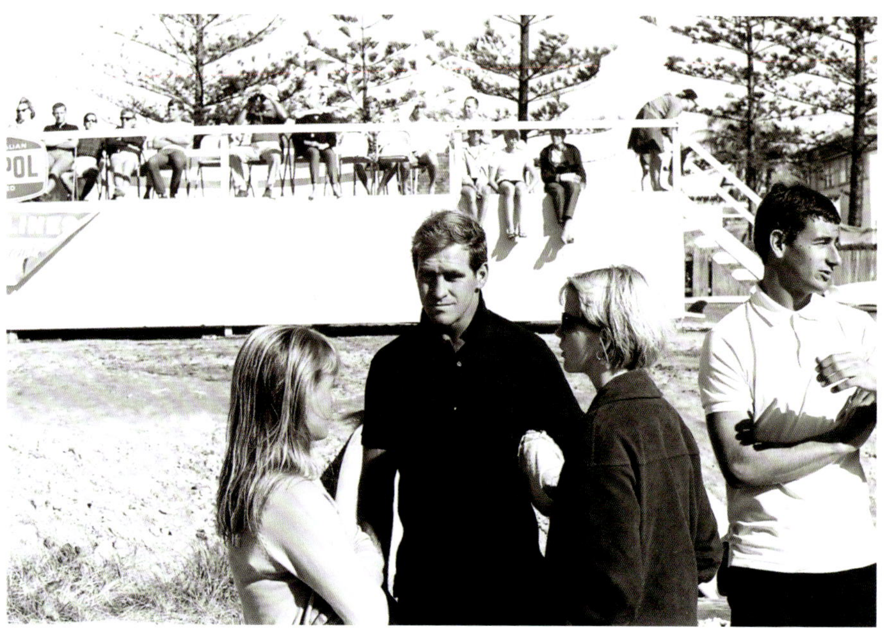

Above: **Nipper Williams** (centre), a Manly surfer, with the judges in the background. **JP**

Opposite: **Bernard 'Midget' Farrelly** (1944–2016) was the first Australian World Surfing champion. In 1962, he won the Makaha International Surfing Championship, the then unofficial world surfing championship. In 1964, he won the inaugural World Surfing Championship at Manly Beach, Sydney.

Here Midget pulls out of a closeout, with Nat Young waiting out the back. **JP** competition – cadets (under 15), juniors (under 18), A and B grade open men's, senior men's (over 28), women's and kneeboarders.

Many surfers of the era used their competition experience to develop a more aggressive and competitive approach in the water. Some thrived on competition and became world champions – 'Midget' Farrelly (1944–2016), 'Nat' Young, Bob McTavish, Peter Drouyn, Peter Troy (1940–2008), Ted Spencer, WA's Ian Cairns and not to forget Phyllis O'Donell, (Australia's first female champion) and Victoria's Gail Couper. Others used this new competitive style to catch the best wave of the day as they battled the increasing influx of riders which made surfing resemble more and more the 'rat race' people were actually trying to escape.

In 1965, the first ever World Surfing Championships were held in Sydney at Manly Beach in front of a crowd of 65,000, with Midget Farrelly and Phyllis O'Donell crowned the first ever World Surfing Champions (1964). It wasn't until the '70s, however, that Australia experienced truly professional surfing competitions taking place. Australia supported three major world championship

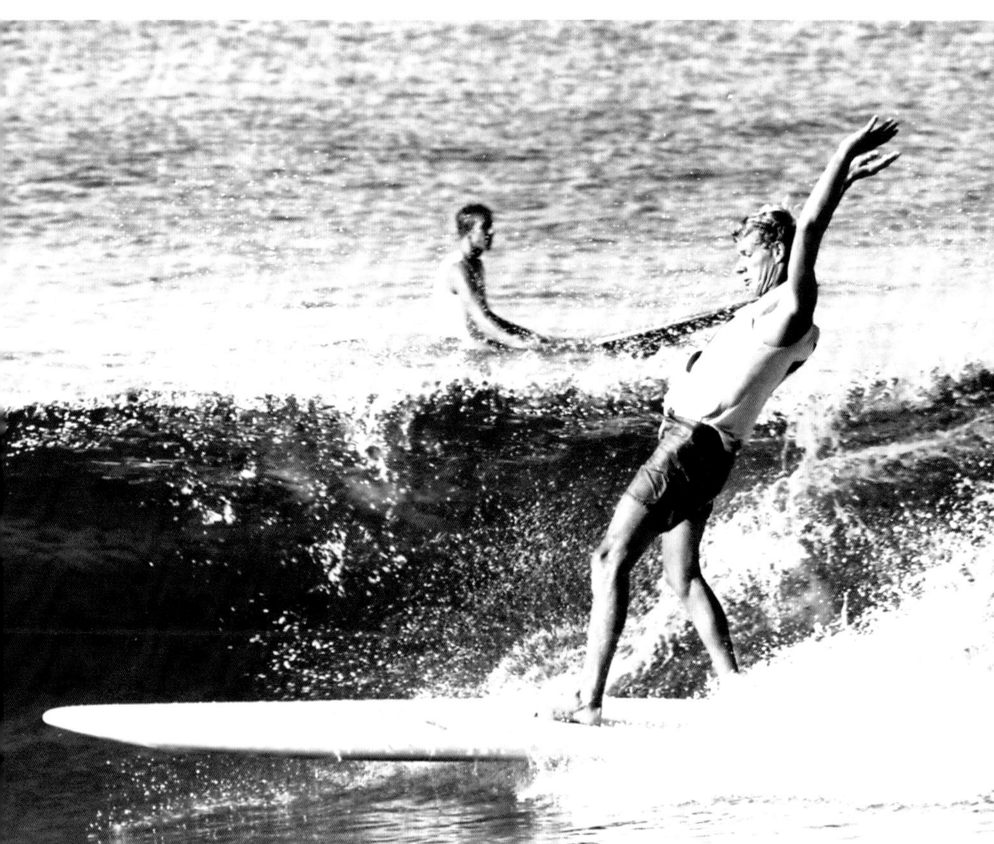

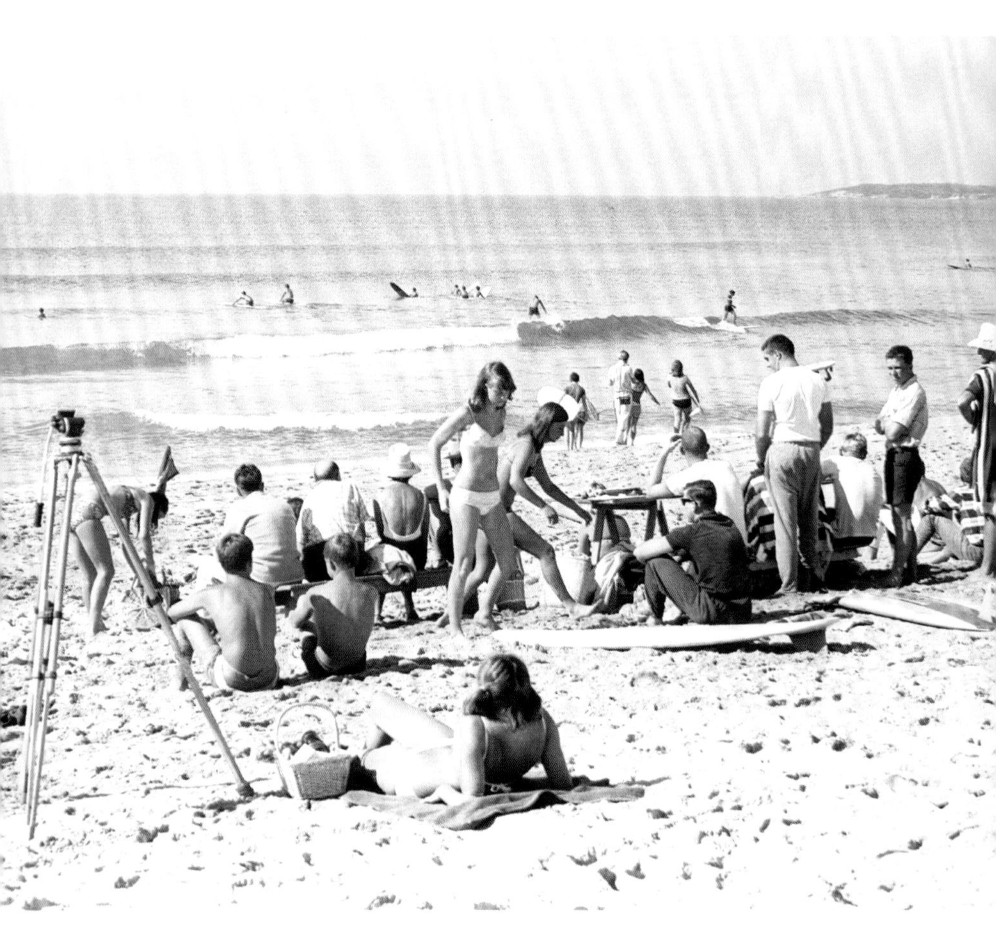

Above: Judges and spectators at the Kurranulla Wahines surfing comp at Wanda, 1966. **BW**

Opposite: 'Snowy' McAlister talking to female competitors before Australian Titles at Coolangatta in 1966. **JP**

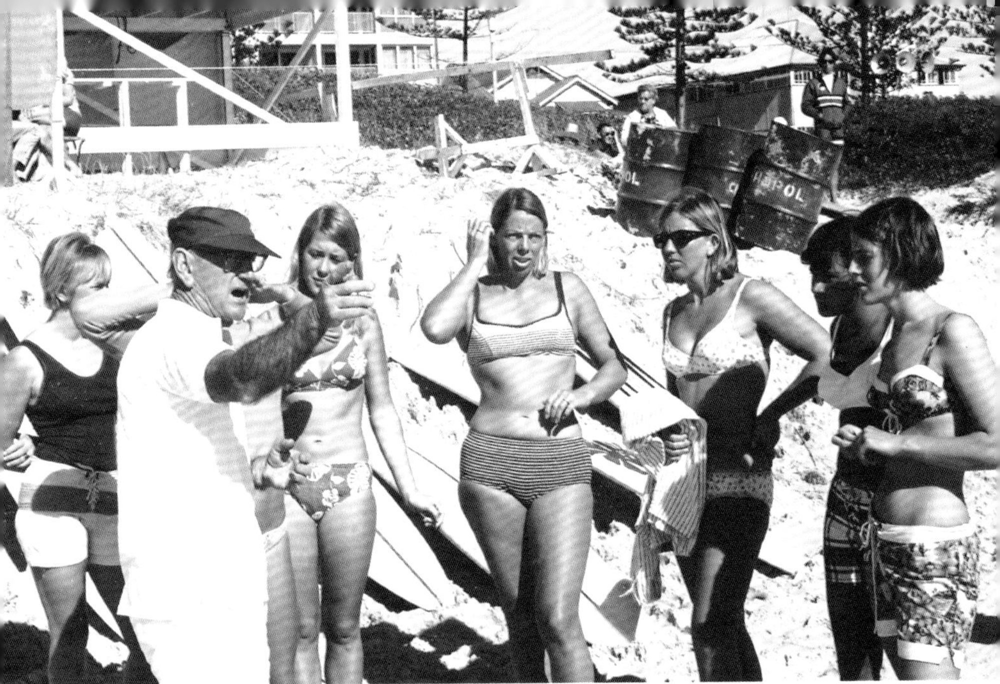

events – the Open Surf Classic at Burleigh Heads (now the Quiksilver Pro Gold Coast), the Bells Beach Classic at Easter (now the Rip Curl Pro) and the Coke-2SM Surfabout in Sydney (now the Drug Aware Margaret River Pro).

The judging of surfing had a difficult infancy, however. The main issue was that the judges' interpretation of events in the water was subjective, and many believe this hasn't changed too much in the fifty years since. In the early days, a panel of surfing peers simply watched the whole event unfold on the water and chose a winner. This method had its share of problems of course – even when it was later refined to compel judges to offer a point score out of 20. Judges were accused of bias, but the real flaw in the system was that they were constantly accused of favouring a particular style … there was no place for innovation and interpretation in a surfing contest. As Nat Young later observed, 'The fashionable style of surfing at any given time became the fashionable style of judging. One person's way of surfing became the measure of what was good, and heaven help you if you didn't conform.'

In the late 1970s, Peter Drouyn, a veteran competitor himself, devised a point-scoring system designed to bring some objectivity into the process. Centred on the concept of there being only two surfers in the water at the same time being judged against each other, five judges scored points out of ten for such qualities as style and co-ordination, close-to-the-wall manoeuvring, split-second positioning and the way in which each surfer used the wave to the fullest extent. The new rules made for an exciting battle between surfers of almost equal ability and most observers believed surfing finally had a system that encouraged individuality and high performance.

It's been that way ever since.

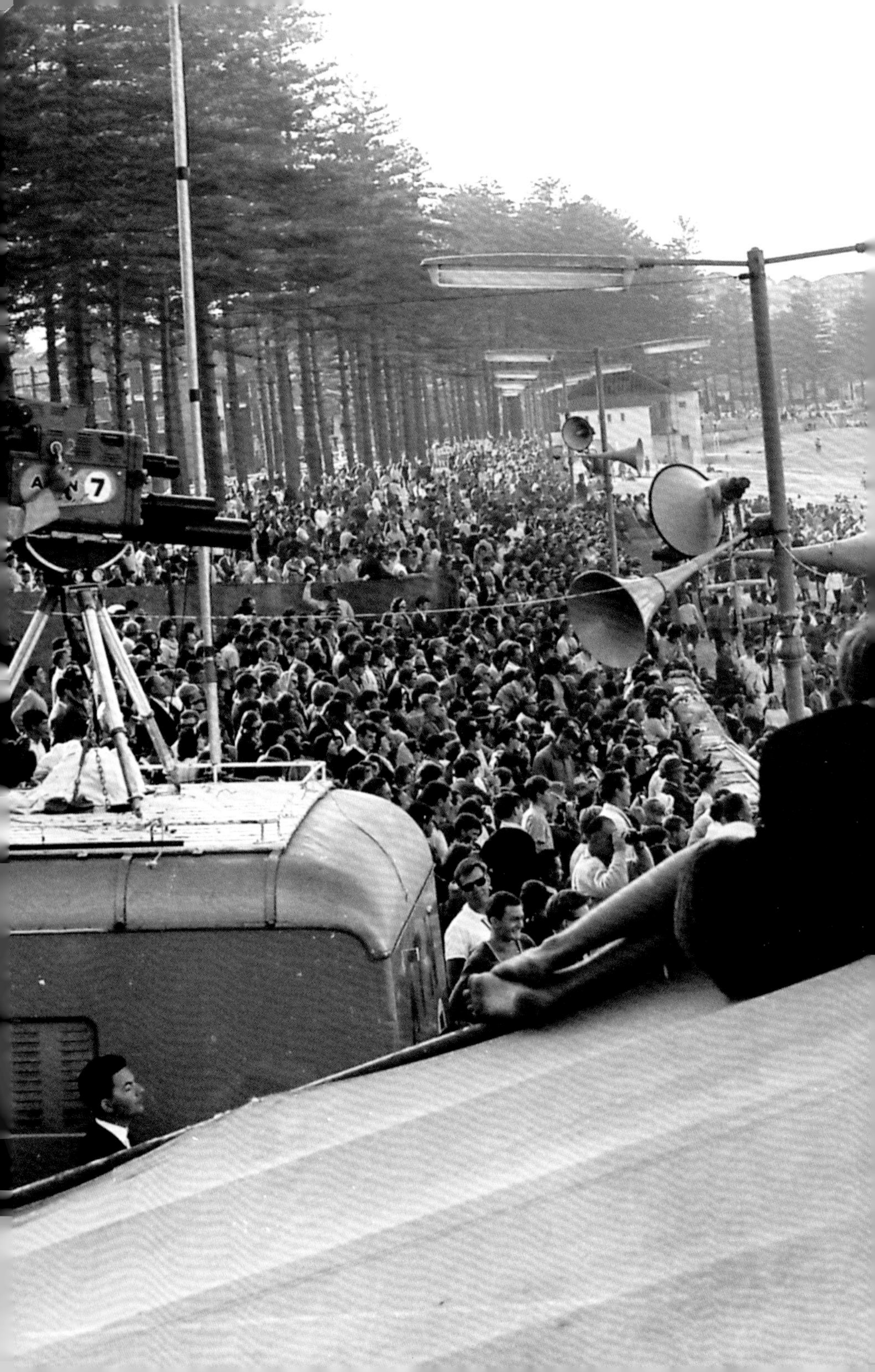
ATN 7

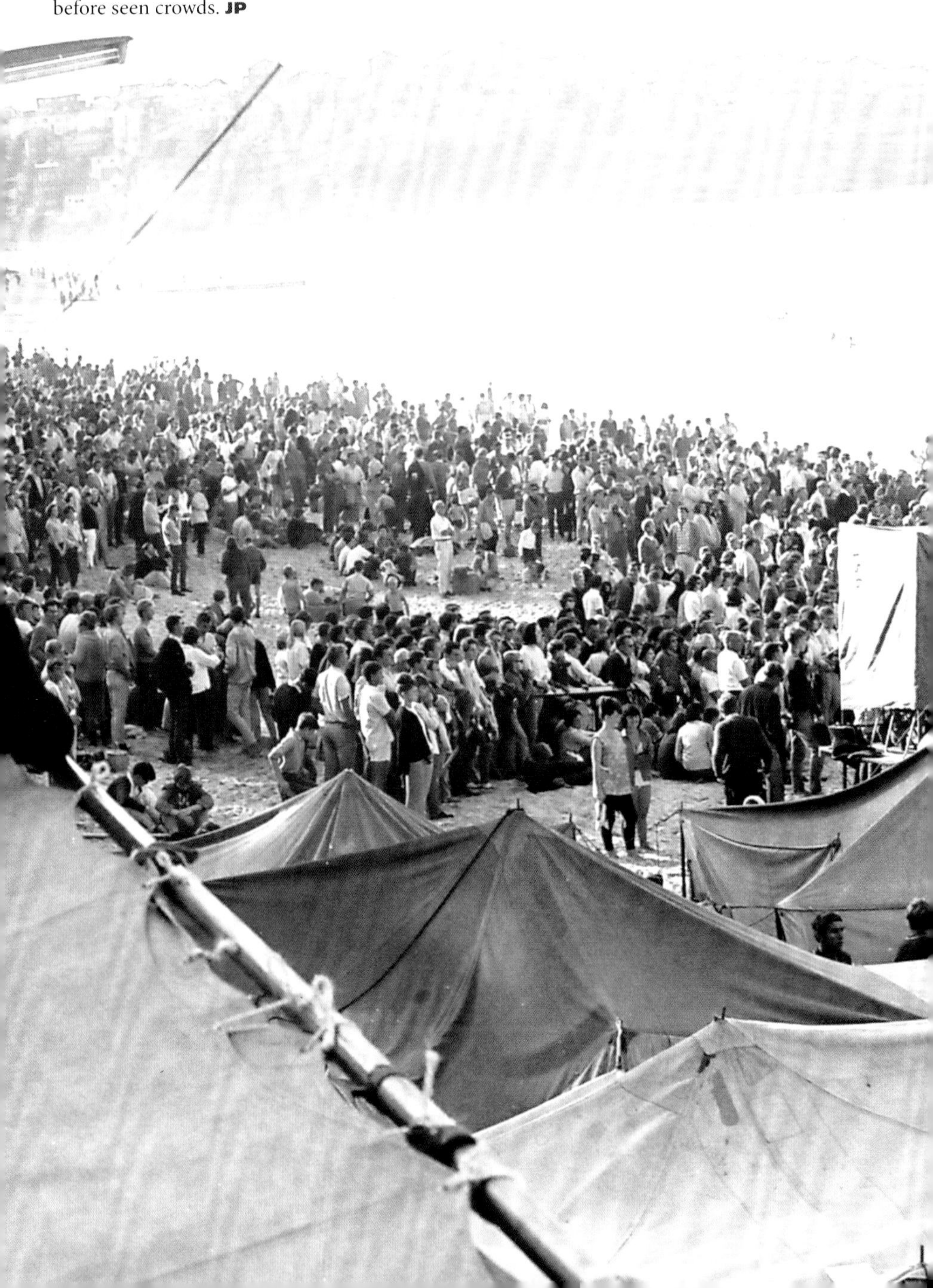

Manly, 1964. Photo taken above the judge's stand at the presentation of the winners of the First World titles conducted at Manly. You can sense the excitement of this event. Everyone wanted a closer look. The event was televised on mainstream news outlets and drew never before seen crowds. **JP**

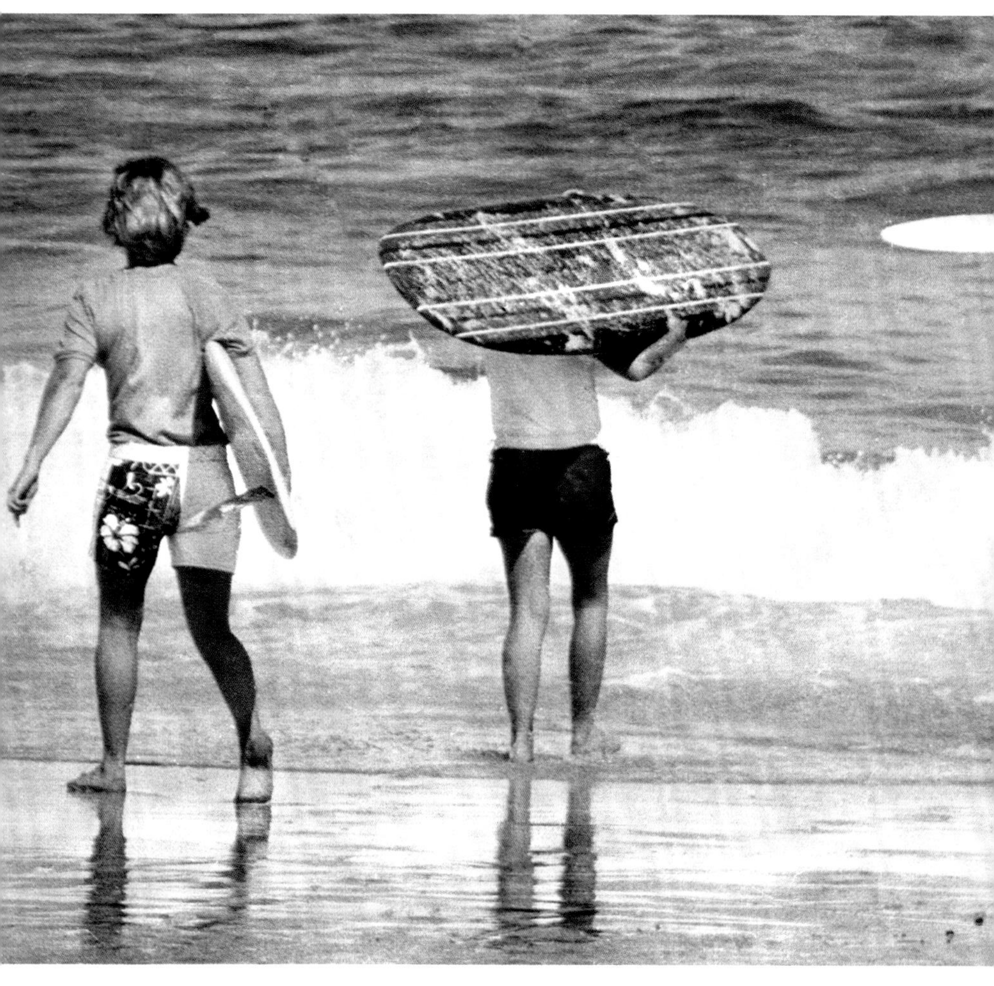

Bondi, 1963. Ladies entering the surf for the finals of the Woman's Invitational Championships. The heavy 'mals' in the early sixties made it difficult for girl surfers (and some of the boys too) carrying the boards and handling them in the waves. **BW**

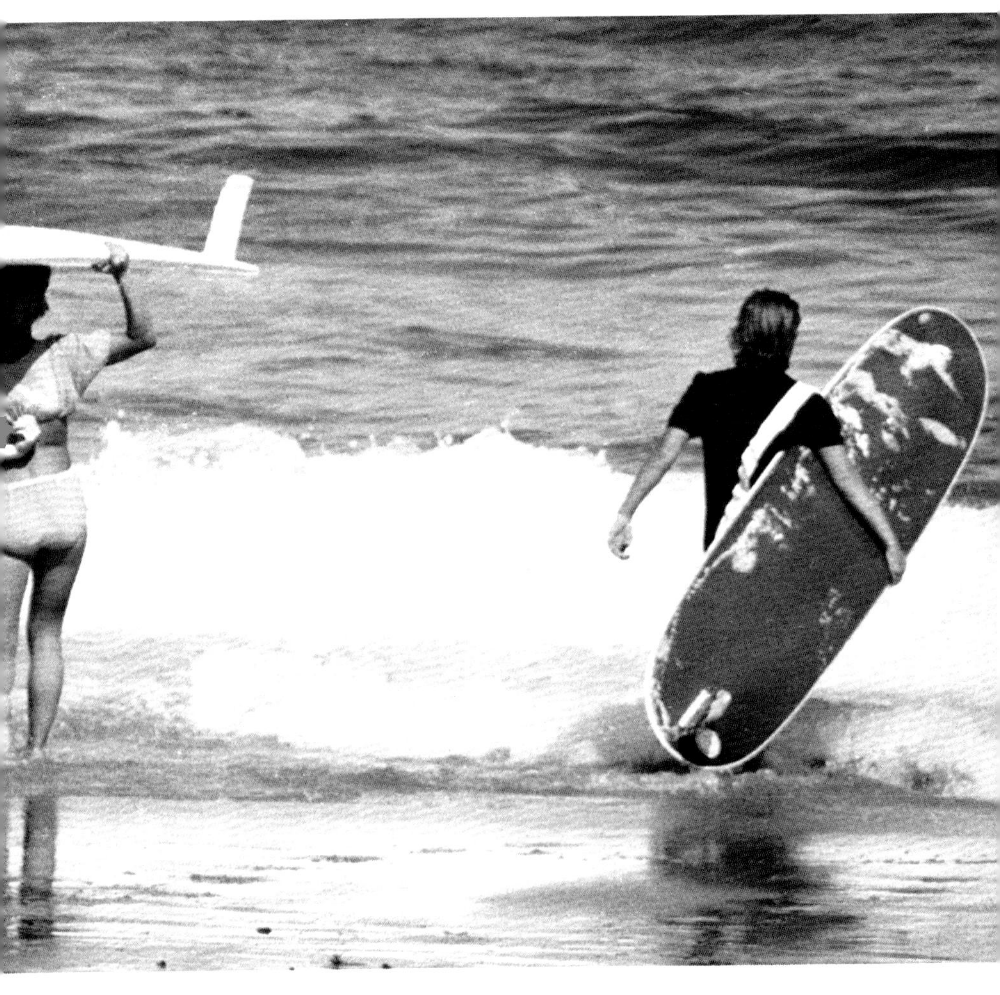

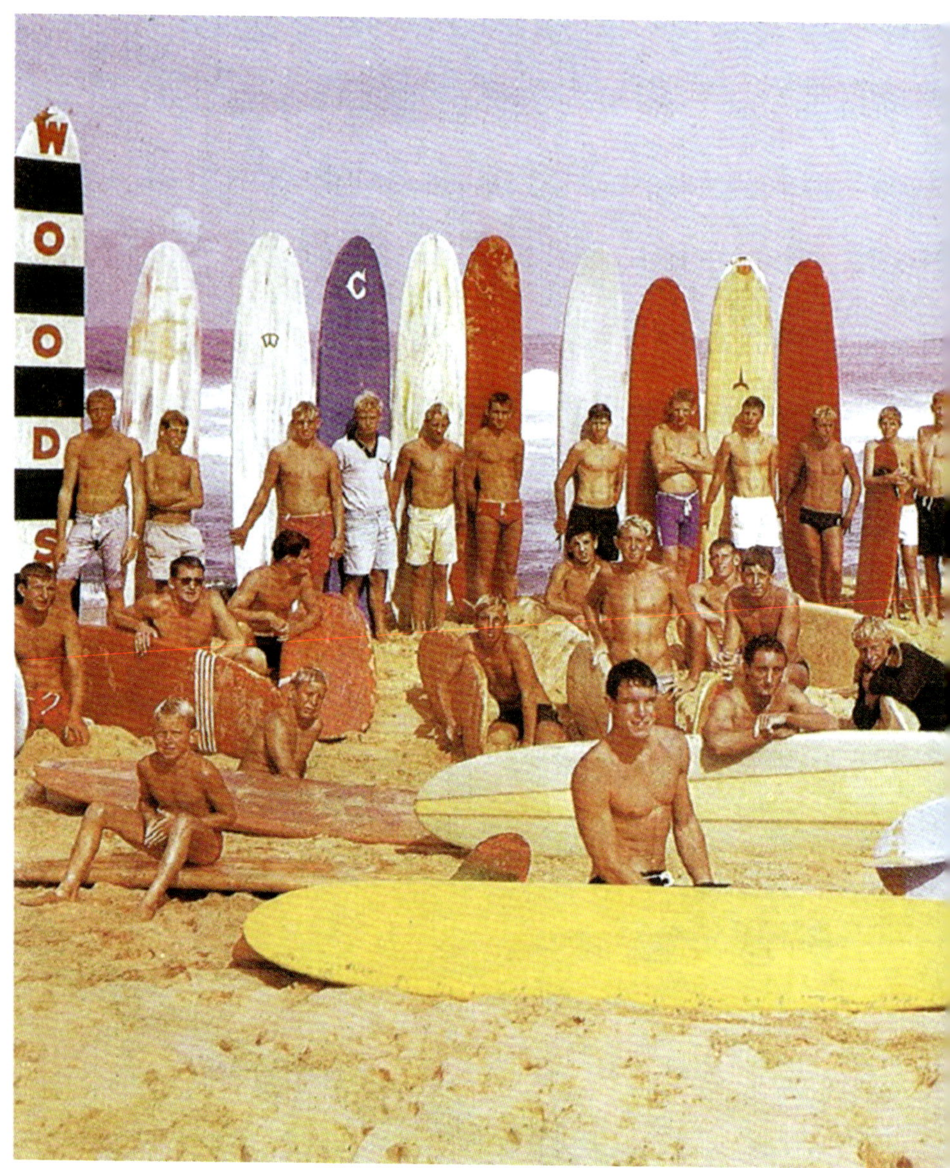

Narrabeen surf-meet, 1962. An alternate photo taken for the Teenagers' Weekly supplement in *Australian Woman's Weekly* 22 August 1962. John Knobel, Bondi local in the '50s and '60s, is standing in front of the second red balsa malibu from the left wearing his home-made blue board shorts with a snazzy rope belt. John surfed on a Norm Casey hollow 16 foot 'toothpick' before the malibus arrived in Sydney in 1956.

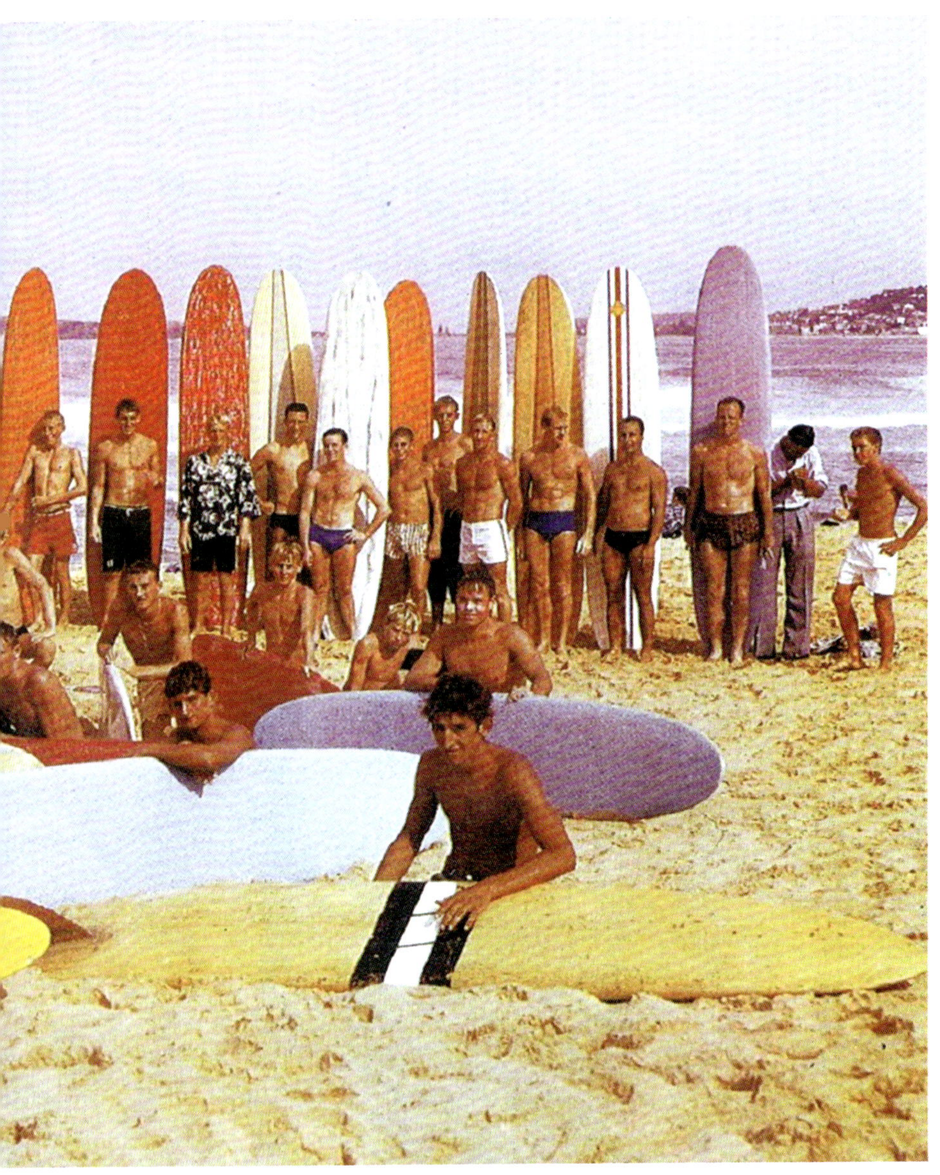

Also pictured: Top, from left: Denis Lindsay, unknown, Peter St. John, Ken McKnight, Jim Pike, Barry Watson, Peter Menzies, John Boylan, Ross Gibson and then Mick Dooley (in Hawaiian shirt). Middle row: John Mater (blue Speedo's), Steve Try (squatting to the right behind Midget Farrelly) Jimmy Ingham, Dave Standen (middle row right, with spikey hair), Midget Farrelly (in black wetsuit), unknown, Bob Fell. Also pictured: 'Puppy Dog' Paton (front row, right).

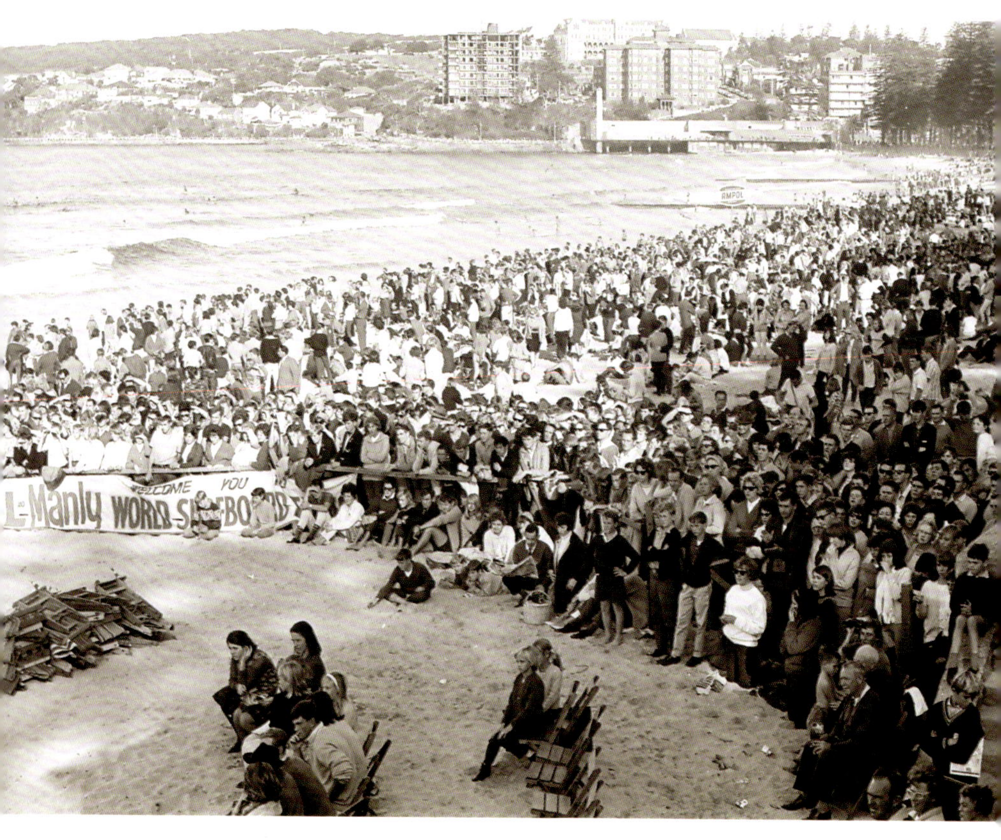

Manly, 1964. Crowds of up to 60,000 watched a memorable day's events. **JP**

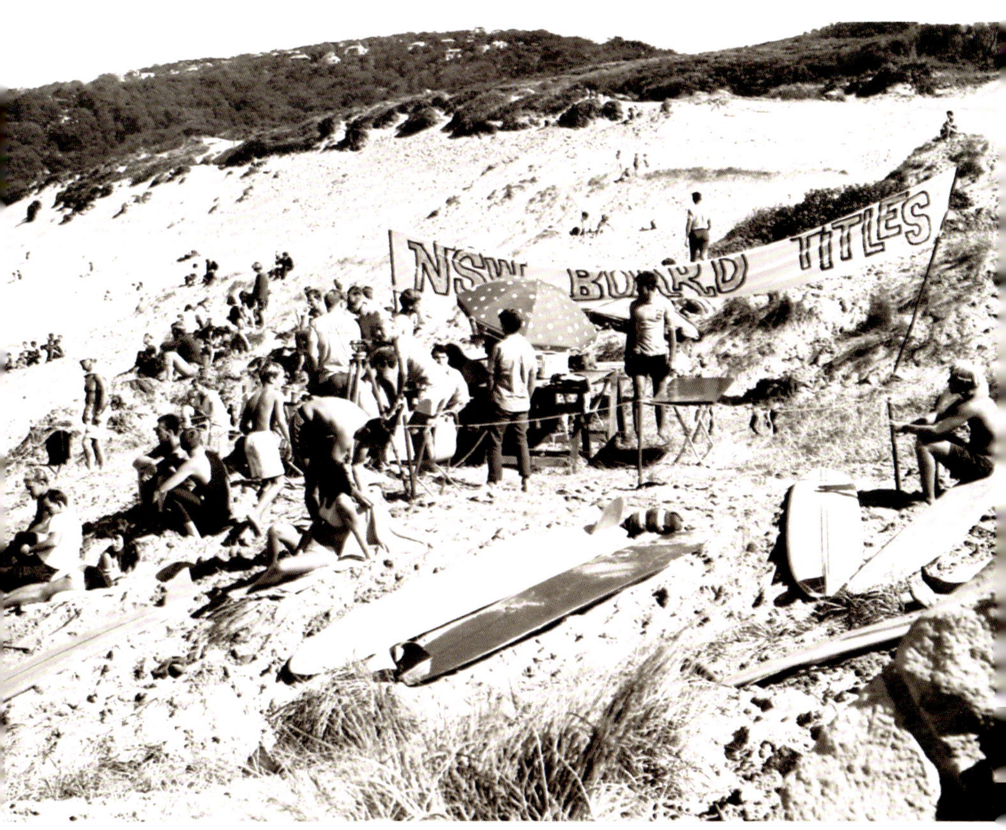

NSW Board Titles, c. 1965. Dated by the fins on the surfboards. **JP**

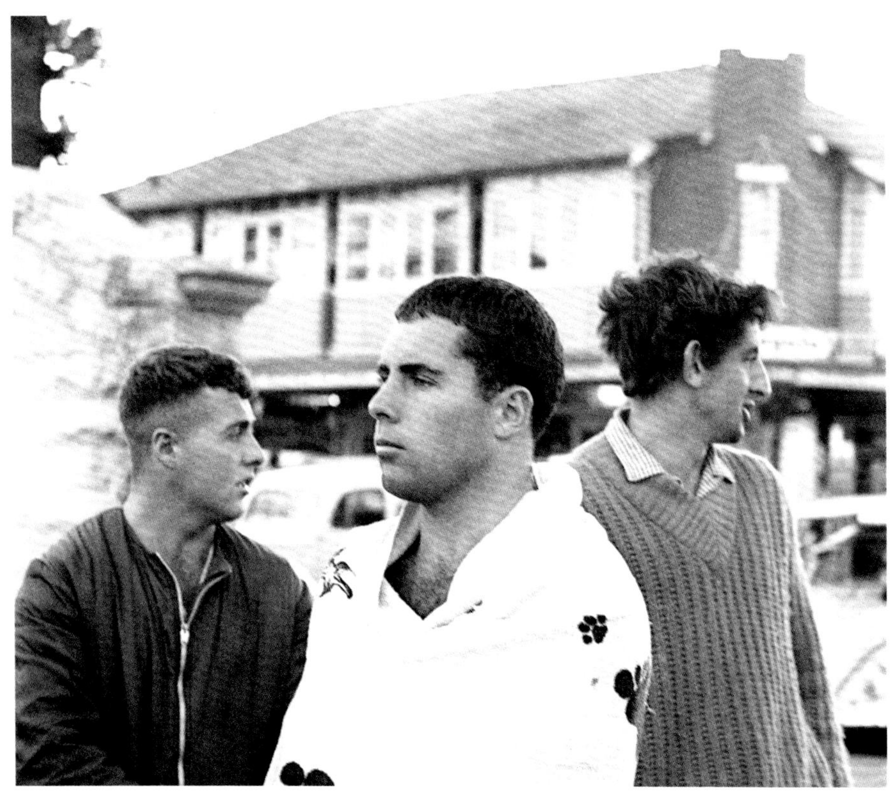

Bob Pike (1940–1999) (centre). Big wave rider Bob Pike warming himself after a session at Dee Why Point in 1962. Bob travelled overseas in the early 1960s to surf the big wave breaks in Hawaii. A legend of big wave surfing. R.I.P. **BW**

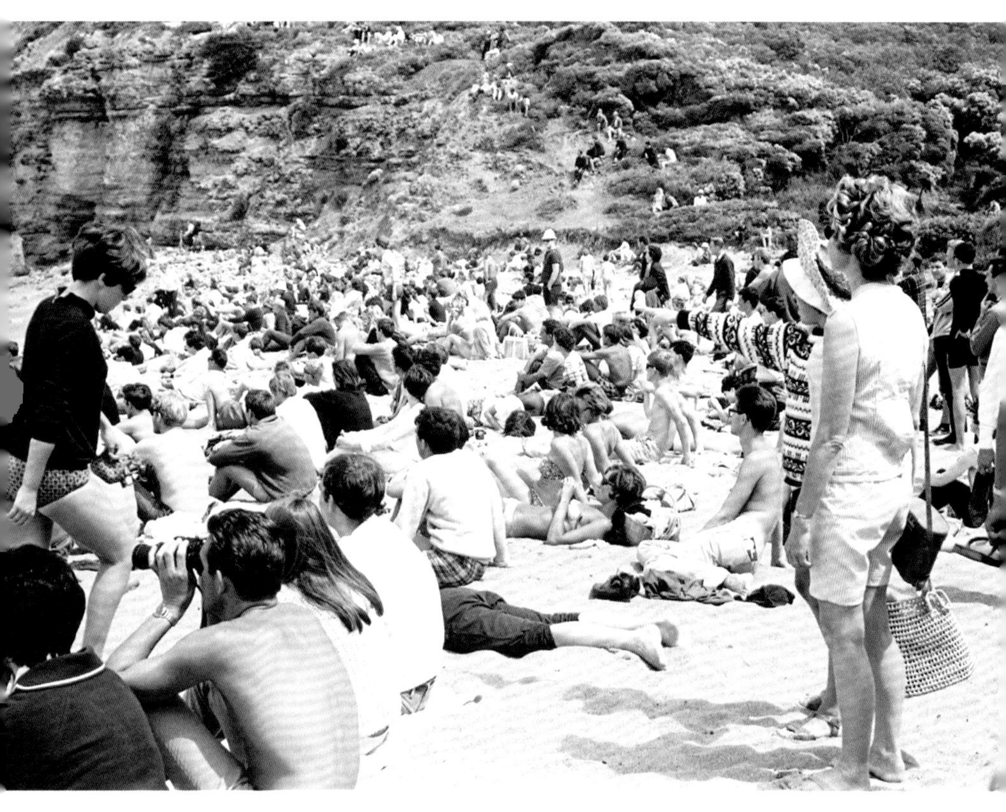

Spectators, Victorian Titles, Bells Beach, February 1967. **BS**

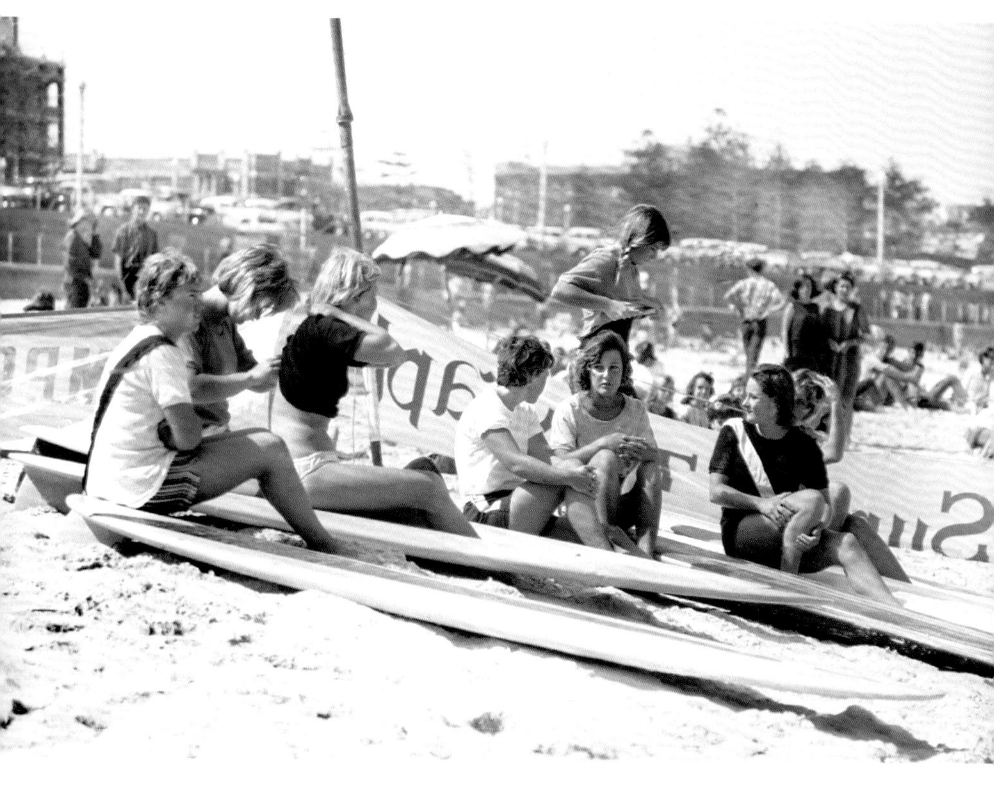

Bondi, November 1963. A group of ladies waiting for their heat at the finals of the women's section of the Invitational Championships. **BW**

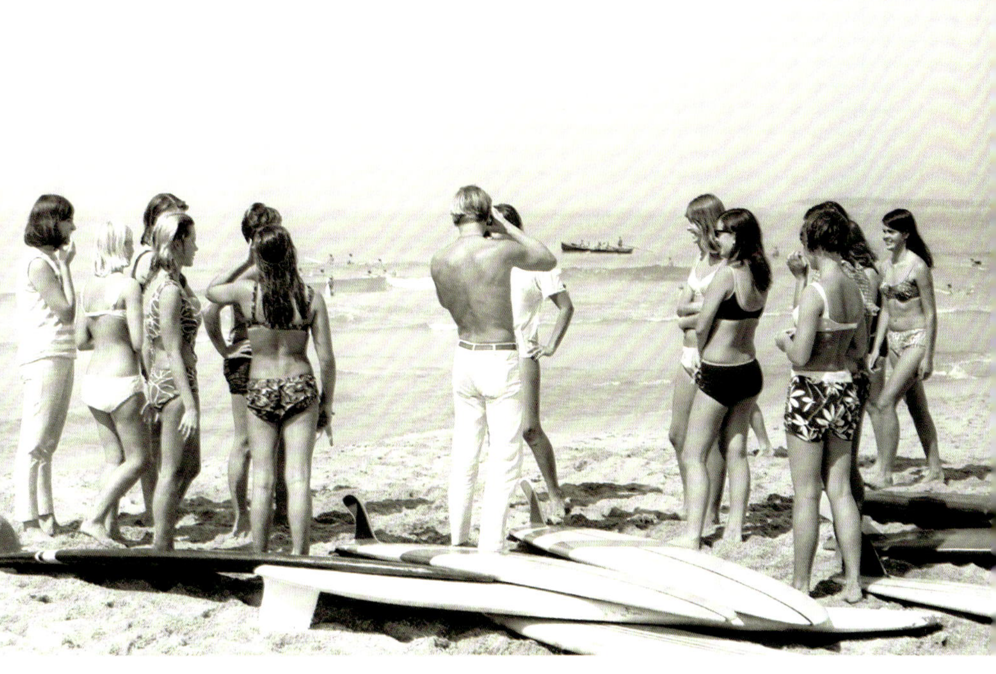

Wanda Beach Competiton, 1966. The Kurranulla Wahines at their first comp. **BW**

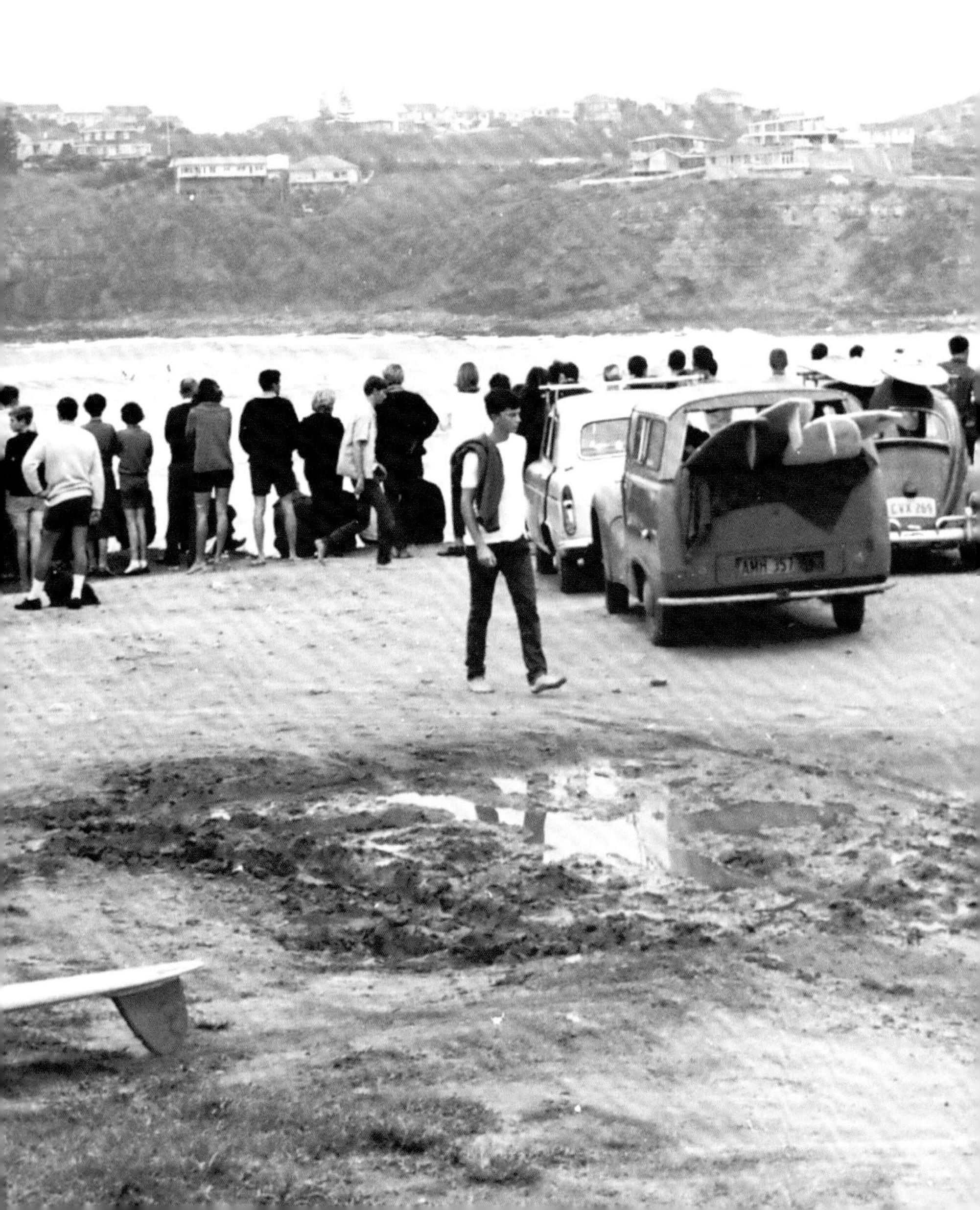

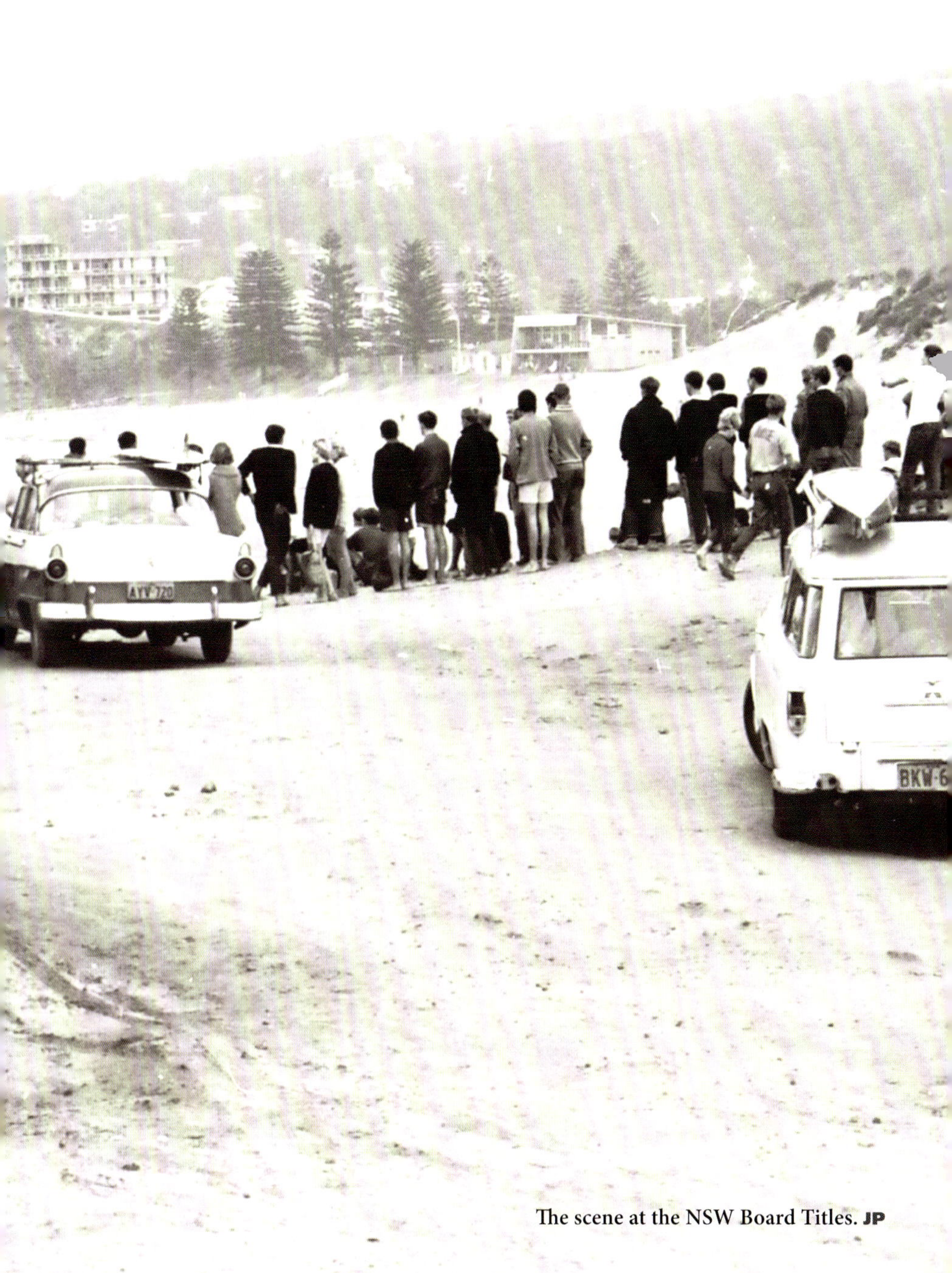

The scene at the NSW Board Titles. **JP**

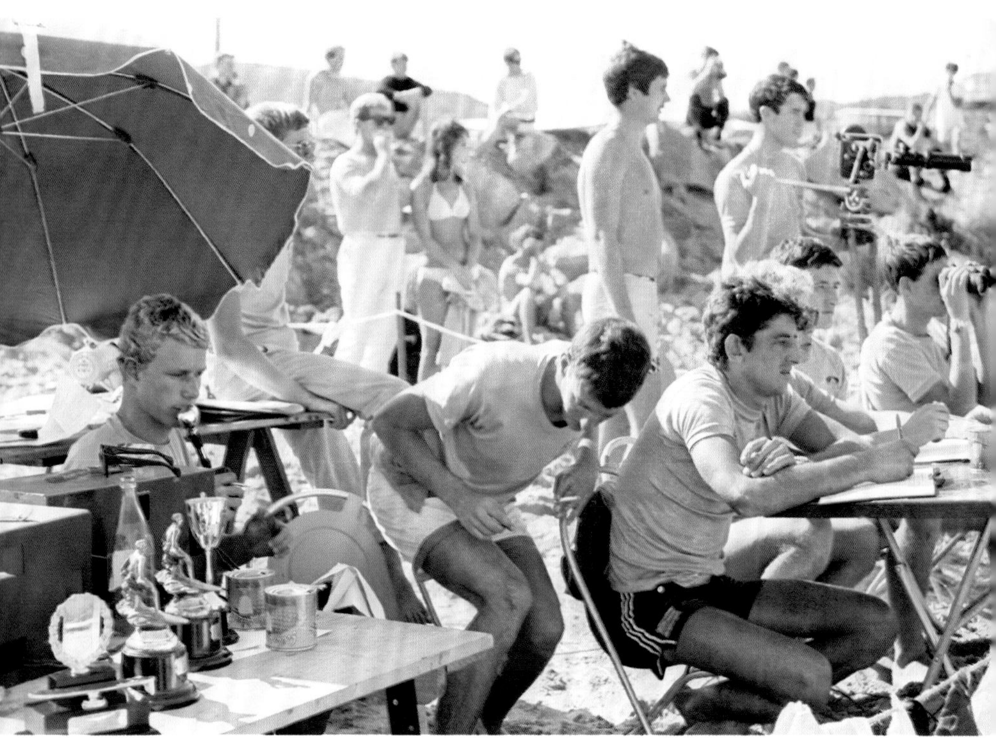

Officials and judges at the interstate surf meet at Avalon, NSW, 1963. **BW**

Open Mens Finalists, Australian Titles, Bells Beach, March 1967.
Peter Drouyn, Robert 'Nat' Young, Bernard 'Midget' Farrelly, **BS**

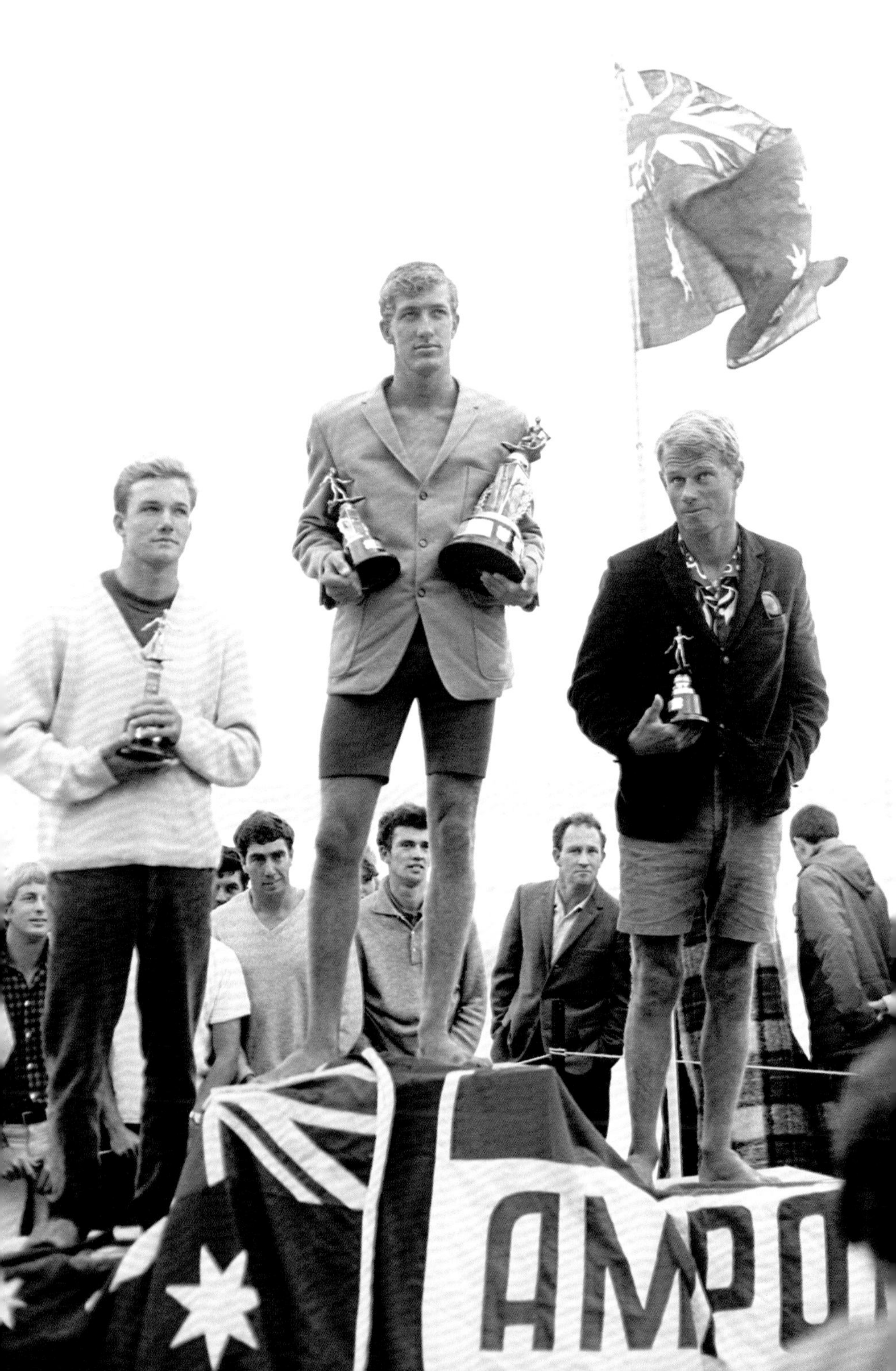
AMPO

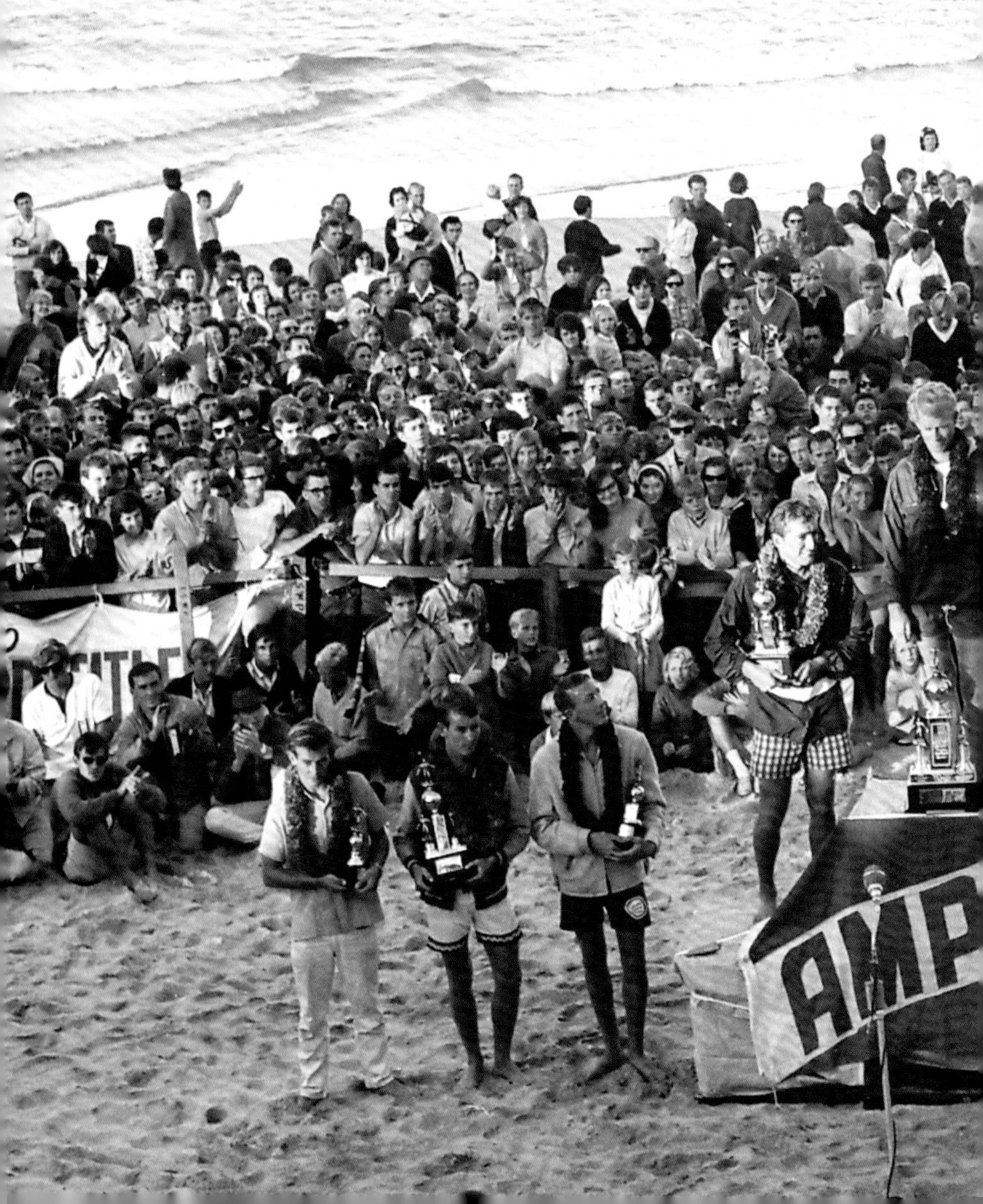

The view from the judges tent of the presentation of the 1964 World Titles. Australian Midget Farrelly made history by becoming the first ever world champion surfer. Also on the podium are Americans Mike Doyle (2nd) and Joey Cabell (3rd). Australia's Phyliss O'Donell on the right won the Women's Division. Australian Robert Conneeley won the Junior Division. **JP**

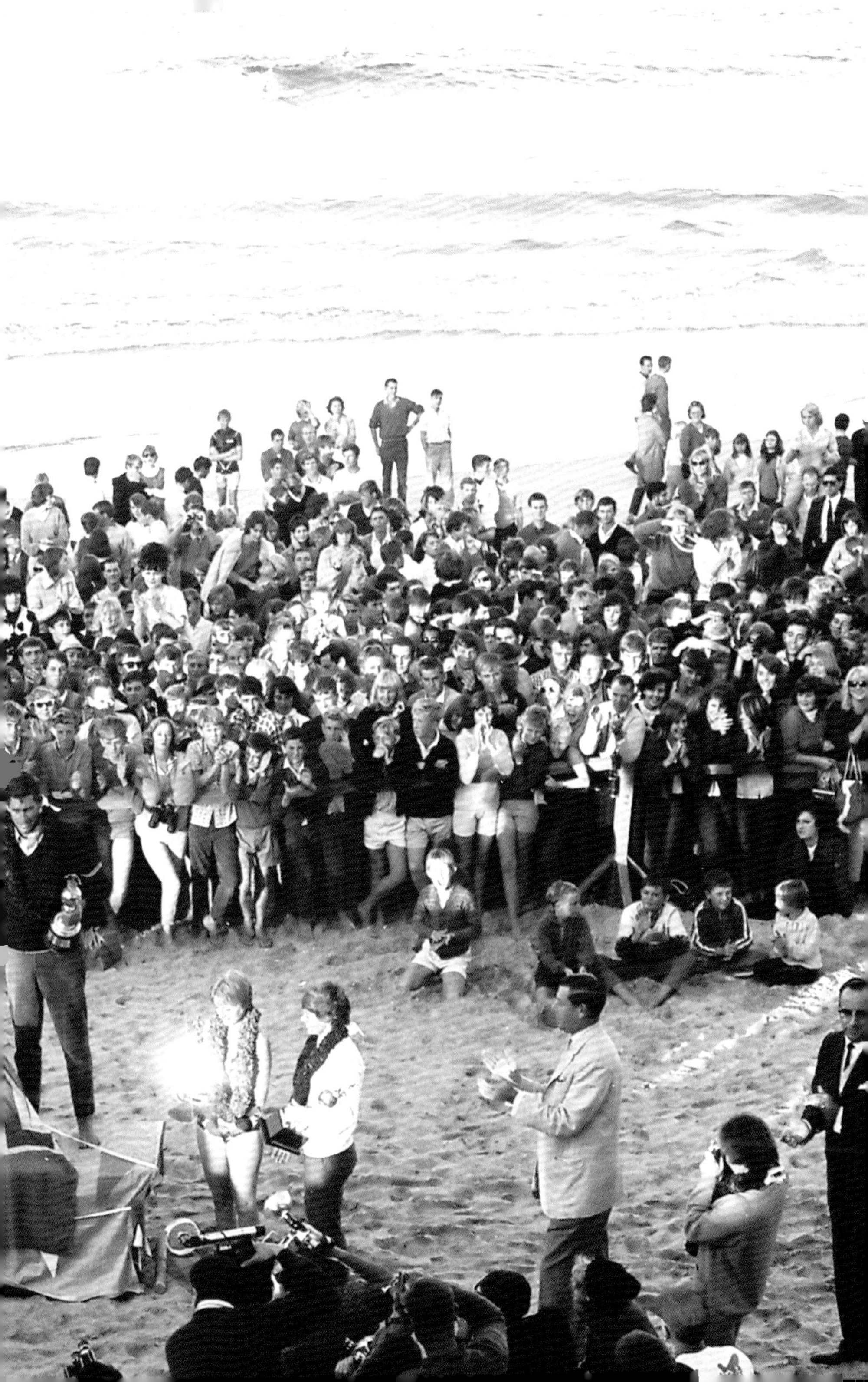

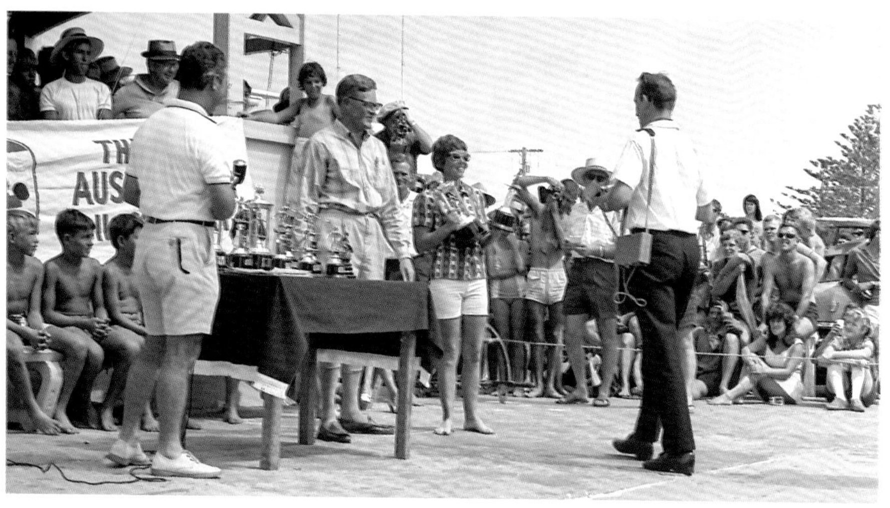

Phyllis O'Donell

- \# 8 times Queensland Champion
- \# 1964 – World Champion
- \# 1967 – 1st place Newcastle
- \# 1969 – 2nd place Bells Beach
- \# 1963/64/65 – Australian Champion
- \# 1966 – 3rd place Makaha Championships
- \# 1968 – 3rd place Porto Rico
- \# 1996 – Inducted into the Surfing Hall of Fame

Originally from Sydney, where she had been mentored by the great 'Snowy' McAllister and Bob Evans, Phyllis moved the Gold Coast in the early '60s. Phyllis was by far the best woman surfer of her era, she surfed aggressively and was not intimidated by the size of the surf, or male surfers, and was well respected by all who surfed with her. A founding committee member of the ASAQ (now Surfing Queensland) in 1964, she still maintains her interest in surfing and is in regular contact with the top women professionals of today. **MS**

Gail Couper and Phyllis O'Donell. 1964. Gail (left) has won more Australian Titles and Bells Pro events than anyone else. It's an incredible legacy for the girls. **JP**

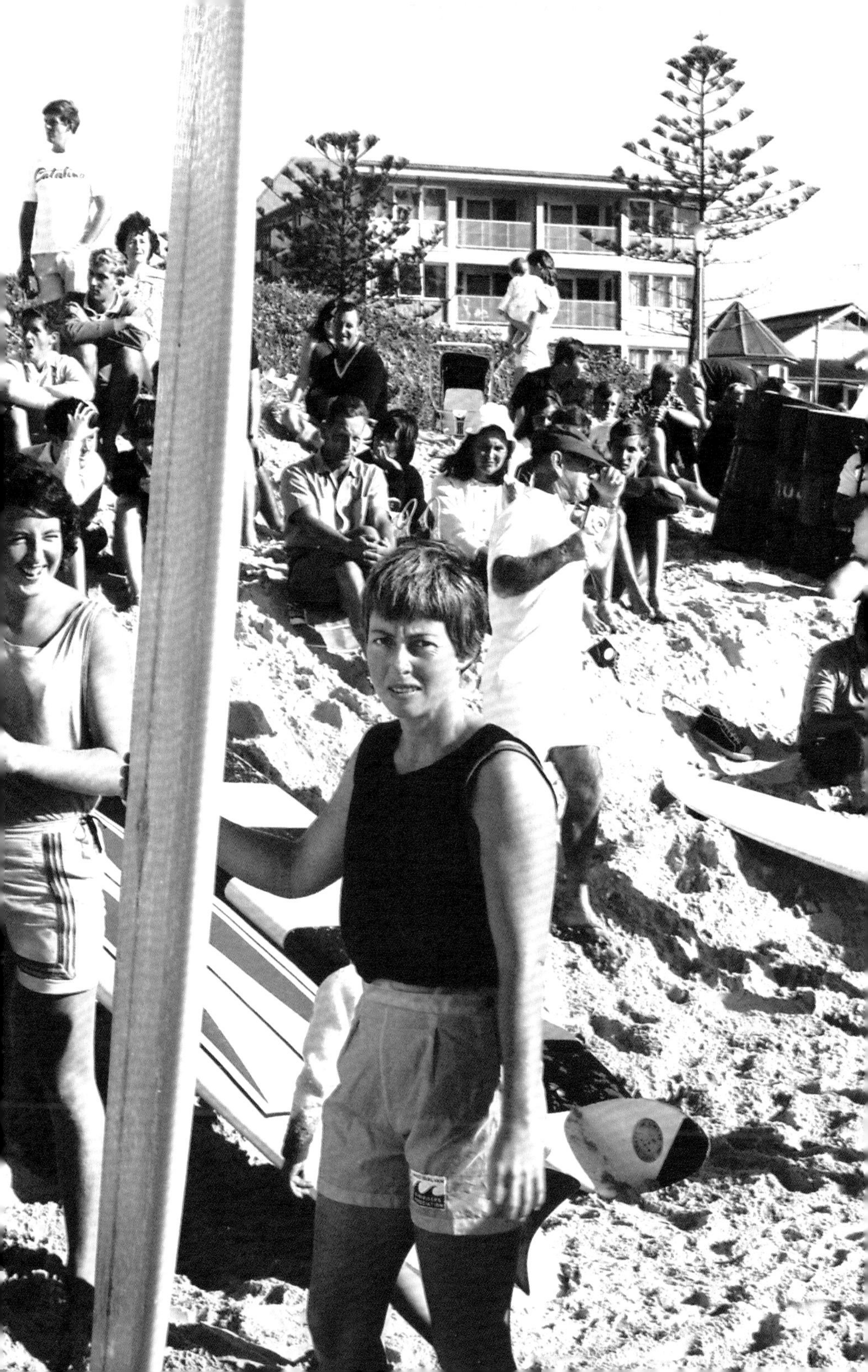

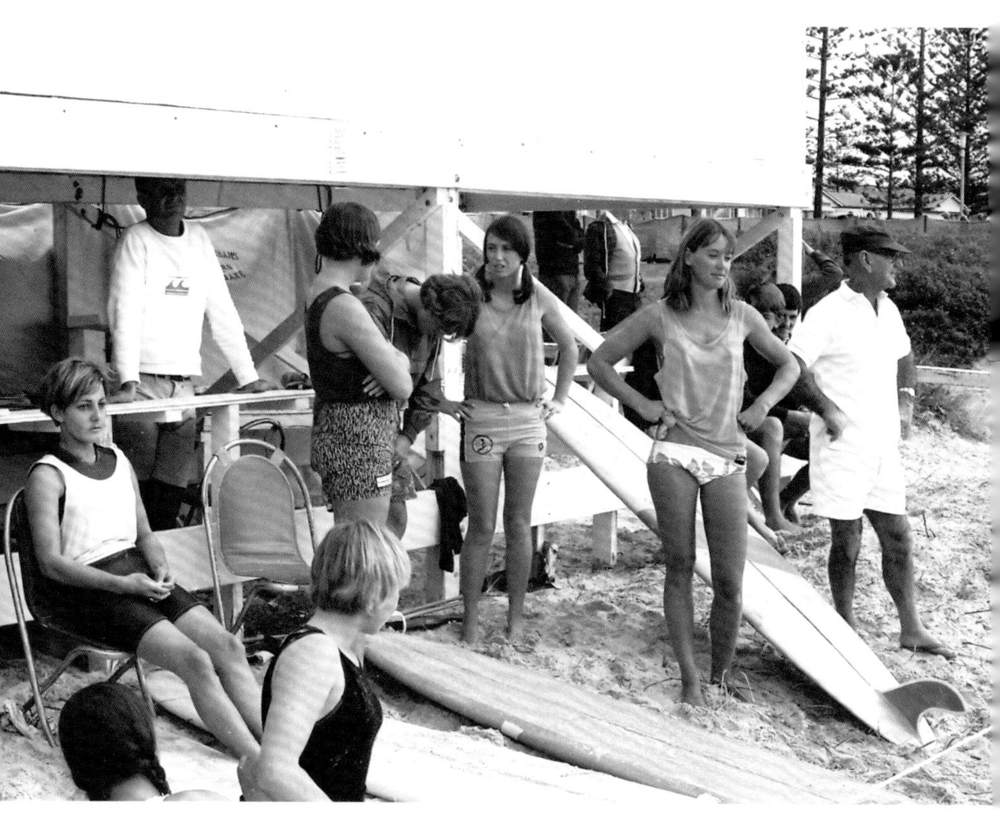

Lady competitors at the NSW State Titles, 1967. Australian surfing legend 'Snowy' McAlister (1904–1988) on the right in white. He was always active helping to bring the surfing events together. R.I.P. **JP**

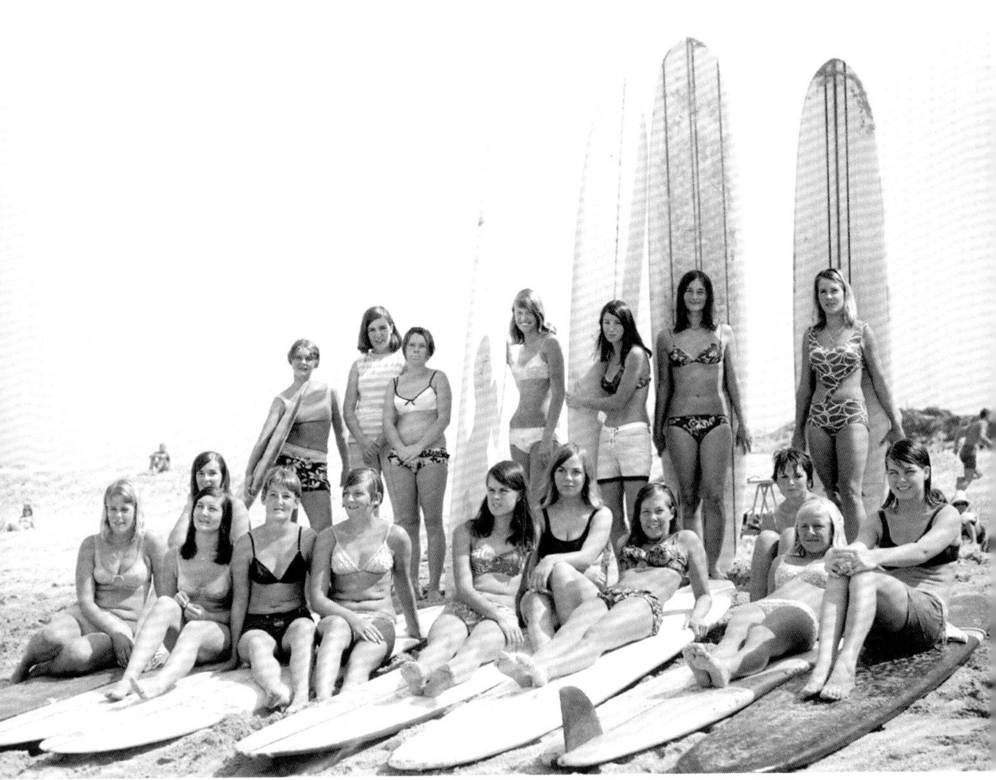

Kurranulla Wahines, Cronulla 1966. The Kurranulla Wahines were formed in 1966 so girls could have their own group to travel to the beaches and also compete in club competitions. After this shot was taken, the girls held their own surf contest in ideal conditions. **BW**

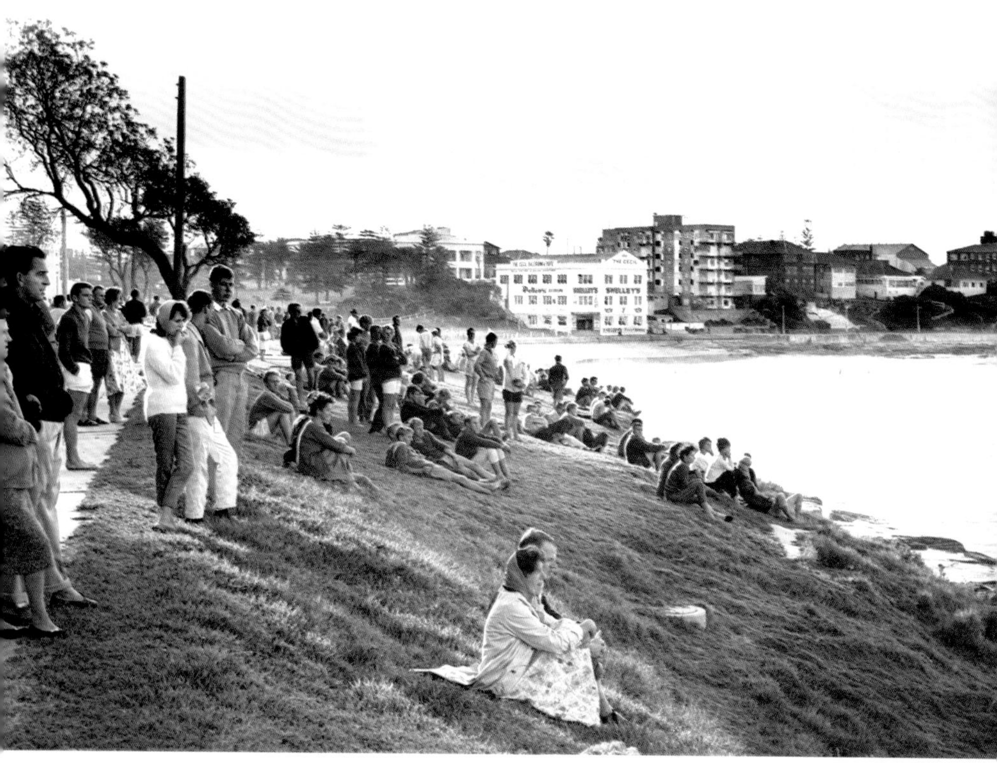

Spectators crowd the headland at Cronulla Point, 1962. **BW**

Victorian Surfing Titles, Bells Beach, February 1967. **BS**

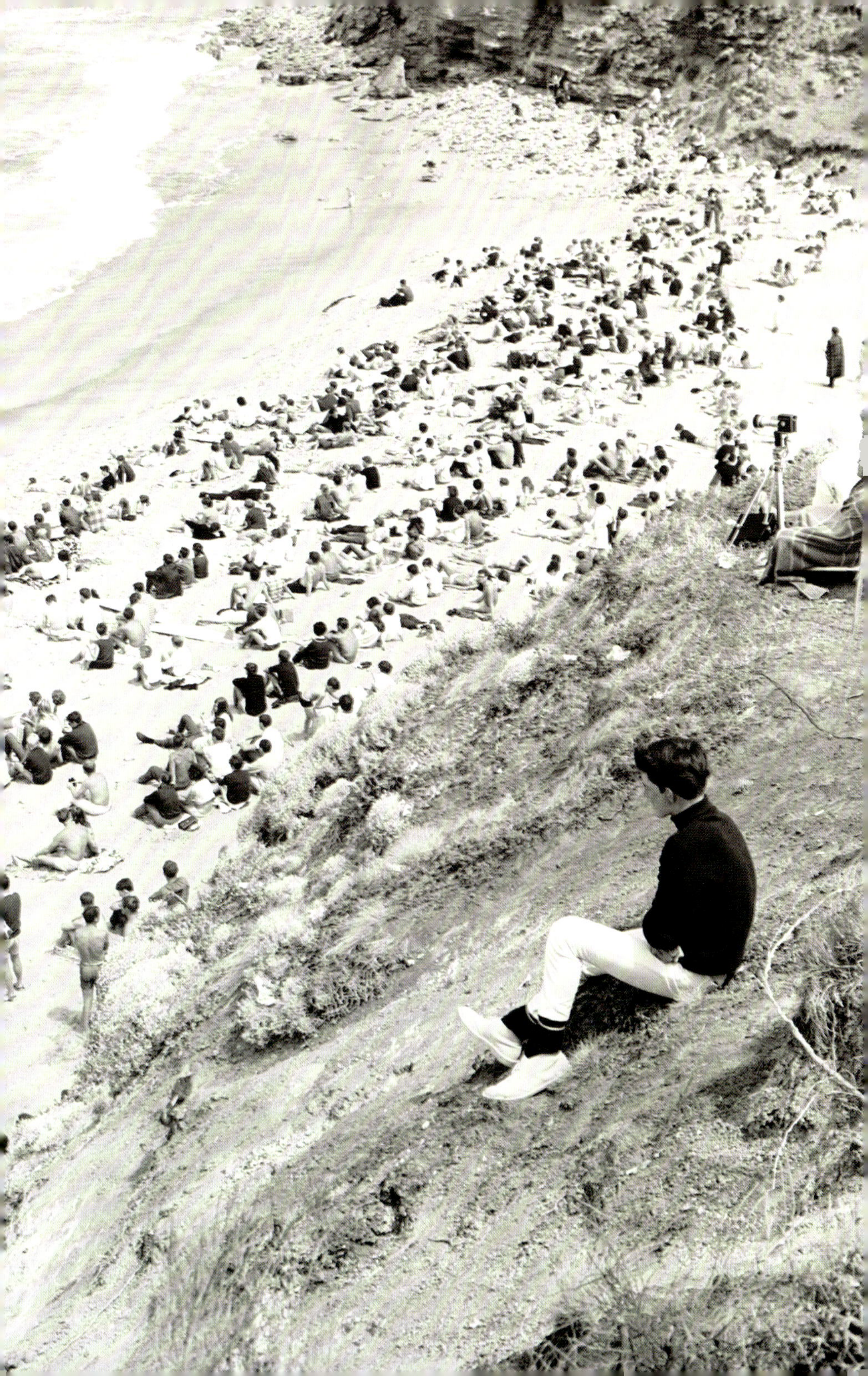

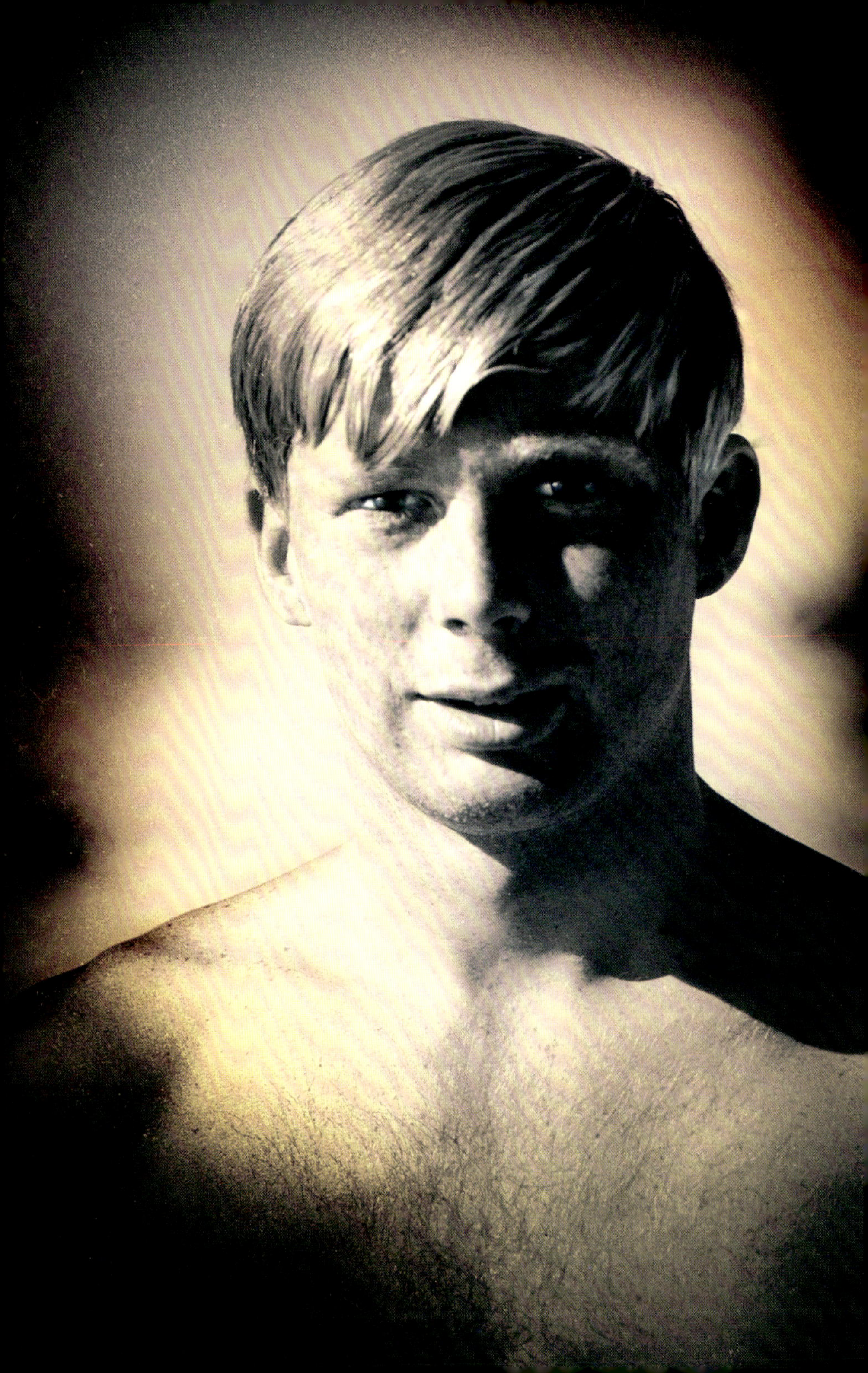

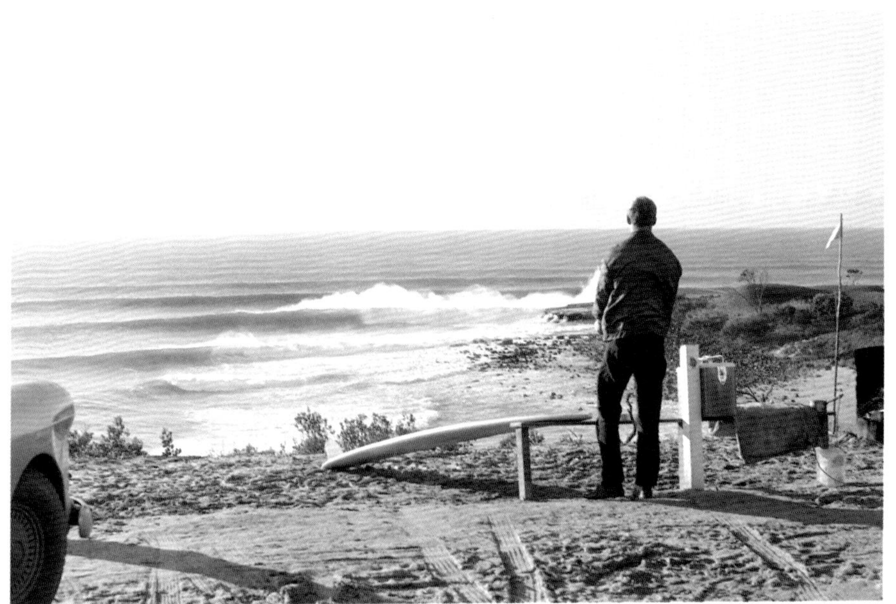

Above: **Gordon Burgis at Angourie, 1965.** Gordon's attention was diverted from doing a patch up on his board by this large set pounding into the surf break. **BW**

Opposite: **Portrait of Gordon Burgis, 1965.** Gordon is a native of Jersey, one of the channel isles and was revisiting Australia on a surfing trip around the world. He participated in the world titles at Manly in 1964 and became the first European surf champion in the late sixties. **BW**

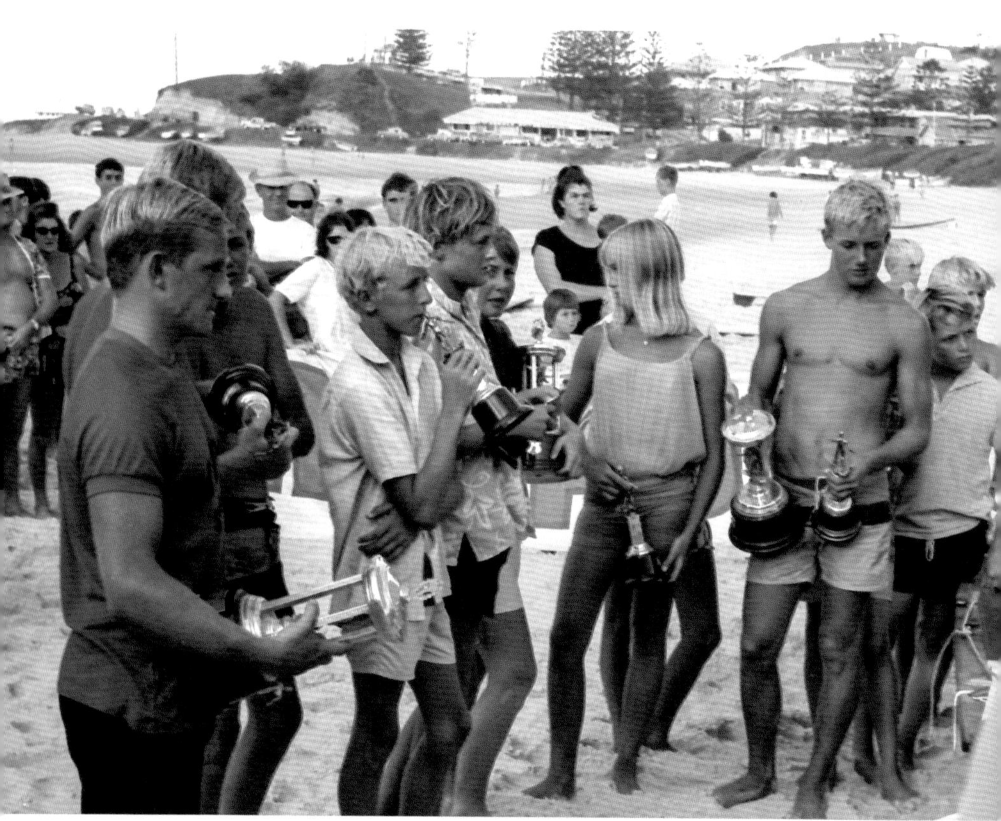

Queensland Title winners, 1965. Bob McTavish, obscured, obscured, Harry Allen, Graham Black, Phyllis O'Donell, Carol Charlton, Peter Drouyn. **MS**

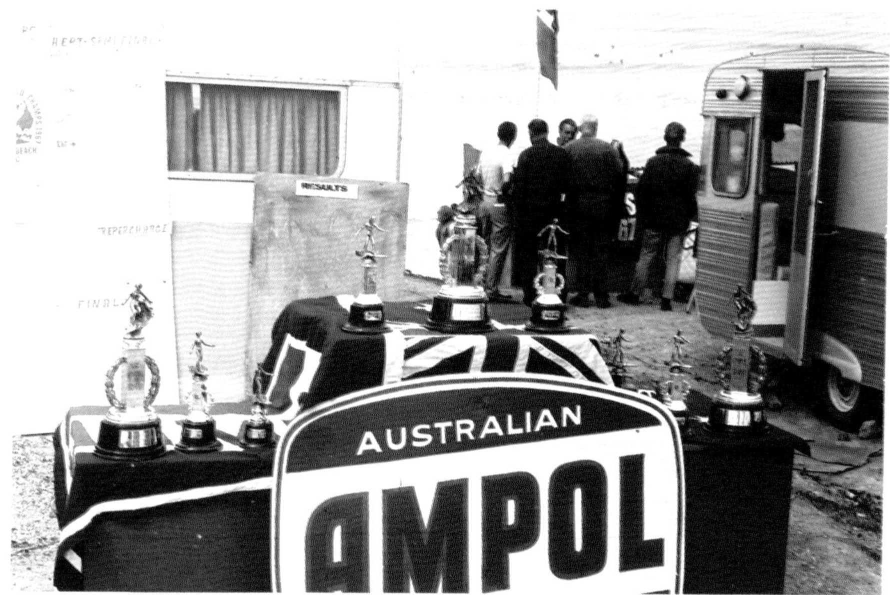

Ampol, sponsors of early surfing competitions in the 1960s. Note the modest trophies and the draw written on cardboard on the side of the official caravan! **JP**

Kirra Surfriders Club trophies made by Barry Sutherland, 1965. **MS**

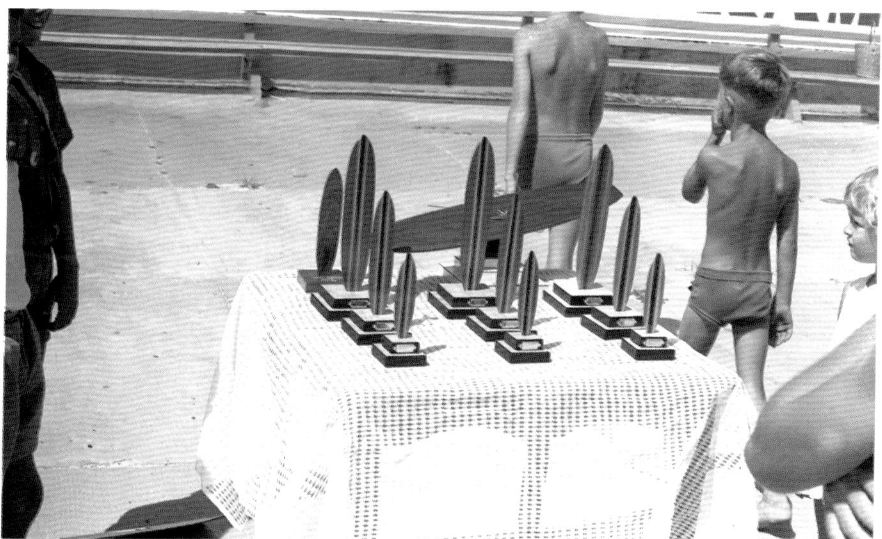

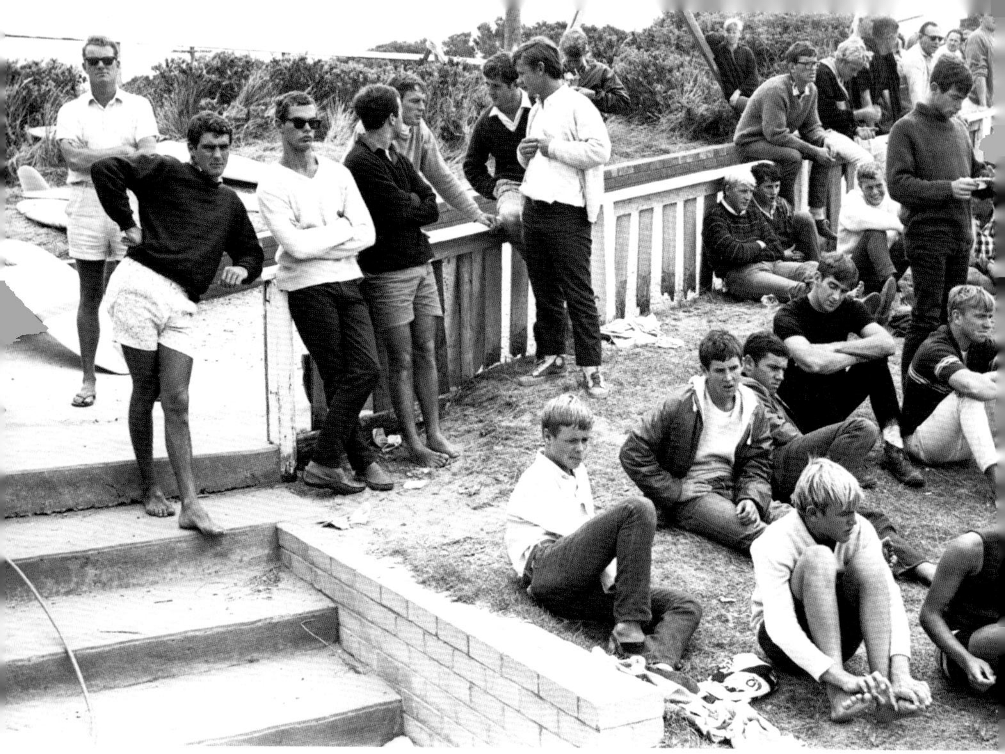

Above and below: Competitors and spectators, Victorian Titles, Torquay Surfclub, February 1966. **BS**

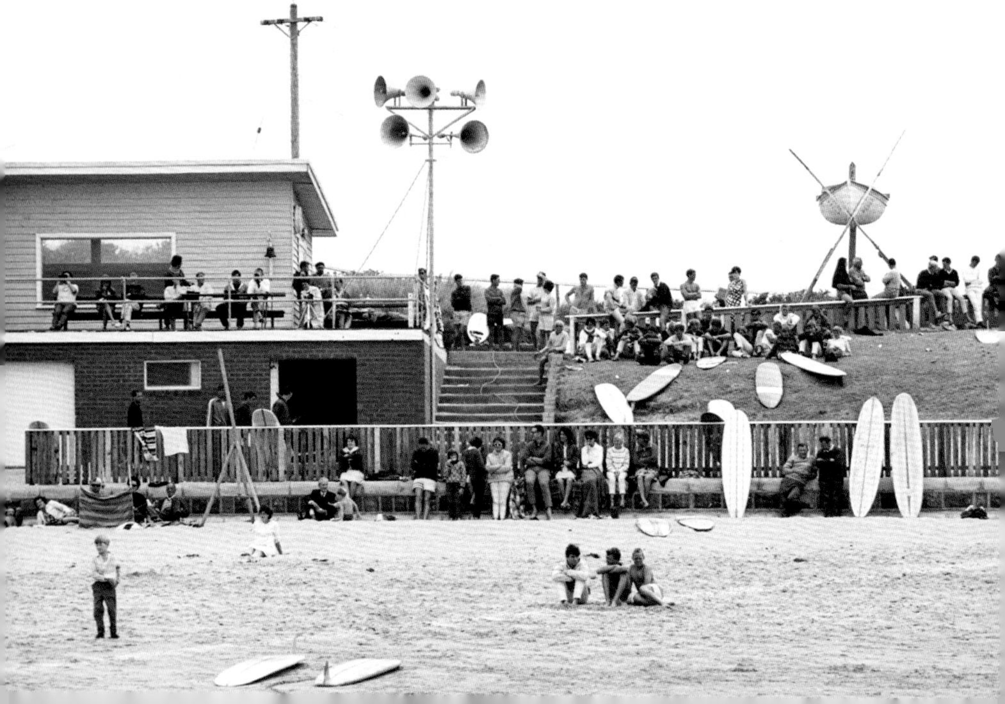

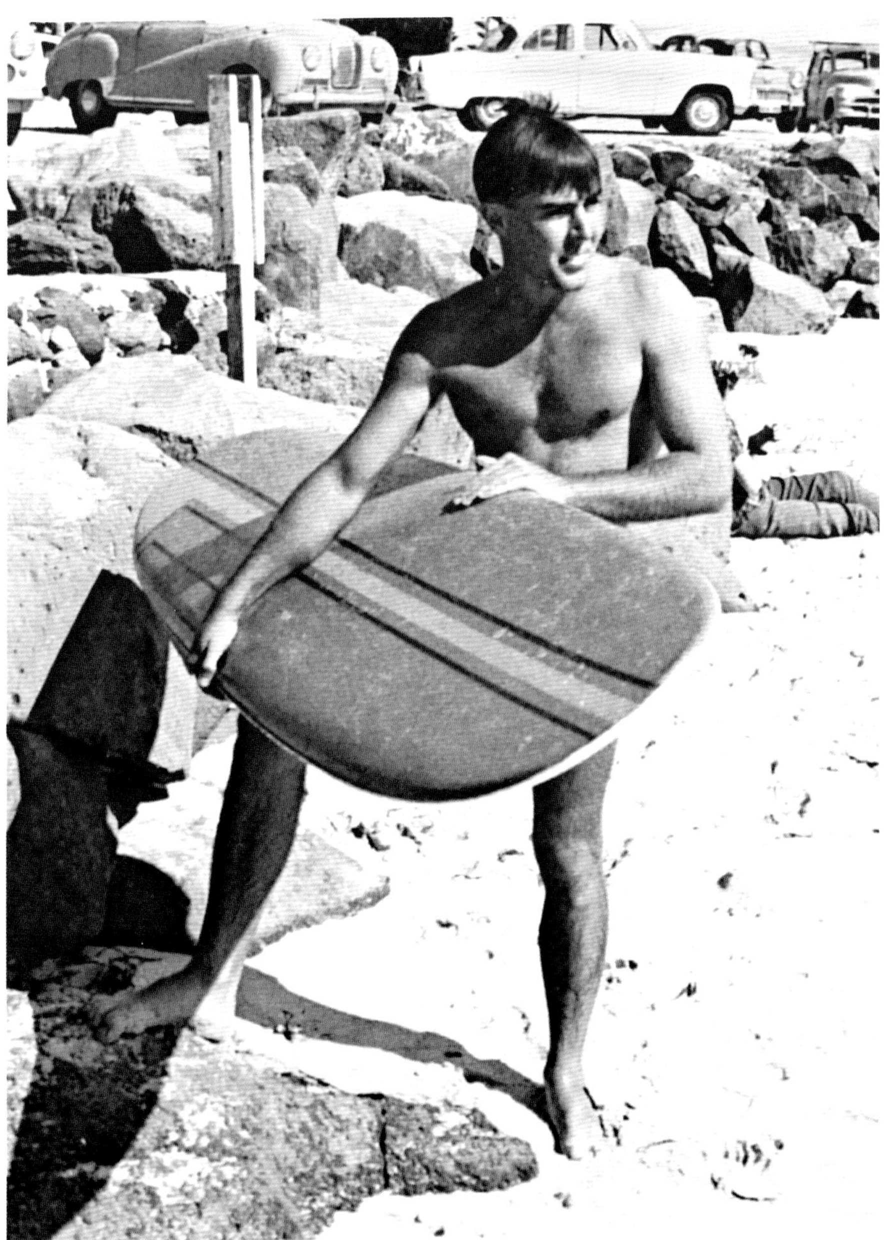

Tony Sutton, 1963. Tony was a Coolangatta local who's father owned Jazzland Dance Hall in McLean Street (the Antique shop). He was an excellent surfer who placed 3rd in the Mens division of the 1964 Queensland Titles. Like others from that era he will remain largely unknown. **MS**

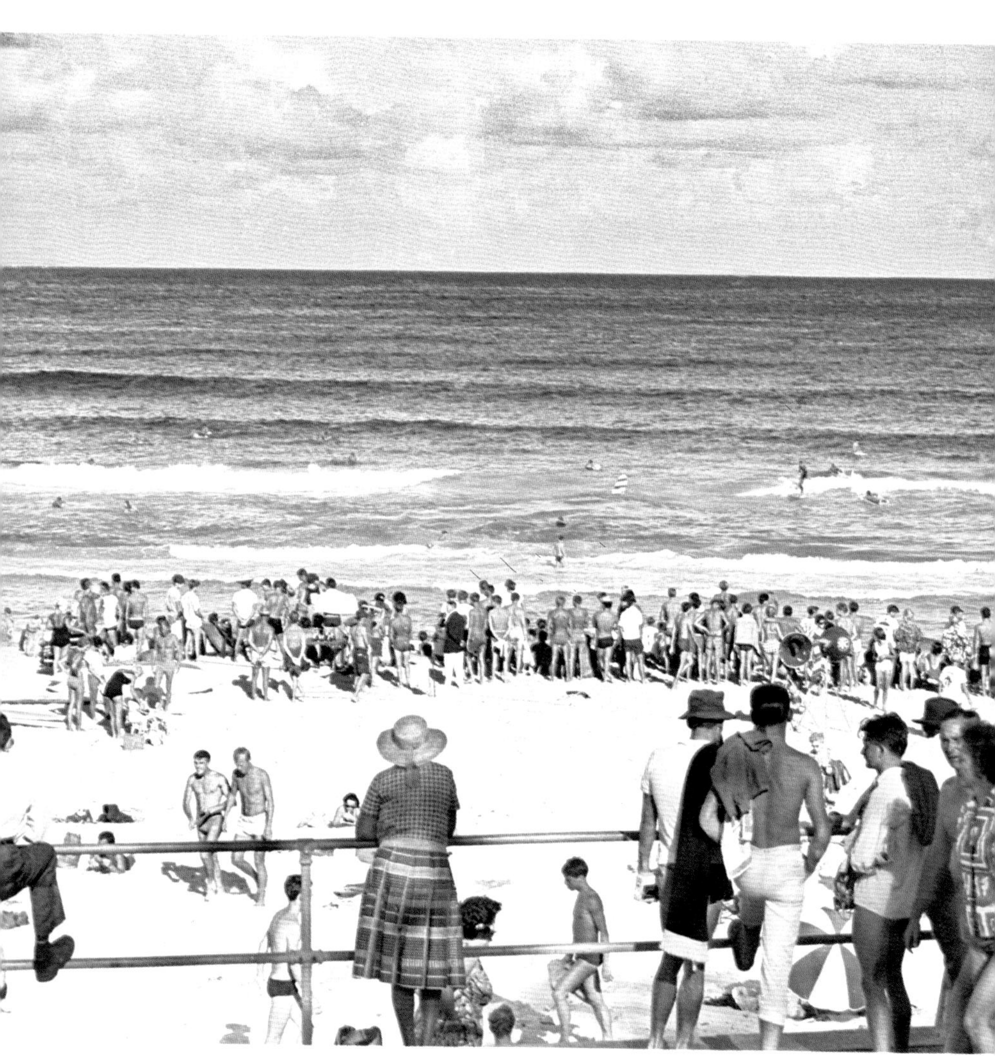

Spectators at the Women's Finals of the Invitational Championships at Bondi, 1962. **BW**

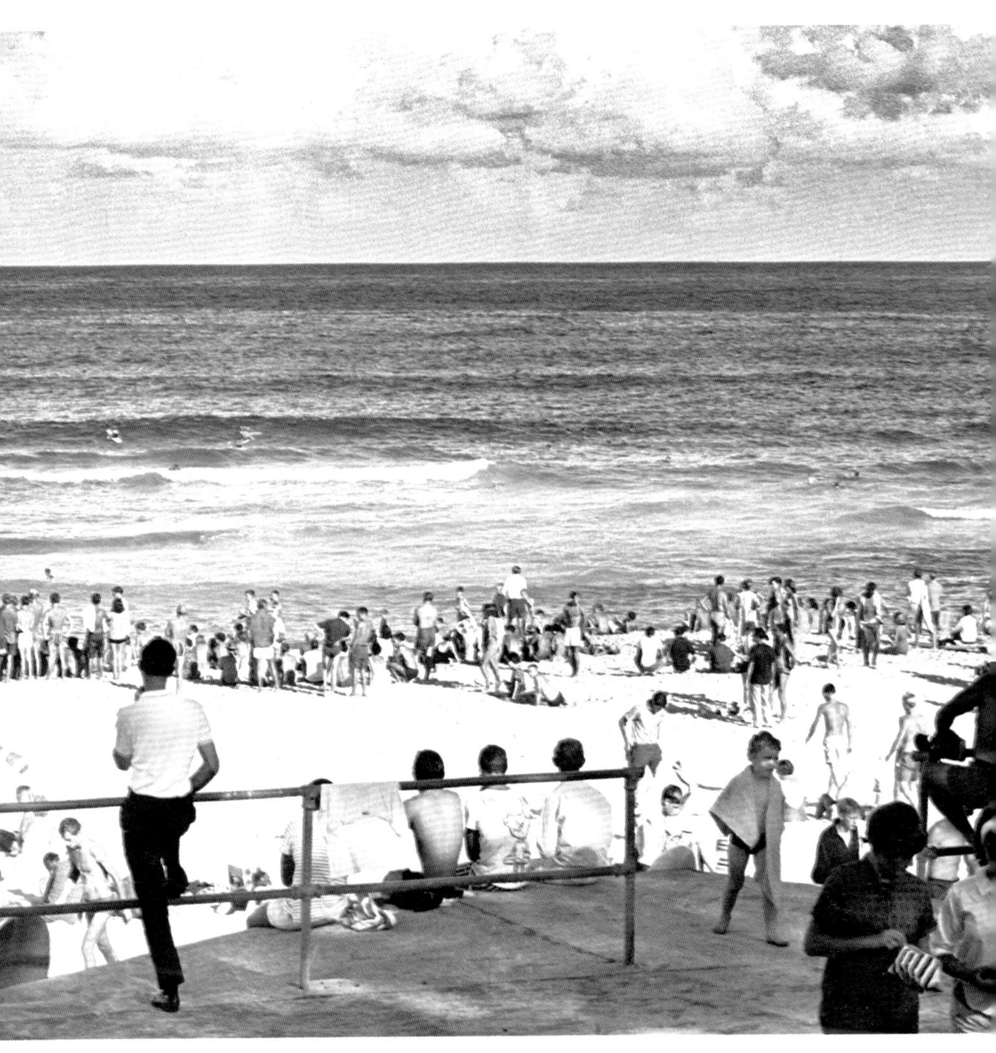

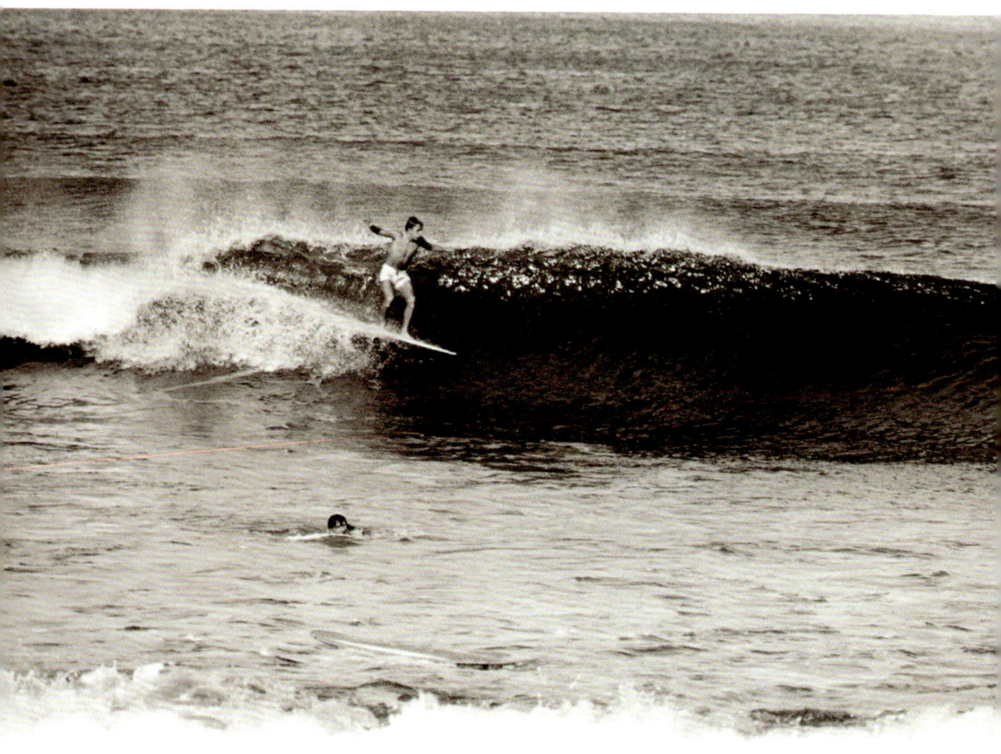

Rod Brooks, Southside Bells, July 1964. Years after I'd taken this shot of Rod Brooks at Southside Bells, I wondered whether I'd got the date right because he wasn't wearing a wetsuit. When I checked with Rod he assured me I did have the correct date. July is pretty cold in Victoria and when the wind chill factor is taken into account, surfing without a wetsuit is quite an amazing feat. **BS**

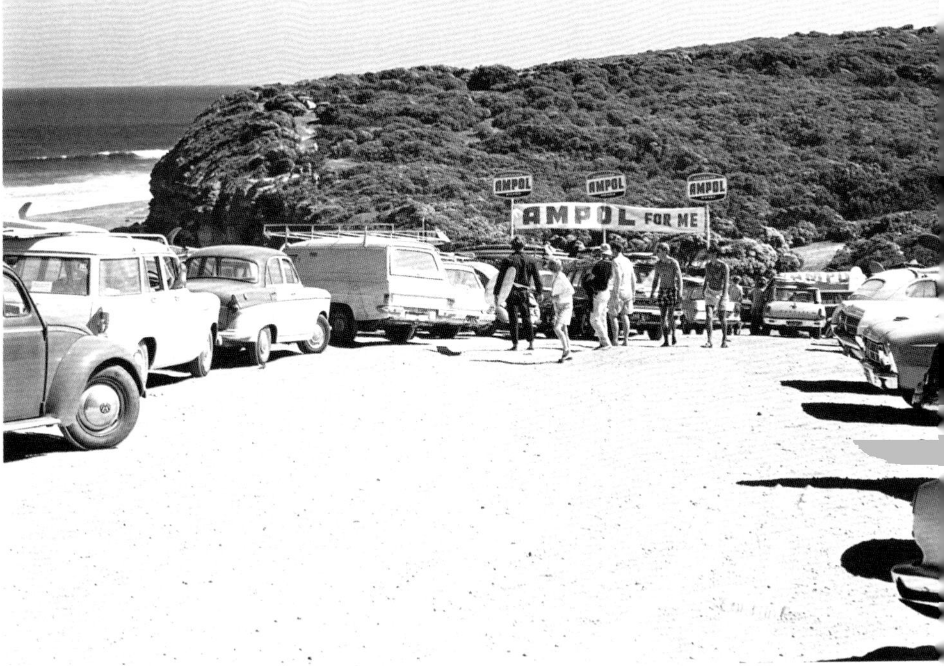

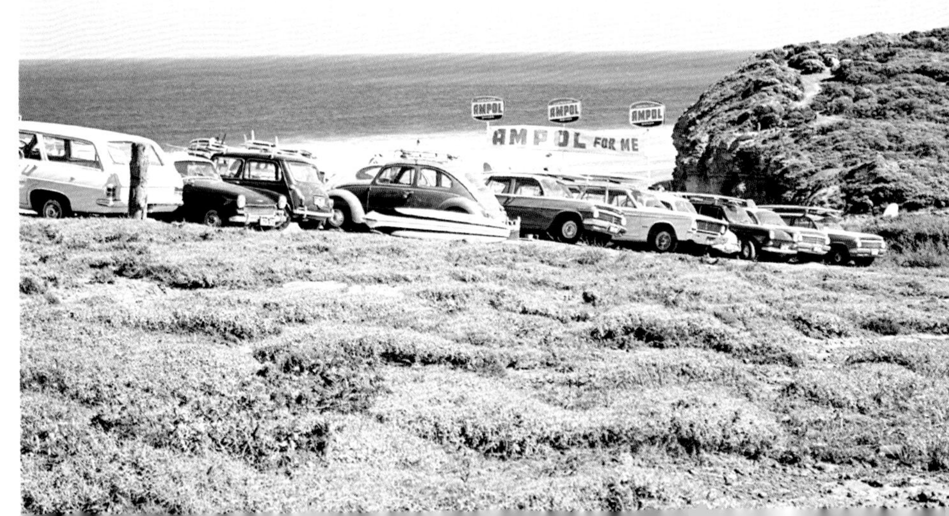

Car park, Victorian Titles, Bell family Farm fence post (below) in foreground, Bells Beach, February 1967. At Bells it was safe to drive to the bottom of the carpark if it was dry. When it had rained there was no way you could drive out unless you had a 4-wheel drive (rare in the 1960s). Many days were spent parking higher up and walking thru the squelching mud. OK when you were going down to the water but messy coming back up and changing from wet gear into dry clothes and trying to get the mud from between your toes. **BS**

Bells Beach contest

Bob Evans, 1965 *Surfing World* editorial, 'The Greatest Contest Ever' put the stamp on Bells as Australia's premier contest. It elevated Bells to the world stage and led to it be proclaimed in the cult movie, *Point Break*, starring Patrick Swayze and Keanu Reeves. Massive contest waves in 1965 and 1981 were key milestones in Australian surfing. 1965 as the biggest and most dangerous contest surf ever seen or ridden in Australia, destroyed longboards as we knew them then. They simply were unable to cope with the giant waves. Change was initiated and Nat Young with a thinner lighter board powered his way to a world title in San Diego one year later in 1966. Every subsequent year at Bells we witnessed the NSW and Qld contingents bringing newer design shorter boards. Stand-out designs that had major impacts were Bob McTavish's fantastic plastic machine, Peter Drouyn's 8' lighter board, Midget Farrelly's stringer-less board, Keith Paul's transition boards, Ted Spencer's White Kite and Baddy Treloar's classic *Morning of the Earth* board. Finally we had Wayne Lynch with his Evolution design until we arrived at sub-6'0" boards that proved just too short in the 1970 World Titles at Bells and Joanna. The Americans hadn't gone sub-6'0" and outgunned us with longer performance boards that had speed.

The Bells Beach contest had an enormous impact on Australian surfing. It became the contest of choice everyone wanted to win. It was integral to surfboard design and performance, a proving ground amphitheatre for Australians to move onto the world stage. The Bowl's big heavy waves were the stage for surfboard designs for the forthcoming Hawaiian winter season later in the year. Australia's top surfers came to Bells each Easter with new designs (especially during the short board revolution period). Sometimes the boards worked, other times they didn't on the solid Bells waves. What worked was refined during the Australian winter in Sydney and along the NSW coast to Queensland. There were stand-out manoeuvres that changed us, John Monie charging down big Bells walls in switch-foot mode, Glen Ritchie belting the lip with his re-entries, Bobby Brown performing rail edge slashes, Keith Paul surfing deep in his power crouch, and Wayne Lynch going vertical on his Evolution boards.

The contest was the inspiration of Torquay surfers Peter Troy and Vic Tantau, originating under the banner, 'Find the best surfer in Victoria'. Ampol were the first major sponsors, followed by Rip Curl in 1973 when it became a pro-contest with prize money awarded.

Australian Titles, Bells Beach, March 1967.
Beach crowd. **BS**

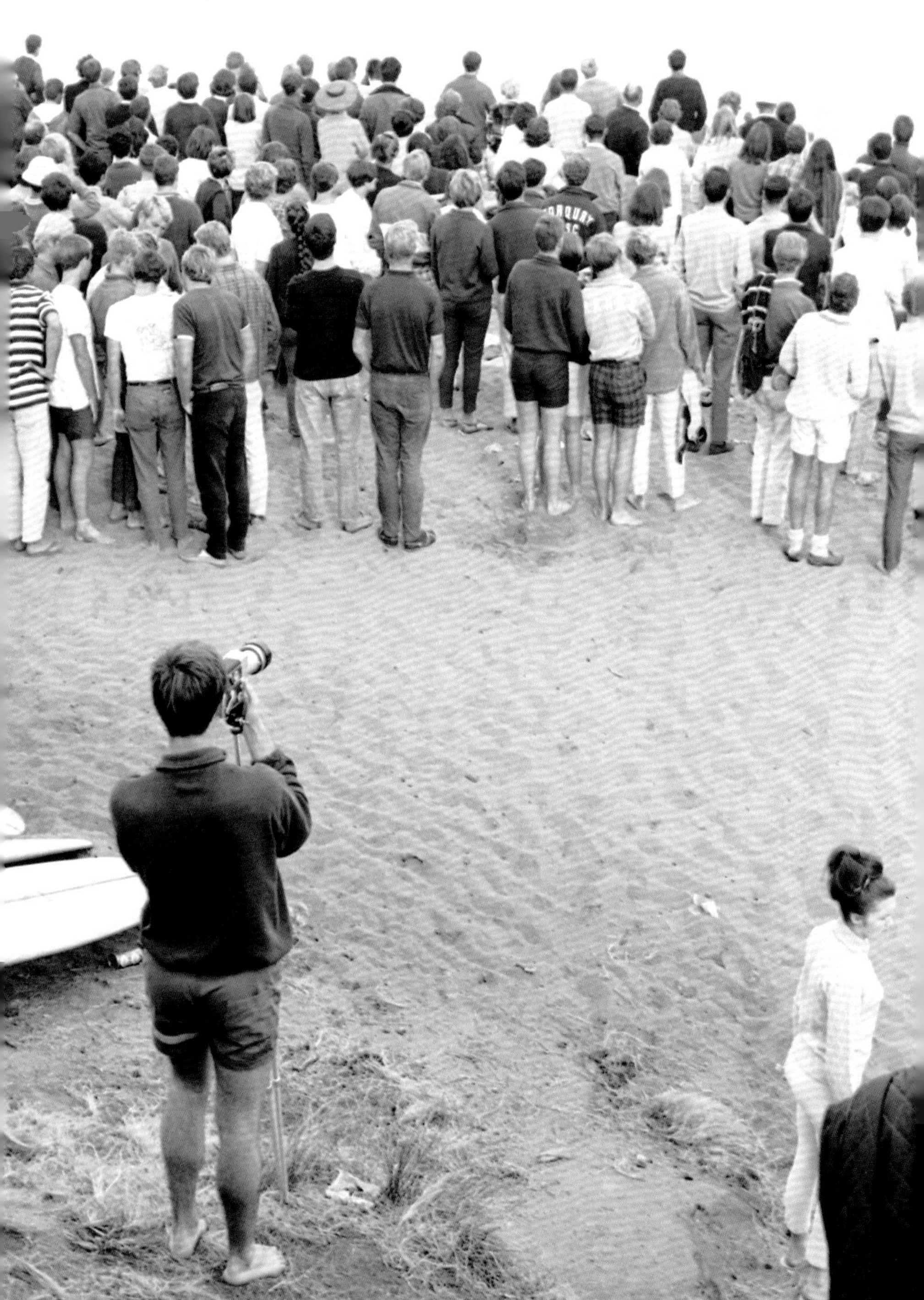

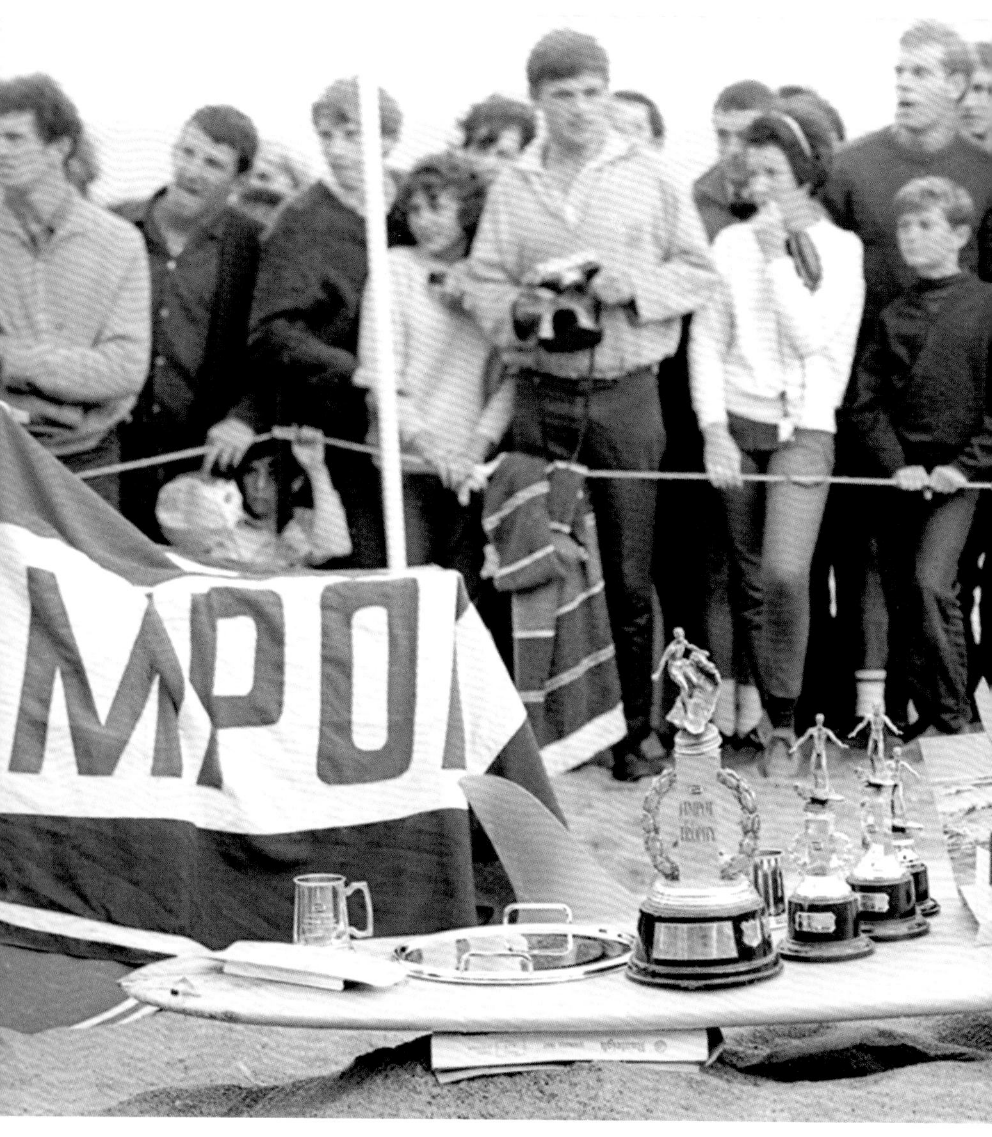

When I look at my catalogue of surfers who recorded wins, top 3 placings or were finalists during the 1960s it's a roll call of Australia's best – Doug Andrews, Mick Dooley, Nat Young, Bernard 'Midget' Farrelly, Rob Conneeley, Glen Ritchie, Bob Pike, John 'Nipper' Williams, Peter Drouyn, Bobby Brown, Bob McTavish, Russell Hughes, John Monie, Lester Brian, Bruce Channon, Ted Spencer, Keith Paul, David 'Baddy' Treloar, Terry Wall, Jeff Watt, Rod Brooks, Wayne Lynch, Butch Cooney, Brian Hughes, Kevin Parkinson, Richard Kavanaugh and Gail Couper (10 wins, the most by any surfer). **BS**

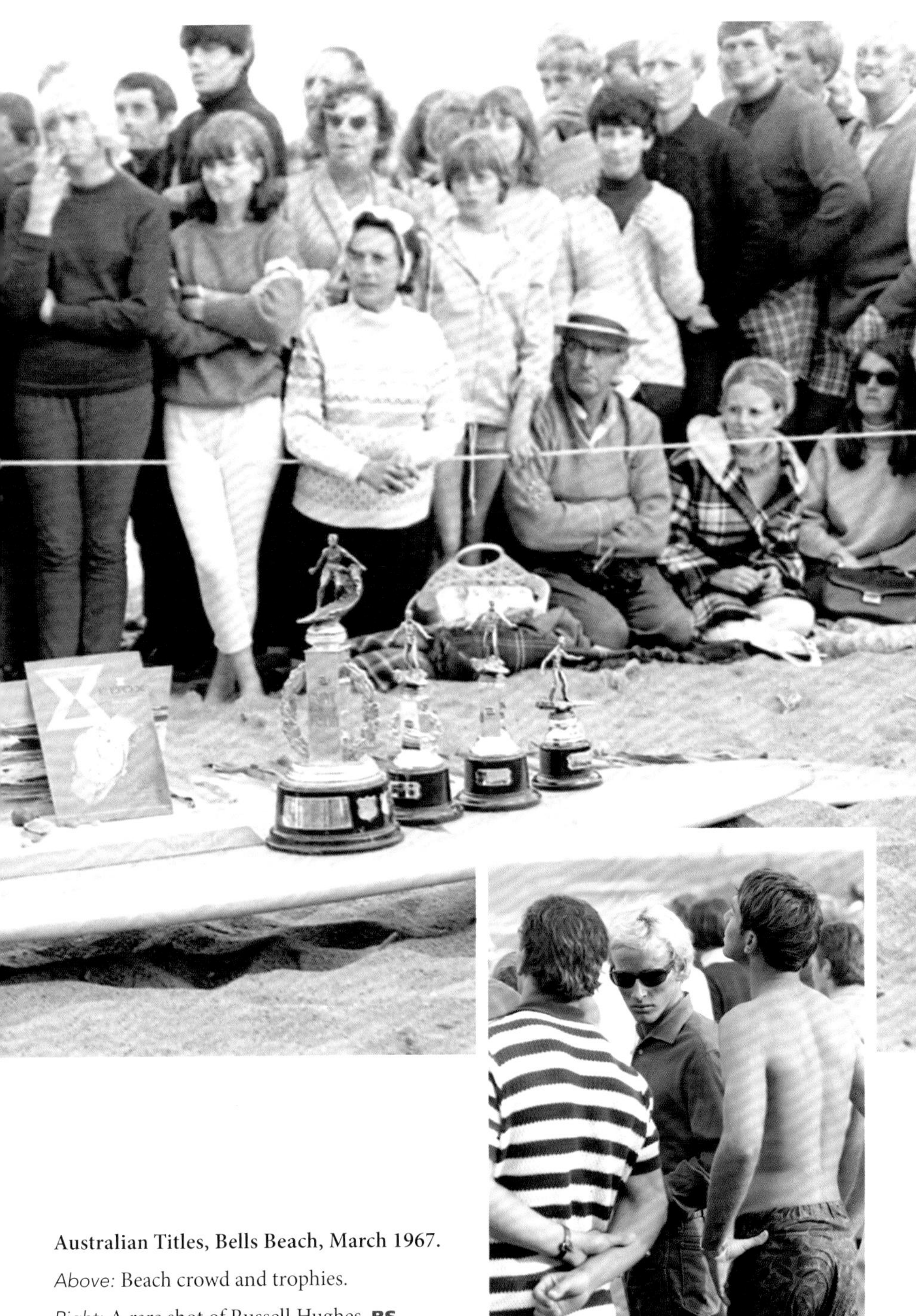

Australian Titles, Bells Beach, March 1967.

Above: Beach crowd and trophies.

Right: A rare shot of Russell Hughes. **BS**

Surfmobiles

Surfers love to travel … Particularly, they love to find surfing places that have perfect waves. The 'surfmobile' became a vital surfer accessory in the 1960s and they came in many shapes and sizes, mostly made in Australia.

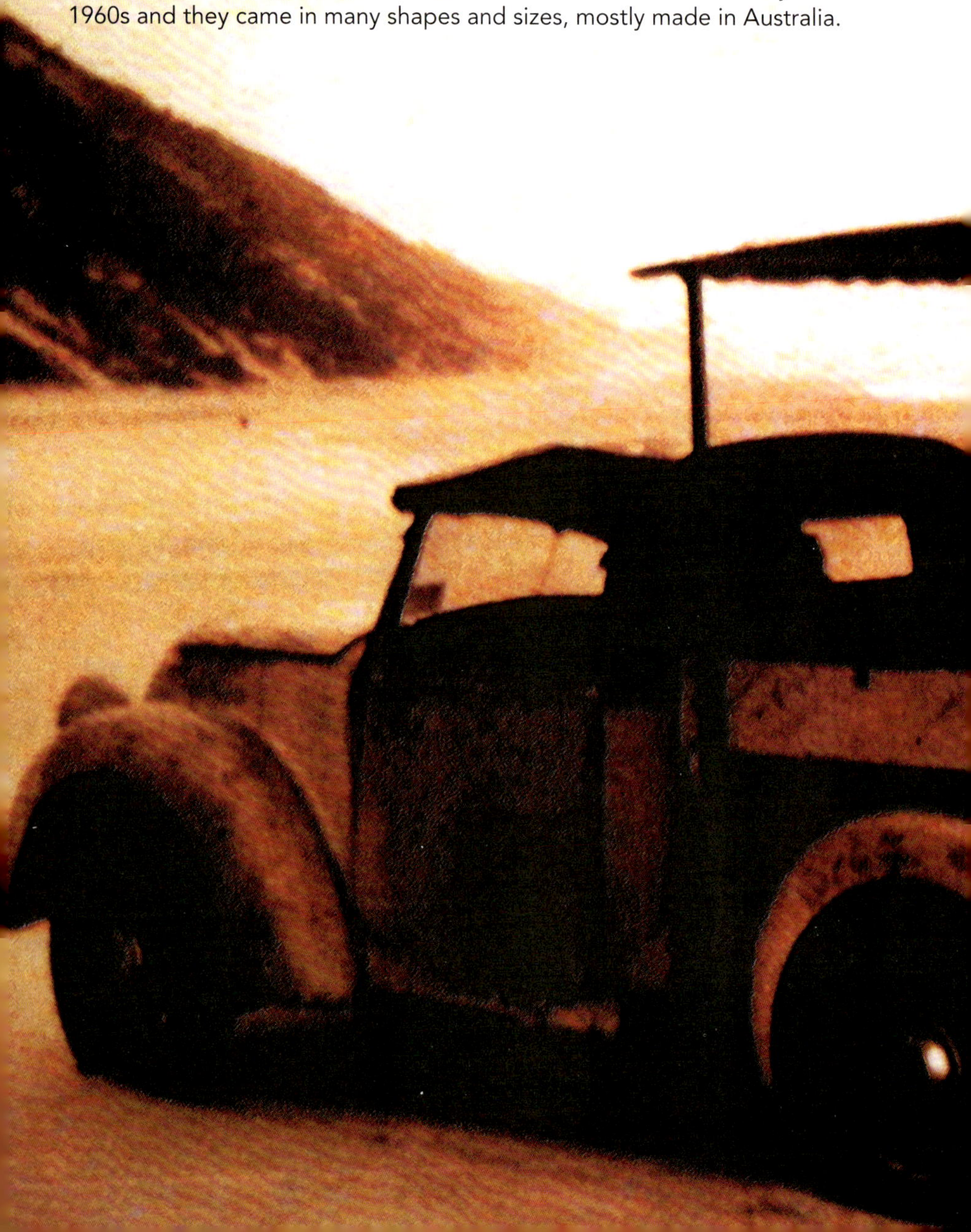

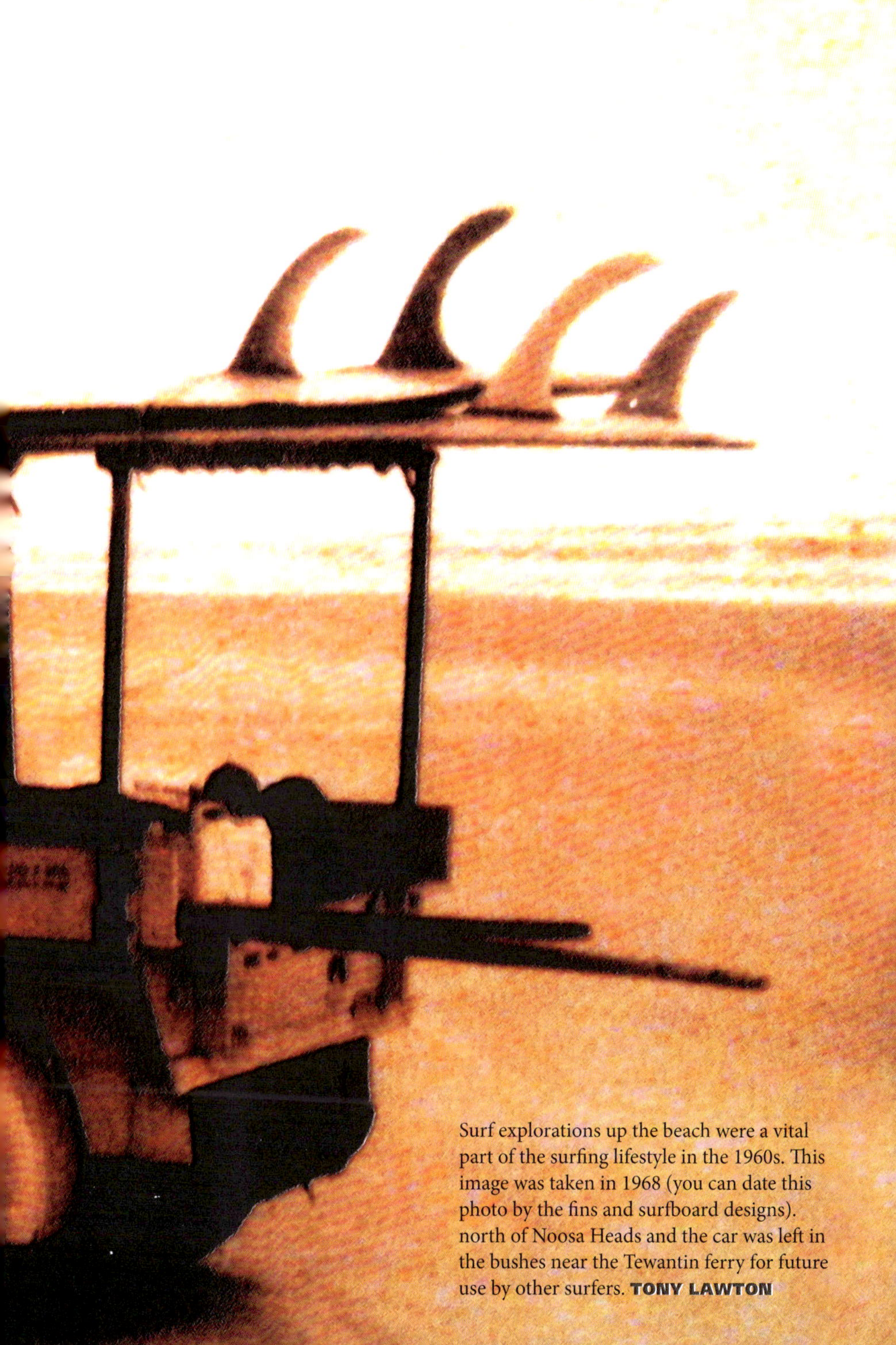

Surf explorations up the beach were a vital part of the surfing lifestyle in the 1960s. This image was taken in 1968 (you can date this photo by the fins and surfboard designs). north of Noosa Heads and the car was left in the bushes near the Tewantin ferry for future use by other surfers. **TONY LAWTON**

Surfers traditionally have a function-first attitude towards cars, the primary function being to house the surfboards and potentially be a nesting place for surfers to sleep … often for weeks at a time. Vans and wagons were the ultimate, with aesthetics an after-thought. Whatever the chosen ride, decay is always around the corner with the harsh coastal environs; sand, damp towels, wax, fermenting wetsuits and salt air sure to rust even the most hardened Australian-milled steel.

In Australia, there was not the wide variety of cars available in 1960 … well, nothing like the proliferation of car ownership of the modern era. Less than one in five people owned a car in the early 1960s, but that number almost doubled during the decade and 'surfers' took up the freedom that came with car ownership as much as any other demographic. Travelling north and south out of Sydney, surfers were a rare sight on the highways of the era, so much so that a fully-loaded surf car travelling in one direction would often pull over and chat to a group of surfers heading in the other direction, their identity and purpose given away by the surfboards on the roof. Meeting fellow surfers on the road was a novelty and they wanted to talk, find out which places were worth visiting, inspect each other's surfboards and jive about the latest surfing styles.

Modification of cars was prolific in the 1960s, with many stories of surfers buying old cars for as little as $50 and ripping the backseat out so they could fit more boards, or install a comfortable bed. Throw in a mattress, some cheap blankets, a bag of oranges, some oats and a box of baked beans and the surfer was good for a week or more. Often times, a bunch of surfers would all throw in $10 to buy a car together and they might drive it up and down the coast all summer, then sell it again in another part of the country, often times getting their money back with a bit more to spend.

'Surfmobile innovation' was evident too with surfers often doing some dodgy wiring jobs to fit out cars with cassette playing stereos on the dashboard and putting the speakers on the roof blaring out the tunes of the era until the battery went flat. The need for 'roll starting' and the likelihood of getting bogged on sandy tracks somewhere was always a reminder to come prepared, as often surfers would disappear for weeks at a time with as little as $10 in their pocket. The surf mechanics were as simple as the engine bays of the cars in the 1960s … all you needed was a set of spanners, some lubrication and perhaps a spare set of spark plugs and timing points. If the windscreen wipers didn't work, no problem, just smear a bit of oil on the glass and hope for the best. The old cars may have had some gears not working, blown-out tail lights and even headlights, but all the surfer wanted was for the car to get them to the beach … their comfort was in the waves.

As the culture of surfing blossomed in the mid to late 1960s, there emerged the cult surf cars … vehicles known to be associated with surfing and surfers, the 'woody' station wagon and the split-window VW bus two of the most obvious shapes. The Volkswagon beetle and bus had the added

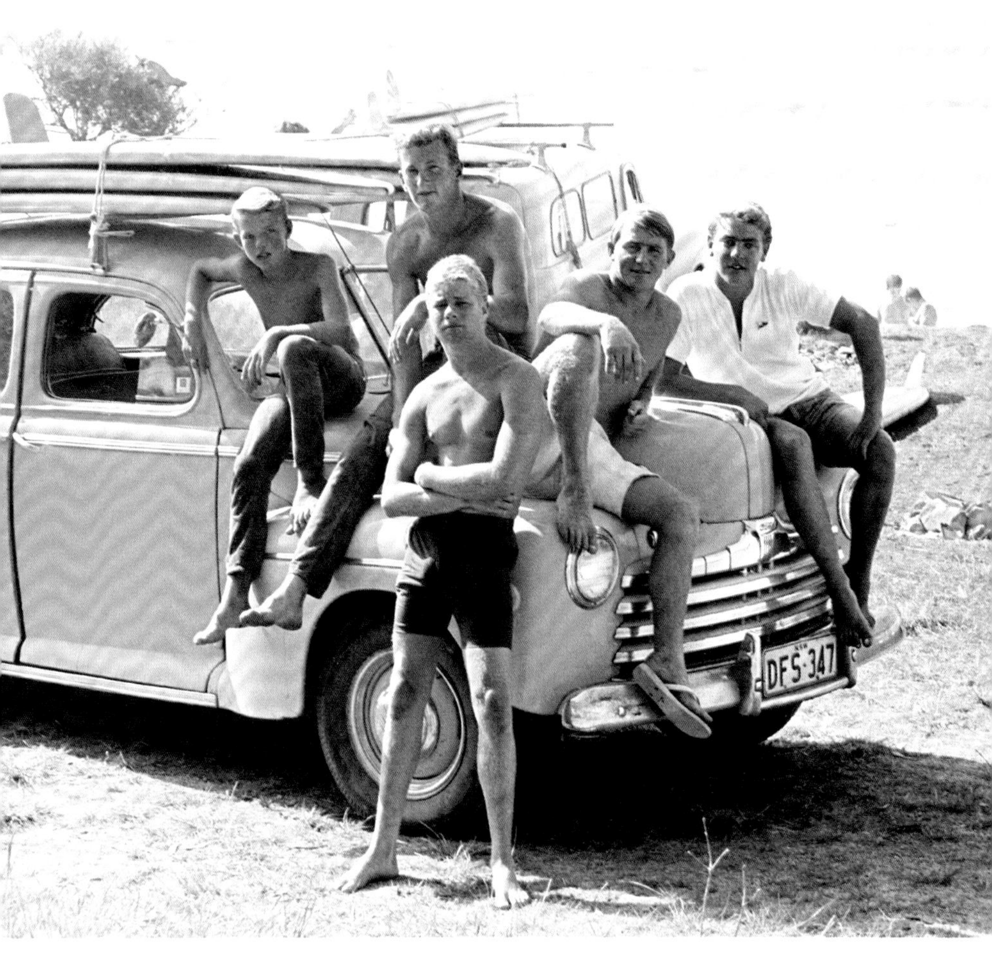

Golf Course, NSW South Coast, 1964. The Cronulla crew poses on the bonnet of John Gittens' car while the surfboards do some posing too on the car roofs. **BW**

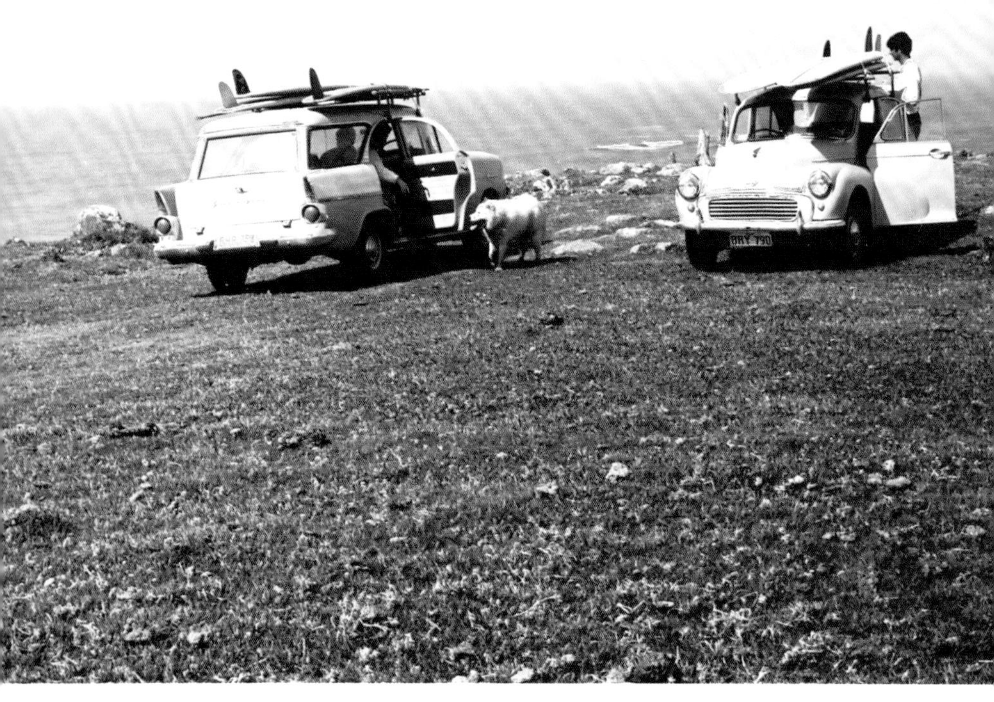

advantage of being so easy and cheap to fix that it became a natural attraction for surfers with little or no money.

In Australia it was all about old Holden, particularly the Holden Wagon; EH, EK and the sophisticated FC wagon. Surfers, inherently broke, would get the cheapest car they could find. Dilapidated older cars of any shape or form have always been popular with surfers; cultural statements of a kind were made as surfers often added hand-painted flourishes to doors, the bonnet and even the roof. These cars were built tough, it was hard to put a dent in one, but surfers had a lot of fun denting them deliberately and giving them an identity all of their own.

Visiting surfers from other countries could land at a major airport and find a second-hand car suitable for the journey ahead. The car would become their home, kitchen and living room, with the surfboard often living on the roof. Roof racks were arbitrary, but the function was important … to hold the surfboards on the roof. However, many a story is told of surfboards flying off and in some cases the roofracks dislodging altogether and a whole rack of surfboards leaving the roof of the car.

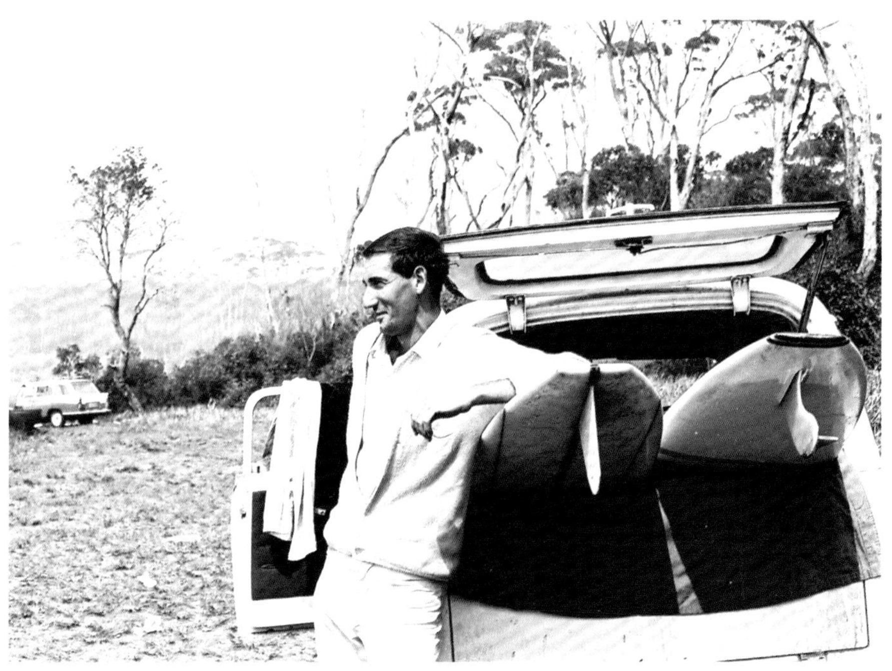

Above: **Photographer John Pennings, 1965.** John posing while on a trip to the south coast. **JP**

Opposite: **Surfing safari, 1965.** John Penning and friends. **JP**

Surfers would often attempt to take their heavy two-wheel drive car onto the sandy tracks, trying desperately to get to previously unsurfed destinations, only to get their car bogged in sand and have to walk out and find help…the old car was sometimes left to rust there until a rescue vehicle could tow it out to safety or a nearby wrecking yard.

Some of the more isolated surfing spots were accessed by sand only and surfers sometimes had a dedicated beach car that they would leave at the beach, disguised in the bushes after it was used, sure to be restarted the following 'surfari'. The surf car and the surfari were unique to surfers and often the adventure was undertaken in pouring rain, as delivered by offshore weather patterns, cyclones and low pressure systems. Driving through flooded rivers, drowning the engine or watching your car get washed downstream were all very real events that took place back then … and all part of the adventure of the sixties.

For some, the adventure went so far as to witness the creation of the next generation on the back seat of the van! Yes, some lives were changed, forever.

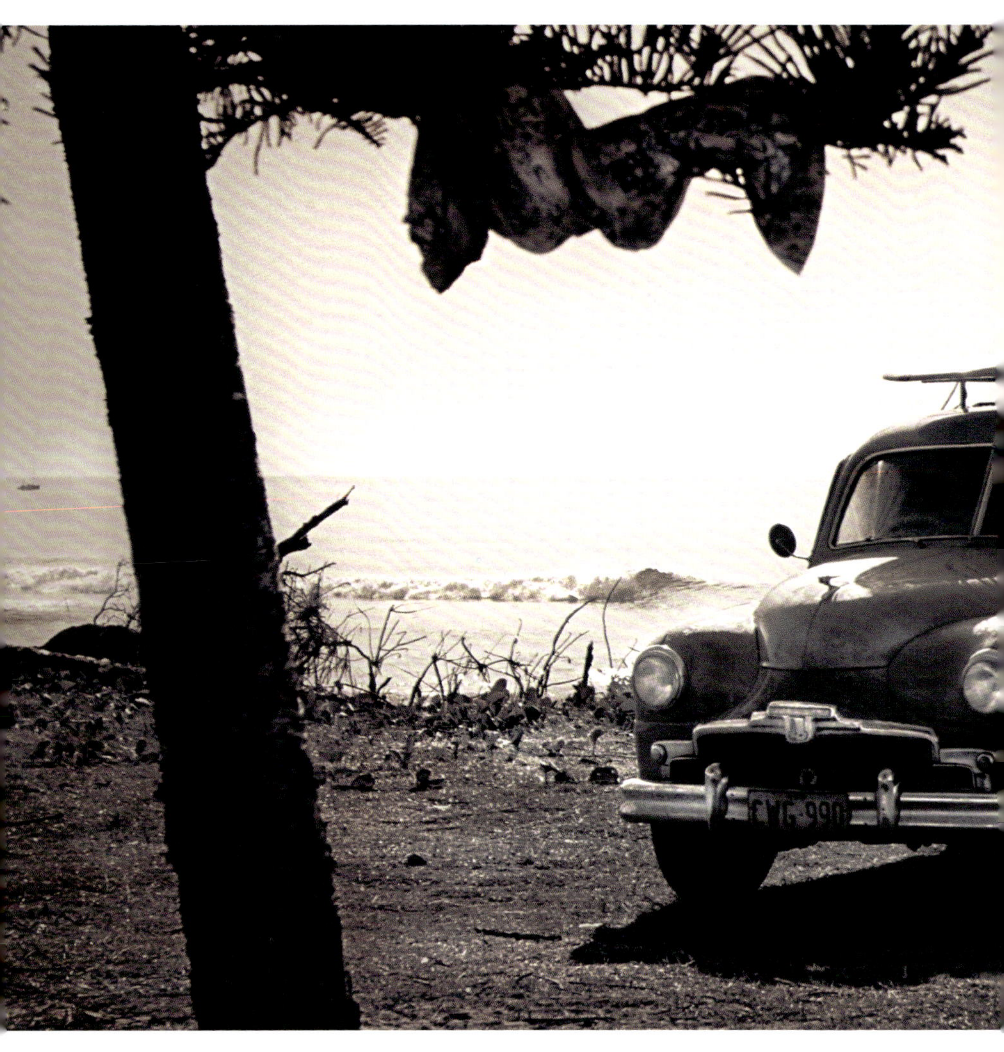

Maroochydore morning, 1964. Bob
Weeks standing beside his van after an
early morning surf. **BW**

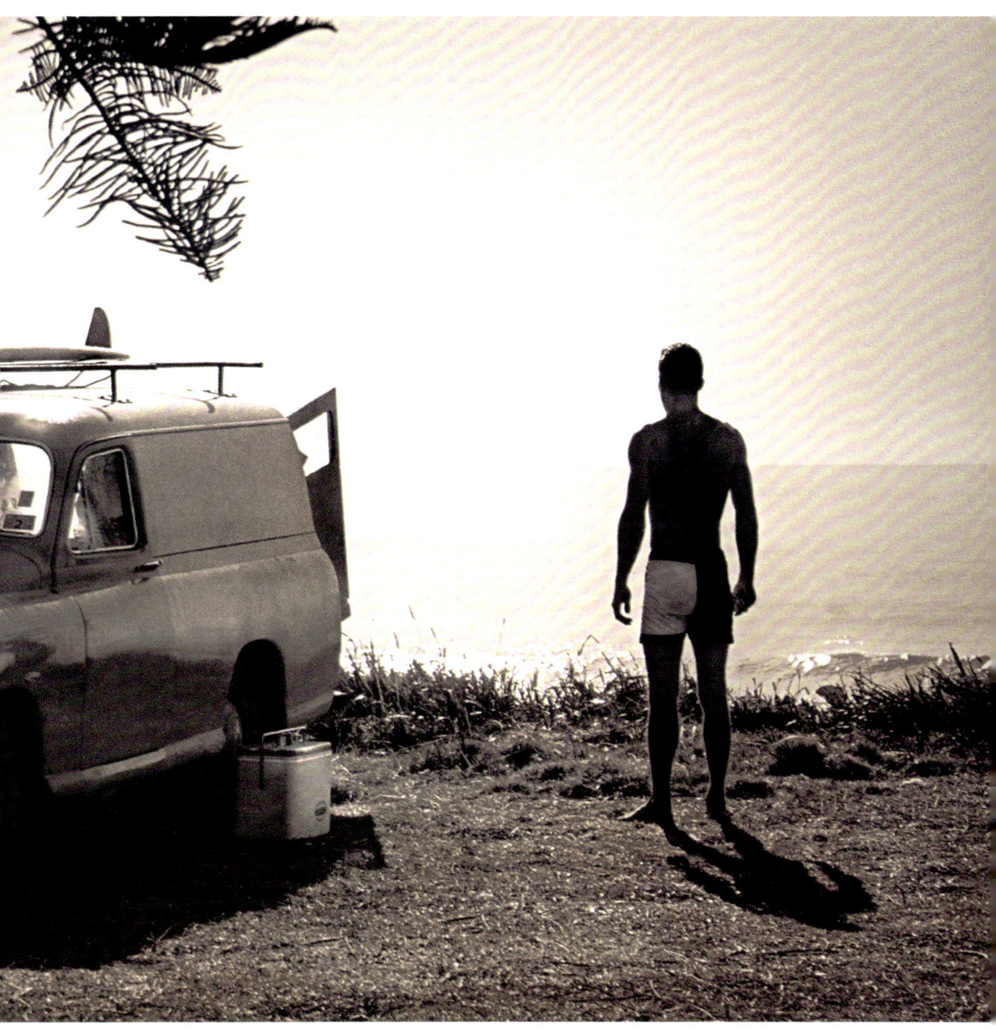

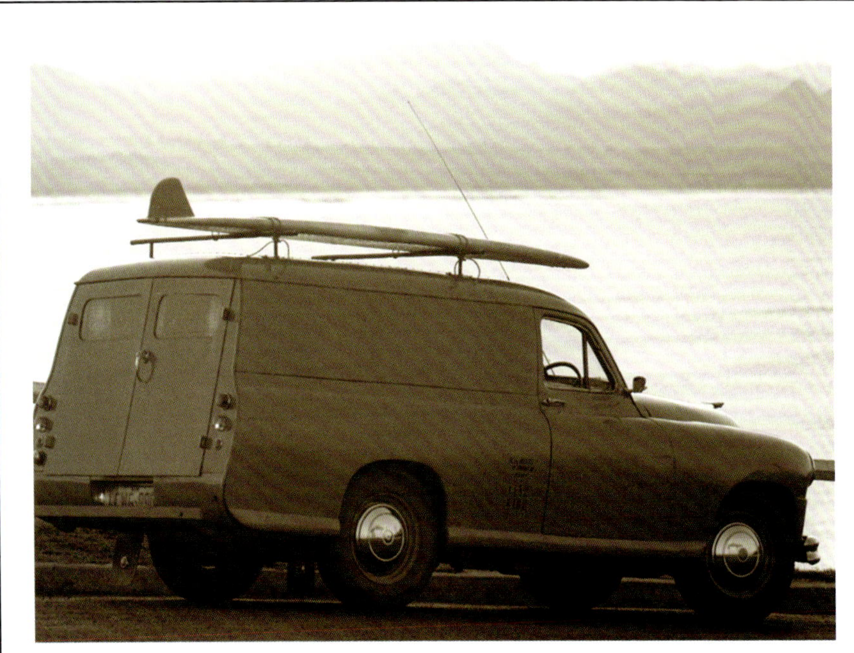

Vanguard panel van on Byron Bay headland, 1965. **BW**

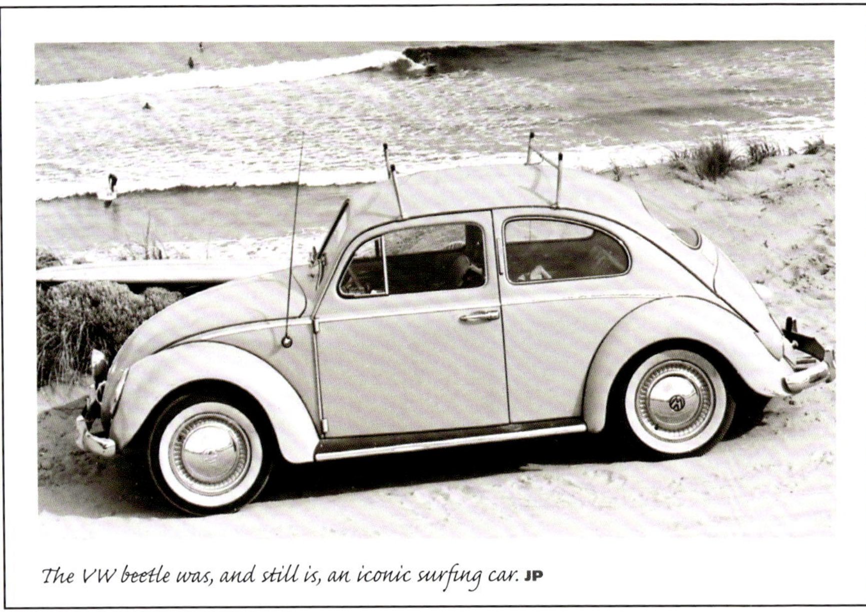

The VW beetle was, and still is, an iconic surfing car. **JP**

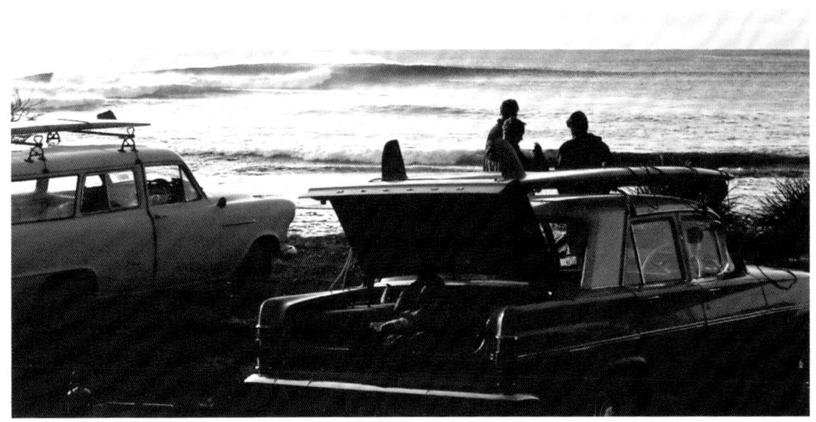

Australia, surfing and Holden – the perfect waves in the background make this one of JP's most treasured photos. **JP**

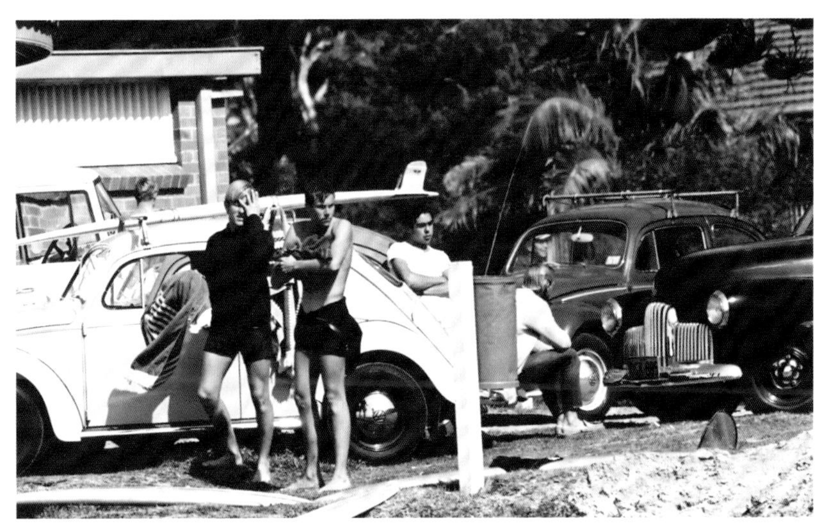

Surfers towelling off after a surf with their Vee-Dubs. **JP**

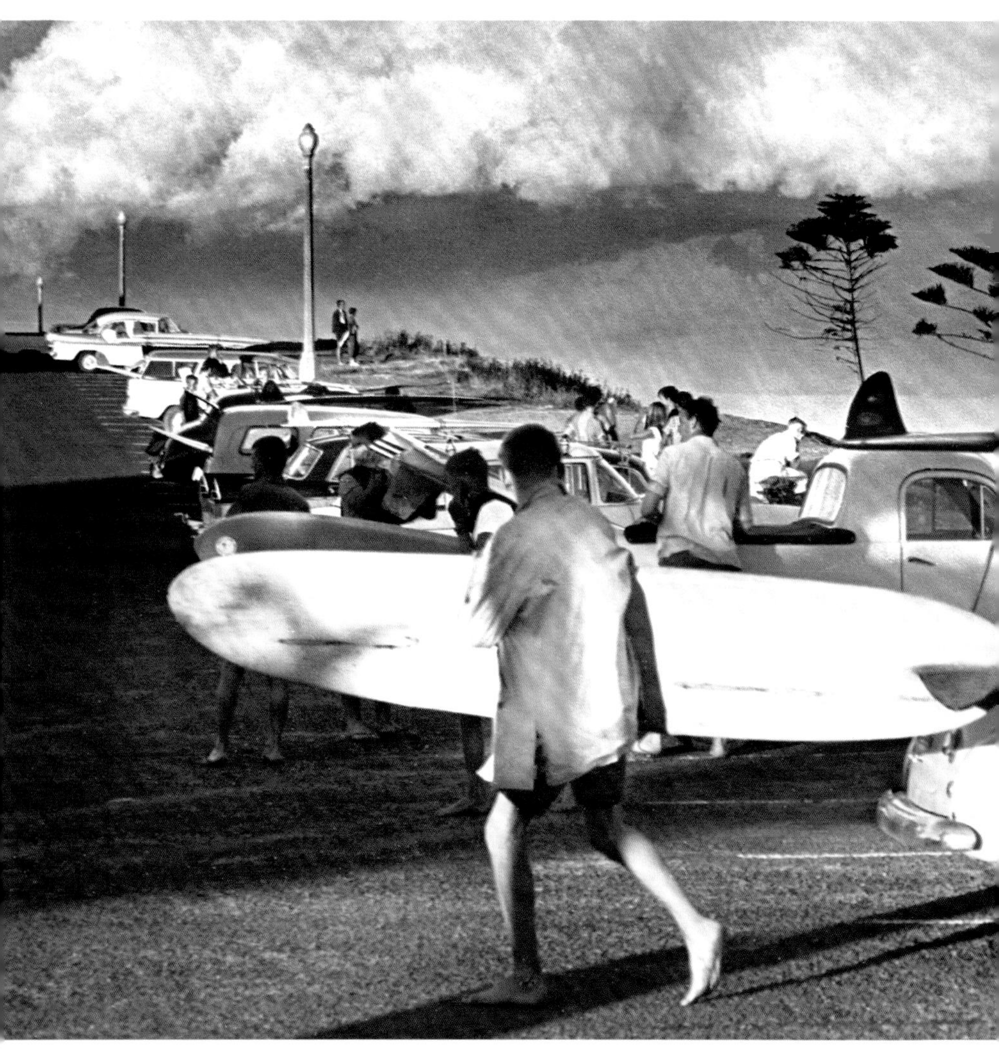

North Cronulla, 1962. The late afternoon
sun makes some interesting patterns on cars
belonging to the surfing fraternity. **BW**

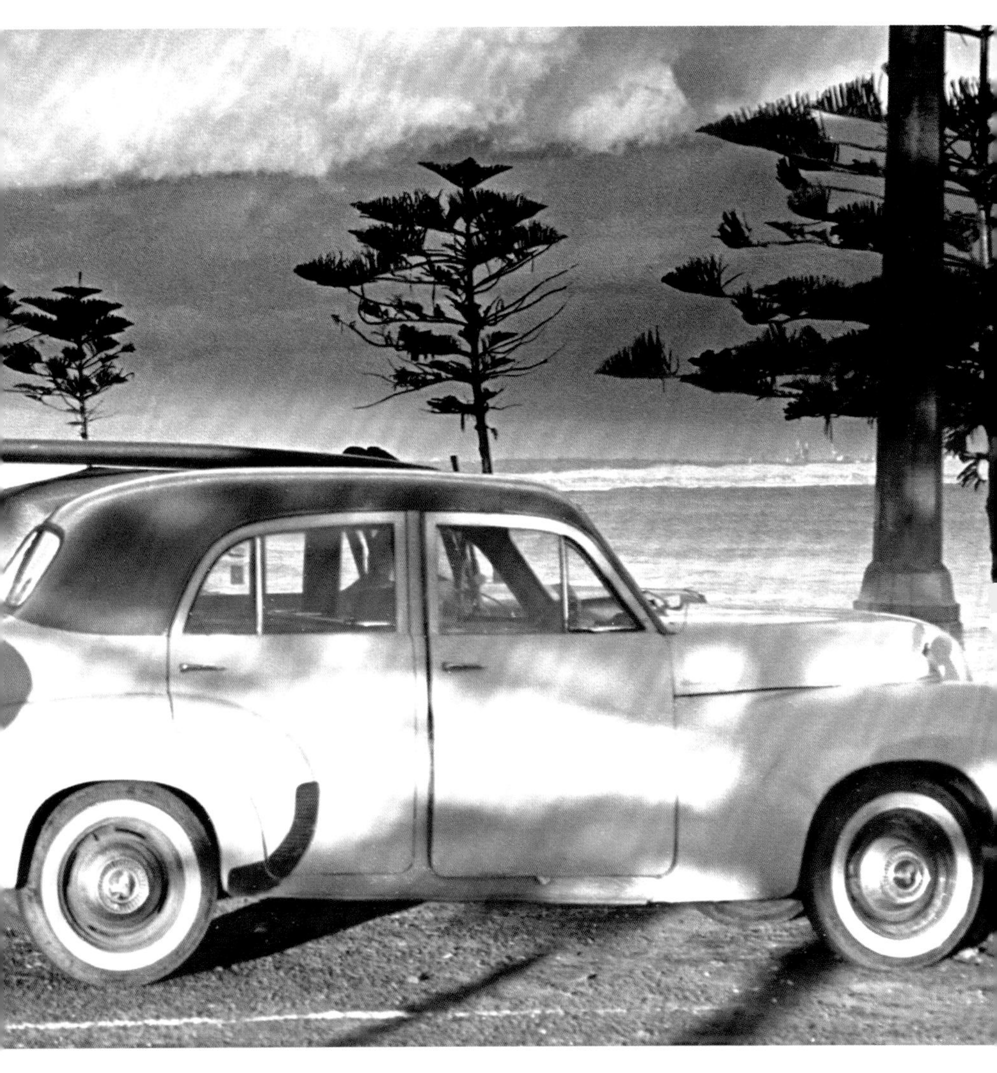

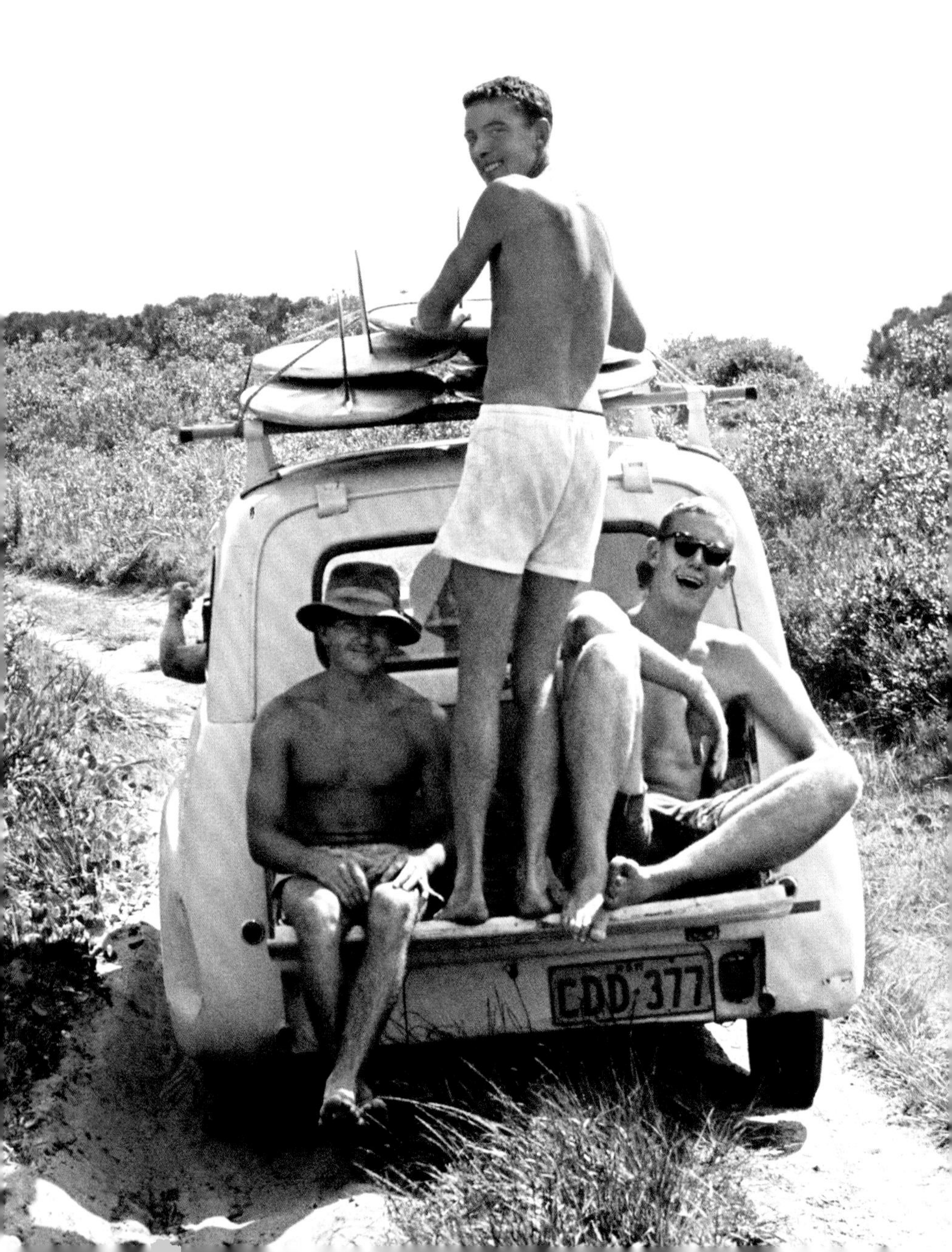

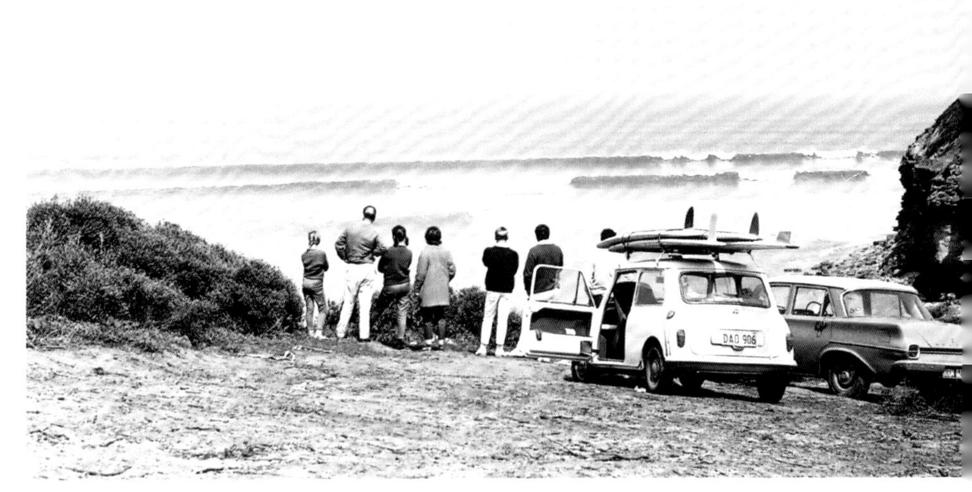

Above: **Bells Beach, 1965. JP**

Opposite: Cronulla surfers Gordon Hill, John Griffiths and Billy Dews getting a lift along the sandy track from 'Voodoo', 1963. **BW**

The adventure south of Sydney sometimes offered surfers a welcome respite from the city crowds. **JP**

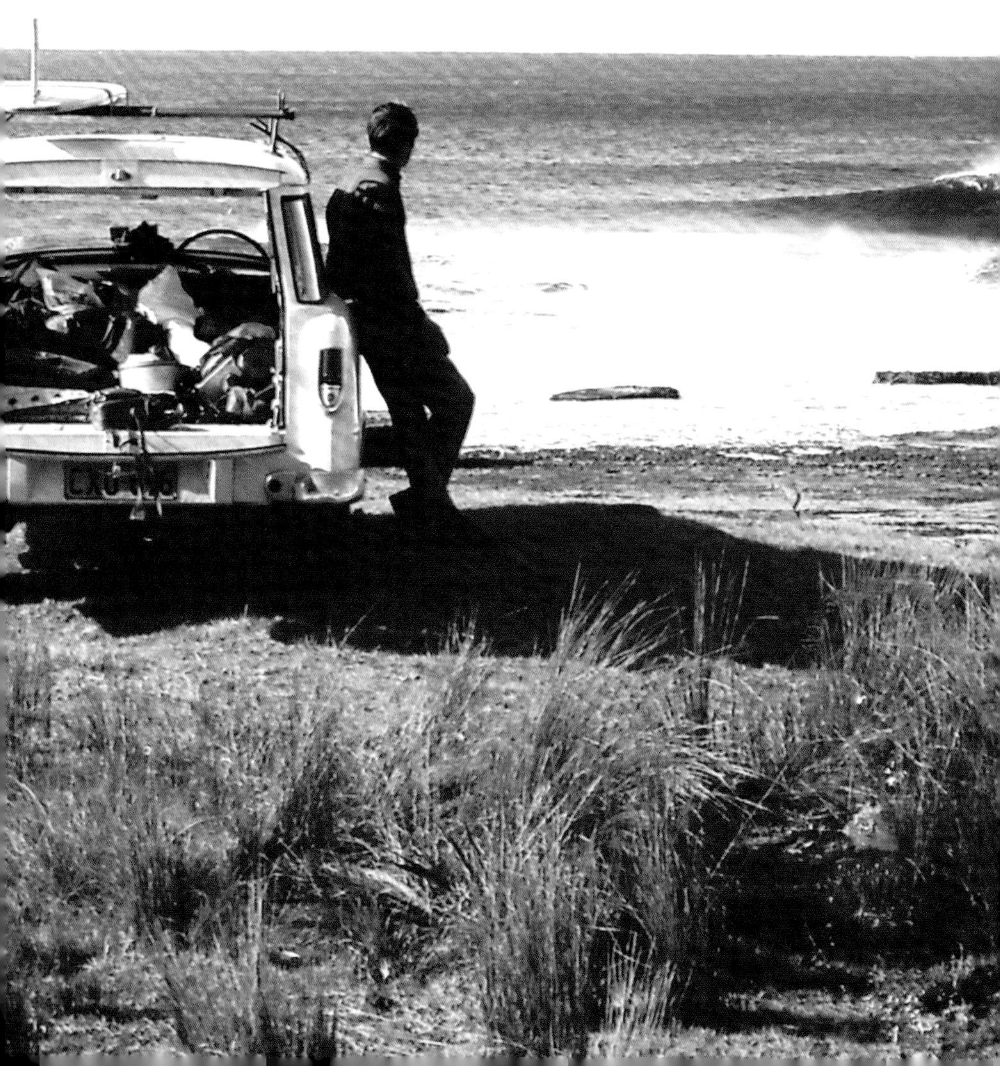

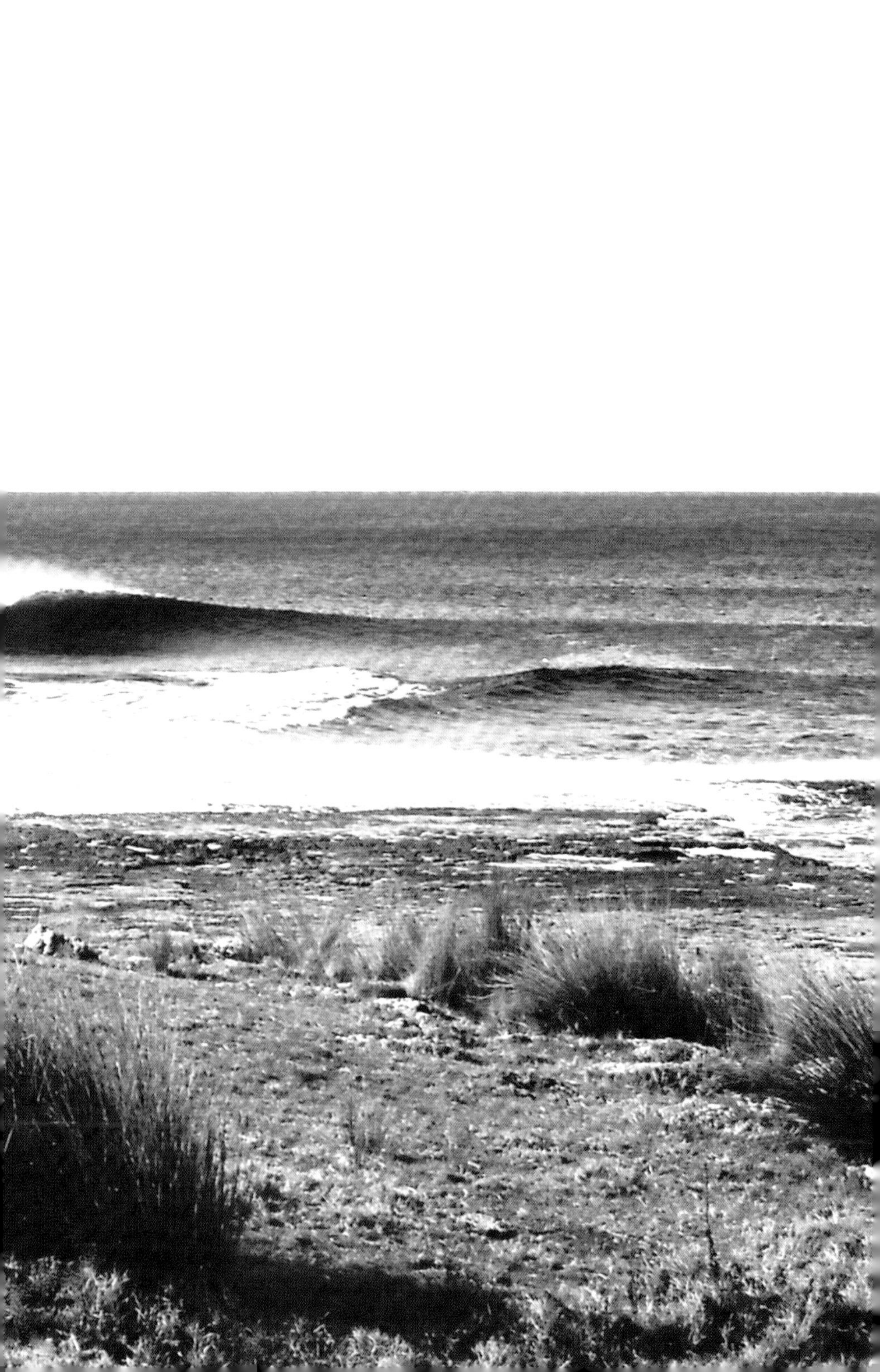

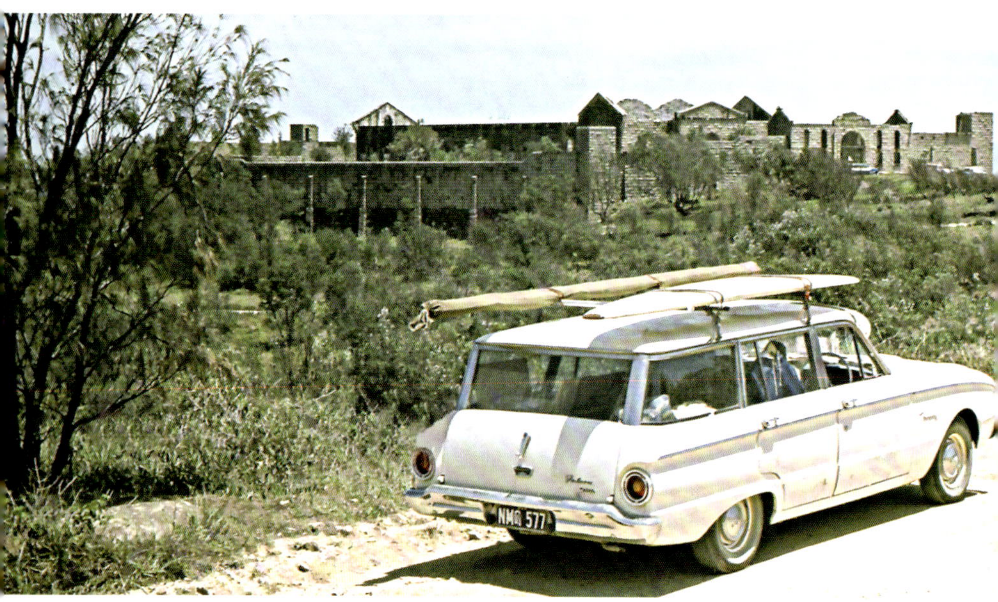

Falcon at Trial Bay, 1963. Taken on one of my trips showing surf movies for Bob Evans. When Bob was unable to travel with the movies because of work commitments, I would collect the projector and screen from Taree and show the movies in theatres or halls up as far as Bundaberg and back to Kempsey, where I would put the equipment on a plane for showings in Sydney that night. **MS**

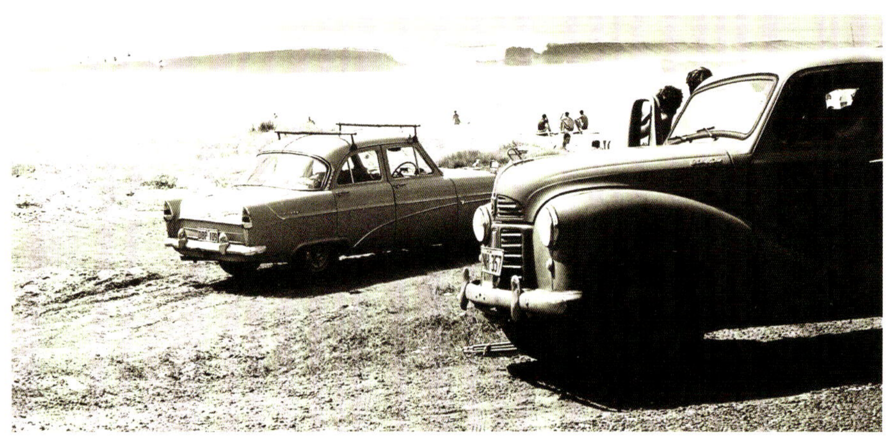

Mollymook carpark. With the John Pennings' Austin ute. **JP**

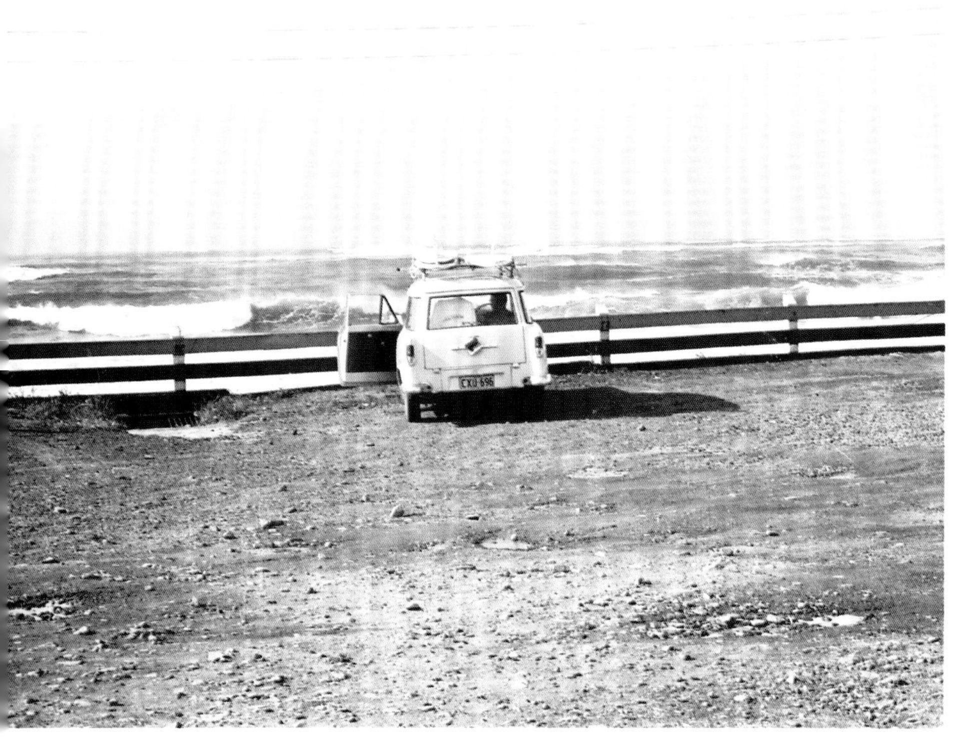

Byron Bay, 1965. Main beach during a cyclone swell. **JP**

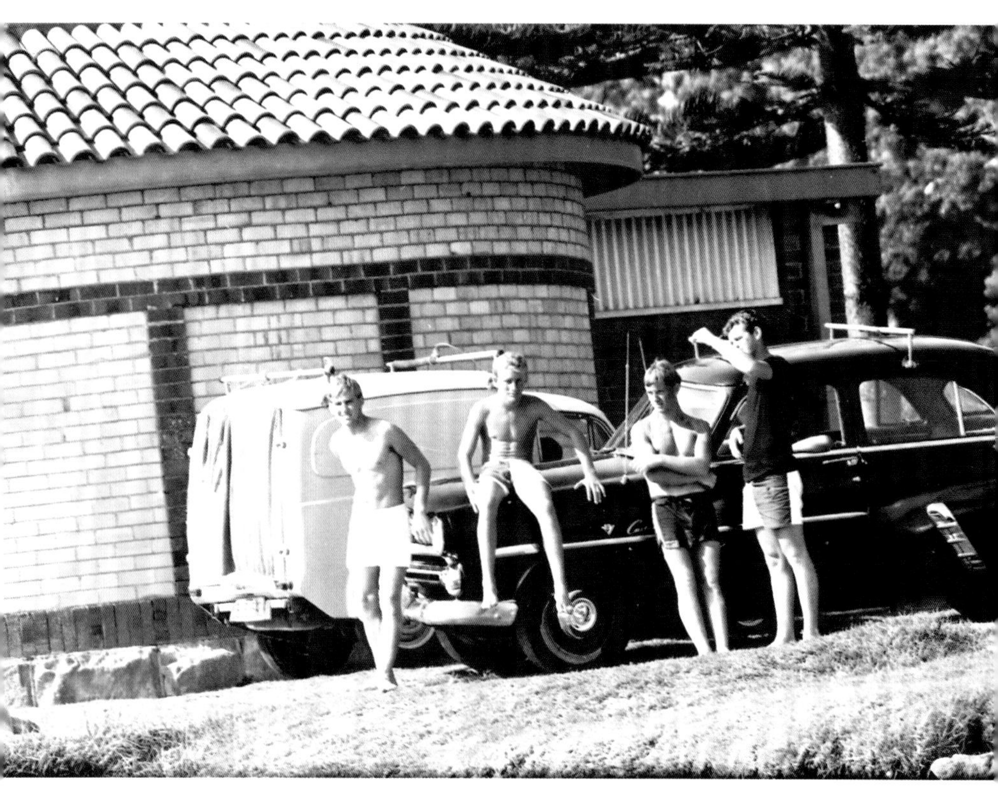

Russell Hughes on the bonnet, outside the Palm Beach dressing sheds. 1965. Russell Hughes 1946–2011 was an outstanding surfer through the 1960s and into the 70s, one of Australia's best. R.I.P. **JP**

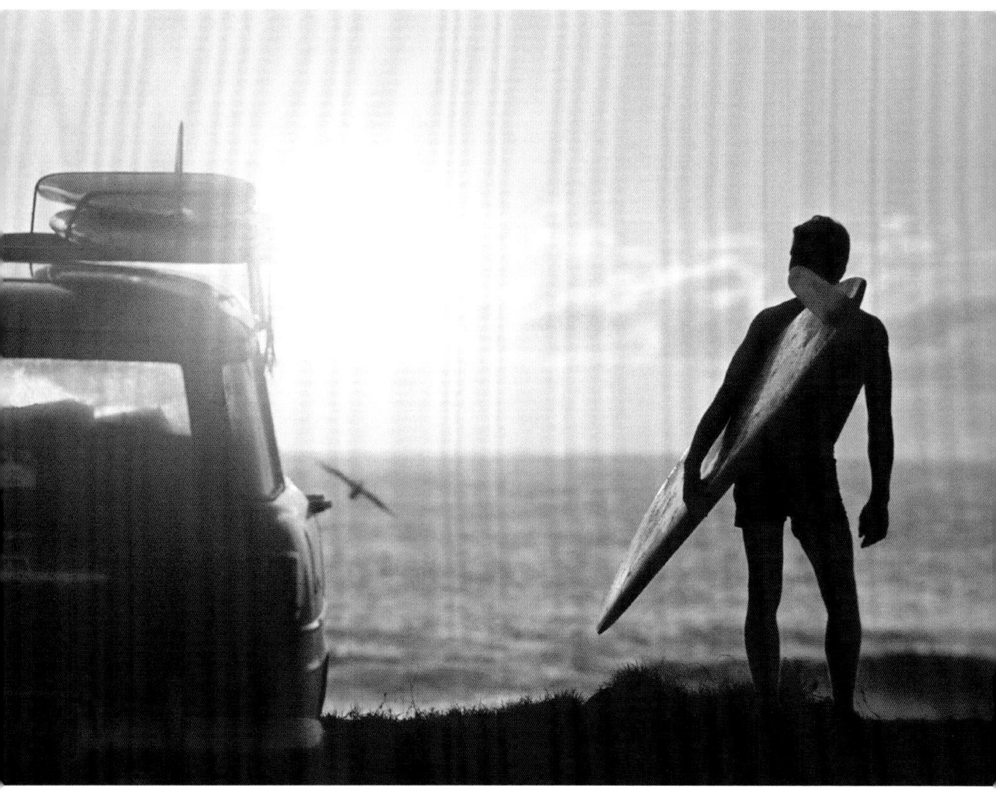

Keith Paull (1946–2004), Crescent Head, 1964. **BW**

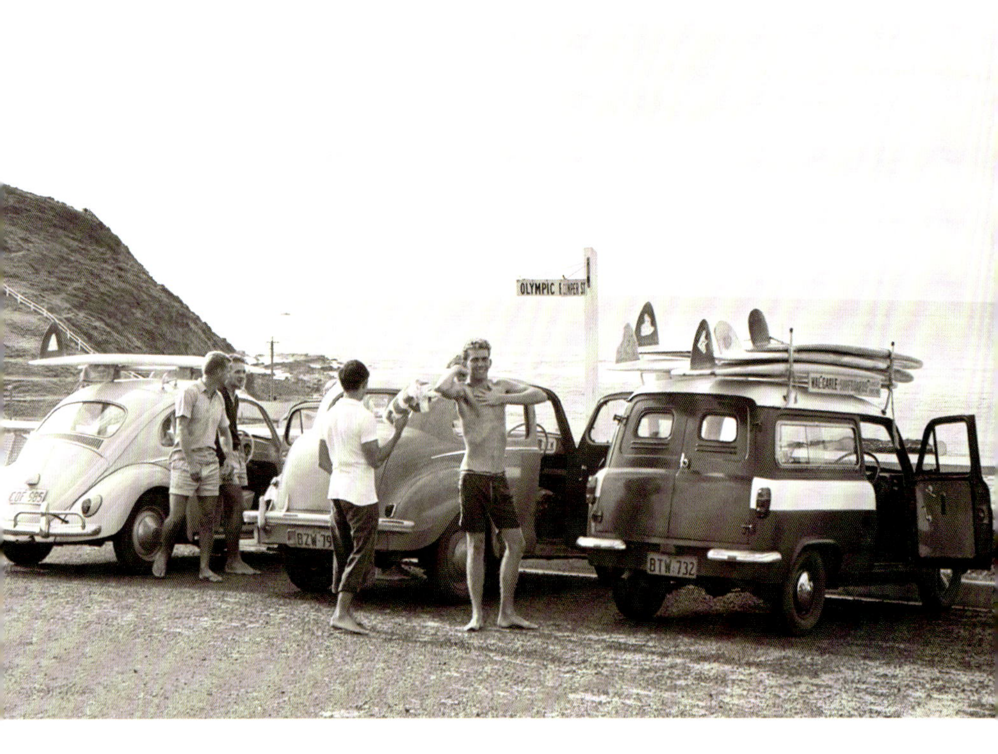

A few Cronulla surfers having just arrived at the Port Kembla carpark, 1962. **BW**

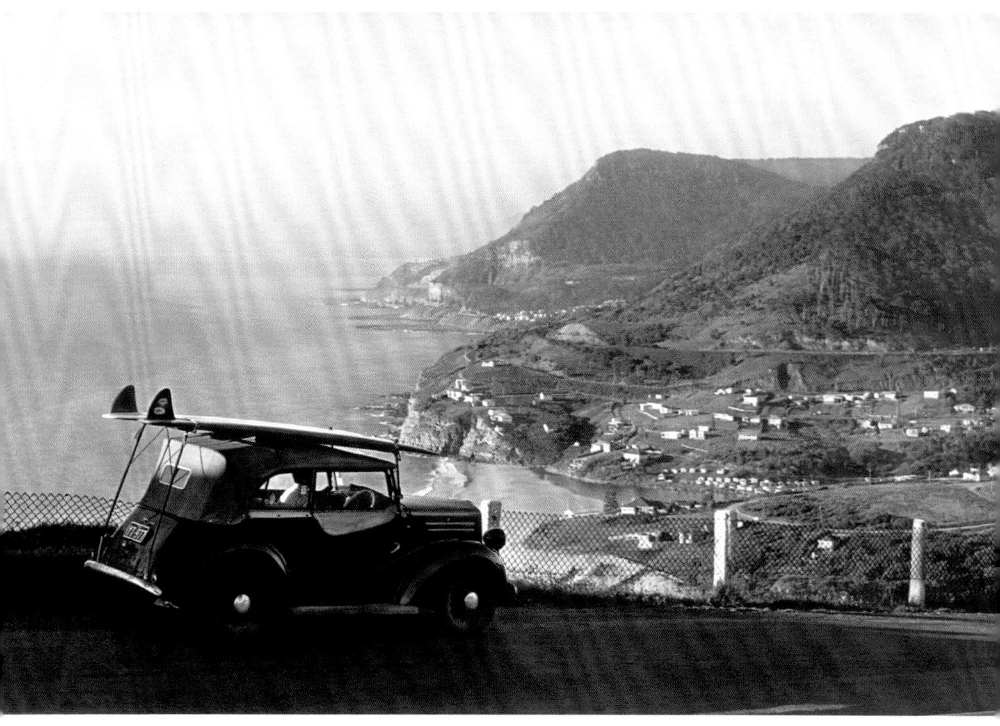

A 1948 Ford Anglia overlooking
Stanwell Park, NSW, in 1962. **BW**

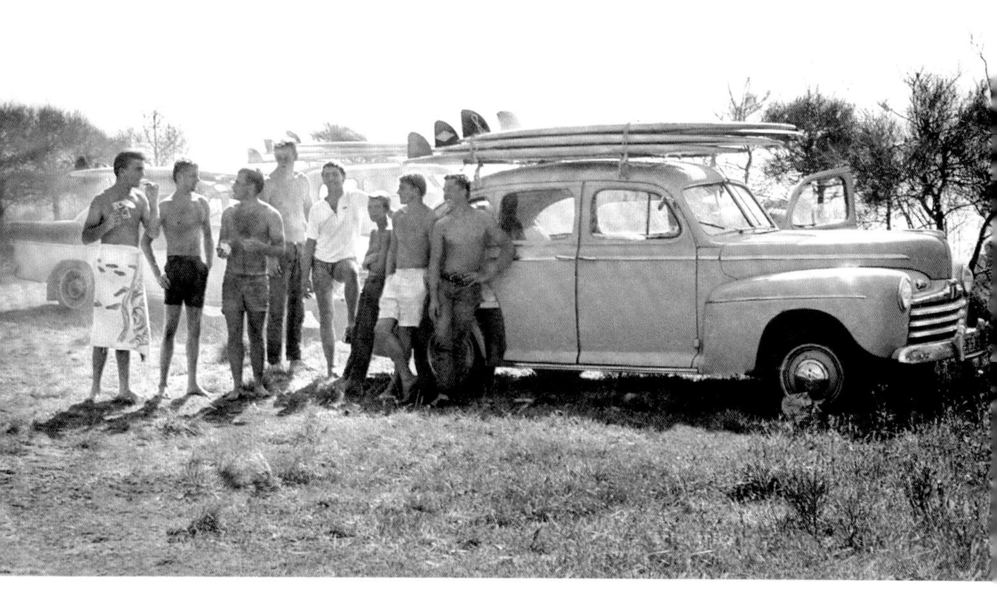

A group of Cronulla surfers at Golf Course Surf break on
the South Coast of NSW, near Mollymook 1964. **BW**

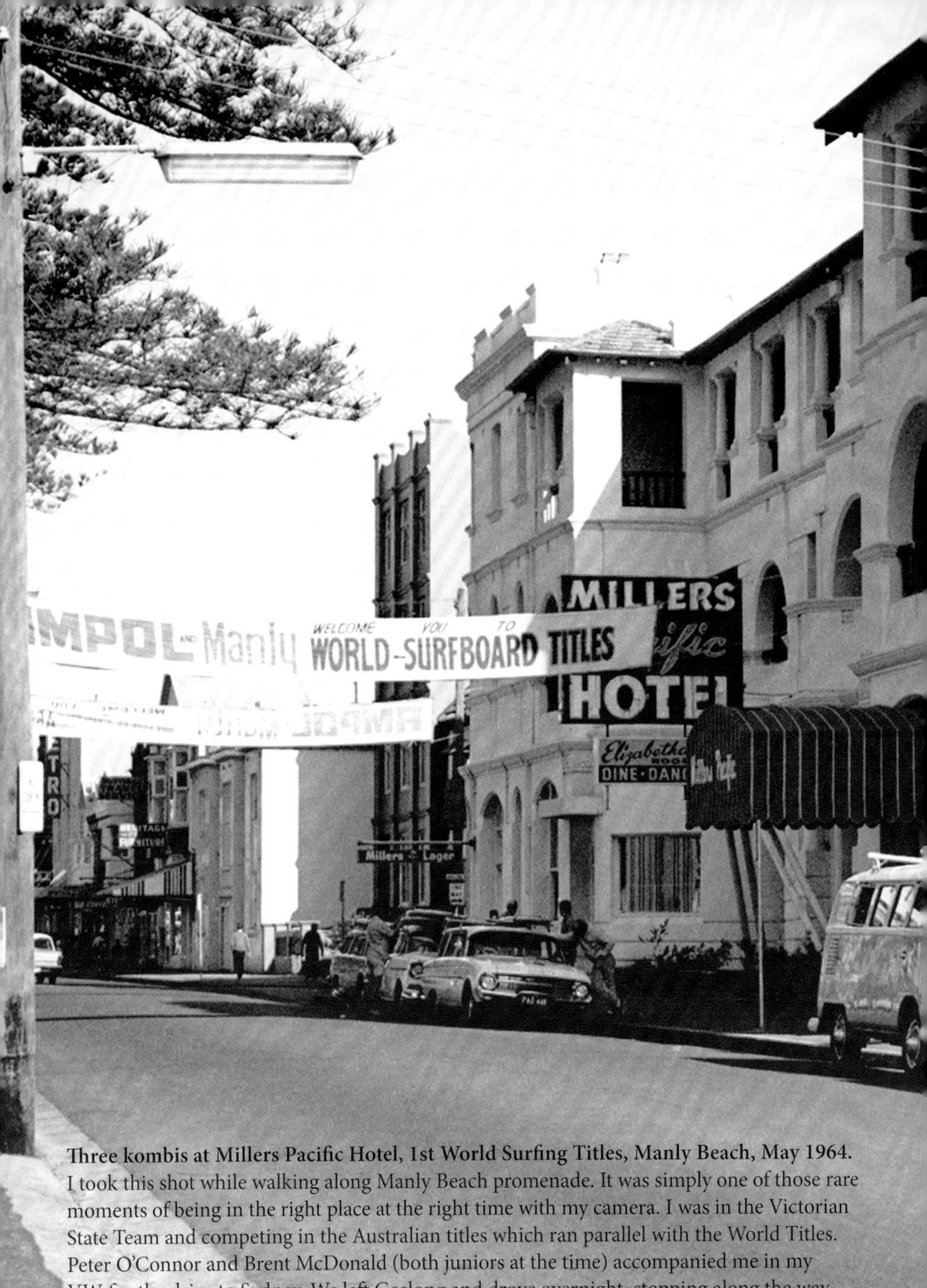

Three kombis at Millers Pacific Hotel, 1st World Surfing Titles, Manly Beach, May 1964. I took this shot while walking along Manly Beach promenade. It was simply one of those rare moments of being in the right place at the right time with my camera. I was in the Victorian State Team and competing in the Australian titles which ran parallel with the World Titles. Peter O'Connor and Brent McDonald (both juniors at the time) accompanied me in my VW for the drive to Sydney. We left Geelong and drove overnight, stopping along the way for refuelling and meals at road stations. Our accommodation was at Queenscliff Surf Club where we encamped in sleeping bags and mattresses on the floor. For meals we dined at a little restaurant on the beach in Manly. It was a few doors along from the Corso and quickly became a popular spot for the interstate surfers. Apart from our meals and some beers at Millers

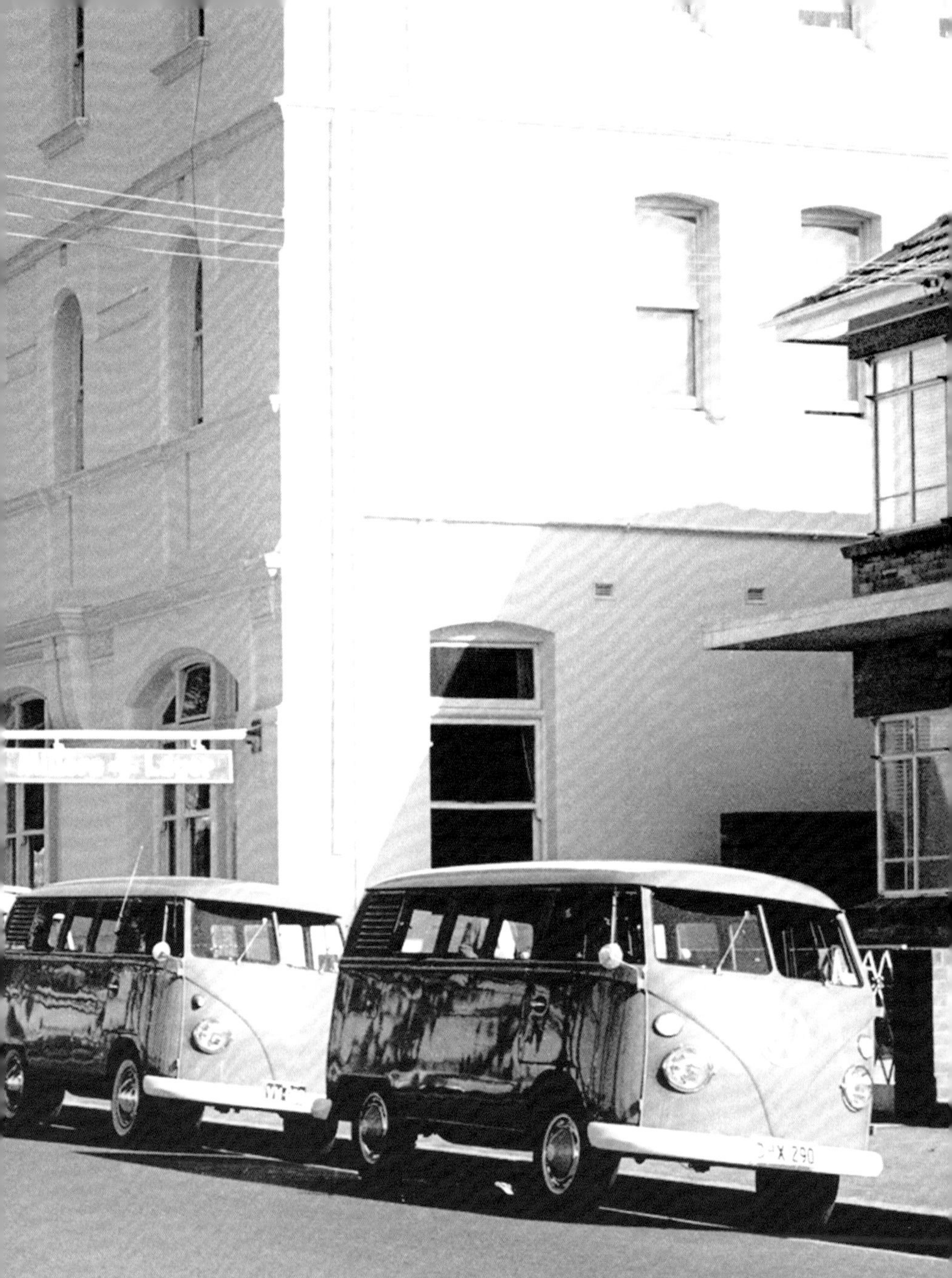

Pacific Hotel, we spent every daylight hour surfing. It was an awesome experience surfing among the best surfers in the world and sometimes perhaps a little intimidating. Here we were in the water with surfers we had only read about in *Surfer Magazine* or seen on Bruce Browne's surf movies. From our perspective they were the elite. One evening I was surfing North Steyne and as I took off on a wave I passed Joey Cabel paddling out. I almost fell off with awe! That's how it was for us. **BS**

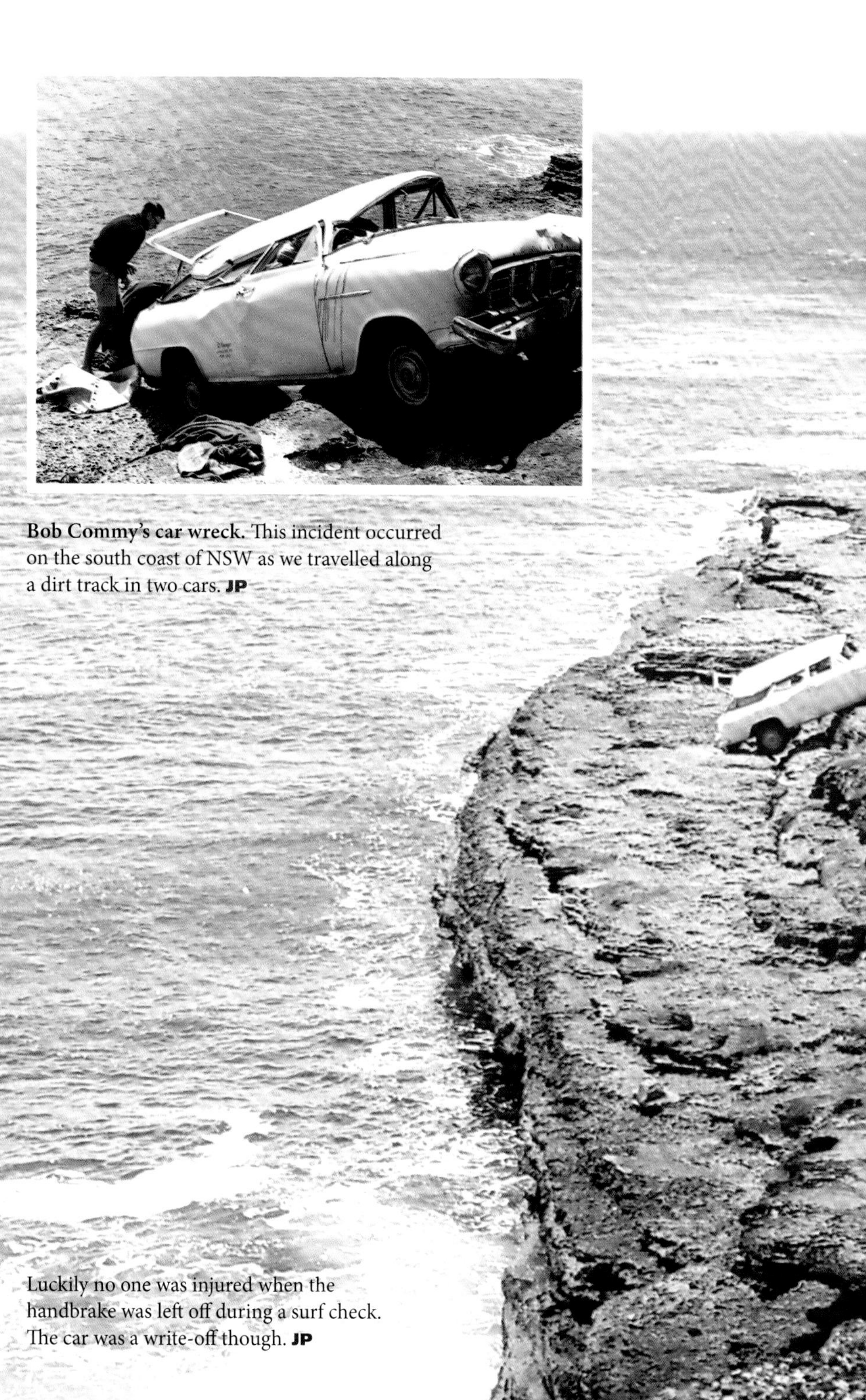

Bob Commy's car wreck. This incident occurred on the south coast of NSW as we travelled along a dirt track in two cars. **JP**

Luckily no one was injured when the handbrake was left off during a surf check. The car was a write-off though. **JP**

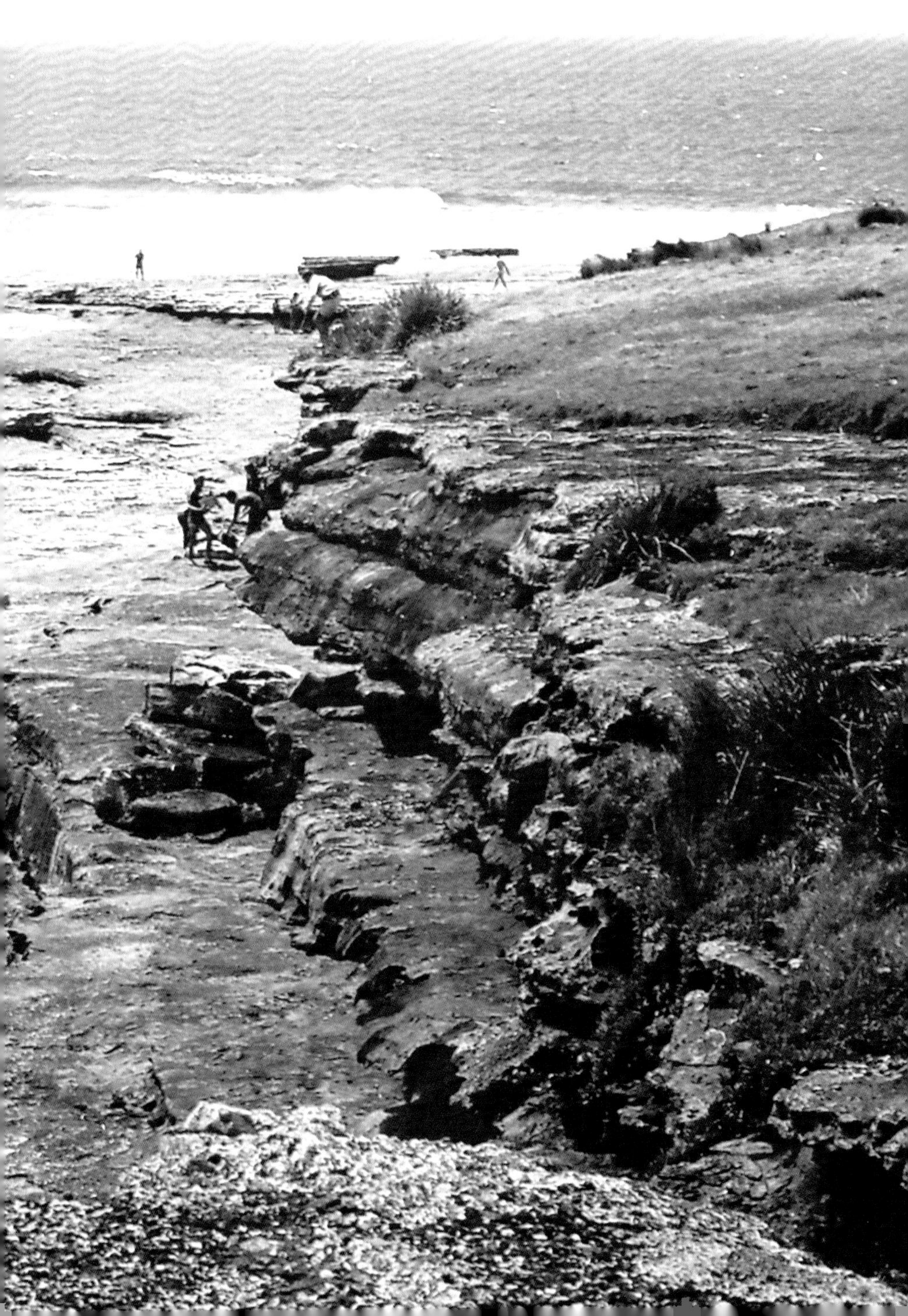

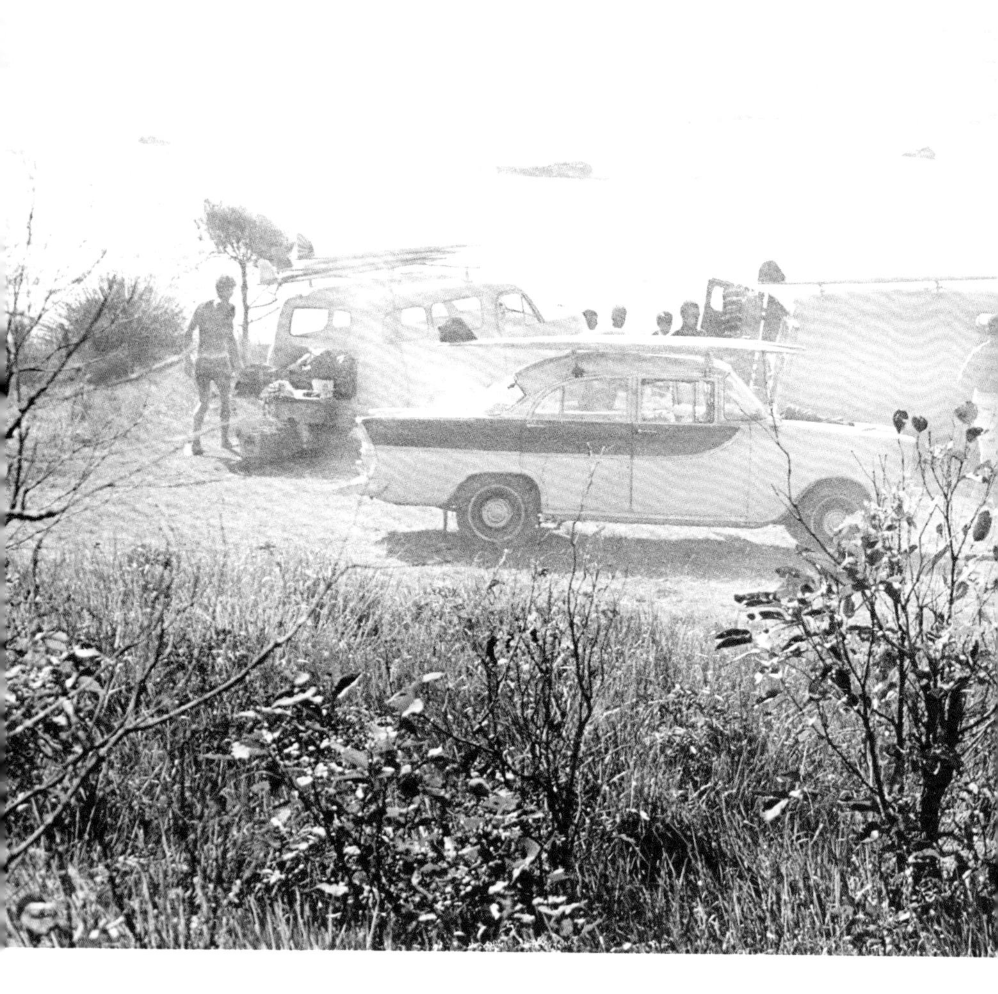

The friendly camping area at Golf Course, 1964. Just for surfers! **BW**

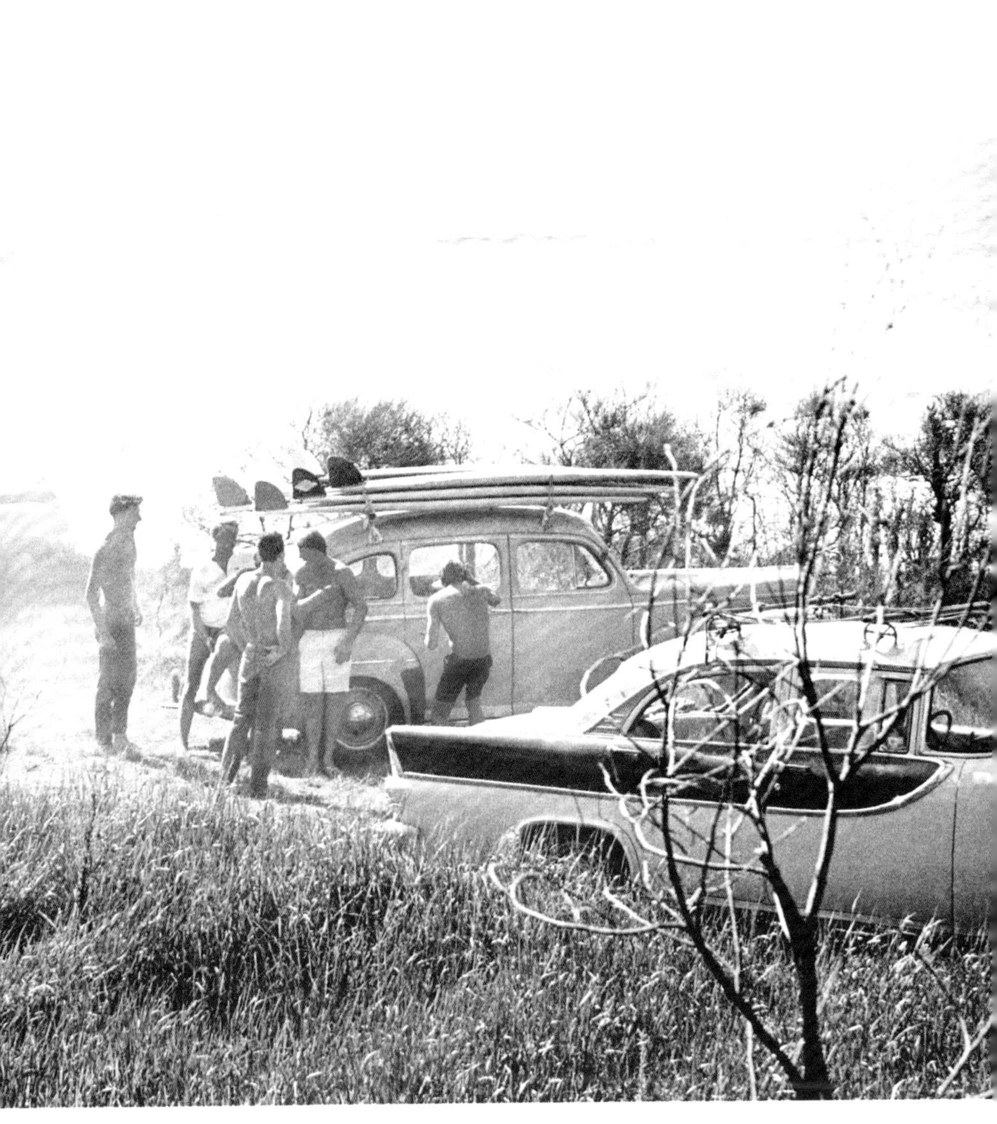

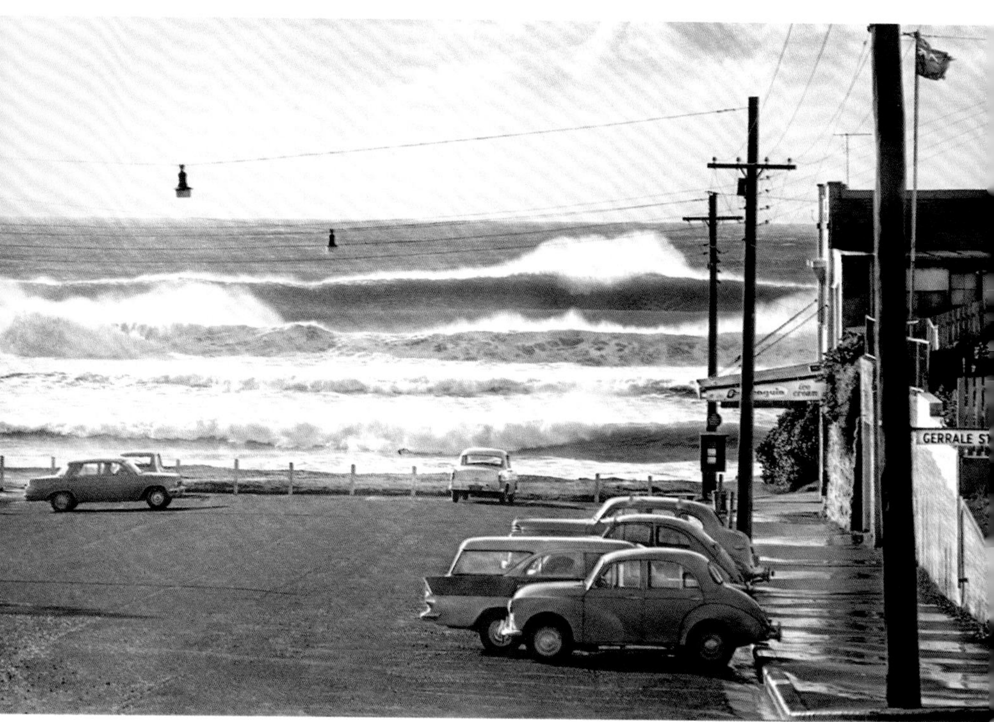

The Alley, Cronulla, 1963. This was the scene that greeted me as I arrived at Cronulla for an early surf one morning. The swell had jumped up overnight and produced these powerful waves and the strong off-shore wind made for a dramatic effect. **BW**

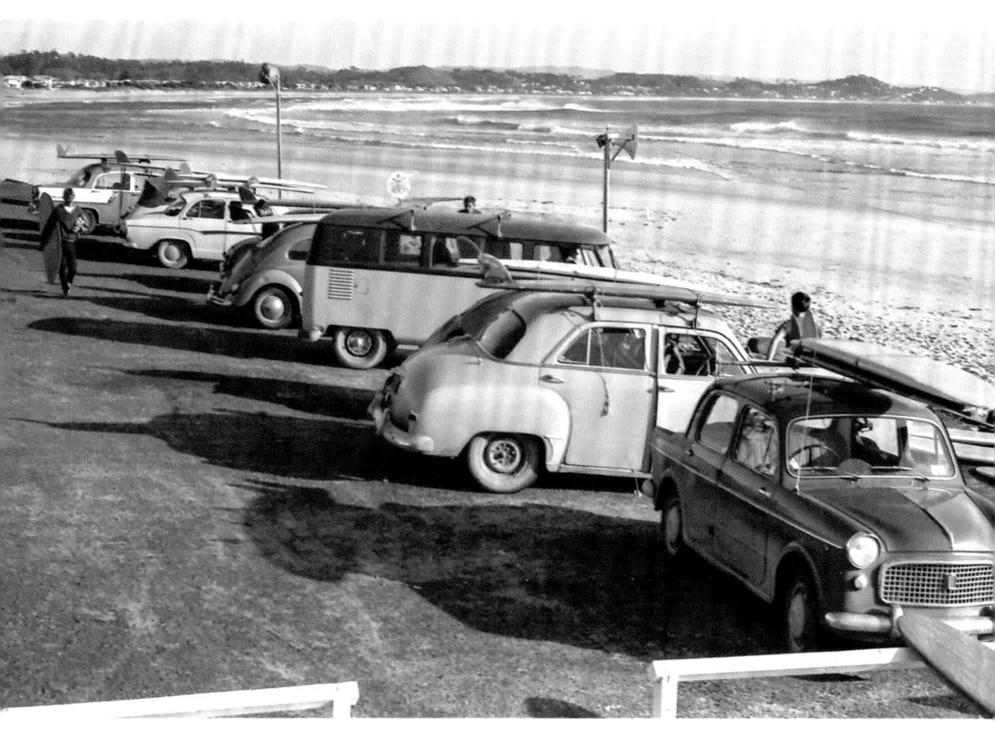

Kirra car park, 1962. Fiat – Bob 'Rughead' Hancock / Dodge – Errol Wright / VW Beetle – Peter Barrett / VW Kombi – Brian 'Furry' Austen / VW Beetle – Tony Sutton / Standard – 'Fungus' / Simca – Col Gallagher / Anglia – Garry Birdsall / Holden – Unknown / Walking – Alan Balmer. **MS**

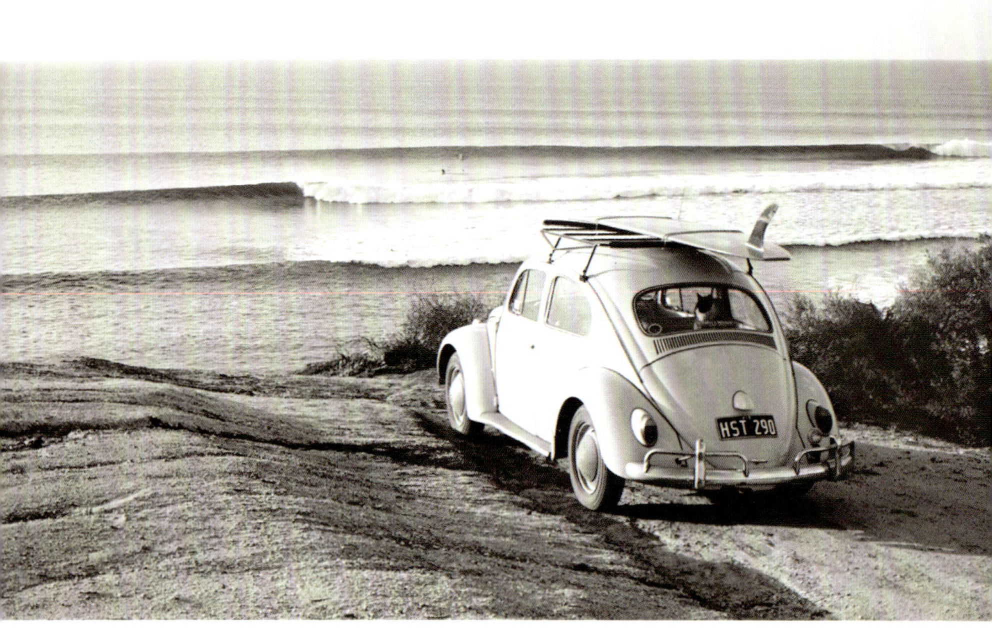

My VW and faithful Siamese cat in the back. He often accompanied me surfing, loved going for a run along the beach and wasn't intimidated by strangers or dogs! Bells Beach, September 1967. **BS**

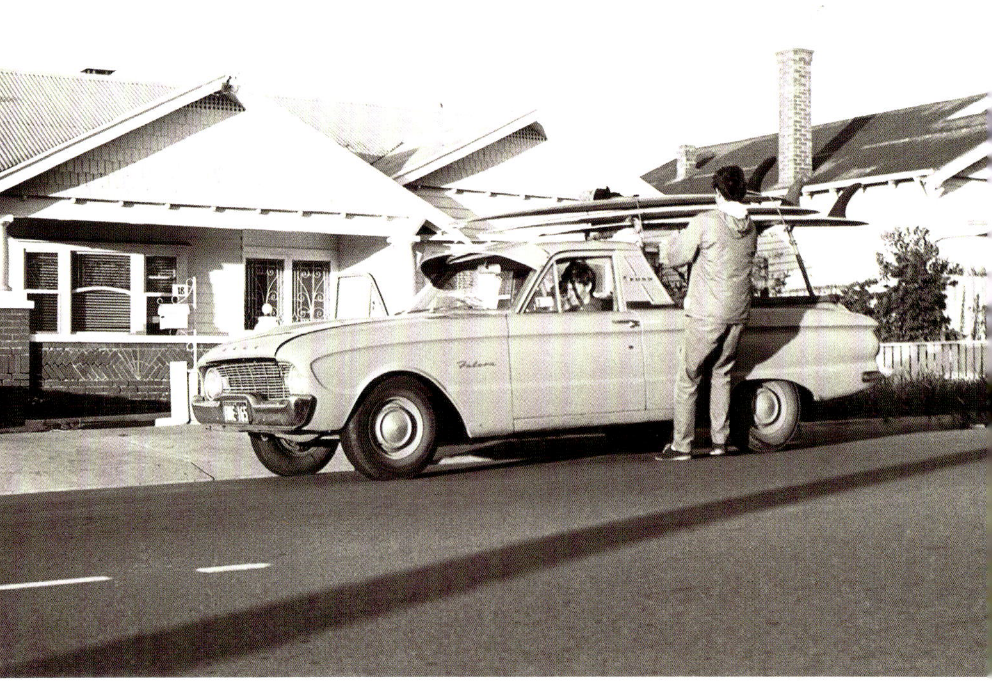

Ted Thornley with Tom McDougal loading my board on Ted's Falcon ute, Corio Street come Torquay Road, Belmont, December 1967. **BS**

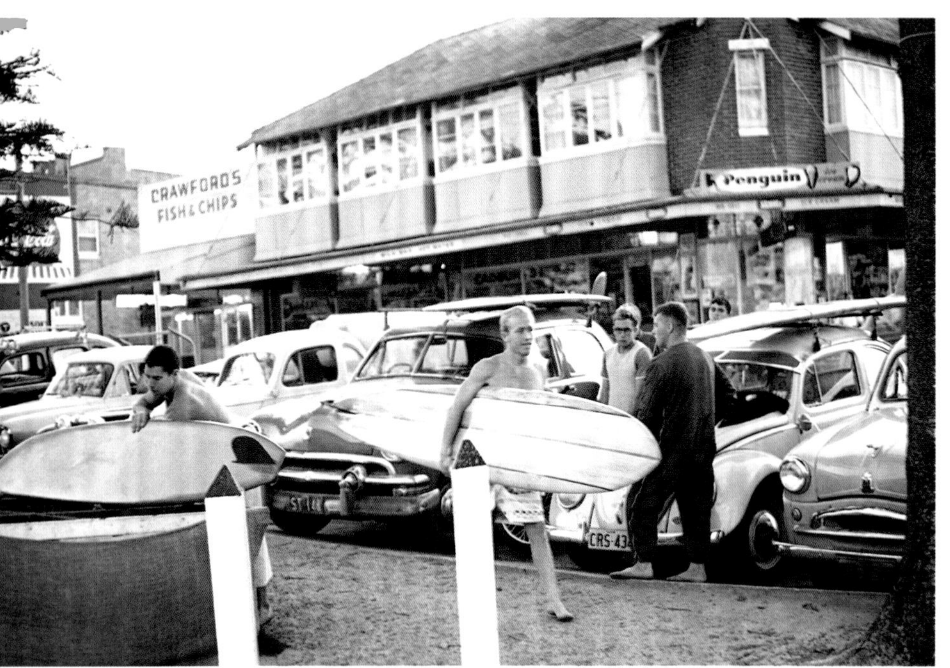

Dave Jackman with his balsa gun at Dee Why, 1962. Bob Pike is laying his board down on the left of the photo. Bob and Dave were pioneers of Australian Big Wave Riding – the first to surf the Fairy Bower when it was big. They later went to Hawaii and showed the world that Australians can surf mountains in the sea. **BW**

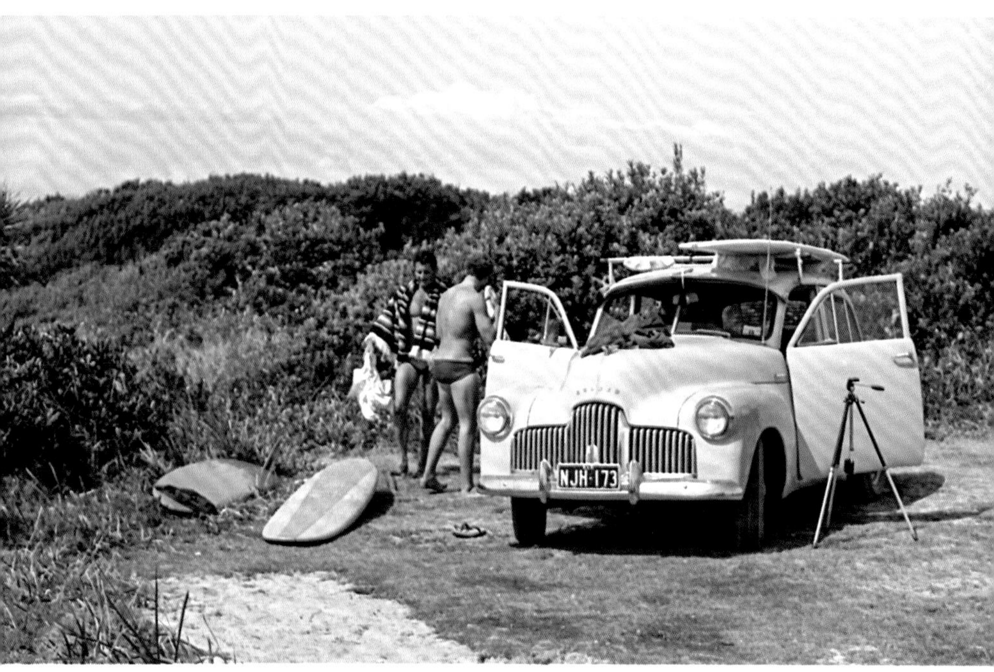

Dave Haynes and Laurie 'Curley' Pinniger, Flat Rock, 1963. The area around Flat Rock was virgin coastal scrub when we first surfed there and the road between Byron Bay and Lennox Head was unsealed and mostly rough dirt.

A road between Lennox and Ballina didn't exist except for an unmade sand track through the scrub. To surf there we often had to remove obstacles from the track and be prepared to push when the car got bogged. **MS**

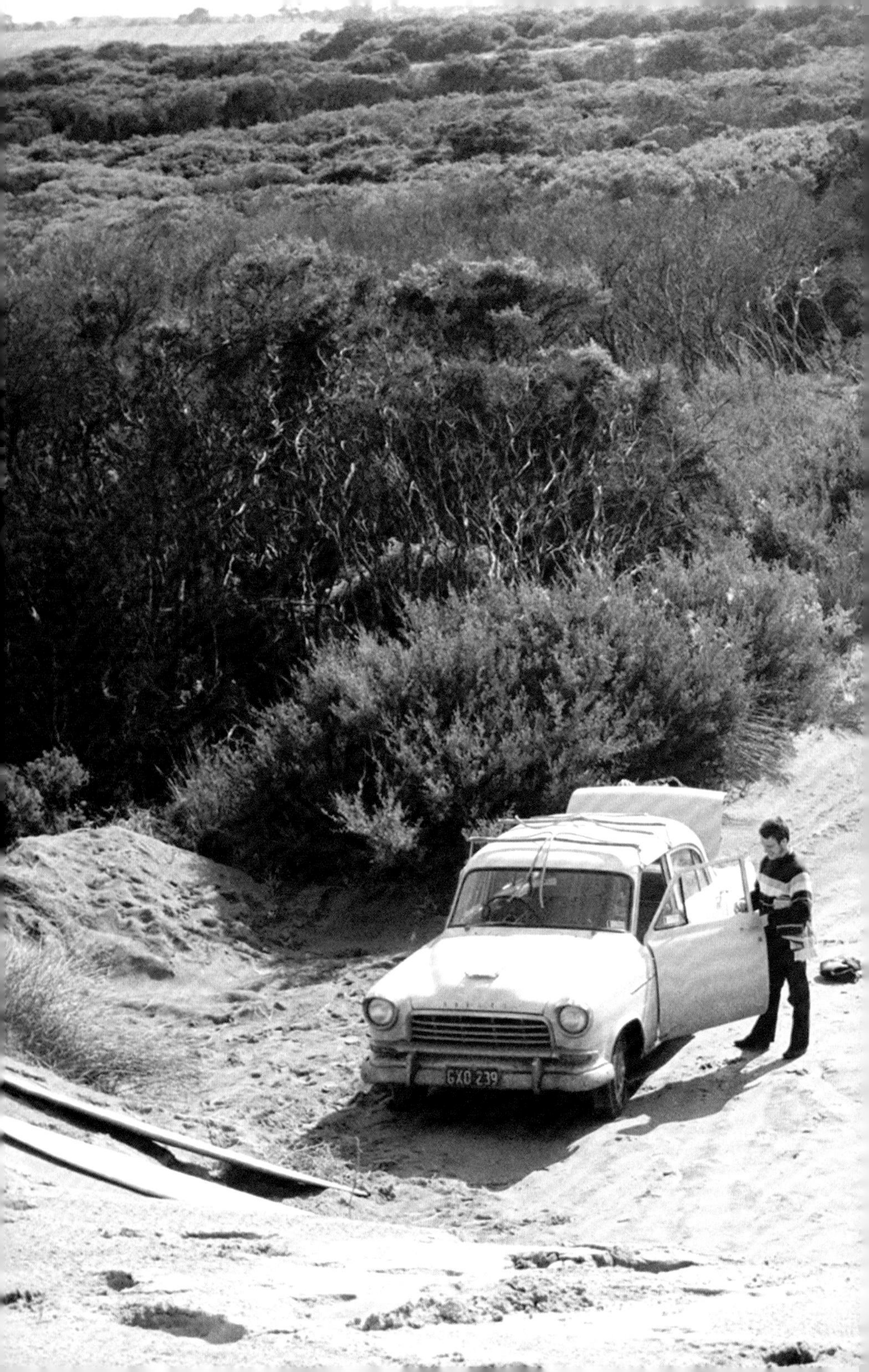

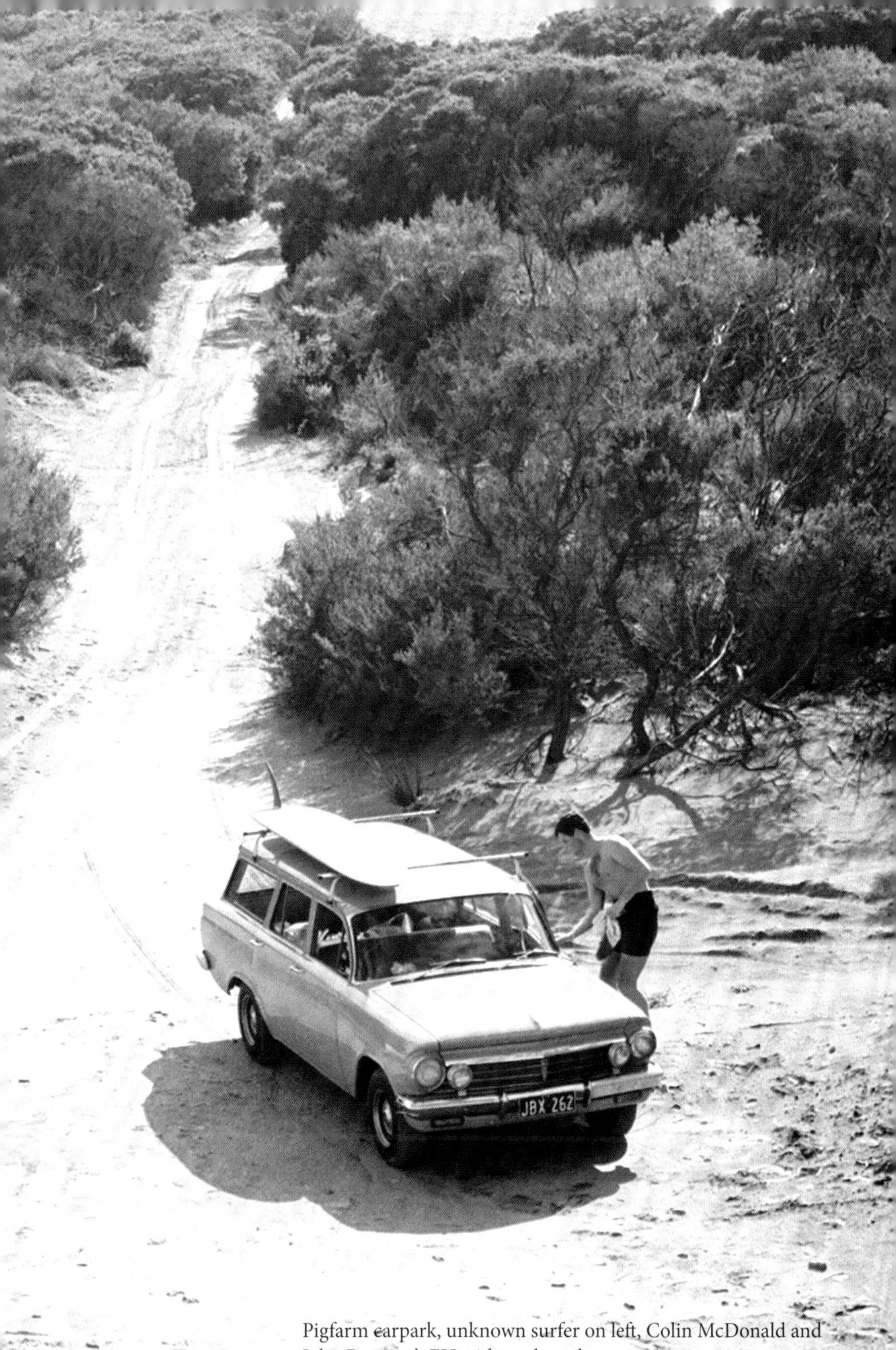

Pigfarm carpark, unknown surfer on left, Colin McDonald and John Panozzo's EH with my board on top. August 1967. **BS**

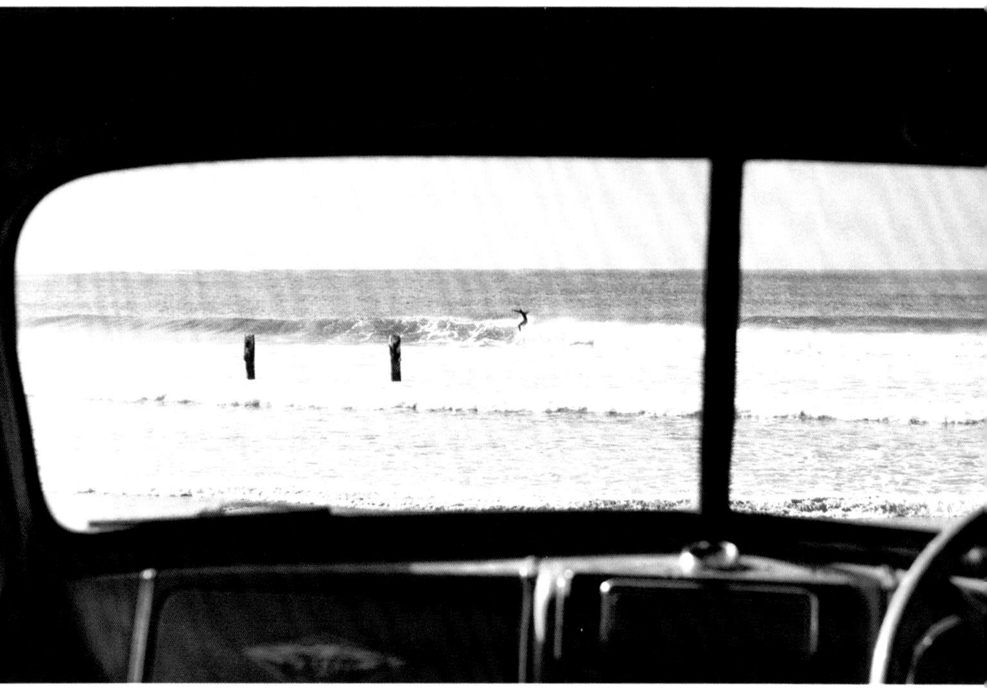

Billy Dews surfing at Woolgoolga, NSW, 1966. The pylons are the remains of the old jetty. **BW**

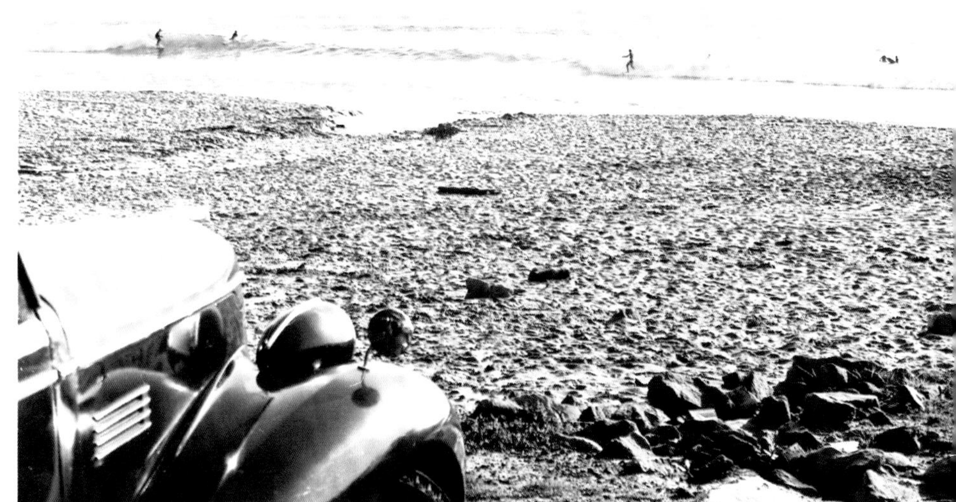

An isolated beach scene. **JP**

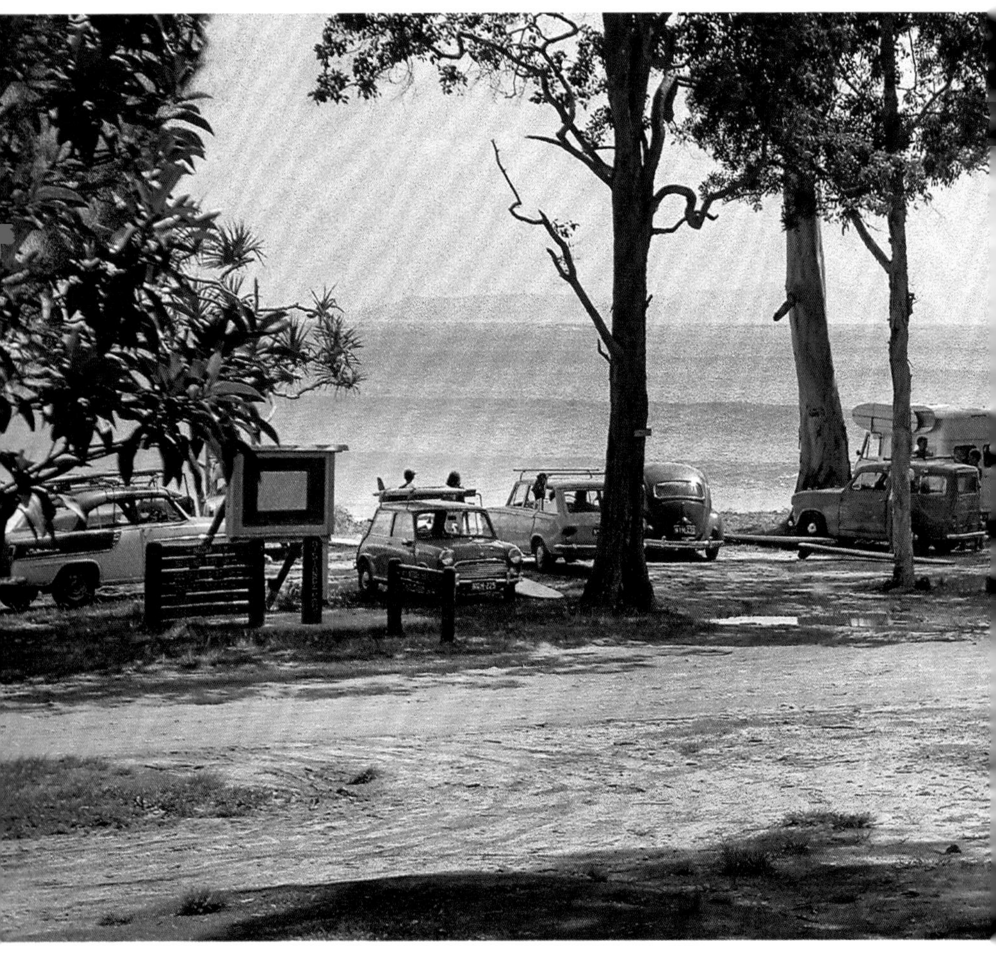

Noosa National Park, 1964. In the early '60s Noosa was a sleepy holiday village usually only frequented by people from Gympie and Brisbane during Christmas and school holiday periods until it was discovered by surfers. I first surfed Noosa in 1961 usually alone or with one other surfer. Photographs that I took then and in following years didn't in my opinion capture the feel of the era as they were mostly of the line-up or surfers on waves. This photo

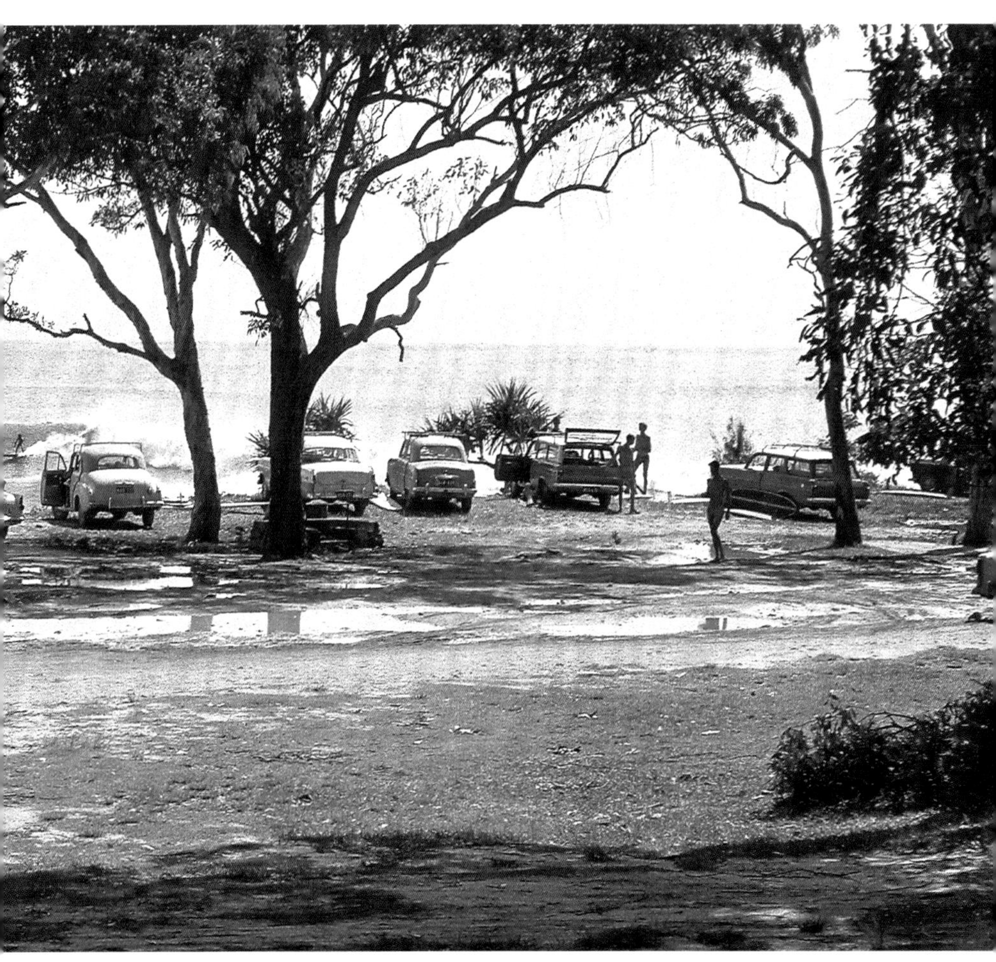

taken in March 1964 shows National Park at its unrestricted best, good surf, random parking and the general laid back feeling of the area. National Park wasn't locked at night and you could camp overnight in your car or on the ground without fear of the Ranger moving you on. The van with board racks on the side in the centre of the photo was owned by Sunshine Coast characters Ma and Pa Bendall. **MS**

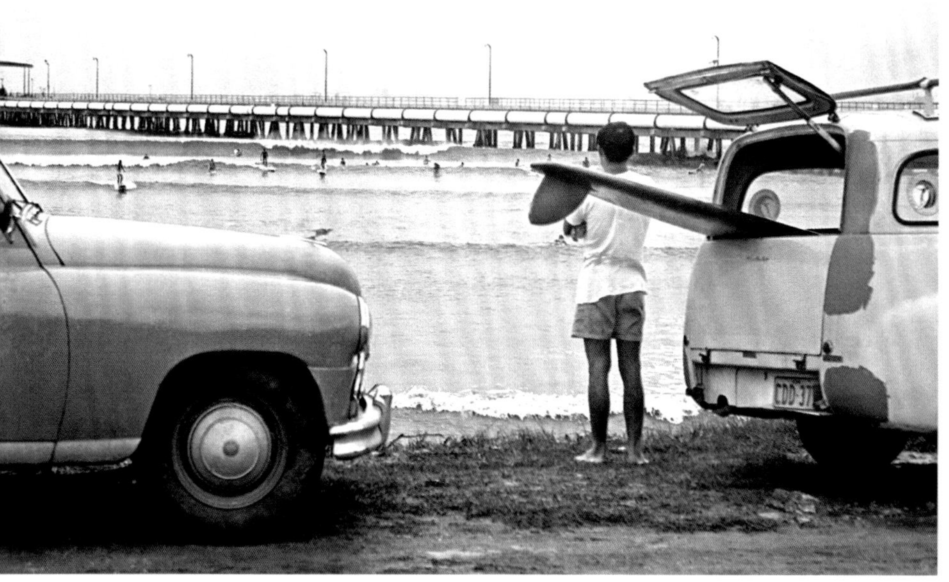

Kurnell, 1964. This was the only place we could ride a few waves when the surf was too big and dangerous on the beaches. **BW**

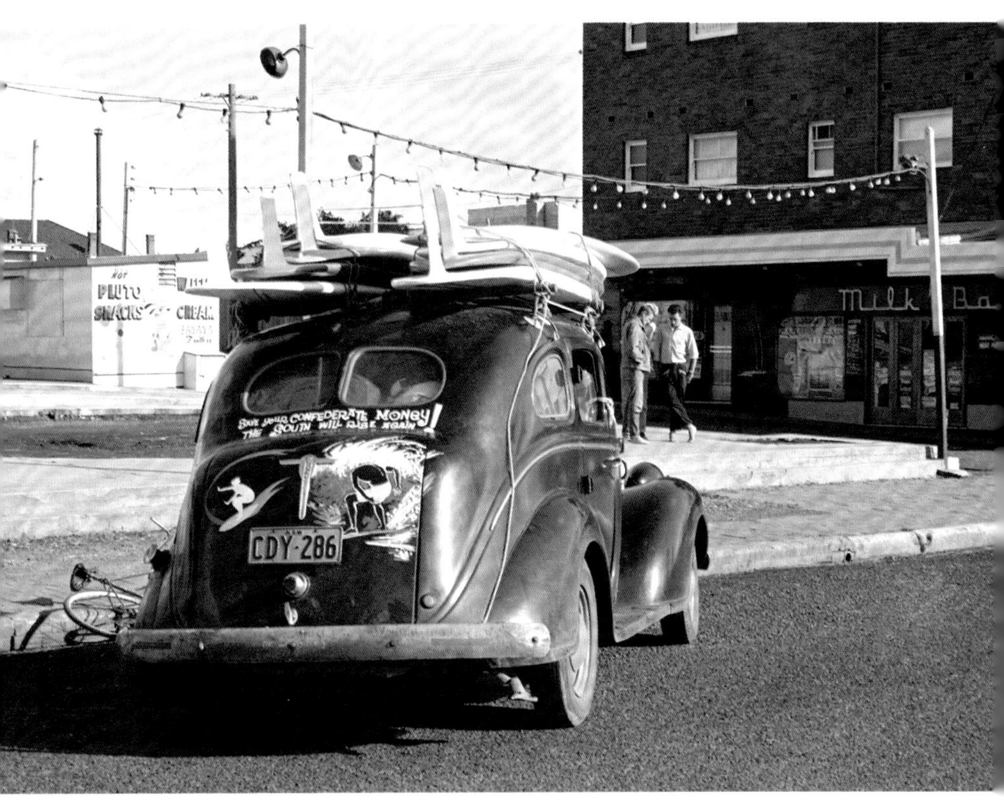

A DeSoto 'surfmobile', Cronulla, 1962. The artwork on the back of the car was painted by 'Nikko', one of the DeSoto Crew. **BW**

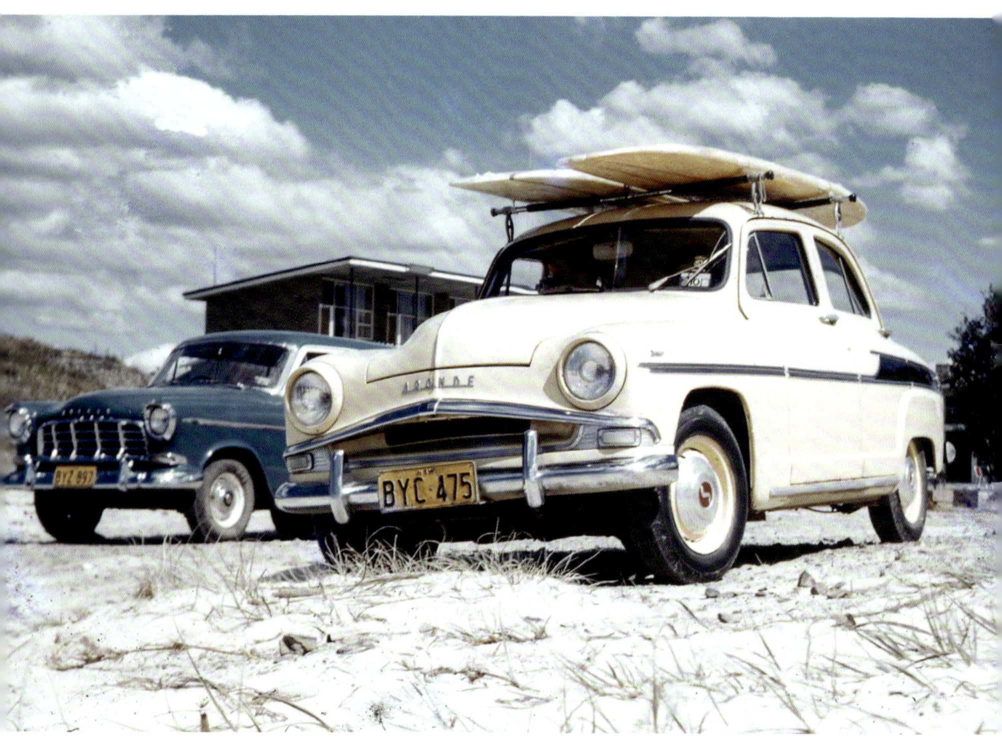

Cabarita, 1961. When you could drive onto the beach on the unmade road. The original Cabarita Hotel, the site of a few wild nights, is in the background. **MS**

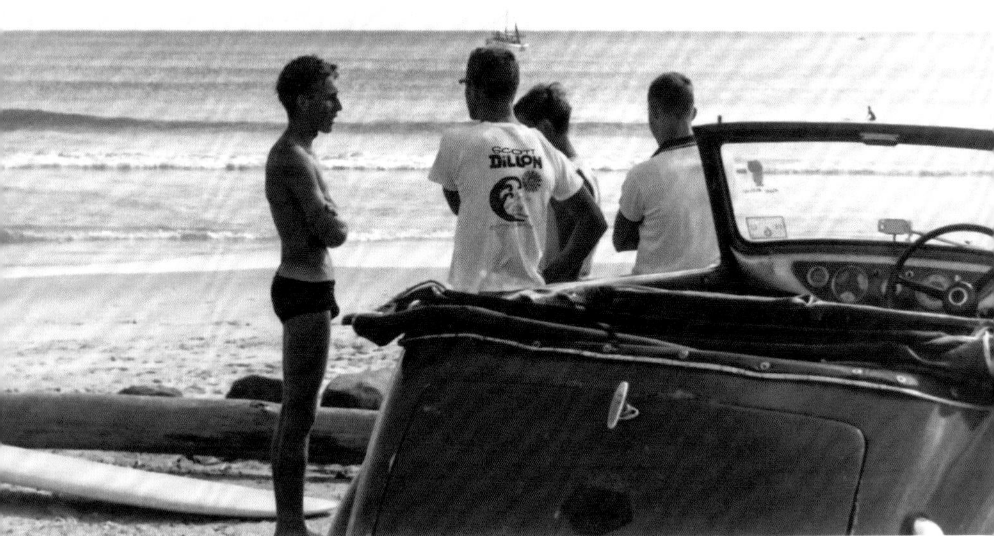

Kirra, 1961. Shoulda been here yesterday. Peter Barrett, 'Horrie' Budd, Ron Wort discuss how good the surf was yesterday. **MS**

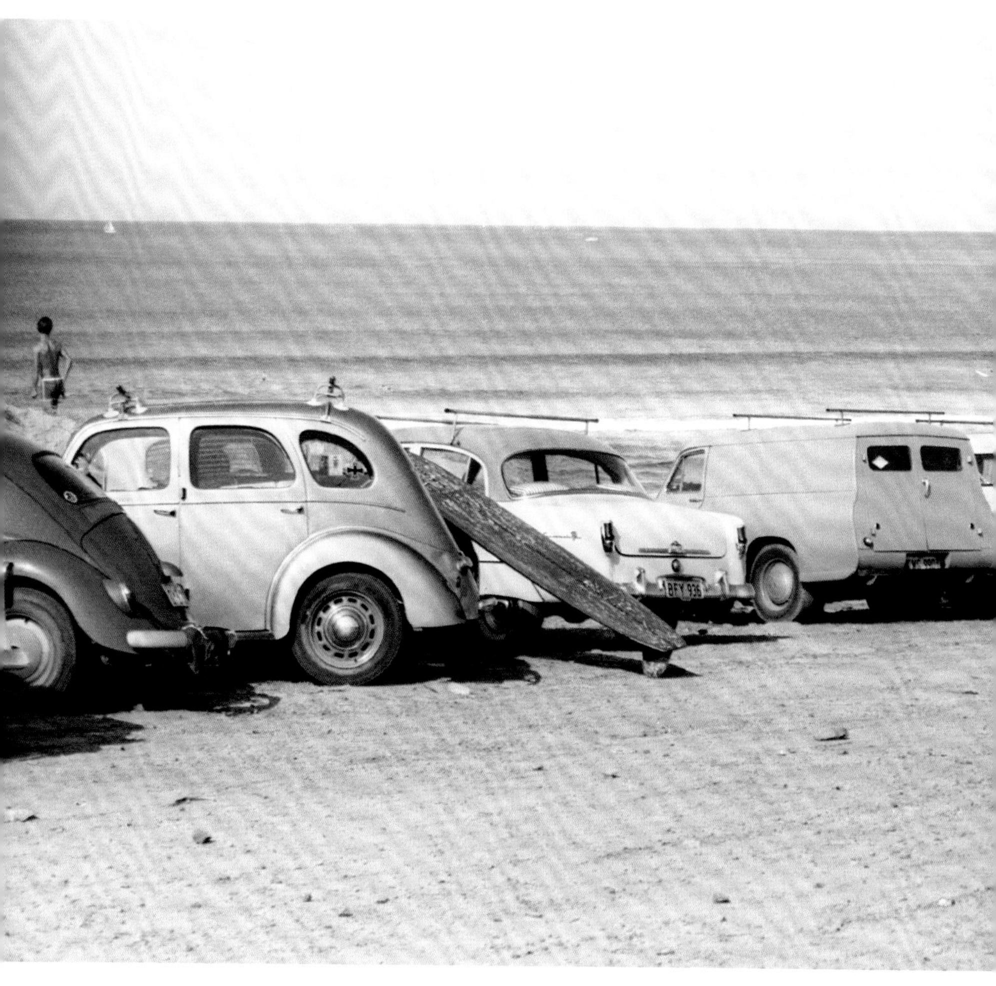

The crowded carpark at Wanda, 1962. **BW**

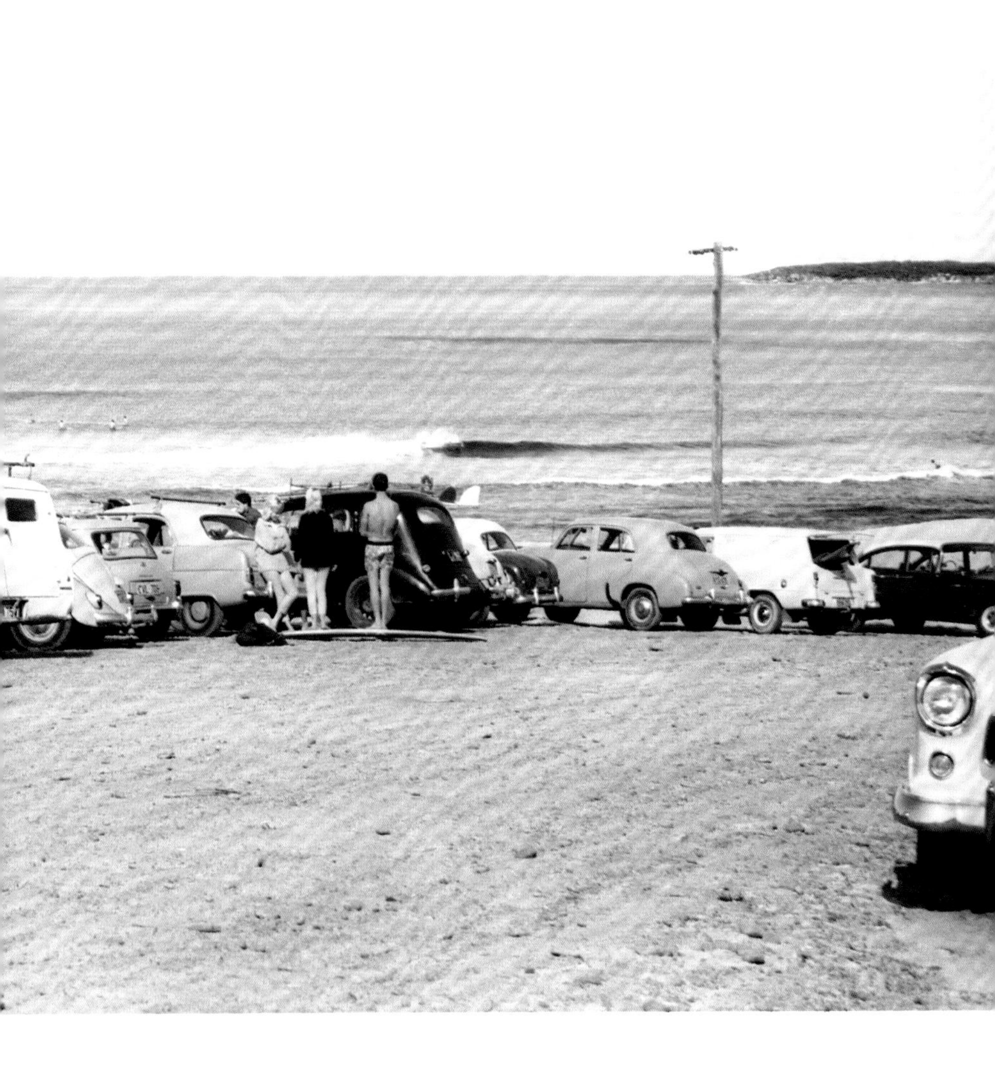

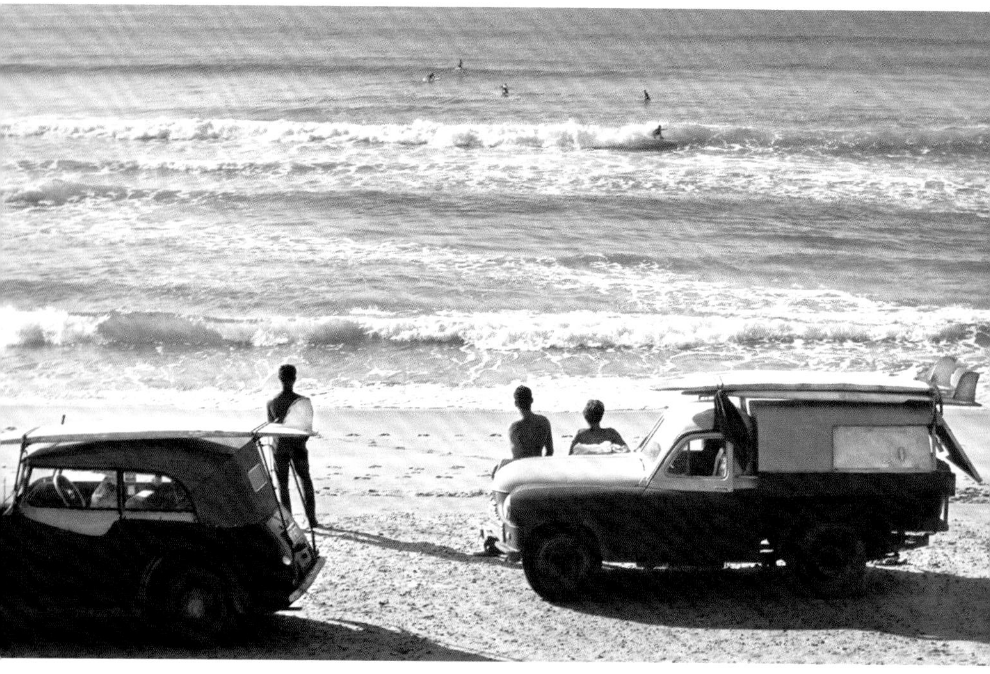

Red House surf break, 1962. The cars are parked on the top of the wall. **BW**

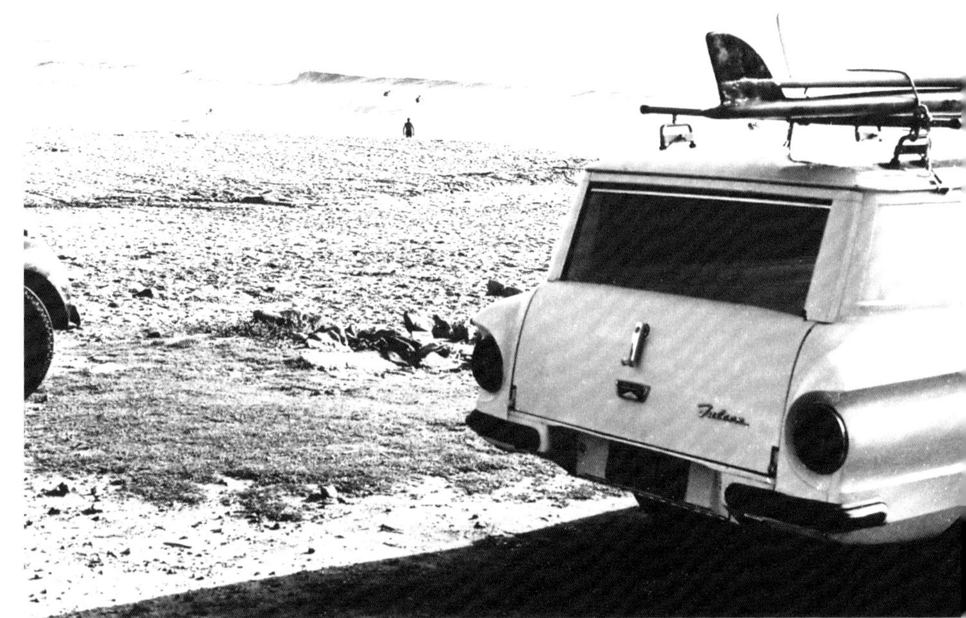

1965. The iconic XP Falcon on the beach. **JP**

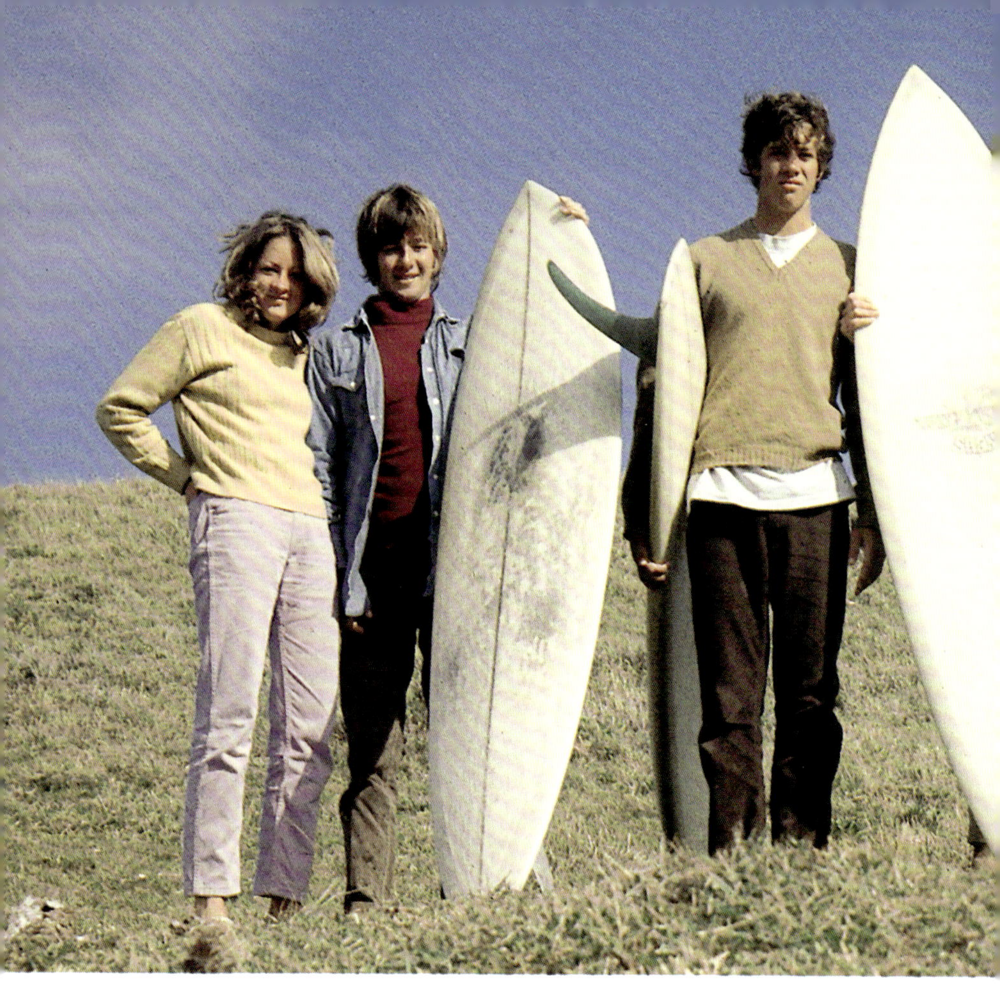

The Shortboard Revolution

Australian surfing came onto the map in the early 1960s largely thanks to the classic surfing of Midget Farrelly, who took his Australian style to the world, garnering respect in Hawaii alongside his Australian peers, including big wave pioneers Bob Pike and Dave Jackman. Midget became the first World Surfing Champion in 1964 at Manly Beach, Australia and he will always be remembered as a fine surfer, surfboard shaper and ambassador of Australian surfing.

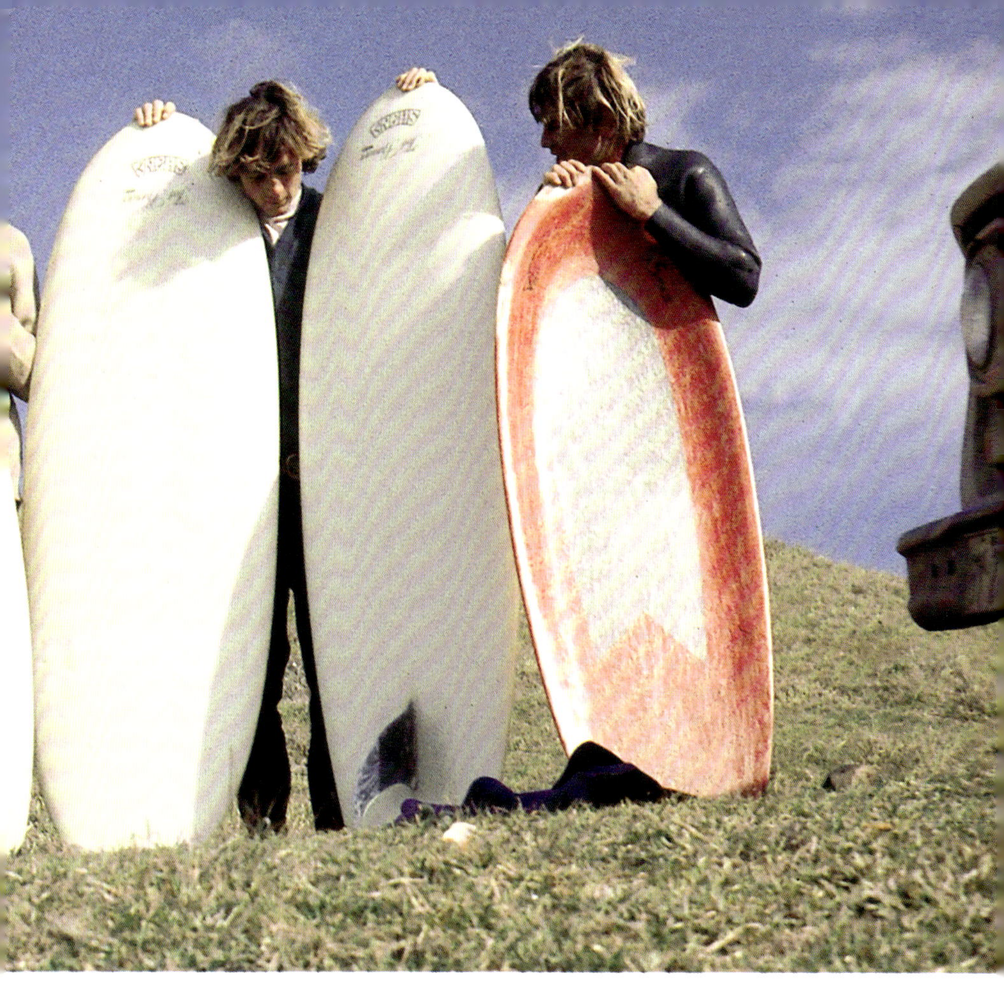

Gary and Terry Keyes, Paul Witzig (centre), Ted Spencer
and George Greenough, 1969. **CHRIS BROCK**

Thanks to Midget Farrelly's lead, and some clever promotion by the late Bob
Evans, Australian surfing quickly became the talking point of surfers all over the
world; they wanted to visit Australia to surf the perfect waves.

Inventor George Greenough, born in America in 1941, spent considerable
time in Australia in the 1960s. In 1965 he arrived in Australia with a kneeboard/
surfboard that was under 5 feet in length, complete with a dorsal fin. At this

time the 'best' surfers in the world were riding heavy 9'6" longboards complete with a cumbersome 'D' fin. The way Greenough surfed the waves was completely different to anyone else in the water. He chose to look for the tube on his short, high-performance surfboards and this was a completely new approach to surfing. For everyone who was privileged enough to be in the sphere of George Greenough, it changed their mindset entirely and a revolution happened in the world of surfing.

By 1966 the new style of surfing was about to hit the world and the roots of the change came from Australia through the innovations of George Greenough and, later, the competitive surfing of Nat Young (colloquially known as 'The Animal'.) Nat Young, with the assistance of a dorsal fin from George Greenough and the surfing inspiration of Midget Farrelly, Peter Drouyn, Bob McTavish, Ted Spencer, Keith Paull and other Australian maestros, went to America and won The World Surfing Championships in San Diego.

Significantly, Nat Young was riding a surfboard (he shaped himself) with an entirely different fin to every other competitor in the contest; a fin that enabled the surfer to do more radical turns. Just as important, Nat's board was much thinner and lighter than those ridden by the other competitors. Australia was further magnified on the world surfing map that was previously dominated by California and Hawaii. Change was in the air and it was set to amplify in coming years, thanks to the surfboard innovations of a number of notable Australian surfers and surfboard shapers.

Surfers discarded their 9'6" longboards and switched to short boards, virtually overnight. Surfboard designer Bob McTavish was spending a lot of time with George Greenough during this time and, coupled with McTavish's curious mind and experimental nature, it wouldn't be long until Bob McTavish would have a shorter board that (in his own words) 'enabled us to draw lines similar to Greenough.'

While Australian surfing was a furnace of board design change in the late 1960s, a similar thing was happening in Hawaii under the guide of Dick Brewer, Ben Aipa, Bill Fury and other notable Hawaiian surfboard designers. By 1967 the world at large was starting to experiment with shorter surfboards but the way surfers perceived the wave was totally changing too.

For many years a good ride had been undertaken on a hollow plywood board with no fin, with the surfer often riding the wave straight to shore in the whitewater. With the invention and introduction of the fin/skeg, in Australia, surfers had started to navigate the face of the wave, albeit cautiously, but it wasn't long until Australian surfers threw caution to the wind and started to push their surfing skills to new heights, ushering in a new era of what has now become known as 'power surfing'. Nat Young, Bob McTavish, Wayne Lynch and Peter Drouyn were among the more well-known Australia surfers who associated with this transitional phase. Some people say Wayne Lynch was the prodigy who, all by himself, ushered in a whole new way of surfing. Other historians look back to Hawaii and the surfing of Ben Aipa and the surfboard

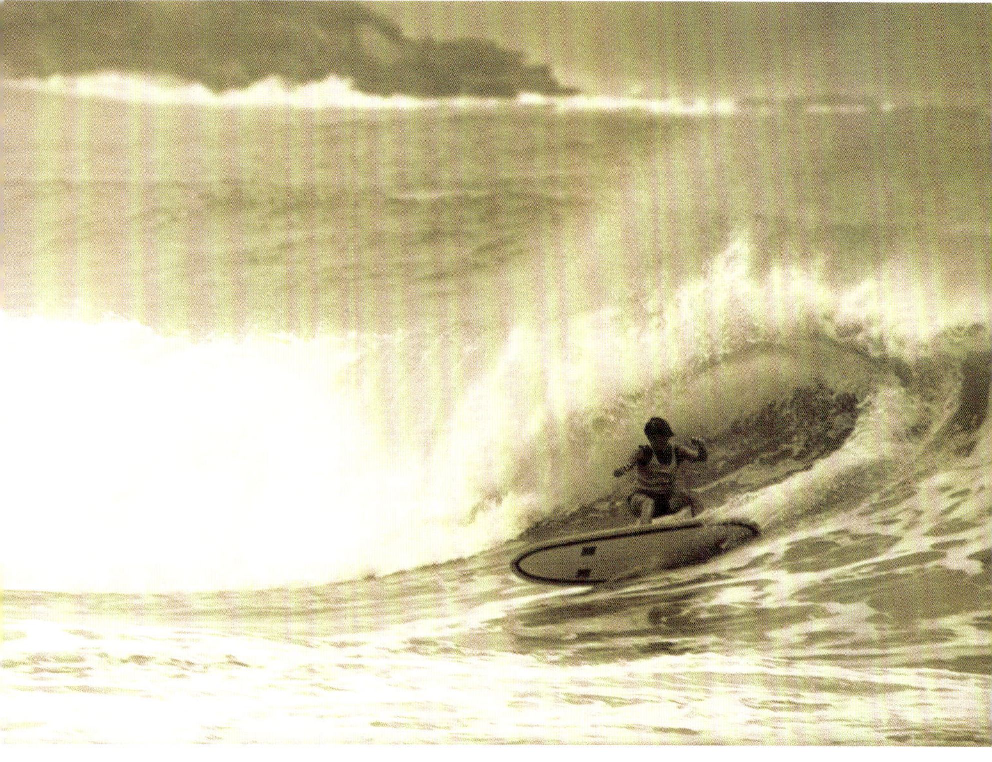

Palm Beach, 1968 Australian Titles. The iconic cutback photo of Wayne Lynch that was used as the cover of the '60s surf film *Evolution*. Wayne burst onto the surfing scene and introduced a radical new approach to surfing that saw surfing go from jazz to Rock 'n' Roll. The surfboard was 7'10". **JP**

designs of Dick Brewer. What came first, the chicken or the egg? The jury is still out, but the fact is that surfing changed in the late 1960s and getting the surfer into the tube was perhaps the biggest innovation in surfing history.

By the winter of 1968, shortboards were the norm and the innovations in surfboard design at this time, and for the next decade, were more prolific than any other era in surfing, before or since. Readers will also note that there are no legropes in any of the photographs. This is because the legrope was not invented until years later. Surfers in the 1960s had to be strong swimmers and surf the wave with flow and harmony. Falling off often had the serious consequence of losing your surfboard onto the rocks and then needing to repair it.

Talking to some of the surfers who were there during the radical transformation in surfboard design you get the feeling that there were a lot of people pushing for change and eventually getting it.

"The kids that I knew and I saw. You think of Michael (Peterson) and Peter Townend. Their brains were whizzing around and every time I saw them, every day they were saying 'we gotta try this'. It was like every day they had a different board. They just kept experimenting for themselves and eventually they got a good board for everyone. They would come in to the factory and go straight to the shaping bay with some new idea."

Joe Larkin, surfboard building pioneer

Michael Peterson (1952–2012) took surfing to new heights and he did it riding surfboards that he handshaped himself. **DICK HOOLE**

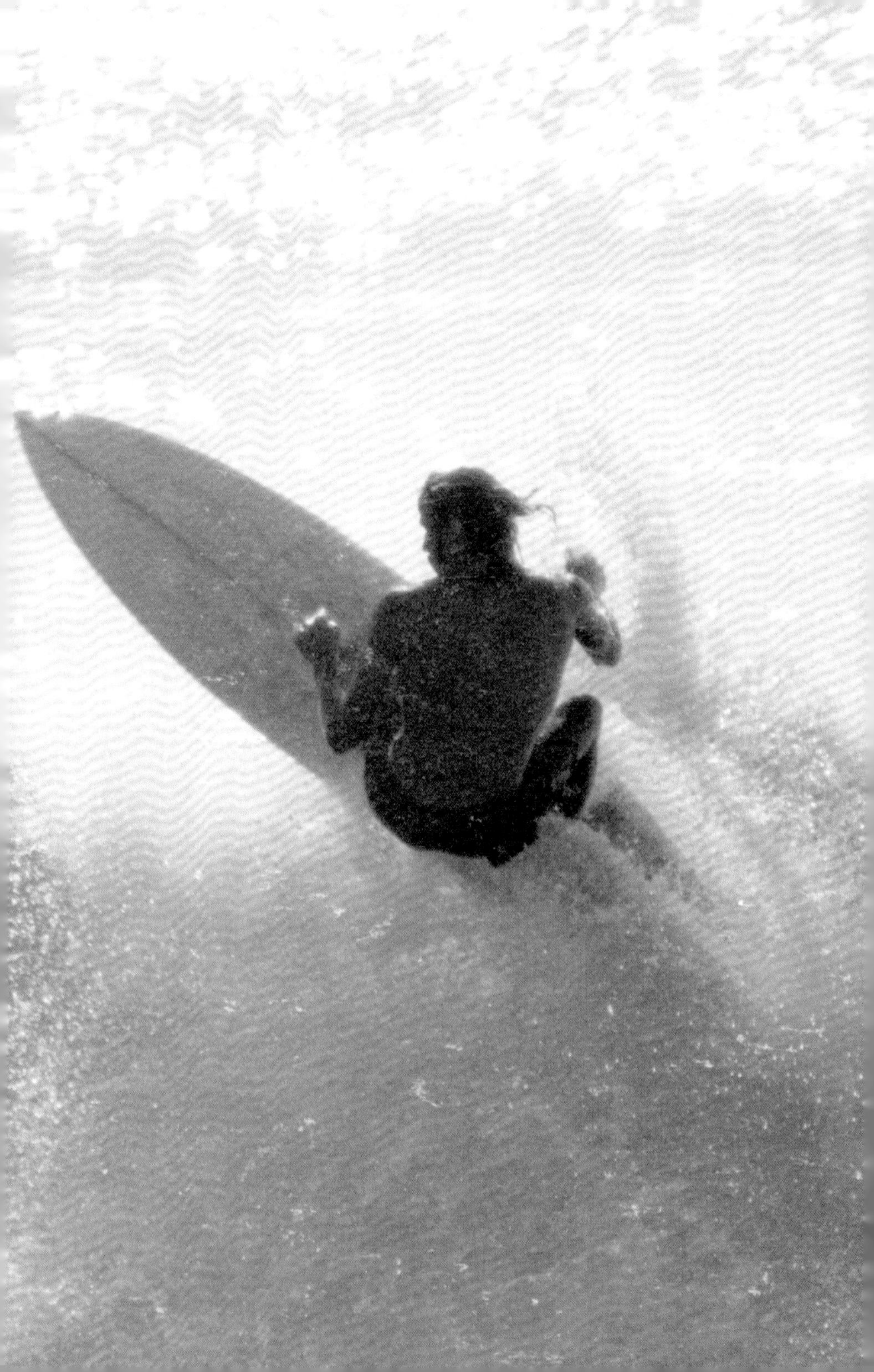

"There is no question that Bob McTavish was inspirational and at a point around the 'Plastic Machine' really did do something that made us all think. After that moment there was quite a few people who picked up and evolved design and surfing beyond Bob McTavish."

Wayne Lynch

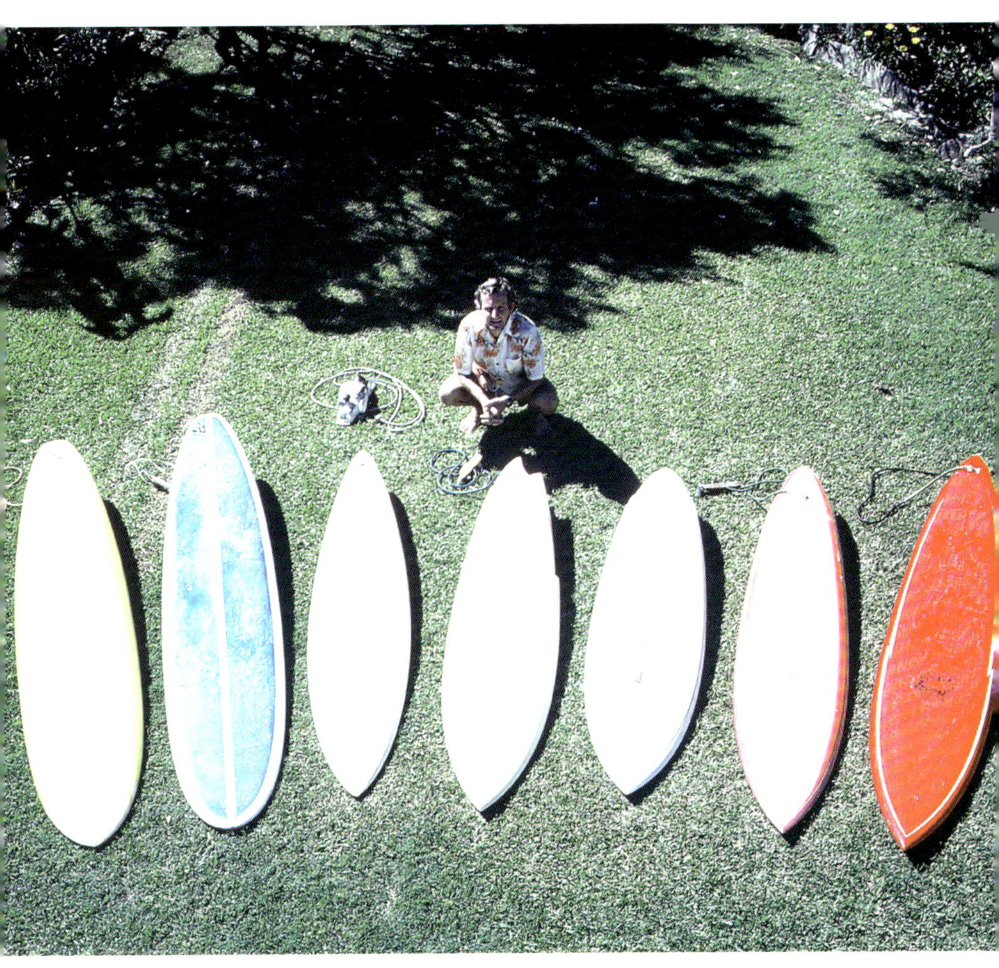

Always innovating, Bob McTavish quiver. **PETER GREEN**

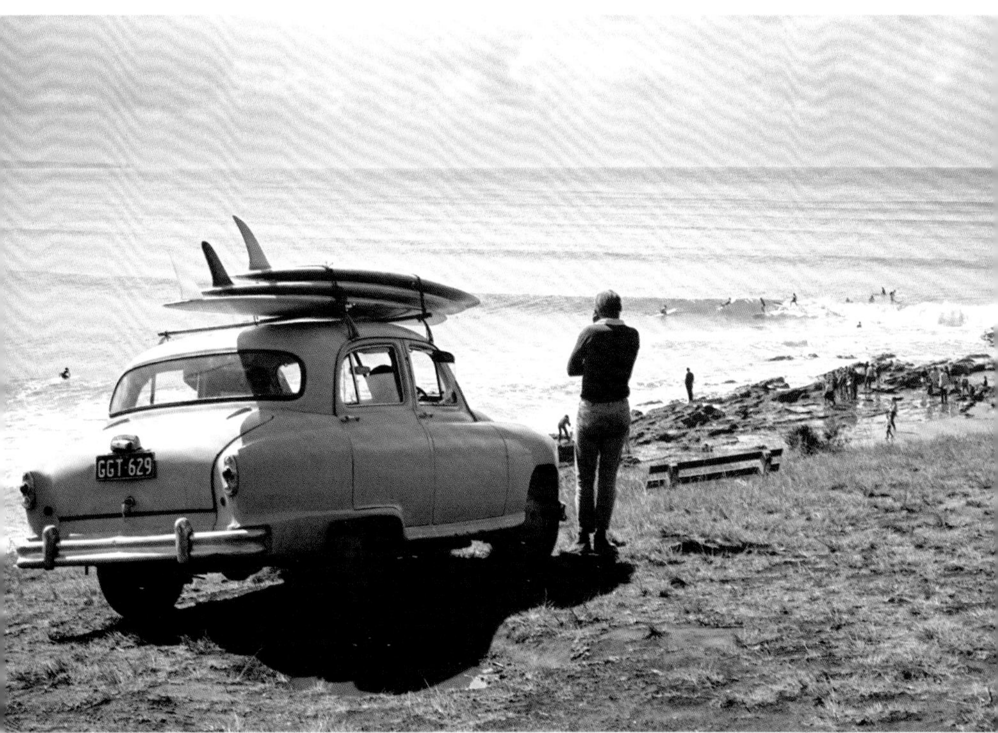

First shortboard – snapped it at Winky Pop

I've often been told this photo (taken at the 1967 Australian Titles) captures the transition from Malibus to the first short boards. The single fin boards (about 8' or slightly longer) on Rod Brooks' Vanguard with Peter Troy standing guard were a dramatic change. I had come down from a 9' Malibu the previous year after I'd seen Peter Drouyn surfing Currumbin. Madeleine and I had taken a holiday to the Gold Coast in July.

One day we drove to Currumbin to visit the sanctuary, like all good tourists did at the time, and then to the beach to surf and relax in the sunshine. As I paddled out to the take-off zone on my trusty 9' Malibu, Peter Drouyn was ripping the waves apart. I watched him coming down the line with speed and intensity that I'd never seen before. His surfing impacted on me so much, that mentally, the longboard was obsolete. I just couldn't ride it anymore and struggled for the remainder of our holiday. I felt so embarrassed each time I paddled out.

When we returned home, I went to see Fred Pyke in Torquay with some notes that I had scribbled together on the Currumbin experience. I had no idea of the actual dimensions and shape of Peter's board, other than, 'Fred it was much shorter and thinner than my Mal'. I left it with Fred and within a week he'd made me a radically different board. It was a nice blue with a black single fin. I couldn't wait to try it out. The first time I put it in the water and attempted to knee paddle was a disaster. I quickly discovered I had to lie on it to gain stability and paddle an entirely different way. With a few 'pit stops' for rests I finally made it to the Bowl take-off zone. Then the fun began! I kept missing waves until I figured out I had to go deeper and take-off later. When I finally managed to get my first wave, take the drop and complete the bottom I turn I was, virtually, somewhat out of control. It took me several sessions to master that board, including a whole new set of shoulder muscles coming into play.

It was a favourite board in that transition out of longboards. Unfortunately I later snapped it at Winky Pop after clipping the reef on a hard bottom turn. Fred repaired it well enough for me to sell and move to the next level shorter board. It was in the 7' plus range and so another challenge began. That was my experience through to the 1970s when I switched to Midget Farrelly boards. Why? I found they suited my surfing and where I wanted to be. Midget's boards were beautiful. They had a look and feel that was different to the boards other shapers were making. There was much experimentation, most of which I didn't like or try. My Civil Engineering experience with fluid dynamics basically told me many of the radical designs simply wouldn't work. I left them alone preferring Midget's craftsmanship. His boards stood out with their curves, rocker and rail profiles. Perfect for down the line speed surfing at Bells and Winky Pop. **BS**

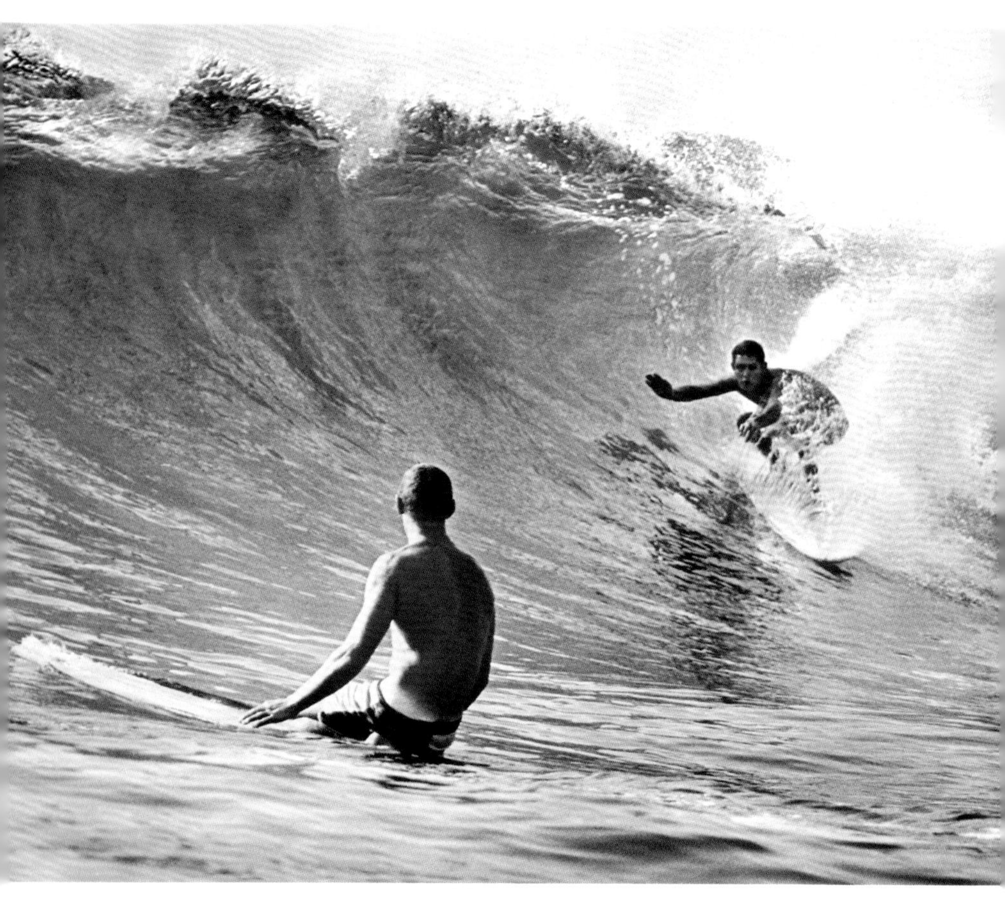

Ken 'Major' Williams watching Bill Penrue cruising down
the face of a smooth Cronulla Point Wave in 1964. **BW**

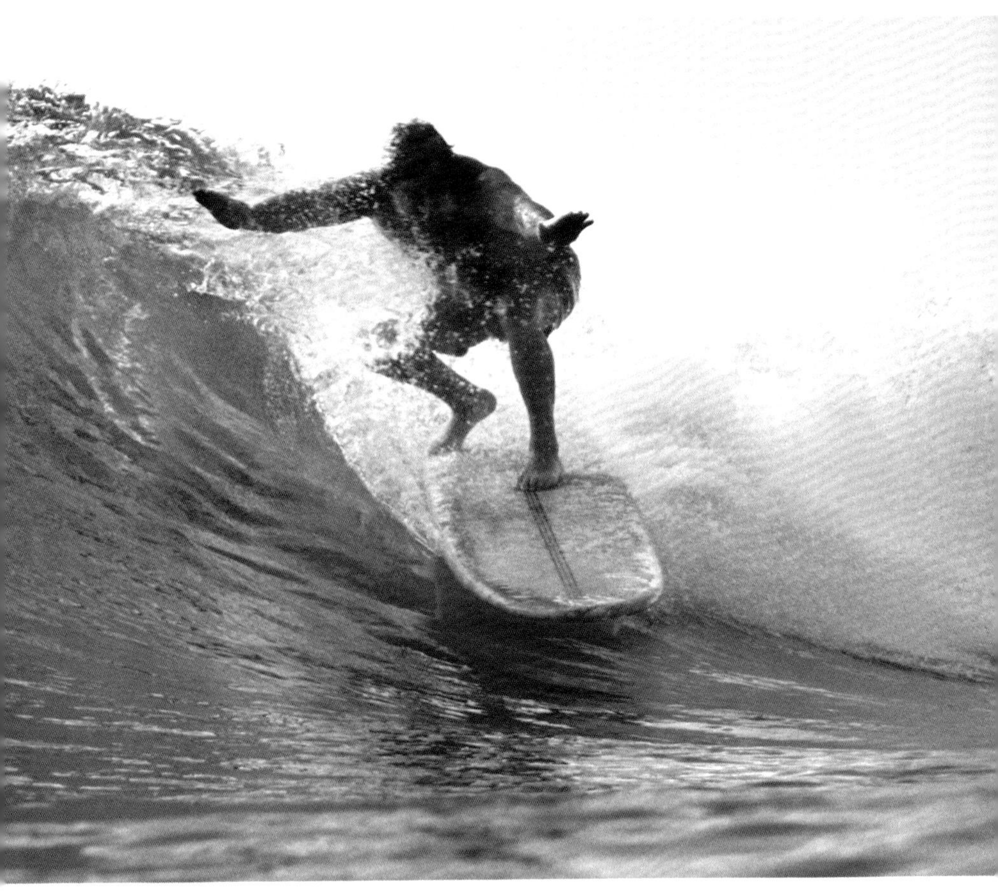

Brian Jackson kicking in with some fancy footwork at 'Sandshoes', 1964. **BW**

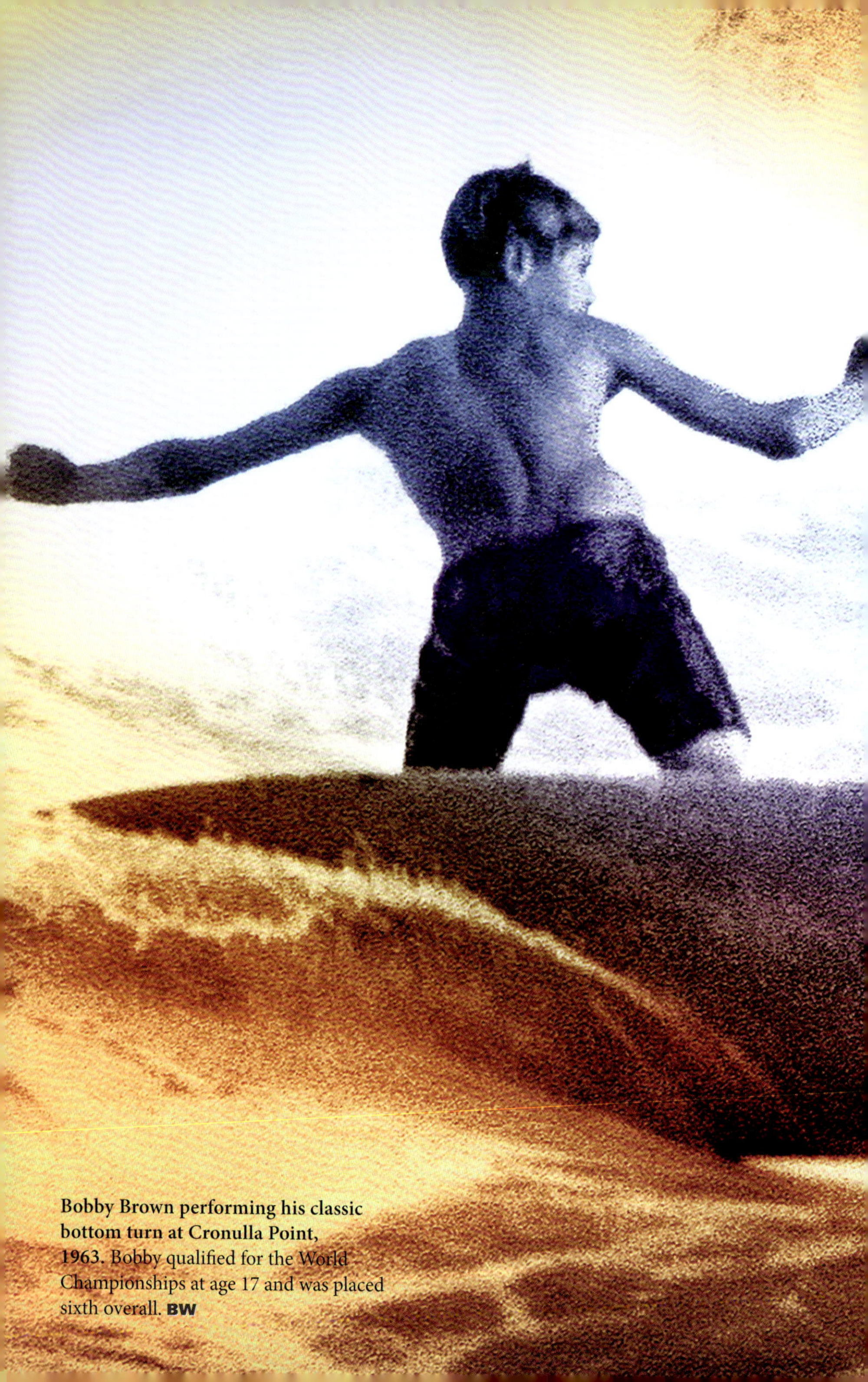

Bobby Brown performing his classic
bottom turn at Cronulla Point,
1963. Bobby qualified for the World
Championships at age 17 and was placed
sixth overall. **BW**

Pop Culture

The 1959 film *Gidget*, starring Sandra Dee as a surf-obsessed teenage girl who takes on the local boys at their own game, changed everything almost overnight. By promoting the surfing lifestyle on screen, it influenced a whole generation and surfing effectively boomed overnight. By the end of 1960, thousands of kids were flocking to the beach.

But then there was a huge American influence on Australia at the start of the Sixties … the music, the fashion, movies and on black and white TV. For an English-centric nation such as Australia, it was a huge culture shock to have waves of American influences hit our shores. 'It took off quite quickly on the beach,' remembers Mal Sutherland, 'and everyone started to dress like the "Yanks" – the jeans and hats, thongs and tennis shoes, and floral shirts and sunglasses.' There was a change in attitude as well … as far as being a conservative country, Australia embraced the brashness of the American teenage scene and the language that came with it.

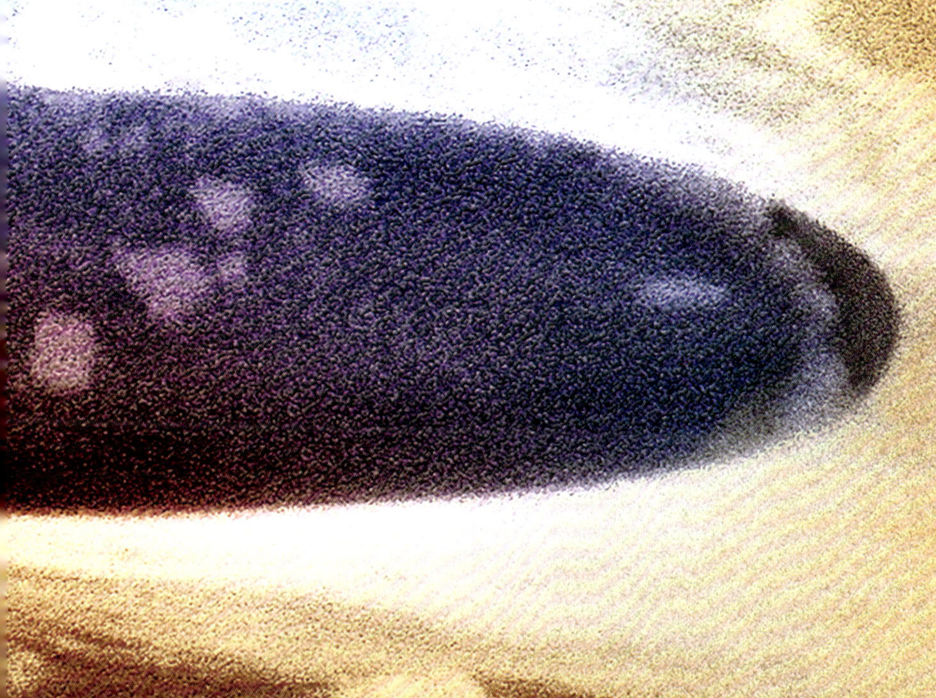

'Once we saw how the guys in the movies carried on the beach, we were quick to follow suite,' says Mal. 'It was a very rebellious era.' Then there was the music of course – rock and roll and then 'beach music' movement came and went. The Beach Boys and Jan & Dean started the surf music craze but it didn't last that long. They virtually went out overnight when The Beatles hit these shores in 1964.

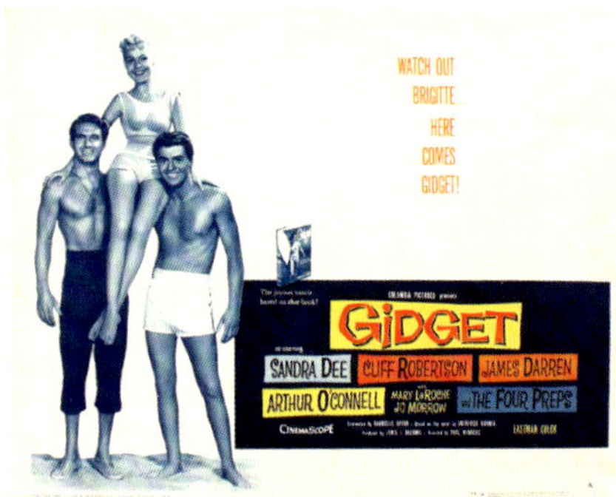

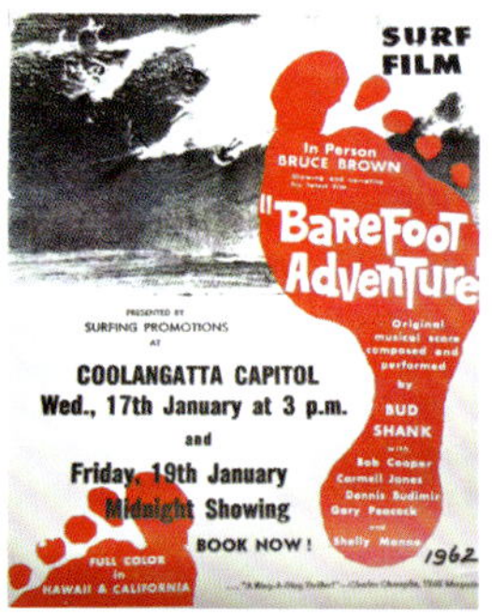

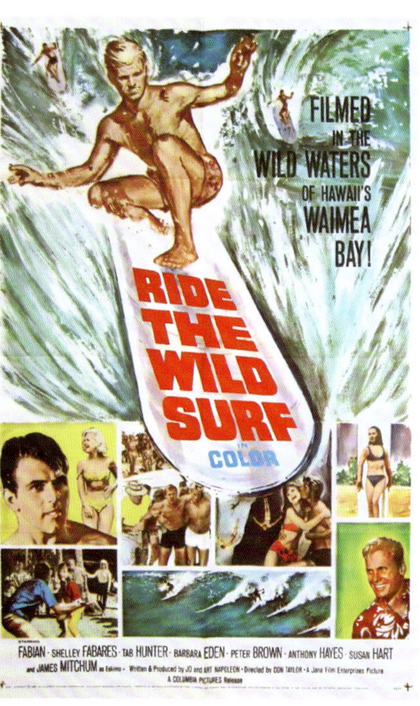

Above: **Gidget poster. The movie that started the craze.** *Gidget* (1959) brought Hollywood's version of the surfing lifestyle of the late 1950s to the big screen. Generally ridiculed by the surfers of the day, it had a huge and almost instantaneous impact on teenagers of the time. Suddenly, beaches were invaded by carloads of would be surfers with all manner of equipment strapped to the roof of their cars. Beaches that usually only had a few local board riders virtually overnight became crowded with novices, initially creating resentment among some of the local surfers.

Right: **Ride The Wild Surf, 1964.** Not as influential as *Gidget, Ride the Wild Surf* nevertheless had all the successful elements of a successful 'beach' movie of the era without the kitsch of the Beach Party movies. With authentic surfing action filmed by directors Art and Jo Napoleon at Hawaii's Waimea Bay, the film starred Fabian, Shelley Fabres, Tab Hunter and a pre-*I Dreamed of Jeannie* Barbara Eden. The film also featured a title song co-written by Beach Boy Brian Wilson and sung by Jan & Dean, and a cameo appearance by Australian Olympian Murray Rose playing – what else? – an Australian surfer.

The first *Surfer* magazine only had stills from the John Severson film *Surf Fever* (1960) and yet it sold 10,000 copies. Publishers quickly realised the popularity of surfing images and sought original photographs from the surfing fraternity. Not that every surfer became a photographer ... most were rank amateurs, in fact, but it was the birth of a new art form.

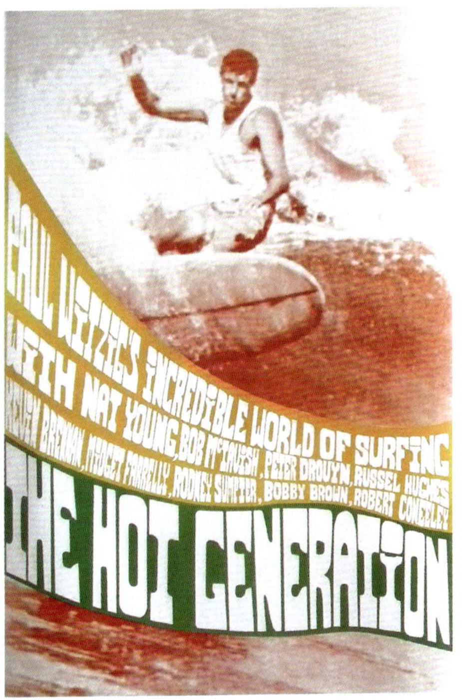

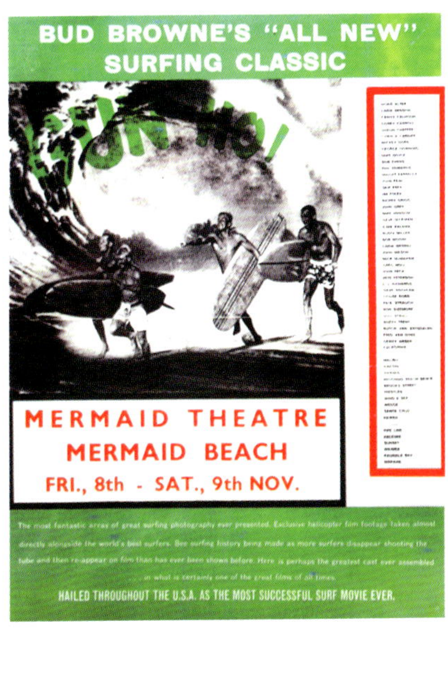

Surf movies. Queensland surfers had their first experience of movies dedicated solely to surfing in January of 1962 when Paul Witzig's Surfing Promotions introduced Bruce Brown's movies *Barefoot Adventure, Slippery When Wet* and *Surf Crazy* at the Capitol Theatre in Coolangatta and the Astor Theatre at New Farm in Brisbane.

The movies only had a musical sound track and after being introduced to the audience Bruce Brown sat on stage and personally narrated each show.

Response to the movies was amazing. In Coolangatta people queued up along Griffith Street for tickets. The theatre seated 1100 and people were turned away at every show with similar scenes in Brisbane.

Bruce had come to Australia with Phil Edwards to film sequences for his new movie to be titled *Surfing Hollow Days*, which eventually featured clips of Phil and Paul Witzig surfing at Wategos Beach, Byron Bay. **MS**

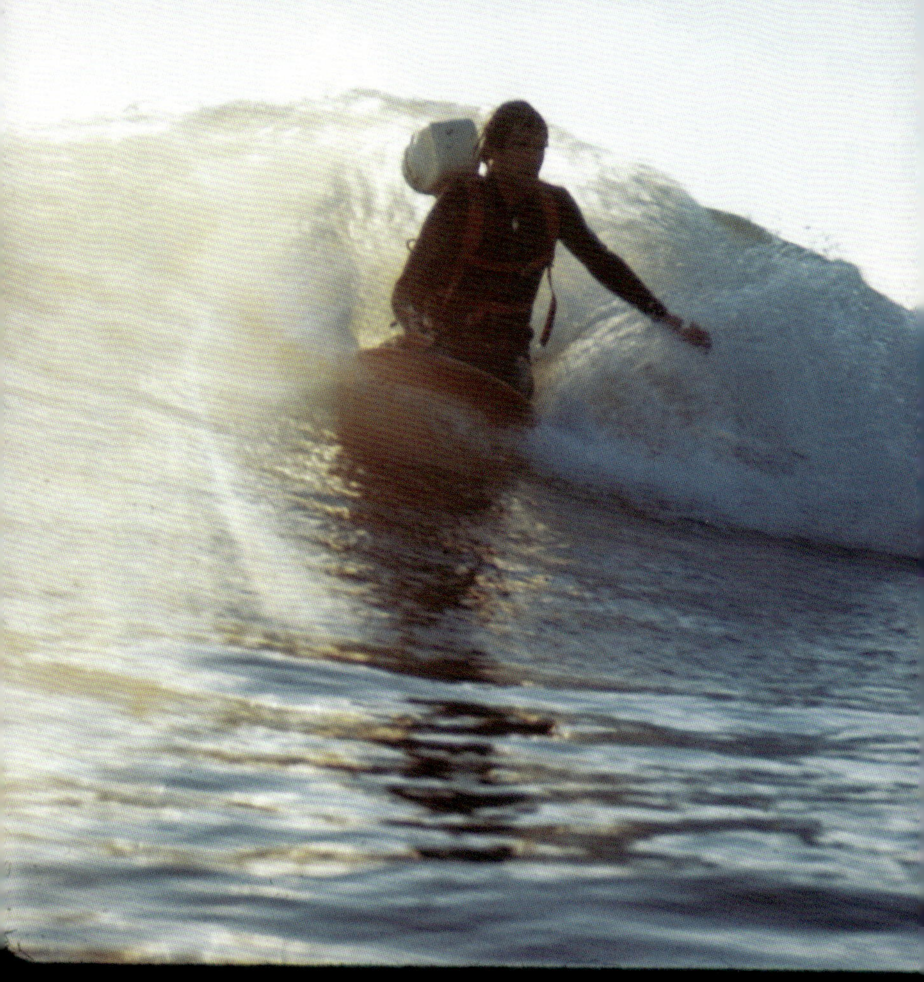

American surfer and cinematographer George Greenough (born 1941) was an innovative kneeboard surfer whose 'spoon' board measured 1.5m by .5m wide. On his 1967 trip to Australia, Greenough turned many people on to kneeboarding, the advantage being that it allowed the surfer to fit into smaller places inside the wave and gave the added sensation of being surrounded by the wave. This 1969 image shows his kneeboard and shoulder camera mould that enabled him to take photos insider the hollow of a wave (*next page*).

One of George Greenough's most significant contributions was the development of the shortboard fin. The theory behind Greenough's design was borrowed from his observations of schools of fish – he found that fibreglass fins had the ability to store energy and hold it for a ime before snapping back upright. The fins he developed for his surfboards enabled surfers to ain acceleration coming out of turns. **GEORGE GREENOUGH ARCHIVES**

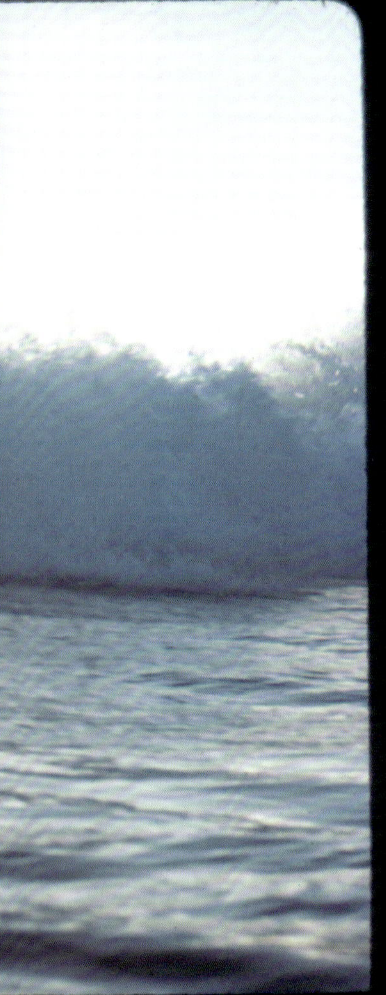

"*Obviously, [George] Greenough and the Australians come to mind, because they gave shortboards the initial launch. They were so smoking hot when they surfed those early shortboards, the rest of the world had to sit up and take notice.*"

Paul Gross, US-based air mattress builder

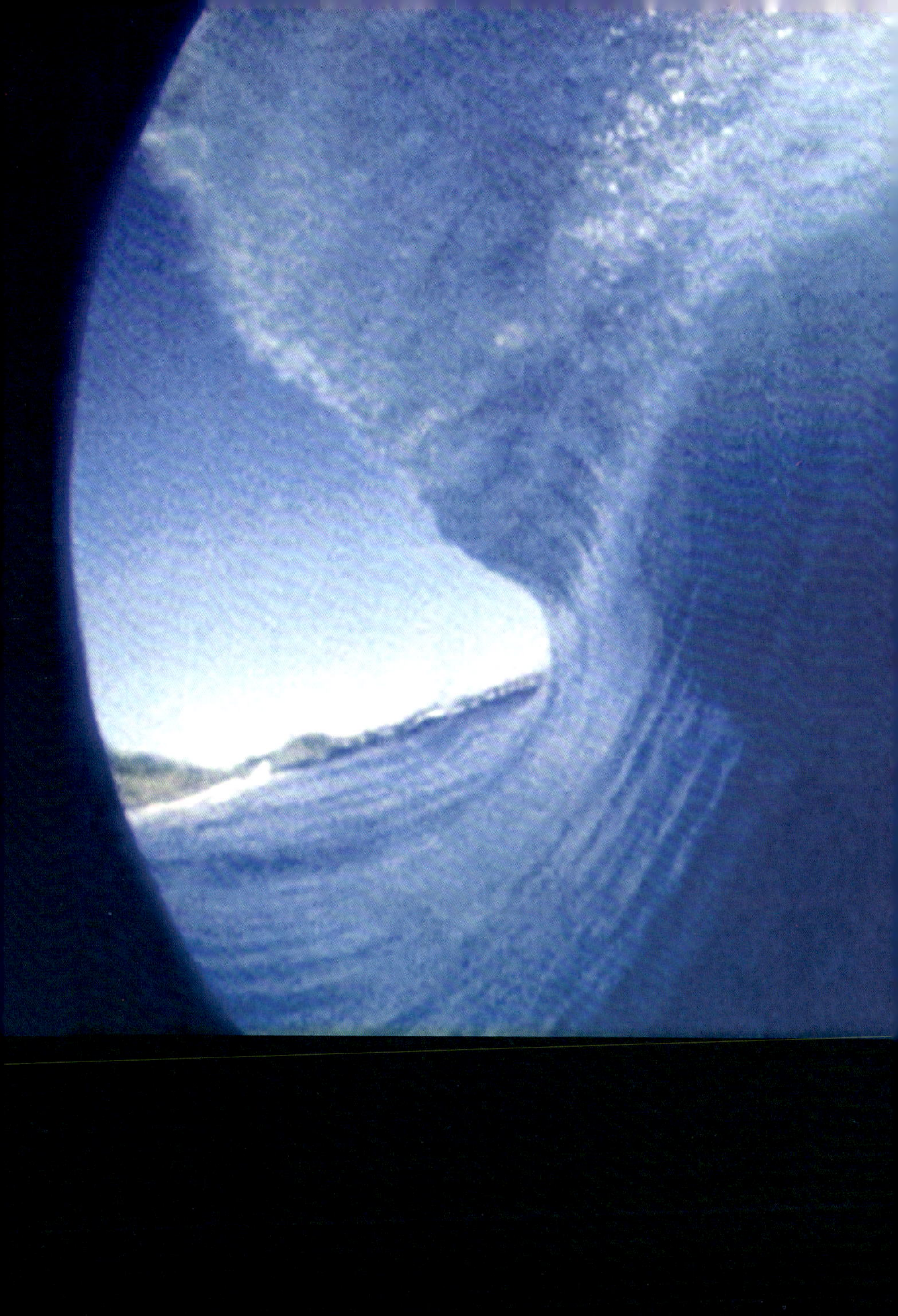

George Greenough's revolutionary in the tube footage. GEORGE GREENOUGH ARCHIVES

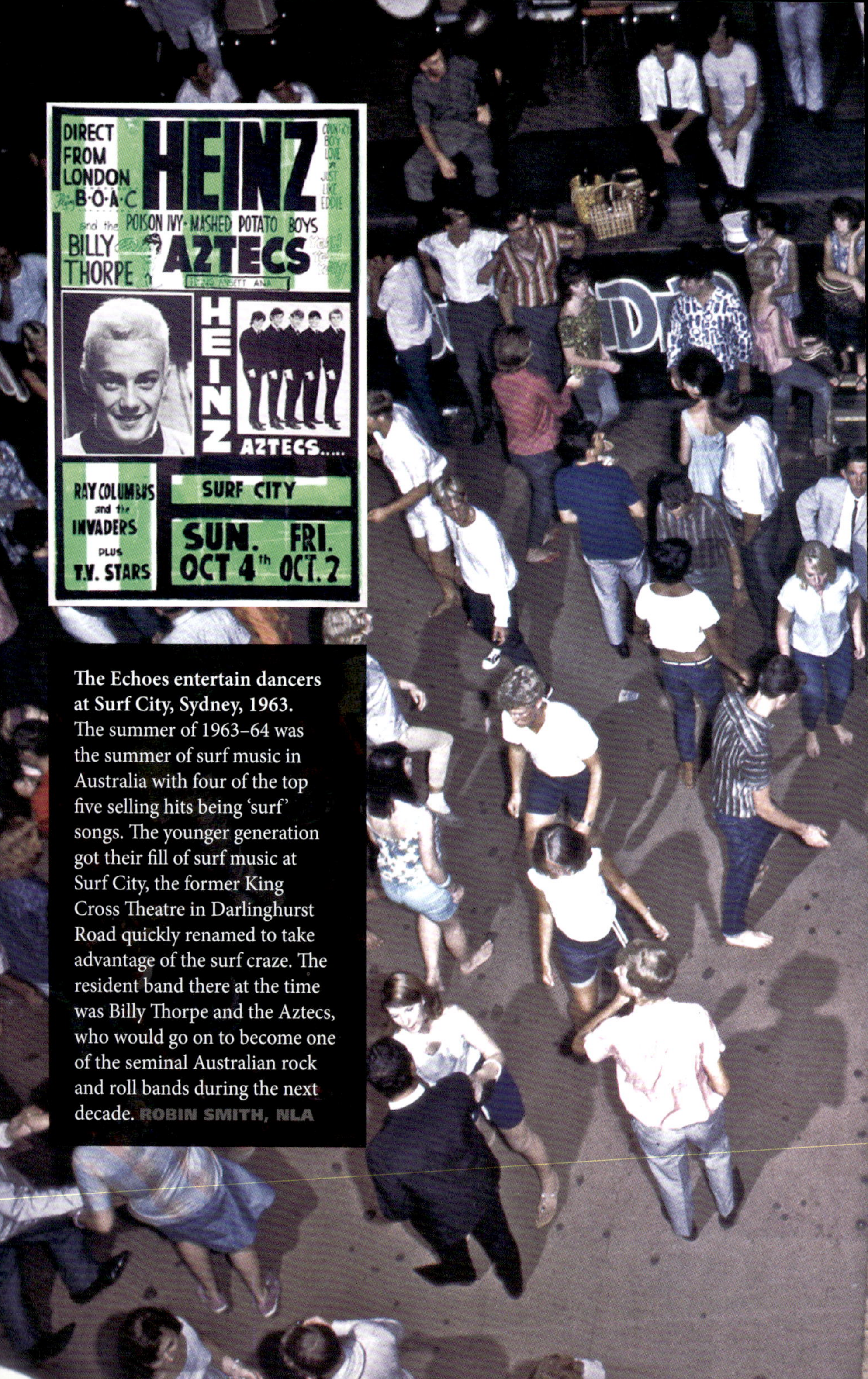

The Echoes entertain dancers at Surf City, Sydney, 1963. The summer of 1963–64 was the summer of surf music in Australia with four of the top five selling hits being 'surf' songs. The younger generation got their fill of surf music at Surf City, the former King Cross Theatre in Darlinghurst Road quickly renamed to take advantage of the surf craze. The resident band there at the time was Billy Thorpe and the Aztecs, who would go on to become one of the seminal Australian rock and roll bands during the next decade. ROBIN SMITH, NLA

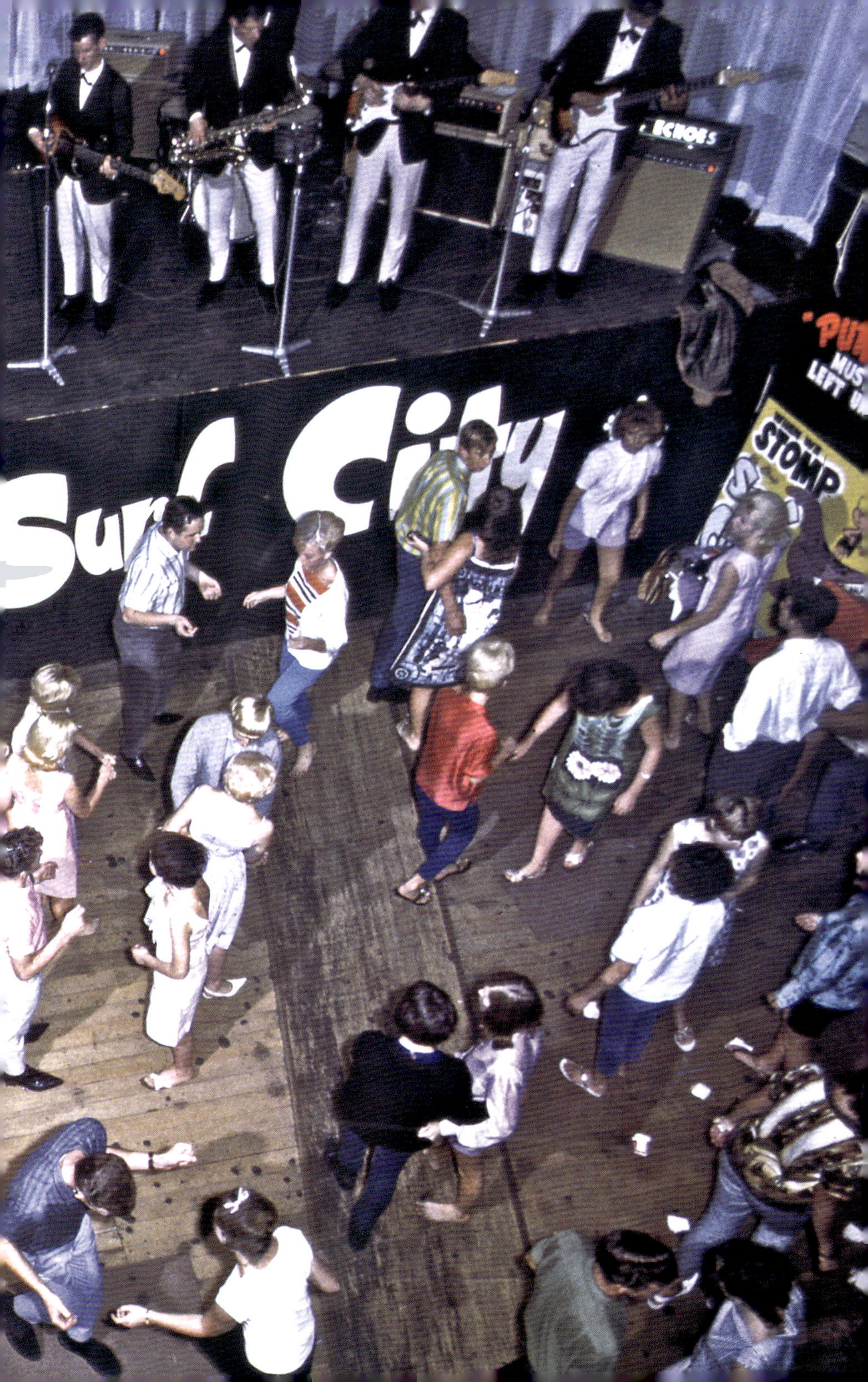

ECHOES
Surf City
STOMP
"PU
MUS
LEFT U

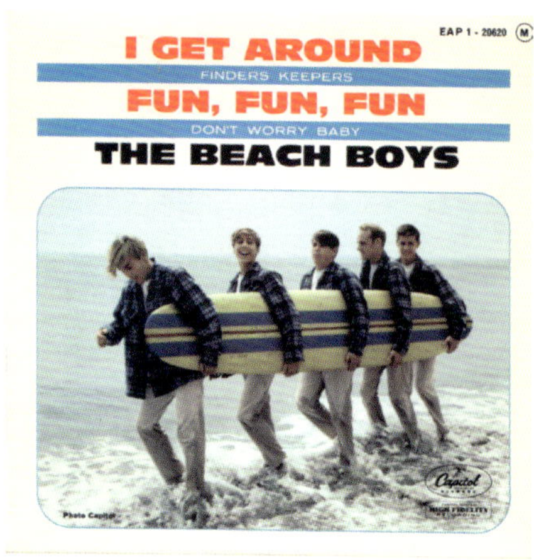

When surf music topped the charts, 1960–1962.

Left: The Beach Boys set the gold standard for beach music in the years immediately before the advent of The Beatles. Originally comprising brothers Brian, Carl and Dennis Wilson, their cousin Mike love and neighbourhood friend David Marks (later replaced by Al Jardine), The Beach Boys hailed from suburban California but (apart from Dennis) none of the members actually surfed. This didn't stop the band from recording the soundtrack to a wonderful era.

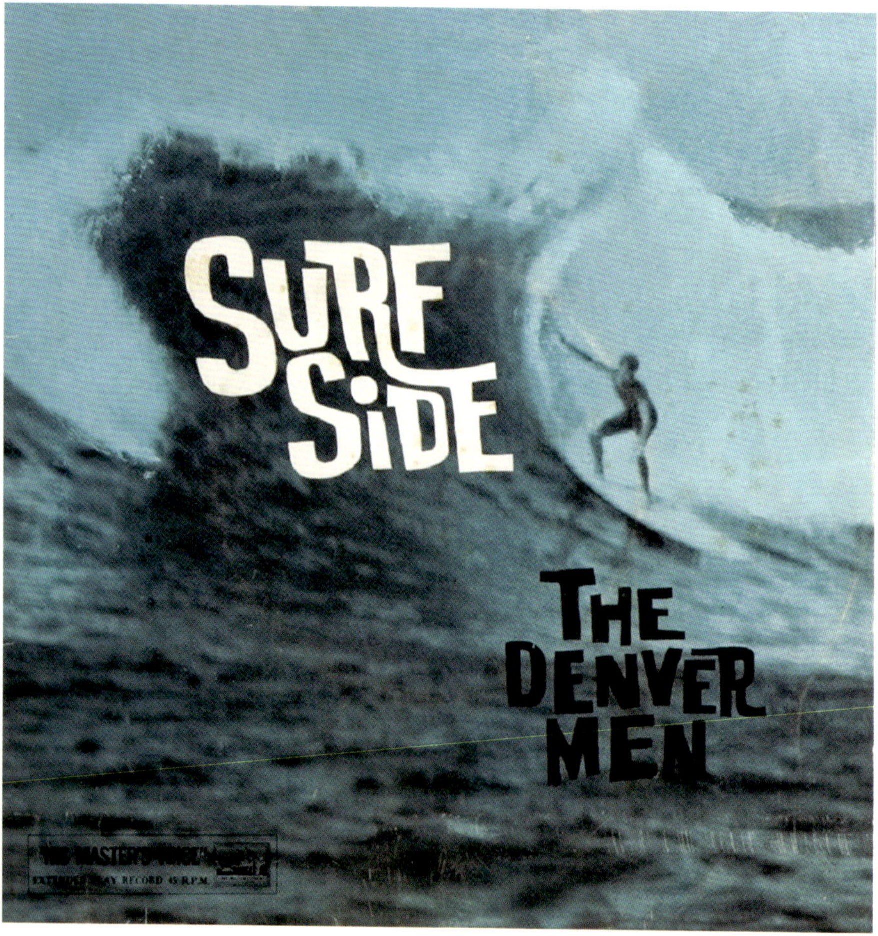

Top right: The Atlantics LP *Now It's Stompin' Time* released later in 1963, took advantage of the dance craze 'The Stomp'.

Middle right: The Atlantics most popular album *Bombora* (1963). A bombora is an aboriginal word for large sea waves that break over a shallow reef or rock formation. The Atlantics were still playing the tune 'Bombora' in 2007 at the Noosa Festival. The surfer on the wave on the cover is Gary Birdsall.

Below right: Little Pattie, born Patricia Amphlett in Sydney in 1949, had her first hit – the wonderfully titled 'He's My Blonde-Headed, Stompie Wompie, Real Gone Surfer Boy' – at the age of 14 in 1963. The diminutive blond-haired moppet headed into the Australian mainstream pop scene after the 'surf music' craze faded in the mid-1960s.

Below left: Vocal group The Delltones had a number of 'surf' inspired hits including 'Surf 'n Stomp', 'Hangin' Five' and 'Surf City' (all 1963).

Opposite: *Surfside* by The Denver Men was one of the first Australian recording to mine the 'surf music' craze in the early 1960s. The Denver Men were led by local favourite Digger Revell.

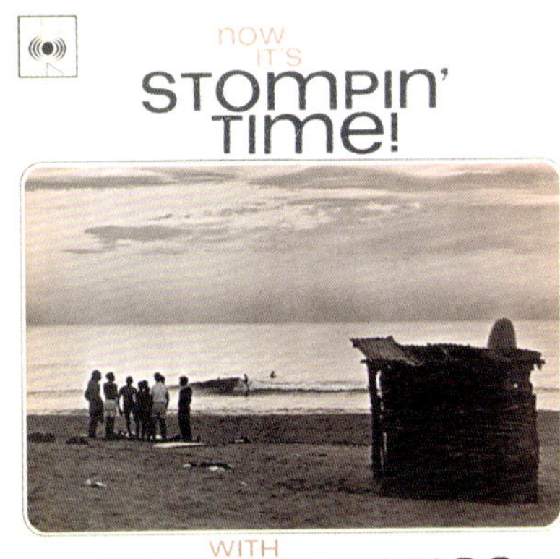

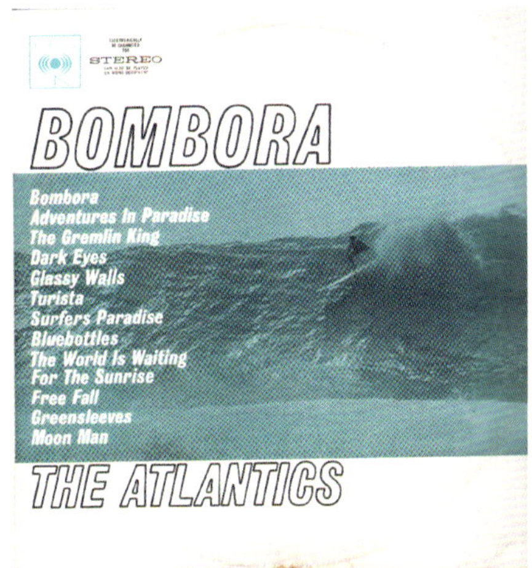

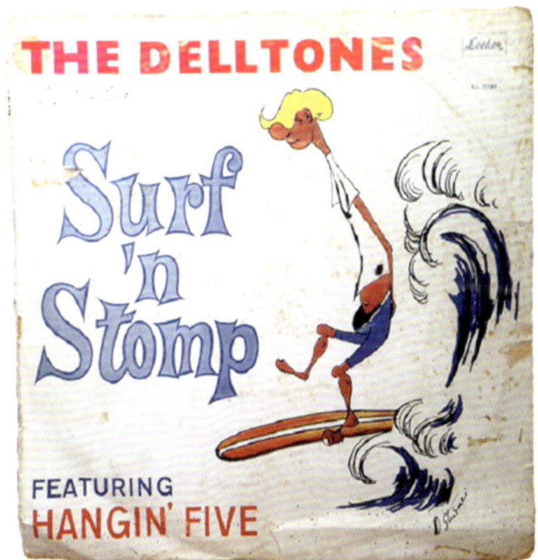

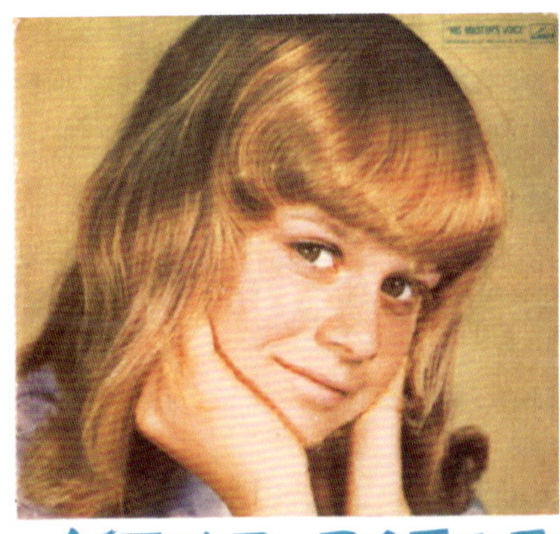

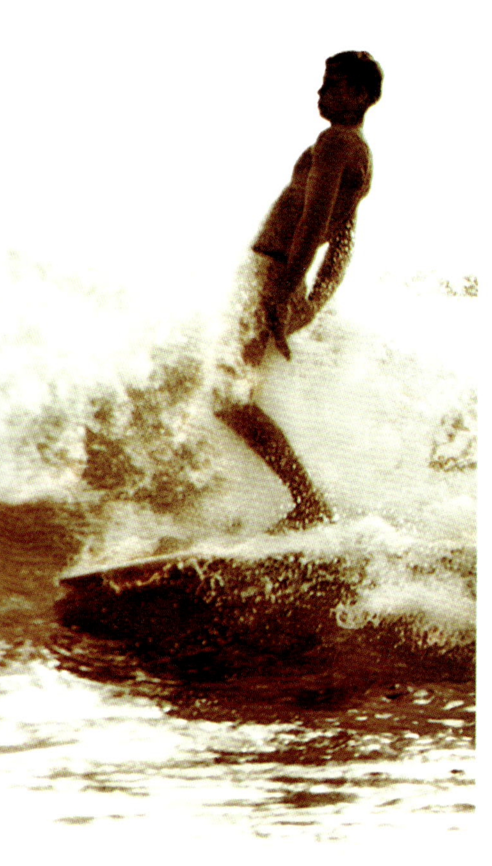

A very relaxed Frank Latta in 1963. **BW**

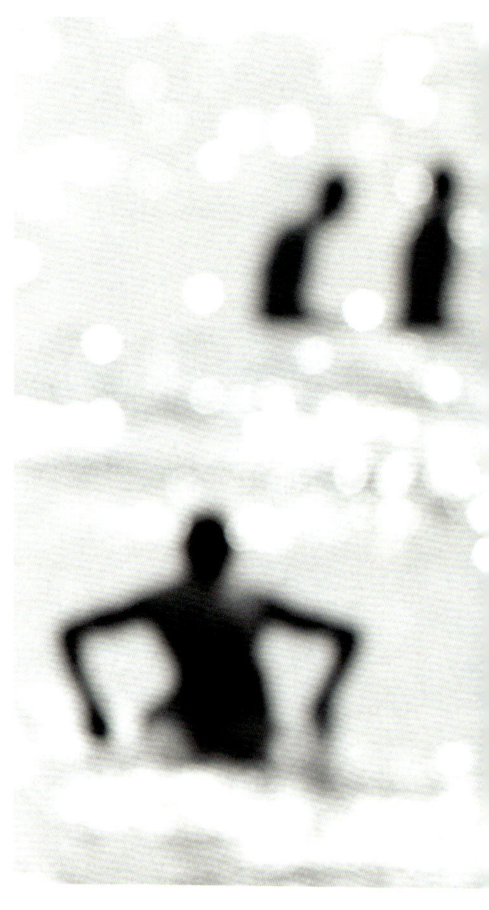

Abstract surfers, 1963. **BW**

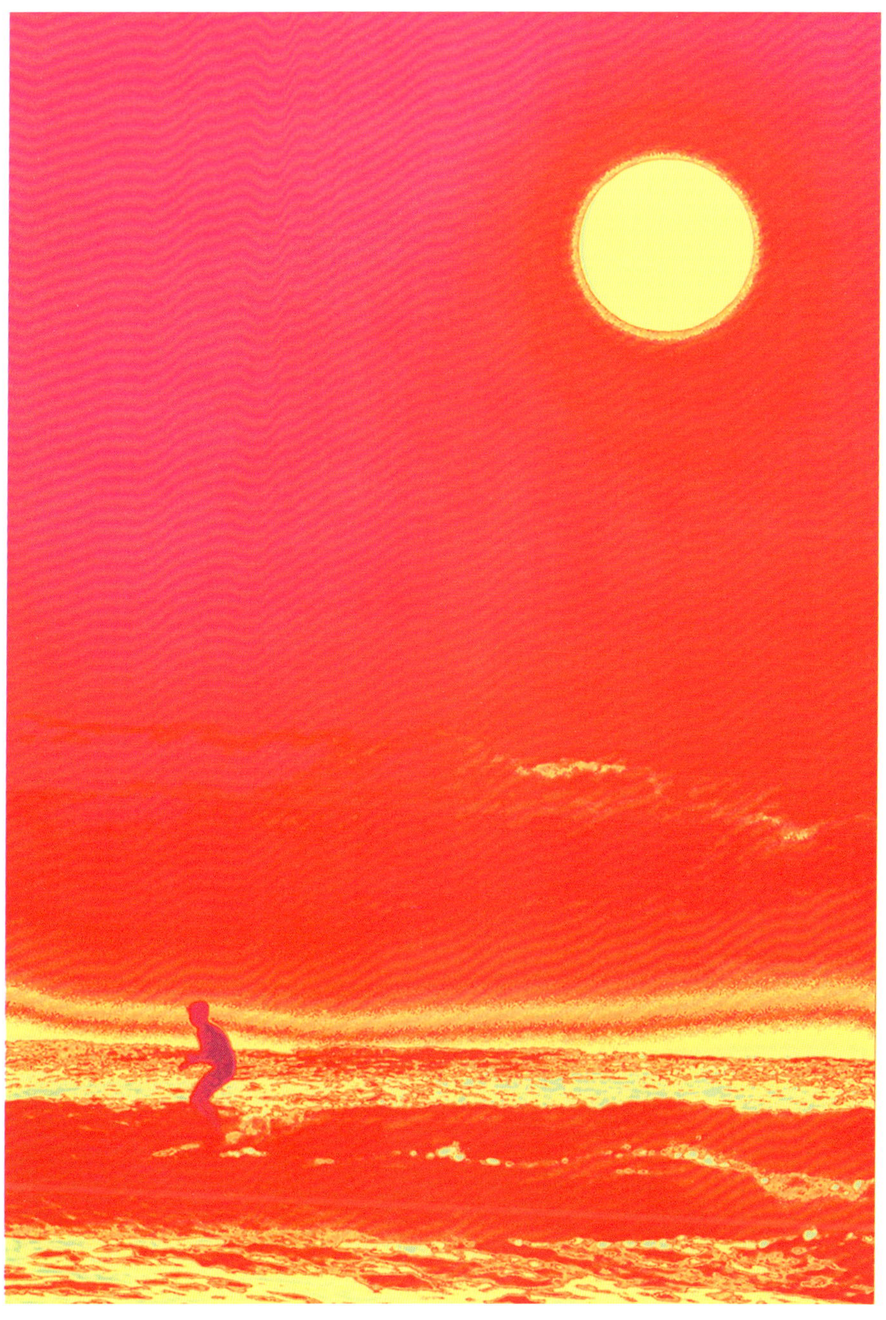

Keith Paull lit by a bright sun at Crescent Head, 1964. **BW**

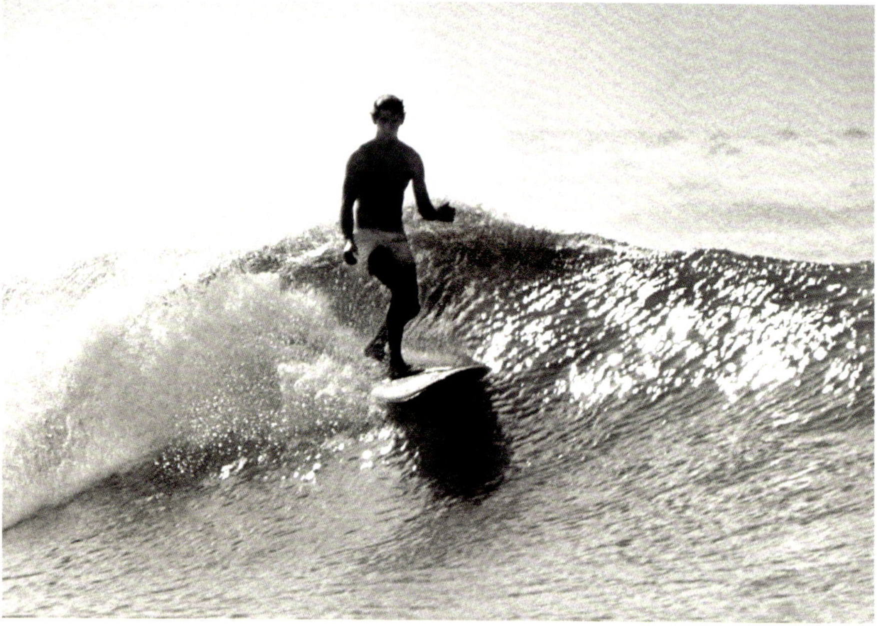

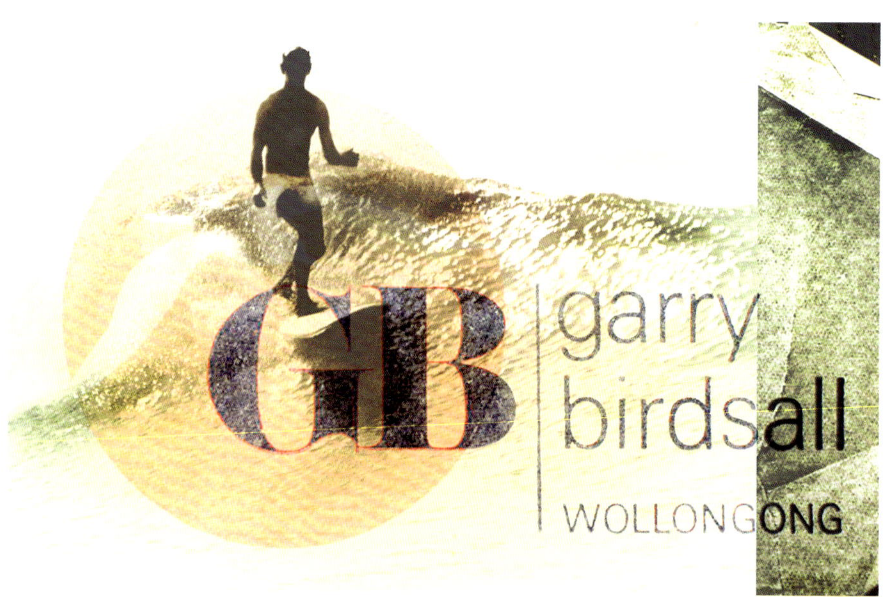

Above: **Garry Birdsall, South Cronulla, 1960s.** Gary began surfing mals around 1958 at Cronulla and became one of the area's most talented surfers. A photo of Gary on a large Cronulla Point wave graced the cover of The Atlantics' 1963 album *Bombora*. Gary worked for a number of boardmakers and in 1966 set up Wollongong's first surfboard manufacturing operation. *Below:* Gary Birdsall's board sticker. **BW**

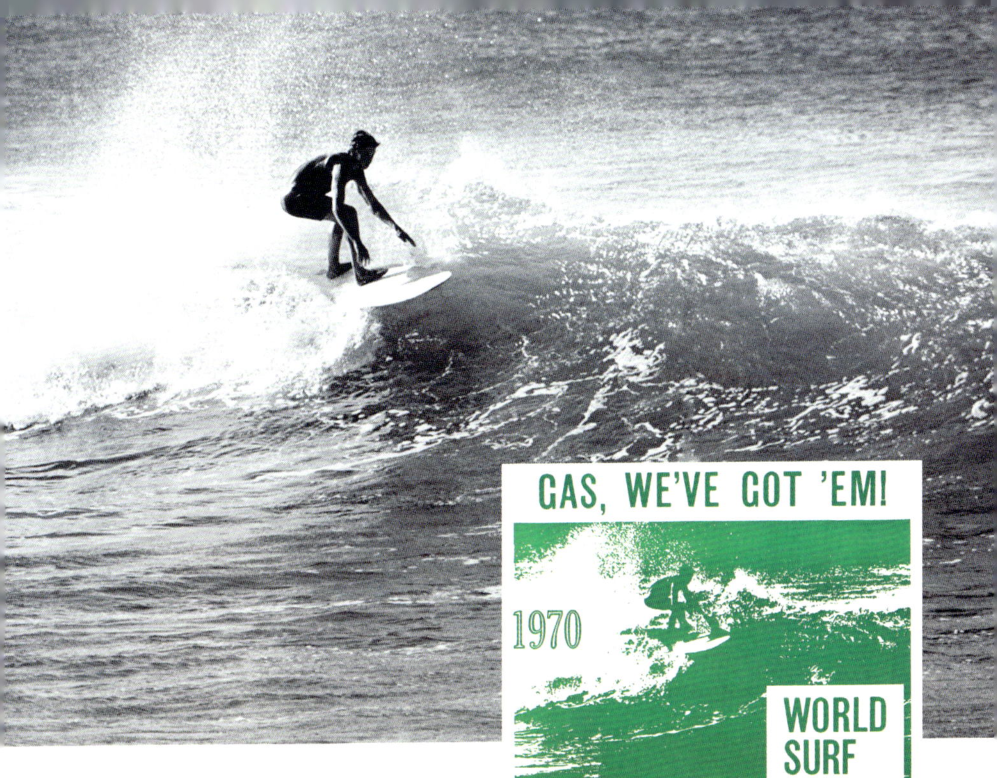

Above: **Wayne Lynch, Bells Beach, June 1968.**

Inset: **1970 World Titles poster image.**

Very occasionally, Bells Bowl waves will reform into the shore-break corner and create a hint of a left-hander on mid-tide. Rarely will they turn into a very good left-hander! So it came as a surprise one day when Wayne Lynch turned off the end of a typical right-hander in the Bowl and back into a perfectly reforming left-hander. Thankfully I'd been following Wayne on the wave through the Bowl and had him in my sights, and was able to capture this shot. It all happened so quickly I was only able to get one shot just as Wayne came out of a bottom turn at high speed into the top of the wave and my focus realm. Because of the angle there was beautiful backlighting to give the photograph an edge with really nice tones. In 1970 I was approached by Bakers Barn for a picture to use on a poster for the World Titles at Bells Beach in May that year. They'd managed to secure the refreshments and food contract for the world titles. Bakers Barn made the most delicious ice cream, operating from a big shed on the Torquay Road at Mount Duneed. The 'Barn' was a 'must stop for an ice cream' destination for surfers and beachgoers travelling back to Geelong and Melbourne. It was always packed late Sunday afternoons on warm sunny days. I met with one of their daughters to go through some prints I'd recently made in the darkroom. She liked the Wayne Lynch one and we proceeded from there. All I asked for was for my name to be on the poster. I saw it as a way of helping the World Titles in a sponsorship sort of way. Well they produced 100s of posters and distributed them at Torquay and along the coast. They forgot to put my name on them! I managed to keep two which to my knowledge are the only surviving ones. Torquay's National Surfing Museum has one (on loan), I've got the other! **BS**

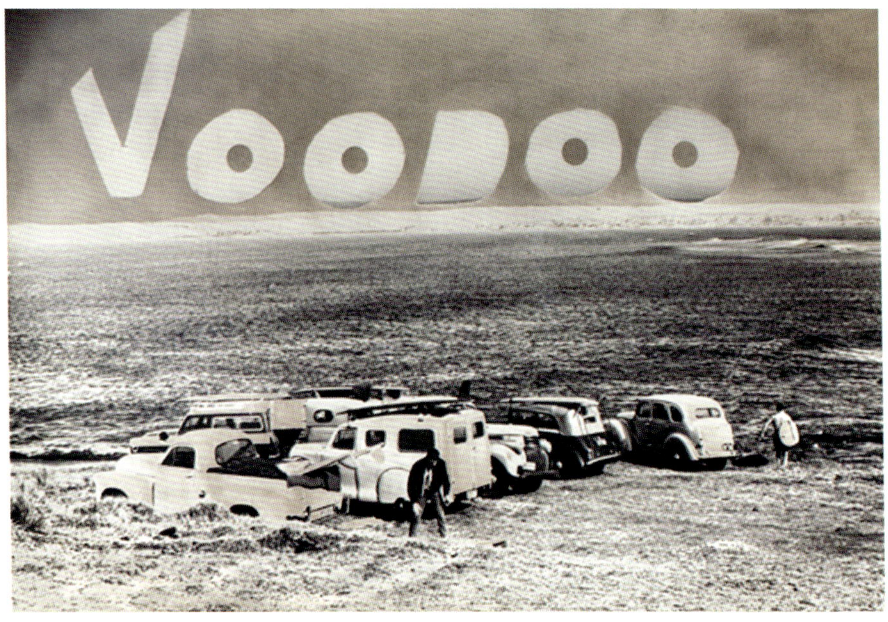

Surfing as art, 1960s. Many surfing photographers used visual effects to enhance their images, including Bob Waters.

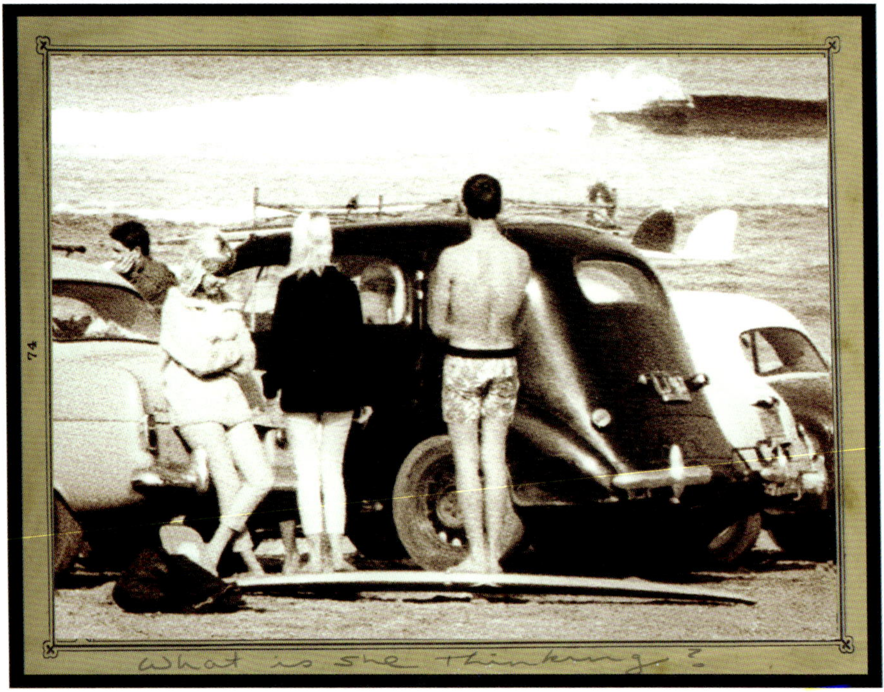

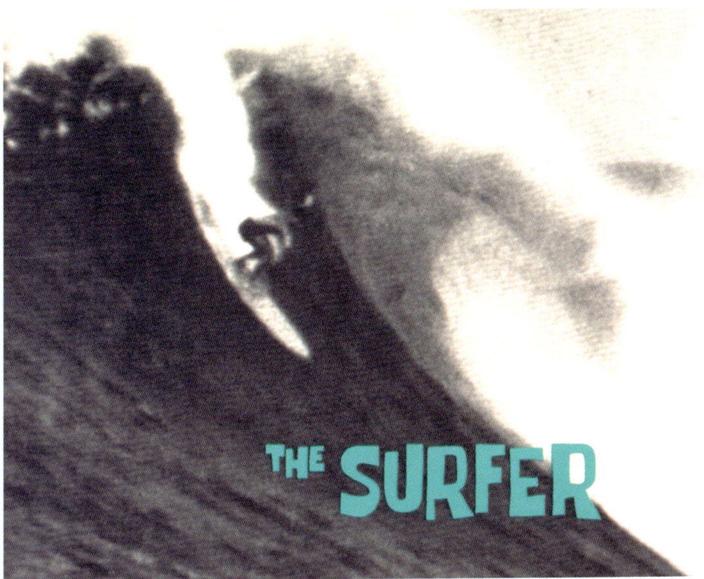

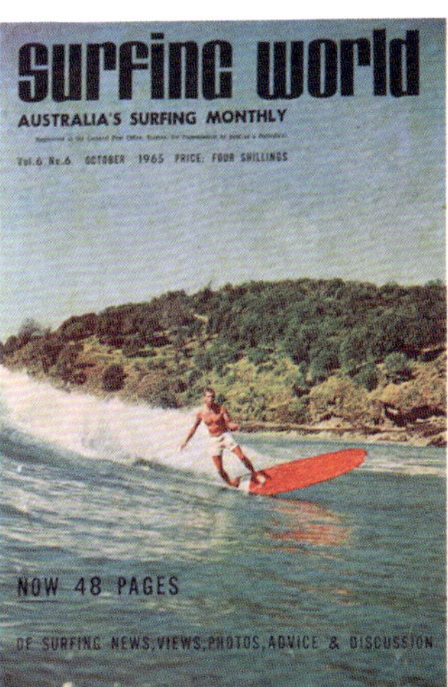

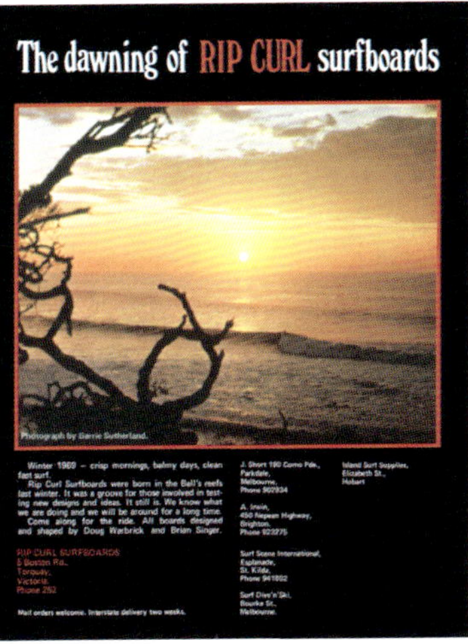

Top: The Surfer, Vol.1 No.1 January 1960, published by John Severson. Severson worked on the magazine while he was filming *Surf Fever* in Hawaii and California, filling the pages with stills from his film. The magazine sold 10,000 copies and was re-released in 1973 and 1985, and has since become a collector's item.

Bottom left: Surfing World magazine was founded by Bob Evans in September 1962 and is still going to this day, making it the second longest running surfing publication in the world.

Bottom right: Barrie Sutherland's 'Dawn Seascape, Bells Beach', the first Rip Curl advertisement, February 1969.

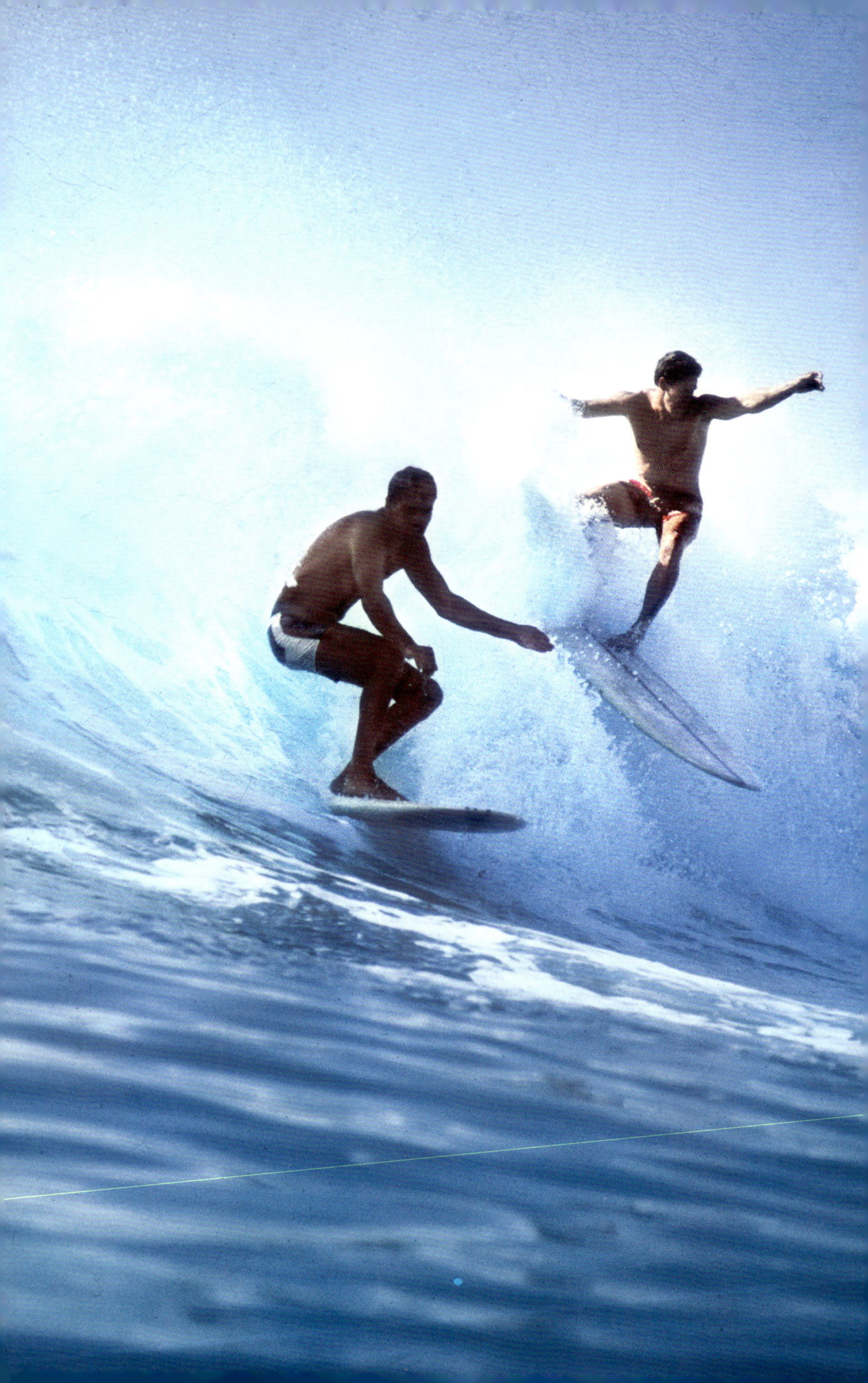

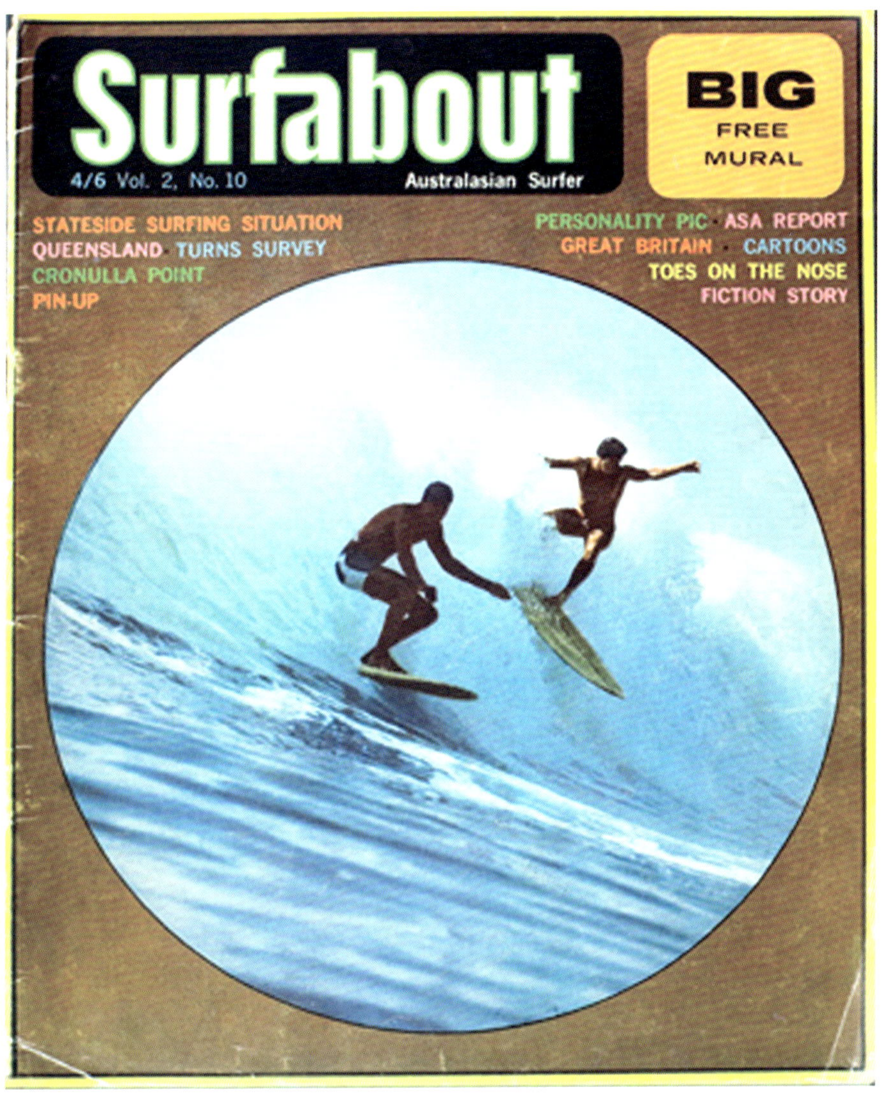

Steve Fowler and Tony McSweeney, Cronulla 1964. This image was became the cover for *Surfabout* magazine that year (*above*). **BW**

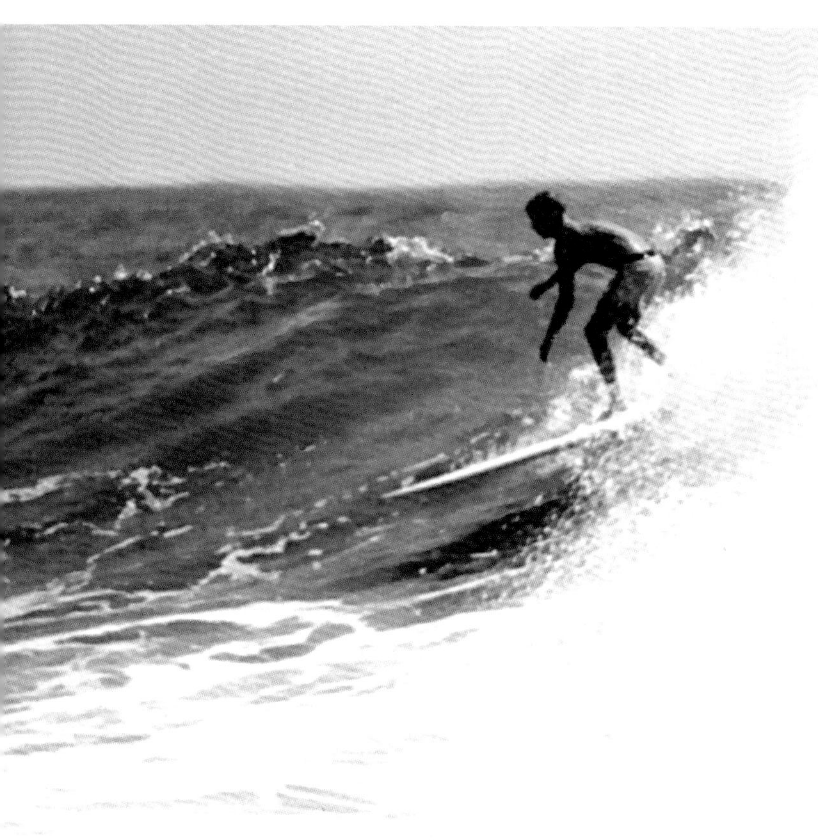

Allan Balmer. Allan was one of the new generation of surfers in the early '60s who had been influenced by surf movies. He quickly progressed to the stage where by 1964 he was generally accepted as one of the best in his age group. A founding member of Kirra Surfriders Club he placed 2nd in the Junior division of the 1st Queensland Titles in 1964.

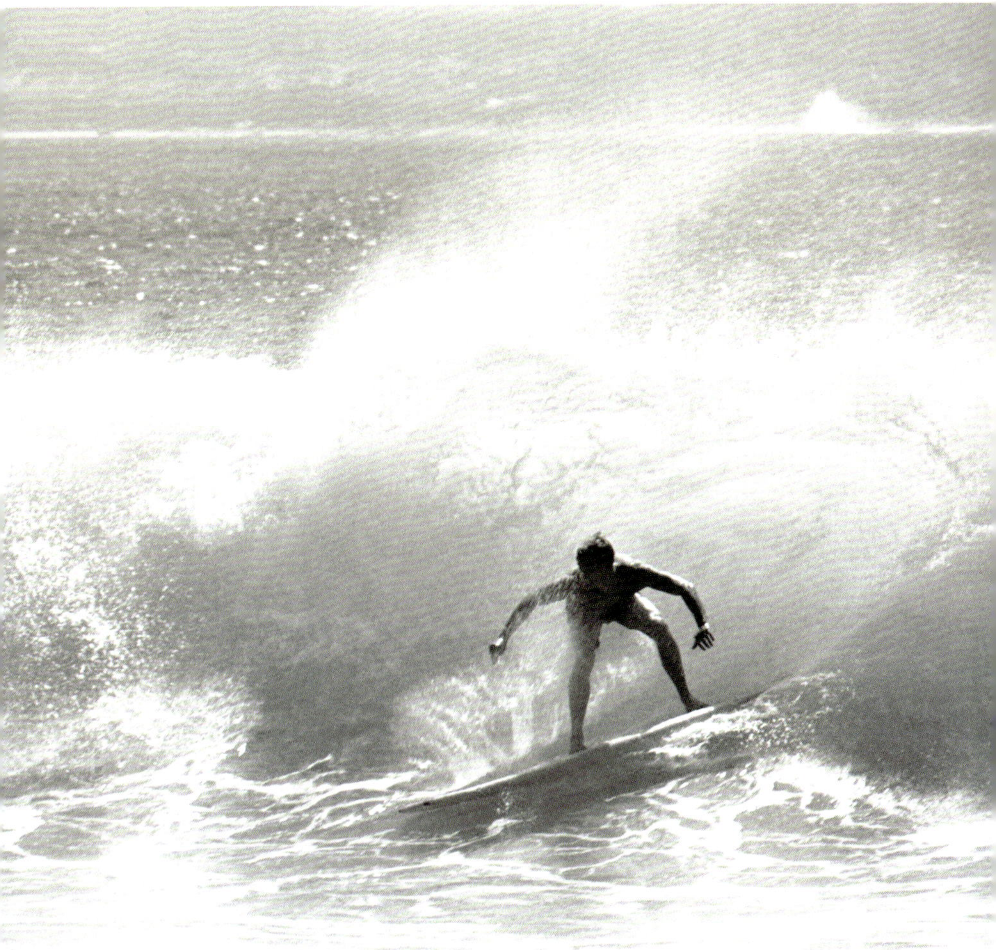

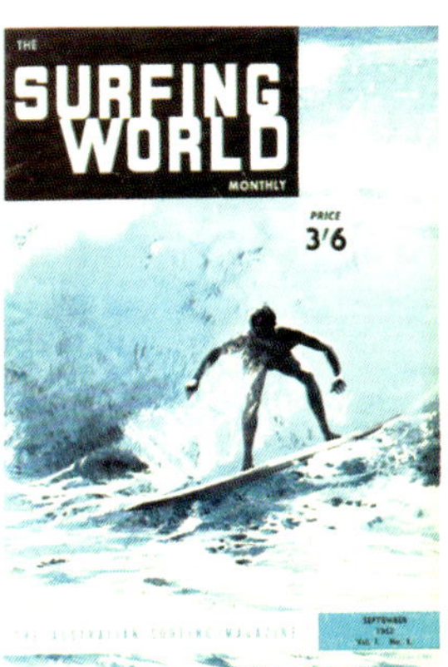

Unknown surfer, Cronulla Point, 1961. This image was the cover shot for the first issue of *Surfing World* magazine in 1962. **BW**

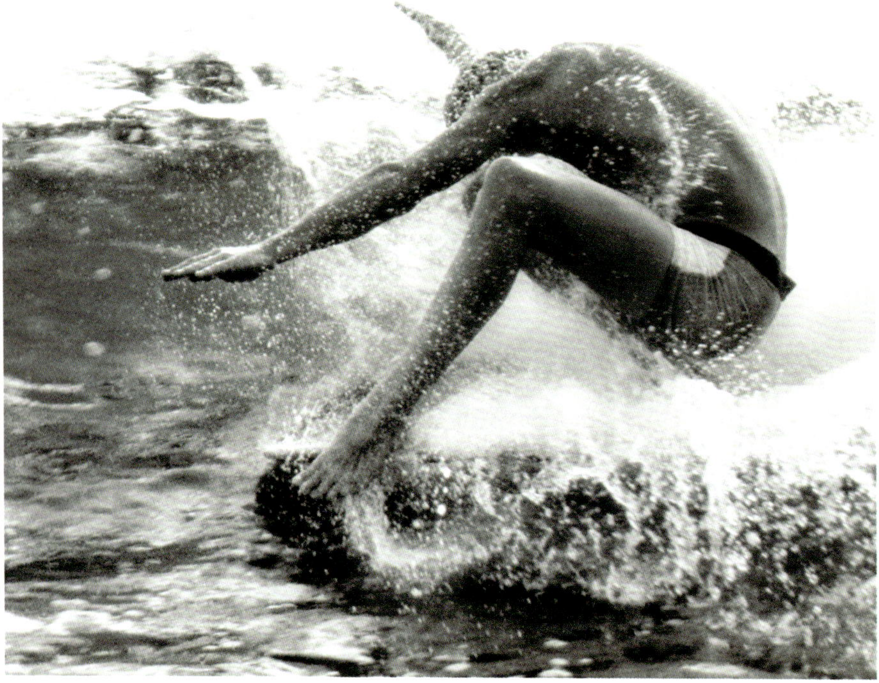

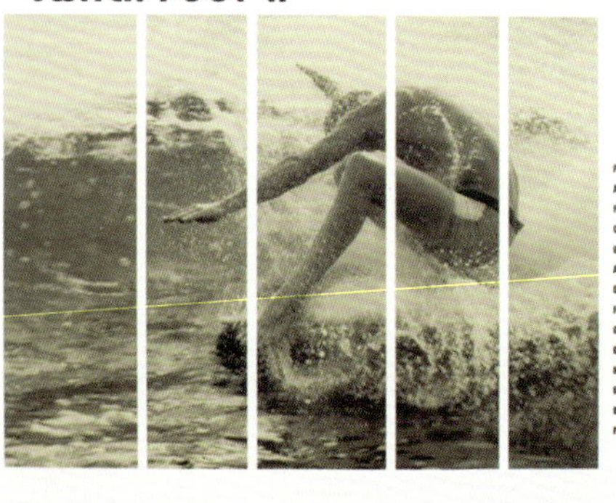

Above: **Frank Latta, Cronulla, 1963.** Frank Latta hangs his toes – and most of his left foot! – off the front edge of his board while performing a head dip on a small shorebreak wave. Frank was a fine surfer and surfboard designer. His surfboards under the iconic San Juan label are now quite collectible. Frank Latta was a pool shark! In 2009 he died in the surf at his housebreak in NSW. R.I.P. **BW**

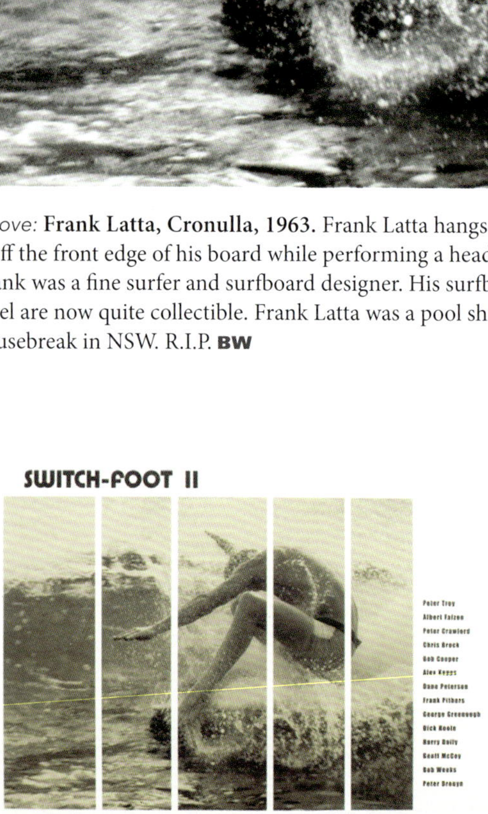

SWITCH-FOOT II

Left: Switch-Foot II followed on from the cult favourite *Switch-Foot: Surfing, Art & Music* a subculture all to itself. The Switch-Foot trilogy of books are a testament to the elders of surfing and the photographers who captured the surfing lifestyle of the 1960s and 1970s. The three coffee table books are available at hodaddy.com.au and a must-have for surfers that are keen on history.

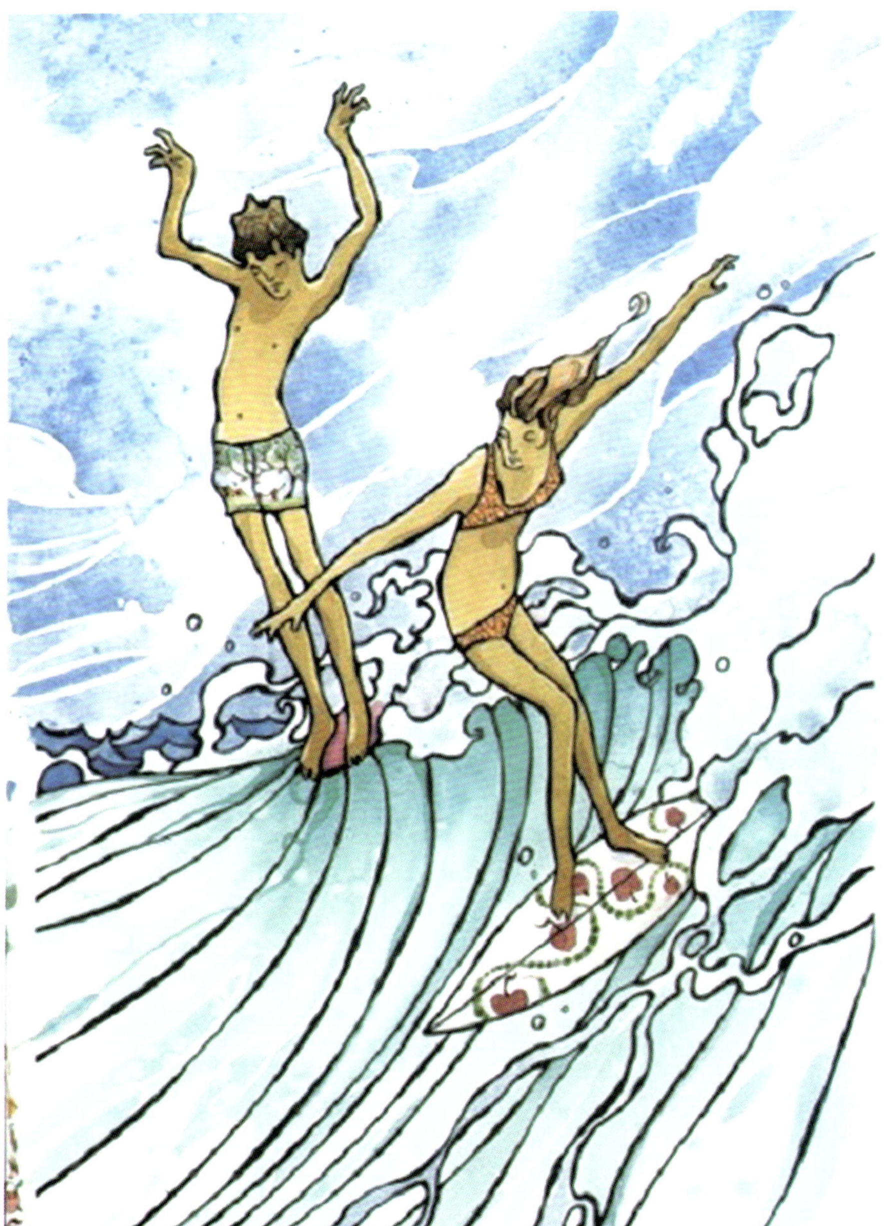

The art of Harry Daily, aka Sketch Holiday, made a formidable entrance into Australian surfing culture in the early 2000s. His iconic 'Adam & Eve' watercolour cryptically points to everything beautiful about surfing, while at the same time the reference to the 'Garden Of Eden' suggests that it could all end with the wrong bite of the forbidden fruit. COURTESY ANDREW CROCKETT, HODADDY.

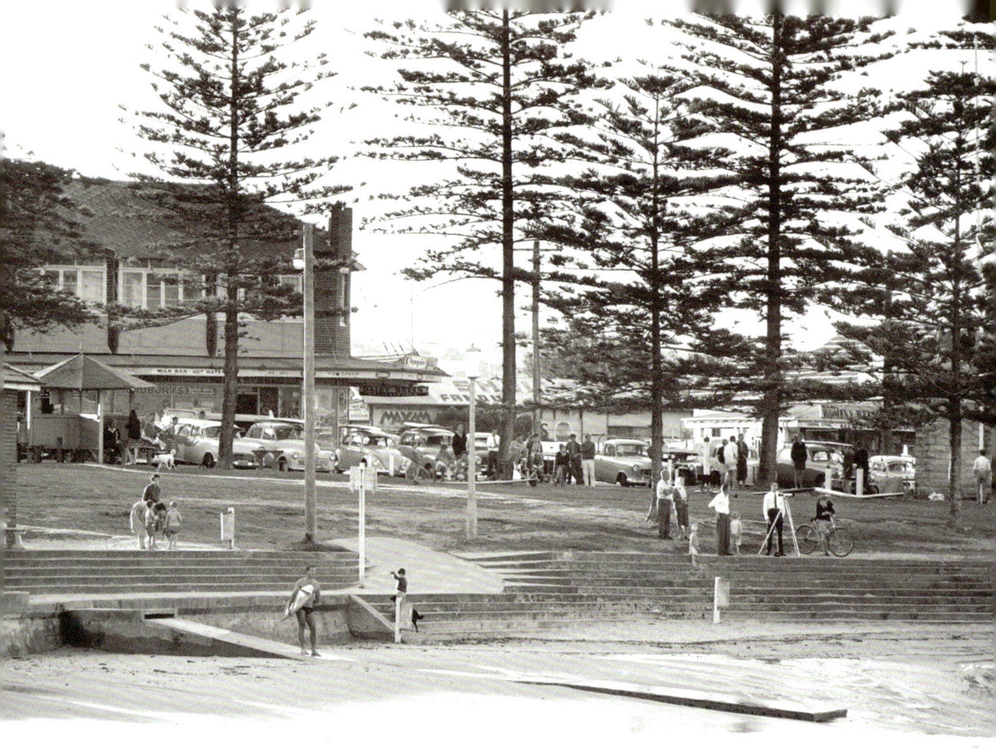

Bob Evans – A Man on a Mission

Few people have contributed so much to the establishment and development of a sport and yet gained so little recognition for his efforts as Bob Evans.

Already a dedicated surfer before he witnessed first-hand the American team performance at Avalon and Torquay in 1956, Bob embraced the introduction of the Malibu like few others.

The crowd reaction to the Yanks demonstration at that carnival left an impression on him and having worked in marketing in the fashion industry Bob saw the potential of promoting board riding as a public spectacle long before any others. In the late '50s, with Joe Larkin as friend and partner, they started making what only could be described as home surf movies. From this humble beginning Bob became the voice of surfing and chronicled the changing face of surfing in the late '50s and '60s.

He became the first person to produce commercial surf movies in Australia and from this he travelled the world filming surfers at sometimes never before seen locations including South America, Europe, Africa and Bali. The establishment of *Surfing World* magazine was also another of his firsts and a number of people owe their careers today from having worked with or for him. It is to the credit of those that followed that Surfing World is still published today.

Apart from promoting surfing commercially via movies and the magazine Bob was a behind the scenes man and pioneered surfing in many ways. He was an instrumental figure in the establishment of the first board riding club (the South Pacific Boardriders Club and the purchase of a house at North Narrabeen as a club house) and the driving force behind the formation of the Australian Surfriders Association (now Surfing Australia). From that and his ability to communicate with business leaders he was the motivator behind the organising of the first World Titles at Manly in 1964.

Bob moved to the U.S. in 1975 and was promoting his last movie *Drouyn and Friends* on the East Coast. Sadly, he passed away from a massive brain haemorrhage in Jacksonville, Florida on 12th October 1976 causing shockwaves among a surfing community who at that time knew him so well. Unfortunately, he never really benefited financially from the effort that he put into promoting the sport. He would be amazed to see how surfing has grown and become the giant commercial enterprise it has become today.

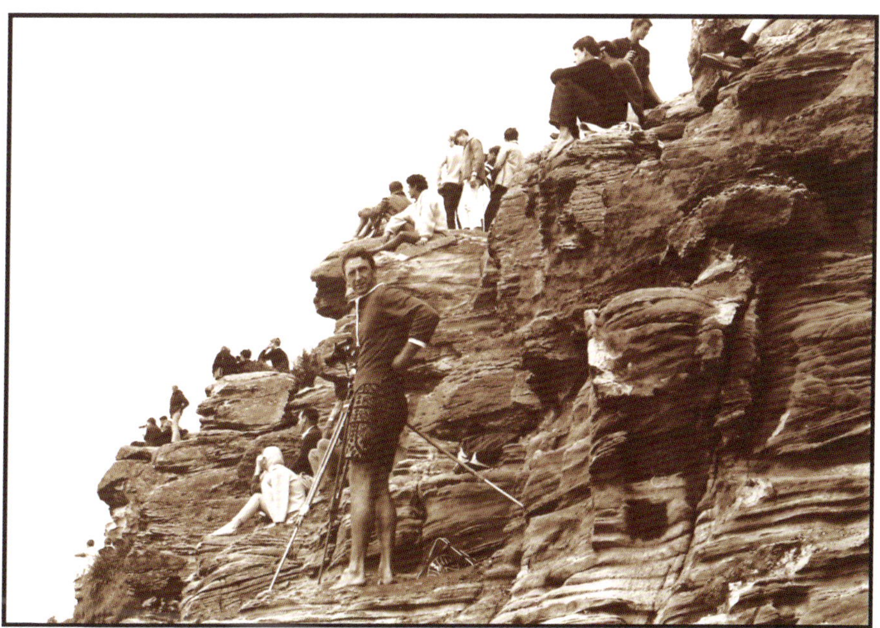

Above: **Bob Evans shooting film in Sydney. JP**

Opposite: **Dee Why, 1962.** Dee Why Beach with filmmaker and surf icon Bob Evans standing behind his tripod mounted camera capturing some classic large wave moments in 1962. Bob was one of the earliest documentors of Australian surfing. He founded *Surfing World* magazine in 1962 and produced a dozen surfing films. **BW**

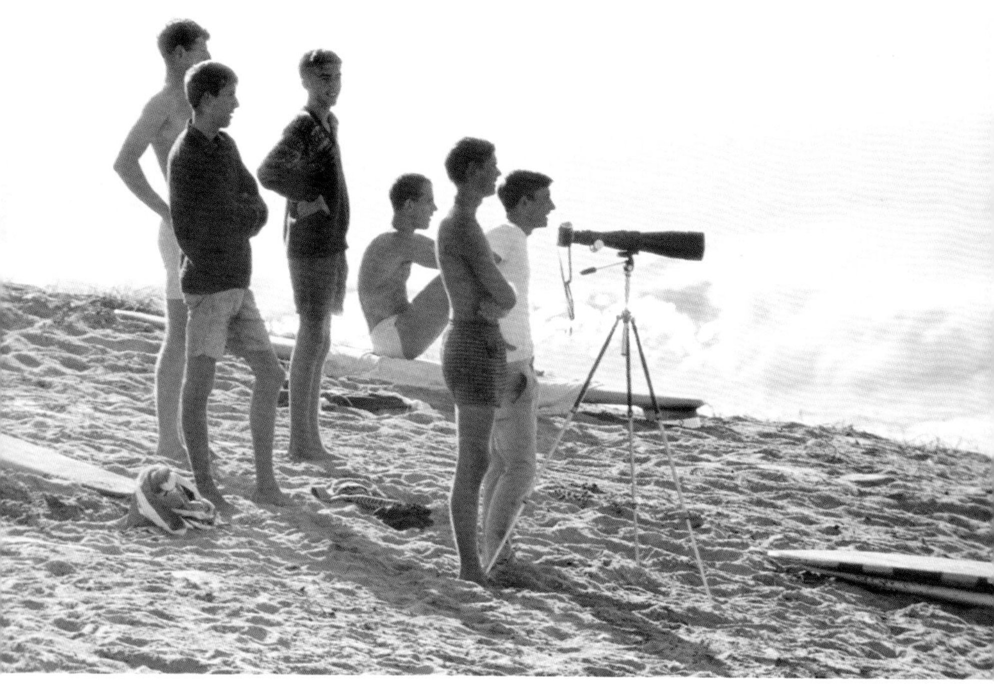

Alby Falzon behind the lens at Shelley Beach in 1963. Alby is famous for his production of the iconic film *Morning of the Earth* (1971). **BW**

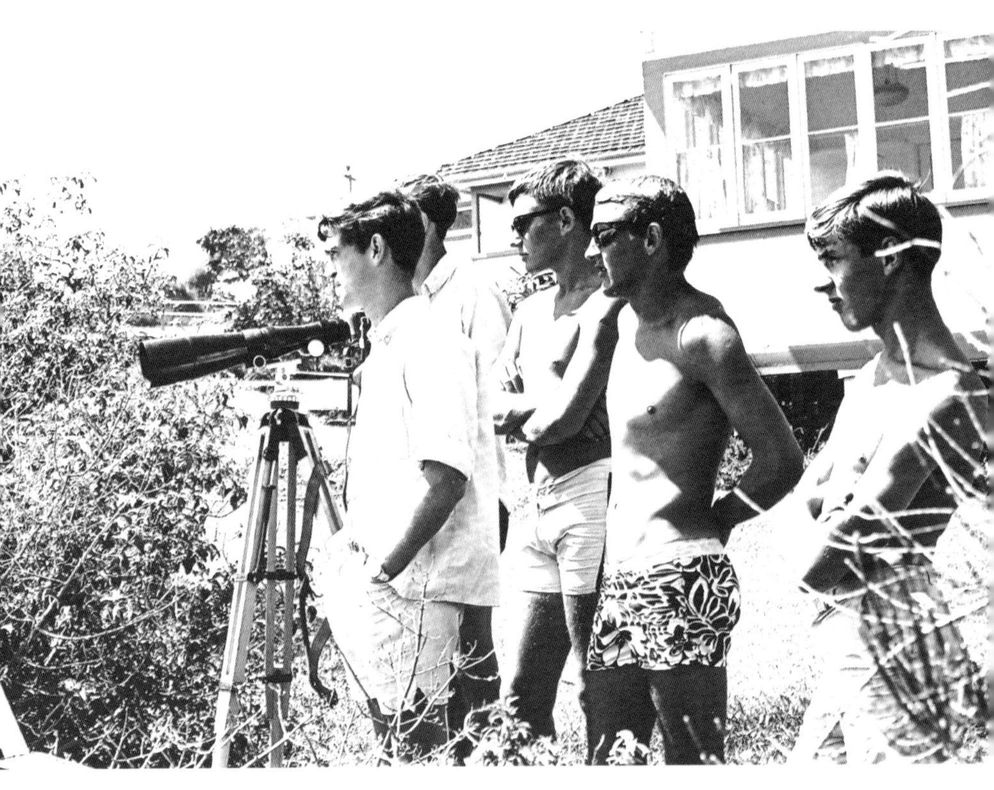

Taking photos from the front yard of a nearby cottage. **JP**

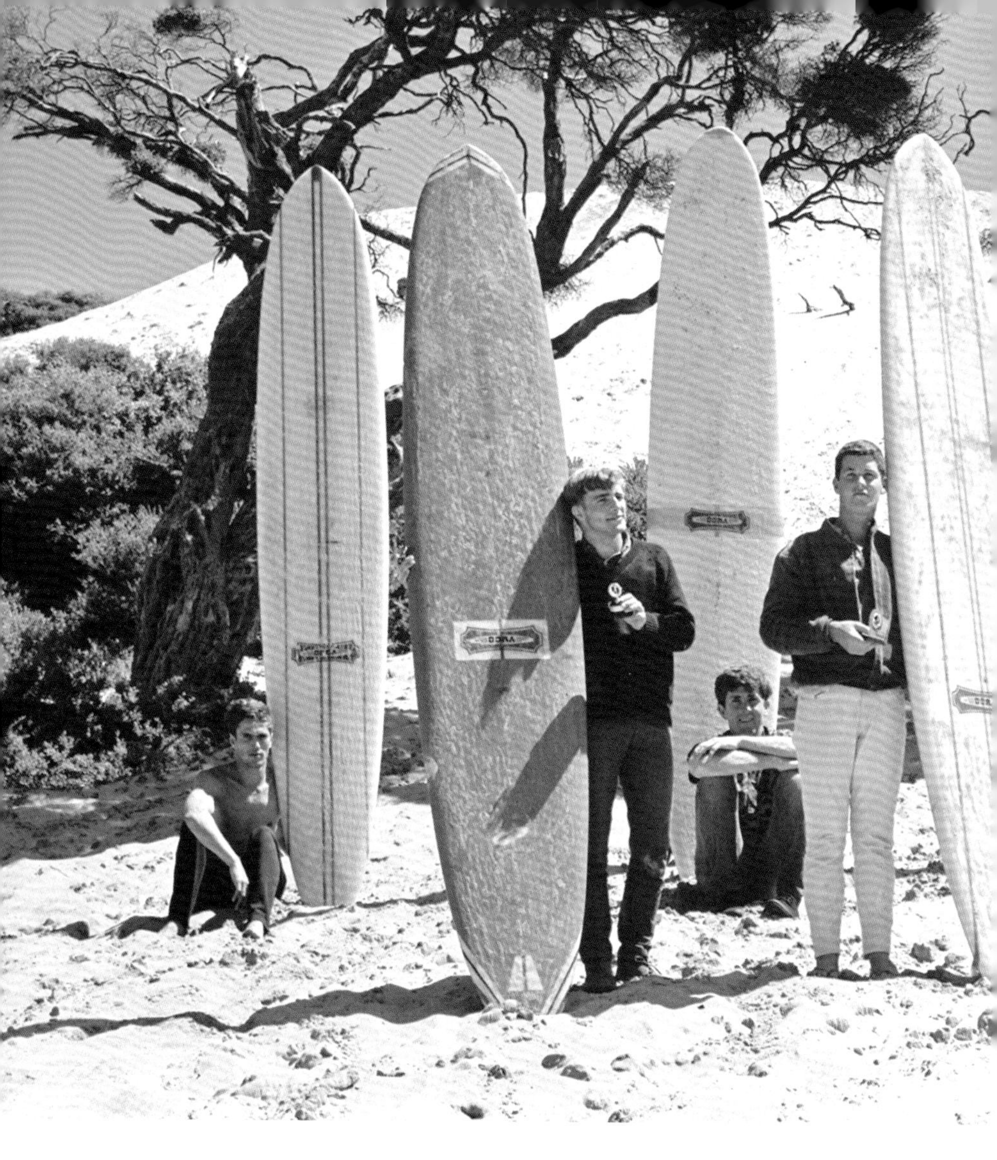

'Dora Surfboards' advertising photo shoot, Point Lonsdale, December 1966. The Dora Team, Point Lonsdale, December 1965 The Dora Team was the brainchild of Doug 'Claw' Warbrick, Pat Morgan and Rod Brooks. George Rice and Pat Morgan made the boards while Claw and Rod handled the sales side of things. I took the photograph for a planned advertising campaign that never eventuated. The venture, looking very rosy, ceased operating overnight after a letter was received from Mickey Dora's lawyer. Like many other startup surf industry ventures at the time, there was little understanding of branding and copyright issues. Obviously Dora understood and was quick to act. Just 25 Dora boards were made by the team! From left: Unknown, Rod Brooks, Pat Morgan, Colin McDonald, Doug 'Claw' Warbrick. **BS**

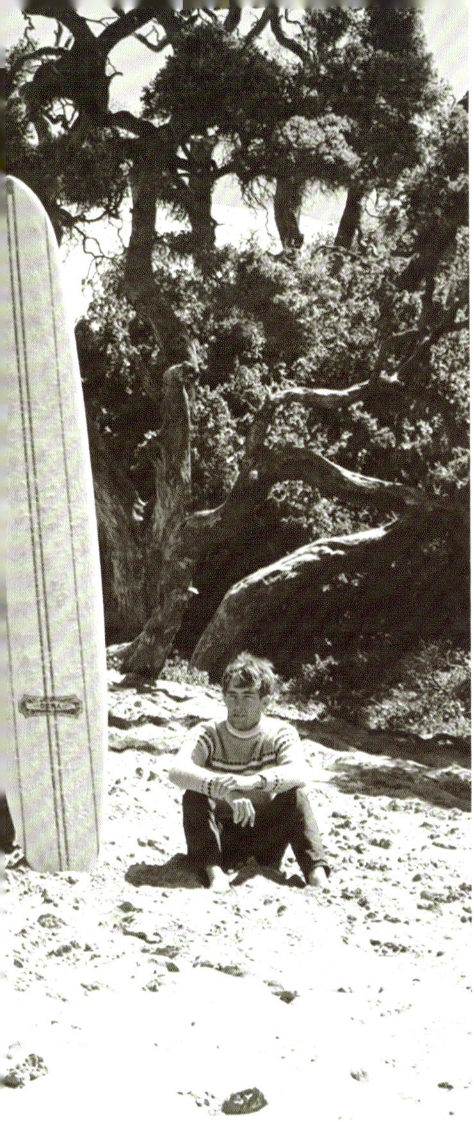

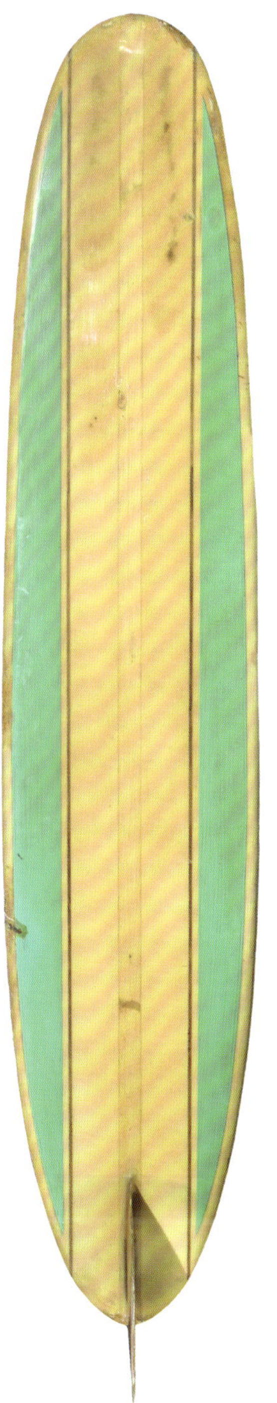

Favourite Places

1960s surfers regularly visited their favourite beaches up and down the east coast of Australia, round to the south in Victoria and all the way across to

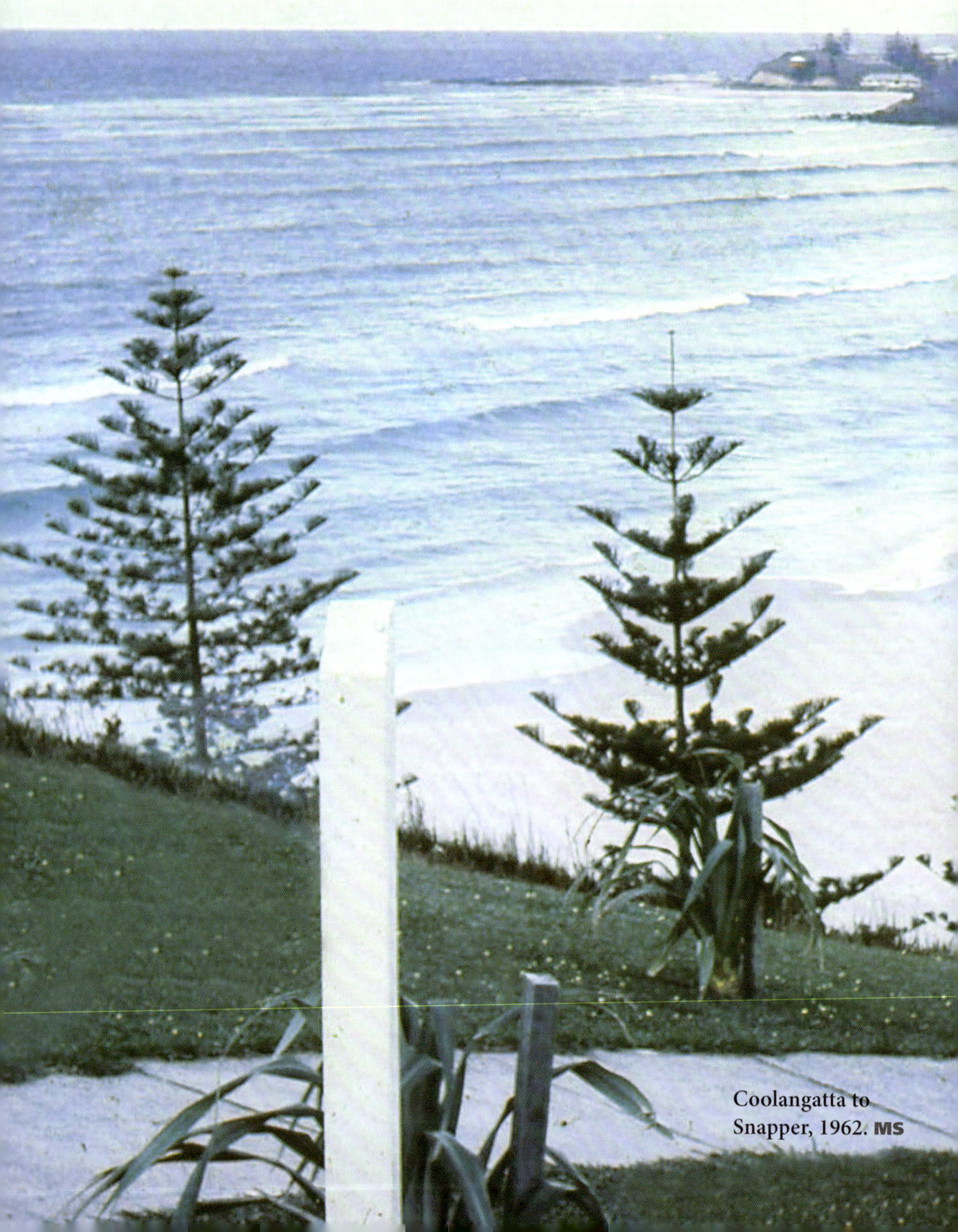

Coolangatta to Snapper, 1962. **MS**

Western Australia. Good surfers grew to know every rock on a beach, every idiosyncrasy of the conditions and the change the waves made. Some of these places grew to be incredible popular during the decade, while others remained carefully guarded secrets within the tightknit surfing community. Here are a few of the best, and how the beaches used to surf in the 1960s:

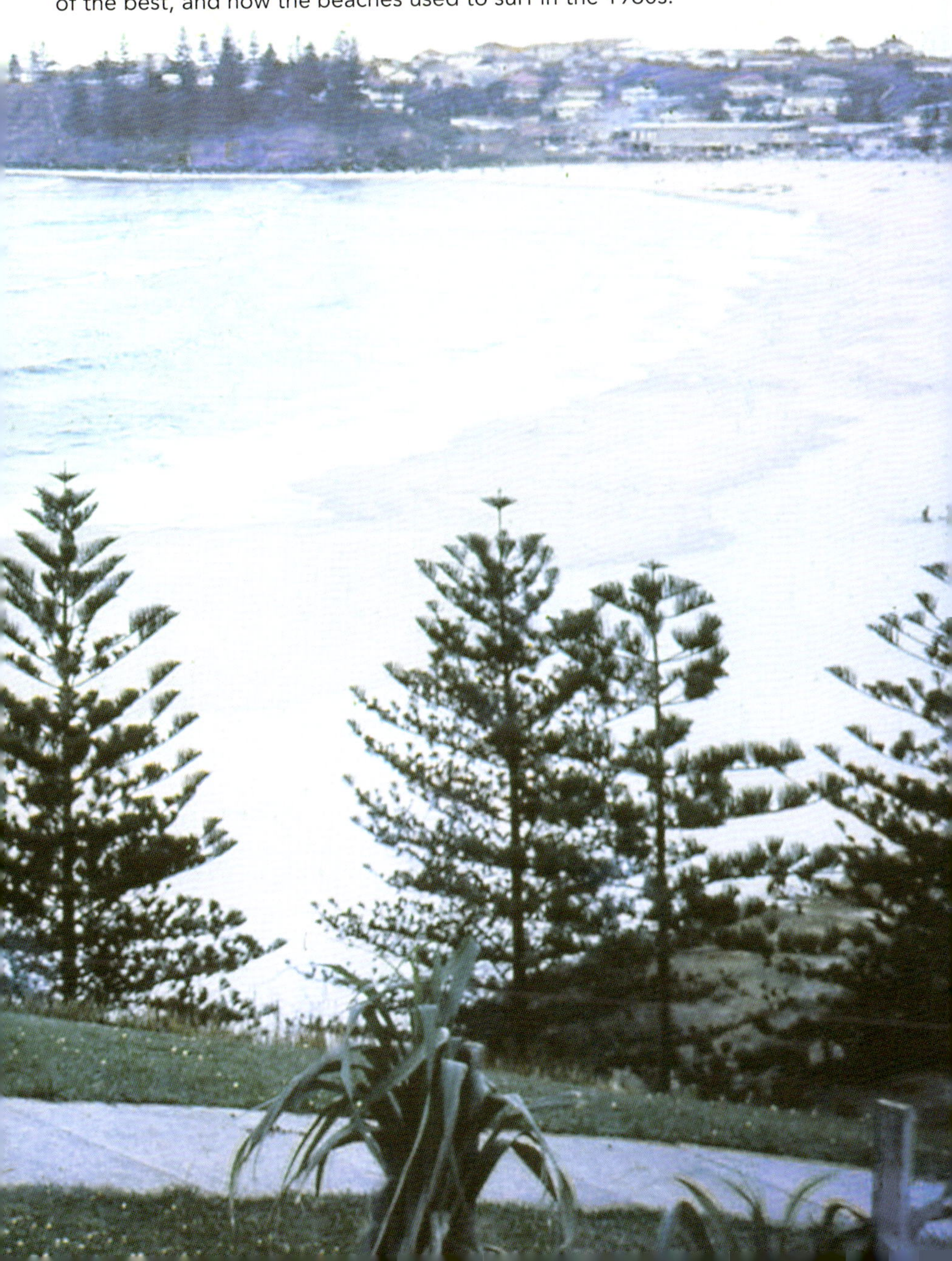

Noosa Heads is the northernmost part of the east coast of Australia, some 136 kilometres north of Brisbane. Noosa was home to Queensland's first surfing scene (Bob McTavish hails from Noosa) with Main Beach, Johnsons, National Park, Tea Tree and Granite Bay popular surfing spots in the 1960s, Today, Noosa boasts one of the few National Surfing Reserves in Queensland. All of these beaches break right at sizes from 1 to 3 metres, depending on the amount of sand built up in the bays.

The Gold Coast has two exceptional breaks, at Kirra and at Burleigh Heads. Currumbin Alley was also popular for a time, but government development interfered with the estuary in the 1970s and affected the waves there before the area was redeveloped and reclaimed in the 1980s. Burleigh Heads, which was the only spot on the Gold Coast that featured a south or southeast swell, was particularly hard to surf, with entry into the water from the rocks often difficult. Kirra takes a north or east swell, but despite the introduction of sand stabilising breakwaters, the waves there were also affected by local government decisions.

Byron Bay showcases 30 km of pristine beaches at the most eastern point of the Australian coastline. Little Wategos and Wategos Beaches, directly below Cape Byron lighthouse, were undeveloped favourites in the 1960s, as was Tallows Beach with its incredible left breaks. A few kilometres south of Byron Bay can be found the hollow waves of Broken Head. Broken Head worked best on north and east swells, with the wind coming anywhere from west to south. At certain times you would think that the waves almost stood still.

Lennox Head is a further ten kilometres down the coast from Byron Bay. The waves at Lennox Head were always more dependent on swell than sand movement (rounded stones form the base of the beach). Because it is on the outside edge of a vast bay, Lennox Head always picked up the south swell extremely well, once making it the most consistent winter wave on the far north coast.

Angourie, on the north coast of New South Wales, once produced almost the perfect wave for surfing. Originally, the beach was very isolated and surfers had to walk along a sandy path where there was once three fishing shacks nestled in the lee of the grassy headland. Emus and kangaroos would look up startled at the sight of young surfers in the area, then bound away down the track. Later the track became a road, and years after the road was sealed. Although the Yamba area had a number of popular beaches in the 1960s, many were only accessible via four-wheel drive.

On the NSW Central Coast in between Newcastle and Gosford, great surfing conditions could be found at Forrester's Beach, once a big wave spot with its submerged reef 100 metres off the beach; Box Head beach, near Ocean Beach, and Terrigal, especially during winter. Swell direction was critical on the Central Coast, because the break forms inside the mouth of Brisbane Water, a wave-dominated barrier estuary that travels 18 kilometres in

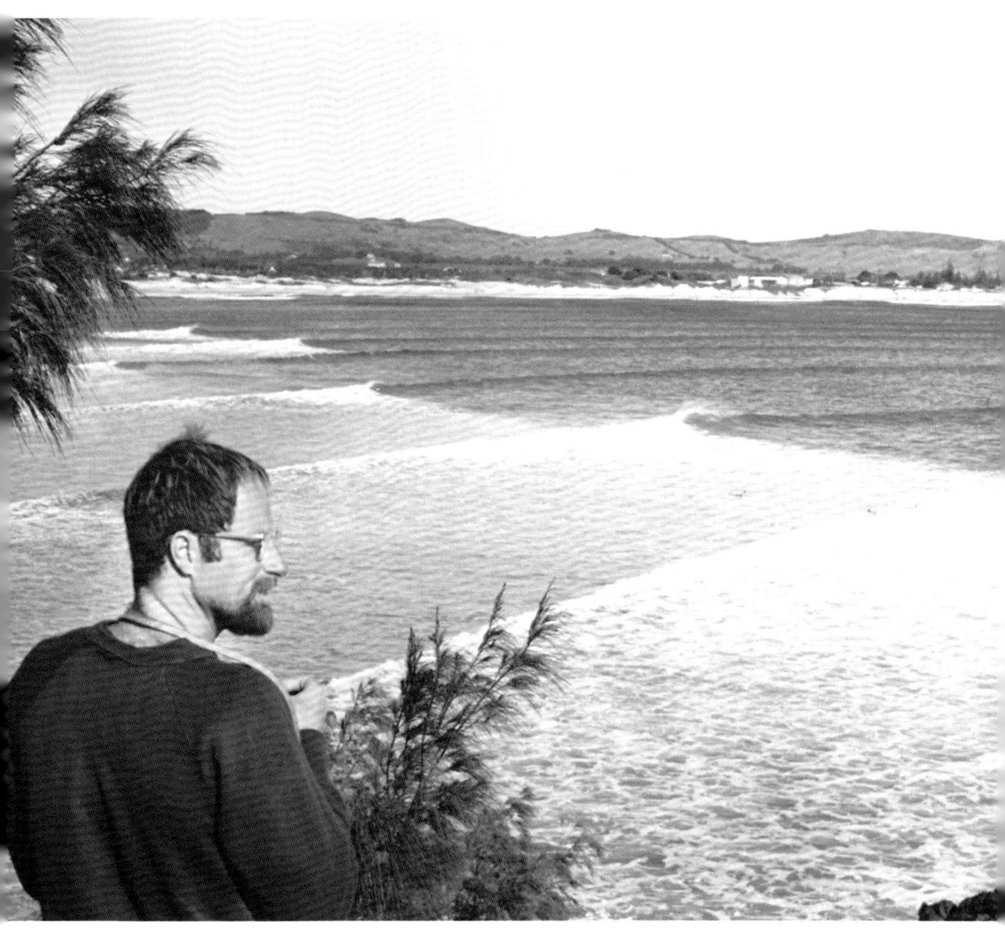

Bob Cooper at the pass, 1964. Bob was the first American surfer to tour the east coast of Australia extensively and had a strong influence on our surfing in those early years (1959/60). He made several trips to Australia before settling here permanently in 1964, citing that California was losing its freedom. He worked for some of the major board manufacturers in California and Sydney before moving north and working at Haydens on the Sunshine Coast.

Bob eventually opened his own surf shop in Coffs Harbour which he and wife Wils ran successfully for many years. Photographs of him surfing first appeared in *Surfer Magazine* Vol.1 No.1 in 1960 and his life has been extensively covered in various surfing publications up to the present day. Ever the purist Bob made a life in surfing with Cooper Surfboards. Bob is now retired to the Sunshine Coast, still surfs and is enjoying life to the full. **MS**

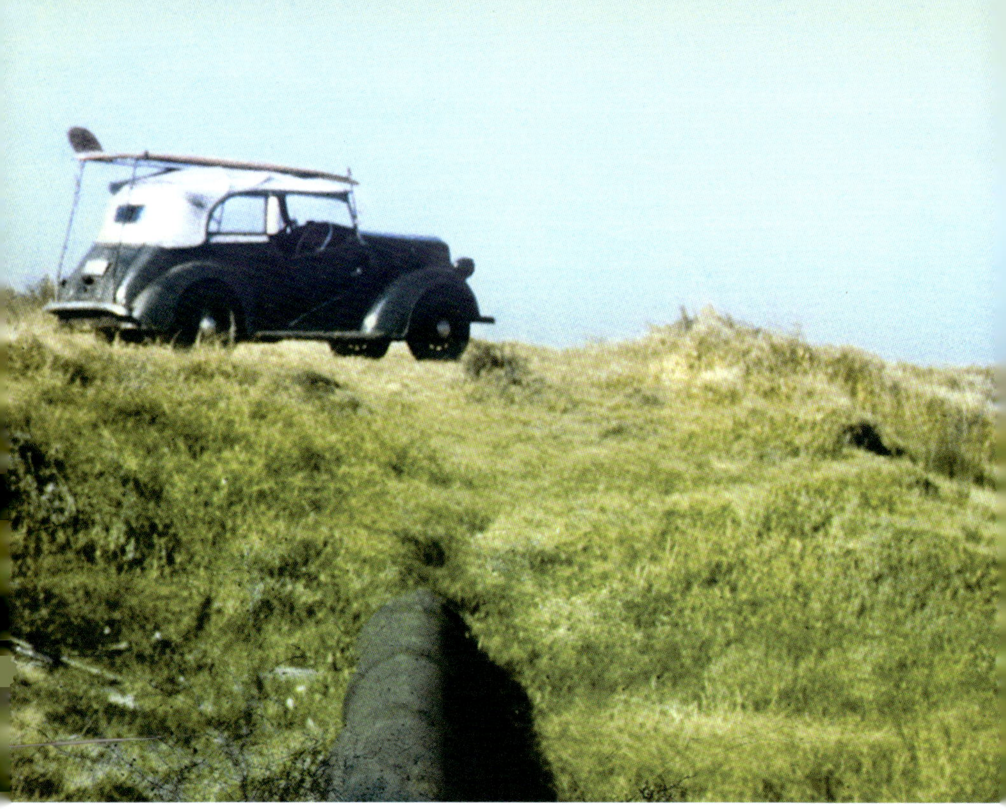

a southerly direction to its mouth at Broken Bay, and will not break in anything but a south-east swell.

In Sydney, **Narrabeen** on the northside of the city had the most consistent break, working on both north and south swells with the wind from west to northeast. On the southside of the city is Cronulla, on the southern end of Bate Bay. Cronulla Point is a rock shelf onto which south to southeast swells pound consistently. At the other end of Cronulla, 'Voodoo' (as the locals called the area near Kurnell) produced excellent left-handers at the secluded reef break at the top of the bay.

South of Wollongong, which boasted Corrimal, Bellambi and Sandon Point, numerous beaches with right and left breaks were found all the way to the Victorian border. 'Pipeline' or Wreck Bay, near Jervis Bay, had an amazing left-hand reef break on a south swell and north-east wind. Ulladulla, 87 km further south, also boasted quality breaks, as did Mollymook, Broulee and Dalmeny.

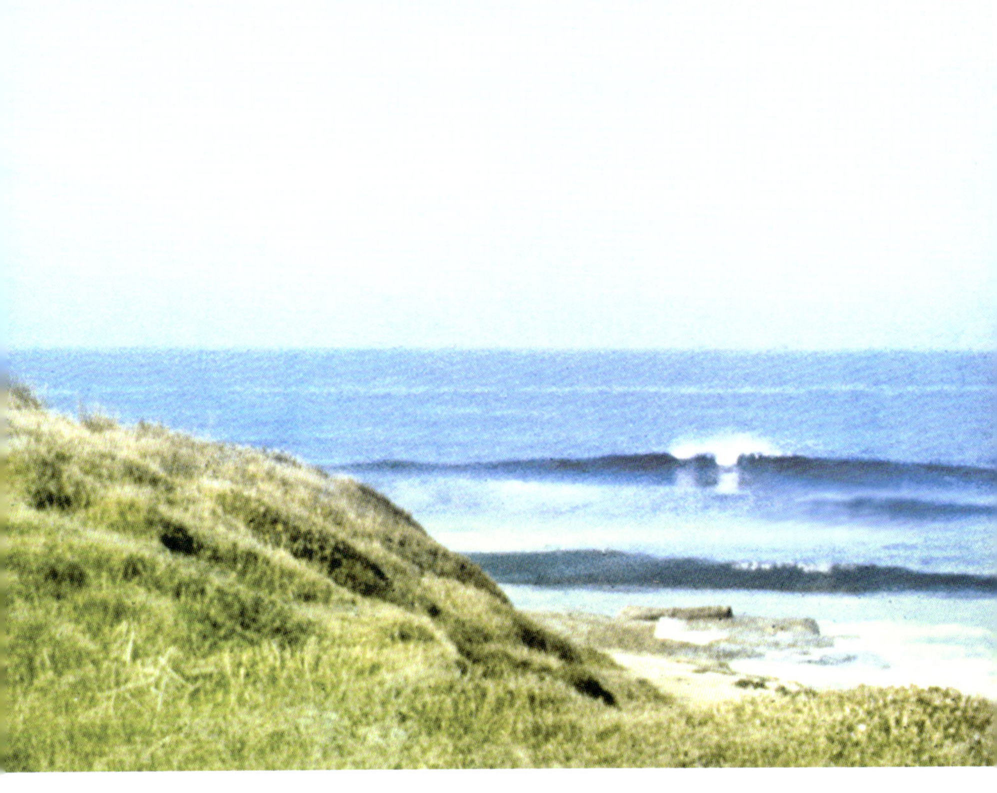

In Victoria, **Phillip Island**, northeast of Melbourne produced some good breaks, as did Flynns Reef (rights) and Cats Bay (lefts). On the other side of Port Phillip Bay, near Torquey, is Bells Beach, home of the annual Easter surfing contest. Although not a particularly hollow wave, Bell's is extremely powerful during the autumn and winter months.

The Bight, along Australia's southern coastline, has some of the most terrifying waves in the world. All the way from Port Campbell in Victoria to Albany in Western Australia there was good surf to be found. The desolate Cactus area on the edge of the Nullarbor Plan had three excellent reef breaks – Caves, Castles and Cactus itself.

In **Western Australia**, 200 kilometres south of the state capital Perth, the most famous and consistent wave can be found at Margaret River. All along the southern coastline are submerged reefs jutting out into the ocean. With the right swell and wind direction, all were capable of producing quality surf, especially during the autumn months.

Voodoo Reef Break, 1961. **BW**

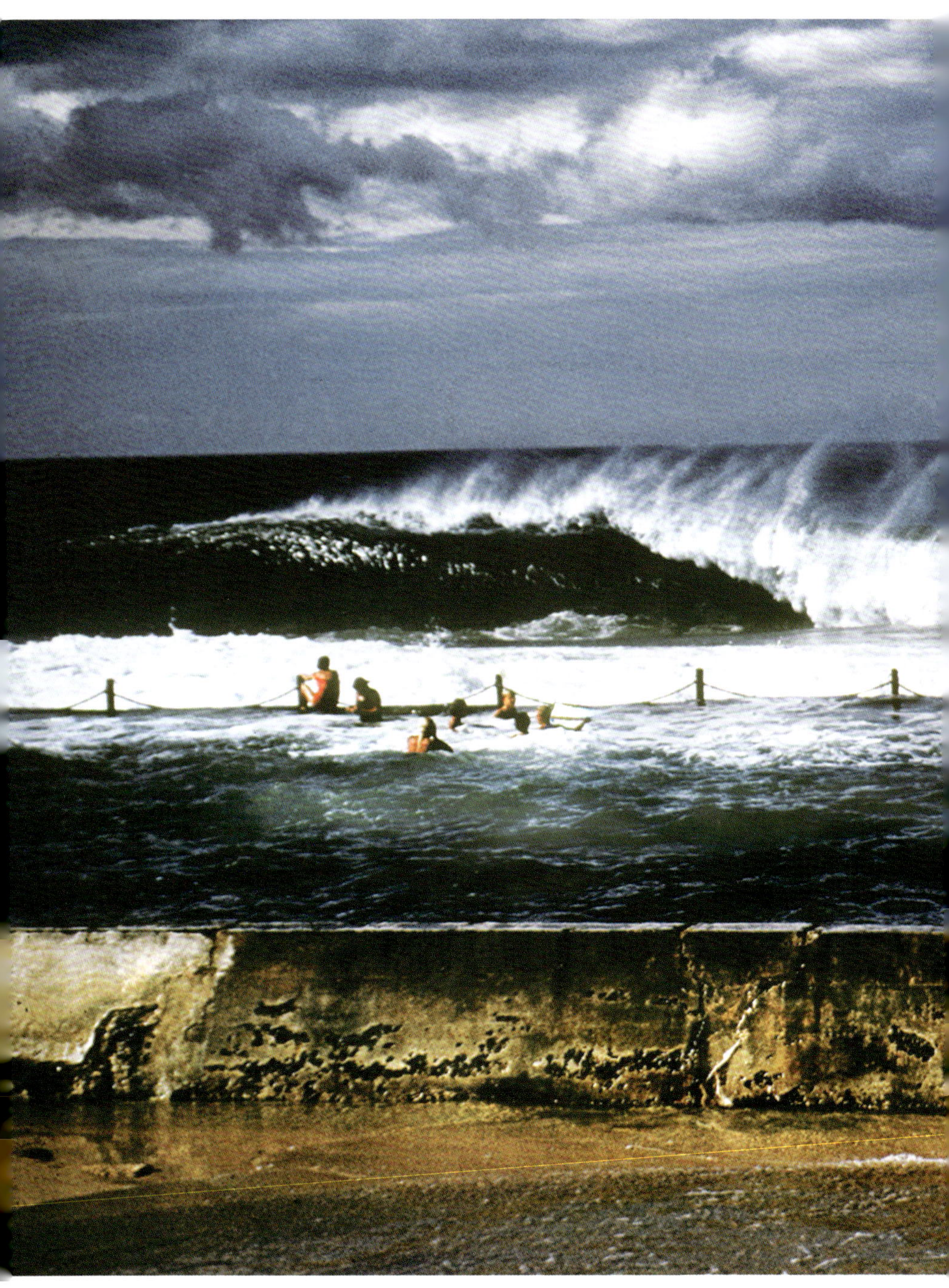

Cronulla Pool, 1960. **BW**

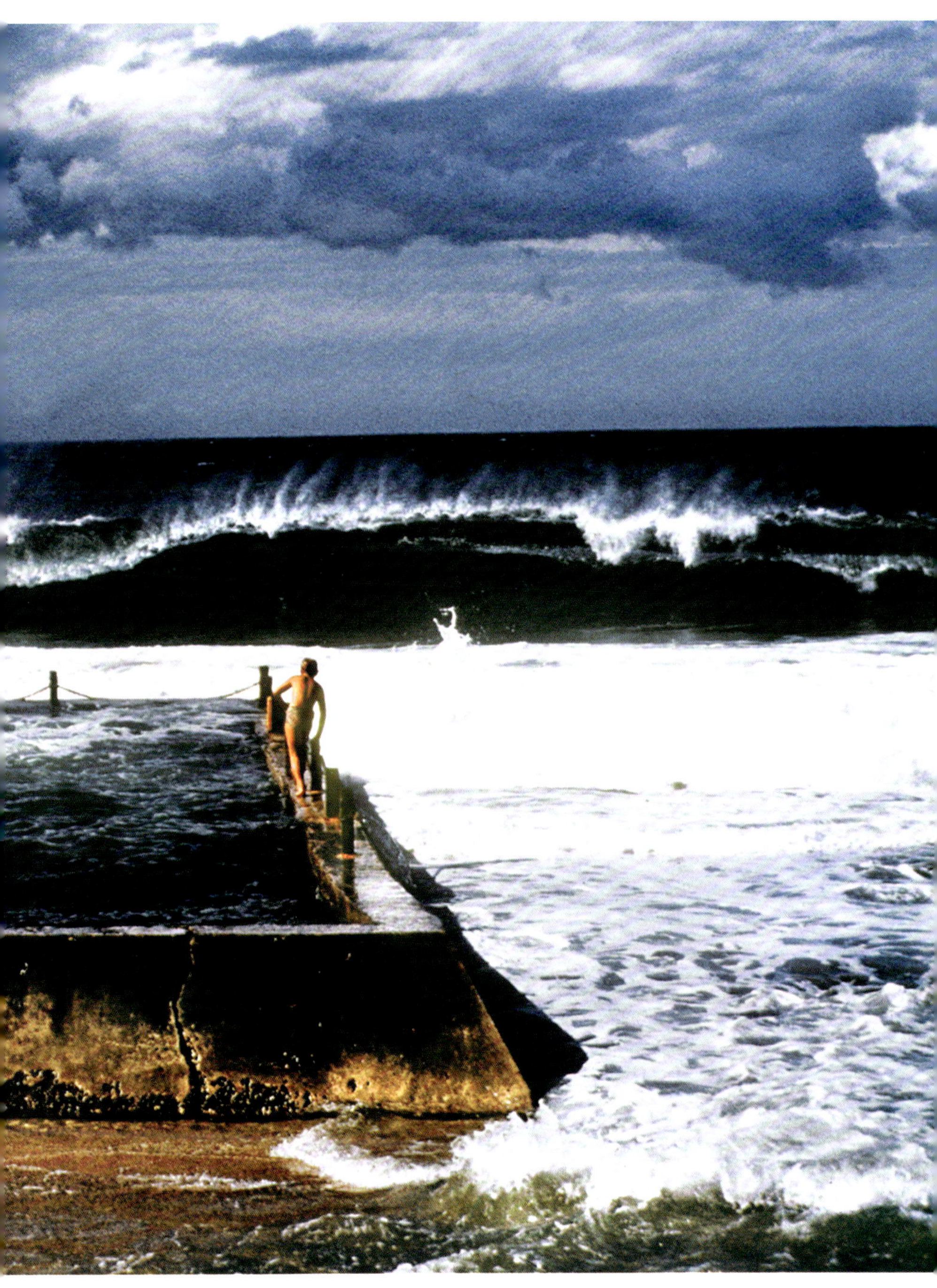

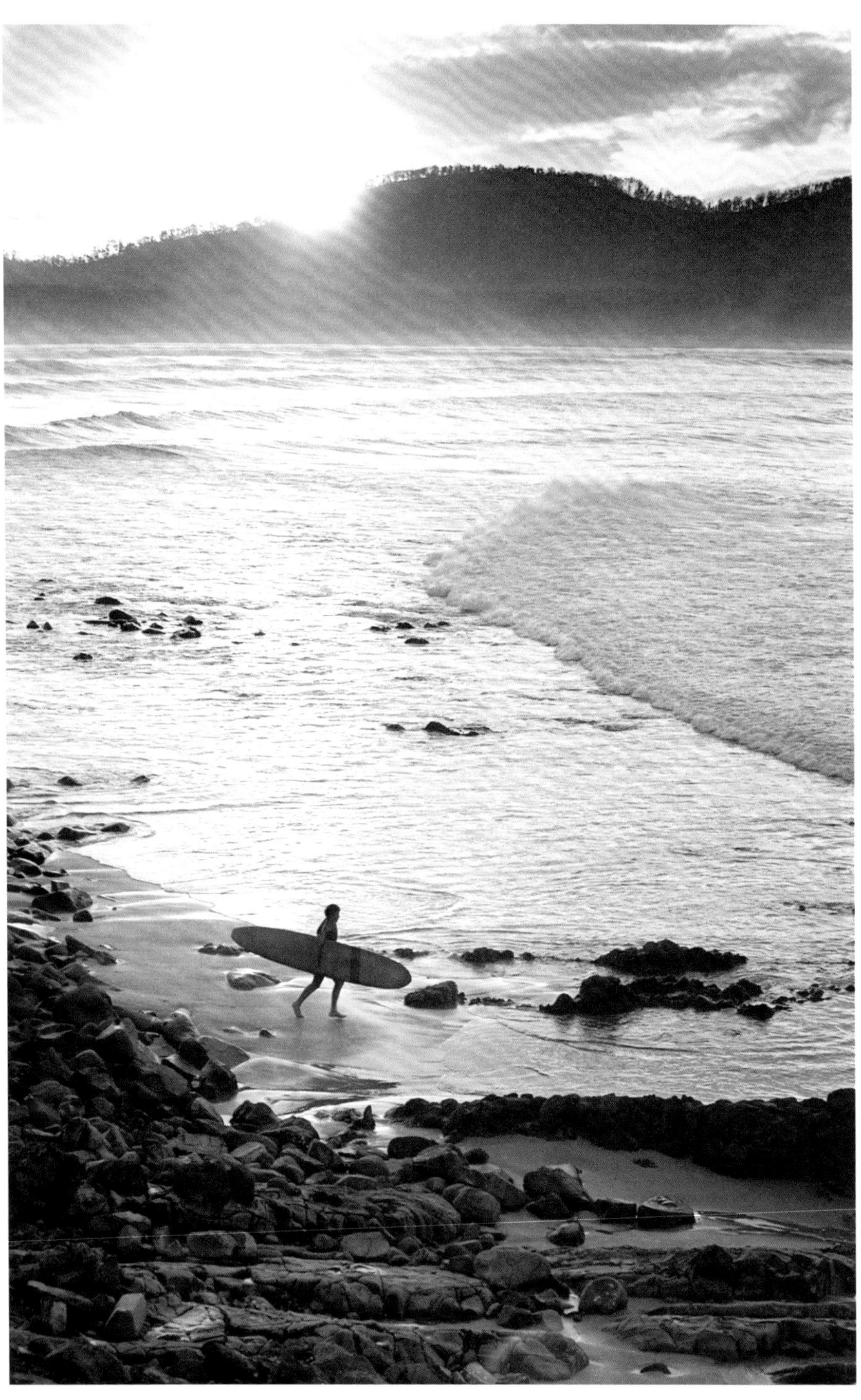

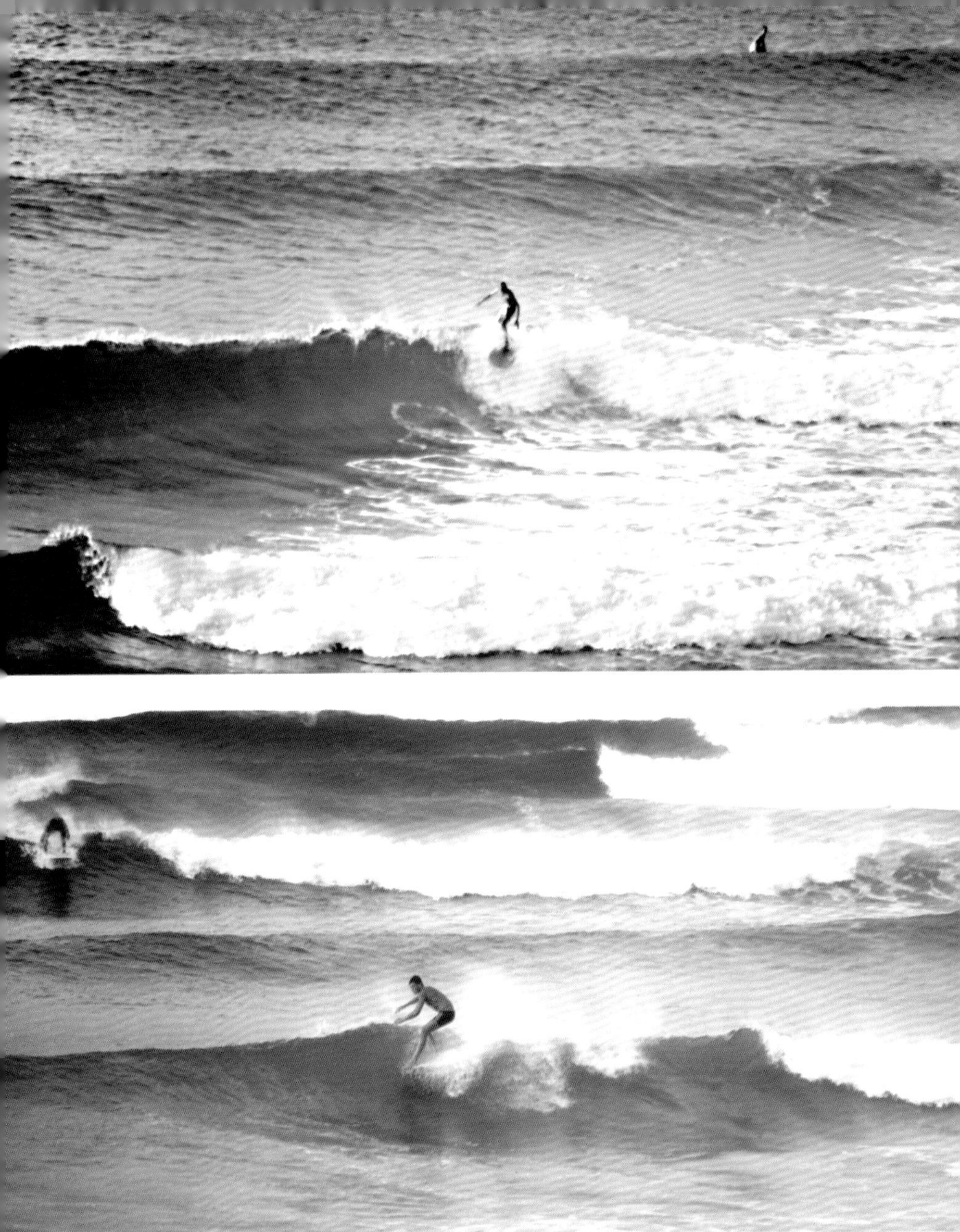

Above: Tony Butler, Coolangatta Beach from Kirra Hill **MS**

Below: Stewart Adams, Rainbow Bay, 1965. **MS**

Opposite: A surfer entering the water for a late afternoon surf at Crescent Head, 1965. Crescent Head was the first surfbreak to grab a few waves for Sydney surfers on their safaris up the north coast from Sydney in winter. **BW**

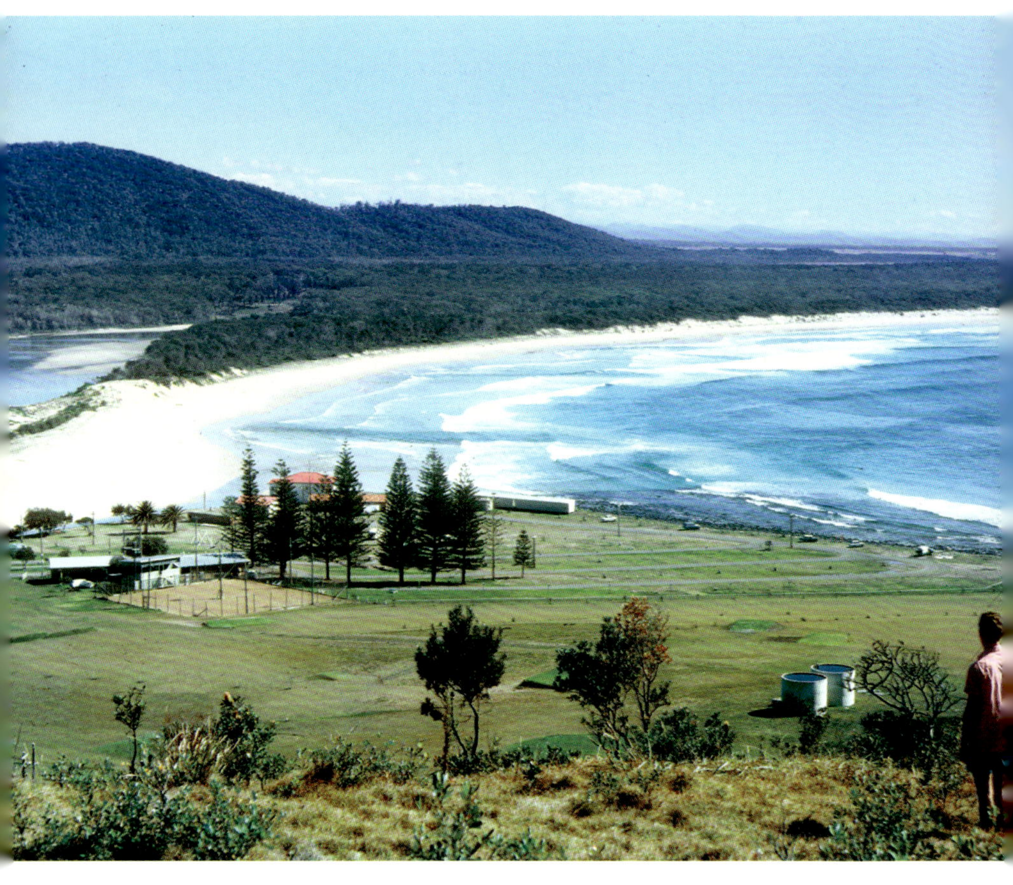

Crescent Head, 1966. Crescent Head was the first surf break to grab a few waves for Sydney surfers on their safaris up the north coast from Sydney in winter. **BW**

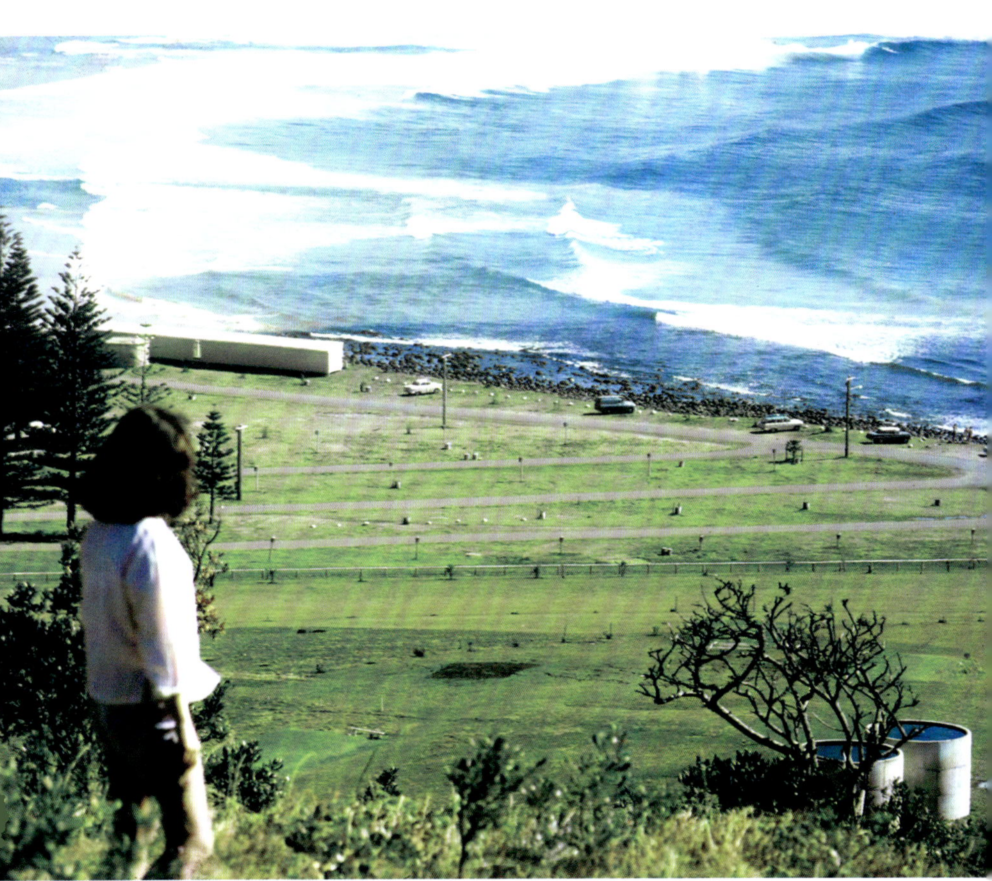

Looking down on the shed and parking area at Crescent Head in 1965. The Shed, with its tables and benches, was a great place to hang out and camp overnight. **BW**

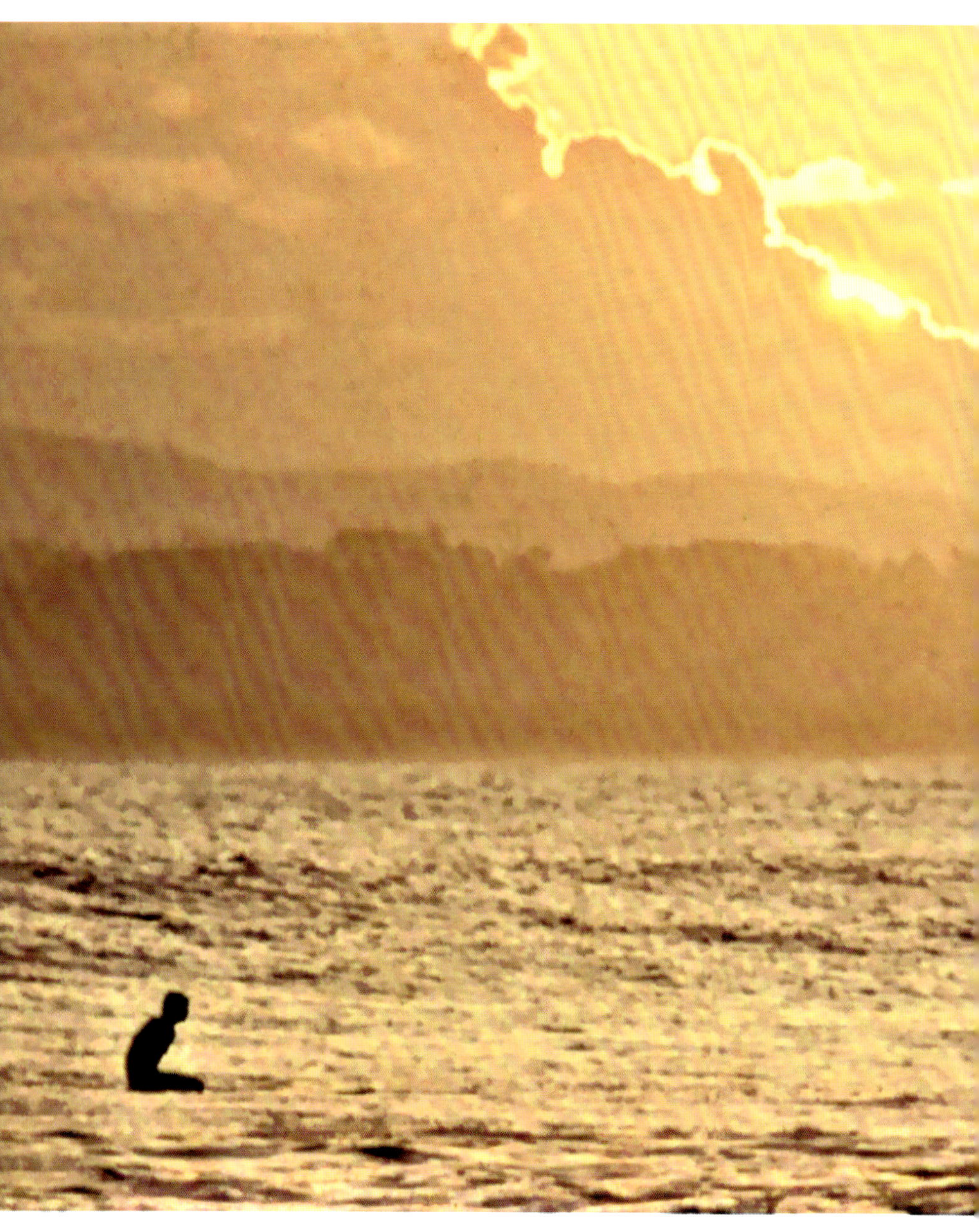

Kirra sunset, 1961. Errol Wright paddles out for the last wave of the day. **MS**

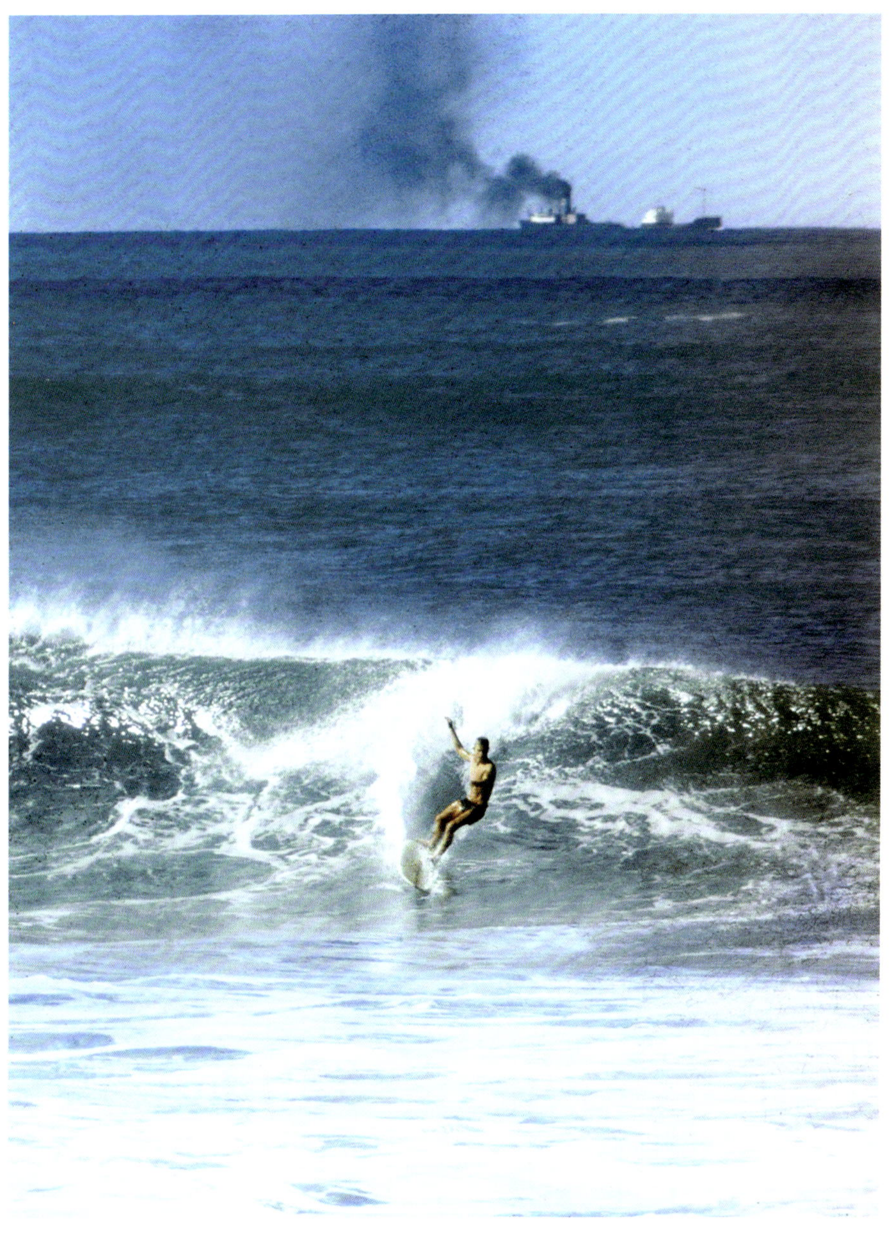

Midget, North Narrabeen, 1963. **BW**

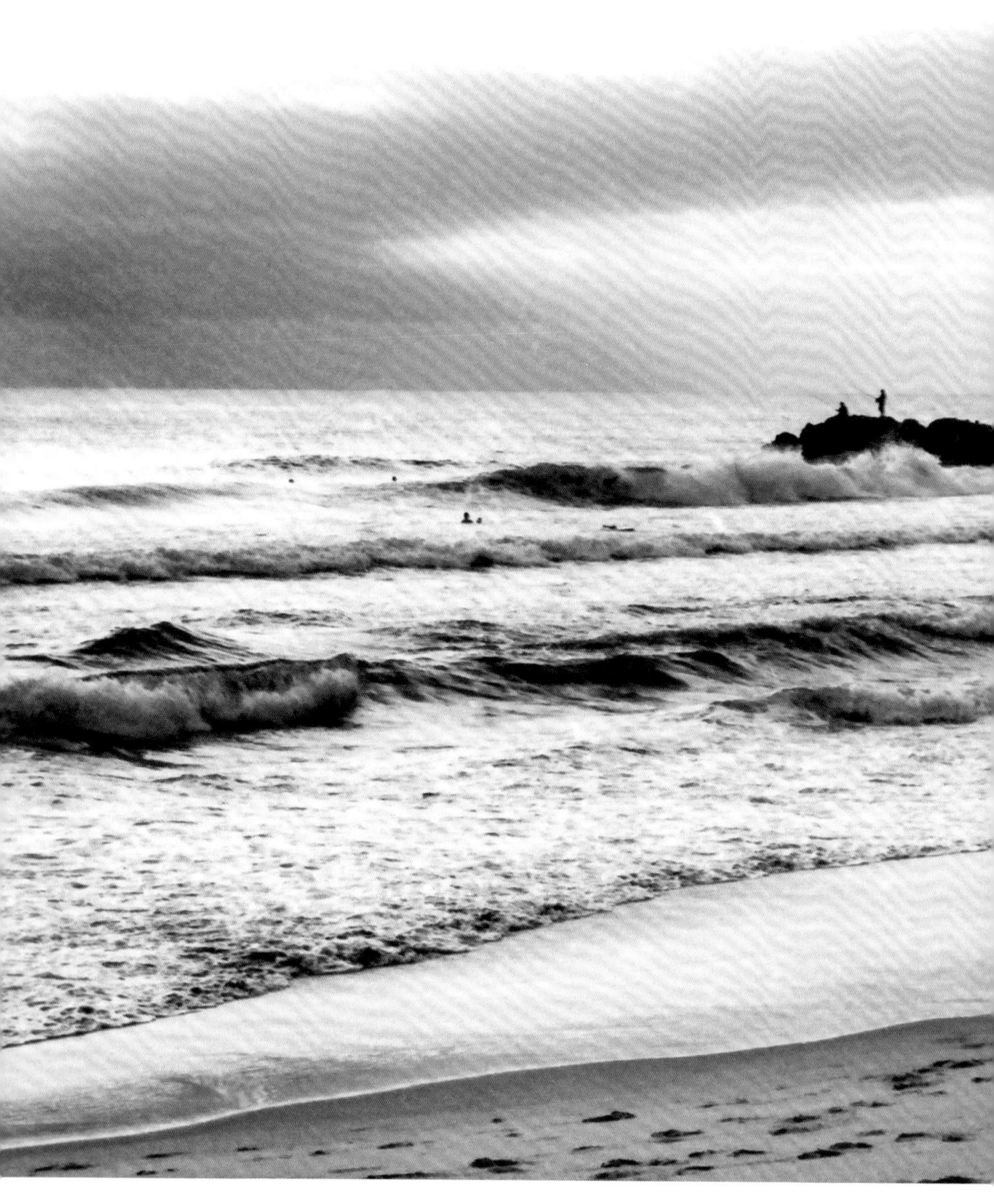

Elephant Rock, 1963. The wave break in these photos will probably never be seen again. Construction of the rock wall from the mainland to Currumbin Rock caused the sand build up we see today. Rocks in the foreground of the photo are now under the foreshore park. **MS**

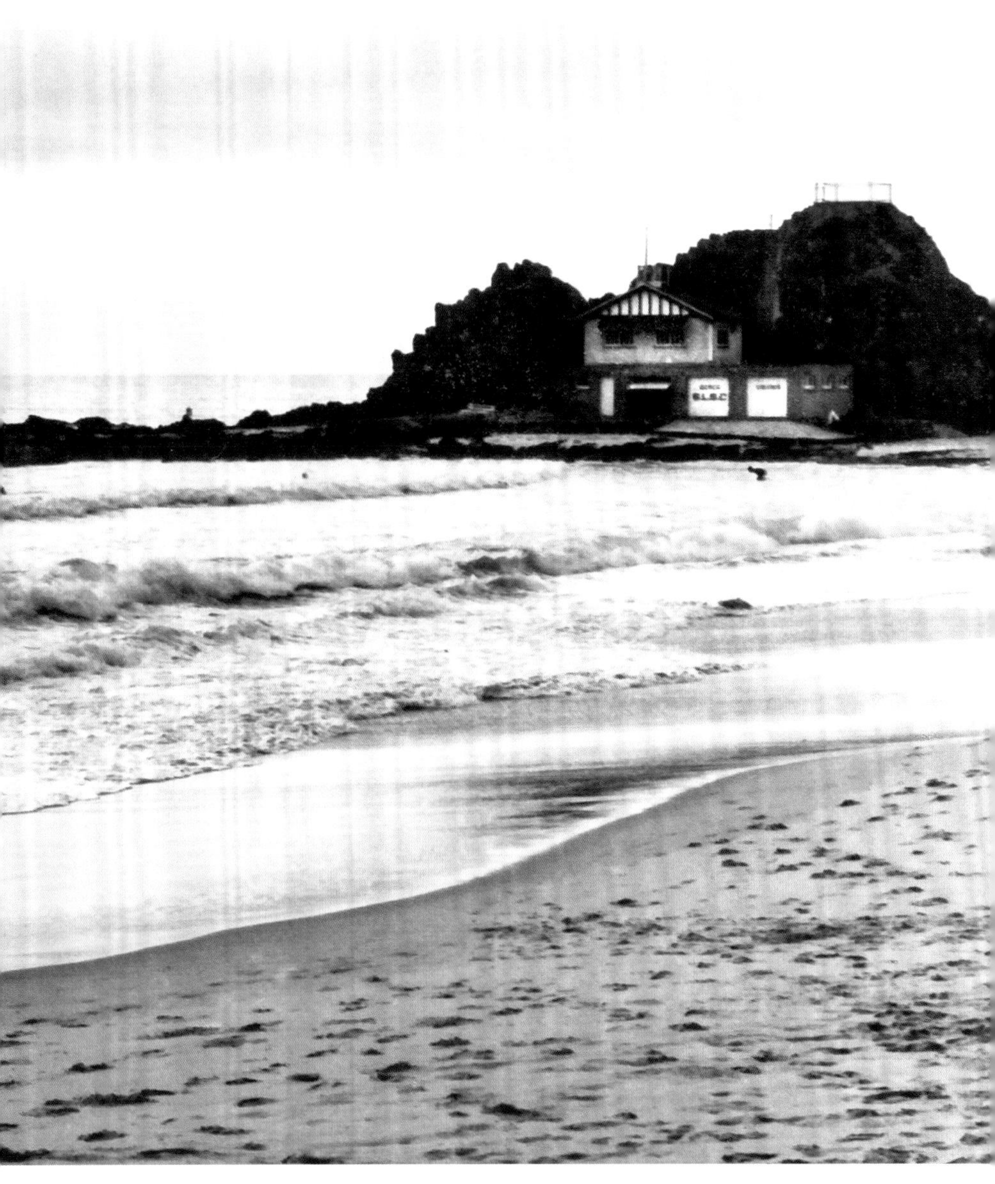

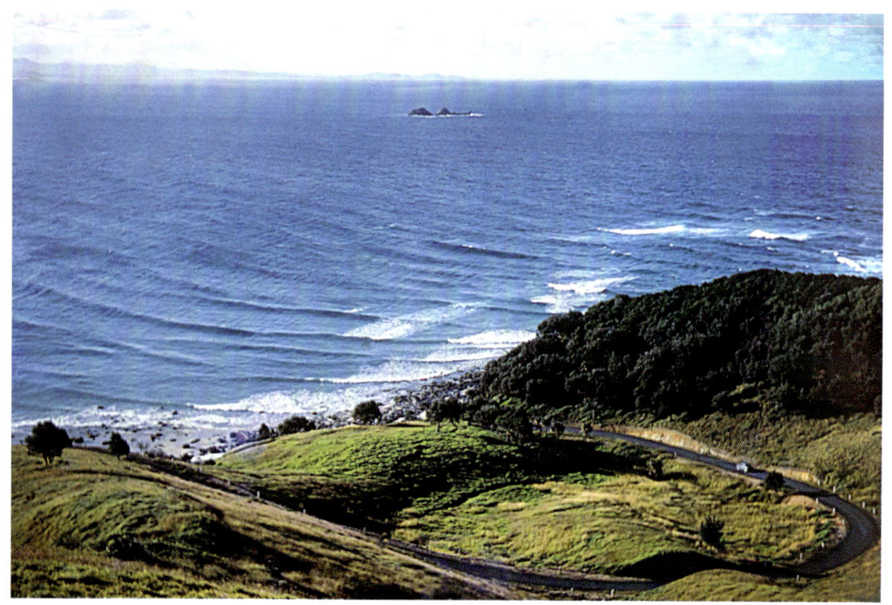

Above: **Wategos Beach, Byron Bay, 1963. MS**

Opposite: **Joe Larkin, National Park, 1963.** Taken on a trip up to Bundaberg showing a movie for Bob Evans. Along the way Joe and I surfed a perfect National Park for over two hours by ourselves with dozens of Portuguese Man O' War for company. I managed to talk Joe into staying out a while longer by himself while I took a few photos. Joe remembers the session well because he thought he was dead when he saw what he thought was a shark surfacing beside him only to realise it was a large turtle. **MS**

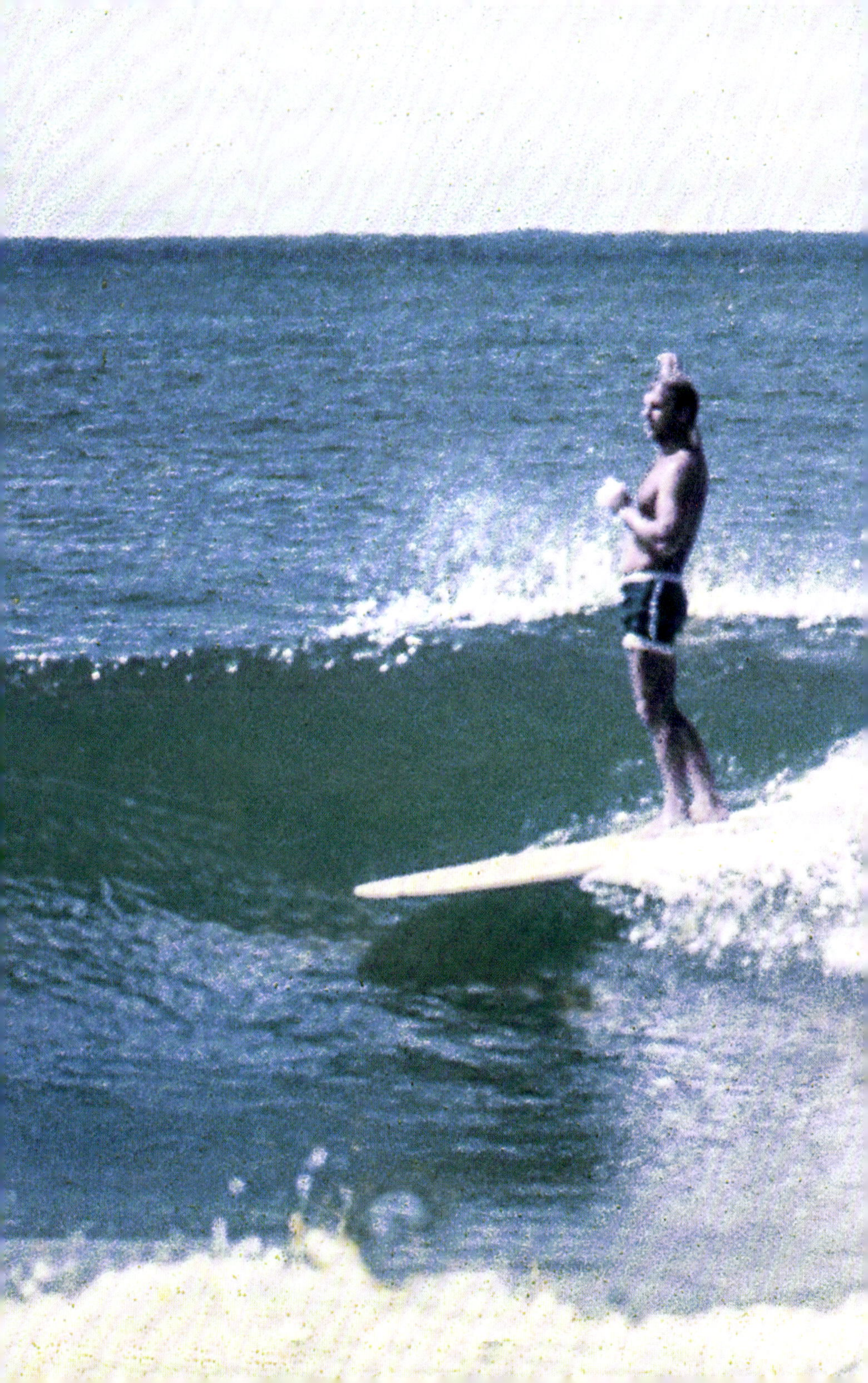

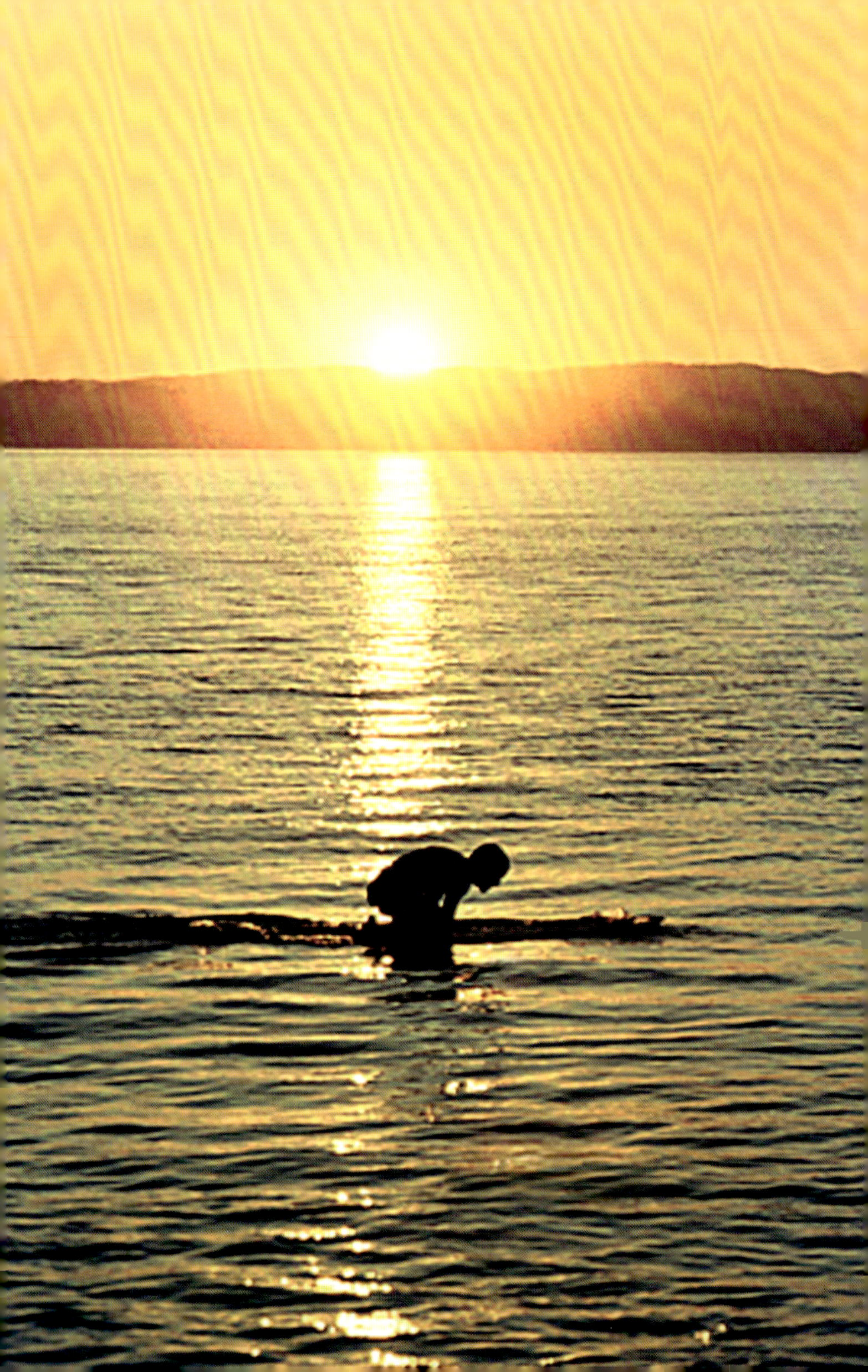

Gold Coast Holiday

July 1966 we holidayed on the Gold Coast again and enjoyed beautiful sunshiny days at my favourite spot, Greenmount beach in Coolangatta. I was always happy to lay on the beach and soak up the sun while Barrie surfed. This late afternoon I picked up his Minolta camera to take some shots of him as he caught a few late afternoon waves. The balmy conditions and proximity of the breaks from the sand enabled me to easily shoot away as he paddled out and caught the last waves of the day. I rarely used the camera but must have remembered this time how to adjust the lens and the light meter correctly before clicking away.

No digital photos or convenient multiple tries those days. Each shot had to be measured and carefully planned. Rolls of colour film weren't cheap so every shot counted. How easy it is today to shoot away with digital cameras, iPhones and iPads ... check each picture as you go and correct the next one if needed! Bingo! No waiting days or a week for the film to be processed to finally see how those shots turned out.

I was stoked to see the results of my casual photo shoot and we especially loved the sunset silhouette ... this one has been a significant trophy ... a lucky hole in one! Composition, timing, a great Minolta camera and relaxed luck of the moment and the result ... another beautiful sunset and some iconic shots for history to enjoy. **MADELEINE SUTHERLAND**

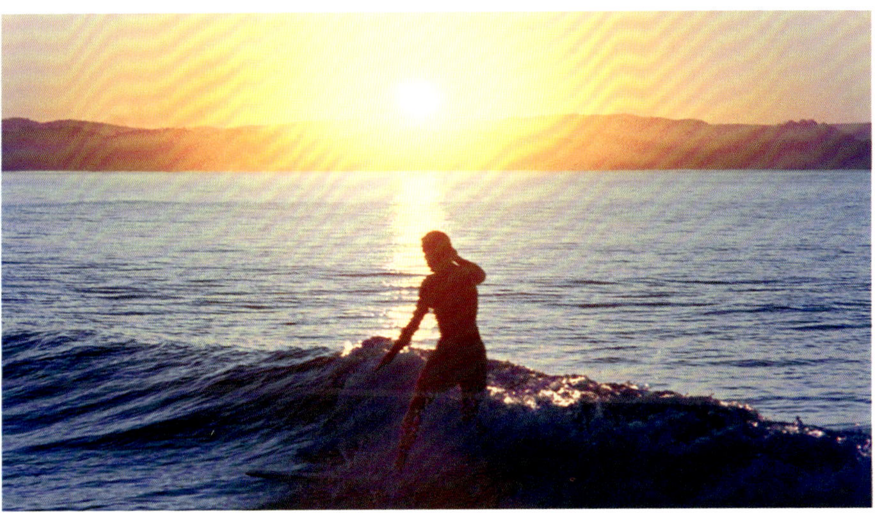

Above: **Barrie Sutherland cruising at Greenmount Point, July 1966.**
MADELEINE SUTHERLAND

Opposite: **Sunset wave.** Barrie Sutherland paddling back out, Greenmount Point, July 1966. **MADELEINE SUTHERLAND**

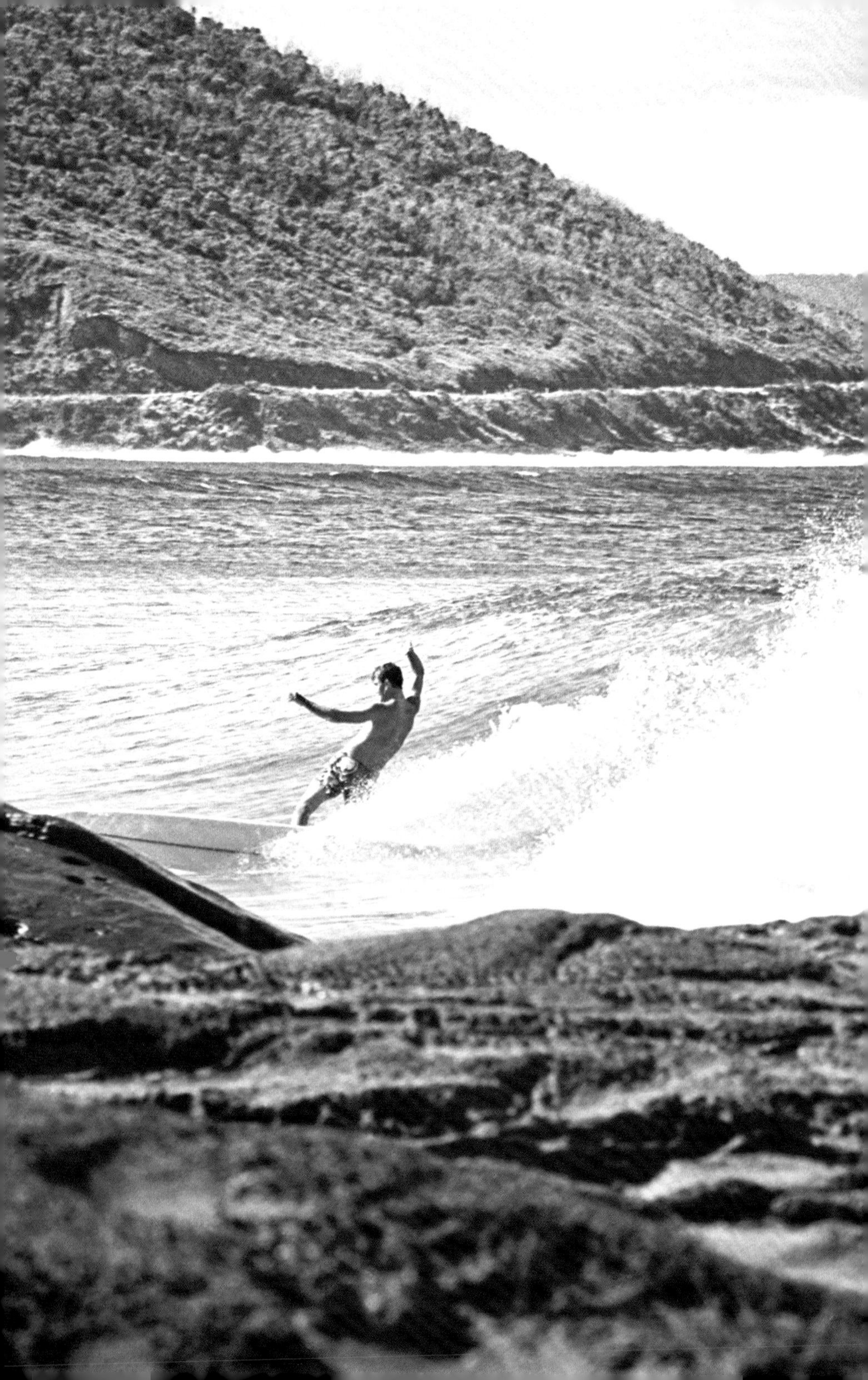

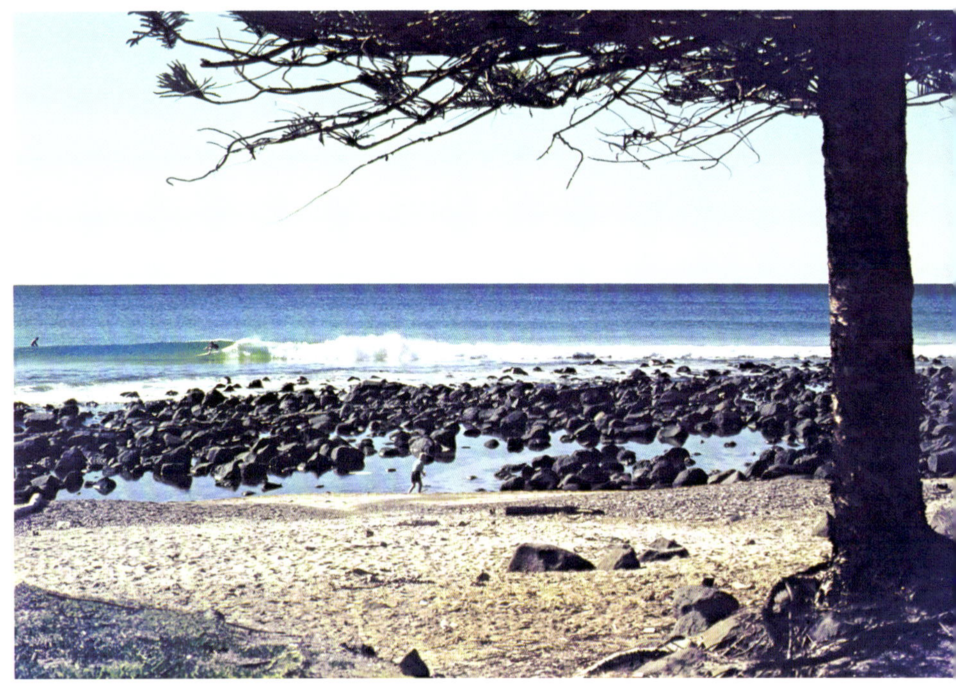

Seascape, Burleigh Heads, July 1966. **BS**

Richard Kavanaugh, Wye River. **BS**

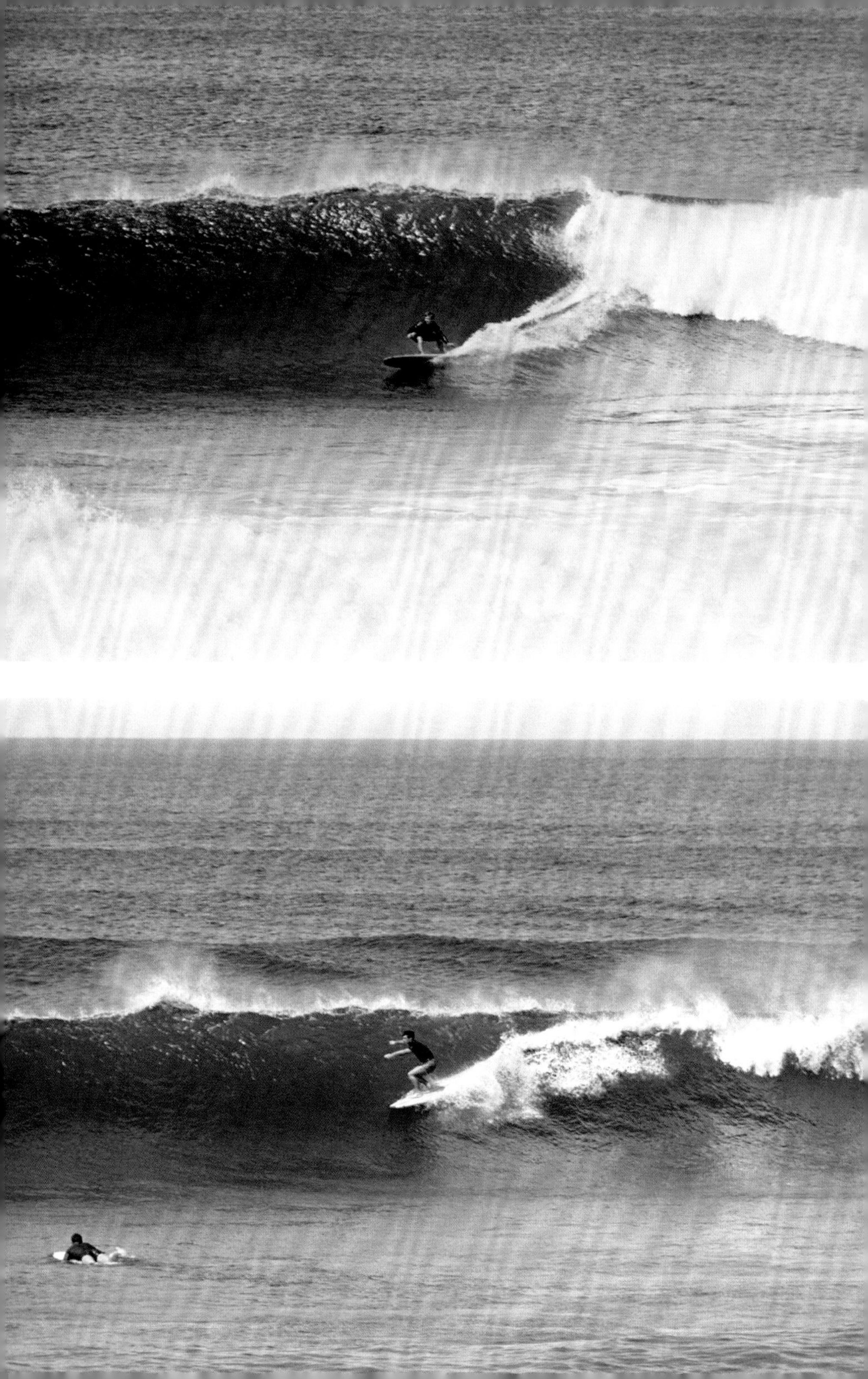

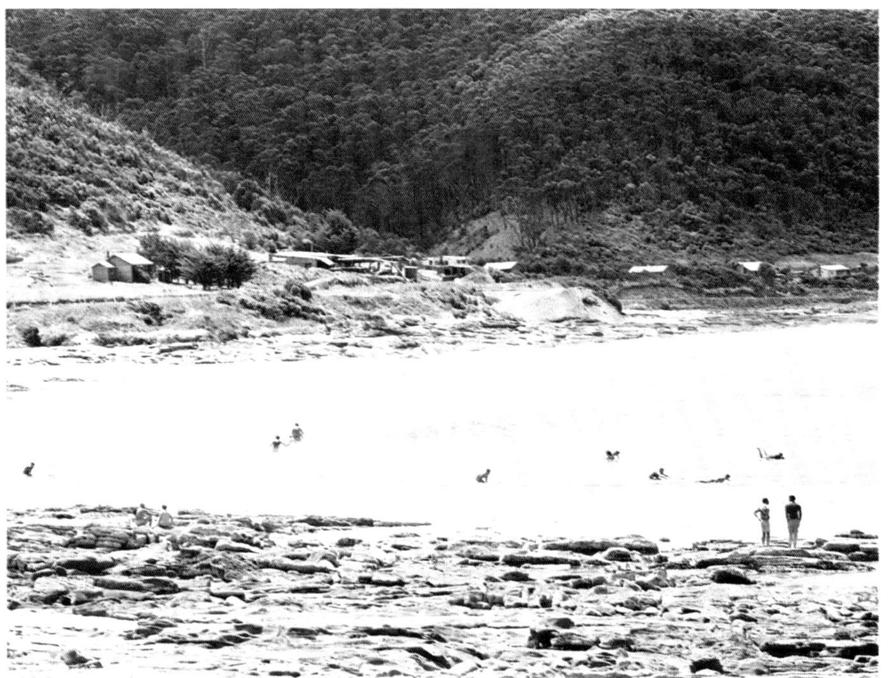

Above: **Kennett River, Victoria. BS**

Opposite top: **Marcus Shaw, Bells Beach, September 1964.** Marcus was one of the original Bells surfers. He had been spear fishing and surfing around the place for some time before I'd visited it in the summer of 1959. Marcus simply stood out in the lineout with his fearless attacking style of surfing. The biggest waves were always stamped with Marcus's trademark backhand attack – deep carving turns, low centre of gravity and huge acceleration off the bottom on his big gun boards. Way ahead of his time. **BS**

Opposite below: **Robbie Lane, Bells Beach, September 1964.** In the early publications of *Surfing World* magazine there are pictures of the Bower Boys who dominated Fairy Bower in the early 1960s. They were Robbie Lane and Glen Ritchie who were very good, strong surfers. Robbie loved Bells. When he came down in Easter 1964 he decided to stay for a season. He powered his way around Bells that winter and made a tremendous contribution to Victorian surfing. Robbie's surfing harmonised with Bells and laid the foundation for the emerging younger stars. He was a likeable and popular person. The Torquay crew adopted Robbie as one of their favourite sons. **BS**

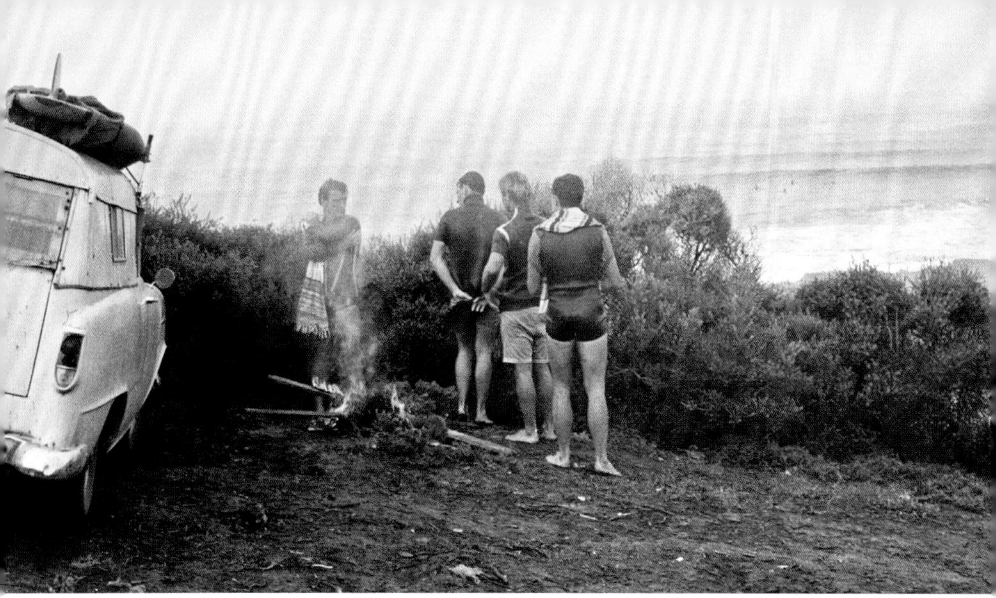

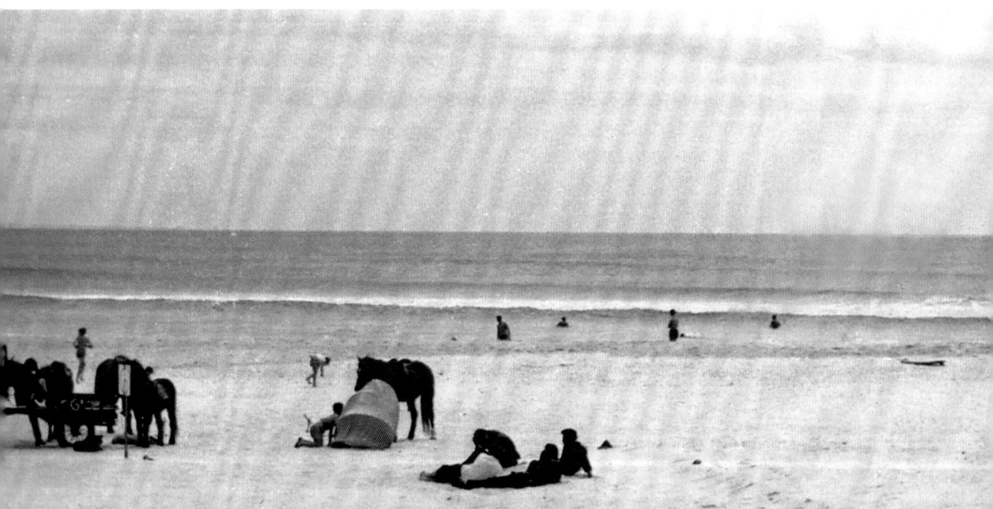

Above: **The car park fire, Bells Beach, Winter 1963.** Fires on the beach at Bells were common in the 1960s. Winters and were an integral part of our winter surfing culture. The Southern Ocean water is cold and the winds icy in late winter. The 1960s Bells surfers were a tough and dedicated crew, braving the Victorian winters to scale new heights of big wave surfing year after year. I took this photo of Marcus Shaw and his mates on an ordinary day at Bells, small swell and light north wind blowing across the wave faces, clearing the fog. It was very cold, hence the fire. From left Bryan Poynton, John Keilor, Marcus Shaw, Bernie Gebbie and Marcus's ute, balsa gun strapped on top! **BS**

Below: **Lone surfer, Greenmount Beach, 1961.** One of Mal's early surf photos using an unknown brand of rangefinder camera. The ponies on the left of the photo were owned by Stewart and Pansy McLean who gave pony rides along Kirra, Greenmount and Rainbow Bay beaches in the 1940s, '50s and early '60s. Sadly, colourful beach characters like the McLeans, Jack Evans, Johnny Charlton, Fred Lang and John (The Mutton Bird Man) Patterson, who became icons of the era, have disappeared from our beaches. **MS**

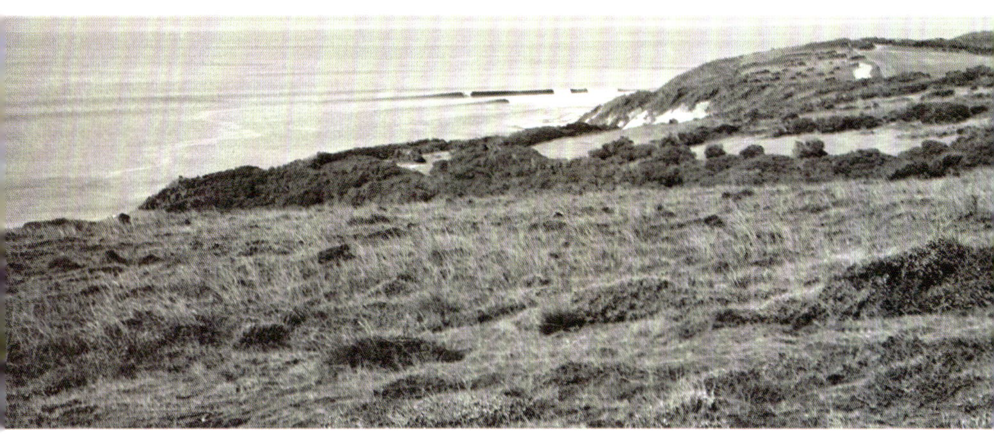

Winki Pop and Old Bells Track, June 1963. My first visit to Bells came via the Jarosite track in February 1959. At the time I was a first year civil engineering student. Wednesday afternoons was allocated for sport and it just so happened there were several of us who were surfers! Naturally we'd travel to Torquay for surfing. There was always a student who had access to a vehicle. In the early 1960s, Torquay surfing elder and legend Joe Sweeney raised the money and organised a local farmer to bulldoze the first access road. It ran west from Jan Juc along the cliff tops to Bells Beach. In summers it was dry, dusty and rough, in winters wet, muddy and easy (for the uninitiated drivers) to get bogged in some sections. **BS**

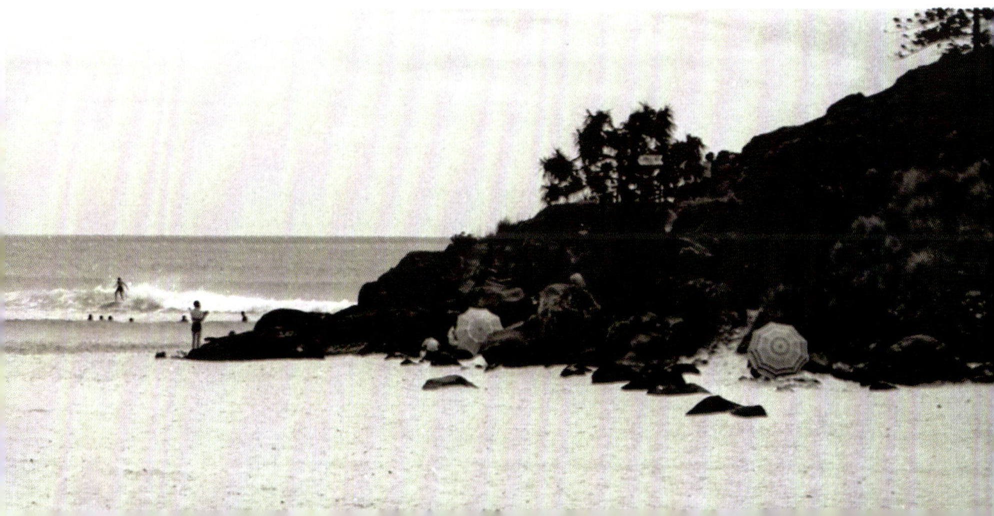

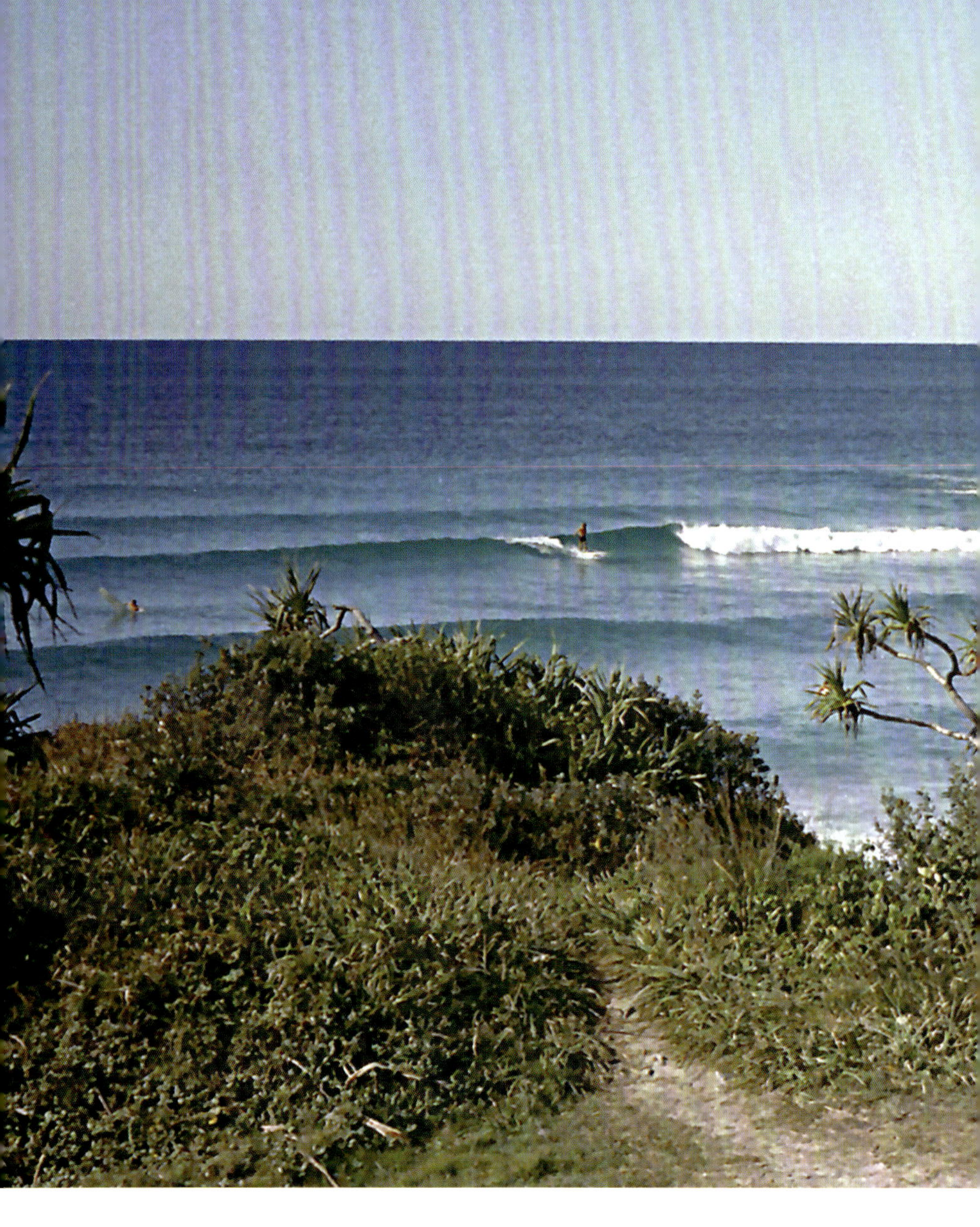

Cabarita, 1962. The Kirra crew were told about Cabarita or Bogangar as we knew it by two local spearfishermen in 1957 and were probably the first to surf there. Access at that time was partially by a sand track constructed by the sand mining companies. It became one of our favoured winter surf locations.

When this photo was taken in 1962 it was still unspoiled and uncrowded. **MS**

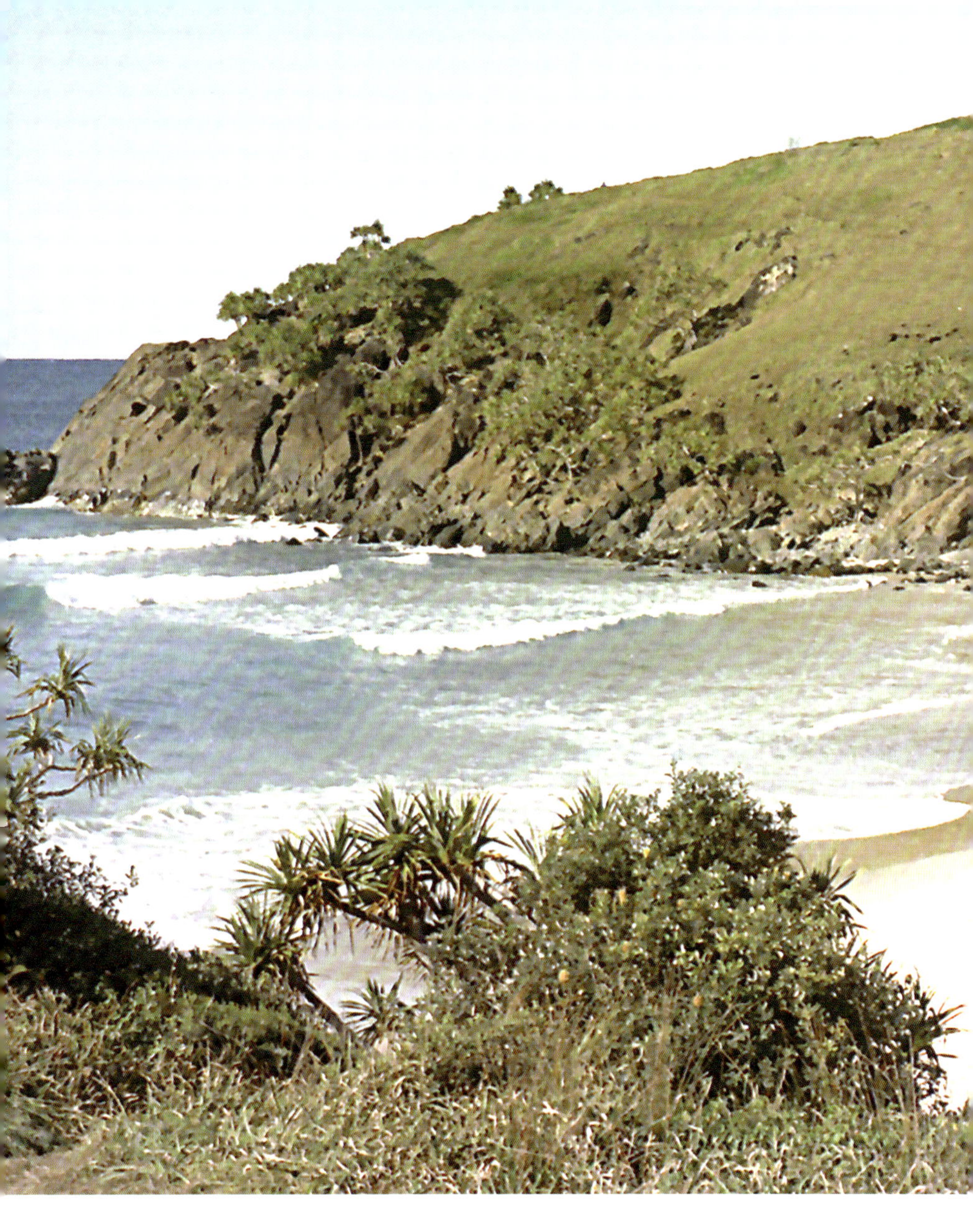

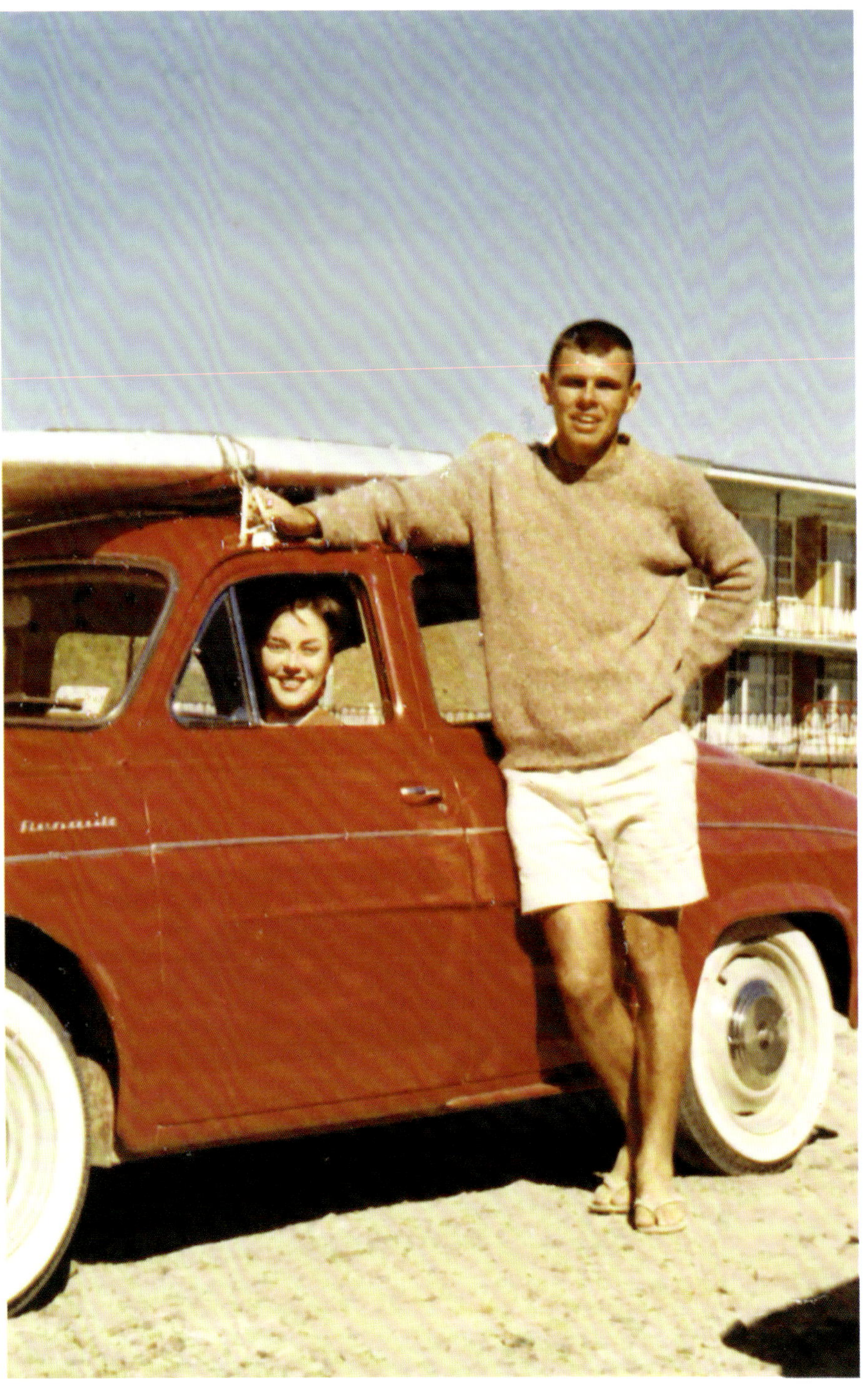

Mal Sutherland

From the age of four Kirra Beach was Mal's playground. In his youth he rode surf-o-planes courtesy of Jack Evans who had the hire concession for Kirra Beach at the time. He purchased the first of two 16ft ply paddle boards in 1953 at age 13 and in late 1956 obtained one of the first hollow-ply Okanui boards to come to Queensland. This was followed by two balsa boards, the first made by Noel Ward and Scott Dillon and the second by Gordon Woods and in 1960 changed to the first of many foam and fibreglass boards.

In 1961 Mal became Queensland agent for Scott Dillon Surfboards and sold many boards to the up and coming surfers of the era.

Because of his interest in photography, in 1962 he was invited by Jack Eden to be Queensland correspondent for the newly launched *Surfabout* magazine and had his first article published in Vol.1 No.3. Later in the 1960s he supplied a number of photographs for Bob Evans' *Surfing World*.

Through surfing contacts he had made he was asked by Paul Witzigs' Surfing Promotions to organize theatre bookings and poster distribution for Bruce Browns' *Barefoot Adventure*, *Slippery When Wet* and *Surf Crazy* the first Surf Movies to be shown in Queensland in January 1962. This led to a long association with Bob Evans Films. At times when Bob was unavailable to travel he showed Bob's movies and those Bob imported from the USA and Hawaiian film makers Bud Browne, Dale Davis and MacGillivary and Freeman, up and down the coast from Taree to Bundaberg, generally surfing and taking his still photos along the way.

He still maintains his interest in photography and in 2005 won the Animal Portrait Division of The ANZANG Wild Life Photographer of the Year awards run by the West Australian Museum. Since the resurgence of the longboard and resulting interest in our surfing heritage Mal's photos have been featured in *Pacific Longboarder Magazine*, Japanese surfing magazines Nalu and Blue, several German tourism magazines, *Rolling Stone Magazine* and a number of hard-cover books on surfing including *Switchfoot* 1, 2 and 3 and *Stoked* by Bob McTavish. In addition, he has written several articles on past legends of the industry for *Pacific Longboarder Magazine*.

Mal has held successful exhibitions of his photographs in the Gold Coast and Noosa Art Galleries and the Bribie Island Museum and has been involved in the establishment of Surf World Gold Coast and held the position of Chairperson for 7 years and Vice Chair for one year.

Mal is a foundation member and life member of both the Kirra Surfriders Club and the Australian Surfriders Association of Queensland (now Surfing Queensland) and was runner up in the open Mens' Division of the inaugural ASAQ Queensland Titles in 1964.

John Pennings

From the inception of surfing media in Australia (1960), the profession of 'Surf Photographer' has always been an elusive livelihood. We hear many stories from the older photographers who 'had to get a real job' and leave surfing photography behind in order to support themselves and their families. 'It would be just enough to pay for the film and the processing', says 74-year-old Sydney-based photographer John Pennings when asked about the pay rates in the early 1960s, when he was working for Bob Evans at the fledgling *Surfing World* magazine. Taking these photographs was a passion project. He made his own darkroom/processing lab and learned all the skills.

'I set up my own little darkroom where I was living in Newport, Sydney. In the darkroom you take the film out of the camera and load it into a spool. You mix your processing solutions (chemicals) up in a tank put your film in and then hang your film up to dry once it is processed. You would put it through the enlarger once it is dried and print off that. I processed my own film for eight years while I was taking surfing photographs from 1962–1970. By 1970 my interest turned to courting women and my trade as a builder, where I could earn enough money to support my family.'

In 2010 the archives of John Pennings were sitting in shoeboxes in his garage in Sydney. It was only through the incessant pestering of *SwitchFoot* author Andrew Crockett, that those shoeboxes were eventually dusted off and taken to a digital scanning lab.

'I am very glad I did,' he says. 'It has been a pleasure signing prints and things and reliving that chapter of my life. Surfing sure has changed.'

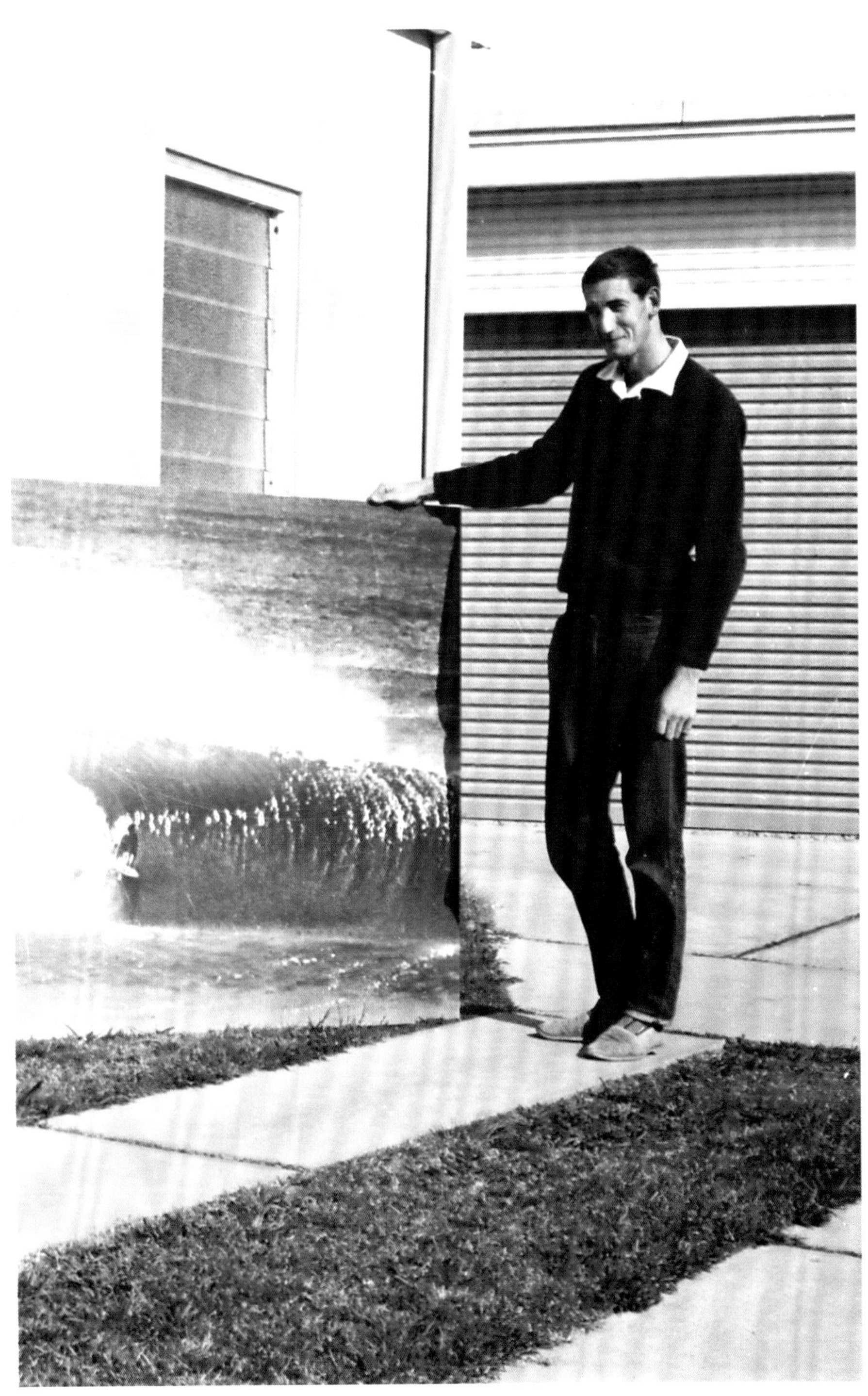

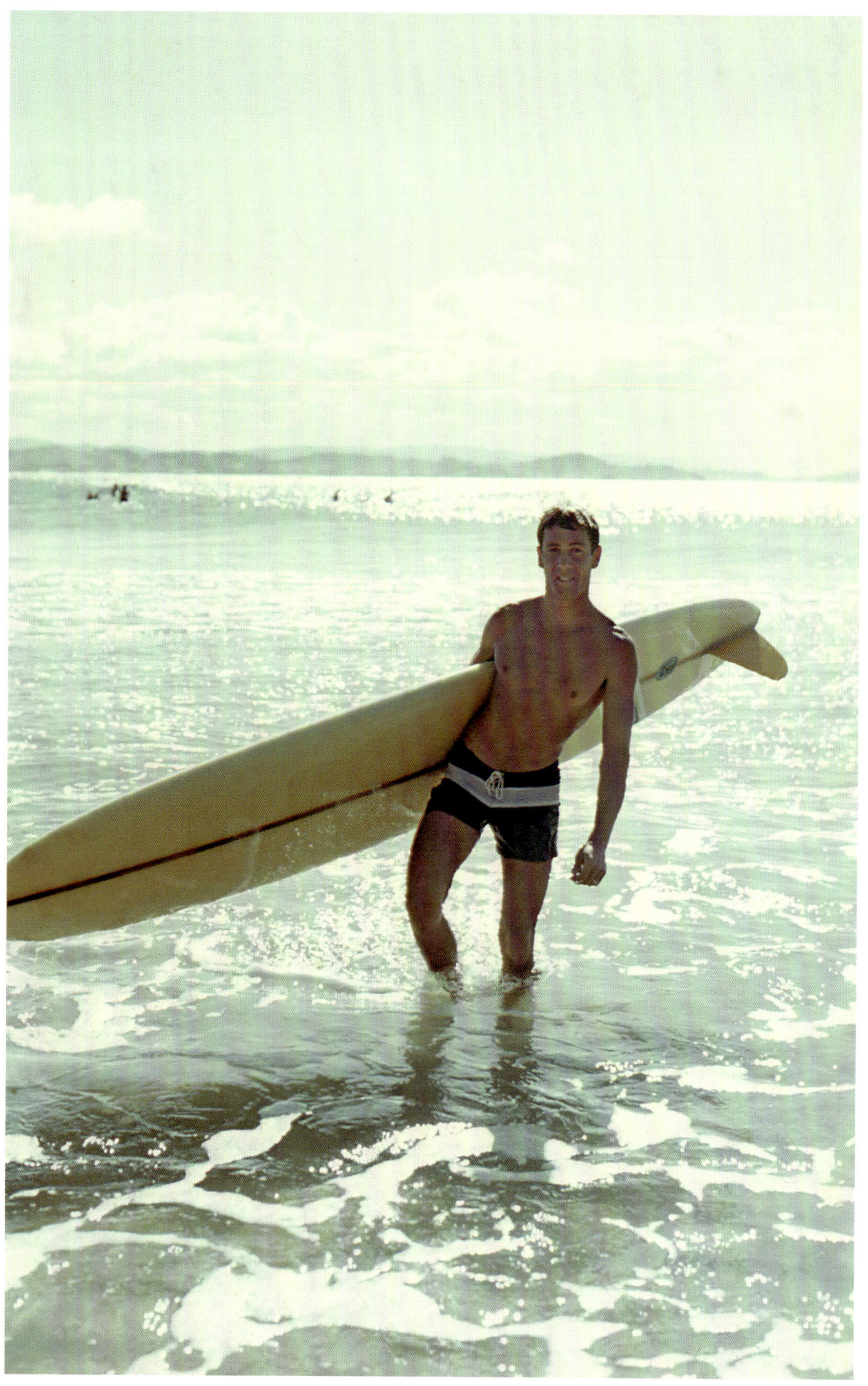

Barrie Sutherland

Barrie Sutherland is an Australian pioneer surf photographer who surfed and photographed the Victorian Surf Coast and Great Ocean Road throughout the 1960s. He was part of the 1960s Torquay-Bells Beach surfing community, a foundation member of the Torquay Board-riders and respected for his surfing ability. Surfing came first and photography second. The combination produced one of Australia's finest portfolios of surfing photographs. It contains many of the legends of Australian surfing in some of the best-quality competition surf captured in the country.

Dave Swan, *Smorgasboarder Magazine*, says, 'It's perhaps at times a title too easily bestowed upon people, but Victorian photographer Barrie Sutherland truly is a living legend of the lens. His celebrated work literally spans the last half a century of surfing, all starting when he first picked up a Kodak Box Brownie back in the late 1950s.'

Throughout the 1960s, Barrie worked with the major Australian surfing magazines – *Surfabout* staff photographer, *Surfing World* contributing photographer. His coverage of the Bells Easter contest is renowned for its historical significance, capturing a special time and place in the evolution of Australian surfing. Easter Sunday 1965 was the most dangerous and heaviest swell ever experienced in an Australian Surfing contest. Barrie captured that epic event on the one roll of film he had with him. Many years' later author and journalist Phil Jarratt wrote in *Australian Surfer's Journal* (Vol 1 No.2), 'As competitors struggled to get out into the line-up through a 12–15 foot roaring forties swell, a lone photographer, Barrie Sutherland, shot the drama of the event. Robert Conneeley won the event and Sutherland's photos forever fixed Bells in the mind of many as Australia's Waimea Bay'.

Barrie retired from surfing photography in 1970 after he joined mining giant, Alcoa of Australia in Geelong. He transferred to WA in 1974 where he honed his surfing skills on the solid WA left breaks from Yallingup to Margaret River. 30 years later and in retirement, Barrie and his wife Madeleine returned to Torquay in 2006 where they opened WaterMarks Gallery. His home surfing break is Bells Beach about 5 minutes from he lives today. He surfs as often as he can.

Bob Weeks

Bob Weeks began taking photographs, developing and printing them when he was 10 years old, way back in 1950s Sydney. The photos featured in this book are from Bob's iconic 1960s surfing collection, which form part of his vast photographic portfolio, and today are regarded as some of the finest in Australian surfing history. Back in 1962, keen photographer and surfer Jack Eden approached Bob and artist Garry Birdsall to join him in planning a new surfing magazine. After a number of meetings, the magazine was designed and printed. Bob's choice of name was agreed on and *Surfabout* was launched.

Bob moved on from 'surfing photography' in the late 1960s, realising that 'things change'. A professional photographer, he has an award-winning collection that traverses many genres and six decades of passion … 'the sort of passion that keeps you awake at night tinkering with the possibilities' he says.

Bob has won many awards as a member of the AIPP including the black and white section in the Nikon 1992/1993 International Photo Contest. There were over 34,000 entries in both the colour and black and white sections. As recently as September 2016 he won the photography section of his local art festival and shared the 'Grand Champion' Award with a local wood carver!

Today, Bob is just as stoked about photography as he's ever been and knows his way around modern equipment and post production techniques like he was born in the technological age. From the early 1950s to today, the passion still burns. Bob's commitment to high-quality photographic restoration and archival quality prints is a testament to his old school way of life … 'take your time and build things that will stand the test of time!'

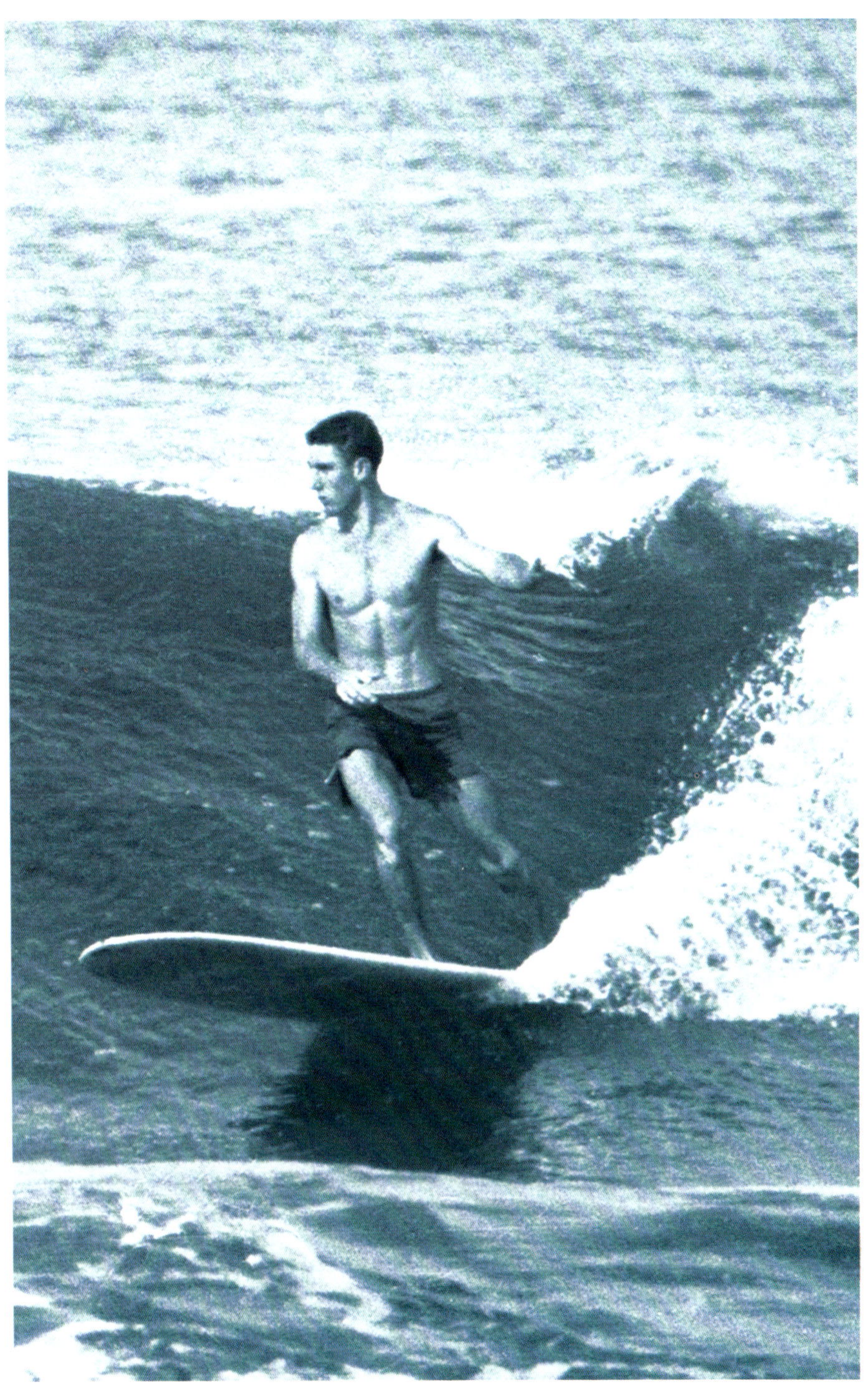

Geelong, Victoria's largest provincial city was the gateway to the coast and Great Ocean Road in the 1960s. Today the city and CBD is by-passed on the sleek M1 linking Melbourne to the coast and Western District. For me it's a one hour drive from home (a few kilometres inland from Bells) to Melbourne and no traffic lights!

I took the photo on Christmas Eve at 8:10pm after a rain storm had passed over the CBD. Waited for a break in traffic and walked onto the road and took it with my trusty Minolta SR1, hand held. It tells a story of Geelong's CBD changed, long gone as the main thoroughfare to the coast.

Moorabool Street is still the main North-South street in the CBD with its strip shopping, but over 50 years later it has changed. Gone are the streams of traffic (and congestion) with vehicles carrying surfboards on their way home to Melbourne on Sunday evenings. Now it's much quieter than those days when it was sunny, warm and clean grounds swells rolling into Bells. The surfers made their way to the coast via Moorabool Street and returned tired, eager to get home. The long drive to Melbourne confronted them.

It was the way home!

BARRIE SUTHERLAND

Moorabool Street, Geelong. The route to Torquay and the Great Ocean Road, Christmas Eve, December 1966. **BS**

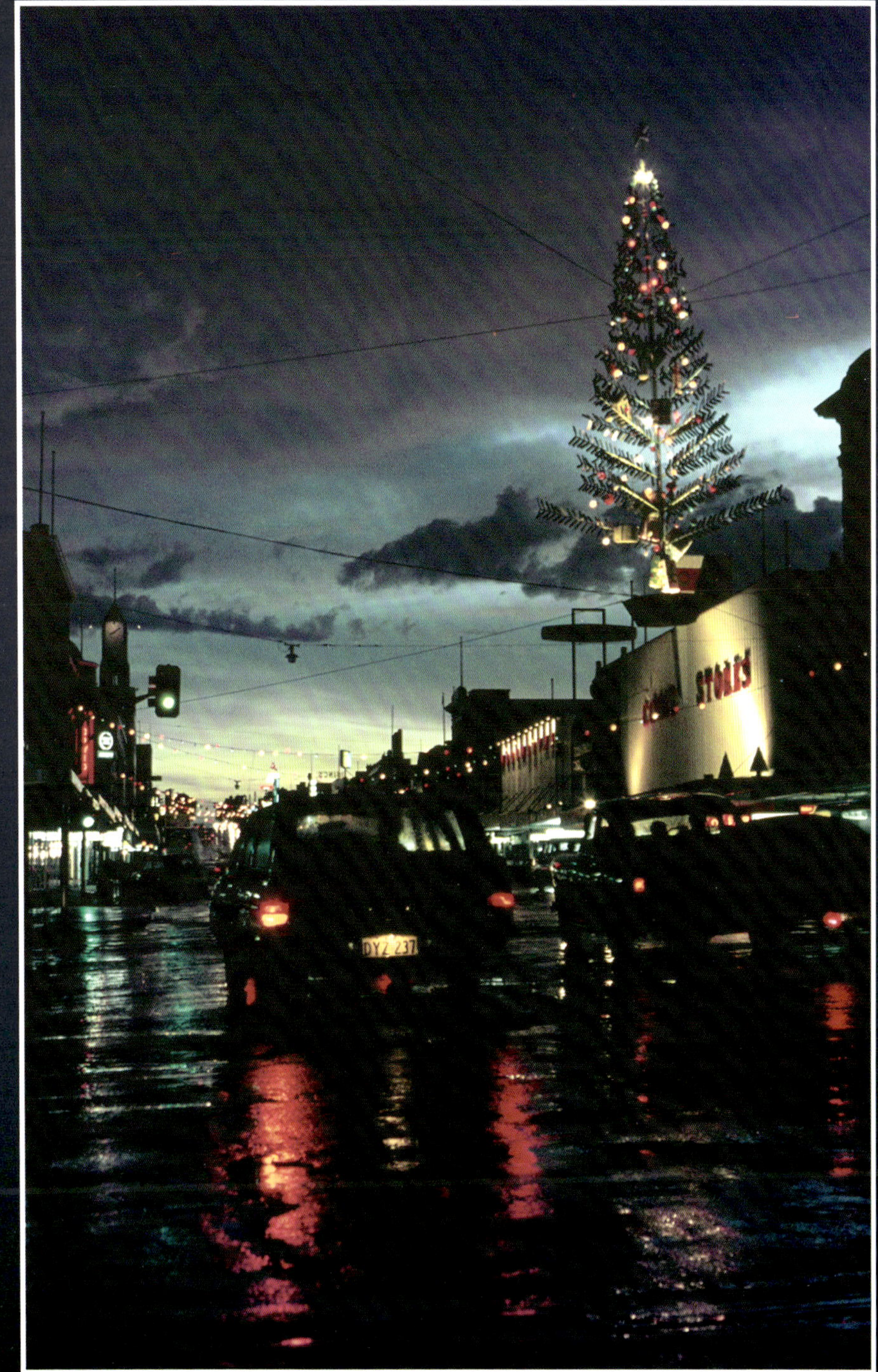
STOTTS
DYZ 237

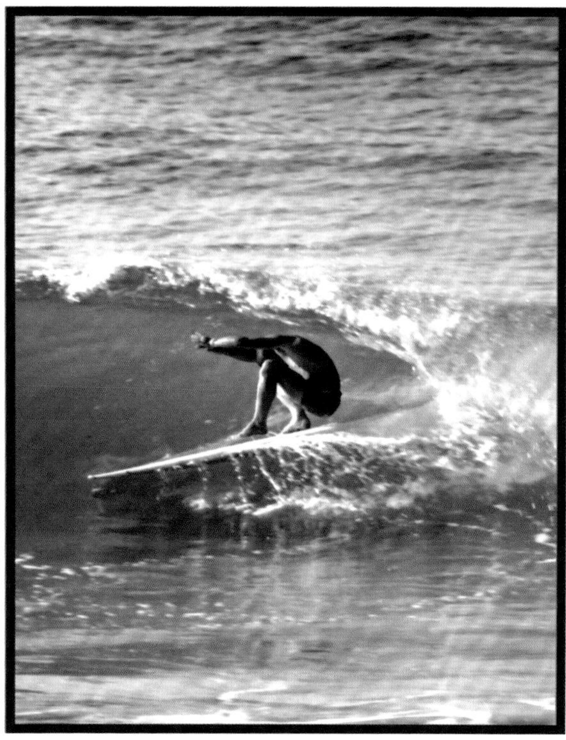

Greenmount Point, 1965. **MS**

First published in 2016 by New Holland Publishers
This edition published in 2023 by New Holland Publishers
Sydney

Level 1, 178 Fox Valley Road, Wahroonga, NSW 2076, Australia

newhollandpublishers.com

A record of this book is held at the National Library of Australia.

ISBN 9781760790882

Managing Director: Fiona Schultz
Publisher: Alan Whiticker
Designer: Andrew Davies
Production Director: Arlene Gippert

Printed in China

10 9 8 7 6 5 4 3 2 1

Keep up with New Holland Publishers:

NewHollandPublishers

@newhollandpublishers

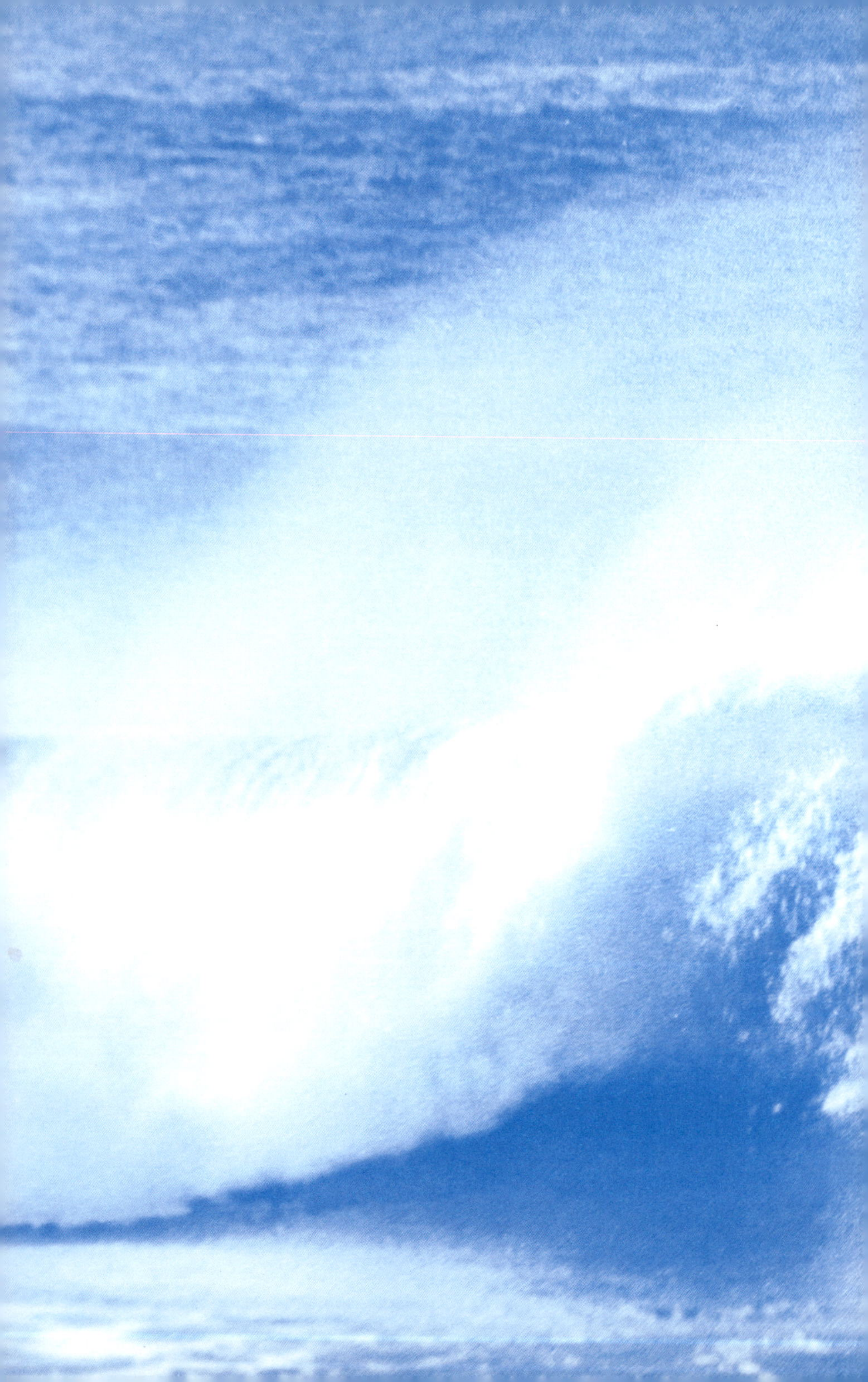